OTHER A TO Z GUIDES FROM THE SCARECROW PRESS, INC.

1. *The A to Z of Buddhism* by Charles S. Prebish, 2001.
2. *The A to Z of Catholicism* by William J. Collinge, 2001.
3. *The A to Z of Hinduism* by Bruce M. Sullivan, 2001.
4. *The A to Z of Islam* by Ludwig W. Adamec, 2002.
5. *The A to Z of Slavery & Abolition* by Martin A. Klein, 2002.
6. *Terrorism: Assassins to Zealots* by Sean Kendall Anderson and Stephen Sloan, 2003.
7. *The A to Z of the Korean War* by Paul M. Edwards, 2005.
8. *The A to Z of the Cold War* by Joseph Smith and Simon Davis, 2005.
9. *The A to Z of the Vietnam War* by Edwin E. Moise, 2005.
10. *The A to Z of Science Fiction Literature* by Brian Stableford, 2005.
11. *The A to Z of the Holocaust* by Jack R. Fischel, 2005.
12. *The A to Z of Washington, D.C.* by Robert Benedetto, Jane Donovan, and Kathleen DuVall, 2005.
13. *The A to Z of Taoism* by Julian F. Pas, 2006.
14. *The A to Z of the Renaissance* by Charles G. Nauert, 2006.
15. *The A to Z of Shinto* by Stuart D. B. Picken, 2006.
16. *The A to Z of Byzantium* by John H. Rosser, 2006.
17. *The A to Z of the Civil War* by Terry L. Jones, 2006.
18. *The A to Z of the Friends (Quakers)* by Margery Post Abbott, Mary Ellen Chijioke, Pink Dandelion, and John William Oliver Jr., 2006
19. *The A to Z of Feminism* by Janet K. Boles and Diane Long Hoeveler, 2006.
20. *The A to Z of New Religious Movements* by George D. Chryssides, 2006.
21. *The A to Z of Multinational Peacekeeping* by Terry M. Mays, 2006.
22. *The A to Z of Lutheranism* by Günther Gassmann with Duane H. Larson and Mark W. Oldenburg, 2007.
23. *The A to Z of the French Revolution* by Paul R. Hanson, 2007.
24. *The A to Z of the Persian Gulf War 1990–1991* by Clayton R. Newell, 2007.
25. *The A to Z of Revolutionary America* by Terry M. Mays, 2007.
26. *The A to Z of the Olympic Movement* by Bill Mallon with Ian Buchanan, 2007.

27. *The A to Z of the Discovery and Exploration of Australia* by Alan Day, 2009.
28. *The A to Z of the United Nations* by Jacques Fomerand. 2009.
29. *The A to Z of the "Dirty Wars"* by David Kohut, Olga Vilella, and Beatrice Julian, 2009.
30. *The A to Z of the Vikings* by Katherine Holman, 2009.
31. *The A to Z from the Great War to the Great Depression* by Neil A. Wynn, 2009.
32. *The A to Z of the Crusades* by Corliss K. Slack, 2009.
33. *The A to Z of New Age Movements* by Michael York, 2009.
34. *The A to Z of Unitarian Universalism* by Mark W. Harris, 2009.
35. *The A to Z of the Kurds* by Michael M. Gunter, 2009.
36. *The A to Z of Utopianism* by James M. Morris and Andrea L. Kross, 2009.
37. *The A to Z of the Civil War and Reconstruction* by William L. Richter, 2009.
38. *The A to Z of Jainism* by Kristi L. Wiley, 2009.
39. *The A to Z of the Inuit* by Pamela K. Stern, 2009.
40. *The A to Z of Early North America* by Cameron B. Wesson, 2009.
41. *The A to Z of the Enlightenment* by Harvey Chisick, 2009.
42. *The A to Z of Methodism* edited by Charles Yrigoyen Jr. and Susan E. Warrick, 2009.
43. *The A to Z of the Seventh-day Adventists* by Gary Land, 2009.
44. *The A to Z of Sufism* by John Renard, 2009.
45. *The A to Z of Sikhism* by W. H. McLeod, 2009.
46. *The A to Z of Fantasy Literature* by Brian Stableford, 2009.
47. *The A to Z of the Discovery and Exploration of the Pacific Islands* by Max Quanchi and John Robson, 2009.
48. *The A to Z of Australian and New Zealand Cinema* by Albert Moran and Errol Vieth, 2009.
49. *The A to Z of African-American Television* by Kathleen Fearn-Banks, 2009.
50. *The A to Z of American Radio Soap Operas* by Jim Cox, 2009.
51. *The A to Z of the Old South* by William L. Richter, 2009.
52. *The A to Z of the Discovery and Exploration of the Northwest Passage* by Alan Day, 2009.
53. *The A to Z of the Druzes* by Samy S. Swayd, 2009.
54. *The A to Z of the Welfare State* by Bent Greve, 2009.

55. *The A to Z of the War of 1812* by Robert Malcomson, 2009.
56. *The A to Z of Feminist Philosophy* by Catherine Villanueva Gardner, 2009.
57. *The A to Z of the Early American Republic* by Richard Buel Jr., 2009.
58. *The A to Z of the Russo–Japanese War* by Rotem Kowner, 2009.
59. *The A to Z of Anglicanism* by Colin Buchanan, 2009.
60. *The A to Z of Scandinavian Literature and Theater* by Jan Sjåvik, 2009.
61. *The A to Z of the Peoples of the Southeast Asian Massif* by Jean Michaud, 2009.
62. *The A to Z of Judaism* by Norman Solomon, 2009.
63. *The A to Z of the Berbers (Imazighen)* by Hsain Ilahiane, 2009.
64. *The A to Z of British Radio* by Seán Street, 2009.
65. *The A to Z of The Salvation Army* by Major John G. Merritt, 2009.
66. *The A to Z of the Arab–Israeli Conflict* by P R Kumaraswamy, 2009.
67. *The A to Z of the Jacksonian Era and Manifest Destiny* by Terry Corps, 2009.
68. *The A to Z of Socialism* by Peter Lamb and James C. Docherty, 2009.
69. *The A to Z of Marxism* by David Walker and Daniel Gray, 2009.
70. *The A to Z of the Bahá'í Faith* by Hugh C. Adamson, 2009.
71. *The A to Z of Postmodernist Literature and Theater* by Fran Mason, 2009.
72. *The A to Z of Australian Radio and Television* by Albert Moran and Chris Keating, 2009.
73. *The A to Z of the Lesbian Liberation Movement: Still the Rage* by JoAnne Myers, 2009.
74. *The A to Z of the United States–Mexican War* by Edward H. Moseley and Paul C. Clark Jr., 2009.
75. *The A to Z of World War I* by Ian V. Hogg, 2009.
76. *The A to Z of World War II: The War Against Japan* by Anne Sharp Wells, 2009.
77. *The A to Z of Witchcraft* by Michael D. Bailey, 2009.
78. *The A to Z of British Intelligence* by Nigel West, 2009.
79. *The A to Z of United States Intelligence* by Michael A. Turner, 2009.

80. *The A to Z of the League of Nations* by Anique H. M. van Ginneken, 2009.
81. *The A to Z of Israeli Intelligence* by Ephraim Kahana, 2009.
82. *The A to Z of the European Union* by Joaquín Roy and Aimee Kanner, 2009.
83. *The A to Z of the Chinese Cultural Revolution* by Guo Jian, Yongyi Song, and Yuan Zhou, 2009.
84. *The A to Z of African American Cinema* by S. Torriano Berry and Venise T. Berry, 2009.
85. *The A to Z of Japanese Business* by Stuart D. B. Picken, 2009.
86. *The A to Z of the Reagan–Bush Era* by Richard S. Conley, 2009.
87. *The A to Z of Human Rights and Humanitarian Organizations* by Robert F. Gorman and Edward S. Mihalkanin, 2009.
88. *The A to Z of French Cinema* by Dayna Oscherwitz and MaryEllen Higgins, 2009.
89. *The A to Z of the Puritans* by Charles Pastoor and Galen K. Johnson, 2009.
90. *The A to Z of Nuclear, Biological, and Chemical Warfare* by Benjamin C. Garrett and John Hart, 2009.
91. *The A to Z of the Green Movement* by Miranda Schreurs and Elim Papadakis, 2009.
92. *The A to Z of the Kennedy–Johnson Era* by Richard Dean Burns and Joseph M. Siracusa, 2009.
93. *The A to Z of Renaissance Art* by Lilian H. Zirpolo, 2009.
94. *The A to Z of the Broadway Musical* by William A. Everett and Paul R. Laird, 2009.
95. *The A to Z of the Northern Ireland Conflict* by Gordon Gillespie, 2009.
96. *The A to Z of the Fashion Industry* by Francesca Sterlacci and Joanne Arbuckle, 2009.
97. *The A to Z of American Theater: Modernism* by James Fisher and Felicia Hardison Londré, 2009.
98. *The A to Z of Civil Wars in Africa* by Guy Arnold, 2009.
99. *The A to Z of the Nixon–Ford Era* by Mitchell K. Hall, 2009.
100. *The A to Z of Horror Cinema* by Peter Hutchings, 2009.
101. *The A to Z of Westerns in Cinema* by Paul Varner, 2009.
102. *The A to Z of Zionism* by Rafael Medoff and Chaim I. Waxman, 2009.

103. *The A to Z of the Roosevelt–Truman Era* by Neil A. Wynn, 2009.
104. *The A to Z of Jehovah's Witnesses* by George D. Chryssides, 2009.
105. *The A to Z of Native American Movements* by Todd Leahy and Raymond Wilson, 2009.
106. *The A to Z of the Shakers* by Stephen J. Paterwic, 2009.
107. *The A to Z of the Coptic Church* by Gawdat Gabra, 2009.
108. *The A to Z of Architecture* by Allison Lee Palmer, 2009.
109. *The A to Z of Italian Cinema* by Gino Moliterno, 2009.
110. *The A to Z of Mormonism* by Davis Bitton and Thomas G. Alexander, 2009.
111. *The A to Z of African American Theater* by Anthony D. Hill with Douglas Q. Barnett, 2009.
112. *The A to Z of NATO and Other International Security Organizations* by Marco Rimanelli, 2009.
113. *The A to Z of the Eisenhower Era* by Burton I. Kaufman and Diane Kaufman, 2009.
114. *The A to Z of Sexspionage* by Nigel West, 2009.
115. *The A to Z of Environmentalism* by Peter Dauvergne, 2009.
116. *The A to Z of the Petroleum Industry* by M. S. Vassiliou, 2009.
117. *The A to Z of Journalism* by Ross Eaman, 2009.
118. *The A to Z of the Gilded Age* by T. Adams Upchurch, 2009.
119. *The A to Z of the Progressive Era* by Catherine Cocks, Peter C. Holloran, and Alan Lessoff, 2009.
120. *The A to Z of Middle Eastern Intelligence* by Ephraim Kahana and Muhammad Suwaed, 2009.
121. *The A to Z of the Baptists* William H. Brackney, 2009.
122. *The A to Z of Homosexuality* by Brent L. Pickett, 2009.

The A to Z of Mormonism

Davis Bitton and Thomas G. Alexander

The A to Z Guide Series, No. 110

The Scarecrow Press, Inc.
Lanham • Toronto • Plymouth, UK
2009

Published by Scarecrow Press, Inc.
A wholly owned subsidiary of
The Rowman & Littlefield Publishing Group, Inc.
4501 Forbes Boulevard, Suite 200, Lanham, Maryland 20706
http://www.scarecrowpress.com

Estover Road, Plymouth PL6 7PY, United Kingdom

This book is a paperback edition of *Historical Dictionary of Mormonism: Third Edition*

British Library Cataloguing in Publication Information Available

Library of Congress Cataloging-in-Publication Data

The hardback version of this book was cataloged by the Library of Congress as follows:

Bitton, Davis, 1930–
Historical dictionary of Mormonism / Davis Bitton and Thomas G. Alexander. — 3rd ed.
p. cm. — (Historical dictionaries of religions, philosophies, and movements ; no. 89)
Includes bibliographical references.
1. Mormon Church—Dictionaries. 2. Mormons—Biography—Dictionaries. I. Alexander, Thomas G. II. Title.
BX8605.5.B558 2008
289.303—dc22 2008014759

ISBN 978-0-8108-6897-7 (pbk. : alk. paper)
ISBN 978-0-8108-7060-4 (ebook)

™ The paper used in this publication meets the minimum requirements of American National Standard for Information Sciences—Permanence of Paper for Printed Library Materials, ANSI/NISO Z39.48-1992.

Printed in the United States of America

Contents

Preface to *Historical Dictionary of Mormonism: Third Edition*

From one point of view, Mormons are but one relatively small group within the contemporary religious spectrum. They see themselves as "God's chosen people," as the "only true and living church," not unlike several other religious groups. Those curious about such a religion might need no further excuse for reading about it. But since its formal organization in 1830, Mormons have had a colorful, exciting history. In the 20th century, while melding into the larger society and achieving respectability in the eyes of most people, Mormonism continued to grow. Especially during the past 30 or 40 years, that growth has been dramatic, which not surprisingly has evoked opposition and denunciation from some quarters. This is not a quiet, dull religion undifferentiated from the many Christian denominations.

Other works of reference exist, but they are pitched exclusively to the Mormon audience or are, in the case of older biographical and historical encyclopedias or the five-volume *Encyclopedia of Mormonism*, library works of reference rather than a handbook that can be easily carried and used. We have benefited from these other works and have supplied a bibliography for those wishing more, but the current dictionary should be more than sufficient as a preliminary orientation to Mormon history, beliefs, practices, and terminology.

We are all familiar enough with encyclopedias arranged in the irrational but convenient alphabetical order that little explanation is required. Part of the fun is in random browsing. At the same time, readers new to the subject might want an overview of Mormon history. Other than the chronology and introduction in the beginning of this book, the entries on New York Period, Ohio Period, Missouri Period, Illinois Period, Exodus, Utah Period, and Colonization can be read in order. Alternatively, the biographical sketches of the presidents of the Church from the beginning can be read in sequence: Joseph Smith, Brigham

Young, John Taylor, Wilford Woodruff, Lorenzo Snow, Joseph F. Smith, Heber J. Grant, George Albert Smith, David O. McKay, Joseph Fielding Smith, Harold B. Lee, Spencer W. Kimball, Ezra Taft Benson, Howard W. Hunter, Gordon B. Hinckley, and Thomas S. Monson. Other articles often include historical information.

In the preface to the second edition of this book, Davis Bitton wrote, "I wish to thank my wife, JoAn, who encouraged me in this project; librarians who assisted me in finding specific details; and general editor Jon Woronoff, whose kindly supervision has made this series the valuable resource it is." After Davis died, JoAn asked me to complete the work that he had so ably begun. I agreed to do this. I thank her for trusting me with the task. I also thank Lyn Clayton for previous help on some of the biographies he prepared for an earlier work.

Most especially, I thank my wife, Marilyn, whose unflagging support for a life that is far too full of projects in various states of completion has added to the joy of nearly a half century of marriage.

Thomas G. Alexander

List of Acronyms and Abbreviations

AML	Association for Mormon Letters
BYU	Brigham Young University
CEBA	Centro Escolar Benemerito de las Americas
CPART	Center for the Preservation of Ancient Religious Texts
FARMS	Foundation for Ancient Research and Mormon Studies
JST	Joseph Smith Translation
JWHA	John Whitmer Historical Association
LDS	Latter-day Saint, often used as a substitute for Mormon or for Church of Jesus Christ of Latter-day Saints in English-speaking countries
LDSSA	Latter-day Saint Students Association
METI	Middle Eastern Text Initiative
MHA	Mormon History Association
MIT	Massachusetts Institute of Technology
MYSC	Mormon Youth Symphony and Chorus
NRI	Nauvoo Restoration, Inc.
RLDS	Reorganized Church of Jesus Christ of Latter Day Saints
UCLA	University of California at Los Angeles
YMMIA	Young Men's Mutual Improvement Association, superseded by Young Men
YWMIA	Young Women's Mutual Improvement Association, superseded by Young Women

Chronology

1805 23 December: Joseph Smith Jr. born in Sharon, Windsor County, Vermont.

1830 26 March: The *Book of Mormon* published in Palmyra, New York. **6 April:** Joseph Smith organized the Church of Christ in Fayette, New York. **30 December:** Church members instructed to gather in Ohio (*Doctrine and Covenants*, section 37).

1831 2 August: Missouri dedicated as the Land of Zion.

1833 20 July: Mob destroyed Mormon printing office in Independence, Missouri. **November:** Mormons left Jackson County, Missouri, due to mob opposition.

1834 8 May: Small "army" known as Zion's Camp began its march from Ohio to Missouri to assist beleaguered Mormons. **30 June:** The group dispersed.

1835 14 February: Quorum of Twelve Apostles organized. **28 February:** First Council of the Seventy organized. **17 August:** Meeting agreed on contents to be included in the *Doctrine and Covenants*, which became the third book of scripture (the "standard works"). **September:** *Doctrine and Covenants* published. **14 September:** Emma Smith appointed to select hymns.

1836 27 March: Kirtland (Ohio) Temple dedicated.

1837 13 June: Two Mormon apostles left Ohio on mission to England, the first proselytizing outside North America. **30 July:** Nine persons baptized in the River Ribble at Preston, England.

1838 6 July: Most Mormons depart from Kirtland, Ohio. **27 October:** Missouri governor Lilburn W. Boggs ordered extermination or expulsion of the Mormons from the state. **30 October:** Seventeen Mormons killed at Haun's Mill in Missouri.

1839 January: Exodus of Mormons from Missouri began. **25 April:** Land purchased in Illinois at site soon renamed Nauvoo. **8 August:** John Taylor and Wilford Woodruff left for mission to England.

1840 6 June: Forty-one converts set sail from England. **15 August:** Baptism for the dead officially announced. **16 December:** Nauvoo Charter signed by Illinois governor.

1841 24 October: Palestine dedicated for the return of the Jews by Apostle Orson Hyde.

1842 1 March: Articles of Faith written by Joseph Smith in letter to John Wentworth and published in Nauvoo newspaper. **17 March:** Female Relief Society organized.

1843 23 May: Missionaries left Nauvoo for Pacific islands. **12 July:** Revelation on marriage recorded, instituting the possibility of plural marriage, or polygamy.

1844 27 June: Joseph and Hyrum Smith killed by a mob in Carthage, Illinois. **8 August:** Leadership of the Church by the twelve under Brigham Young approved by vote in a large conference in Nauvoo.

1846 4 February: Evacuation of Nauvoo began. **1 May:** Nauvoo Temple dedicated. **13 July:** Volunteers began to enlist in the Mormon Battalion of the U.S. Army.

1847 22–24 July: Pioneer company under Brigham Young arrived in the Salt Lake Valley. **5 December:** First Presidency reorganized with Brigham Young as president of the Church.

1848 June: Crops saved when flocks of gulls devour crickets.

1849 6 October: Missionaries called to preach in Continental Europe.

1850 28 February: University of Deseret, predecessor of University of Utah, founded. **15 June:** *Deseret News* began publication. **9 September:** Congress organized Utah Territory. **20 September:** Brigham Young appointed governor of Utah Territory.

1851 **11 July:** *Pearl of Great Price* (fourth volume of scripture) published as a pamphlet in England.

1852 **28–29 August:** Plural marriage first publicly announced.

1857 **24 July:** Definite news received that a U.S. Army regiment had been ordered to Utah. Rumors had reached Utah earlier. **7–11 September:** Mountain Meadows Massacre.

1858 **11 June:** Peace commissioners resolved dispute and brought an end to the Utah War.

1859 **10–17 July:** Horace Greeley interviewed Brigham Young.

1860 **24 August–10 September:** English explorer Richard F. Burton visited Utah.

1861 **18 October:** Telegraph line reached Utah.

1862 **8 July:** Lincoln signed Morrill Anti-bigamy Act, prohibiting polygamy and limiting property ownership by religious organizations in the territories.

1869 **10 May:** Transcontinental railroad completed.

1870 **12–14 June:** Rev. J. P. Newman and Mormon apostle Orson Pratt debated the question "Does the Bible sanction polygamy?"

1874 **23 June:** Poland Act passed by Congress, restricting local government in Utah.

1875 **3 October:** U.S. president Ulysses S. Grant began visit to Utah. **16 October:** Brigham Young Academy founded in Provo, Utah (predecessor of Brigham Young University).

1877 **1 January:** St. George Temple dedicated. **29 August:** Brigham Young died. **4 September:** Twelve apostles under President John Taylor presided over the Church.

1878 **25 August:** Primary organization for children founded by Aurelia Spencer Rogers.

1879 **6 January:** Reynolds decision handed down. U.S. Supreme Court upheld constitutionality of the Morrill Anti-bigamy Act and confirmed conviction of polygamist George Reynolds. **21 July:** Joseph Standing, Mormon missionary, killed by a mob in Georgia.

1880 19 August: Mormon missionaries arrested for preaching in Berlin and ordered out of Germany. **5–6 September:** U.S. president Rutherford B. Hayes and party visited Utah. **10 October:** *Pearl of Great Price* officially accepted as a standard work. First Presidency of the Church reorganized with John Taylor as president.

1882 22 March: Edmunds Act against polygamy passed by Congress.

1887 3 March: Edmunds-Tucker Act, intensifying penalties for polygamy and allowing for confiscation of LDS Church property, became law without presidential signature. **25 July:** Death of Church president John Taylor. Twelve apostles presided over the Church.

1888 21 May: Manti (Utah) Temple dedicated.

1889 7 April: Wilford Woodruff became president of the Church.

1890 24 September: Manifesto issued by Church president Wilford Woodruff. **6 October:** Manifesto approved by vote in general conference.

1891 9 May: U.S. president Benjamin Harrison and party visited Salt Lake City.

1893 6 April: Salt Lake Temple dedicated. **8 September:** Mormon Tabernacle Choir won second prize at Chicago World's Fair (the Columbian Exposition).

1894 13 November: Genealogical Society of Utah organized.

1895 8 May: Constitutional convention completed its work in drafting a state constitution for Utah.

1896 4 January: Utah became a state.

1897 24 July: Fiftieth anniversary of entrance of Mormon pioneers into Salt Lake Valley celebrated. **November:** *Improvement Era* began publication.

1898 2 September: Church president Wilford Woodruff died. **13 September:** Lorenzo Snow sustained by apostles as president of the

Church. **9 October:** Lorenzo Snow and other authorities sustained by vote of general Church conference. **8 November:** B. H. Roberts elected Utah's congressman (he was accused of polygamy and not allowed to take his seat).

1903 15 October: Brigham Young Academy became Brigham Young University.

1904 5 April: "Second manifesto" ended plural marriage.

1913 21 May: Boy Scout program officially adopted for boys of the Church.

1915 January: *Relief Society Magazine* for women began publication.

1929 15 July: Mormon Tabernacle Choir started weekly radio broadcast.

1930 6 April: Centennial of the organization of the Church celebrated.

1933 5 November: Chapel in Washington, D.C., dedicated.

1936 7 April: Welfare program introduced.

1937 July: Outdoor pageant, "America's Witness for Christ," began at Hill Cumorah in New York.

1947 24 July: Centennial of the arrival of pioneers in the Salt Lake Valley celebrated.

1954 July: Indian Placement Program inaugurated. **21 July:** Church College of Hawaii announced.

1963 12 October: Polynesian Cultural Center dedicated in Laie, Hawaii.

1966 1 May: First stake in South America organized in São Paulo, Brazil.

1969 3–8 August: World Conference on Records took place in Salt Lake City.

1970 15 March: First stake in Asia organized in Tokyo. **22 March:** First stake in Africa organized in Transvaal, South Africa.

1971 January: New Church magazines began publication: *Ensign* (for adults), *New Era* (for youths), and the *Friend* (for children).

1972 14 January: Establishment of the Historical Department of the Church announced, replacing the Church Historian's Office.

1974 1 September: Church College of Hawaii renamed Brigham Young University–Hawaii campus.

1975 19–21 June: Open house for new 28-story Church office building in Salt Lake City.

1976 25 June: Missouri governor Christopher S. Bond rescinded 1838 extermination order.

1978 9 June: First Presidency announced that worthy men of all races would be eligible to receive the priesthood. **9 September:** Missionary Training Center replaced Mission Home in Salt Lake City and Language Training Mission.

1979 29 September: New edition of the King James Version of the Bible published.

1980 6 April: Centennial of the organization of the Church.

1981 26 September: New editions of *Book of Mormon*, *Doctrine and Covenants*, and *Pearl of Great Price* published.

1982 1 April: Church membership reached 5 million. **3 October:** New subtitle announced for *Book of Mormon*: *Another Testament of Jesus Christ*.

1984 28 October: The 1,500th stake organized: the Ciudad Obregon Mexico Yaqui Stake.

1985 27 January: Church members participated in a fast in order to raise funds ($11 million) for famine victims in Africa. **2 August:** Revised hymn book published. **23 October:** Family History Library dedicated. **10 November:** Ezra Taft Benson became 13th president of the Church.

1988 12 November: Centennial of Ricks College, Rexburg, Idaho.

1989 16 May: Brigham Young University Jerusalem Center dedicated.

1991 **26 May:** San Francisco de Macoris Dominican Republic Stake organized as the 1,800th stake of the Church. **31 May:** Church membership reached 8 million. **8–29 June:** Mormon Tabernacle Choir toured Eastern Europe. **December:** *Encyclopedia of Mormonism* published by Macmillan.

1992 **30 August:** The 1,900th stake created: Orlando Florida South Stake. **26 December:** Mormon Tabernacle Choir began tour of Israel.

1993 **1 January:** India Bangalore Mission opened, with Gurcharan Singh Gill as president. **6 January:** Mormon Tabernacle Choir concluded tour of Israel.

1994 **5 June:** Howard W. Hunter became 14th president of the Church. **17 November:** Future Church president Thomas S. Monson honored by Catholic Community Services of Utah for humanitarian care. **3 December:** More than 20,000 food packages prepared for families in Bosnia, Croatia, and Albania. **11 December:** Church's 2,000th stake created in Mexico City.

1995 **21 February:** Gordon B. Hinckley honored for promoting high moral values by National Conference of Christians and Jews (Utah Region). **12 March:** Gordon B. Hinckley becomes 15th president of the Church. **1 April:** Position of regional representative replaced by new position of area authority. **23 September:** Proclamation on the family issued by the First Presidency. See appendix 2. **18 December:** President Gordon B. Hinckley interviewed for the CBS television program *60 Minutes* by Mike Wallace.

1996 **18 January:** General authorities announced withdrawal from boards of directors of business corporations. **28 February:** More than half of Church membership lived outside the United States. **29 June:** President Gordon B. Hinckley awarded the Golden Plate Award for exceptional accomplishment in public service by the American Academy of Achievement.

1997 **April:** Organization of Third, Fourth, and Fifth Quorums of the Seventy announced. **19–21 April:** Mormon Trail Wagon Train departed from Iowa and Nebraska to reenact the overland journey to the Salt Lake Valley that occurred in 1847. **28 May:** New nine-story headquarters building for the *Deseret News* dedicated in Salt Lake City, Utah. **9**

July: Smithsonian Institution's National Museum of American History at Washington, D.C., opened an exhibit on the Mormon Pioneer Trail. **4 October:** Plan announced to construct "small" temples in areas whose population would not justify larger ones.

1998 February: President Gordon B. Hinckley toured Nigeria, Ghana, Kenya, Zimbabwe, and South Africa and announced plans to construct a temple in Ghana. **26 April:** President Gordon B. Hinckley addressed 20,000 people in Madison Square Garden, New York City. **7–10 June:** Dedication of temple in Preston, England, site of first English baptisms in 1837. **14 June–2 July:** Mormon Tabernacle Choir toured England, Belgium, Switzerland, Italy, France, Spain, and Portugal. **28 June:** First meetinghouse dedicated in Ukraine at Donetsk. **8 September:** President Gordon B. Hinckley interviewed on the network TV show *Larry King Live*.

1999 9 February: Deseret Management Corporation, the Church's holding company for commercial entities, acquired Bookcraft, Inc. **11 February 1999:** Leonard J. Arrington, the Church's most prolific and respected historian, died. **1 April:** Sesquicentennial of organization of the Sunday school celebrated. **25 April:** President Gordon B. Hinckley addressed 57,500 in Santiago, Chile. **29–30 April:** Women's Conference at Brigham Young University attended by 20,000 women. **13 May:** President Gordon B. Hinckley addressed Los Angeles World Affairs Council. **24 May:** Free website for genealogical research, familysearch.org, launched. **25 September:** Relief Society declaration on roles and values of women announced. **26 November:** *American Prophet: The Story of Joseph Smith*, a television documentary, made its national debut over the Public Broadcasting System. **24 December:** President Gordon B. Hinckley interviewed again on *Larry King Live*.

2000 8 March: President Gordon B. Hinckley addressed National Press Club Newsmakers Luncheon in Washington, D.C. **22 April:** The 100 millionth copy of the *Book of Mormon* printed. **21 June:** Announced that Ricks College would become a four-year institution and would be renamed Brigham Young University–Idaho. **7–8 October:** New 21,000-seat Conference Center in Salt Lake City, Utah, dedicated.

2001 20 January: Mormon Tabernacle Choir sang at the inauguration of President George W. Bush.

2002 **22 May:** First Missionary Training Center in Africa opened in Ghana. **27 June:** Rebuilt Nauvoo Temple dedicated in Nauvoo, Illinois. **8 December:** Hispanic Christmas fireside held in the Conference Center for 13,000 Spanish-speaking members.

2003 **12 November:** Mormon Tabernacle Choir was awarded the National Medal of Arts by President George W. Bush at the White House in Washington, D.C.

2004 **24 March:** Illinois House of Representatives passed a resolution expressing regret for the expulsion of the Latter-day Saints from Illinois following the murder of Joseph and Hyrum Smith in June 1844. **29–30 April:** Annual Women's Conference at Brigham Young University attended by 17,000 women. **27 May:** Elder Russell M. Nelson addressed an international conference on religious freedom in Kiev, Ukraine. **23 June:** President Gordon B. Hinckley received the Presidential Medal of Freedom at the White House in Washington, D.C. **19 October:** First Presidency issued a statement defending the definition of marriage as the union of a man and a woman. **26 December:** President Gordon B. Hinckley was interviewed for the third time on the television talk show *Larry King Live*.

2005 Bicentennial year of Joseph Smith's birth on 23 December 1805. Throughout the year programs, pageants, plays, and concerts commemorated his life and ministry. The Museum of Church History and Art offered an exhibit on "Joseph Smith: Prophet of the Restoration" attended by some 430,000 visitors during the year. **1 January:** More than 70 tons of relief supplies sent (in partnership with Islamic Relief Worldwide) to Indonesia to assist victims of tsunamis in southern Asia. Later additional containers of supplies were sent to Indonesia and Sri Lanka. **6–7 May:** Academic conference, "The Worlds of Joseph Smith," was held at the Library of Congress in Washington, D.C. **31 March:** Perpetual Education Fund announced to assist young people in selected countries complete an education leading to satisfactory employment. **July:** Website, josephsmith.net, launched by Family and Church History Department. **10 August:** Ricks College, in Rexburg, Idaho, was officially renamed Brigham Young University–Idaho, a four-year university. **September–October:** To aid victims of hurricanes Rita and Katrina, the Church sent 200 truckloads of supplies; 300,000 hygeine kits; and

60,000 cleanup buckets. Volunteer hurricane relief work on site totaled 35,000 man days. **17 December:** Release of film *Joseph Smith: Prophet of the Restoration* for showing in visitors centers.

2006 February: American Red Cross gave the Church its Circle of Humanitarians award for substantial aid to the Measles Initiative in Africa, where local members assisted in vaccinating millions. **30 April:** Mormon Tabernacle Choir performed its 4,000th broadcast. **May–August:** Church celebrated 50 years on Taiwan with concerts, youth conference, and 50-mile bike ride. **21–15 August:** Brigham Young University Education Week offered more than 200 classes to thousands of participants; many of the classes were disseminated worldwide through the Church's satellite system. **September–December:** Museum of Church History and Art held exhibit honoring Willie and Martin Handcart companies. **September:** Spanish edition of LDS scriptures released on the Internet. **21 October:** Annual Latino cultural celebration in Conference Center for Spanish-speaking members included songs and folk dancing. **November:** Mormon Tabernacle Choir received Mother Teresa award from St. Bernadette Institute for Sacred Art.

2007 4 February: Fireside service for young adults broadcast or rebroadcast in up to 32 languages. **10 February:** Worldwide leadership training session broadcast over the Church's satellite system. **31 March:** Salt Lake Tabernacle rededicated after several years of restoration and seismic stabilization. **31 March 2007–January 2011:** Museum of Church History and Art exhibit documented the Salt Lake Tabernacle. **Spring:** Members provided charitable assistance by responding to disasters including a flood in Argentina, tornadoes in the central and southwestern United States, landslides on the island of Hispaniola, an earthquake in Japan, and flooding in Jakarta. **30 April–1 May:** *The Mormons*, a four-hour documentary by Helen Whitney that examined the history, beliefs, and practices of the Church of Jesus Christ of Latter-day Saints, broadcast on PBS. The broadcast elicited considerable discussion and commentary. **25 June:** Church membership reached 13 million members. **26 June:** Announcement that the 1 millionth missionary since 1830 had been called. **10 August:** President James E. Faust died in Salt Lake City. **7 September:** Elder Marlin K. Jensen participated in a memorial service for those murdered by southern Utah Mormon militiamen in 1857. **2 October:** Church held its first online news conference. **6 October:** Henry B. Eyring sustained as second counselor in the First Presidency. Elder Quentin L. Cook sustained as a member of the Quorum of Twelve Apostles. **15 December:** Elder M. Russell Ballard urged members to use new media such as Internet blogs to defend the church.

2008 **27 January:** President Gordon B. Hinckley died at his home in Salt Lake City. **4 February:** Thomas S. Monson called as president of the Church with Henry B. Eyring as first counselor and Dieter F. Uctdorf as second counselor. **10 February:** Rexburg Temple in Idaho dedicated by President Thomas S. Monson.

Introduction

Many people have heard of Mormonism, if only vaguely. They may have seen Mormon missionaries with white shirt and tie and identifying name tags. A newspaper headline or a television news item tells of a Mormon politician. Perhaps one discovers that a classmate at school or a colleague at work belongs to this religion. But many know nothing at all about Mormonism. Sociologists conducting interviews or producers of documentaries asking questions of people on the street demonstrate rampant ignorance and misinformation. Even those with no particular bias in favor of or against Mormonism often understand virtually nothing about its beliefs, the obstacles it has faced, and its achievements.

Compared to other world religions, Mormonism has a short history. Members celebrated the Church's centennial in 1930. Not until 2030 will it reach its bicentennial. But those few generations covering less than two centuries compress a tremendous amount of human experience, with a cast of colorful characters and a series of dramatic confrontations. Like it or not, agree or disagree with its beliefs, one who seeks to understand Mormonism, its beliefs, its leading people, its way of looking at life—in short what makes it tick—must first have at least a general sense of its history.

THE 19TH CENTURY

The Church of Jesus Christ of Latter-day Saints—the official name, Mormonism being a nickname—was organized on 6 April 1830 in western New York. The religious toleration of early America allowed a multiplicity of competing churches. One strain of thinking about Christianity in the early 19th century was restorationism—essentially the idea that Christianity needed to return to the norms and usages of the primitive church. Not the only church grounded in such thinking, Mormonism was, at least in part, based on this understanding. It was also a prophetic religion. Those who joined the Church accepted its founder, Joseph Smith, as a prophet of God in the same way that Jeremiah and Ezekiel were prophets of God. Not claiming to be divine or to displace Jesus Christ as redeemer, Joseph mediated God's will to his followers. Such a claim made the new religion appear ominous. Who could know what he might say or do or what his followers might do under the assumption that they were performing God's will?

Like other Christians, Mormons believed the Bible. But they also accepted other books as scripture, most particularly the *Book of Mormon*. Without question, such an open-ended view seemed dangerous to many. Who knew how far it would go? Was there any limit? "Give me that old-time religion. . . . It's good enough for me." This refrain from a popular religious song expressed a common feeling. Never mind that it was directed against modernist impulses in Protestantism or that "old-time religion" might require careful defining. In this instance, the attitude simply meant that the Bible was inerrant and sufficient. There was no need, most people thought, for any other book to home in on the unique territory already occupied by the Holy Bible.

A third feature of the new religion was its missionaries. Those who believed carried the word to others. Mormon missionaries would hit the road and preach wherever they could. They called on friends and neighbors, relatives, and anyone who might listen. Full of conviction, they saw themselves as continuing the injunction of Christ to go into all the world and preach the gospel. Not surprisingly, many spurned their overtures. Those who did looked on the missionaries as disturbers of the peace. Pastors of existing churches saw them as "sheep stealers."

A fourth feature of Mormonism was the doctrine of gathering, preached in the 19th and early 20th centuries. As people joined the new church, they moved to join their fellow believers in covenant communities. A declared gathering place brought converts from near and far. By coming together, Mormons gathered in sufficient numbers to seem a threat to others. The older inhabitants would see the newcomers arrive individually, in families, in small wagon companies. When, the old settlers wondered, would the Mormons outnumber the others? When would they dominate the economy and the politics of the city or county?

Such fearful reactions led to street meetings, demonstrations, riots, and eventually mobs who burned the barns and homes of Mormons. This drama replayed itself in Ohio, Missouri, and Illinois. Finally, on the dark night of 27 June 1844, amid the shrieks and yells of a militia turned into a lawless mob, the founding prophet, Joseph Smith, and his brother, Hyrum—while incarcerated in jail awaiting trial—fell dead in a hail of bullets. Those who committed the brutal murders saw them as a justifiable lynching, perfectly consistent with the traditions of 19th-century America. The Mormons, stunned and grief-stricken, saw it as martyrdom.

In less than two years, still the victims of persecution, Mormons fled their cities, crossed the Mississippi, and headed westward into the Iowa territory. A bird's eye view during the next months would have seen wagon trains of refugees slowly moving westward, with camps established at intervals for rest, resupplying, and regrouping. It was another exodus. Fighting weather conditions and a lack of supplies, fearful of their persecutors, these "displaced persons" were strung out over several hundred miles. After a halt for the winter of 1846–47, they pushed on to the Great Basin on the western slope of the Rocky Mountains—a journey that required several months of painful, persistent travel across a wilderness with no cities along the way to serve as supply stations.

The geographical scope of the Mormon movement was vast. In addition to many believers who stayed where they were in Illinois, Iowa, Ohio, and other states, hundreds organized in wagon-train companies moved along the trail from Illinois to Utah. At the same time another company under Samuel Brannan sailed from New York around the southern cape of South America and then northward to Yerba Buena (later San Francisco) in California. And the federal government recruited 500 Mormons into the U.S. Army during the Mexican-American War. They marched as an infantry battalion on a seemingly interminable journey to Kansas, New Mexico, and across the dry wastes of Arizona to the Southern California coast at San Diego.

The refugees arrived in Utah beginning in late July 1947. They came from different directions. The main group crossed the plains through what is now Nebraska and Wyoming. Some came eastward from California. Others from the South crossed to what is now Colorado, then struck north to the California-Oregon-Mormon trail. Interrupted briefly by a clash with federal troops in 1857, the refugees embarked on an ambitious program of colonization, founding settlement after settlement—more than 500—throughout an immense empire that stretched from southern Canada to northern Mexico and from Colorado to California. The pioneering so central to the American experience as part of the great westward movement was inescapably part of what it meant to be Mormon in the 19th century.

What is amazing, perhaps, is that the Mormon religion continued to attract followers. Joining it meant unpopularity, sacrifice, and perhaps even death. In the face of such a stark reality, why did people flock to Mormonism at the beginning and why did they continue to declare their allegiance to it right through the times of troubles? Motives are not easy to decipher, but let us recognize the explanations that have been offered.

First, Mormons themselves said quite simply that they knew the Church was true and was guided by God's prophet. Therefore they had to follow it, whatever the cost. Such is the faith and testimony of religious believers.

Second, quite a few people in America and Europe were dissatisfied with the established churches. They longed for something different. Some of them were disaffiliated, unchurched "seekers." Others were still members of the existing churches but reluctant and dissatisfied communicants. Whether on the level of beliefs or mode of worship or organizational forms, they hoped and prayed for a change. When the Mormon missionaries came along, such people were ready to listen and respond. This was not the attitude of everybody, to be sure, or even a majority of Christians, but some people constituted a prepared audience, receptive to the new message.

Third, some joined the Mormons because they wanted to improve their situation. Bored or lacking opportunity where they were, they signed on in anticipation that moving to the place of gathering would give them a fresh start. Leaving the streets of industrial England, for example, people saw themselves as prosperous farmers or shop owners in America. Theology may have been secondary to these folks. Although they did not necessarily reject the new beliefs, their interest was more practical. Such workings of the human mind are difficult to measure even among contemporaries.

Fourth, Mormonism satisfied many human needs. In 1830, 1880, 1930, and right up to the present, there are people abroad in the land—all lands—who are hurting, depressed, very much alone, down in their luck, needing human contact. Maybe all of us fall into these categories at different times. Mormonism is not the only religion to provide for such needs, but from its beginning the Church has been very good at it. One could receive a helping hand, a leg up, an arm around the shoulder. What the Church provided was not simply a handout, for sacrifice and unpopularity came with the package. In addition, perhaps more important, Mormonism offered involvement, a feeling of doing something that mattered, a chance to help others even worse off than oneself—one of the best remedies known to health care professionals. For many, the Church congregation became the primary locus of interaction with others.

However the conversions are explained, people continued to join up. And since members of the Church tended to have many children, high birth rate played a part in Mormonism's growth. Six members formed the initial membership in 1830. By 1840 there were 16,000; by 1850, 51,000. By the end of the 19th century the Church had 283,000 members.

From 1841 on, something new was added—the practice of polygamy. Practiced by perhaps a quarter of the families, it was kept quiet at first, although rumors circulated and exposés were written. In 1852, ensconced in their new home in the Rocky Mountains, Church leaders publicly acknowledged and defended polygamy as a biblical practice that was part of the restoration of all things. Many considered it essential for the ultimate degree of salvation. Not normally justified, they said, the unusual marriage arrangement had been permitted by God under special circumstances, as with the patriarchs Abraham, Isaac, and Jacob, and now themselves. Since marriage was a religious sacrament, Church leaders also thought they were protected by the First Amendment.

For one man to have two or more wives at the same time was, to say the least, a departure from the norm in Western society. Polygamy was something one read about in *Arabian Nights* but did not witness in real life; it was not the prosaic monogamous marriage of Christian tradition. For several decades polygamy was the publicist's "hook," the feature of the Mormon religion that could be counted on to attract interest. Lacking the stimulation of today's explicit television and movie fare, many let their imaginations run wild. Appealing to prurient interest, polygamy became the most sensational thing about Mormons. It defined their public image.

With practically all of its leading men being polygamists, the Church was most easily caricatured in marital terms. Yet even for the half century of its practice in the Mormon community—roughly the second half of the 19th century—polygamy was a minority phenomenon. Anything less than half is a minority, and certainly less than half of Mormons lived in polygamous marriages or were the children of such marriages. Yet it was prominent, especially among the leaders, and attracted shocked attention.

Opponents mounted a national campaign. They denounced the Church in the press, from the pulpit, in the halls of Congress. The anti-polygamy crusaders were, in their own view, simply defending the American home. If there were not laws sufficiently explicit to bar polygamy, they argued, let them be passed. Anti-polygamy statutes appeared on the books, reaching a culmination in the 1880s. Then those laws had to be enforced, which required decisions by the courts. Especially after 1884, hundreds of Mormon husbands and a few plural wives were hauled off to prison. The government dissolved the Church as a corporation and in large part escheated its property. In Idaho, a test oath was imposed to disenfranchise not only polygamists but all Church members.

Mormons living during the second half of the 19th century could not help but be aware of the strident negative press. Superstitious, contemptible lawbreakers, followers of a religion that was patently absurd—this was the verbal labeling followers were subjected to. Not distinguishing between the practice of polygamy and the entire community, some blunt preachers called for Mormonism's extermination. Naturally, especially within their own ranks, Latter-day Saints spoke back, defended themselves, and accused their enemies of hypocrisy.

EARLY 20TH CENTURY

Then everything changed. The transformation did not occur suddenly in the year 1900. It started a few years earlier and required the first decade of the 20th century to run its course. But transformation did take place.

The Church abandoned polygamy, ceasing to promote the practice. Those who know only what they read in the newspapers or see on television may be surprised at this, for occasional cases of polygamy continue to attract public attention. Those who still practice polygamy, however, have abandoned the Church; such marriages are performed by dissidents who have rejected the Latter-day Saint tradition. Nevertheless, for the Church, such cases are a public relations nightmare. Church members wince and feel they are being wrongly represented to the public, tarred for a practice long ago forsaken. For more than a century the Church itself has not advocated, taught, or performed such illegal marriages. Continuing to the present, no Church president or general authority, no local leader, no missionary is involved in the practice. In its 20th-century embodiment and up to the present, Mormonism has been a strong advocate of monogamy and traditional morality.

Economic and political practices of the past also faded. With the coming of the national political parties to Utah in the 1890s, the political stand-off based on religion disappeared, for both Republicans and Democrats courted both Mormons and non-Mormons. Differing religiously, they cooperated politically.

In many respects, Mormonism had become respectable. This is not to say that Mormon theology was accepted by others. But the Latter-day Saints appeared to follow a middle-class morality. They attended the same sports and recreational events as other people. They demonstrated their patriotism over and over again. Side-currents and subsurface eddies complicated this cheerful picture, but for six or seven decades, as we can verify by an analysis of press reports, a general spirit of good feelings prevailed. In some ways this attitude continues.

During the same years, through natural increase as well as conversions, the Church continued to grow. From 283,000 in 1900, membership ascended to 1 million by 1947. Membership doubled to 2 million by 1963 and to 4 million by 1979.

LATE 20TH AND EARLY 21ST CENTURIES

As always in the history of nations and institutions, we find both continuity and change. In noticing some distinguishing characteristics of the generation leading up to the present, we acknowledge that these individuals had raised their heads earlier, with hints of what was to come. Nevertheless, in attempting to understand the recent past and the present, the following deserve specific mention.

Burgeoning Growth

The Church continued to grow in number of members and also according to other important indices. In 1947, it was 1 million; 1963, 2 million; 1979, 4 million; 1991, 8 million. Just when the 16 million figure will be reached is unknown, but at the end of 2007 total membership was 12,868,606. During the same time period, from 1947 to 2007, the number of stakes (comparable to dioceses) grew from 169 to 2,745. A stake offers the complete program of the Church. The number of congregations, known as wards and branches, grew from 1,425 to 27,475. The number of missionaries out preaching to those willing to listen grew from less than 5,000 to 53,164.

Globalization

Raw membership figures fail to reveal some important facts. One is the movement of Mormonism into new countries. Missions are not established where forbidden by the government. The Muslim world has not been receptive to Christians of any kind, and the huge country of China places stringent limitations on worship and proselytizing. But where possible the Church has sent its missionaries, divided among 347 missions as of 2007. All missions succeed in converting people, but such success varies greatly from country to country. Especially fruitful mission fields have been Mexico, Central America, South America, Africa, and the Philippines. Although headquarters remained in the United States, at Salt Lake City, Utah, the Church membership became steadily more diverse. On 28 February 1996, a milestone was reached with more than half of all members living outside the United States, and that trend has continued.

Militating against establishing strong congregations around the world during the early decades of the Church's history was the doctrine of gathering. Small congregations were routinely depleted of their most committed members who emigrated to Utah. Then, starting early in the 20th century, or even before, those contemplating emigration were reminded of the limited employment opportunities that might await them. Discouragement of gathering was made stronger after World War II. On 1 December 1999, repeating advice uttered several times before, the

Church's First Presidency again stated that members should "remain in their homelands rather than immigrate to the United States."

Not well understood by many people are Mormon temples, edifices that are not ordinary meetinghouses but instead sacred spaces for the administering of ordinances to Church members. Throughout much of its history, the Church's temples were very few and confined to North America. Then temples were dedicated in England and Switzerland. The generation leading up to the present has been a generation of temple building. As temples have increased in number, all the ordinances have become more accessible to people in all parts of the world. From the 1980s to the present, temples have been erected every year until the number passed 100 and then 120. In simple terms, the construction of temples is institutional evidence of maturity, of putting down roots in many states and countries.

Opposition

We have noted the persecution of the 19th century. During the closing decades of the 20th century, after a half century or more of relative quiescence and presumably provoked by the growth and expansion already described, opposition by foes of the Church resumed. Attacking the Mormons were radio programs, newspaper and magazine articles, movies, and books carried by Christian bookstores. Some respectful dialogue occasionally occurred when spokesmen for Mormonism and conventional Christianity clarified their respective positions and even noted areas of agreement. But the name-calling was widespread. Anyone wishing to bash the Church had ample opportunity and ample resources. In its most repellant form, the opposition waved signs, desecrated sacred symbols, and shouted epithets at peaceable people attending conferences, pageants, and even weddings. Relying on law enforcement officers for protection, Mormons simply continued their activities and moved forward.

Increasing Prominence

Occupying headlines and being mentioned by news commentators is not a goal pursued by the Church. But increasing visibility is indicated by documentary television programs, movies produced by Latter-day Saint cinematographers, sports stars, popular entertainers, and politicians. At this writing, a Mormon, former governor Michael Leavitt of Utah, is secretary of health and human services. Another, Senator Harry Reed of Nevada, is majority leader of the U.S. Senate. Another, former governor Mitt Romney of Massachusetts, was a contender for the Republican nomination for president of the United States. The former president of the Church, Gordon B. Hinckley, appeared on national radio and television shows to explain the position of the Church. His successor, President Thomas S. Monson, indicated in an interview following his call that he would continue to meet with the press. Many Church members no doubt would prefer the quiet of obscurity, but the Church of Jesus Christ of Latter-day Saints will presumably continue its dynamic growth and be considered newsworthy, even if only as a decidedly non-trendy example of a group that stands athwart many of the trends of the age.

After all this time—after all the supposed accommodation and middle-class respectability of many members—Mormons continue to be a counterculture. In an age of increasing secularism in the Western world, Mormons believe in God. In a cynical age, they are idealistic. They scorn the values of the Hollywood elite and the mass media. Traditional morality remains their commitment. While some conservative Christians and Jews, or other believers in natural law and traditional values, might find their presence uncomfortable, in Mormons they have allies on these basic matters. Resisting the spirit of the age, Mormons continue to advance their religion. Finding themselves at odds with the larger culture is not a new experience for them.

The Dictionary

– A –

AARONIC PRIESTHOOD. The lower of the two major divisions of **priesthood**, the other being the **Melchizedek Priesthood**. As part of the **restoration**, the Aaronic Priesthood was conferred upon **Joseph Smith** and **Oliver Cowdery** by the resurrected John the Baptist (***Doctrine and Covenants***, section 13). The offices within the Aaronic Priesthood, from the bottom, are **deacon**, **teacher**, and **priest**.

ABEL, ELIJAH (1810–1884). African American member, **priesthood** holder, **missionary**. Born 25 July 1810 in Washington County, Maryland, he was baptized in 1832, one of a small number of African Americans who joined the church in the 19th century. He was ordained an **elder** in 1836 and ordained a member of the Third **Quorum** of the **Seventy** in Kirtland, Ohio, the same year. He served a mission in Canada and New York in 1838. He served as undertaker for the city of Nauvoo, Illinois, in 1840, and became a partner in the House Carpenters of Nauvoo in 1841. Married to Mary Ann Adams, he served as manager of the Farnham Hotel in Salt Lake City, Utah, from 1853. He served again as a missionary in Canada from 1883 to 1884. He died in Salt Lake City in 1884.

ABORTION. The following statement by the **First Presidency** was issued in 1973: "The Church opposes abortion and counsels its members not to submit to or perform an abortion except in the rare cases where, in the opinion of competent medical counsel, the life or good health of the mother is seriously endangered or where pregnancy was caused by rape and produces serious emotional trauma in the mother. Even then it should be done only after counseling with the local presiding priesthood authority and after receiving divine confirmation through prayer."

ACTIVITY. Regular participation in church worship and **callings**. In common usage, an "active" **member** is one who faithfully attends meetings, pays **tithing** and makes fast offerings, follows the **Word of Wisdom**, and in all respects tries to exemplify the standards of the Church. Obviously, there are degrees of activity. *See also* INACTIVITY.

ADOPTION. Young single mothers are encouraged to place newborns in a stable, two-parent home. **LDS Family Services** assists in making adoptive arrangements and provides counseling for the mother. The decision is the mother's. Adopted children may be sealed to parents in the **temple**, thus becoming permanent members of the **family** not only in this life but eternally. *See also* SEALING.

AFRICA. At the end of 2005 there were 237,401 Mormons and 42 **stakes** in sub-Saharan Africa. (The countries of North Africa have not proved congenial to Christian proselytizing.) South Africa contributed early converts and, after a 40-year hiatus, **missionary** proselytizing was resumed there in 1903. Since 1978 missionary work has been promulgated in other African countries where possible, with the greatest success in Nigeria, Ghana, and the Democratic Republic of the Congo. The first black African stake was created at Aba, Nigeria, in 1988. At the end of 2005 there were 11 stakes and 62 **wards** in South Africa, 14 stakes and 109 wards in Nigeria, and 5 stakes and 41 wards in Ghana. Also considered part of the African area for administrative purposes are Madagascar, Mauritius, and Reunion. **Temples** in Africa have been dedicated at Johannesburg, South Africa (1985), Accra, Ghana (2004), and Aba, Nigeria (2005).

AFRICAN AMERICANS. Standard designation for Americans of African ancestry. Since the term obviously does not include the millions who live in Africa or who have emigrated from **Africa** to **Europe** and other countries, or people of African ancestry born in Brazil and elsewhere, the encompassing racial label is **blacks**.

AFTERLIFE. *See* PLAN OF SALVATION.

AMADO, CARLOS H. (1944–). General Authority. Born on 25 September 1944 in Guatemala City, Guatemala, he was 11 when his parents joined the Church. He graduated from a technical college and then worked as a draftsman for four years. From 1965 to 1967 he served as a **missionary** in Peru, then served as branch **president**, **bishop**, **stake** president, and mission president in both Guatemala and El Salvador. He was a **seminary** teacher and then director for the Church Educational System in **Central America**. In 1989, he became a member of the Second **Quorum** of the **Seventy** and in 1992 a member of the First Quorum of the Seventy. He and his wife, Mayavel, have six children.

ANDERSEN, NEIL L. (1951–). General authority. Born on 9 August 1951 in Logan, Utah, he graduated with a bachelor's degree from **Brigham Young University (BYU)**. He earned a master's degree in business from Harvard University. In Florida his business interests included advertising, real estate development, and health care. He served as **stake** president and **president** of the France Bordeaux Mission. In 1993 he was called to serve in the First **Quorum** of the **Seventy** and in 2005 became a member of its presidency. He and his wife, Kathy Sue, are parents of four children.

ANDERSON, RICHARD LLOYD (1926–). Missionary, lawyer, historian. Born in Salt Lake City, Utah, on 9 May 1926, Anderson completed his early education in Utah, became a Navy radioman during World War II, and from 1946 to 1949 served as a missionary in the Northwestern states. Anderson authored *A Plan for Effective Missionary Work*, known as the Anderson Plan, which was widely used in many of the Church's missions in the early 1950s. After receiving a B.A. in History at **BYU** in 1951, Anderson attended Harvard Law School, earning the J.D. degree in 1954. After one year as a **seminary** and **institute of religion** teacher he entered the graduate program in ancient history at the University of California at Berkeley, completing the Ph.D. in 1962. At BYU, Anderson was named honors professor of the year. Teacher of the New Testament, he cultivated a special interest in Paul, leading to a book, *Understanding Paul* (1983). The acknowledged authority on the **witnesses of the *Book of Mormon***, he published many articles and in 1981 a book entitled *Investigating the* Book of Mormon *Witnesses*. He and his wife, Carma, have four children.

ANTHON TRANSCRIPT. Characters copied from the original ***Book of Mormon*** plates shown by **Martin Harris** in February 1828 to Professor Charles Anthon, of Columbia College (later University) in New York City. Anthon declared the characters genuine but, when told of their miraculous origin, recanted his authentication. He later gave two contradictory accounts of the interview. Whatever was said, Harris was sufficiently convinced that he put up most of the funds for the publication of the first edition of the *Book of Mormon* in 1830. The characters of the transcript, as they survive in a handwritten version, have been ridiculed as clumsy scrawls, but parallels have been found in Demotic Egyptian, Old South Arabian, Old North Arabian, Micmac, and a script carved on Olmec baked clay seals.

ANTI-MORMONISM. Rejection of Mormonism's claims is not anti-Mormonism, but militant, repeated, and organized opposition is. The earliest examples occurred just before and soon after the inception of the Church in 1830. Public demonstrations against the early Mormons often degenerated to looting and lynching. Many publications denouncing Mormons were filled with inaccuracies, oversimplification, and stereotyping typical of hate movements in general.

Publications and lectures against the Church can be found during every decade of Mormon history. Showing renewed vigor since the 1960s, anti-Mormonism at its worst is shamefully inaccurate and irresponsible, willing to use any means to accomplish its ends. When anti-Mormons try to document their assertions, they tend to ignore context and the question of typicality. They seem determined to portray Mormons and Mormonism in the worst possible light. In a similar vein, students of anti-Semitism have delineated all the key features of this mentality: scapegoating, obsession, stereotyping, caricaturing, overgeneralizing, and so forth.

Consider the many bases for anti-Mormonism. Atheists and foes of organized religion; those who dislike the Judeo-Christian ethic or belief in God; those who regard all Christians as unacceptable; **Catholics** who reject those outside their own faith; **Protestants**, especially evangelicals, who disapprove of Christians who are not "born again"; ex-Mormons who lash out at the religion they once embraced—from all these groups and sometimes from interaction between them ridicule and hatred gush forth. Short of ceasing to exist, the Latter-day Saints can do nothing that would satisfy their opponents.

A key factor in provoking such opposition is the success, or expansionist thrust, of Mormonism. A religion that was static or dwindling would more likely be ignored. A few individual Mormons have written and spoken out in defense of their faith, and some websites attempt to counter defamation and misrepresentation. However, the Church as such seldom responds to anti-Mormons, preferring to keep attention focused on its positive goals.

APOCRYPHA. The 14 books included in Catholic Bibles but excluded from most Protestant versions. They were included in the original edition of the King James Version as a separate section but later removed. A larger definition of the term would include extra-canonical works produced by early Christians, for which the term *pseudepigrapha* is more commonly used. Since they do not believe in a closed canon, Mormons have been interested in these works. "There are many things contained therein that are true, and it is mostly translated correctly," wrote **Joseph Smith** of the Old Testament apocrypha. "There are many things contained therein that are not true, which are interpolations by the hands of men. . . . Therefore, whoso readeth it, let him understand, for the Spirit manifesteth truth" (***Doctrine and Covenants***, section 91).

APOSTASY. Sometimes called the Great Apostasy. The falling away from the truths, principles, and authority of original **Christianity**. In the Mormon view, the beginnings of this process are discernible in the New Testament itself. At some point, probably as early as the second century, the Christian church no longer adequately represented God's work on earth. Of the multiple "Christianities" none remained pure or true to the original teaching. None had unqualified divine endorsement. Despite their claims, none possessed authority from God.

Any digressions from the teachings of **Jesus Christ**, whether theological under the influence of Greek philosophy or organizational under the influence of Roman law, are seen as manifestations of apostasy. Christians of the late Roman Empire and the Middle Ages were the victims of this process, not necessarily its perpetrators. Despite some individual lives of sincerity and even faithfulness, the Church as an institution was devoid of divine authority. The changes in teachings and ordinances were not minor but fatal.

Protestants of the Reformation era had a similar view of Christian history, differing on their dating of the process and their prescription for a remedy. For Mormons the Great Apostasy preceded the church councils and creeds of the patristic era. Therefore they do not regard those doctrinal pronouncements as authoritative or consistent with the New Testament norm. Most importantly, the loss of the true church in doctrine, organization, **sacraments**, and authority necessitated not a reformation but the **restoration** that occurred beginning with God's call to **Joseph Smith**.

APOSTATE. Someone who has abandoned the faith, especially one who has become belligerent or teaches doctrines condemned by the Church. An "inactive" **member**, one who does not participate in the meetings and programs of the Church, is not so described, and more than a few Church members, after spending some months or even years in **inactivity**, resume participation. The apostasy *from* the Church of an apostate is not the same as the **apostasy** *of* the Church, or the Great Apostasy. *See also* ACTIVITY; APOSTASY.

APOSTLE. *See* TWELVE APOSTLES, QUORUM OF THE.

AREA. Since 1984 the Church has been divided into geographical "areas" for administrative purposes. Division into geographical areas was a response to the growth of Church **membership** in different parts of the world and to the difficulty of coordinating everything from Church headquarters in Salt Lake City, Utah. Presidencies for areas outside the United States and Canada live in their areas, where they devote full time to planning, calling of leaders, training, and supervision.

Areas at the end of 2005 were Africa Southeast, Africa West, Asia, Asia North, Philippines, Pacific Islands, Australia New Zealand/ Pacific Islands, South America South, Chile, South America West,

Brazil North, Brazil South, South America North, Central America, Mexico North, Mexico South, Europe West, Europe North, Europe East, North America Northwest, North America Southwest, North America West, North America Central, North America Northeast, North America East, North America Southeast, Utah North, Utah South, Utah Salt Lake City, Idaho, Europe West, Europe East, and Europe Central areas. Rather than having separate articles on each of these, the present dictionary groups them as follows: **North America**, **Central America and Mexico**, **South America**, **Europe**, **Africa**, **Asia**, and the **Pacific**. The presidency over an area is made up of three members of the **quorums** of the **seventy**. On 1 April 1995 the new administrative position of **area authority seventy** was created and the position of **regional representative** discontinued.

AREA AUTHORITY SEVENTIES. Experienced Church leaders who are members of the third and subsequent **quorums** of the **seventy.** Not designated as **general authorities**, they continue their regular employment and reside in their own homes. They train **stake** presidencies, serve in **area** presidencies, tour **missions**, train mission **presidents**, and complete other assigned duties (*Ensign*, 2004).

ARRINGTON, LEONARD J. (1917–1999). Historian, economist, intellectual leader. Born on 2 July 1917 on a farm near Twin Falls, Idaho, Arrington received a B.A. at the University of Idaho, joined the U.S. Army during World War II, serving in North Africa and Italy, and after the war earned a Ph.D. in economics at the University of North Carolina. His academic appointments were at Utah State University and **BYU**. He had appointments as visiting professor at the University of Bologna and the University of California at Los Angeles (UCLA). Arrington has served as president of the Western History Association, the Agricultural History Society, and the Pacific Coast Branch of the American History Association. In 1986 he was named a fellow of the Society of American Historians.

A leader among loyal Mormon intellectuals, Arrington was founding president of the **Mormon History Association (MHA)** in 1965 and from 1966 was an advisory editor of ***Dialogue: A Journal of Mormon Thought***. In 1972 he was appointed Church historian, serving until

1982 (with a change of title in 1977 to director of History Division), and for 10 years supervised a team of professional historians who produced books, articles, oral histories, and working papers. When this History Division was abolished in 1982, Arrington and his team of historians were transferred to the **Joseph Fielding Smith Institute for Church History** at BYU, which he directed until his retirement in 1987. After 12 more years of productivity, he died in 1999. Arrington influenced a generation of historians working on the Mormon past. See his bibliography as compiled by David J. Whittaker in *Journal of Mormon History* 25 (Fall 1999): 11–45.

ART. Not possessed of elaborate meetinghouses and with a worship service that is simple rather than highly symbolic or liturgical, the Church would not appear to be a likely patron of the arts. Mormon artists, like others, make their way by seeking commissions or selling their work in the private sector. Still, in the visual arts there have been occasions when the Church has been a sponsor. First, architects have designed **ward** meetinghouses and especially **temples**, some of which are architecturally significant. Sculptors have produced works displayed on **Temple Square** or at historic monuments. A series of sculptures known as the Relief Society Monument to Women can be seen in a garden adjacent to the visitors' center at Nauvoo, Illinois. Paintings and murals have been important in the temples. At the end of the 19th century, several Mormon painters were sent to study in France in order to prepare them for this task. Other paintings hang in meetinghouses and visitors centers.

In 1984 the **Museum of Church History and Art** was dedicated in Salt Lake City, Utah. In addition to historical exhibits, it has both standing and temporary exhibits of Mormon art and intermittently holds Church-wide competitions. Hundreds of submissions of paintings, bas-reliefs, weaving, metalwork, and so on are submitted on Mormon religious subjects. Some of the most interesting of these come from areas of the world where the Mormon presence is relatively recent, such as Indonesia or Haiti, where native artistic traditions are employed to convey concepts of the Mormon religion. Besides overtly religious subjects, of course, Mormon artists do portraits, landscapes, pottery, and the like. *See also* LITERATURE; MUSIC.

ARTICLES OF FAITH. Thirteen statements of belief that appeared in an 1842 letter from **Joseph Smith** to John Wentworth, editor of the *Chicago Democrat.* While similar listings had been drafted earlier by **Orson Pratt** and others, this 1842 version became authoritative, as it was later incorporated into the ***Pearl of Great Price*** and thus canonized. For many years Mormon children have memorized these statements as part of their **Primary** training. Often printed on small cards and distributed as a means of introducing Mormonism to interested parties, the Articles of Faith are technically not considered a creed.

1. We believe in God, the Eternal Father, and in His Son, Jesus Christ, and in the Holy Ghost.
2. We believe that men will be punished for their own sins, and not for Adam's transgression.
3. We believe that through the Atonement of Christ, all mankind may be saved, by obedience to the laws and ordinances of the Gospel.
4. We believe that the first principles and ordinances of the Gospel are: first, Faith in the Lord Jesus Christ; second, Repentance; third, Baptism by immersion for the remission of sins; fourth, Laying on of hands for the gift of the Holy Ghost.
5. We believe that a man must be called of God, by prophecy, and by the laying on of hands by those who are in authority, to preach the Gospel and administer in the ordinances thereof.
6. We believe in the same organization that existed in the Primitive Church, namely, apostles, prophets, pastors, teachers, evangelists, and so forth.
7. We believe in the gift of tongues, prophecy, revelation, visions, healing, interpretation of tongues, and so forth.
8. We believe the Bible to be the word of God as far as it is translated correctly; we also believe the *Book of Mormon* to be the word of God.
9. We believe all that God has revealed, all that He does now reveal, and we believe that He will yet reveal many great and important things pertaining to the Kingdom of God.
10. We believe in the literal gathering of Israel and in the restoration of the Ten Tribes; that Zion (the New Jerusalem) will be built upon the American continent; that Christ will

reign personally upon the earth; and, that the earth will be renewed and receive its paradisiacal glory.

11. We claim the privilege of worshiping Almighty God according to the dictates of our own conscience, and allow all men the same privilege, let them worship how, where, or what they may.
12. We believe in being subject to kings, presidents, rulers, and magistrates, in obeying, honoring, and sustaining the law.
13. We believe in being honest, true, chaste, benevolent, virtuous, and in doing good to all men; indeed, we may say that we follow the admonition of Paul—We believe all things, we hope all things, we have endured many things, and hope to be able to endure all things. If there is anything virtuous, lovely, or of good report or praiseworthy, we seek after these things.

While some important aspects of theology are not included in these articles, which is consistent with article 9, the Articles of Faith provide a good point of departure for understanding the Mormon position. Books discussing each of these statements in detail have been published by **James E. Talmage** and **Bruce R. McConkie**.

ASIA. Although there were **missionaries** in India during the1850s, virtually all progress in Asia has occurred since World War II. At the end of 2005, the Asia and North Asia **areas** had 330,770 Mormons, with 63 **stakes**; Taiwan had 42,881 Mormons, 9 stakes, one **temple**; Hong Kong had 22,263 Mormons, 5 stakes, one temple; India had about 6,000 **members** in 26 branches with no official prosleytizing activity; China had less than a thousand members.

The Asia North administrative area is comprised of Korea and Japan. Early missionary efforts in Japan started in 1901 but had negligible results. After World War II, conversions were more numerous, reaching 211 by 1949. Continuing expansion led to the organization of stakes and temples in Tokyo (1980) and Fukuoka (2000). Yoshihiko Kikuchi became a **general authority** in 1977. By the end of 2005 Japan had 121,068 members in 30 stakes and 167 **wards**.

Kim Ho Jik, studying for a doctorate at Cornell University, joined the Church in 1951 and upon returning to South Korea, helped lay the foundations for missionary work in his country. In 1956 two missionaries were sent from Japan. Growing rapidly, the Church in South Korea had its first stake in 1973, with Rhee Ho Nam as **president**. In 1985 a temple was dedicated at Seoul. Han In Sang became the first Korean general authority. At the end of 2005 there were 78,646 Korean members, divided into 17 stakes and 98 wards.

Perhaps the most striking Mormon success in Asia has taken place in the Philippines. The fact that most Filipinos were Christian and many spoke English facilitated proselytizing. The first mission was established in 1967 and the first stake founded in 1973. In 1984 a temple was dedicated in Manila. At the end of 2005 there were 553,121 members in 76 stakes and 466 wards. Over 80 percent of the missionaries in the Philippines are young Filipino men and women. After their missionary experience, they have been a major source of leadership for the Church in the Philippines.

ASSISTANTS TO THE TWELVE. A small group, starting in 1941 with five individuals called as **general authorities** to assist the Quorum of the **Twelve Apostles**. Under the direction of the twelve, they visited **stake conferences** and assisted in directing **missionary** activity. In 1976 this designation was terminated. The functions were assumed by the **quorums** of the **seventy**.

ASSOCIATION FOR MORMON LETTERS (AML). A private organization dedicated to the encouragement of Mormon **literature**. Founded in 1976, the AML holds an annual meeting with papers critically examining Mormon literature, sponsors readings, and gives awards in fiction, poetry, essay, and criticism. A newsletter and an annual publication are received by dues-paying **members**.

AUDITORS. A committee of professional auditors examines church financial records each year and issues a formal statement attesting to the fact that proper procedures are followed and accountability maintained. Businesses owned or controlled by the Church are audited by the Church's internal auditors, independent professional auditing firms, or government regulatory agencies.

AUSTRALIA. *See* PACIFIC.

AUXILIARIES. Organizations within the Church with programs for specific age or gender groups. Developed in response to perceived needs, mostly in the latter half of the 19th century, they have been modified as necessary in the 20th. In principle, the auxiliaries could be abolished, added to, or again modified, and the Church itself would go on. The principal auxiliary organizations are **Relief Society**, **Primary**, **Sunday School**, **Young Men**, and **Young Women**. The **priesthood** is not considered an auxiliary. Although the details of **quorum** organization and age-group divisions are subject to change as directed by **general authorities**, priesthood authority is prerequisite to the Church itself.

– B –

BABBITT, ALMON WHITING (1813–1856). Lawyer, politician, public official. Born in Cheshire, Massachusetts, Babbitt moved to western New York and joined the Church shortly after its organization in 1830. He served as a **missionary** for the Church in New York in 1831, married Julia Ann Hills Johnson in 1833, and served as a missionary for the Church in Canada in 1834, the same year he participated in **Zion's Camp**. Babbitt served as presiding **elder** for the Church in Kirtland, Ohio, in 1840–1841 and as lawyer for the Church in Nauvoo from 1843 to 1845. In 1842 Babbitt attended the University of Cincinnati and served as a member of the Illinois legislature in 1844. In 1945 he served as a member of the committee to petition the federal government on behalf of the Mormons in 1845. After the bulk of the members had evacuated Nauvoo in 1946, Babbitt remained in the city on assignment for the Church to help in selling properties. Chosen as congressional delegate for the provincial state of Deseret in 1849, he worked unsuccessfully for admission of the state into the union. After this service, Babbitt worked as an agent for the territory in Washington and was appointed secretary of Utah Territory, where he served from 1853 to 1856. He worked concurrently as a lawyer in Utah Territory from 1849 to 1856. Babbitt was killed by Cheyennes on his return to Utah in 1856.

BALLANTYNE, RICHARD (1817–1898). Teacher, **Sunday School** organizer. Credited with founding the first Sunday School in Utah at his home on 9 December 1849, Ballantyne was a convert from Scotland who emigrated to Nauvoo, Illinois, in 1843 and subsequently crossed the plains to Utah. In 1853–1854 he preached Mormonism as a **missionary** in Calcutta, India. An astute businessman and supporter of education, Ballantyne lived in Ogden, Utah.

BALLARD, M. RUSSELL (1928–). Businessman and **general authority**. Born in Salt Lake City, Utah, on 8 October 1928, Ballard attended primary and secondary schools as well as the University of Utah. From 1948 to 1950 he served in the British Mission. Outside the Church, Ballard acquired interests in automotive, real estate, and investment businesses, while his Church responsibilities included being a **counselor** in a bishopric, **bishop**, and **stake high councilman**. In 1974 Ballard became **president** of the Canada Toronto Mission. Two years later he was called to the First **Quorum** of the **Seventy**, of which he was a member of the presidency from 1980 to 1985. In October 1985 he became a member of the Quorum of the **Twelve Apostles**. He served on the Missionary Executive Council, Leadership Training, Personnel, and Information Communications Systems committees. He and his wife, Barbara, have seven children.

BAPTISM. Latter-day Saints regard baptism as an essential **ordinance** for entrance into the Kingdom of God, for **membership** in the Church, and as a condition for a remission of sins. Consistent with the original root meaning of the word and the symbolism of death and rebirth, baptism is by complete immersion in water. Infants, incapable of exercising faith, are not baptized. Adult converts who decide to accept Mormonism are baptized. Children who are raised by Mormon parents and instructed are baptized at age eight, considered the age of accountability.

BAPTISM FOR THE DEAD. Baptism of a living person who serves as a proxy for a deceased person. The practice is referred to in 1 Corinthians 15:29, where Paul cites it as evidence for the reality of the resurrection: "Else what shall they do which are baptized for the dead, if the dead rise not at all? why are they then baptized for the dead?" Reinstituted by a revelation to **Joseph Smith** in 1841, baptism for the dead is carried out only in **temples**. The rationale underlying the practice rests on the following propositions: that baptism is essential to salvation, that God would not be so unjust as to condemn someone for failing to accept a gospel never presented to him or her, that preaching and conversion go on in the spirit world, and that baptism, an earthly ordinance, can be accomplished vicariously. It is not believed that post-mortal spirits will be forced to accept immersion, as coerced baptism is contrary to agency, but for those who wish it, the means for satisfying all requirements is established. One result of belief in vicarious work for the dead has been much research in **genealogy** and the establishment of a notable Family History Library.

BATEMAN, MERRILL J. (1936–). Economist, educator, **general authority**. Born on 19 June 1936 in Lehi, Utah, Bateman served as a **missionary** in the British Mission. He earned a bachelor's degree in economics from the University of Utah and a Ph.D. from the Massachusetts Institute of Technology (MIT). After three years on the faculty of the Air Force Academy, he accepted a position as professor of economics and director of the Center for Business and Economic Research at **BYU** in 1967. He was then hired by Mars Corporation and simultaneously acted as consultant for the U.S. Departments of State and Commerce, the World Bank, and other agencies. In 1975 he became dean of the BYU Graduate School of Management and College of Business. He was president of BYU from 1996 to 2003. Bateman served as **bishop**, **stake president**, and **regional representative**. He was called to the Second **Quorum** of the **Seventy** in 1992, as **presiding bishop** in 1994, and to the First Quorum of the Seventy in 1995, becoming a member of its presidency in 2003. In 2007 he was called as president of the Provo Temple. He and his wife, Marilyn, are the parents of seven children.

BAXTER, DAVID S. (1955–). General authority. Born on 7 February 1955 in Stirling, Scotland, Baxter grew up in circumstances of poverty. When **missionaries** knocked on their door, the mother let them come in out of pity. Appreciating the spirit brought by the missionaries, the family studied and then joined the Church. David was not yet 13 when he was baptized in January 1968. The family moved to Surrey, England, and became active members of the **branch** there. David completed his primary education and then matriculated at the University of Wales, where he earned a bachelor's degree in business management in 1976. He was a missionary in Scotland from 1976 to 1978, serving for 10 months on the Shetland Islands. He became a senior executive for British Telecom. At the age of 25, he was called to be **bishop**. He was also **stake president**. From 2002 to 2006 he served as an **area seventy** and was second **counselor** in the presidency of the Europe West area. In April 2006, he was sustained a member of the First **Quorum** of the Seventy. He and his wife, Dianne, have four children.

BECK, JULIE B. (1954–). Counselor in **Young Women** presidency, **Relief Society** general president. Born on 29 September 1954, Beck attended Dixie College and **BYU** where she earned a degree in family science. She served as **ward** Young Women and **Primary** president and counselor in a **stake** Relief Society presidency. She was **called** in April 2007 as Relief Society general president. Julie married Ramon P. Beck in 1970 and they have three children.

BEDNAR, DAVID A. (1952–). Educator, **general authority**. Born on 15 June 1952 in Oakland, California, Bednar earned bachelor's and master's degrees from **BYU** and a Ph.D. from Purdue University. He has held faculty positions in business management at Texas Tech University and the University of Arkansas at Fayetteville, Arkansas. Author of books on organizational behavior, Bednar was named outstanding teacher by the College of Business Administration. He served as a **bishop**, **stake president**, **area authority seventy**, and **regional representative**. After serving as president of **BYU**–Idaho from 1997 to 2004, he became a member of the **Quorum** of the **Twelve Apostles**. He and his wife, Susan, have three sons.

BENNION, LOWELL L. (1908–1996). Educator, humanitarian. After growing up in the Salt Lake City, Utah, area, Bennion graduated from the University of Utah in 1928. He married Merle Colton and one month later departed for a **mission** to Germany. After his mission, joined by his wife, he remained to study at Erlangen, Vienna, and

Strasbourg, completing a doctoral dissertation under Maurice Halbwachs on the methodology of Max Weber.

He briefly worked for the Civilian Conservation Corps—jobs were not plentiful in 1934—before accepting the assignment as director of the **institutes of religion** adjacent to the University of Utah. He taught University of Utah students, ultimately thousands of them, on subjects ranging from the **scripture** to courtship and **marriage**, always with a strong emphasis on practical ethics.

Bennion authored many lesson manuals for use in **seminary** and institute classes, articles for Church magazines, a **Sunday School** manual, and an introductory book for college students entitled *The Religion of the Latter-day Saints*. In 1962 he became assistant dean of students and professor of sociology at the University of Utah. He founded a boys ranch in Idaho that provided a setting where urban youths could have a break from their stressful routine, learn to work in the outdoors, and come under the influence of a kindly mentor.

After retiring from the university, Bennion became executive director of the private Community Services Council, which aided hundreds of indigent and senior citizens. His favorite passage of scripture—Micah 6:8: "What does the Lord require of thee? But to do justly, to love mercy, and to walk humbly with thy God."—was placed on his grave after his death in 1996.

BENSON, EZRA TAFT (1899–1994). Agriculture leader, U.S. secretary of agriculture, **general authority**, Church **president**. Born on 4 August 1899 on a farm in Whitney, Idaho, Benson attended Utah State Agricultural College (now Utah State University), graduated from **BYU**, and earned a master's degree in agricultural economics at Iowa State College. He served as a county agricultural agent and was extension economist and marketing specialist for nine years in Boise with the University of Idaho.

His Church experience included service as a scoutmaster, **missionary** in England, **counselor** in the **stake** presidency, and from 1938 as a stake president in Boise. Becoming executive secretary of the National Council of Farmer Cooperatives in 1939, he moved to Washington, D.C., and became president of the Washington, D.C., Stake. In 1943 he was called to be a member of the **Quorum** of the **Twelve Apostles**. After the war he became president of the European

Mission and supervised a massive distribution of welfare supplies. He was a member of the national executive board of the **Boy Scouts** and received the Silver Beaver, Silver Antelope, and Silver Buffalo awards.

After the election of Dwight D. Eisenhower as president of the United States in1952, Benson was named secretary of agriculture. Under constant criticism, he stayed in office for Eisenhower's two terms, the first clergyman to serve in a cabinet position.

Back in full-time Church service, Benson supervised work in **Europe** (1964–1965) and **Asia** (1968–1971). In 1973, he became president of the Quorum of the Twelve Apostles. Known for his love of country, he warned of the dangers of Communism. When he became Church president in 1985, however, he studiously avoided making narrow political pronouncements. His presidency lasted until his death on 30 May 1994. He emphasized missionary proselytizing and the simplification of programs through **correlation**. He urged people to read the ***Book of Mormon***.

BERNHISEL, JOHN MILTON (MARTIN) (1799–1881). Church leader, territorial delegate. Born in Perry, Cumberland County, Pennsylvania, Bernhisel received a medical certificate from the University of Pennsylvania in 1819. He graduated from the University of Pennsylvania medical department in 1827. He served as attending physician in Herculaneum, Missouri, in 1818 and 1819 and as a general practitioner in Pennsylvania from 1827 to 1832. In 1832, Bernhisel moved his medical practice to New York City and remained there until 1943, when he moved to Nauvoo. Bernhisel joined the **LDS** Church in 1837, during his time in New York. He became a member of the Council of Fifty in 1844. In 1845 he married Julia Ann Haight Van Orden. He remained in Nauvoo during the 1846 **exodus** to try to dispose of property left at the abandonment. He married plural wives Dolly Ranson, Catherine Paine, Fanny Spafford, Melissa Lott Smith, Catherine Burgess Barker, and Elizabeth Barker. He served as Utah territorial congressional delegate from 1851 to 1859 and again from 1861 to 1863. From 1859 through 1861 and from 1863 through 1879 he served as a general medical practitioner in Salt Lake City, Utah. He was also a vice president of Zion's Cooperative Mercantile Institution from 1868 to 1873.

BIBLE. Accepted as **scripture**, the Bible is one of the four standard works. The King James, or Authorized, Version is used in English-speaking countries. Other translations may be consulted for individual study and comparison. For non-English readers the Church decides on the best existing translation for its purpose.

Mormons are quite traditional and even literal in their acceptance of the Bible as the word of God. Although scholars at **BYU** and others are familiar with biblical scholarship, they have been reluctant to accept any criticism that would undermine the authority of the sacred text. Young people study the Bible in **seminary** and **institute** programs. In the adult study course in **Sunday School** both the Old Testament and the New Testament are systematically read and discussed every four years.

During the early 1830s **Joseph Smith** prepared a revision of the Bible by going through a copy of the King James Version and making hundreds of changes and additions. The resulting work was first published in the 1860s. In the majoritarian Mormon Church the JST (Joseph Smith Translation) has never superseded the King James translation, but for comparison the current Church-sponsored editions of the Bible include many of the JST emendations in footnotes and an appendix.

Mormons find themselves in an isolated position. Their approach to the Bible is too literal and traditional for most modern Bible scholars and mainstream Christian churches. Yet **Protestant** evangelicals, themselves literalist and conservative, find it impossible to accept the Mormon concepts of an open canon, continuing revelation, or "inspired" improvements of the sacred text.

BICKERTONITES. After **Joseph Smith**'s assassination in June 1844, one who claimed the right to succeed him as **president** of the Church was **Sidney Rigdon**, a **counselor** in the **First Presidency**. When his proposal was rejected by a nearly unanimous vote of a conference of Church members on 8 August 1844, he moved to Pennsylvania and established his own church. By the time of Rigdon's death in 1876, he had only one disciple left, William Bickerton. Membership of the Bickertonites remained small and was threatened by internal dissension. Thirty-five or 40 families followed Bickerton to Kansas, where their settlement became the town of St. John. The church has continued to grow to approximately 15,000 members, of whom about 3,000 live in the United States. Rejecting not only the Church under **Brigham Young** but also the doctrines and **ordinances** introduced by Joseph Smith at Nauvoo, the Bickertonites accept as **scriptures** the **Bible**, ***Book of Mormon***, and ***Doctrine and Covenants*** in their own edition, including later revelations that were pronounced legitimate by their own presiding authorities. Often designated as the Church of Jesus Christ (Bickertonite), the denomination's official name is "the Church of Jesus Christ with Headquarters in Monongahela, Pennsylvania." *See also* SCHISMS; SUCCESSION.

BIRTH CONTROL. Believing that preexistent spirits are waiting to be born into mortality, Mormon parents have historically had families larger than the American average. Decisions about **family** size are left up to parents, who consider among other things the family's financial resources and the physical and mental health of both the father and mother.

BISHOP. The head of a congregation, or **ward**, the bishop is closer to the level of a pastor or parish priest than to the bishops familiar to **Catholics**, Anglicans, and others. A layman called to preside over his congregation, the bishop is sustained by raised hand at a meeting of **ward** members. This call comes only to a male Latter-day Saint who has demonstrated faithfulness and who passes standards of **worthiness**.

The bishop calls **members** to fill the many lay positions in the ward; determines the worthiness of members for attending the **temple**; visits the sick; counsels; and in general concerns himself with the spiritual and temporal welfare of ward members. He has the assistance of two **counselors**, the three constituting a bishopric. Also assisting are an executive secretary, a ward clerk, and usually assistant clerks. Working in close conjunction with the bishop to meet the needs of ward members is the female president of the **Relief Society**.

Although men who serve are ordained as bishops, service as a bishop of a particular ward is temporary. Since the position pays no salary, a bishop continues his regular vocation. After a few years the bishop is released along with his two counselors, to be then replaced by another ward member called to this responsibility. *See also* CALLING; SUSTAINING.

BLACKS. In the 19th century, Mormons had little interaction with blacks. Although identified with abolitionism to some extent, which contributed to their persecutions by pro-slavery Missourians, Mormons did not take a consistent anti-slavery position, and among those who settled Utah before the Civil War there were a few slave holders. With few exceptions, **African Americans** were eligible for **membership** in the Church but not for **priesthood** and leadership. Only a few African Americans became Latter-day Saints during the first century and a half of the Church's history.

Although members speculated on the doctrinal reasons for the failure to ordain blacks, President David O. McKay said that it was a practice rather than a doctrine. Presently available evidence indicates that some **general authorities** like McKay's **counselor** Hugh B. Brown would like to have seen the policy changed. He gave talks indicating that the Church believed in full civil rights for all people, including blacks.

A great divide occurred in 1978, when President **Spencer W. Kimball**, with the support of his counselors and the **twelve apostles**, proclaimed that "every faithful, worthy man in the Church" (with no exclusion based on race) might hold the priesthood (***Doctrine and Covenants***, official declaration 2). Since then proselytizing has been carried out in several countries in **Africa**. In the United States, Brazil, Zaire, Nigeria, various European countries, and elsewhere, blacks have joined the Church, served as **missionaries**, participated in **ordinances** of the **temple**, and filled leadership positions. Since membership records do not indicate race, it is impossible to give the exact number of black members. *See also* GENESIS GROUP.

BLESSING OF INFANTS. An **ordinance** or ceremony in which the infant is brought to church by the parents and, during a Sunday meeting, given a name and a blessing. A group of **priesthood** holders form a circle, with one priest holding the baby, and a designated person, usually the father, formally declares the child's name and pronounces words of blessing to be enjoyed during the course of the child's life on condition of faithfulness. Infants are not eligible for **baptism**.

BONNEVILLE INTERNATIONAL CORPORATION. A corporation of Church-owned radio and television stations, including KSL in Salt Lake City, Utah. Other television and radio stations have been acquired and a production/advertising company created. As commercial enterprises, these all pay taxes. They do not proselytize but do broadcast public service announcements promoting **family** and community values.

BOOK OF COMMANDMENTS. First compilation of the **revelations** of **Joseph Smith** in published book form. A printing press had been established in Independence, Missouri, and in December 1832 the book was at press. Before the entire book could be printed, a mob stormed the printing office, destroyed the press and type, and scattered what had been printed. Some of the printed sheets were salvaged and later bound. Many of the revelations had already been published in *Evening and Morning Star*, a Church newspaper. In 1835, a larger collection of the revelations was published as ***Doctrine and Covenants***.

BOOK OF MORMON. One of the four canonical or standard works of **scripture** of the Church. First published in 1830 in English, the *Book of Mormon* has since appeared in many editions, including translations into other languages (77 in its entirety, 28 others in an abbreviated version entitled *Selections*). Although listed on the 1830 title page as "author," **Joseph Smith** consistently declared that the work was a translation from hieroglyphic inscriptions on ancient metal plates. Since he made no pretense of understanding the "reformed," or modified, Egyptian language, the process was possible only "by the gift and power of God."

Recounting the experiences of an Israelite colony that migrated from Jerusalem around 600 BC, the *Book of Mormon* tells of their settlement in the Western Hemisphere; their divisions; their wars, prophets, and religious teachings. After his death and resurrection in Jerusalem, **Jesus Christ** appeared to these "other sheep" and gave them a condensed version of his ministry as recounted in the **Bible**. After a period of peace and harmony these people degenerated once again, participated in a series of bloody wars, and finally clashed in a struggle in which one major group was exterminated.

The survivors were among the ancestors of those later identified as the American Indians. One of the final **prophets**, **Mormon**, abridged a vast quantity of earlier records; it is the abridger's proper name that gives the title to the book as a whole. One of the "books" within the *Book of Mormon* also gives a highly compressed version of the history of an earlier colony that migrated to the Western Hemisphere as early as the third millennium BC.

On this historical framework, selective and "abridged" from more complete records, the *Book of Mormon* presents its religious message. At its heart is the repeated presentation, by anticipatory prophecy or later preaching, of Jesus Christ and his saving gospel as the divine means provided for human salvation. Looking forward to a future time, thought by Mormons to be the "dispensation" that started with Joseph Smith in the 19th century, the book also foretells the gathering of the Jews to Israel, the redemption of other tribes of Israel, and the **restoration** of the Christian gospel.

Critics began to ridicule the *Book of Mormon* even before it was published and continued afterward. It was denounced as a patent forgery, full of references to 19th-century concerns. Its use of an English style borrowed from the Authorized, or King James, Version of the Bible and undisguised lengthy quotations from Isaiah and the Sermon on the Mount were pointed to as obvious giveaways. References to horses, elephants, and steel were trumpeted as anachronisms. Mark Twain, unimpressed, called it "chloroform in print." Two major obstacles prevent many modern people from taking the book seriously. Those from Christian backgrounds, especially **Protestants**, proclaim the Bible to be unique as scripture and on the face of it cannot accept the claims of an additional scripture. Those of a secular bent, increasingly numerous, find it impossible to think in terms of prophets, angels, and an intervening God.

Such obstacles notwithstanding, the *Book of Mormon* has a rather impressive record. Those who read it prayerfully and carefully testify in large numbers that it teaches them, inspires them, and speaks peace to their souls. Their conviction that it is true, they say, comes from the Holy Ghost. It continues to be taught in adult **Sunday School** classes on a regular basis along with the other standard works.

Non-Mormon reaction continues, on the whole, to be negative. Archaeologists and anthropologists find no support for a Hebrew population in the Western Hemisphere. Other critics emphasize the environment of 19th-century New York as the formative matrix for the book. Against this, Mormon scholars continue their work on several parallel paths, including the Near Eastern setting of the first 40 pages of the *Book of Mormon*; the possible geographical fit of the book's account with actual places in the Western Hemisphere; refuting or explaining the claimed anachronisms; studying the book's proper names against their alleged background; discovering Hebraisms through analysis of the book's complex literary forms, including poetry, sermons, speeches, letters, typology, and others; and highlighting cultural and biological evidences of ancient contact between the earth's two hemispheres. Of particular interest has been the discovery of several outstanding examples of chiasmus (a parallel pattern of Near Eastern origins following the structure a-b-c-c-b-a). Defenders of the *Book of Mormon* find it implausible that a 23-year-old of Joseph Smith's minimal educational background could have produced such a work. *See also* INSTITUTES OF RELIGION; MAXWELL, NEAL A.; NATIVE AMERICANS.

BOOK OF REMEMBRANCE. A volume of **family** records containing **genealogy**, **patriarchal blessings**, personal histories, biographies, or autobiographies. Encouraged to keep such records, **members** of the Church are also motivated by an interest in genealogy.

BOY SCOUTS. In 1913, just a few years after the beginning of the Scouting movement, the Church began sponsoring troops. Soon the percentage of participation by Mormon boys in Scouting far exceeded the national average. In the United States Mormons are a prominent and respected component of the Boy Scouts of America. In other countries, where possible, troops are sponsored in conjunction with the Scouting organizations there.

BRANCH. A congregation presided over by a branch **president** and two **counselors.** Either because the group is too small or because no **stake** has been organized in the surrounding area, a branch is not raised to the status of a **ward.** It is a ward in embryo, awaiting the necessary conditions.

BRANNAN, SAMUEL (1819–1889). Church leader, **apostate**, businessman. Samuel Brannan was an apostate Mormon who led a group to California, helping to found San Francisco. Born in Saco, Maine, Brannan was converted to Mormonism as a teenager and worked as a printer's apprentice in Kirtland, Ohio. In 1844 this early experience, which had been reinforced by work on newspapers, helped qualify him to assist in editing *The Prophet*, a Mormon newspaper in New York City. He got into trouble with Church authorities for the unauthorized, premature preaching of **polygamy**. After being disfellowshipped, he was reinstated and assisted **Parley P. Pratt** in editing *The Messenger*.

In 1846, while **Brigham Young** led the main body of Mormons overland to the mountain West, Brannan led 238 Mormons aboard the ship *Brooklyn*, which sailed around Cape Horn. On July 29 the *Brooklyn* arrived at Yerba Buena (San Francisco). Brannan and his group founded a community, which they called New Hope. He published the first newspaper and preached the first sermon in the new settlement. In June 1847 he received a letter from Brigham Young stating the intention of the Church leaders to establish a settlement in the Great Basin, not in California. Brannan traveled overland to meet Young and try to convince him of the advantages of the coastal location. Unsuccessful, he returned and used his powers of persuasion on discharged members of the **Mormon Battalion**, urging the advantages of the beautiful California location over the rigors of the Rocky Mountains.

In 1849 Brannan became a promoter of gold mining, thus contributing to the great Gold Rush. Investing in hotels, shipping, and construction, he became California's first millionaire. When asked for a generous contribution to Young and the Church, he refused. Two years later he was **excommunicated** for unchristianlike conduct and neglect of duty. Also cited as a cause of action was his active role in founding a vigilante committee in San Francisco.

In 1859 Brannan established Calistoga, a 2,000-acre ranch, in Napa Valley, California. In addition to raising Merino sheep and beautiful horses he distilled brandy from the harvest of the extensive vineyards. For a few years Brannan seemed to prosper, but he also appeared bent on self-destruction. In 1868 Brannan was wounded in a property argument. Then affairs provoked a divorce suit from his wife, which forced a liquidation of his property holdings. Brannan's alcoholism became more and more severe. After an ambitious plan to colonize Sonora in northern Mexico failed, Brannan became impoverished and spent his final years partially paralyzed and suffering from arthritis. In 1889 he died a pauper.

BRIGHAM YOUNG UNIVERSITY (BYU). Founded at Provo, Utah, in 1875 as the Brigham Young Academy, this institution was named a university in 1903. During the first half of the 20th century its growth was slow but steady. After World War II, BYU experienced spectacular growth, from 1,500 students in 1945 to 25,000 by 1970. A cap enrollment of 27,000 was then established, though the enrollment has reached more than 30,000.

Like other universities, BYU publishes a catalogue that describes its many colleges: Biology and Agriculture; Education; Engineering and Technology; Family, Home, and Social Sciences; Fine Arts and Communications; Humanities; Nursing; Physical and Mathematical Sciences; and Physical Education. There is also a law school and a school of management. BYU is accredited by the Northwest Association of Schools and Colleges. The special aura that sets BYU apart from most other universities is religious. Over 90 percent of the student body and faculty are Mormon. All faculty and students, Mormon and non-Mormon alike, are expected to adhere to an honor code that includes abstinence from tea, coffee, alcohol, and tobacco in keeping with the **Word of Wisdom**. Students are required to take classes in religion. In addition, student **wards,** organized for religious worship, also function as support groups.

Questions of academic freedom have arisen occasionally. One flurry occurred in 1910–1911 over the modernist views of a few professors, three of whom were forced to resign. In the early 1990s sociologists and historians raised questions about the attitude of the university toward their research and participation in certain popular organizations. A statement of the university's position on academic freedom sought to allay fears. The great majority of subjects—mathematics, agriculture, nursing, chemistry, foreign languages, management, and others—raise no problems. As for the rest, both students and faculty are fully aware before going there of BYU's basic commitment to the sponsoring Church. In addition to its on-campus programs, the university sponsors a large, successful distant learning program, with more than 600 courses for students in all parts of the world.

BRIGHAM YOUNG UNIVERSITY–HAWAII (BYU–Hawaii). Founded at Laie on the north shore of Oahu in 1955, the institution was known as the Church College of Hawaii until 1974. BYU–Hawaii offers bachelor's degrees in business, education, information sciences, social sciences, and psychology. Academic programs fall under the College of Arts and Sciences (in addition to traditional majors such as history, English, and political science, there are majors in exercise and sport science, Hawaiian studies, and social work); School of Business (including majors in accounting, hospitality and tourism, and international business); School of Computing; and School of Education (training primary and secondary teachers). In December 2006, BYU–Hawaii's total enrollment of 2,492 students included 1,141 international students, largely from the **Pacific** islands and **Asia**. A large percentage of students are able to pay tuition costs by part-time employment at the adjoining **Polynesian Cultural Center**. Students agree to follow a basic code of behavior and to take required religion classes. BYU–Hawaii is accredited by the Western Association of Schools and Colleges.

BRIGHAM YOUNG UNIVERSITY–IDAHO (BYU–Idaho). Formerly known as **Ricks College**, the institution adopted its current name on 10 August 2001. A four-year institution with degree programs, BYU–Idaho has a cap enrollment of 11,600 students at any one time but during the year serves 15,000 students, who come from all 50 states and more than 50 countries. Students may earn an associate's degree or a bachelor's degree. Most majors require an internship. Academic departments are divided into the following colleges: Agriculture and Life Sciences; Business and Communication; Education and Human Development; Language and Letters; Performing and Visual Arts; Physical Sciences and Engineering.

Restructuring in the interest of efficiency and cutting the cost of education, BYU–Idaho abolished its intercollegiate athletics programs. Instead students were to become participants in the Activities Program, with six core areas: outdoor, service, talent, fitness, sports, and social. A three-semester schedule was adopted to take advantage of campus facilities throughout the year. BYU–Idaho is accredited by the Northwest Commission on Colleges and Universities.

BRIGHAM YOUNG UNIVERSITY STUDIES. A refereed scholarly periodical established at **BYU** in 1959 and published quarterly. Usually called simply *BYU Studies*, this "voice for the community of **LDS** scholars" has included bibliographies, essays, poetry, fiction, and articles from the various disciplines of the humanities and social sciences. Especially prominent have been articles on Mormon history, including primary documents. The journal sponsors the website ldsfaq.byu.edu, which answers over 400 questions about Mormonism.

BROOKS, JUANITA (1898–1989). Folklorist, historian. Born in Bunkerville, Nevada, Brooks experienced the hardships of the frontier as well as the closeness to nature of her rural setting. She became a schoolteacher in Mesquite, an adjacent community, and in 1919 married Ernest John Pulsipher, who died in early 1921. Brooks attended **BYU**, graduating in 1925. She took a position at Dixie Junior College in St. George, Utah, where for a generation she taught English and debate. Later she earned an M.A. degree from Columbia University. In 1933 she married a widower, Sheriff Will Brooks.

As president of the **Relief Society** in her **stake**, Brooks supervised a project of typing early pioneer diaries for preservation. She became a field representative for the Huntington Library and was a major force in building up a Mormon collection there. Over a generation of productivity, often stealing time for writing from her household duties, Brooks produced biographies, a history of Jews in Utah, a memoir, and a thorough study of the **Mountain Meadows Massacre**. She received an honorary doctorate from the University of Utah and a distinguished service award from the Utah Academy.

BROTHER AND SISTER. In addition to the usual biological meaning of these terms, Mormons use them as forms of address for other members of the Church, as in "Brother Smith" or "Sister Hernandez."

The terms connote a feeling of fraternal closeness to fellow Church members. In the strict sense, as children of the one Heavenly Father, all humans are brothers and sisters. *See also* FORMS OF ADDRESS.

BROWN, HUGH B. (1883–1975). Lawyer, educator, **general authority**. Born in Utah on 24 October 1883, Brown was essentially a Canadian, for his family moved to Alberta when he was only six years old. He married Zina Young Card in 1908 and became a major in the Canadian Army during World War I. After studying law, Brown became a barrister and solicitor in Lethbridge, Alberta, as well as **president** of the Lethbridge **Stake**. In 1927 he moved his family to Salt Lake City, Utah, and joined a prominent law firm. Two years later he became president of the Granite Stake.

Politically, Brown was a Democrat. During the 1930s he served as state chairman of the Democratic Party and, after an unsuccessful bid for the U.S. Senate, was appointed chairman of the State Liquor Commission. In 1937 he was called as president of the British Mission. He supervised the downsizing of the mission during World War II, served as coordinator of **LDS** servicemen, and resumed presidency of the mission after the war.

In 1946 he took a position as professor of religion at **BYU**. In 1953 he was called to be one of the **assistants to the twelve**, and in 1958 was named to the **Quorum** of the **Twelve Apostles**. In 1961 he became a **counselor** in the **First Presidency**. An important participant in the expansion associated with the presidency of **David O. McKay**, Brown repeatedly emphasized Church support of civil rights for all Americans, though ordination of **blacks** to the **priesthood** came only later.

BROWN, S. KENT (1940–). Scholar. Born 1 October 1940 in Murray, Utah, Brown earned a bachelor's degree in classical Greek with a minor in Near Eastern languages at the University of California at Berkeley in 1967, followed by a Ph.D. in religious studies from Brown University. Since 1971 he has been a professor of ancient scripture at **BYU**. In 1978 and 1979 Brown was a fellow of the American Research Center in Egypt. In the mid-1980s, he led a project to microfilm more than 1,500 ancient Christian manuscripts in Cairo and Jerusalem. From 1993 to 1996 he was director of the BYU

Jerusalem Center. The author of many articles and several books, Brown was a managing editor for *The Coptic Encyclopedia* and an editor for the *Encyclopedia of Mormonism.* He is director of the **Foundation for Ancient Research and Mormon Studies (FARMS)** and editor of the *Journal of* Book of Mormon *Studies*. His Church **callings** include serving as **bishop** twice and **stake president**. He and his wife, Gayle, have five children.

BURTON, H. DAVID (1938–). Businessman, presiding **bishop**. Born on 26 April 1938 in Salt Lake City, Utah, Burton graduated with a bachelor's degree in economics from the University of Utah and then earned a master's degree in business administration from the University of Michigan. He became a **high councilor**, **stake president**, and for 14 years secretary to the **presiding bishopric**. In 1992 he became first **counselor** in the Presiding Bishopric and in 1996 was sustained as presiding bishop. He and his wife, Barbara, are parents of five children.

BYBEE, ARIEL (1943–). Mezzo-soprano. Born 9 January 1943 in Reno, Nevada, Bybee is a graduate of **BYU** and also studied at the University of Southern California. At the Metropolitan Opera in New York City, she performed in a variety of operatic roles.

– C –

CALLING. The basis of service in the Church, a lay organization relying on volunteers for its functioning. **General authority**, **stake president**, **bishop**, **Relief Society** president, **ward** librarian, home teacher, **missionary**, scoutmaster, teacher of 10-year-olds in **Primary**—all of these are callings. **Active** Church **members** fill many callings during the course of their lives. Although time-consuming, callings are to be performed conscientiously and willingly. Many attest to the value of experiences that without accepting callings they would not have had.

Two characteristics of callings deserve explanation. First, they come from the top down. It is the bishop who must staff the many positions in his ward by issuing calls to ward members. **Presidents** of stakes, general authorities, and **area** authorities similarly staff positions in the areas of their assigned jurisdiction. The expectation is that loyal Church members will respond affirmatively when asked to fulfill a specific responsibility. One does not apply. Second, callings are temporary. With the exception of the 15 general authorities who make up the **First Presidency** and the **Quorum** of the **Twelve Apostles**, callings are for a limited period of time. Full-time missionaries serve for 18 months, two years, or, in the case of mission presidents, three years. Other positions are more flexible in their duration.

The conception of the calling occasions some adjustment for those who are accustomed to the upward mobility of business and government. In the Church, empire building is not welcomed. One who has been a bishop or stake president can suddenly find that his calling is that of a choir director or **Sunday School** teacher. Those who have seen Mormon missionaries in different locations may not be aware that missions, too, are callings. One may indicate a willingness to serve and must pass standards of **worthiness**, but the call itself comes from Church headquarters, at which time one discovers where the missionary service will be. *See also* MISSIONARY PROGRAM.

CANADA. *See* NORTH AMERICA.

CANNON, ELAINE A. (1922–2003). Journalist, author, **Young Women** leader. Born in Salt Lake City, Utah, on 9 April 1922, Cannon grew up and attended school there. Starting as a teenager, she wrote a daily column for the ***Deseret News*** and edited the women's section. In 1942 she married D. James Cannon and became the mother of six children. She became a radio artist for both NBC and CBS while locally hosting a TV talk show. She wrote for national magazines like *Better Homes and Gardens* and *Seventeen.* From 1950 to 1954 she served on the president's White House Committee on Children and Youth. For the Church magazine ***The Improvement Era*** she coedited with **Marion D. Hanks** a section addressed to youth. In 1960 she was named to the general board of Young Women and from 1978 to 1984 served as general president. In the 1980s she was vice-president of the National Council of Women. She wrote many self-help and inspirational books as well as one on Mormon artist Minerva Teichert.

CANNON, FRANK JENNE (1859–1933). Newspaperman, politician, territorial delegate, U.S. senator. A son of George Q. Cannon and Martha Jenne Cannon, Cannon grew up in Salt Lake City, Utah. He served as a reporter for the *San Francisco Chronicle* in 1880. In 1882 he was appointed deputy clerk and recorder for the city of Ogden, Utah. He moved to Washington, D.C., in 1883, and during 1883 and 1884 he served as private secretary for territorial delegate John T. Caine. Returning to Ogden, Cannon was elected county recorder for Weber County in 1882. From 1887 to 1893 he served as editor of the *Ogden Herald*, a Mormon-affiliated newspaper. In 1886 he wrote *Life of Joseph Smith the Prophet*, but because of a controversy concerning his personal life, the authorship was attributed to his father, George Q. Cannon. After the 1891 division of the Mormon people into the two national political parties, Cannon served as delegate to the Republican National Convention in 1892. In 1894 he was elected as Utah's territorial delegate to Congress, and he served from 1895 until Utah's admission as a state in 1896. In 1896 the legislature elected Cannon as one of Utah's first senators, and under the system then in force, he served four years from 1896 to 1900. In 1896 he bolted the Republican Party to support the Silver Republican Ticket in opposition to the Gold Standard and William McKinley's election. He remained in the Republican Party during his senatorial term, but in 1900 he joined the Democrats and served as chair of the Utah state Democratic Party convention in 1900. In 1902 he was elected chair of the Utah state Democratic Party, and in 1903 he served as editor of a Democratic Party organ, the *Utah State Journal*. He served as delegate to the national Democratic Party convention in 1904.

In 1905 Cannon broke with the **LDS** Church and became editor of the *Salt Lake Tribune*, which was then owned by Thomas Kearns and a virulently anti-Mormon journal. This led to his **excommunication** from the LDS Church. He moved to Denver, Colorado, in 1909 to serve as editor of the *Rocky Mountain News*. In 1911 he and Harvey J. O'Higgins published an attack on church **president** Joseph F. Smith in *Under the Prophet in Utah*, which he followed up in 1913 with *Brigham Young and His Mormon Empire.* In 1878 Cannon married Martha Brown. He died in Denver in 1933.

CANNON, GEORGE Q. (1827–1901). Journalist, delegate to Congress, **general authority**. Born on 11 January 1827 in Liverpool, England, Cannon was a teenager in 1842 when his family was converted to Mormonism by his uncle **John Taylor**. They emigrated to Nauvoo, Illinois. Left an orphan by the death of his mother during the journey and of his father shortly after their arrival, George was taken in by John Taylor and assisted him in editing the ***Times and Seasons***.

After crossing the plains during the Mormon **exodus**, Cannon was sent to mine gold in California in 1849 and the following year was called as a **missionary** to Hawaii. He mastered the Hawaiian language and, with his fellow missionaries, succeeded on converting many natives to the Church. With assistance, he translated the ***Book of Mormon*** into the Hawaiian language.

Returning to the mainland, Cannon married Elizabeth Hoagland, published the *Book of Mormon* in Hawaiian at San Francisco, and edited the Mormon newspaper *Western Standard.* In 1858 he was named editor of the ***Deseret News***. He was assigned to provide information to newspaper editors and preside over Latter-day Saints in the eastern states. In 1860, he was ordained a member of the **Quorum** of the **Twelve Apostles** and sent to England to preside over the European Mission, returning in 1864. In 1872 he was elected delegate to Congress from Utah Territory.

A **polygamist**, Cannon was expelled from Congress in 1882 for violating the new Edmunds Act. In 1888 he was imprisoned for unlawful cohabitation; like other Mormons in the same situation, he saw himself "a prisoner for conscience' sake." He owned a publishing company and was a director of several businesses. He was a **counselor** to Presidents **Brigham Young**, John Taylor, **Wilford Woodruff**, and **Lorenzo Snow**.

CANNON, MARTHA HUGHES (1857–1932). Physician, politician. Martha Hughes Cannon was the second daughter of Peter Hughes and Elizabeth Evans. Shortly after Cannon's birth in Wales her family joined the Church of Jesus Christ of Latter-day Saints and emigrated to the United States in 1858. After a two-year stay in New

York City, due to the poor health of her father, the family then emigrated to Utah. Her sister, Annie, died during the overland journey while her father died three days after reaching the Salt Lake Valley. Her mother remarried James P. Paul, a widower with four children of his own.

At a very young age, Cannon displayed unusual intelligence and strong individuality. She always dreamed of becoming a doctor and constantly worked toward this goal. At 14, with apparently little education, Cannon began teaching school. Unfortunately, she experienced difficulty in maintaining discipline with some of the bigger students. The following year she found a job as a typesetter for the ***Deseret News*** and the *Woman's Exponent*. Cannon saved almost all of her money and applied it to her medical school fund. Eventually, she enrolled in the University of Deseret (University of Utah) in preparation for medical school. In 1878, she entered the medical school at the University of Michigan. She received her M.D. in 1880 and continued her education at the University of Pennsylvania and the National School of Elocution and Oratory. Cannon returned to Salt Lake City, Utah, and opened a private medical practice. She also worked as a resident doctor at the Deseret Hospital. While at the hospital, she met her future husband, Angus Cannon, a member of the board of directors and **president** of the Salt Lake Stake. In 1884, she married Cannon, becoming his fourth wife. Cannon lived abroad during each of her pregnancies to prevent her husband from going to jail. She lived in England between 1886 and 1887 and used the services of many facilities in France, England, and Switzerland.

Cannon worked in the political sphere as well. She constantly championed women's voting rights for various suffrage organizations. In one of the most dramatic state senator races, Martha, one of five Democratic candidates, vied for one of five senatorial seats. Her husband ran for the same seats on the Republican ticket. The Cannons did not directly run against each other, and each could possibly have gained a seat in the state senate. Only Martha garnered this prize. While in the position, she introduced many important and progressive acts of legislation that included a bill establishing the State Board of Health, the Pure Food Law, and the State School for the Deaf, Dumb, and Blind. She also served as a member of the State Board of Health, the board of directors of the State Deaf and Dumb

Institute, and vice president of the American Congress of Tuberculosis. In 1915 her husband of thirty-one years died in Salt Lake City. The last twelve years of her life, Cannon worked at the Graves' Clinic in Los Angeles. She died in Los Angeles on 10 July 1932.

CANNON, SYLVESTER Q. (1877–1943). Businessman, engineer, **general authority**. A son of **George Q. Cannon**, Sylvester was born on 10 June 1877 in Salt Lake City, Utah. His graduation from the University of Utah was followed by completion of an engineering degree at MIT. From 1899 to 1902 he served as a **missionary** in the Netherlands and Belgium. In 1904 he married Winifred Saville.

After directing a land and irrigation survey of Weber River in Utah, Cannon returned to Holland as mission **president** for two years. From 1912 to 1925 he was engineer for Salt Lake City. Among the projects he supervised was a major reservoir and control of air pollution. He was **counselor** in a **stake** presidency and in 1917 became president of the Pioneer Stake. In 1925 he was named **presiding bishop**, thus a key figure in the administration of **Heber J. Grant**. Among many other construction projects Cannon supervised plans for the construction of the Idaho Falls Temple. In 1939 he joined the ranks of the **Quorum** of the **Twelve Apostles**.

CARD, ORSON SCOTT (1951–). Writer. Born in Richland, Washington, Card served as a **missionary** in Brazil. He earned degrees at **BYU** and the University of Utah. Best known for his science fiction, Card received the Hugo and Nebula awards for best novel in 1986 and 1987. A series of American fantasy, the Alvin Maker series, is set in a magical version of the American frontier and contains many parallels and echoes of the **prophet Joseph Smith**. His Homecoming Saga recasts Mormon **scripture** as science fiction. A novelized historical biography *Saints* touches upon many events of early Mormon history. *A Storyteller in Zion* presents the challenges of being a writer in the Mormon culture setting. Several contemporary novels emphasize character and moral dilemmas. Card's works have been translated into Catalan, Danish, Dutch, Finnish, French, Polish, Japanese, and other languages. He and his wife, Kristine, live in Greensboro, North Carolina. They have five children.

CARMACK, JOHN K. (1931–). Lawyer, businessman, **general authority**. Born on 10 May 1931 in Winslow, Arizona, Carmack was a **missionary** in the West Central States Mission and served in the U.S. Army during the Korean War. He received a B.A. degree from **BYU** and a law degree from UCLA. Carmack was a legislative assistant in the California legislature, president of a Los Angeles law firm, and president of the Westwood Bar Association. In West Los Angeles he was chairman of the board of the Chamber of Commerce and member of the executive council for Los Angeles council of Boy Scouts of America.

In the Church, Carmack was a **bishop**'s **counselor**, **high councilor**, **stake** president, **regional representative**, and **president** of the Idaho Boise Mission. In 1984 he became a member of the First **Quorum** of the **Seventy**. Named an emeritus general authority in 2001, Carmack was named director of the Perpetual Education Fund.

CATHOLICISM. Although neither group accepts the ultimate authority claims of the other, Mormons and Catholics are similar in their insistence on the need for legal authority in the church; on the importance of **sacraments**, or **ordinances**; and on basic social values. Despite examples of cooperation and sometimes even mutual admiration, however, opinions of one another have not always been positive. The Mormon perception of Catholicism has sometimes been very critical because most converts to Mormonism come from **Protestant** backgrounds with a traditional anti-Catholic animus. At the same time, until the breakthroughs in Central and South America, predominantly Catholic countries proved especially unreceptive to the Mormon message. These two details explain both the make-up of the Mormon population and the frustrations encountered by Mormon proselytizing. It is not entirely surprising, then, to find references in some early Mormon sermons and writings to the tyranny of the pope and the superstition of Catholics. Biblical expressions such as "whore of Babylon," which Protestants had long put to polemical purposes against the Catholic Church, were repeated by some Mormons, along with counterparts in the Mormon scriptures such as "the great and abominable church." Some Mormon accounts of the Great **Apostasy** were in effect indictments of historical Catholicism.

Since the latter part of the 20th century the attitude toward Catholics has considerably softened. In 1958 a reference by a Mormon **general authority** to the Catholic Church as "most abominable above all other churches" was removed in a revised edition of the book. Articles in Mormon magazines more carefully described the apostasy as occurring in the first and second centuries, exculpating later Catholics, who were victims, not villains. Some publications even began emphasizing the many basic points on which Mormons and Catholics agreed or at least shared similar positions. Contributing to the more amicable attitude are the proselytizing successes in largely Catholic countries; an awareness that Mormons and Catholics can make common cause against an overwhelmingly secular world; and more sophisticated historical and theological scholarship that discourages the demonizing of such a large part of Christianity.

Catholic views of Mormons remain negative. Rome sees Mormons as one of the "sects," or "**cults**," which a more neutral usage has labeled "new religious movements." Catholic works on Mormons are few and range from the irresponsible and inaccurate to a few works containing fairly reliable history and sociology.

CELIBACY. Mormons do not consider celibacy a requirement for the **priesthood**. Indeed, the married state is considered to be on a higher level and essential to the highest degree of salvation. On the other hand, in the sense of abstinence from sexual intercourse as long as one is unmarried, celibacy is in fact an expectation. *See also* MARRIAGE.

CENTRAL AMERICA AND MEXICO. In 1875 the first Mormon **missionaries** entered Mexico and arranged for the publication of a pamphlet in Spanish. A few converts were made, but most of them were unsteady. The next phase occurred with the colonization of northern Mexico by Anglo Mormons. Many of these settlers were driven out during the Mexican Revolution, but some of them returned. A few hundred native Mexicans rallied to the Mormon religion as well.

After World War II the Church grew rapidly. Many young Mexicans were instructed in Church-owned schools and served as **missionaries**. **Stakes** and **wards** were organized. A **temple** was built in

Mexico City in 1983. At the end of 2005 there were 1,043,718 **members** in 206 stakes and 1,408 wards with 12 temples. Not until 1947 did missionaries enter Guatemala. By the end of 2005 there were 200,537 members in 40 stakes and 236 wards, and a temple was constructed in 1984. Other Central American countries also saw rather dramatic increases. At the end of 2005 membership totals were as follows:

Country	Members	Stakes
Costa Rica	33,036	5
El Salvador	94,296	16
Honduras	116,416	20
Nicaragua	52,184	7
Panama	40,897	7

CENTRO ESCOLAR BENEMERITO DE LAS AMERICAS. Church-owned preparatory school on the northern outskirts of Mexico City founded in 1963. Starting with 15 teachers and 125 students, the school had 120 teachers and 2,100 students in 1999. Housing is provided for 1,065 students. **Seminary** classes are taken by all students. The library contains 90,000 volumes. In addition to college preparatory courses, many students participate in sports or artistic pursuits. Sponsored performing groups include the Banda de Guerra, Porristas, the Rondalla, the Symphony Orchestra, the Choir, and Ballet Folklorico. In 1994 the Agricultural Institute was established, a one-year program in horticulture. About 80 percent of the students continue their education on the university level.

CHAPLAINS. During World War I, **B. H. Roberts** was a chaplain in the Utah National Guard and later one of three chaplains with the American troops in France. During World War II, 46 Mormon chaplains served. Mormon chaplains have continued to serve with the U.S. military, holding general worship services, counseling with military personnel, and performing duties for Latter-day Saint military personnel. In 1995 Kay Schwendiman, former chaplain for the 96th Army Reserve Command, became chairman of the United States National Conference on Ministry to the Armed Forces, representing 250 faith groups in providing assistance to chaplains. In part because of the requirement that chaplains have a degree in religious education, the number of Mormon chaplains in the armed services does not equal the percentage of Mormons serving.

CHASTITY. A term little understood in the late 20th century, chastity refers to abstaining from sexual relations outside of **marriage**. The increased chance of unwanted pregnancy, sexually transmitted diseases, and emotional scars that linger are among the practical reasons for rejecting promiscuity and choosing a chaste pattern of behavior. Ultimately, chastity is one of the commandments of God. Although violations inevitably occur, they are to be deplored, not shrugged off. The appropriate response for violation is **repentance**.

"CHOOSE THE RIGHT." Title of a popular Mormon hymn, with words by Joseph L. Townsend and music by a Salt Lake City, Utah, candy maker named Henry A. Tuckett, first printed in a song book of 1909. In the final generation of the 20th century the three words assumed greater prominence when used in awards given to children in **Primary** and, even more, when the letters CTR were widely used as a logogram on pins, rings, and other examples of Mormon kitsch.

CHRISTENSEN, CLAYTON M. (1952–). Scholar, **area authority seventy**. Born on 6 April 1952 in Salt Lake City, Utah, Christensen served as a missionary in Korea from 1971 to 1973. After earning a bachelor's degree in economics at **BYU** in 1975, he attended Oxford University as a Rhodes Scholar, earning an M.Phil. in applied econometrics in 1977. He then earned an MBA degree at Harvard Business School in 1979. Later, in 1992, he was awarded a doctorate in business administration by Harvard and then became a faculty member at the Harvard Business School.

Christensen founded three successful companies. He was named a White House fellow in 1982, serving as an assistant to the secretary of transportation. He served as an advisor to the Brigham and Women's Hospital in Boston and was a member and chairman of the board of directors of the Massachusetts Affiliate of the American Diabetes Association. He was elected a member of the Town Meeting in Belmont, Massachusetts. For the Boy Scouts of America, Christensen was scoutmaster, den leader, and chairman of the troop committee. His **callings** in the Church included that of **bishop** and **counselor** in the presidency of the Massachusetts Boston Mission. In April 2002 he became an area authority seventy. His statement "Why I Believe," found on his website, emphasizes the opportunities to serve afforded by the Church. He and his wife, Christine, have five children.

CHRISTENSEN, JOE J. (1929–). Educator, **general authority**. Christensen was born on 21 July 1929 in Banida, a farming community in southeastern Idaho. As a young man, he served as a **missionary** in Mexico and Costa Rica. His college training was at Utah State University and **BYU**. After a tour of duty in the U.S. Air Force and completion of his university degrees, he was employed as a **seminary** and **institute** teacher.

With his wife and six children, Christensen went to Mexico in 1970 to preside over the Mexico City Mission. Called as associate Church commissioner of education, he spent the next several years establishing seminary and institute programs in many countries. For four years he was **president** of the **Missionary Training Center** in Provo, Utah. In 1985, he was appointed president of **Ricks College**. In 1989, he became a general authority as a member of the First **Quorum** of the **Seventy** and in 1993 was sustained a member of its presidency. He became an emeritus general authority in 1999.

CHRISTIANITY. Mormons have an inclusive definition of Christianity, including within its boundaries **Catholics**, **Protestants**, Orthodox, and, of course, themselves. This does not mean they consider all forms equally valid or all ideas right. The term is not therefore a declaration of total agreement but a simple way of designating those who accept **Jesus Christ** as the Savior. On the other hand, some of their opponents deny that Mormons are Christians on the grounds that they do not accept the creeds of historic Christianity starting in the fourth century. By such a definition, some Mormons have responded, the original Christians of Bible times would be excluded. Whatever others may say, Mormons declare their faith in Jesus Christ as Creator, Redeemer, Lord, and Master, now physically resurrected, one of the three persons in the Godhead. Some whose claim to Christian identity has not been challenged believe far less about Christ.

CHRISTOFFERSON, D. TODD (1945–). Attorney, **general authority**. Born on 24 January 1945 in American Fork, Utah, Christofferson majored in English and international relations at **BYU**. After serving as a **missionary** in Argentina from 1964 to 1966, he earned a juris doctorate from Duke University. A law clerk for U.S. District Court Judge John J. Sirica during the Watergate hearings, he then joined a Washington law firm, specializing in legal work for financial institutions. Christofferson lived in Tennessee, Virginia, and North Carolina. He participated in interfaith organizations, received the Silver Beaver Award of the **Boy Scouts** of America, and served as chairman of the Middle Tennessee Literacy Coalition and chairman of Affordable Housing of Nashville.

In the Church, Christofferson's **callings** have included **seminary** teacher, **high councilor**, **bishop**, **stake president**, and **regional representative**. In 1993 he was called to the First **Quorum** of the **Seventy** and in 1998 became a member of its presidency. He and his wife, Kathy, have five children.

THE CHURCH OF JESUS CHRIST OF LATTER-DAY SAINTS. Official name of the Church popularly known as the Mormon Church with its headquarters in Salt Lake City, Utah. It is a world Church with members in all inhabited continents. When formed in 1830, the organization was known as the Church of Christ and for a brief period by some as the Church of the Latter-day Saints, but in 1838 the present name was given by revelation (***Doctrine and Covenants*** 115:4): "For thus shall my church be called, even The Church of Jesus Christ of Latter-day Saints."

Although long, the name admirably conveys important ideas. The definite article "the," capitalized and included as part of the name, is significantly not the indefinite article "a." Mormons see theirs as God's church on earth, uniquely authorized and recognized by Him. Although such exclusivity appears arrogant and does not encourage ecumenism, Mormons answer that the designation is not their own but God's and that they fully acknowledge sincerity, goodness, and truth wherever found.

The term *church* conveys the importance and value of organization. Mormons believe that **Jesus Christ** deliberately founded an organization—both at the time of his earthly ministry in Palestine and at the time of the **restoration** in 1830. The desire of some to "go it alone" without institutional religion is incompatible with the human need for instruction, support, and especially the **sacrament** of the Lord's Supper and other **ordinances** of salvation, for all of which the Church is vital.

"Of Jesus Christ"—these words indicate the "ownership" of the Church, whose it is, the source of its authority. It is not the prerogative of human beings on their own to organize the Lord's church. They can go through the motions, of course, even for the crass motive of obtaining a tax-exempt status, but without divine authorization a church is not his. Careless librarians and others who classify works on Mormonism as non-Christian, perhaps because of a surface similarity between "Mormon" and "Muslim," have probably paid little attention to the official name.

"Of Latter-day Saints" refers to the members of the Church. For many people, the word ***saints*** designates those from Mary and the original apostles to the person most recently elevated through the Catholic Church's canonization procedures. As used in the New Testament, the word referred simply to members of the church, as when Paul wrote to the saints at Corinth or Ephesus. To differentiate themselves from such original, or early-day, saints, Mormons call themselves Latter-day Saints. While the Church derives its authority from above, it is here pronounced also to be "*of* the Latter-day Saints." It belongs to them as well as to God. As a lay organization each **ward** or **stake** requires the services of many unpaid laborers. Those named to positions, from the **president** of the Church on down, receive the approval of the members by a **sustaining** vote. *See also* FIRST VISION; MISSION OF THE CHURCH.

CLARK, J(OSHUA) REUBEN (1871–1961). International lawyer, ambassador, and **general authority**. Born in Grantsville, Utah, on 1 September 1871, J. Reuben Clark grew up in a small town environment. He attended Latter-day Saints' College in Salt Lake City, Utah, and came under the influence of its president, **James E. Talmage**. In 1898 he graduated as valedictorian from the University of Utah.

Clark moved east to attend Columbia Law School. An appointment as assistant solicitor in the U.S. State Department and then as solicitor in 1910 led him to work on problems with Mexico. Although he left the State Department with the election of Woodrow Wilson, Clark continued to accept such government appointments as general counsel for the American-British Claims Commission, special assistant to the attorney general, executive officer to the judge advocate general, and special counsel for the U.S. negotiators at the Washington Arms Conference of 1921–1922. After returning to Utah for a period, J. Reuben Clark was again called into government service. From counsel to the U.S. commission pressing claims against Mexico he went on to become undersecretary of state and then special advisor to Dwight W. Morrow, U.S. ambassador to Mexico. From 1930 to 1933 Clark was U.S. ambassador to Mexico.

In 1933, even though he had never held any high Church office, Clark was named a **counselor** in the **First Presidency**. For 28 years he served in sequence as counselor to Presidents **Heber J. Grant**, **George Albert Smith**, and **David O. McKay**. Because of his extensive experience and strong will, he made a significant contribution to all of these **presidents**. When, from 1951 to 1959, Clark became second instead of first counselor, his memorable statement was, "In the service of the Lord, it is not where you serve but how" (*Conference Reports*, April 1951, 154).

Clark was intimately involved with the introduction of the **welfare program**, the evacuation of **missionaries** from **Europe** in 1939, the reopening of the missions after World War II, and the building of many chapels. A student of the scriptures, he produced his own harmonization of the gospels and a series of radio lectures on the Great **Apostasy**. After studying the implications of modern translations of the **Bible**, he spoke in favor of the Church's continued use of the King James Version. As the Church's educational system of **seminaries** and **institutes of religion** expanded, Clark insisted that all teachers must adhere to belief in the atonement of **Jesus Christ**, the divine calling of **Joseph Smith** as **prophet**, and the continued legitimate leadership of the successive Church presidents.

A conservative Republican, Clark was less than enthusiastic about U.S. participation in World War II, deplored the use of the atomic bomb, warned against the power of the military-industrial elite, made some comments construed as anti-Semitic, and lamented "our dwindling sovereignty." At the same time, he acknowledged that these were personal opinions, not official Church positions.

CLARK, KIM B. (1949–). Educator. Born on 20 March 1949 in Salt Lake City, Utah, Clark grew up in Spokane, Washington, and then served a two-year **mission** in Germany. In 1974 he earned a B.A. degree at Harvard University, followed by an M.A. in 1977 and the Ph.D. in 1978. He became George F. Baker professor of business administration, and, in 1995, dean of the Harvard Business School. He was inaugurated as president of **BYU–Idaho** on 12 October 2005. He and his wife, Sue, have seven children.

CLAYTON, WILLIAM (1814–1879). Clerk, musician. Born 17 July 1814, in Preston, Lancashire, England, Clayton joined the **LDS** Church in 1837, as part of the first group converted in England. The following year **Elders** Heber C. Kimball and **Orson Hyde**, who had led the missionary effort, returned to Kirtland, Ohio, and they ordained Clayton as second **counselor** in the English mission presidency. He served in this **calling** until emigrating to Nauvoo, Illinois, in 1840. In Nauvoo, Clayton served as private secretary to **Joseph Smith** and clerk for the **Nauvoo Temple**. In addition to recording Joseph Smith's revelation on celestial marriage, Clayton performed the ceremonies for four of Smith's plural marriages. Clayton also held several civic positions, including Nauvoo city treasurer, recorder for the Nauvoo city council, and member of the Nauvoo Legion band. At a camp in Iowa after Mormons were driven from Nauvoo, Clayton wrote *Come, Come, Ye Saints*, which has become a favorite LDS hymn. While a member of the 1847 pioneer company, Clayton invented a "roadmeter," which measured the distance traveled by a wagon wheel. In Utah, Clayton acted as the auditor of public accounts for the Provisional State of Deseret. When Congress organized Utah as a territory, Clayton also served as territorial auditor of public accounts and territorial recorder of marks and brands. Besides his civic duties, Clayton also served as secretary for Zion's Cooperative Mercantile Institution for a number of years. On 4 December 1879, Clayton died in his Salt Lake City, Utah, home.

CLERGY. In the usual sense, the Church has no clergy, except possibly **general authorities**. It is a lay organization. With no divinity schools and no paid ministry, the **LDS** Church does not follow the practice of other churches. No young Mormon looks forward to becoming a full-time clergyman in the Church; the concept does not exist. With the expansion of **membership**, of course, there are those who are employed by the Church. These include teachers in the **seminaries** and **institutes of religion**, editors of magazines, librarians, and professionals and secretaries in many different departments. These full-time positions are regarded as employment, not **callings**.

On the level of the congregation, or **ward**, interaction is between fellow members, all amateurs or laity, although some occupy positions of responsibility. Visitors are sometimes surprised to find that the person conducting a meeting is actually a barber or a grocer. In the Church, however, he may be the **bishop**. **Missionaries** serve full-time during their 18-month or two-year calling, but they are not paid for this. Their sustenance-level stipend comes from their own savings, support of their families, or, in some cases, funds donated to the missionary program. Never do these young men and women think of themselves as professional clergymen in the sense of having chosen a life's career.

COLONIZATION. If colonization refers to the establishment of new settlements, Mormons have been in the forefront of colonization. Looking at the different phases of Mormon history, we discover the beginnings of such conscious establishment of settlements in Missouri. The same process was repeated in Illinois with the build-up at Nauvoo and the establishment of several settlements in the region.

But it was in the west that Mormon colonization moved into high gear. The initial establishment of Salt Lake City, Utah, in the Great Salt Lake Valley (1847) was followed by the deliberate peopling of the region as pioneers were sent out to establish communities in designated locations. Dots appeared on the map, as it were, as new settlements were founded north and south of Salt Lake City. Ambitious plans for a far-flung empire led to Mormon communities as far away as the Salmon River in Idaho and San Bernardino, California, but the political and military pressures of the mid-1850s led to a pull-back from these most distant outposts.

Partially because of the population pressure caused by a high birth rate and a steady flow of new immigrants, the settlement expansion continued. By the death of **Brigham Young** in 1877, more than 300 settlements had been founded. (These are listed in Milton R. Hunter,

Brigham Young the Colonizer.) By the end of the 19th century, more than 500 had been founded. If the Mormon colonization was any different from that taking place all across the American landscape, it was in its organization and advance planning. Sites were selected on the basis of preliminary reconnaissance that assured a supply of water and soil that was cultivable. A leader was named and people were called to join the new settlement on the basis of needed skills. Madcap individualism was suppressed in favor of the community interest, as lots were assigned and work assignments handed out.

Of course there was the initial phase of confronting an environment devoid of amenities or even minimal shelter. Living in tents or wagon boxes was followed by putting up simple shacks or cabins. If necessary, a wall to provide protection against Indians was built. Planting, irrigating, cultivating, and the initial harvest were always an arduous, suspenseful drama. The extreme hardship of the initial phase often led to premature deaths, sometimes to defections. As time went on, however, homes were improved, the community became larger and more adequate in providing basic needs, and civic pride manifested itself in parades and celebrations.

Although the completion of the transcontinental railroad in 1869 ended Utah's isolation in some respects, it did not mean the end of colonization. And those who left the more settled areas to strike out in their wagons for a new site several hundred miles away were pioneers as much as were those who first came to the Salt Lake Valley in 1847. Each place had its heroic leaders, its founding fathers and mothers. Some of the settlements and their dates follow: Little Colorado River in Arizona (1876); Bunkerville, Nevada (1877); Star Valley, Wyoming (1879); St. Johns, Arizona (1879); Rexburg, Idaho (1882); Colonia Juarez, Mexico (1885); Cardston, Alberta, Canada (1887). *See also* ILLINOIS PERIOD; MISSOURI PERIOD.

COMMANDMENTS. Mormons are often urged to "keep the commandments." This is meant to include not only the Ten Commandments (but not the detailed dietary proscriptions of the Mosaic law) and such commands from Jesus as to preach the gospel unto all the world, but also instructions from the Lord in modern revelation. The **Word of Wisdom** has been construed as a commandment. The specific covenants of **baptism** and the **temple**—generally to live a life of Christian service and unselfishness—also become obligations one should keep. To those who might see such an emphasis as legalism, a failure to understand the liberty with which Christ made humans free, Mormons would reply that **Jesus Christ** said, "If ye love me, keep my commandments" (John 14:15), and that his yoke is easy and his burden light (Matt. 11:30). They fully recognize that without the grace of God their efforts would be meaningless.

COMMUNITY OF CHRIST. Current name of the organization formerly named the **Reorganized Church of Jesus Christ of Latter Day Saints (RLDS)**. Because of having constantly to explain that they were not Mormons, not members of the **Church of Jesus Christ of Latter-day Saints** (the primary focus of this dictionary), members of the RLDS Church assembled at world conference in April 2000 decided by a vote of 1,979 to 561 to adopt a new name, **Community of Christ**. Membership is close to 250,000 in about 50 countries and has remained relatively static for the past several decades. The history of this church up to 2001 is treated under its official name to that point, Reorganized Church of Jesus Christ of Latter Day Saints.

To give an accurate current picture that differentiates the Community of Christ from the Church of Jesus Christ of Latter-day Saints, several points deserve mention. Both groups reject the practice of **polygamy**, but the Church of Jesus Christ of Latter-day Saints, starting with **Joseph Smith** no later than 1841, allowed it until the **Manifesto** of 1890. Administratively, at the top of the Community of Christ are a presidency of three and a quorum of twelve apostles. The president of the Community of Christ is no longer required to be a descendant of Joseph Smith. Starting in 1984, women can be ordained to the **priesthood**. Several women are apostles. The Community of Christ has a paid ministry, including not only general officers but pastors in its congregations and missionaries. Tithing, the major source of income for sustaining church operations, is defined as 10 percent of income after taxes and after "what is needed for basic living needs." The Community of Christ accepts as scripture the **Bible**, ***Book of Mormon***, and ***Doctrine and Covenants*** (its own version) but not the ***Pearl of Great Price.*** Revelation is not confined to these works. According to the Community of Christ, "God is revealed to us through scripture, the faith community, prayer, nature, and in human history."

The Community of Christ owns two **temples**: (1) one at Kirtland, Ohio, which is viewed as a historic site and is open to tourists who wish to view its interior as well as exterior; and (2) one at Independence, Missouri, dedicated in 1994. The ceremonies and **ordinances** associated with Latter-day Saint temples, including endowments and **baptism for the dead**, are not administered by the Community of Christ. The Independence temple, striking architecturally, is a center of education, meditation, and peace.

On 14 June 2006 the Community of Christ announced a downsizing within the organization. Through "early retirements, voluntary separations and involuntary separations," about 80 people would be let go. More than 400 people, including ministers at churches and workers at headquarters in Independence, Missouri, remained on the payroll. *See also* MCMURRAY, W. GRANT; SCHISMS; SUCCESSION; VEAZEY, STEPHEN M.

COMMUNITY SERVICE. Church members are encouraged to participate in their communities, volunteering when possible to assist deserving programs. **Wards** and **stakes** often organize themselves to assist in community projects. The full-time **missionaries** throughout the world also assist the communities to which they are assigned on a regular basis. *See also* HUMANITARIAN AID; WELFARE PROGRAM.

CONFERENCE CENTER. Large assembly hall in Salt Lake City, Utah, completed in April 2000. The fan-shaped auditorium has a capacity of 21,000 and is used for **conference** sessions, pageants, and other public events. In addition to the auditorium, the building has over 60 translation booths, a theater with 900 upholstered seats, and underground parking for 1,300 vehicles. The roof is landscaped with fountains, trees, and flowers. The center was constructed to meet the highest seismic standards.

CONFERENCES, GENERAL. Gatherings in April and October of each year at the **Conference Center** (after a century and a quarter of meeting in the **Tabernacle**) in Salt Lake City, Utah, where members and officers listen to addresses from the **general authorities** and women leaders of **auxiliaries**. A report by **auditors** is presented and the names of current general authorities are presented for the **sustaining** vote of the congregation. Through some 2,600 satellite dishes, radio and television broadcasts of conference proceedings reach a world-wide audience. In addition, the conference meetings can be accessed by personal computers. The proceedings are published in the ***Ensign*** each May and November and also in a series entitled *Conference Reports*.

CONFERENCES, STAKE. Gatherings of members in a **stake** that until 1979 occurred every three months. Then they were reduced to two per year. During a two-day period several meetings, or sessions, are held. **General authorities** and stake authorities are sustained by vote, and instructional and inspirational addresses are given. Visiting general authorities address the stake every other year. *See also* SUSTAINING.

CONFIRMATION. A sacred **ordinance** following **baptism**. Seated in a chair, the recipient has hands laid on his or her head by one or more individuals who hold the **Melchizedek Priesthood** authority. By the authority of that **priesthood** and in the name of **Jesus Christ**, the officiator confirms the recipient a member of the **Church of Jesus Christ of Latter-day Saints**, bestows the Holy Ghost, and adds additional words of blessing and counsel.

CONSTITUTION OF THE UNITED STATES. This foundational document is commonly referred to as "inspired." "And for this purpose have I established the Constitution of this land, by the hands of wise men whom I raised up unto this very purpose, and redeemed the land by the shedding of blood" (***Doctrine and Covenants*** 101:80). The primary concern in the 19th century was protection in the free exercise of religion. From the public announcement of **polygamy** in 1852 through the next generation, Mormons claimed protection of the practice as part of their religion, but this claim was struck down by the Reynolds decision (1879), in which the Supreme Court made a distinction between protected belief and not-necessarily-protected action. An 1839 statement by **Joseph Smith** that the Constitution would be imperiled, hanging as it were by a thread, but would be saved by the elders of the Church, is at least partially explained by his frustration at the unwillingness or inability of the federal government to protect the persecuted Latter-day Saints. Individuals and groups within the Church have cited the statement at different points in time in explanation of their political views.

COOK, QUENTIN L. (1940–). Attorney, **seventy**, **general authority**. Born in Logan, Utah, to J. Vernon and Bernice Kimball Cook, he served as a missionary in England from 1960 to 1962. After returning to Logan, Cook married Mary Gaddie. They are the parents of three children. He earned a bachelor's degree in political science in 1963 from Utah State University and a J.D. from Stanford Law School in 1966. Living in Hillsborough, California, he worked for 27 years as a corporate attorney, serving as managing partner of Carr, McClellan, Ingersoll, Thompson, and Horn. He served as president and CEO of the California Healthcare System and for a time as vice chairman of Sutter Health System.

In the Church, Cook served as a member of the presidency and as **president** of the San Francisco Stake, a **regional representative**, and an **area authority seventy**. He served as a member of the Second **Quorum** of the Seventy and was called to the First Quorum of the Seventy on 5 April 1998 and to the Presidency of the Seventy on August 1, 2007. On the call of Henry B. Eyring to the **First Presidency**, Cook was called to the Quorum of the **Twelve Apostles** on October 6, 2007.

CORRELATION. In 1960, building on earlier efforts, the **First Presidency** started a review of Church programs. Three coordinating committees were created, one each for children, youth, and adults. A permanent Correlation Department was established in 1972. The purposes of correlation have been to assure that **auxiliaries** and other Church programs function to support the **family** rather than displace it; to maintain order among the different auxiliaries and programs; to assure that lesson materials and other publications of the Church are doctrinally sound; to simplify Church programs; and to bring all Church-sponsored activities under the direction of the **priesthood**.

The entire curriculum of the Church was reviewed, reorganized, and rewritten so that the **gospel** would be taught at the three stages of life—childhood, youth, and adulthood—in a coherent way, at the appropriate level, and with proper reinforcement and review. Care was exercised to avoid overemphasizing some points and leaving out others. This revised, systematic curriculum has been translated into many languages. Also shaped by correlation have been Church magazines and the weekly **family home evening**. Scheduled Church meetings were consolidated so that only one trip to church on Sunday would be required. In short, the ongoing correlation program attempts to assure that the Church will function with maximum efficiency in achieving its purposes. *See also* MISSION OF THE CHURCH.

COSTA, CLAUDIO ROBERTO MENDES (1949–). General authority. Born on 25 March 1949 in Santos, Brazil, Costa and his family lived in poverty. To supplement the family's meager income, he shined shoes on the street. When he was 12 years old, he met Mormon **missionaries** and took them home to meet his family. Most of the family joined the Church, but Claudio held out.

By age 17, he was manager of a shoe store. Then he left home to complete his military obligation, after which he moved to Sao Paulo. He worked in the mail room of a bank and rose to become manager. Accumulating a record of successful leadership, Costa successively became manager of five different companies.

At age 27, he was baptized a **member** of the Church. After studying at the Paulista Institute for Gems and Precious Metals, he became manager of a jewelry store. Three years later, at a significant reduction in pay, Costa accepted full-time employment with the Church as associate area manager over **seminaries** and **institutes.** From 1990 to 1993 he was **president** of the Brazil Manaus Mission. In April 1994, he was called to be a member of the Second **Quorum** of the **Seventy.** In 2001, he became a member of the First Quorum of the Seventy. He and his wife, Margareth, have four children.

COUNCIL OF FIFTY. *See* FIFTY, COUNCIL OF.

COUNCIL OF TWELVE APOSTLES. *See* TWELVE APOSTLES, QUORUM OF THE.

COUNSELOR. An important, easily overlooked position, or **calling**, in the functioning of the Church at all levels. Soon after the organization of the Church in 1830, **Joseph Smith** became **president** and had two **counselors**, the three making up the **First Presidency**. In time, the same kind of three-person executive body appeared throughout the Church organization. The **presiding bishop** has two counselors. Presidents of the general **Relief Society**, **Sunday School**, **Young Men**, **Young Women**, and **Primary** each have their two counselors. **Area** presidencies, **stake** presidencies, and **ward** bishoprics are similarly constituted, as are the presidencies of **priesthood quorums** and stake and ward **auxiliary** organizations. Over each of the 344-plus **missions** a president is assisted by two counselors, and the same is true of each **temple**.

At meetings of these three-person groups decisions are made. Although the counselors give advice, their role is not thus limited. The counselors function as sounding boards and sources of information. They also lighten the load of the president or bishop by taking on specific responsibilities assigned to them. Counselors accumulate training and experience. Many who are called to the position of bishop or president, including women in Primary, Young Women, and Relief Society, served previously as counselors.

COVEY, STEPHEN R. (1932–). Popular lecturer, author, business consultant. Born on 24 October 1932 in Salt Lake City, Utah, Covey earned a B.S. in business administration from the University of Utah, a master's degree in business administration from Harvard, and a doctor's degree from **BYU**. From teaching business management and organizational behavior, Covey expanded his scope through lectures, training programs, and consulting for private businesses. In 1997 he organized the Franklin-Covey Company, a worldwide management consulting firm. He is the author of several best-selling books, including *Seven Habits of Highly Effective People* and *First Things First*.

An active member of the Church, Covey has served as **bishop, mission president**, and **regional representative**. He wrote *Spiritual Roots of Human Relations* and *The Divine Center.* In 1994 he received the International Entrepreneur of the Year award. *Time Magazine* named him one of 25 most influential Americans. In 2003 he received the National Fatherhood Award. He is on the board of directors of the Points of Light Foundation, which mobilizes volunteers in many communities. He and his wife, Sandra, have nine children.

COWDERY, OLIVER (1806–1850). Attorney, **general authority,** one of the **witnesses of the *Book of Mormon***. Born at Wells, Vermont, on 3 October 1806, Cowdery remained there and received basic education. In 1826 he moved to New York to join his older brothers. He took a job as a schoolteacher in 1829. Boarding with the parents of **Joseph Smith**, Cowdery found out about the translation of metal plates and, after receiving a **revelation**, worked as scribe and copyist in 1829–1830. Cowdery testified of several miraculous experiences: the appearance of John the Baptist to restore the **Aaronic Priesthood**; the appearance of Peter, James, and John to restore the **Melchizedek Priesthood**; and being one of the witnesses of the *Book of Mormon*. His testimony is printed in all editions of the book. At the Church's organization in 1830, Cowdery was called as "second **elder**." When a presidency was organized, he became an associate **president**. He also had the title of Church recorder in 1830–1831 and 1835–1837. He assisted in preparing some of the early revelations for printing and wrote a series of letters that remain a basic primary source.

In 1838 Cowdery joined others in disputing some of the Church's organizational, economic, and political policies. He was **excommunicated** along with some other dissidents. For 10 years he was out of the Church, practicing law in Kirtland, Ohio, before moving to Tiffin, Ohio, in 1840. In 1847 he moved to Wisconsin. Despite a good reputation in the community, he was defeated in a bid for the state legislature. In 1848 he rejoined the Church at Council Bluffs, Iowa, reaffirming his earlier testimonies. Failing in health and short of funds, he was unable to proceed directly to Utah but remained near relatives in Richmond, Missouri. There he died on 3 March 1850 at age 43.

COWLEY, MATTHEW (1897–1953). General authority, **missionary** to the **Polynesians**. Born 2 August 1897 at Preston, Idaho, the son of Apostle Matthias Cowley, who soon moved his family to Salt Lake City, Utah, Matthew left on a mission to the New Zealand

Maoris at age 17. During his five years there he learned the language, preached, translated **scriptures**, and developed a great love for the people.

After graduating from the University of Utah, Cowley attended law school at George Washington University. He married Elva Taylor in 1922 and worked in the office of Utah senator **Reed Smoot**. He practiced law in Salt Lake City, serving twice as county attorney.

In 1938 he was called to be mission **president** in New Zealand. Beloved by the Maori people as *Tumuaki*, Cowley knew them by name and often stayed in their homes. When the other American missionaries returned to the United States because of World War II, he remained in order to look after the Church members in New Zealand. In all, this mission lasted nearly eight years.

In 1945 Cowley was called to the **Quorum** of the **Twelve Apostles**. The next year he was made president of the Church's Pacific missions. Traveling by air, he visited not only New Zealand but also Samoa, Tonga, the Cook Islands, and Hawaii. In 1949 he also visited Japan and China, holding conferences and helping establish the Church there. A down-to-earth man who related easily to people, Cowley was a favorite speaker wherever he went. He died on 13 December 1953.

CREATION. In the general sense that they believe the world is not a product of chance but of deliberate creation by God, Mormons are creationists. But they do not insist on a limited time frame for the process, regarding the "days" spoken of in Genesis as creative periods of indefinite length. Nor do they consider creation to be ex nihilo, the bringing of the world into existence from nothing. Rather, reasoned **Joseph Smith** on the basis of the Hebrew verb, creation could mean causing the world to come into existence by assembling or organizing existing material elements into a new combination. The creation of humans could likewise mean the combining of physical bodies with an immortal spirit; the individual spirit was not created on earth but had existed in a pre-mortal state. As far as earth and the mortal phase of existence are concerned, the emphasis is not on the imperfectly understood process but on the fact of God's intentionality and divine purpose. *See also* PLAN OF SALVATION.

CROSS. The symbol found throughout the Christian world is not used in Mormon worship or architecture. President **Gordon B. Hinckley** explained that "the cross is the symbol of the dying Christ, while our message is a declaration of the living Christ." Absence of the cross among Mormons by no means signifies denial of the atoning sacrifice of Jesus Christ through the suffering that began in Gethsemane and was completed on Golgotha.

CULT. Term used by some sociologists of religion to describe churches not part of "historical" or "orthodox" **Catholicism** or **Protestantism** or that reject all or some of the historic Christian creeds. Although used dispassionately by Max Weber and others, the term is often used as a term of disparagement, even contempt, by those who see themselves as superior to upstart religions. Recognizing the unfortunate polemical uses of the term, some recent scholars have preferred the term *new religious movements* to describe groups of relatively recent origin. Objecting to being defamed by avowed enemies or to being excluded from **Christianity**, some Mormon defenders have pointed out inconsistencies in usage of the term and have argued that primitive **Christianity** itself possessed all the supposed criteria of a cult.

– D –

DAHLQUIST, CHARLES W., II (1947–). Attorney, Church leader. Born on 5 August 1947, he grew up in Boise, Idaho, earned a bachelor's degree from **BYU** in 1971, and received a juris doctorate from the University of Utah in 1974. He served as scoutmaster, **ward Young Men** president, branch **president**, **high councilman**, **stake** president, and president of the Germany Hamburg Mission. Winner of the Silver Beaver Award, he served on the executive board of the **Boy Scouts** of America. In 2004 he became general president of Young Men. He and his wife, Zella, have five daughters.

DANCE. Unlike some religions of a Puritan or Pietist tradition, Mormons have welcomed dancing as a legitimate form of recreation, even worship. Crossing the plains during the **exodus** from Illinois, they would often rejuvenate themselves around the campfire in the evening by getting out the fiddles and kicking up their heels in reels and schottisches. In the West every community found that dances provided necessary recreational relief.

As new dance fashions were introduced, they were often perceived as suggestive or improper. Thus at social events sponsored by the Church, leaders did not welcome the new dance styles, starting with the waltz in the late 19th century and continuing through the foxtrot and, after the middle of the 20th century, the jitterbug, swing, the twist, and various styles associated with rock and roll. At first the new dance step was forbidden. Then it was often gradually accepted as long as certain guidelines were followed. Adult leaders supervising social events did not wish to encourage behavior that seemed tasteless or sexually provocative. At the same time they realized that a strict exclusion of current dance steps would render their sponsored activities unpopular among young people.

Throughout the Mormon communities of the West and in **ward** and **stake** recreational activities, social dances—square, country, and ballroom dancing—have continued in the 20th century. For many years the **Young Men** and **Young Women** sponsored dance instruction and put on a giant dance festival in the University of Utah stadium. The church has also sponsored dance festivals in various regions.

DANITES. (1) A controversial paramilitary organization among the Mormons in 1838–1839 during the **Missouri Period**. Some Danites engaged in illegal activities against some Missourians, no doubt rationalized in their own minds as self-defense, a justified reaction to the persecution they were experiencing. To determine the extent of this violence requires sifting through contradictory accounts by participants in the events. On balance, however, it seems clear that Mormons suffered far more than they inflicted. It is unclear whether the group was initially sponsored by **Joseph Smith** or whether it was an unauthorized group started privately by Church member Sampson Avard. The evidence is mixed. Joseph Smith and others of the **First Presidency** knew of the organization and much of its activity. In the 1980s the discovery of early diaries and letters from the Missouri Period indicated the existence of a public Danite organization that assumed responsibility not only for the defense of the community but also for the construction of homes and providing supplies.

(2) In the **Illinois Period**, during the **exodus**, and during the subsequent **Utah Period**, the Danite organization did not exist, but the legend took on a life of its own in 50 or more novels portraying the Danites as sinister night riders who intimidated and brutalized ordinary people. John D. Lee or his editor, J. H. Beadle, used the term in *Lee's Confessions*, whether accurately or hyperbolically is not known. The various discussions helped produce a highly negative stereotype of Mormonism.

DEACON. At the age of 12, **worthy** male Church **members** are ordained deacons, an office in the **Aaronic Priesthood**. They perform such assignments as passing the emblems of the **sacrament** (called Eucharist in some other churches) to Church members, collecting **fast offering**, and assisting in the maintenance of the building and grounds. Deacons are grouped into **quorums** of 12 or fewer members. A **president**, two **counselors**, and a secretary are called. An adult adviser teaches and trains. This is the first level, or office, of priesthood service. At age 14 comes ordination to the office of a **teacher**.

DEAD SEA SCROLLS. Discovered in 1947, the Dead Sea Scrolls consist of materials produced and copied between 200 BC and 70 AD by the separatist Jewish settlement of Qumran. The community was annihilated by the Romans, but these records had been placed in sealed earthenware jars. Because of their great significance for understanding the Judeo-Christian world of the first century, Mormons have been interested in them. Some popular speakers and writers claimed striking parallels between the scrolls and Mormonism, but serious Mormon scholars, while interested, have been appropriately cautious. In 1996 the Provo International Conference on the Dead Sea Scrolls brought scholars from many different countries to **BYU**. **FARMS** produced a database on CD-ROM that contains a fully integrated and computerized collection of Dead Sea Scrolls texts.

DESERET. (1) A ***Book of Mormon*** term meaning "honeybee." (2) The first name chosen for the new territory Mormons hoped would become a state in the West. It was rejected in favor of Utah but remained attached to several businesses and activities.

DESERET ALPHABET. A phonetic alphabet promoted by **Brigham Young** and others in the 1850s. Partially modeled on Pitman shorthand by George Watt and Wilford Woodruff, the new alphabet was supposed to be easier to learn by foreigners. A few books were published in the Deseret Alphabet, but because of the prohibitive cost of putting all publications of the territory into this new type, it was abandoned.

DESERET BOOK COMPANY. A book company owned by the Church's Deseret Management Corporation. Its publishing arm publishes many of the writings about and for Mormons. Its retail arm, consisting of stores in several Western states, sells its own publications, works by other publishers, and general trade books. In 1999 it produced a compact disc called GospeLink (since updated), which included conference addresses, Church periodicals, and hundreds of books by **general authorities** and other writers. In 2006, Deseret Book announced separate mergers with Bookcraft and Seagull Books, publishers of books for the Mormon market.

DESERET INDUSTRIES. A thrift store and rehabilitation center. There are 49 such stores in the western United States. Any surplus clothing is shipped to the **Humanitarian Center**, where it is sorted and baled for sending where needed anywhere in the world.

DESERET MORNING NEWS. Daily newspaper owned by the Church and published in Salt Lake City, Utah. Started in 1850 and taking its name from the ***Book of Mormon*** word meaning "honeybee" that had been proposed as the name of the territory, the *Deseret News* was originally a weekly. Later a semiweekly edition was produced and from 1867 also a daily. Changing from an evening to a morning publication in 2001, the newspaper's name became *Deseret Morning News.* It contains the sections found in other newspapers: news, editorials, comics, and classifieds. It subscribes to national news services. Editorially it has expressed a conservative to moderate position with special attention to moral values. Of special interest is the section entitled *Church News*, published weekly in the Saturday edition, which enables readers to keep abreast of news of the Church worldwide. In 1997, a new nine-story building to house the editorial and production departments was dedicated in Salt Lake City.

DESERET TRUST COMPANY. Established in 1972, it assists donors by providing professional trust services, including administering trusts established for the benefit of the Church and its entities. Deseret Trust Company reports to the **presiding bishopric**.

DEW, SHERI L. (1953–). Editor, publisher, women's leader. Born on 21 November 1953 in Ulysses, Kansas, Dew graduated from **BYU** in 1977. After taking courses on the graduate level and working as an assistant editor with Bookcraft, she became editor and associate publisher of *This People* magazine. Employed by **Deseret Book Company** in 1988, she was associate editor, director of publishing, vice president of publishing, and finally from 2002 president. She wrote biographies of **Ezra Taft Benson** and **Gordon B. Hinckley** and other books. She was a **ward** and **stake Relief Society** president before becoming a member of the Relief Society general board. From 1907 to 2002, she was second **counselor** in the general Relief Society presidency.

DIALOGUE: A JOURNAL OF MORMON THOUGHT. Quarterly periodical started in 1966 by editors **G. Eugene England** and G. Wesley Johnson, then graduate students at Stanford University. *Dialogue* includes historical articles, essays, fiction, poetry, photography, art, book reviews, and letters to the editor. Not sponsored by the Church, *Dialogue* has served as an outlet for a range of opinion and scholarship about Mormonism.

DIDIER, CHARLES (1935–). General authority. Born on 5 October 1935 in Ixelles, Belgium, Didier became fluent in French, Flemish, English, Spanish, and German. After earning a bachelor's degree in economics at the University of Liege, he became an officer in the Belgian Air Force Reserve. A convert, he was baptized in 1957. Didier served as **president** of the France Switzerland Mission, **regional representative,** and **Sunday School** general president. In 1975 he became a member of the First **Quorum** of the **Seventy**, serving in its presidency from 1992 to 1995 and again from 2001 to the present. He and his wife, Lucie, have two children.

DISPENSATION. Mormons have a view of salvation history that includes a series of dispensations, efforts by God to reach humankind through the divine saving gospel. Each of these efforts, represented by such figures as Adam, Noah, Abraham, and Moses, was followed by a declension, or **apostasy**. This dispensational pattern includes certain corollaries. For instance, the gospel of **Jesus Christ** did not originate in first century Palestine but instead goes back to the creation. Indeed, it had been spelled out and agreed to in the pre-mortal existence. The mission of Jesus Christ on earth included the unique, infinite atonement for the sins of all humans, but the Church he then founded carried no guarantees of permanence. The warnings of a "falling away" were part of the teaching of both Jesus and the original apostles (2 Thess. 2:3). The Great Apostasy merely repeated a process that had occurred repeatedly before.

The restoration of the gospel by **Joseph Smith** marked the beginning of the final dispensation. The time had come in the divine economy for the final act, the dispensation of the fullness of times. By contrast, the Christian church of the first and second centuries represented the dispensation of the meridian of time. If the geographical sweep of Mormonism included all the world, at least in the intention to carry the message to all people, the temporal sweep is equally extensive. In a sense, therefore, it is incorrect to see Mormonism as a new religion less than two centuries old. In the view of its adherents, it is the "eternal gospel" restored to earth in the culminating phase of human history. *See also* PLAN OF SALVATION.

DISSENT. The Church has not insisted on the kind of uniformity that denies human nature, the natural process of growing in knowledge, or legitimate differences of opinion. Those who become **inactive** are not the objects of persecution. In due course many such individuals resume full participation. **Excommunication** is more often for behavior than belief.

But belief is not a matter of indifference, especially if one is teaching or influencing others. **J. Reuben Clark** declared that those who teach in Church classes must accept three things: the divinity of **Jesus Christ**; the divine calling of **Joseph Smith** as a **prophet**; and the legitimacy of the present head of the Church as the holder of **priesthood** keys. A teacher in the Church setting who rejects any of these fundamentals would be transgressing the limits of dissent. How, Clark asked, could a person presume to teach as a representative of the Church while undermining its basic position?

Anyone who wishes to pursue interests outside the curricula of the Church may of course do so in individual conversation, study groups, meetings of professional associations, or private reading and research. But members are cautioned to avoid acrimony, to maintain perspective, and to be patient. The meetings of the Church are intended to accomplish certain goals. They are not to be disrupted or turned into free-for-all discussions, with impassioned statements of private views on controversial historical and theological issues. "He that hath the spirit of contention is not of me, but is of the devil, who is the father of contention" (*Book of Mormon*, 3 Nephi 11:29). The unity sought within the Church derives from sustaining the **general authorities**, a feeling of love and mutual respect among members, a shared vision of life and its purposes, fidelity to covenants, and the access of all to the inspiration of the Holy Spirit. *See also* ACTIVITY; POLITICS; SCHISMS; SUCCESSION.

DISTRIBUTION CENTERS. Church-owned stores throughout the world that sell authorized literature, **temple** clothing, and curricular materials in many languages. Included are **scriptures**, lesson manuals, handbooks, forms, audiovisual materials, hymn books, and video and cassette types. Using order forms printed in the ***Ensign***, people may order such material by mail. **Garments** may also be purchased at these centers.

DIVORCE. Although regarded as an evil, divorce is permitted by the Church. The rate of divorce among U.S. Mormons is slightly lower than in the general population. Those who marry in the **temple**, because of a shared religious commitment, have far fewer divorces. When temple marriages fail, the parties may, after a civil divorce, request from Church authorities a "cancellation of **sealing**," which has the effect of rescinding the relationship after death. *See also* MARRIAGE.

DOCTRINE AND COVENANTS. One of the four standard works or **scriptures** of the Church. Mostly made up of **revelations** issued by **Joseph Smith**, the work also contains prayers, letters, and official declarations by other **prophets**. Although the subject matter has to do with specific problems that arose in the early years, the principles are broadly applicable. The work is divided into 138 sections, equivalent to chapters, which in turn are subdivided into verses. Examples of the subject matter include: the atonement of **Jesus Christ** (section 19), **baptism** (section 22), **sabbath** day (section 59), the three levels or glories that await humans after death (section 76), **priesthood** (sections 84, 107, 121), the code of health known as the **Word of Wisdom** (section 89), the **manifesto** officially ending **polygamy** in 1890 (official declaration 1), and the granting in 1978 of the priesthood to all **worthy** males of whatever race (official declaration 2).

The revelations issued by Joseph Smith were first circulated in handwritten copies or printed in Church newspapers. As early as 1833 an effort was made to compile them into a work entitled ***Book of Commandments***, but its printing was stopped by mob action in Missouri and very few copies were salvaged. In 1835 the first edition of *Doctrine and Covenants* included the revelations from the ill-fated earlier work and others received since. The most important later editions, edited and expanded, appeared in 1844, 1876, 1921, and 1981. Twenty or more editions in translation have appeared.

DRUGS. In the period before the medical breakthroughs at the end of the 19th century, Mormons were not different from other people in seeking relief from suffering by means of patent medicines. Various home remedies were also used. With the improvements in medicine starting at the end of the 19th century and extending to the present, Mormons were glad to experience the benefits. This meant taking advantage of improved anesthetics and using prescription drugs according to the recommendation of their doctor. The substantial increase in medicines made available by drug companies and the willingness of doctors to prescribe these, including anti-inflammatory and mood-altering pills, affected the entire population. The **Word of Wisdom** bars the use of alcohol, tobacco, tea, and coffee. By extension, it would also preclude drug dependency. The "recreational" use of marijuana, LSD, rave, meth, and other "hard" drugs is considered foolish, self-destructive, and a callous mistreatment of one's physical body. To assist individuals in breaking such addictions, and those to alcohol and tobacco, **LDS Family Services** offers a 12-step program of recovery.

– E –

ECCLES, MARRINER STODDARD (1890–1977). Businessman, Federal Reserve official, treasury official. Marriner Eccles was the oldest child of David Eccles and his plural wife, Ellen Stoddard. Ellen and her children spent time in both Baker, Oregon, and Logan, Utah, because of her husband's business interests in both areas. Eccles briefly attended Brigham Young College; however, he left school in 1909. His father did not encourage his children to attend college for he found it unnecessary for a profitable business career. The following year, Eccles served a **mission** to Scotland. Two years later, he returned home, and his father died shortly thereafter. Not only did Eccles assume responsibility for his mother, brothers, and sister, but served as executor of his mother's share of his father's large estate. Although David Eccles' legal wife, Bertha Eccles, received the widow's share of his property, Marriner and the other children received a child's share. In 1913 Marriner married Maysie Campbell Young. Eccles worked as the president of the Hyrum State Bank and the director of the Thatcher Brothers Bank. In 1916 he organized the Eccles Investment Company, a holding firm, to manage his father's legacy left to the Logan Eccles family. By 1920, Eccles assumed control of various businesses, including Stoddard Lumber, Sego Milk, and Anderson Lumber. He served as president of Ogden First National Bank and of Utah Construction Company. During the Great Depression, Eccles recommended increased federal deficit spending to weather the financial difficulties. Impressed with the young man, President Roosevelt asked Eccles to join his staff as the assistant to Secretary of Treasury Henry Morgenthau Jr. The following year President Roosevelt nominated Eccles as the head of the Federal Reserve System. In this capacity, Eccles orchestrated two important pieces of legislation, the Federal Housing Act of 1934 and the Banking Act of 1935. Eventually, President Truman removed Eccles as the chair of the board of governors of the Federal Reserve System. Marriner spent much of his remaining years writing and speaking about world overpopulation and against the U.S. military intervention in Vietnam.

ECUMENICAL MOVEMENT. A loosely defined movement to bring Christian denominations together, ultimately, according to the hopes of some, to erase distinctions and restore the unity that existed prior to the Protestant Reformation or even prior to the "great schism" between the Eastern and Western church. By their own choice as well as that of the ecumenists, Mormons have not participated in meetings of the ecumenical movement. Similarly, Mormons do not belong to the National Council of Churches or the World Council of Churches. The basis for the **restoration** expressed in the **First Vision**—that the existing churches were wrong, meaning that they lacked authority and taught as doctrine the commandments of men—leaves little room for compromise on basic theological positions. On the other hand, Church leaders have recognized a broad commonality among people of faith, as opposed to secularists. Friendships have been formed across denominational lines, and mutual good wishes have been expressed. In disaster relief and different forms of humanitarian aid the Church has worked effectively with others.

EDUCATION. Although often limited by poverty and practical exigencies, the Church from its beginning advocated the pursuit of knowledge both formally through schooling and informally through personal effort. Literacy is essential for reading the **scriptures**. To be ignorant and uninformed is to be handicapped if not disqualified as a citizen, a parent, and a **missionary**. During the **Illinois Period**, in addition to primary schools operated by individual teachers, Church leaders at Nauvoo planned to establish a university but their efforts were derailed by **persecution** and the **exodus**.

In the Great Basin, the schooling of children began almost immediately and expanded through public and private primary schools. Thousands of students learned the rudiments, the three Rs, and other subjects as well. The **Sunday School** mainly taught religion, including basic morality and the scriptures, but through its periodical, *The Juvenile Instructor*, also expanded awareness of the natural world, geography, and literary and historical figures. Compulsory education was not yet standard in America, and most students stopped attending school after a few years. To provide opportunity for a high school education, the Church began establishing "academies" in the 1870s. Eventually there were academies throughout the Mountain West and in the colonies in Canada and Mexico. With the advent of compulsory public schooling, the Church-sponsored academies were closed, turned over to the state, or developed into institutions of higher learning.

In the 20th century, Church schools, essentially high schools, were established in New Zealand, Tonga, Samoa, Mexico, and several South American countries. As **membership** continued to increase, these were scaled back or closed. Young people were encouraged to obtain an education through public schools. To provide basic skills and open doors of opportunity, the **Relief Society** sponsored a literacy program.

On the level of higher education the Church operates **BYU, BYU–Idaho, BYU–Hawaii**, and **LDS Business College**. Students from throughout the United States and from many other countries attend these institutions. However, these institutions cannot accommodate all Latter-day Saint college students and cannot accept all those who apply for admission. To supplement public schools and universities the Church provides **seminaries** and **institutes of religion** where feasible.

EDUCATION WEEK. Each year in August thousands of people gather at **BYU** for a week of educational and religious lectures by prominent speakers, including some **general authorities**. Classes are offered in self-improvement, **family** relations, religious education, history, science, youth interests, health, and literature. Originally called Leadership Week, the first annual meeting, intended for those holding leadership positions in the Church, took place in the winter of 1922 with 2,046 in attendance. Education Week was soon opened up to all interested members 14 years of age and older. Except for when it was canceled during and immediately after World War II, attendance has steadily increased each year. The 1999 Education Week hosted 29,775 registrants. Selected lectures were telecast over the Church satellite system. In 1998, **Ricks College** began sponsoring its own Education Week, starting with 300 classes offered by 45 instructors to about 2,000 people.

EIGHT WITNESSES. *See* WITNESSES OF THE *BOOK OF MORMON.*

ELDER. (1) An office in the **Melchizedek Priesthood**. Male Church members who pass standards of **worthiness** are ordained elders at the age of 18. Adult male converts are ordained as soon as possible after their **baptism**. **Elders** possess authority to perform all the functions of the lesser **Aaronic Priesthood**, including baptism and administering the **sacrament**. In addition, they have the necessary authority to confer the gift of the Holy Ghost in the **ordinance** of **confirmation**. Elders are organized into **quorums** of as many as 96 people with a **president**, two **counselors**, and a secretary. They meet weekly for instruction and the planning and reporting of service projects.

(2) A form of address for male missionaries and for **general authorities** except members of the **First Presidency** and **Presiding Bishopric**.

EMERITUS. Status of **general authorities**, specifically the First **Quorum** of the **Seventy**, who have been honorably released at the age of 70. Members of the Second Quorum of the Seventy serve for a five-year term and are then released, but are not considered to have emeritus status. Members of the **First Presidency** and Quorum of the **Twelve Apostles** have lifetime tenure.

EMPLOYMENT RESOURCE CENTERS. Devoted to assisting the unemployed, underemployed, self-employed, and unskilled, local centers help patrons to set goals, obtain practical training, prepare résumés, and master interview skills. Computer and Internet connections assist in pursuing job leads. For the self-employed, workshops are provided. The centers work in close cooperation with the Perpetual Education Fund in countries where it is established. In 2006, 286 centers operated in more than 50 countries. The previous year the centers helped more than 222,000 people.

ENDOWMENT. *See* TEMPLES.

ENGLAND, G. EUGENE, JR. (1933–2001). Essayist, poet, founder of private Mormon organizations and periodicals. Born in Logan, Utah, on 22 July 1933, Eugene England received the usual primary and secondary education. He married Charlotte Hawkins, and the two of them served as **missionaries** in Samoa from 1954 to 1956. They went on to have six children.

After graduating from the University of Utah in 1958, England attended MIT for one year and then entered the graduate program in English at Stanford University, receiving his M.A. in 1969 and a Ph.D. in 1974. His professional career has taken him to St. Olaf College in Minnesota and, in 1977, to **BYU**, where he won several coveted teaching awards. After retirement, he continued teaching at Utah Valley State College.

Along with G. Wesley Johnson, England was founding editor of ***Dialogue: A Journal of Mormon Thought*** in 1965. He promoted Mormon creative writing through his own poetry and essays, critical reviews and anthologies, and the **AML**, which he cofounded in 1977. He served as **counselor** in four bishoprics, and as branch **president**, **bishop**, and **high councilor**.

***ENSIGN*.** Official magazine of the Church, published monthly beginning in January 1971. The *Ensign* includes editorials, nonfiction articles in history and doctrine, fiction, poetry, news of events in the Church, and even some humor. Especially important are the May and November issues, which publish the proceedings of the April and October **general conference**.

ESPECIALLY FOR YOUTH. A summer program, started in 1976 at the **BYU** campus, where 172 young people ages 14 to 18 gather. Directed by 15 counselors, they participate in recreational, cultural, and devotional activities. In 2004 1,400 participants met. The program has expanded to 34 states, Canada, the United Kingdom, and Ireland. Selected speakers from these sessions tour other **stakes** by request.

EUROPE. The first preaching of Mormonism in Europe began with the mission to Great Britain in 1837. The ***Millennial Star***, which started publication in 1840, was filled with the details of conversion and emigration, first to Nauvoo, Illinois, then to the Great Basin in the West. By the middle of the 19th century, **missionaries** were proselytizing in various parts of the continent. Except for scattered individual conversions, the area of success on the continent was limited to Scandinavia. By 1900, close to 100,000 European Mormons had emigrated.

In the 20th century, proselytizing was extended to France, the Netherlands, and Germany. A preliminary effort leading to a few converts was made in Czechoslovakia. However, all European missionary efforts were interrupted by World War II. When missionaries returned to Europe after the war, they looked up the scattered surviving **members** and added to their number by conversions. Success increased in the 1960s and after. Where numbers were sufficient, **wards** and **stakes** were established, local members were called to positions of responsibility, and **temples** were constructed. It was a generation of growth and maturation. Long kept out of Eastern Europe by the conditions of the cold war, Mormon missionaries began to gain access during the 1980s. Missions have been established in the Czech Republic, Poland, states of the former Yugoslavia, Bulgaria, Romania, Greece, the Ukraine, Armenia, and Russia. At the end of 2005 membership for the different European countries stood as follows:

Country	Members	Stakes	Wards	Temples
Armenia	2,083			
Austria	4,138	2	13	
Belgium	6,267	2	11	
Bulgaria	2,084			
Czech Republic	1,981			
Finland	4,500	2	15	1
France	33,200	9	60	
Germany	37,149	14	91	2
Greece	631			
Hungary	4,147			
Iceland	225			
Italy	21,791	4	26	

Netherlands	8,286	3	19	1
Norway	4,134	1	7	
Poland	1,531			
Portugal	37,812	6	35	
Romania	2,483			
Russia	18,785			
Spain	39,784	9	56	1
Sweden	8,862	4	24	1
Switzerland	7,699	4	23	1
UK	181,872	46	284	2
Ukraine	9,951			

Although the percentage growth in Europe was not so rapid as in **South America** or **Asia**, it has been steady. Second- and third-generation Mormon families in Europe have demonstrated tenacity. Many young members study in **seminary** and **institute of religion** classes, after which they serve full-time missions. In 2003 the church began the establishment of outreach centers at institutes of religion in Western Europe to assist in reactivation and fellowshipping young single adults. Experienced leadership has been built up. **General authorities** of European origin have included F. Enzio Busche, Dieter F. Uchtdorf, and Erich W. Kopischke (Germany); Charles A. Didier (Belgium); Derek A. Cuthbert (England); Jacob de Jager (Netherlands); and Hans B. Ringger (Switzerland).

EVANS, RICHARD LOUIS (1906–1971). Radio announcer, civic leader, **general authority**. Born on 23 March 1906 in Salt Lake City, Utah, Evans served as a **missionary** to England as a young man and gained experience as an assistant editor of the ***Millennial Star***. In 1928 he became an announcer for KSL radio in Salt Lake City and the following year began announcing for the weekly broadcast of the **Mormon Tabernacle Choir**. "Once more we welcome you within these walls, with music and the spoken word, from the Crossroads of the West"; "May peace be with you, this day and always"—such expressions became readily recognized throughout the country. Evans's short talks, or "sermonettes," were widely appreciated. Many of them were published in books, including *This Day and Always*. He also wrote a newspaper column for King Features Syndicate.

In 1937 Evans began a long career as managing editor and later senior editor of the ***Improvement Era***. The next year, only 32 years old, he became a **general authority** as one of the **presidents** of the First Council of **Seventy**. In 1947 he was appointed director of **Temple Square**. In 1953, at age 47, he became one of the **twelve apostles**. He was president of the Utah Alumni Association, president of the Knife and Fork Club, and, in 1949, president of the Salt Lake Rotary Club. He later became president of Rotary International. Evans died in 1971 at the age of 65.

EXCOMMUNICATION. A formal action that deprives a person of Church membership. Careful procedures are described in the ***General Handbook of Instructions***. Grounds for such an action vary from flagrant moral infractions to the deliberate teaching of false doctrine or belonging to **apostate** groups. Exercising considerable latitude in addressing such problems, **bishops** also have the option of imposing lesser penalties of disfellowshipment or a temporary suspension of some privileges. Previously called church courts, such procedures are currently called disciplinary councils. **Melchizedek Priesthood** holders may be excommunicated only by a disciplinary council convened by a **stake president**. When excommunication proceedings are instituted, the person charged is allowed the opportunity for a hearing, records are kept, and appeals are allowed. These proceedings are regarded as confidential. While attempting to maintain the integrity of the Church and its purposes, bishops are urged to be solicitous and kind in order, where possible, to bring the offender back into fully participating membership. *See also* DISSENT.

EXODUS. After the **prophet Joseph Smith** was assassinated in June 1844, most Mormons accepted the leadership of **Brigham Young** and the **Quorum** of the **Twelve Apostles** in August. The attempt to remain in Nauvoo, Illinois, signaled by continued in-migration and construction on the **temple**, had to be given up under the insistent and increasingly violent pressure of the **anti-Mormons**. In February 1846 the wagons started moving out from the city, across the Mississippi River, and to the plains of Iowa. By fall, only a few inhabitants remained in Nauvoo.

Under Brigham Young's direction, leaders organized these 10,000 or so refugees into companies; provided protection and nourishment during whatever period of time they would be en route; determined a place of ultimate settlement; got the people to that destination in good order; and established them there in such a way that an ugly competition for property claims would be avoided. Of some help was the recruitment of 500 males into the **Mormon Battalion**, which, although it seemed oppressive to many at the time, did get one group to the West under government direction and provided a payroll to aid the others.

By the late fall of 1846 and early winter of 1847, Mormons were strung out in various encampments throughout Iowa. Along the banks of the Missouri River near present-day Omaha, Nebraska, and Council Bluffs, Iowa, they built temporary settlements for the winter, which remained inhabited for several years as a mustering and jumping-off place for the westward migrants. On 14 January 1847 Brigham Young issued a set of instructions called "The Word and Will of the Lord" (*Doctrine and Covenants*, section 136). Organized into companies, the people were to cooperate in helping one another, raising crops, building houses, and sending a company of **pioneers** westward to locate a place of settlement and put in crops.

The pioneer company of 143 men, 3 women, and 2 children set out in mid-April. In their number were Young and seven other apostles. A detailed account of the journey was kept by diarists William Clayton and Thomas Bullock, carefully recording the distance traveled each day, as calculated by a mechanical odometer constructed for the purpose and attached to a wagon wheel. Their destination was already known, Young and his colleagues having studied various accounts and maps made by mountain men and explorers, including John C. Frémont. They regarded this exodus as the fulfillment of earlier plans and prophecies of Joseph Smith. One effort to dissuade them was reportedly made by Jim Bridger. Another was made by **Samuel Brannan**, who came from California in a vain effort to persuade Young to settle there.

On 21 July advance scouts entered the Salt Lake Valley, and the party began plowing and planting on 23 July. Brigham Young entered with the remainder of the company on 24 July. He pronounced it as indeed the right place. For the next few weeks members of the advance company explored, surveyed, established simple shelters, coaxed water from the stream onto the dry soil, and planted crops. Then many returned eastward to get their families.

This original exodus consisted of more than just one small exploring company. Joining the advance company in a kind of convergence were Mississippi converts, one contingent that had been detached from the Mormon Battalion because of poor health, and soon from California other discharged soldiers from the battalion. Behind the advance company other groups had been moving westward and over several weeks, company after company entered the Valley. By December 1847 something close to 2,000 were trying to establish themselves in their promised land.

By the 1850 census 11,380 people inhabited Great Salt Lake City, Utah, and the small settlements in the immediate vicinity. Others making their way westward, or temporarily halted in Missouri, were still experiencing their own "exodus." The comparison with the children of Israel led by Moses from Egypt to their promised land could not be avoided. In January 1847 Brigham Young had a revelation and proclaimed, "I [God] am he who led the children of Israel out of the land of Egypt; and my arm is stretched out in the last days, to save my people Israel" (***Doctrine and Covenants*** 136:22.) Although pioneering and **colonization** did not stop with the original westward thrust, the initial exodus had saved the destitute Mormons and established them in their land of refuge. *See also* ILLINOIS PERIOD; SUCCESSION; "THIS IS THE PLACE" MONUMENT.

EYRING, HENRY (1901–1981). Scientist. Born on 20 February 1901 of Mormon parents in Colonia Jaurez, Mexico, Henry moved with his family to Arizona. Along with the usual rough and tumble of boyhood in rural America, Henry did well in his schooling, graduating from Gila Academy in Thatcher, Arizona. When he went off to attend the University of Arizona at Tucson on scholarship, as Eyring often recounted in later years, his father told him that his religion did not require him to believe anything untrue. Graduating with a bachelor's degree and completing a master's degree the following year, Eyring pursued his doctorate at the University of California at Berkeley, receiving a Ph.D. in 1927.

After a year as an instructor at the University of Wisconsin, a year in **Europe** working with Michael Polanyi and others, and a one-year lectureship at Berkeley, Eyring accepted an appointment at Princeton University. He advanced to the rank of full professor and became director of the Textile Research Institute. In 1946, he became professor of chemistry and dean of the graduate school at the University of Utah, his professional home for the remainder of his life. A prolific scholar, Eyring produced more than 350 publications, including four books. Professional associations included the American Chemical Society, of which he served as president, the National Science Board, and the American Association for the Advancement of Science. Recipient of the National Medal of Science, the Joseph Priestley Celebration Award, the Berzelins Gold Medal from the Swedish Academy of Science, and the Wolf Prize in Chemistry from the Wolf Foundation in Israel, Eyring also received honorary degrees from 15 different universities. One colleague listed the following as scientific disciplines to which Eyring was a significant contributor: mining engineering, metallurgy, ceramics, fuels, explosives, geology, plastics, fibers, lubricants, organic chemistry, molecular biology, analytical chemistry, radiation chemistry, electrolytic chemistry, quantum chemistry, and statistical mechanics. Perhaps his most basic discovery was the absolute rate theory of treating chemical reaction kinetics and other rate processes.

Always a devout member of the Church, Eyring served on the general board of the **Sunday School** for many years. In addition to articles in Church magazines, he wrote *The Faith of a Scientist* (1967). He and his wife, Mildred Bennion Eyring, had three sons: Edward M., Henry B., and Harden. Mildred died in 1969, and in 1971 Eyring married Winifred Brennan. Until nearly the end of his life he participated in an annual 50-yard dash with his graduate students.

EYRING, HENRY B. (1933–). General authority, second **counselor** in the **First Presidency**. Second son of the eminent scientist **Henry Eyring**, Henry B. Eyring was born on 31 May 1933 in Princeton, New Jersey. He received a bachelor's degree in physics from the University of Utah. After serving as an officer in the U.S. Air Force, he attended the Harvard Graduate School of Business, receiving his MBA and a doctorate in business administration. He married Kathleen Johnson. Accepting a position at the Stanford Graduate School of Business, he taught but also entered the business world as founder and director of a computer manufacturing company. In 1971, he was named president of **Ricks College**.

In the Church, Eyring served as **bishop**, **regional representative**, member of the **Sunday School** general board, and commissioner of the Church Educational System. In 1985, he became a general authority as first counselor in the **Presiding Bishopric**. In 1992 he became a member of the First **Quorum** of the **Seventy** and in 1995 a member of the Quorum of the **Twelve Apostles**. In October 2007 he was called as second counselor in the First Presidency. On 4 February 2007 he was called as first counselor to President Thomas S. Monson of the First Presidency.

– F –

FAMILY. In an age of family breakdown, Mormons are among those fighting to preserve the nuclear family as the best assurance of safety and fulfillment for individuals and the best protection against social disintegration. Not sealed off from the larger society, Mormons have their share of dysfunctional families, divorce, and other signs of tension. To combat these problems, principles are taught in all of the **auxiliary** organizations as well as **seminaries** and **institutes of religion.** Members are encouraged to participate in a weekly **family home evening**. Each **ward** provides support through **home teaching** and **visiting teaching**. In addition to whatever community assistance might be available, the resources of the **welfare program** and **LDS Family Services** assist the Church in strengthening its families.

As part of their belief in the **ordinances** of the **temple**, Mormons have faith that righteous families will endure beyond the grave. "Families can be together forever"—these words begin the chorus of one of their hymns. Such an eternal union of husband and wife, parents and children, is dependent on receiving the **sealing** ordinances of the temples either in this life or, if one has not had the opportunity, vicariously after death, and living in faithful obedience to the **commandments**.

Considering that strong families are a benefit to all of society, the Church sponsors public service announcements that have been widely used by radio and television stations. Nondenominational in application, these announcements stress principles such as spending time with children. On 23 September 1995 the **First Presidency** issued the proclamation on the family, reaffirming traditional values (see appendix 2). *See also* MARRIAGE.

FAMILY AND CHURCH HISTORY DEPARTMENT. In 2000 the Historical Department of the Church merged with the Family History Department of the Church to form the Family and Church History Department, in order to better serve the expanding membership of the Church.

Head of the Family and Church History Department is the Church historian and recorder. As has been true throughout most of the history of the Church, this individual is a **general authority**. His role is not that of a working research historian or genealogist but of administering and coordinating history-related activities.

Family History creates online products and seeks to deliver indexes and images to personal home computers or family history centers. Both the Family History Library and a division called Worldwide Support assist researchers directly and train local family history consultants. The Family History Library, in Salt Lake City, Utah, is one of the premier research libraries for genealogical research, with books and records and especially microfilm rolls of primary sources from all over the world.

Church History adopted a horizontal reorganization of its staff, resulting in the department-wide functions of collections development, preservation, and public programs being integrated across the traditional institutional boundaries of archives, library, and museum. A new 250,000-square-foot facility called the Church History Library will be completed in 2009 to provide state-of-the-art storage, preservation, and public research services for the ever-expanding historical collections of the Church.

A long-range project of Church History is the publication in approximately 30 volumes of the papers of **Joseph Smith**, edited and annotated according to professional standards. In addition to collecting diaries, oral histories, and local records from throughout the

Church, the department makes them available to researchers through organizing and cataloging; selective printed publication; compact discs of certain collections, including census and immigration records; and selective digitalized online publications. *See also* GENEALOGY.

FAMILY HISTORY. *See* GENEALOGY.

FAMILY HOME EVENING. A regularly scheduled time once a week in which families enjoy recreation and some form of instruction or spiritual enhancement. To some extent such activities occur naturally within families, but the urbanization and intensified pace of life in the 20th century has combined with evidence of **family** breakdown to increase concern among Church leaders. Building on earlier programs going back to the 1910s, the program as it now exists was instituted in 1965. Manuals were issued containing lessons and suggested activities. To assure time for holding family home evening, no Church meetings were scheduled on Monday. Responding to interest from others, the Church has publicized the family home evening program broadly and has readily shared its resource materials.

FAMILYSEARCH. Provider of **family** history and **genealogy** resources, FamilySearch.org, launched on 24 May 1999, allows free access to the Church's searchable database of 81 million names. More than 100,000 hits a day attest to the fact that people throughout the world utilize this resource. The long-range goal is to make images and indexes as widely available as possible.

FARNSWORTH, PHILO (1906–1971). Father of television. Born near Beaver, Utah, Farnsworth early showed an aptitude for mathematics and technology. As early as age 13, he won a national contest with an invention related to automobiles. Living in Idaho at the time, interested in electricity and radio, he drew an "image dissector" for his teacher, Justin Tolman. Tolman copied the drawings in his notebook, which later turned out to be crucial evidence in a battle over the television patent.

In 1921, the Farnsworths moved to Provo, Utah, where Philo attended **BYU**, married Elma "Pem" Gardner, and aroused the enthusiasm of a few collaborators for his television scheme. In 1926, he moved to San Francisco to work on the project. Overcoming obstacles one at a time, Farnsworth and his friends finally produced an electronically transmitted image. "In 1927 when I first saw a television image transmitted without any moving parts," he said, "I believe I felt the greatest thrill of my lifetime before or since, and I have had quite a lot of them."

When a Russian scientist, Vladimir Zworykin, showed up at the laboratory and claimed to represent Westinghouse, Farnsworth showed him everything. Later Zworykin, who actually worked for RCA, fought Farnsworth for the patent rights. Examining the evidence, including Tolman's earlier notebooks, the U.S. Patent Office upheld Farnsworth's claims. Farnsworth died on 11 March 1971. About 20 years later, his statue was placed in the rotunda of the nation's capitol, joining **Brigham Young**'s to represent the state of Utah.

FASTING. Abstaining from food and drink. Combined with **prayer**, fasting contributes to feeling close to God. Often people requesting special blessings or inspiration in making personal decisions will fast. In addition, **members** are urged to fast from two meals on the first Sunday of each month and to pay a generous **fast offering.** On this day a meeting is devoted to the expression of personal **testimony**.

FAST OFFERING. A donation to the Church on the first Sunday of each month, the equivalent of the meals one has abstained from. These funds are specifically designated for helping the poor and needy. Increased poverty and the expansion of the Church into areas of the world where many people live close to the subsistence level have increased the need for assistance. Church **president Spencer W. Kimball** urged members to donate not merely the cost of two meals but substantially more when possible. Unlike many relief programs, the fast offering program results in 100 percent of the donation going to the assistance of the needy.

FAUST, JAMES E. (1920–2007). Attorney, legislator, **general authority**. Born on 31 July 1920 in Delta, Utah, James E. Faust attended school in Salt Lake City, Utah. He served as a **missionary** in Brazil and afterwards entered the U.S. Air Force, reaching the rank of first lieutenant. After World War II, Faust entered law school at the University of Utah and received the J.D. degree in 1948. As a lawyer, he was president of the Utah Bar Association in 1962–1963. He was elected to the state legislature as a Democrat from 1949 to 1951. President John F. Kennedy appointed him to the Lawyers Committee for Civil Rights and Racial Unrest.

In the Church he served as **bishop**, **high councilor**, **stake** president, and **regional representative**. In 1972 he became an **assistant to the twelve** and **area** supervisor in **South America**. In 1976 he was named one of the presidency of the First **Quorum** of the **Seventy**, and in 1978 became a member of the Quorum of the **Twelve Apostles**. As **president** of the International Mission, with responsibility for members and **investigators** in parts of the world without organized missions, he traveled widely, displaying an ability to relate to people of all races and nationalities. In 1995 he became second **counselor** in the **First Presidency**. He and his wife, Ruth, had five children.

FEMINISM. As the term was understood in the 19th century, Mormons were feminists. Mormon women were among the first to vote and participated in the national movement for female suffrage. Basic spiritual equality between women and men has always been assumed: both men and women may achieve salvation in the fullest sense of the word. In the **Relief Society** and other **auxiliary** organizations women exercised leadership roles from nearly the beginning of the Church.

The current women's liberation movement has led to some complications. Some militant feminists have disparaged the role of wife and mother, some going so far as to advocate abolition or restructuring of the **family**. While a few Mormon women were caught up in the rhetoric of national and world feminism in its extreme form, other Mormon feminists, less extreme, have expressed concern about such issues as education and employment, child care, and male abuse of power. Church leaders, including the women leaders in the Relief Society, try to show sensitivity to legitimate concerns. That female education and professional accomplishment are valued is evident from the women selected to serve in leadership positions. Several thousand young women serve as full-time **missionaries.** At the same time, Church leaders have insisted on the importance of the family. Rather than putting males and females into opposition, they pursue a partnership on the general Church level, in the **stakes** and **wards** and in the family. *See also* WOMEN, ROLES OF.

FIFTY, COUNCIL OF. A council formed by **Joseph Smith** in the spring of 1844. At its origin, this body appeared to be intended as the basis for establishing the political Kingdom of God on earth as part of the onset of the **millennium**. Three nonmembers of the Church were included. In practical terms the fifty (whose membership overlapped in part with the **Quorum** of the **Twelve Apostles**) helped organize Joseph Smith's presidential campaign in 1844, supervised the migration to the West, and in territorial Utah met at infrequent intervals. Since it was not an essential body of government in church or state, it lapsed.

FIRESIDE SERVICE. A Church-sponsored meeting outside the regular scheduled meetings of the Church, sometimes held in private homes, more often in a **ward** meetinghouse or **stake** center. Typically, all the youth of a stake are invited to hear a musical presentation or a talk that will be of special interest to them. There is greater latitude in choice of subject matter than in a **sacrament** meeting.

FIRST PRESIDENCY. The **president** of the Church and his two **counselors**. Upon the death of the president, the First Presidency is dissolved, the two counselors resuming their place in the **Quorum** of the **Twelve Apostles**. Historically, the First Presidency was organized in 1832 with **Joseph Smith** as president. Although on different occasions additional counselors, or assistants, were added to the First Presidency, the standard pattern was that of three individuals: the president and two counselors. Counselors who have been especially influential in the First Presidency, not including those who became president of the Church, are **Sidney Rigdon**, **Hyrum Smith**, **George Q. Cannon**, **J. Reuben Clark**, **Hugh B. Brown**, **N. Eldon Tanner**, **Thomas S. Monson**, and **James E. Faust.** As with all bishoprics and presidencies, the First Presidency functions as a unit, and the counselors, besides acting as advisers, perform many of the necessary functions.

FIRST PRINCIPLES. Faith in **Jesus Christ**, **repentance**, **baptism**, and laying on of hands for the gift of the Holy Ghost. Based on Acts 2:37–38, with the assumption of faith on the part of those addressed, these are the basics taught throughout the Mormon **scriptures**. Although faith is given priority, this is not a salvation-by-faith-alone doctrine. Nor is it an approach to salvation that disparages organized religion, for the **ordinances** of baptism and **confirmation** require the authority of **priesthood.** Although not usually listed as one of the first principles, enduring to the end is implicitly the fifth principle. Without continued faithfulness, the whole process is frustrated. The first principles and ordinances are not the whole of the **gospel**. To them are added other covenants and ordinances, such as those of the **temples**. But the first principles are foundational. They are never superseded. One's entire life is to be one of faith, repentance, and enduring. The commitments made at baptism and confirmation are renewed by regularly partaking of the **sacrament** throughout life.

FIRST VISION. The first **revelation** received by **Joseph Smith**. The setting was upper New York State, where competition between the different Christian denominations was intense. Some members of the Smith family, living just outside Palmyra, became Presbyterians. Young Joseph, not yet 15, was attracted to the Methodists but was confused by the "war of words and tumult of opinions" (***Pearl of Great Price***, Joseph Smith History 1:10). A reading of James 1:5 prompted him to take his dilemma directly to God in prayer, which he did in the spring of 1820. After an evil power tried to stop his effort, a great vision came: a pillar of light and two divine beings, one of them referring to the other as his son. Joseph was told that his sins were forgiven, that he should join none of the existing churches, and that in the future, if faithful, he might be the means of bringing back the true Christian faith. Local ministers reacted to Joseph's experience with ridicule and **persecution**. Such things may have happened in the days of the **Bible**, they said, but not now.

In the 20th century, some historians claimed there was no evidence of any religious revivals in Palmyra, New York, in the year 1820, but historians Milton Backman and D. Michael Quinn have discovered several examples of such activity in the immediate area, as Joseph said. For Mormons the First Vision is God's declaration, unequivocally and utterly authoritative, of the results of the Great **Apostasy** and the need for a **restoration.** Joseph Smith was only 14 years of age at the time. Not for another 10 years, in 1830, would the time be ripe to establish the Church.

FOLKLORE. Like all peoples, Mormons convey stories orally. Many of the stories told and passed on from generation to generation have to do with miracles of healing or dreams. The modernization associated with the 20th century has perhaps modified Mormon popular storytelling, but it still occurs in the form of "urban folklore." One recurring tale in the Mormon oral tradition recounts appearances of "the Three Nephites," characters from the ***Book of Mormon*** who were promised that they could remain on earth and not taste of death. Prominent in the study of Mormon folklore have been folklorists Hector Lee, Austin and Alta Fife, Thomas E. Cheney, and **William A. Wilson**. Others, such as Jan Harold Brunvaand, have supervised collecting and published articles on Mormon folklore.

FORMS OF ADDRESS. In any culture, one of the usages that has to be learned is the proper forms of address. For example, do you address the monarch as "King" or "Your Majesty"? Is the local parish priest properly addressed as "Reverend" or "Father"? Mormons are no exception, having their own standard usage. The following is descriptive—not an attempt to lay down rules, in other words, but to describe how Mormons do it.

The most widely used titles are "Brother" and "Sister," used for adult Church members of the male and female gender, respectively. Children are not addressed in this way, nor are nonmembers. Although occasionally heard in isolation, these words usually accompany the last name, as "Brother Smith" or "Sister Martinez."

A **bishop** and two **counselors** preside over a **ward**. The bishop is referred to as "Bishop Jones," for example, or often simply "Bishop," while the counselors are "Brother Taylor" or "Brother Gonzales." Among the **general authorities** there is a **presiding bishop**. He is known as "Bishop Burton." His counselors are also addressed as "Bishop."

The term ***president*** applies most importantly to the president of the Church, who is properly addressed or referred to as President **Gordon B. Hinckley** or President Hinckley. His two counselors have the same title, being addressed as President Monson or President Faust. Note that the term *bishop* is not attached to the counselors in a **ward** bishopric, but the term *president* is used for counselors in **stake** presidencies and the counselors in the First Presidency.

There are many presidents in the Church. On the stake level the presiding triumvirate is a stake presidency, all three of whom are addressed and referred to as "President." There are also presidents of general, stake, and ward **auxiliary** organizations, and of the many **priesthood quorums** throughout the Church. While it is not improper to address all of these by the title of president, it is common usage to employ the terms *Brother* or *Sister*.

Another term often used is **elder**. All worthy male members are ordained to the office of elder in the **Melchizedek Priesthood** at the age of 18 or 19. Yet all such elders are not usually addressed by this title. Those properly so addressed are all general authorities, with the exception of those in the **First Presidency** and **Presiding Bishopric,** and all male **missionaries** during their two-year missions. Female missionaries are "Sister," as in Sister Lambson.

Examples of well-meant but awkward and improper usage include the following: Prophet Hinckley (although sustained as "prophet, seer, revelator" and referred to in the third person as "the prophet," the term is not used as a form of address); Apostle Oaks (although those in the **Quorum** of the **Twelve Apostles** are apostles, the term is not used as a form of address); and Mr. Hinckley (which comes across as lacking in respect). First names are used by Mormons like everyone else, but in formal settings, as **conferences** or other Church meetings, even individuals who are close friends use the appropriate titles.

FOUNDATION FOR ANCIENT RESEARCH AND MORMON STUDIES (FARMS). An independent research and service organization established in 1979 as a nonprofit, tax-exempt, educational corporation. Dedicated to scholarly research having to do with the history, culture, language, geography, politics, and law of the ***Book of Mormon*** and other ancient **scriptures**, FARMS published a widely circulated newsletter, *FARMS Review of Books*, a semiannual *Journal of* Book of Mormon *Studies*, and other books and research papers. In 1999 FARMS established the Center for the Preservation of Ancient Texts (CPAT), which sponsored an electronic **Dead Sea Scrolls** database and a series of Islamic texts. In 2006, FARMS was brought under the umbrella of the **Neal A. Maxwell Institute for Religious Scholarship**.

THE FRIEND. A monthly magazine published for the children of the Church since 1971. In addition to stories and puzzles, *The Friend* publishes accounts of children's activities and achievements from throughout the Church. Instruction about leaders, history, and religious teachings is pitched at a simple level. Its predecessor magazine for children was entitled *The Children's Friend.*

FUNDAMENTALISTS. (1) In general, those who are seeking to return to the "fundamentals" of something, as with the **Protestant** fundamentalists of the early 20th century. Martin Marty and other scholars have applied the term more widely as they study "fundamentalisms" not only in **Christianity** but also in Islam and other world religions. Just how Mormonism fits into this broad terminology is not simply stated, for in their own conception Mormons have returned to the basics of primitive Christianity, while in the eyes of their detractors they have deviated from the norms of historic Christianity.

(2) Within the context of Mormon history, fundamentalists, according to current usage, are those who still cling to the practice of **polygamy**, and in some cases, versions of the **United Order**. They are **excommunicated** from the Church when discovered. Some have never been members of the Church. The use of the term *Mormon* to refer to these groups is frequently misleading because the uninformed often confuse them with members of the Church of Jesus Christ of Latter-day Saints. The Church office of public affairs, attempting to convey to the reality of what the Church teaches and practices, deplores the use of the term *Mormon fundamentalists*, as it so readily leads to misunderstanding.

Several fundamentalist groups exist more or less clandestinely. Estimates of their number living in the West vary from 20,000 to 30,000, but, according to scholar Brian C. Hales, this number may be too high. Prosecutions of the illegal activity of polygamy are few, partly because of the practical problem of providing for the children if parents are imprisoned or deprived of income, and partly because of a changed climate of opinion that tolerates many kinds of behavior by consenting adults. In recent years, however, extensive prosecutions have occurred for child abuse and underage marriages. *See also* MANIFESTO.

– G –

GARMENTS. White underwear worn by adult Mormons after receiving their endowments in the **temples**. This conservative underclothing has simple, unobtrusive markings symbolic of **gospel** ideals. Garments are not available in the general retail market but are purchased through Church **distribution centers**.

GATES, SUSA YOUNG (1856–1933). Suffragist, women's leader. The second daughter of Lucy Bigelow and **Brigham Young**, Susa Young Gates attended the University of Deseret (University of Utah) where she completed courses in stenography and telegraphy. In 1870, Gates, her mother, and her sister, Eudora, moved to St. George, Utah. There, she arranged various activities that involved organizing the Union Club, a social group for the local young men and women, and worked in the St. George temple as a recorder. Shortly thereafter, she married Alma Dunford, a local dentist. However, marriage responsibilities and her husband's alcoholism quickly overwhelmed the 16-year-old Gates. She divorced her husband in 1877. Three years later, much better prepared for marriage, she married Jacob Gates. In 1885, she accompanied her husband on his **mission** to Hawaii. The family remained there for the next five years. She also served on the general board of the Young Ladies Mutual Improvement Association (YLMIA) and the general board of the **Relief Society**, and she edited several Mormon publications for women. Gates continually participated in political, educational, and social causes. She continually championed the causes specific to women, which consisted of women's suffrage, genealogy, history, and education. She annually attended the National Council for Women on behalf of the YLMIA and served as the Press Committee chair for three years, and on two occasions, she represented the National Council of Women at its international conference. In educational matters, Gates organized the Brigham Young Academy's (now BYU) Music Department and Domestic Science Department. Utah's governor John C. Cutler appointed Gates to a six-year term on the board of directors of the Agricultural College of Utah (now Utah State University). While serving in this capacity, she initiated the Domestic Science Department here also. Gates created the Utah chapter of the Daughters of the American Revolution. While serving as president of the Daughters of the Utah Pioneers, she established the Hall of Relics. Finally, she worked as the head librarian of the Genealogical Society of Utah. She died in 1933 after suffering from cancer.

GATHERING. The "gathering of Israel" (**Articles of Faith**, no. 10) included not only the return of the Jews to the Holy Land but the concentration of Church members in a location in the Western Hemisphere where they would build a temple to God.

Early gathering places in Ohio, Missouri, and Illinois attracted converts. As they joined the Church in other parts of the United States, **members** would, where possible, migrate to the current gathering place, often called the Latter-day **Zion.** After the **exodus** to the West, it was the Salt Lake Valley in Utah that drew members in by the thousands, many of them converts from **Europe**, year after year through the second half of the 19th century.

Due to population pressures, limited job opportunities, and a desire to build up the Church in many parts of the world, the gathering in Utah slowed down in the 20th century. Church leaders urged members to remain where they were. But longing for the opportunities that drew other immigrants to America, many Mormons continued to move to the Salt Lake Valley if possible. Wishing to live in the midst of fellow believers, they continued to move to Utah and other mountain states, although at a slower rate. It was a time of transition.

After World War II, especially since the 1960s, the pattern of growth through **missionary** proselytizing greatly increased Mormon members and **wards, stakes,** and **temples** in all of the 50 states and in **Europe**, **Central America and Mexico**, **South America**, **Asia**, and **Africa**. On 1 December 1999, the **First Presidency** repeated "the long-standing counsel to remain in their homelands rather than immigrate to the United States." Individuals are considered gathered into the Church and Kingdom of God when they are baptized.

GENEALOGY. The discipline or activity of searching ancestry, including the preparation of pedigree charts and **family** reconstitution, or family group, sheets. Motivated by the doctrine of **baptism for the dead**, Mormons have been diligent genealogists since the 1840s. The vicarious **ordinance** work performed in the **temples** was based upon the genealogical research that allowed members to perform proxy service for their deceased ancestors.

In 1894 a genealogical society was organized. As an official designation, the name was changed to Family History Department in 1987, although the previous term was still used for some of the activities. From the 1930s, and especially after World War II, an ambitious microfilming project was launched. In many countries of the world, wherever permission could be obtained, ecclesiastical records and vital statistics were filmed.

The Family History Library in Salt Lake City, Utah, houses a vast collection of volumes and, most importantly, microfilm and microfiche records from many countries of the world. Through 4,500 branch libraries these materials are available to researchers in more than 40 countries. The Family History Library is just one part of the **Family and Church History Department** that is in the process of creating new products that will assist people in doing genealogical research and will contribute substantially to the delivery of genealogical information anywhere it is desired. In 2005, digital cameras began to be used and a massive program launched to digitize the 2.4 million rolls of microfilm. The long-range goal is to make all this material available through the Internet. *See also* FAMILYSEARCH.

GENERAL AUTHORITIES. Leaders of the Church on the general, as opposed to the local, level. When the Church was organized in 1830, the organization was simple: **Joseph Smith** was first **elder** and **Oliver Cowdery** was second elder. Soon Smith became **president**;

he and his two **counselors** constituted the **First Presidency**. In 1835 the **Quorum** of the **Twelve Apostles** was organized. When a quorum of the **seventy** was created, its seven leaders were known as the First Council of the **Seventy**. A **presiding bishop** was appointed very early, and, finally, a **patriarch** to the entire Church was designated. From the 1830s to the recent past these have been the Mormon general authorities.

During the past generation this basic structure has been adjusted according to needs. In 1941, in order to visit the increasing number of **stakes, assistants to the twelve** were appointed. In 1967 **regional representatives** were established—not considered general authorities—as a kind of intermediate supervisory level. In 1976 the First Council of the Seventy and the assistants to the twelve were released and called to the new First Quorum of the Seventy. In 1989 a Second Quorum of the Seventy was established, appointments to which were for a five-year term. These seventies are all general authorities and, among other responsibilities, are typically assigned to the presidencies of specific geographical **areas**. On the grounds that his functions were now adequately performed by stake patriarchs, the general Church patriarch was declared emeritus in 1979 and the position left unfilled.

The total number of general authorities thus has enlarged, consisting of the First Presidency (3), Quorum of the Twelve Apostles (12), presidency of the seventy (7), First Quorum of Seventy (52), Second Quorum of Seventy (28), and Presiding Bishopric (3).

GENERAL HANDBOOK OF INSTRUCTIONS. Official guide containing instructions for local leaders such as **stake presidents** and **bishops**. Given the lay nature of the Church organization, such guidance is helpful in answering questions ranging from the keeping of records to the care of buildings. Although local leaders must exercise judgment according to the varying circumstances that arise, the handbook helps assure a minimum uniformity. Not available in bookstores, the handbook is distributed to the Church officials it is intended to assist.

GENESIS GROUP. In 1970, three **African American** Latter-day Saint men met together to discuss common needs and issues. Assigned to meet with them were three of the **twelve apostles**: **Gordon B. Hinckley**, **Thomas S. Monson**, and **Boyd K. Packer.** As a result of those meetings, the **First Presidency** and the twelve apostles decided that an organization should be established as a support group for African American Latter-day Saints in and around Salt Lake City, Utah. The outcome of that decision was a dependent branch, organized in October 1971. The name *Genesis*, meaning beginning, was chosen by the African American members. President was Ruffin Bridgeforth; first **counselor**, Darius Gray; and second counselor, Eugene Orr. After the death of Bridgeforth in 1997, Darius Gray became president. Membership is approximately 60 percent nonwhite—African Americans, Africans, African Carribean, Latinos, Polynesians—and 40 percent white, including parents of adopted African American children and several biracial couples. Members of the Genesis Group maintain membership in their home **wards**. Meetings are held monthly and do not conflict with regularly scheduled church meetings. *See also* BLACKS.

GENTILE. (1) Generally, in Jewish usage, a non-Jew. (2) In informal Mormon usage uncommon now, but frequently used in the 19th century for a non-Mormon. In the 19th century both Mormons and non-Mormons generally used the term. More recently, its use is generally confined to humor and anecdotes. It has been humorously remarked that Salt Lake City is the only place where a Jew is a Gentile.

GODHEAD. God the Eternal Father, his son **Jesus Christ**, and the Holy Ghost. Mormons prefer the term Godhead to Trinity because of the creedal terminology associated with the latter. Mormons consider the three divine beings as separate individuals whose unity is one of purpose and intent. When Jesus was baptized by John the Baptist, the Father's voice was heard from heaven, and the Holy Ghost descended like a dove (Matt. 3:16). When Jesus was in Gethsemane, he prayed to his Father, not to himself. When **Joseph Smith** received the **First Vision** in answer to prayer, two beings appeared to him, God the Father and God the Son. Jesus Christ, the Son, has a glorified, resurrected body of flesh and bones, as does the Father, while the Holy Ghost is a personage of spirit (***Doctrine and Covenants***, section 130).

GOSPEL. The good news of **Jesus Christ** and the atonement wrought by him that brings immortality and, on condition of **repentance**, saves humans from their sins. As Mormons use this word, it refers to the *restored* gospel, or the *fullness* of the gospel, as taught in the **scriptures** and by the modern **prophets** from **Joseph Smith** to the present. A more complete view of the "good news" is embodied in the **plan of salvation**, which explains life and its meaning, including the blessings that are in store for those who love God and keep his **commandments**. Basic essentials are the **First Principles** of faith in the Lord Jesus Christ, repentance, **baptism,** and the gift of the Holy Ghost, which along with **resurrection** and judgment are sometimes collectively defined in the scriptures as the gospel. Indispensable to achieving the fullness of salvation, according to the gospel plan, is the **priesthood**, the power to administer the saving **ordinances.**

GRACELAND UNIVERSITY. Founded in 1895 as Graceland College at Lamoni, Iowa, Graceland is sponsored by the **Community of Christ**. Its current enrollment is close to 2,400 students. An urban campus in Independence, Missouri, houses a school of nursing, programs in education, and a seminary. Offering 60 degree programs, it is accredited by the North Central Association of Colleges and Schools.

GRANT, HEBER J. (1856–1945). Businessman, **general authority**, **president** of the Church. Born on 22 November 1856, the son of Jedediah Grant, a **counselor** in the **First Presidency** who died when the boy was still an infant, Heber was raised by his mother, Rachel Ivins Grant. His upbringing included a good basic education and activity in the Young Men's Mutual Improvement Association (YMMIA). Tall and lanky, he learned to throw a baseball by persistent practice against a barn door and later went on to play on a team that won the territorial championship. Grant's life was a story ideal for author Horatio Alger Jr. Grant learned to write a beautiful Spencerian hand, sold insurance, worked as a bank cashier, saved his money, and bought the Ogden Vinegar Works. The future seemed auspicious.

But he also faced difficulties. After he married Lucy Stringham, she developed serious health problems, which led to her death 12 years later. When Grant became a **stake** president at the young age of

23, the travel and worry so sapped his strength that he suffered from extreme depression and recurrent insomnia. The decline of his business income and the loss of his Ogden factory to a fire added to his burdens.

Called to the **Quorum** of the **Twelve Apostles** in 1882, Grant was assigned to work with the **Sunday School** and the YMMIA. Like other apostles, he traveled, especially to Arizona and Mexico, where he labored among the Yaqui Indians. He remained active in business as owner of a bank, an insurance company, a newspaper, a livery stable, and retail companies. He was also one of the owners of the Salt Lake Theater and the Utah Sugar Company. A crisis came in 1893 with the national depression that led to the loss of his business empire. Still, Grant was able to negotiate loans and assist the Church to survive its financial plight.

He married two additional wives, both of whom had been schoolteachers. Twelve children came from these marriages. Despite his frequent absences, surviving letters give every indication of tender, supportive, and respectful relationships.

Since he had become an apostle at the relatively young age of 26, it was not entirely surprising that he outlived his colleagues to become president of the twelve apostles and, in 1918, president of the Church. Grant's presidency, from 1918 to 1945, included the post–World War I years, the Great Depression, and World War II. Serving on the board of directors of national corporations, he promoted good will for the Church. He was influential in promoting two Hollywood movie productions, *Union Pacific* and *Brigham Young*. Not given to heavy theological discourse, Grant advocated faithfulness and obedience to the **commandments**. He was especially emphatic in urging adherence to the **Word of Wisdom**. He sprinkled his sermons with quotations from popular poet Edgar A. Guest and the essayist and university president David Starr Jordan.

The Church was challenged by the moral laxity of the 1920s and by the economic crisis of the '30s (which for many Mormon farmers was just a further burden added to the agricultural depression they had been experiencing ever since the war). Responding to the former, Grant stressed the old-time virtues, which he exemplified. Although a Democrat, he was extremely critical of the New Deal. The widespread unemployment following the crash of 1929 prompted Grant to introduce the **welfare program** and call a young **stake** president, **Harold B. Lee**, to administer it.

The Church grew steadily. Hundreds of chapels were constructed. Temples were built in Hawaii, Canada, and Arizona. An imposing chapel, still standing although no longer owned by the Church, went up in Washington, D.C. **Missionary** work continued. In 1937 Grant traveled to England to attend meetings commemorating the first missionaries' arrival there one century earlier. World War II necessitated a reduction of the missionary force everywhere and, in **Europe**, a closing down of missions.

As always with presidencies, Grant's counselors shared the responsibility. Anthon H. Lund, Charles W. Penrose, and Anthony W. Ivins played this role through the '20s, and Ivins into the early 1930s. For the remainder of Grant's presidency his counselors were **J. Reuben Clark** and **David O. McKay**. During World War II, with many young Mormons in military service, a committee was organized to supervise the calling of **chaplains** and to prepare a miniature newspaper and special editions of Mormon books for servicemen. Not bellicose, President Grant expressed reservations about the war and recognized that Church members in other countries would rightfully serve in their armed forces.

GREAT APOSTASY. *See* APOSTASY.

– H –

HALES, ROBERT D. (1932–). Businessman, **general authority**. Born in New York City, Robert D. Hales earned a bachelor's degree from the University of Utah and a master's of business administration degree from Harvard University. He was a jet fighter pilot in the U.S. Air Force. Then he became an executive with four major national companies. He served as **counselor** in the **stake** presidency, **regional representative**, president of the England London Mission, first **counselor** in the general presidency of the **Sunday School**, **assistant to the twelve**, member of the First **Quorum** of the **Seventy**, and **presiding bishop**. Hales was ordained one of the **twelve apostles** in April 1994. He and his wife, Mary, have two sons.

HANDCART PIONEERS. Mormon immigrants who crossed the plains not in the standard covered wagons but by walking, carrying their belongings in small two-wheeled carts that were either pushed or pulled. Nearly 3,000 made the journey in 10 companies between 1856 and 1860.

Of the 250 deaths, most were in two companies led by James G. Willie and Edward Martin in 1856. A combination of late departure from England and from Florence, Nebraska, and an unusually early winter led to tragedy. In Wyoming, both of these companies were caught in bitter weather, including icy winds and blizzards. Running out of food, they huddled in camps while waiting for help. Fortunately **Brigham Young** learned of their plight and sent relief from Salt Lake City, Utah. Crossing hundreds of miles in heavy snow, horseback riders and wagon trains found the destitute immigrants, brought food and warm clothing and bedding, and helped carry the survivors on the final lap of the journey.

The mistaken judgment behind the late departure in 1856 was obvious. But it was the courage and heroism of the handcart pioneers and their rescuers that came to be emphasized. On **Temple Square** in Salt Lake City a statue by Torlief Knaphus commemorates "The Handcart Family." In December 2006 a documentary entitled *Sweetwater Rescue* aired on public broadcasting stations in the United States. A visitors center at Martin's Cove in Wyoming offers informative exhibits about the handcart experience. *See also* PIONEERS.

HANKS, MARION DUFF (1921–). Educator, community leader, **general authority**. Born on 13 October 1921 in Salt Lake City, Utah, Hanks was raised and educated there. From 1942 to 1944 he was a **missionary** in the Northern States Mission and then enlisted in the U.S. Navy, serving aboard a submarine chaser. He married Maxine Christensen, and they have five children.

Hanks taught in the **seminary** and **institute** system. In 1953 he became a member of the First Council of **Seventy**. From 1962 to 1964 he was president of the British Mission.

A member of the national executive board of the **Boy Scouts** of America, he earned the Silver Beaver, Silver Antelope, and Silver Buffalo awards. With **Elaine Cannon** he edited a section entitled "Era of Youth" for the ***Improvement Era***. For five years he was managing director of the **Latter-day Saints Students Association (LDSSA)** for college students.

He served on the President's Council on Physical Fitness and Sports. Other public service included president of the Salt Lake City Rotary Club and in 1977–1978 district governor; first chairman of the Utah Committee on Children and Youth; chairman of the Salt Lake Cancer Society; chairman of the Mental Health Board; and president of the Community Service Board. He has been on the governing boards of **BYU**, Weber State University, Southern Utah University, and Snow College.

After presiding over the British Mission from 1962 to 1964, he was **area** supervisor for Southeast Asia/Hawaii. From 1980 to 1982 he was executive administrator of the Southeast Asia/Philippines area, living in Hong Kong. He initiated a pioneering effort working with refugees. He chaired the board of the Ouelessebougou Mali–Utah Alliance, which since 1985 assisted with sanitation, agriculture, and literacy in a consortium of 22 villages in Mali.

From 1982 to 1985 Marion D. Hanks was president of the Salt Lake Temple. Then, after serving as executive director of the Priesthood Department of the Church, he was given emeritus status in October 1992.

HARRIS, FRANKLIN STEWART (1884–1960). Agronomist, educator, university president. Born in Benjamin, Utah, on 29 August 1884, Harris moved with his parents and siblings to Juarez, Mexico, in 1889. There, in a rural setting, he grew up. He graduated from Juarez **Stake** Academy in 1903. During his first year at **BYU** his family moved from Mexico to Cardston, Alberta, Canada. Franklin continued pursuing his studies, working as a teaching assistant to **John A. Widtsoe** in soil chemistry, and in 1907 graduated with a B.S. degree. He married Estella Spilsbury in 1908.

After earning a Ph.D. at Cornell University, Harris became a professor of agronomy at Utah Agricultural College (now Utah State University) in 1912, director of the School of Agricultural Engineering and Mechanical Arts, and in 1916 director of the experiment station. He published *The Principles of Agronomy* (1915), *Sugar Beets in America* (1918), and *Soil Alkali* (1920). In 1921 he became president of BYU. At the time the BYU faculty consisted of 78 people, only 10 of whom had doctorates. His was the guiding hand that helped raise the institution to a higher level by building a program, attracting qualified faculty, and in general maintaining high standards.

During the '20s and '30s, Harris was appointed U.S. representative to the Pan Pacific Science Congress in Tokyo in 1926; chairman of a commission to check on conditions among Jews in the Soviet Union in 1929; chairman of the agriculture section of a scientific congress in Mexico City in 1935; and member of an agricultural mission to Iran in 1939 (where later he helped set up the Point Four program). In 1945 he resigned as president of BYU to become president of Utah State University. He retired in 1950 and died in 1960.

HARRIS, MARTIN (1783–1875). One of the three **witnesses of the *Book of Mormon***. Born in 1783 in Easton, New York, he married Lucy Harris (a distant cousin) and the couple had at least six children. A veteran of the War of 1812, he purchased a 320-acre farm near Palmyra, New York. For seven years he was elected road overseer. Religiously he was unaffiliated but looked for a restoration of original Christianity.

Sometime after 1824 Harris heard of **Joseph Smith** and the metal plates. Believing what he heard, Harris helped Smith move to Harmony, Pennsylvania, for safety. In 1828 Harris took a transcription of characters from the plates to two scholars, Charles Anthon and Samuel L. Mitchill, for verification. Whatever took place in the interviews, Harris came away convinced that a prophecy in Isaiah 29 had been fulfilled. For a short period Harris assisted Smith as scribe, but when he borrowed and then lost the first 116 pages of the handwritten manuscript, he was removed from that position. He pled for forgiveness and continued to support the project. His testimony of seeing the plates and an angel, signed along with **Oliver Cowdery** and **David Whitmer**, appeared in the front of the ***Book of Mormon*** when it was published in early 1830. Harris mortgaged part of his farm as security for the printing of the book and later sold part of it to pay the bill.

Harris was baptized the day the Church was organized, 6 April 1830. A year later he moved to Kirtland, Ohio; traveled with Smith to Missouri; and preached Mormonism as a **missionary**. He was a member of the first **high council** at Kirtland. After traveling again to Missouri as a member of **Zion's Camp**, Harris returned to Ohio and, with his two fellow *Book of Mormon* witnesses, selected the first **Quorum** of the **Twelve Apostles**. His first marriage having failed, he married a niece of **Brigham Young**.

From 1837 on Harris became more or less disaffected from the Church. Except for one missionary trip to England, he lived in Kirtland, Ohio. His wife and children moved to Utah in 1856. Harris himself moved there and rejoined the Church in 1870. Many times he bore his testimony of the *Book of Mormon*, reaffirming the testimony he had written for the original 1830 publication. He died in Clarkston, Utah, on 10 July 1875.

HIGH COUNCIL. A body of 12 high priests in the **Melchizedek Priesthood** who assist a **stake president**. Holding regular meetings, a stake high council advises the stake president on matters he presents to it, including the selection of individuals for specific **callings** in the stake. In serious disciplinary actions, the high council discusses and evaluates the evidence along with the stake presidency and ratifies the decision of the stake president (***Doctrine and Covenants***, section 102). Individual high councilmen are given different supervisory and training assignments. They represent the stake presidency by speaking in **ward sacrament meetings** and in other assignments. *See also* EXCOMMUNICATION.

HIGH PRIEST. An office in the **Melchizedek Priesthood**. Those called to serve in **bishoprics**, **stake** presidencies, **high councils**, or as **general authorities** are, if they are not already such, ordained to the office of high priest. **Elders** who have served faithfully in other **callings** are often advanced to the high priest office for reasons of age compatibility. All the high priests in a stake constitute the stake high priest **quorum**. Those in a **ward** are called a high priest group and meet each Sunday for instruction and for planning compassionate service and other activities. The **president** of the Church is the presiding high priest in the Church; the stake president, the presiding high priest in the stake; the bishop, the presiding high priest in the ward.

HILLAM, HAROLD G. (1934–). Orthodontist, **general authority**. Born on 1 September 1934 in Sugar City, Idaho, Hillam served as a **missionary** in Brazil, graduated from **BYU**, and attended dental school at Northwestern University, where he later returned for an advanced degree in orthodontics. He practiced his profession in Idaho Falls, Idaho, and was president of the Rocky Mountain Society of Orthodontists.

In the Church, Hillam was a **bishop**'s **counselor**, **high councilor**, **stake president**, and **regional representative**. Then he served as mission president in Portugal. In 1990 he became a member of the Second **Quorum** of the **Seventy**, in 1991 a member of the First Quorum of the Seventy, and in 1995 a member of its presidency. He served as general president of the **Sunday School**. He was named to emeritus status in 2005. He and his wife, Carol, have seven children.

HILL CUMORAH. Near Palmyra, New York, a hill (drumlin) where Mormons believe an ancient prophet buried the inscribed plates later translated and published as the ***Book of Mormon***. The precise spot where the plates were buried is unknown. In 1928, the Church purchased the hill and erected a large monument. Since 1937 the hill has been the site of the annual Hill Cumorah Pageant.

HINCKLEY, GORDON BITNER (1910–2008). General authority, Church **president**. Born on 23 June 1910 in Salt Lake City, Utah, Hinckley graduated from the University of Utah in 1932. He was a **missionary** in Great Britain for two years. Employed by the Church as executive secretary of its Radio, Publicity, and Mission Literature Committee, he became executive secretary of the General Missionary Committee in 1951, managing the entire missionary program. He was president of the East Mill Creek **Stake**.

In 1958 he was called as an **assistant to the twelve** and three years later became a member of the **Quorum** of the **Twelve Apostles**. His assignments included serving on or chairing committees on missionaries, **temples**, **correlation**, and **welfare**. He served on the Church Board of Education and the Board of Trustees of **BYU** and **Ricks College**. Since 1981 he served in the **First Presidency**, as second

counselor to President **Spencer W. Kimball**, and from 1985 as first counselor to President **Ezra Taft Benson**.

Hinckley traveled in **Asia** after World War II and played a key role in establishing the Church in the Philippines, Taiwan, Hong Kong, Japan, and Korea. With the beginning of a major program of constructing temples in many different countries, it was he more than anyone else who traveled to the different locations and dedicated the new sacred edifices.

In 1995 he became president of the Church. Experienced in dealing with the media, Hinckley launched initiatives to improve the image of the Church, encouraged **community service**, and with good humor responded to the questions of Mike Wallace, Larry King, and other interviewers. In 1998 he announced a goal of 100 temples, which was made realizable by scaling back on their size. He and his wife, Marjorie Pay Hinckley (1911–2004), had five children. Hinckley died in his home in Salt Lake City on 27 January 2008.

HISTORICAL DEPARTMENT OF THE CHURCH. In 1972, as part of a broad administrative reorganization, the Church Historian's Office was renamed the Historical Department of the Church. Originally subdivided into Library, Archives, and Historian's Divisions, it was later reorganized into Library-Archives, Arts and Sites, and History Divisions, and still later into Library, Archives, and Museum. The stated mission of the Historical Department of the Church was to acquire, organize, preserve, and oversee the use of records, publications, photographs, artifacts, and other materials having to do with the history of the Church.

The History Division, under the direction of **Leonard J. Arrington**, was a group of about a dozen professional historians who from 1972 prepared bibliographies, established an oral history program, and produced many books and articles on Church history. In 1982 this group was transferred to **BYU** and designated the **Joseph Fielding Smith Institute for Church History.** In 2006 it was disbanded. Most of its historians were hired by the **Family and Church History Department**, current title of what had been the Historical Department of the Church.

HISTORIC SITES. The following historic sites and visitors' centers are staffed by **missionaries**, senior couples whose assignment is to welcome guests and provide basic information: Beehive House, Salt Lake City, Utah; ***Book of Mormon*** Historic Publication Site, Palmyra, New York; Brigham Young winter home, St. George, Utah; Carthage Jail, Carthage, Illinois; Cove Fort, Utah; Hill Cumorah, Manchester Township, New York; Independence Visitors' Center, Independence, Missouri; Jacob Hamblin home, Santa Clara, Utah; John Johnson farmhouse, Hiram, Ohio; Joseph Smith Memorial, Sharon, Vermont; Joseph Smith Sr. farm, Manchester Township, New York; Liberty Jail, Liberty, Missouri; **Mormon Battalion** Visitors' Center, San Diego, California; Mormon Handcart Visitors' Center, Alcova, Wyoming; Mormon Trail Center at Historic Winter Quarters, Omaha, Nebraska; Nauvoo Historic District and Visitors' Center, Nauvoo, Illinois; Newel K. Whitney store and home, Kirtland, Ohio; Peter Whitmer farm, Fayette Township, New York; St. George Tabernacle, St. George, Utah; Temple Square, Salt Lake City, Utah. In addition, visitors' centers are located at **temples** in Mesa, Arizona; Laie, Hawaii; Idaho Falls, Idaho; Los Angeles and Oakland, California; St. George, Utah; Washington, D.C.; Mexico City, Mexico; Hamilton, New Zealand; and others.

HISTORY OF THE CHURCH. Articles in the present volume treating Mormon history include **New York Period**, **Ohio Period**, **Missouri Period**, **Illinois Period**, **Exodus**, and **Utah Period**. Also historical are such topics as **Colonization**, **Polygamy**, the **Mountain Meadows Massacre**, and **Gathering**. Biographical articles relate to different periods of Church history. One recommendation would be to read in sequence the sketches of the presidents of the Church from the beginning to the present: **Joseph Smith**, **Brigham Young**, **John Taylor**, **Wilford Woodruff**, **Lorenzo Snow**, **Joseph F. Smith**, **Heber J. Grant**, **George Albert Smith**, **David O. McKay**, **Joseph Fielding Smith**, **Harold B. Lee**, **Spencer W. Kimball**, **Ezra Taft Benson**, **Howard W. Hunter**, and **Gordon B. Hinckley**. Articles treating different geographical **areas** also provide a historical overview.

HOLLAND, JEFFREY R. (1940–). Educator, president of **BYU**, **general authority**. Named president of BYU in 1980, he presided during a decade of expansion and increased visibility of BYU in scholarship and athletics. In 1989 he became a member of the First **Quorum** of the **Seventy**. In 1994, at age 53, he was sustained to the Quorum of the **Twelve Apostles**.

HOME TEACHING. Church members are called upon each month by a team of two **priesthood** holders. The home teachers are urged to become acquainted with the needs of each **family** or individual and prayerfully seek to be of assistance. They are also encouraged to help the family with temporal needs such as home repairs and caring for the sick. A message of inspiration and instruction is delivered, special needs are ascertained, and friendships are formed. The Church is brought into the lives of the people on the ground level, as it were. The original impetus goes back to the instruction (***Doctrine and Covenants***, section 20) that teachers are to "visit the house of each member and exhort them to pray vocally and in secret and attend to all family duties." *See also* VISITING TEACHING.

HOMOSEXUALITY. Same-gender attraction leading to sexual relations has challenged secular governments and churches up to the present. Until 1973 it was labeled a disorder by the American Psychiatric Association. That year, by a 58 percent vote, homosexuality was removed from the list of disorders. The extent to which the condition is genetic and inborn or the result of social conditioning, or some combination of the two, continues to divide researchers. The extent to which society should accept homosexuality in the form of same-sex marriage, view it as a disqualification for such influential adult positions as **priest** or scoutmaster, or devise some compromise is likewise controversial.

Church leaders do not condone cruelty. "Our doctrines obviously condemn those who engage in so-called 'gay bashing'—physical or verbal attacks on people thought to be involved in homosexual or lesbian behavior," said **Dallin H. Oaks**. Those "struggling with the burden of same-sex attraction are in special need of the love and encouragement that is a clear responsibility of Church members." The Church neither endorses nor condemns treatment programs that attempt to lessen same-sex attraction.

HUMANITARIAN AID. To assist those in need or victims of disasters, a variety of channels are used by Mormons. They volunteer or donate to relief programs of their choice. By the payment of a monthly **fast offering** and specific contributions for humanitarian aid, Mormons create a fund that can be drawn upon by **bishops** and the general Church to meet needs. From the 1990s, Church-service **missionaries** were assigned to low-income areas of the central city to give career counseling, budgeting advice, and other forms of assistance. The Church has established employment centers in cities throughout the globe. A large Humanitarian Center in Salt Lake City, Utah, assembles packets of material to be sent to areas of the world in need of assistance. The center draws upon surplus clothing from **Deseret Industries**; donations from companies and institutions of medical equipment, computers, and school supplies; donations from individuals, including handmade baby clothes and quilts; and humanitarian funds. Donations to the Church's humanitarian fund all go for humanitarian aid, with none of them used for administrative expenses.

In the 20 years following 1985, often teaming with other service and relief organizations, the Church assisted 183 countries, distributing more than 51,000 tons of food; 7,600 tons of medical equipment; 68,000 tons of surplus clothing; and 5,700 tons of educational supplies. In addition teams of Latter-day Saint volunteers labored to assist sufferers following natural disasters. *See also* LDS PHILANTHROPIES.

HUNTER, HOWARD WILLIAM (1907–1995). Lawyer, businessman, **general authority**, Church **president**. Born in Boise, Idaho, on 14 November 1907, Hunter received his early education there and became an Eagle Scout. In 1928 he moved to California, married Clara May Jeffs, and earned a juris doctor degree, graduating cum laude from Southwestern University Law School. Admitted to the California State Bar, he became a leading corporate attorney. He served as **bishop**, **stake high councilor**, and president of the Pasadena Stake. While stake president he also served as chairman of the Southern California Welfare Region and Los Angeles Welfare Region. He was on the **temple** committee during the construction of the Los Angeles Temple.

In 1959, at age 51, he became a member of the **Quorum** of the **Twelve Apostles**. He served on the board of directors of several corporations, including First Security Corporation and the New World Archaeological Foundation. He has been president of the **Polynesian Cultural Center**, the Genealogical Society, and the West European Mission. In 1985 he became acting president and in 1988 president of the Quorum of the Twelve Apostles. Clara, his wife of many years, died in 1983. In 1990 he married Inis Bernice Egan. He became president of the Church in June 1994 at age 86 but died in March 1995. *See also* GENEALOGY.

HUNTSMAN, JON (1937–). Businessman, billionaire, philanthropist. Born on 21 May 1937 in Blackfoot, Idaho, Jon Meade Huntsman Sr. grew up in poverty and worked after-school jobs to help support his family. After earning an undergraduate degree at the Wharton School of Business at the University of Pennsylvania, Huntsman earned an MBA degree from the University of Southern California. He became president of the Huntsman Corporation, the largest privately held chemical company in the nation. He served as special assistant to the president under Richard Nixon and vice president of the U.S. Chamber of Commerce. Huntsman gave $40 million to his alma mater, the Wharton School, and pledged $100 million to create the Huntsman Cancer Institute at the University of Utah. He has also sponsored programs for the homeless and shelters for abused women. He has served as a **stake president** and an **area authority seventy**. He and his wife, Karen, are the parents of nine children.

HYDE, ORSON (1805–1878). Missionary, pioneer, apostle. Hyde was born on 8 January 1805 in Oxford, Connecticut. Left an orphan at age 12, he was raised by neighbors. They moved to Kirtland, Ohio, in 1819. There he worked as a clerk in the Gilbert-Whitney store. He joined the Methodists in 1827, but when he heard the preaching of **Sidney Rigdon**, Hyde joined his congregation. When the first Mormon **missionaries** arrived in the fall of 1830, Rigdon accepted the new religion and Hyde soon followed in early 1831.

Immediately Hyde began preaching Mormonism in Ohio, Missouri, Pennsylvania, New York, Canada, and Indiana. In 1834 he married Marinda Nancy Johnson. After returning from the strenuous expedition of **Zion's Camp**, he became a member of the original **Quorum** of the **Twelve Apostles** in 1835. He was one of the original bearers of the message of Mormonism to England in 1837.

In Missouri during the height of the persecutions there, Hyde briefly defected and was **excommunicated**. When he expressed his strong desire to return six months later, he was reinstated as a member and as an apostle. He had no sooner moved to Nauvoo, Illinois, and established his family there than he was called on a special mission to Palestine. Taking months to make the long journey, he arrived in Jerusalem on 24 October 1841 and dedicated the land for the future return of the Jews.

Back in Nauvoo during the final year of the **Illinois Period**, he was introduced to **polygamy** and, after soul-searching, took two plural wives. Three other wives would be added later, and a total of 32 children were born. In the spring of 1844, Hyde became a member of the **Council of Fifty**. During 1846, the year the **exodus** began, he was sent on another mission to England.

Upon his return, Hyde settled in Utah. As a loyal follower and **pioneer**, he led a group to colonize Fort Supply in Wyoming. In 1855 he led a group to settle Carson Valley, Nevada, serving as a probate judge there. In 1858 Hyde was called to lead the Mormon settlements in south-central Utah. He built a home in Spring City, Utah, and for the final 20 years of his life was the Church leader in the area. Hyde also served on the territorial supreme court and in the legislature. *See also* MISSOURI PERIOD.

– I –

ILLINOIS PERIOD. Western Illinois was the main center of Mormonism from 1839 to 1846. Fleeing from Missouri after the extermination order issued by Governor Lilburn W. Boggs, Mormon refugees were received and cared for in Quincy and other Illinois towns. Jailed in Liberty, Missouri, **Joseph Smith** sent out encouraging and inspiring instructions (***Doctrine and Covenants***, sections 121–123). By spring of 1839, Smith having rejoined his family and people, a site for settlement was selected at Commerce, Illinois, on the east side of a bend in the Mississippi River a few miles north of

Quincy. Rechristened Nauvoo (based on a Hebrew word for "beautiful"), this became the new **gathering** place and the Mormon center.

Nauvoo grew rapidly, eventually reaching a population of some 12,000. (Estimates vary, depending on the year and whether or not the surrounding area is included.) A charter granting the city powers of self-government similar to other Illinois city chargers was granted by the legislature. The Nauvoo Legion, a unit of the state militia, was organized for defense. Two newspapers began publication, a Masonic lodge was formed, even a university was started, although it was one in little more than name.

In a bold stroke, when the Church and its people seemed to be in the depths of persecution and despair, Joseph Smith sent most of the **twelve apostles** to England, where they arrived in 1840. A preliminary proselytizing mission there in 1837 had already started making converts. Nearly 5,000 of these English converts emigrated to Nauvoo, joining other converts from the United States. Even with some loss by attrition, the future of Mormonism in Illinois seemed assured.

Some of the houses erected in the new city were impressive two-story brick structures. Joseph Smith moved his family into a new "mansion house." Funds were raised and construction started on a hotel, the Nauvoo House. A Masonic building served as a cultural hall. Although it is easy to exaggerate the "refinement" of a community still close to its original poverty, this was a town on the rise. The people tried to raise their sights as best they could. Included in the entertainment were dinner parties and balls, circuses, parades, and theater.

In addition to retailing food and clothing, much of the economic life of Nauvoo revolved around the construction of roads, houses, and public buildings. Naturally there was trade with the surrounding area. Located on the banks of the Mississippi, Nauvoo seemed a natural port for whatever trade the river could generate. A manufacturing and agriculture society was established. Plans were put forth for industry and a dam in the river that would greatly enhance its navigability. What was needed to undergird such development was capital, always in short supply.

The Mormon religion experienced important development during this period. Concepts such as eternal progression, the potential deification of humans, and the eternal duration of **family** relationships were enunciated. **Baptism for the dead** was introduced. **Polygamy**, which had been adumbrated earlier, was announced to the inner circle of leaders by a **revelation** in 1843 and began to be practiced by a few of the leading families. The **temple** announced for Independence, Missouri, had been thwarted by persecution and expulsion. Now a new temple, a sacred place for the **ordinance** of endowment and eternal **marriage**, began to rise in Nauvoo, an imposing white edifice on the highest elevation of the city.

Organizationally, **wards** were established as the congregational unit. In 1842 the **Relief Society** was founded as the organization for women. A Council of **Fifty** with ambitious plans for **colonization** and government was initiated. Most importantly, perhaps, the **Quorum** of the **Twelve Apostles**, seasoned after directing the migration from Missouri and by their missionary labors in England, came to occupy the most important administrative role next to the **First Presidency**.

Repeating the pattern of the **Ohio Period**, this doctrinal and institutional creativity aroused opposition. Nearby communities felt threatened by economic, religious, and political competition. As Mormons became numerous, they were a political force, a swing vote if not the dominant vote in the county. Illinois Masons were alarmed by the sudden emergence of a large lodge among the Mormons. Rumors of imperialistic designs and of the new marriage practices began to circulate, sometimes with a kernel of accuracy but often exaggerated and distorted. For a variety of reasons some Mormons defected. Persecution raised its head once again as **anti-Mormons** formed vigilante groups.

Aware of opponents within and fierce enemies without, Joseph Smith did several things simultaneously. He pushed for the continued growth of Nauvoo, especially the completion of the Nauvoo House and the temple—this in the face of the threatened revocation of the city's charter. He initiated an exploring expedition to find an alternative place of settlement in the West. The actual departure of this party was deferred until after the election of 1844. He assigned an apostle, **Lyman Wight**, to lead a company to find a place of settlement in Texas. He gave increased responsibility to the twelve apostles, declaring that they now had all the authority he had. He ran as an independent for president of the United States, sending out the apostles and others to campaign for him.

By late spring of 1844 the opposition mounted in a deafening crescendo. Anti-Mormon newspapers called for the use of violence. Mobs burned Mormon farms and outlying settlements, sending their frightened inhabitants fleeing into Nauvoo for safety. The state of Missouri demanded that Joseph Smith return for trial because of the attempt on former governor Lillburn Boggs's life. Then an opposition newspaper, the *Nauvoo Expositor*, appeared in Nauvoo itself, denouncing Smith and his policies in intemperate terms. The city council declared the newspaper a public nuisance and ordered the destruction of its press, an action that simply fanned the flames. Promised protection by Governor Thomas Ford, Joseph Smith and his brother **Hyrum Smith** were jailed in Carthage, Illinois, where they were assassinated on 27 June 1844. The era of Mormonism's first **prophet** had come to an end, the Church just 14 years old.

The big question now was survival of the Church. Some newspapers expressed confidence that, deprived of their charismatic leader, the Mormons would quickly disperse. **Sidney Rigdon**, who, along with Joseph and Hyrum Smith, had been a member of the First Presidency, put in a bid for the leadership. But at a large gathering of the members at Nauvoo on 8 August 1844 the vote was decisively in favor of the twelve apostles assuming the leadership, with **Brigham Young** as president.

For another year and a half Nauvoo survived. Young and his colleagues provided leadership, continuing the doctrines and policies of Joseph Smith. Construction of houses continued. The temple was finally completed at the beginning of 1846. Although conversion and disaffection continued simultaneously, the balance seemed in favor of continued growth, especially with dramatic successes in England. During 1845, however, anti-Mormon violence in the area combined with demands that the Mormons leave Illinois, which Young and the other leaders agreed to do, hoping first to sell their properties and to have adequate time for preparing wagons and supplies.

By winter of 1845–1846 the writing was on the wall. The capstone of the temple having been laid, more than 6,000 Mormons received their temple ordinances in January and February. With the hoof beats of marauding mobsters raising panic and forcing people from the surrounding settlements to seek protection in the city, and with violence on both sides, the Mormon leaders agreed to depart. Starting in February 1846 refugees moved from the city and across the river—generally by barge, but for a short time on ice—and continued westward into Iowa. Those who required more time continued to be harassed. By the fall of 1846 the Mormons who recognized the leadership of Brigham Young had practically all departed.

Schism and **apostasy** had occurred as early as the 1830s when some refused to follow revelations and policies of Joseph Smith that had not been part of the religion at its beginning, but such dissidents had always been relatively few. Now a larger group, although still a minority, refused or were unable to embark on the arduous journey to the distant Great Basin. Eventually some of these rallied to form the **RLDS** Church.

As a result of renewed proselytizing and growth mostly after the middle of the 20th century, there were 53,047 Church **members** in Illinois at the end of 2005, divided into 12 **stakes** and 90 wards. A temple in a suburb of Chicago was completed and dedicated in 1985. The Nauvoo Temple, closely modeled on the original structure, was rebuilt and dedicated in 2002. In 2004 the Illinois House of Representatives formally expressed regret for the forced expulsion of Mormons from the state in 1846. *See also* EXODUS; MISSOURI PERIOD; NAUVOO RESTORATION, INC.

***IMPROVEMENT ERA*.** Magazine published monthly from 1897 to 1970. At first the official organ of the YMMIA, it enlarged its scope and was effectively the magazine for adults in the Church.

Contents included editorials, doctrine, exhortation, recipes, historical articles, short stories, poetry, and advertisements. Instructions for **priesthood** leaders and messages to be delivered by **ward** teachers, now called **home teachers**, were included. The "Spoken Word" of **Richard L. Evans** was a regular feature. For many years **John A. Widtsoe** published answers to questions under the column title "Evidences and Reconciliations." Addresses by **general authorities** at **general conferences** were printed, selectively for many years and completely from 1942 on. A special section entitled "The Era of Youth," edited by **Elaine Cannon** and **Marion D. Hanks**, appeared from 1960 on. When the final issue of the *Improvement Era* appeared in

December 1970, its circulation was 275,000. Its successor, the ***Ensign***, started publication in January 1971.

INACTIVITY. Inactive Mormons are those, sometimes called "non-practicing" in other traditions, who do not attend Church services. Other indications of this status include failure to observe the **Word of Wisdom** and failure to pay **tithing**. Obviously there are degrees of inactivity, ranging from the person who still has a **testimony** but for a variety of reasons fails to attend the regular meetings to the **apostate** who resents the Church and wants nothing more to do with it. Many from the first group and even some from the second group sooner or later return to full participation. To recognize this variety and to avoid stereotyping, Church leaders now prefer the designation "less active."

INDIANS. *See* NATIVE AMERICANS.

INSTITUTES OF RELIGION. Programs of study in religion for college students. The first of these institutes was established in 1926 at the University of Idaho. When there are sufficient Mormon students, an institute building is usually constructed near a university campus. Courses are offered on the **scriptures**, Church history, world religions, and **marriage** and **family**. Recreational activities, social functions, and worship meetings provide opportunities for Mormon students to interact. Most institute instructors hold the doctorate or a master's degree.

With the expanding Church population and the limited enrollment capacity of **BYU**, institutes have become increasingly important. In 1993, the institute program was made available not only to college and university students but to all young adults between 18 and 30. In 2005, enrollment was 367,034.

INTERNATIONAL MAGAZINES. The *Liahona* is the official international magazine of the Church. The Church publishes the *Liahona* in 50 different languages from monthly to semi-annually, depending on the language. Until 1970, the Church titled international magazines differently in each language, for example, *l'Etoile*, *Der Stern*, *Millennial Star*, *la Stella*, and *Tambuli*. Many articles in the *Liahona* are translated and printed from English-language publications, but other articles are produced by people from the different nations or areas. Eight pages of each issue are filled with news from the country or area served. The *Liahona* is designed "to strengthen the faith of members; to promulgate the truths of the restored gospel; to keep members informed of current and vital Church policies, programs, and events; and to entertain and enrich the lives of Church members" (***Ensign***, September 1986).

INTERNET. The rapid rise of the Internet as a means of communication and a source of information has brought a variety of sites about Mormonism. The official Church website is lds.org. *See also* GENEALOGY.

INVESTIGATOR. Someone who is seriously studying the Mormon religion with a view to possible conversion and **baptism**. When individuals or families indicate a willingness to learn, **missionaries** teach them the restored **gospel** and its requirements in a series of lessons. *See also* REFERRAL.

IVINS, ANTHONY WOODWARD (1852–1934). Businessman, politician, **general authority**. The year following Ivins's birth in Toms River, New Jersey, his family emigrated to the Salt Lake Valley, and they eventually settled in St. George, Utah. At age 23, he participated in an expedition to Arizona and New Mexico to locate sites for possible **colonization**. Later returning as a proselyting **missionary**, he preached the gospel to the Indian and Mexican peoples. In 1882, Ivins presided over the Mexico City mission, learning to speak Spanish fluently. In 1878, Ivins married Elizabeth Ashby Snow, and he engaged in the cattle business as manager of the Mojave Land and Cattle Company and partner in the Kaibab Cattle Company. Politically, he worked as St. George's constable; served as prosecuting attorney for Washington County, Utah; and represented southern Utah counties in the Utah Territorial Legislature. In 1888 he led out in organizing a nascent Democratic Party as the "Sagebrush Democrats." At the same time, he served as St. George **Stake** YMMIA president and as a member of the stake **high council**. In 1888 he became first **counselor** in the stake presidency. As a leader in the Democratic

Party, he served as mayor of St. George and as a member of the Utah state constitutional convention.

For over a decade, Ivins served as the presiding authority in the Mexican colonies. Eight Mormon settlements, located in Sonora and Chihuahua, provided refuge for saints in danger of violating anti-polygamy legislation. The **First Presidency** authorized Ivins to perform plural marriages, illegal in both Mexico and the United States, when proper documentation was presented. He seems to have continued to do so until President **Joseph F. Smith** issued the "second manifesto" in 1904. Ivins returned to Utah when the First Presidency called him as a member of the **Quorum** of the **Twelve Apostles** in 1907. He served in this position until President **Heber J. Grant** called him as second counselor in the First Presidency in 1921. He was called as first counselor in 1925 and remained in that position until his death in 1934.

– J –

JACK, ELAINE LOW (1928–). Leader of **Young Women, Relief Society** general president. After growing up in Cardston, Alberta, Canada, Elaine attended the University of Utah for two years. Marrying medical student Joseph E. Jack in 1948, she moved with him to New York City. His medical training and practice as a surgeon took them to Boston, Alaska, and finally Salt Lake City, Utah. The Jacks have four sons.

Elaine performed community service work for the American Cancer Society and served in medical and auxiliary positions. She served as **ward** Relief Society president, ward Young Women president, **stake** Relief Society president's **counselor**, Relief Society general board member, and counselor to **Ardeth Kapp** in the Young Women general presidency. From 1990 to 1997 she served as general president of the Relief Society.

JACK-MORMON. Colloquial term for someone who is a member of the Church in name only or who never, or hardly ever, attends meetings. (The original usage of the term in the 1840s referred to non-Mormons who were friendly to the Church, but that meaning has lost its currency.) Heard only infrequently now, "Jack-Mormon" has been replaced for most purposes by "inactive" or "less active." *See also* ACTIVITY; INACTIVITY.

JACOBSEN, FLORENCE SMITH (1913–). Youth leader, art curator, historic preservationist. Born on 7 April 1913, Florence Smith was raised in Salt Lake City, Utah. She earned a bachelor's degree in interior design at the University of Utah and in 1935 married Theodore C. Jacobsen. They have three sons.

On the **ward** and **stake** level she worked with the **Primary**, **Boy Scouts**, and **Young Women**. In 1955 the Jacobsens moved to New York City to preside over the Eastern States Mission. Upon their return in 1959, Florence was named to the general board of the Young Women. Two years later she became general president of the organization, serving from 1961 to 1972.

In 1969 Jacobsen directed an ambitious centennial celebration, which included an original movie, *Pioneers and Petticoats*. She played a central role in the production of the musical stage play *Promised Valley* and, growing out of its orchestra and chorus, the establishment of the **Mormon Youth Symphony and Chorus**. Her training in design and historic costume was also called upon when she was assigned to supervise the restoration of the **Joseph Smith** home in Palmyra, New York, and **Brigham Young**'s Lion House in Salt Lake City. She was a member of the National Council of Women and the International Council of Women. She served as a vice president of the National Council of Women.

In 1973 she was appointed Church curator. With a reorganization of the **Historical Department of the Church**, Jacobsen became director of Historic Arts and Sites with responsibility over the many historic sites throughout the United States, serving until 1986. Under her direction, artifacts and works of art that had been poorly displayed or stored in closets and attics were catalogued and restored. Most importantly, the **Museum of Church History and Art** was constructed in order to provide a suitable facility for exhibiting examples of the Church's artistic heritage.

JAMES, JANE ELIZABETH MANNING (1818–1908). African American member. Jane Elizabeth Manning was born to Isaac Manning, a free black, and Phyllis Abbott in Wilton, Connecticut. Isaac Manning died about 1825, and in 1826 Jane was sent to live and work in the household of Joseph Fitch, a wealthy Wilton farmer. She worked here as a servant and was taught some Christian principles, but was given little, if any, educational instruction. She learned to read in her adult years, although she could never write; she signed her name using a mark and "wrote" letters and business items by dictating to friends.

Mormonism was first introduced into southwestern Connecticut during the winter of 1841. Jane heard the message of these **missionaries** in 1842 and was baptized on 14 October 1842. Upon her baptism, she experienced the gifts of speaking in tongues and of healing the sick. In early October 1843, Jane Elizabeth, her son Sylvester (an illegitimate child), her mother Phyllis, two brothers, two sisters, a brother-in-law, and a sister-in-law left Wilton and emigrated to Nauvoo, Illinois. Upon arrival in Nauvoo, she and her family stayed at the Nauvoo House where the **prophet Joseph Smith** provided temporary shelter. Jane Elizabeth remained a member of Smith's household and worked in the Nauvoo House until June 1844.

In 1845 Jane Elizabeth met and married Isaac James, a free black who had been converted in 1839. The two left Nauvoo and moved west across the Mississippi River into Iowa. While traveling through Iowa, Jane Elizabeth gave birth to their first child, Silas F. James on 10 June 1846. Jane Elizabeth and her husband and sons departed their Winter Quarter's encampment on 22 June 1847, and reached the Salt Lake Valley on 22 September 1847.

The James family settled on a farm outside of Salt Lake City, Utah, and raised sheep. Through a community effort, the surrounding farmers, the James family included, slowly prospered and made a decent living. Around 1869, Isaac left his family and divorced Jane Manning James. In 1874, she married Frank Perkins, but this union only lasted two years. She then moved to Salt Lake City and despite a life of poverty she managed her home and raised children and grandchildren. She also remained very active in the **Relief Society** and still found means to donate money for the St. George, Manti, and Logan **temples**. She also contributed to an old folks excursion to Liberty park, to the Lamanite mission, and to the Deseret Hospital.

The biggest trials James faced in life included overcoming racial conflict and the death of her children, as she outlived all of her children and many of her grandchildren. She lived in a society plagued by racial bigotry and was a member of a church whose practices at the time caused her some grief. Because she lived before 1978, she was unable to participate in temple ceremonies, in spite of repeated efforts to do so.

JENSEN, MARLIN K. (1942–). Attorney, **general authority**. Born on 18 May 1842 in Ogden, Utah, Jensen served as a **missionary** in Germany, graduated with a degree in German at **BYU**, and earned the juris doctorate from the University of Utah. Specializing in estate planning with an Ogden law firm, he was also a partner in the Jensen Family Middle Fork Ranch, a 600-head beef operation.

After serving as **bishop**, **stake president**, mission president, and **regional representative**, Jensen was named to the First **Quorum** of the **Seventy** in 1989. He served as Central European area president. In 2004 he was called as executive director of the **Family and Church History Department** of the Church and as Church historian and recorder. He and his wife, Kathleen, are parents of eight children.

JERUSALEM CENTER. BYU's Jerusalem Center for Near Eastern Studies, on Mount Scopus in northeast Jerusalem, was dedicated in 1989. Public protests by ultra orthodox Jews had attempted to stop construction, but an official ruling that all legal requirements had been met allowed the structure to be completed.

Its seven levels and 120,000 square feet include classrooms, a library, a multipurpose room, a cafeteria and dining rooms, two auditoriums, and dormitory rooms. It was designed by Franklin T. Ferguson, a Salt Lake City architect, in cooperation with David Reznik, a Jerusalem architect.

Selected from a pool of applicants, 169 university students study the **Bible**, the history and culture of Islam, Palestine, post-biblical Judaism, and languages. Weekly field trips take students to sites of historical and cultural significance.

The 320-seat auditorium serves as a concert hall for performances on a 3,000-pipe organ and for groups and individual artists from the community. With increasing violence in Israel, concern for the safety of students led to closing the center's academic programs from 2003 to 2007.

JESSOP, CRAIG D. (1949–). Musician, director of **Mormon Tabernacle Choir**. Born in Millville, Utah, Jessop received a bachelor's degree in music from Utah State University, an M.A. degree from **BYU**, and a doctorate of musical arts from Stanford University. A lieutenant colonel in the U.S. Air Force, he was director of the Singing Sergeants, 1980–1987; conductor of the Band of the United States Air Forces in Europe, 1987–1991; and conductor of the Air Combat Command Heartland of America Band, 1991–1995. He also served as musical director of the Maryland Choral Society, the Rhineland-Pfalz International Choir of Germany, and the Omaha Symphonic Chorus. A baritone vocalist, Jessop performed in the Merola Opera Training Program of the San Francisco Opera. He was a member of the Robert Shaw Festival Singers. In 1995, he became associate director of the Mormon Tabernacle Choir. Named music director in 1999, he served until 2008. He and his wife, RaNae, have four children.

JESUS CHRIST. The Savior and Redeemer of the world. Born in Bethlehem, Jesus performed miracles; called apostles; founded a Church; was betrayed, crucified, and resurrected. The second member of the Godhead (**Articles of Faith**, no. 1), by commission the Creator of the earth (John 1:3), Jesus Christ is the "author and finisher of our salvation" (Heb. 12:2; Moroni 6:4) The Church is named after him; baptized Mormons take upon themselves his name; his sacrifice is memorialized weekly in **sacrament** meetings. Mormons accept the virgin birth; that is, the infant was miraculously conceived by Mary. Of a divine Father and a human mother, Jesus had both divine and human attributes. Literally, he is the only begotten Son of God.

To suggest that Mormons do not believe in Christ or that someone other than Jesus of Nazareth is their Savior is not a harmless misunderstanding but a blatant lie. One among many passages in the ***Book of Mormon*** states, "We talk of Christ, we rejoice in Christ, we preach of Christ, we prophesy of Christ, and we write according to our prophecies, that our children may know to what source they may look for a remission of their sins" (2 Nephi 25:26). *See also* CHRISTIANITY.

JEWS, JUDAISM. The relationship between Mormons and Jews is ambiguous. Usually the two groups had little or nothing to do with each other, each facing its own trials.

On the level of ideology, Mormons anticipate that prior to the second coming of Jesus Christ many Jews will recognize Him as messiah. In 1841, long before the rise of organized Zionism, the land of Palestine was dedicated for the return of the Jews by Apostle **Orson Hyde**. For a time, on a small scale, proselytizing was specifically tailored for Jewish **investigators**. With relatively small results, the targeted proselytizing was abandoned.

Down to the present, conversions of Jews to Mormonism have taken place on an individual basis, motivated by family connections, dissatisfaction with their previous religion or secularism, and, as Mormons believe, the Holy Spirit. No record is kept of ethnicity and previous religious affiliation, and therefore it is impossible to state the numbers.

Church leaders have consistently expressed friendship for the state of Israel. A flare-up of hostility to Mormons occurred there with the announcement of the construction of the **Jerusalem Center**, but the demonstrations were by a small minority of orthodox Jews and were overcome by the support of well-wishers, including Jerusalem mayor Teddy Kollek, and the agreement that in Israel the Church would not engage in organized proselytizing.

As part of its efforts in **genealogy**, the Church gathered records of Jews, including victims of the holocaust. These have been freely made available, and Jewish families have expressed appreciation. Upon the discovery that **baptism for the dead** was performed for some of the individual Jews on these records, a few protested that they did not want their ancestors turned into Mormons. The Church's position, as with all such vicarious work, is that acceptance of it is entirely voluntary by the individual in the spirit world, that no harm has been done, and that it should make no difference to those who regard such vicarious work as meaningless. But in consideration for the sensitivity of the protestors, Church representatives agreed that the vicarious work for holocaust victims would be ended unless initiated by direct descendants.

Parallels between the Jewish and Mormon experience include the self-image by Mormon **pioneers** during the **exodus** from Illinois that they were the modern equivalent of the children of Israel fleeing Egypt under Moses. Mormons traversed their wilderness and established their **Zion** in a western region where there was a sea of salt, a fresh-water lake about forty miles away, and a river connecting the two, which to this day is called the Jordan River. An examination of visual images of Mormons and Jews in periodicals of the 19th century reveals that both groups were viciously stereotyped along with other unpopular minorities like Chinese immigrants and American Indians.

Mormons consider themselves to be of the House of Israel either by direct lineage or by adoption. Each individual's connection is declared by a **patriarchal blessing** and is usually through the line of Ephraim, grandson of Jacob/Israel.

JOHN WHITMER HISTORICAL ASSOCIATION (JWHA). Officially organized in 1973, by historians and others from the **RLDS** Church, the JWHA has always included people from different religious and secular backgrounds. It proclaims its area of interest as "the study of early Mormonism, the history of the Reorganized Church of Jesus Christ of Latter Day Saints, and **LDS** factions located in the Midwestern United States." JWHA distributes a newsletter, sponsors an annual meeting, cosponsors (with Graceland College) a spring lecture series, and publishes an annual journal. *See also* MORMON HISTORY ASSOCIATION.

JOSEPH FIELDING SMITH INSTITUTE FOR LATTER-DAY SAINT HISTORY. A group of historians at **BYU** whose primary assignment was the research and writing of Church history. Established in 1982 by the transfer and renaming of the group previously attached to the **Historical Department of the Church**, the Institute edited and published primary sources, and worked on a variety of individual projects, as well as sponsoring grants, fellowships, lectures, and scholarly seminars.

In 2005 the Institute was formally disbanded. Jill Mulvay Derr, director of the Institute, issued this statement: "Many of the Institute's former faculty, senior fellows, and staff are currently forwarding their work in Mormon history under the auspices of the Family and Church History Department in Salt Lake City, Utah, or the History Department at Brigham Young University. Scholarship on Mormon women promoted by the Institute's Women's History Initiative continues under the auspices of the Women's Research Institute at Brigham Young University."

JOSEPH SMITH MEMORIAL BUILDING. A building in downtown Salt Lake City, Utah, known as the Hotel Utah since its completion in 1911. After major restoration and renovation, the building was dedicated in 1993 and renamed. Open to the public are a magnificent lobby, a family history area with computers and assistants, a 500-seat theater, and two top-floor scenic outlooks and restaurants. Office buildings of different Church departments occupy eight floors. On the mezzanine level are a chapel and teaching and leadership rooms. In the basement are found a distribution center and an outlet for the purchase of **temple** clothing.

JOURNAL OF DISCOURSES. A 26-volume work published in Liverpool, England, between 1854 and 1884. Based on the shorthand reporting of George D. Watt and others, the *Journal of Discourses* includes many sermons by Mormon leaders of the latter 19th century. Since these sermons were not canonized, they are not official statements of Mormon doctrine. Nevertheless, they touch on many topics and constitute a valuable primary source for historians. A five-volume addendum made up of sermons delivered by Mormon leaders from 1886 to 1898 has been published by Brian H. Stuy under the title *Collected Discourses* (1987–1992).

– K –

KAPP, ARDETH GREENE (1931–). Leader of **Young Women**. Born on 19 March 1931 in Glenwood, Alberta, Canada, Ardeth Greene had a small-town upbringing. While attending **BYU**, she met Heber Kapp, whom she married in 1950.

Living in Utah and California, the Kapps built a series of seven homes. Ardeth worked for the telephone company for 10 years. Later she earned a bachelor's degree in elementary education at the University of Utah, followed by an M.S. in curriculum development from **BYU**. In addition to teaching school and supervising student teachers, Ardeth Kapp worked as a writer and consultant. She authored several books, articles, and instructional manuals.

In the Church she had experiences ranging from **Primary** and **Sunday School** teacher to board member of the **Relief Society.** Having served as **Young Women** president in three **wards**, she was called to the Church's youth **correlation** committee and then the curriculum development committee. In 1972 she became a **counselor** in the general presidency of the Young Women, and from 1984 to 1992 served as general president of the Young Women. The theme repeated in Young Women under her direction included this affirmation: "We will stand as witnesses of God at all times and in all things, and in all places" (from ***Book of Mormon***, Mosiah 18:9).

Her community service includes membership on a citizens planning commission, the board of trustees for the National Coalition against Pornography, and the executive board of the Mental Health Resource Foundation. She accompanied her husband when he was called as president of the Canada Vancouver Mission. She continued to lecture and publish for the Latter-day Saint audience.

KENNEDY, DAVID M. (1905–1996). Banker, political leader, Church leader. Born in Randolph, Utah, on 21 July 1905, David Kennedy lived in this small rural town and performed all the chores common to ranches. Later the family moved to Ogden, Utah. He attended high school at Weber Academy (later Weber State University). At age 20 he married Lenora Bingham. Within two months, he was on his way to Great Britain to serve a Church **mission**.

Returning to Utah in 1928, Kennedy completed studies at Weber College. Then the couple went east to Washington, D.C. David found employment as a clerk with the Federal Reserve Board. He graduated from the George Washington University Law School in 1935 and continued working for the Federal Reserve. Among their Church associates were **J. Willard Mariott**, Senator **Reed Smoot**, and **Ezra Taft Benson**. In 1942 David became a **counselor** in a **ward** bishopric and in 1944 was made **bishop**.

Still employed by the Federal Reserve Board, Kennedy completed a degree at Rutgers University Graduate School of Banking. In 1946 he accepted a position with the Continental Illinois National Bank and Trust Company of Chicago. He ascended to become president and then chairman. For 22 years the Kennedys were contributors to the Chicago community. In the Church he served for 15 years as a counselor in the **stake** presidency.

While at Chicago he served on the board of **Nauvoo Restoration, Inc. (NRI)**. He was chairman of the mayor's committee for economic development, head of the Citizen's Bond Committee, on the board of trustees for the University of Chicago, and on the board of trustees for the Brookings Institution. He chaired a commission that made recommendations on improving the organization of the federal budget.

In early 1969 Kennedy became U.S. Secretary of the Treasury. In less than two years he resigned but remained ambassador at large, traveling to many countries and negotiating on economic matters. He also became U.S. ambassador to NATO. In 1973 he resigned from government. Kennedy then received another **call** from the Church when he was asked to be an ambassador to the world. Traveling to different countries, meeting with high government officials, he was remarkably successful obtaining unofficial or official recognition of the Church. He thus played a key role in the worldwide expansion of Mormonism in the generation following 1973.

KERR, W. ROLFE (1935–). Educator, **general authority**. Born on 29 June 1935 in Tremonton, Utah, Kerr attended Utah State University receiving a bachelor's degree in agriculture. He also earned a master's degree at Utah State University and a doctorate at the University of Utah.

Kerr served as **counselor** in bishoprics, **stake** president, on the **Sunday School** general board, and as **president** of the Texas Dallas Mission. In 1996 he was called to the Second **Quorum** of the **Seventy** and the following year to the First Quorum of the Seventy. Kerr's experience in educational administration included positions at Utah State University, Weber State College, and the University of Utah. He was president of Dixie State College and commissioner of the Utah System of Higher Education. As commissioner of education for the Church from 2005 through 2008, Kerr directed operations of **BYU, BYU–Idaho, BYU–Hawaii**, LDS Business College, and **seminaries** and **institutes of religion** throughout the world.

KIKUCHI, YOSHIHIKO (1941–). General authority. Born on 25 July 1941 in Hokkaido, Japan, Kikuchi graduated from Asia University of Tokyo and became sales manager and then president of businesses. Converted to the Church in 1955, he served as a **missionary** and later as **stake** president in Tokyo. He served as **president** of the Hawaii Honolulu Mission and president of the **temple** in Tokyo before his call to the First **Quorum** of the **Seventy** in 1977. He and his wife, Toshiko, have four children.

KIMBALL, JONATHAN GOLDEN (1853–1938). General authority, beloved preacher known for his humor. Born in Salt Lake City, Utah, on 26 June 1853, J. Golden Kimball was the son of prominent leader Heber C. Kimball, **counselor** in the **First Presidency** of the Church. Only 15 when his father died, Golden became a mule driver. In addition to making some money and acquiring a skill, he acquired the habit of swearing. "You can't drive mules if you can't swear," he said (Cheney, *The Golden Legacy*, 18). At the time he did not participate in Church activities.

In the 1870s Golden and his mother joined other family members as **pioneers** of the Bear Lake, Utah, area. In 1881, at the age of 28, Golden moved to Provo with his brother to attend Brigham Young Academy (now **BYU**). Inspired by **Karl G. Maeser**, he raised his sights. Two years later he accepted a call to serve a **mission** in the southern states, where his down-to-earth way of expression enabled him to communicate with ordinary people.

After his mission, he married Jennie Knowlton. Kimball was sent back to the southern states as mission **president**. In 1892, he was named as one of the First Council of the **Seventy**. For the nearly half century of his life that remained, he associated with other Church leaders, traveled throughout the **stakes** and **wards**, and spoke at the **general conference**.

Tall and lanky, J. Golden Kimball spoke with a high-pitched voice. He never totally abandoned the swearing habit, using words, he said, that were left over "from a much larger vocabulary" (Cheney, *The Golden* Legacy, 37). He was a distinctive personality, an original.

"A lot of people in the Church believe that men are called to leadership in the Church by revelation and some do not," he said. "But I'll tell you, when the Lord calls an old mule skinner like me to be a General Authority, there's got to be revelation" (Cheney, *The Golden Legacy*, 100).

As stories by and about J. Golden Kimball were passed from person to person, they assumed a life of their own. Some were embellished, others invented. He had become a subject of Mormon **folklore**. He died in a car accident in 1938.

KIMBALL, SPENCER W. (1895–1985). Arizona businessman, civic leader, **general authority**, **president** of the Church. Born in Salt Lake City, Utah, on 28 March 1895, Spencer Kimball moved with his family to southeastern Arizona at the age of three. Raised in Thatcher, where his father was **stake** president, he went through the local schools and from 1914 to 1916 preached Mormonism as a **missionary** in the Central States Mission. After one semester of study at the University of Arizona, Kimball was inducted into the army. He married Camilla Eyring and, when his army service was deferred, took a job at a bank. In 1927 he started his own insurance agency in Safford, Arizona. He was prominent in local politics and community service. In 1936 he became president of the Arizona Rotary Club.

From 1924 he was a **counselor** in the **stake** presidency, and in 1938 he became president of the Mount Graham Stake. In 1943 he was called to the **Quorum** of the **Twelve Apostles** and moved to Salt Lake City. In addition to the usual travels to **stake conferences** throughout the Church, Kimball was given special responsibilities over missionary work and assisting **Native Americans**. Under his direction the Indian Placement Program developed as a means of providing educational opportunity for children. He repeatedly preached against racial prejudice. Kimball suffered from health problems, some serious. After throat cancer he could speak only with a hoarse whisper. But he persisted and the people loved him for it.

It was a surprise when at age 78 he succeeded to the presidency of the Church. At the most, people assumed he would preside very briefly. To the contrary, however, his administration from 1973 to 1985 became the most animated in the history of the Church to that time. He greatly expanded the number of missionaries. Countries hitherto unexposed to Mormonism were opened up to proselytizing. **Temples** were erected in many parts of the world, increasing from 15 to 31. **Area** conferences were held, enabling members in Chile and Finland, Korea and Tonga, and many other places, to see President Kimball personally along with other general authorities and in exciting Saturday programs demonstrate costumes, songs, and dances of their own culture. Administrative changes, notably the organization of the First **Quorum** of the **Seventy**, were made to cope with the rapid growth of **membership**.

A great sense of vigor infused the Church under Kimball's leadership. "Lengthen your stride," he urged the members (***Ensign***, November 1974, 117). His own motto was "Do it." In 1978 a longstanding policy of not ordaining **blacks** to the **priesthood** (although some had been baptized as members) was reversed. The announcement, presented as the will of the Lord, was quickly followed by proselytizing in Nigeria, Ghana, and other parts of **Africa**.

Following cerebral hemorrhage, a third round of brain surgery in 1981 left him so weak that for the last three or four years of his life most of the routine business of administration was carried on by his two **counselors**. His wife, Camilla Eyring Kimball, sister of **Henry Eyring**, was a vivacious woman of high intelligence. They had four children. *See also* PROPHET.

KNIGHT, GLADYS (1944–). Celebrated performing artist. Born in Georgia, Gladys sang as a soloist with the local church choir. At age eight, she won the Ted Mack Original Amateur Hour contest. With her cousins, she formed The Pips, producing such hits as "I Heard It through the Grapevine" and "Midnight Train to Georgia." She won Grammy awards, platinum and gold records, a Clio, a CableACE Award, American Music Awards, and a place in the Rock 'n' Roll Hall of Fame and the Rhythm and Blues Hall of Fame.

When her daughter, Kenya, and her son, Jimmy, joined the **Church of Jesus Christ of Latter-day Saints**, Gladys did not immediately show a personal interest. Eventually she agreed to take the **missionary** lessons and was baptized in 1997. In 1999 she addressed the annual Women's Conference. That same year, her son, Jimmy, died at age 36.

Knight continued to accumulate awards, including Grammy for Best Traditional R&B Vocal Performance in 2002 and Grammy for Best Gospel Performance in 2005. She organized and directed Saints Unified Voices, winning the Grammy Award for Best Gospel Choir in 2006.

KOPISCHKE, ERICH W. (1956–). Businessman, educator, **general authority**. Born 20 October 1956 in Elmshorn, Germany, Kopischke earned a degree in business. After service as a **missionary** and in the military, he worked as an executive in the insurance industry. In 1996 he joined the Church Educational System, and in 2000 he was appointed Europe Central area director. In 2003 he was called to serve as president of the Berlin, Germany, mission. He served as a **bishop**'s **counselor**, **stake high councilor**, district **president**, and stake president. He served as second and first counselor in the Europe Central area presidency. In 2007 he was called to the First **Quorum** of the **Seventy** and assigned to the presidency of the Europe Central Area. He is married to Christiane Glück, and they have seven children.

–L –

LAMANITE. One of the large groupings in the ***Book of Mormon*** account, named after Laman, a member of the original colony that left Jerusalem. A superficial reading sometimes leaves the impression of a long struggle between "good guys" and Lamanite "bad guys," but the history was much more complex than this, as intermingling occurred and both groups showed the ability at different points to achieve a high level of Christian living or descend to an abysmal depravity.

Since the Lamanites were the survivors at the end of the *Book of Mormon* narrative, they were considered to be among the ancestors of the **Native Americans**, sometimes called Lamanites—a usage sometimes extended to include **Polynesians**. A student performing group from **BYU** called the Lamanite Generation put on a lively show of song and dance that drew from both Native American and Polynesian cultures.

Those employing the term with reference to modern peoples intend to emphasize the promised "flowering," the glorious future, of the scriptural references. But non-Mormon Native Americans do not understand or accept the designation, and some Mormon Native Americans deplore its negative connotations. Some scholars follow John

Sorenson in arguing that the designation should belong only to those from a small area in **Central America**.

LANT, CHERYL C. (1944–). Educator; leader of women, children, and youth. Born 30 January 1944, and raised in Utah, Lant attended **BYU**, where she studied human development and family relations. She developed a phonic-based beginning reading program and with her husband became cofounder and co-owner of a private school for children. Her Church service included **ward Relief Society** president, ward **Young Women** president, and member of the **Primary** general board. In 2005 Lant became general president of the Primary. She and her husband, John, are the parents of nine children.

LATTER-DAY SAINT STUDENTS ASSOCIATION (LDSSA). Organization for Mormon college students. At colleges and universities where there are sufficient numbers of Mormons, the LDSSA sponsors social activities and represents the interests of its student members on campus. Its officers are students, but it has a faculty adviser, usually an instructor from the **institute of religion**.

LDS. Latter-day Saint or Saints. In English-speaking settings, Church members often use LDS instead of Mormon.

LDS FAMILY SERVICES. Professional counseling available to assist members dealing with problems ranging from marital conflict to addiction, depression, and same-gender attraction. Members may approach the agency directly. Often they are referred by their bishop. Adoption services assist in bringing together families who desire to adopt and mothers who voluntarily decide that such would be better for their child. In addition to 55 offices located throughout the United States, the agency has nine international offices. Like other such agencies, LDS Family Services charges a fee.

LDS PHILANTHROPIES. Previously known as LDS Foundation, LDS Philanthropies coordinates voluntary contributions to the Church and its different entities and humanitarian projects. Accepting contributions from nonmembers as well as members of the Church,

LDS Philanthropies applies the funds as needed or according to the specific desires of the donor. The contribution goes entirely to the specified recipient program, with zero deducted for overhead (*LDS Church News*, 17 September 2005).

LEADERSHIP TRAINING. In a lay church with a constantly repeating rotation of people in different positions of responsibility, the challenge of training leaders is immense. The ***Handbook of Instructions*** explains procedures and lines of responsibility. One of the functions of **ward** and **stake** conferences is to give instruction and answer questions. Throughout the Church each stake has **auditors** who periodically go over the **membership** and financial records and supervise the clerks who keep the records. Visiting **general authorities** and resident **area authority seventies** provided leadership training sessions. Starting on 11 January 2003 periodic leadership meetings were transmitted via satellite in 56 languages to priesthood leaders all over the world. Presidencies of **areas,** stakes, and wards concern themselves with the training and supervision of leaders in their respective jurisdictions.

In 2005, the Church began using e-learning technology for training record keepers, **Primary** teachers, and **Young Women** leaders. In downloadable slide show format, lessons were posted on the website lds.org. German and Spanish translations of some lessons were available, and the lessons were to be translated into Cantonese, Dutch, French, Italian, Japanese, Korean, Mandarin, Portuguese, Russian, Samoan, Swedish, and Tongan.

In addition to such specific training efforts, it should not be overlooked that the Church itself functions as a giant training machine. Young **missionaries**, having necessarily assumed responsibility in decision making and oversight, are well prepared for other **callings**. Serving in positions lower in the hierarchical scale prepares people for moving up. Especially the huge numbers of **counselors**, having participated in discussions and shared responsibility in bishoprics and presidencies, are ready to assume greater responsibility should the occasion arise.

LEE, HAROLD BINGHAM (1899–1973). Civic leader, **general authority**, **president** of the Church. Born in Clifton, Idaho, on 28

March 1899, Lee had a boyhood of farm work, schooling, and the usual Church activity. Precocious, he attended the state normal school and became a school principal at age 17. At age 21, he served a **mission** in Denver, Colorado, preaching, baptizing, and gaining administrative experience. After his mission he became principal of a school in Salt Lake City, Utah, and married Fern Lucinda Tanner. They had two daughters.

After a series of responsibilities on the **ward** and **stake** level, Harold became president of the Pioneer Stake in 1930. He was also first appointed and then elected to the city commission. To help his stake members face the hardships of the Depression, Lee began welfare and work projects. In 1935, he was appointed full-time organizer and administrator for a Church-wide **welfare program**. Named to the **Quorum** of the **Twelve Apostles** in 1941, Lee took on broader administrative responsibilities. Especially important was his effort in the 1960s to promote **correlation**, a simplification of programs.

The death of his wife and his daughter Maureen in 1962 was a personal tragedy for him. The next year he married Freda Joan Jensen, who often accompanied him on his assignments. In 1970 he became a **counselor** in the **First Presidency**. Thus he was thoroughly prepared when in 1972 he became president of the Church. It was a surprise when he suddenly died of heart failure on 26 December 1973.

LEE, JOHN D. (1812–1877). Colonizer, murderer. After serving in 1828 and afterward as a mail carrier in his home city of Kaskaskia, Illinois, 1828, Lee enlisted in the Illinois Mounted Volunteers during the Black Hawk War of 1832. Afterward, he worked as a clerk in Galena, Illinois. In 1833 he married Aggatha Ann Woolsey, and the two of them joined the **LDS** Church in 1838. They lived in Missouri where Lee became a member of the Danites, a semi-secret militia, in 1838. The same year he served a **mission** to southern Illinois, and in 1841 after the saints had moved to Illinois, he served a mission to Tennessee. He served as a city policeman in Nauvoo in 1843, and in 1844 he left Nauvoo to campaign for Joseph Smith, a candidate for president of the United States. He became one of the original members of the Council of **Fifty** in 1845.

In addition to Aggatha Ann Woolsey, Lee married plural wives Nancy Bean, 1845; Louisa Free, 1845; Sarah Caroline Williams, 1845; Sarah C. Williams, 1845; Abigail Sheffer, 1845; Rachel Woolsey, 1845; Polly Ann Workman, 1845; Deletha Moss, circa 1845; Nancy Ann Vance, 1845; Emeline Vaughn Woolsey, 1846; Nancy Gibbons Armstrong, 1847; Mary Vance Young, 1847; Lavina Young, 1847, Mary Leah Groves, 1853, Mary Ann Williams, 1856; Emma Batchelor, 1858; Teresa Morse Chamberlain, 1859; and Ann Gordge, 1865. He settled in Salt Lake City, Utah, in 1848 and remained there until he was called to settle as part of the Iron Mission in Iron County, Utah, in 1850. In September 1857 he was one of the leaders of a body of Iron County militia and a few Paiute Indians in massacring a party of Arkansas emigrants at Mountain Meadows. He was excommunicated from the **Church of Jesus Christ of Latter-day Saints** for his role in the massacre in October 1870. In 1874 he was arrested for his role in the massacre, convicted in 1876, and executed in 1877. He was reinstated in the LDS Church posthumously in 1961.

LEE, REX E. (1935–1996). Attorney, educator, university president. Born and raised in St. Johns, Arizona, Rex Lee started as a student at **BYU** in 1953, served as a **missionary** in Mexico, and returned to graduate with a bachelor's degree. In 1959 he married Janet Griffin. After graduating from BYU and completing law school at the University of Chicago in 1963, Lee became a law clerk for U.S. Supreme Court justice Byron R. White. Then for eight years he practiced with a law firm in Phoenix, Arizona.

In 1972 he became founding dean of the new J. Reuben Clark Law School at BYU. His job of building a reputable professional school was interrupted by government service in 1975 when he became assistant U.S. attorney general and in 1981 when he became U.S. solicitor general. Representing the government, he argued many cases before the Supreme Court.

In 1989 he was appointed president of BYU. Although fighting a battle with cancer, diagnosed in 1987, he functioned with energy, effectiveness, and good humor until 1995, when he resigned because of failing health. Lee was a **bishop**, **stake president**, and member of the **Young Men** general board. He and his wife, Janet, had seven children.

LITERATURE. Most writing produced by Mormons from the beginning to the death of **Brigham Young** in 1877 is lacking in the literary qualities that would give it lasting interest. This does not mean a total lack of literary production. At the outset the ***Book of Mormon***, a work of over 500 pages, signaled a religion for people who were literate, as did the other **scriptures** and early periodicals. But it was not for their literary qualities that believers valued these writings or the pamphlets written in defense of the new religion.

The hymnal compiled by **Emma Smith** in 1835 included borrowed, adapted, and original hymns appropriate for the new faith; it was revised and expanded in later editions throughout the century. Some poetry, mostly doggerel, appeared in the early periodicals, but poets of greater than average ability, like **Eliza R. Snow** and **John Lyon**, were also expressing themselves. Two professors of English, Richard Cracroft and Neal Lambert, later compiled an anthology, *A Believing People*, in which they show examples of the early poetry but also demonstrate that the literary forte, if there was one for the early Mormons, was probably such personal writings as letters and, more importantly, diaries and autobiographies. A memorable example is *Autobiography of* ***Parley P. Pratt***.

During the final quarter of the 19th century, the existence of the **Young Men** and **Young Women** auxiliary organizations (then known as Mutual Improvement Associations) and the establishment of a periodical, *The Juvenile Instructor*, for the **Sunday School** provided outlets for stories and poems. A poet of ambition, Orson F. Whitney, produced an epic entitled *Elias*. The fiction, highly didactic and moralistic, included a serialized novel based on the ***Book of Mormon***, *Corianton*, by **B. H. Roberts**; stories and novels by Susa Young Gates; and Nephi Anderson's *Added Upon* (1898), which traces the life of its characters from the pre-mortal existence through this life and on into their continued interaction after death.

In the early 20th century Anderson and others continued to write fiction in the genre known as "home literature." Similar moralism characterized the fiction in Church magazines. The ***Relief Society Magazine*** did much to stimulate literary interests through courses in literary history and appreciation and by publishing many stories and poems.

Around midcentury, several works by expatriate Mormons appeared. Vardis Fisher published his Harper Prize novel *Children of God: An American Epic* (1939). Maureen Whipple's *Giant Joshua* (1941) is still considered by some the most distinctively Mormon novel. **Virginia Sorenson** was publishing her Mormon novels, *A Little Lower Than the Angels* and *The Evening and the Morning*. Samuel W. Taylor struck a humorous chord in *Heaven Knows Why* (1948).

Since the 1960s, various circumstances have combined to create a renaissance of Mormon literature. The enlarged **membership** means a larger audience. Church magazines like ***Ensign***, the ***New Era***, and the ***Friend*** have actively sought authors and published them. Independent periodicals, especially ***Dialogue*** and ***Sunstone,*** have provided additional outlets for poetry, essays, and stories as well as reviews making judgments of quality. **Deseret Book Company** has enlarged its publication scope to include fiction, and other publishers have proved receptive to Mormon subjects. The **AML** has provided a forum for discussion and the presentation of new work and has made annual awards. Not least important, **BYU** has become an academic home for several literary historians as well as poets and novelists.

So fertile has been Mormon literature in the present generation—in novels and short stories, drama, poetry, essays, and even religious and devotional pieces—that a listing quickly becomes a bibliography. A few examples must suffice. Productive poets include May Swenson, Clinton F. Larson, Carol Lynn Pearson, Arthur Henry King, Emma Lou Thayne, and Susan Howe. Edward Geary, Mary Bradford, **Eugene England,** and Louise Plummer are notable essayists. Among the many writing Mormon fiction are Levi Peterson (*Canyons of Grace, The Backslider*), Neal Chandler (*Benediction*), Donald R. Marshall (*The Rummage Sale*, *Frost in the Orchard*), Douglas H. Thayer (*Under the Cottonwoods*), Donald S. Smurthwaite (*Fine Old High Priests, A Wise, Blue Autumn*), **Orson Scott Card**, and Tracy Hickman, the last two writers of science fiction.

Some Mormon writers have achieved considerable success outside the field of Mormon literature. Among them are Orson Scott Card and Anne Perry, whose mystery novels set in Victorian England have garnered a wide following.

Persistent tensions in Mormon literature include realism versus idealism, faithfulness versus rebellion, moralism versus open-ended description, seriousness versus humor. In publication there is also tension between sponsored and unsponsored work. Pieces published by Deseret Book or appearing in Church magazines understandably must meet certain standards of the faith. Independent journals and publishers have greater latitude. Significant literature has emanated from both directions.

Largely unrealized is the literary potential of the international Church. Considering the richness of different traditions, one might anticipate Mormon poetry and novels, hymns and essays, biographies and autobiographies from Peru, France, Tonga, Ghana, and Russia, to mention only a few of the possibilities. *See also* MEMBERSHIP; PLAN OF SALVATION; UTAH PERIOD.

LUDLOW, DANIEL HANSEN (1924–). Educator, administrator, writer. Born in Benjamin, Utah, on 17 March 1924, Ludlow was raised and attended school in Spanish Fork, Utah. He graduated from Utah State University in 1946, received an M.A. from Indiana University in 1953, and earned a Ph.D. from Columbia University in 1955. He then accepted a faculty appointment in religious instruction at **BYU**.

In addition to teaching classes, Ludlow served as dean of his college. In 1972 he was called to be the Church's director of **correlation**, continuing until 1988 except for a two-year **mission** presidency in Perth, Australia, from 1981 to 1983.

A gifted teacher, Ludlow became known far beyond his college classrooms. He participated regularly as a lecturer in the extension series "Know Your Religion." He directed semester-abroad programs in Israel and led many tour groups there. He also conducted tours to Mexico and Central America. Author of at least 10 books in addition to many articles and manuals, Ludlow was editor-in-chief of the five-volume *Encyclopedia of Mormonism* published in 1992.

LUND, GERALD N. (1939–). Author, teacher, **general authority**. Lund was born on 12 September 1939 in Fountain Green, Utah. He earned bachelor's and master's degrees in sociology at **BYU** and did postgraduate work in theology and Hebrew at Pepperdine University.

From 1965 he taught **seminary** and **institute** and served as a curriculum writer for the Church Educational System (CES).

He wrote *The Work and the Glory,* a popular multivolume historical novel that follows a fictional family through its experiences in the opening decades of Church history. Transferred to the screen, it achieved some note. Lund also wrote a number of other books, including a series of fictional books on the life and ministry of Christ. He served as branch **president**, **stake missionary**, **counselor** in bishopric, **bishop**, stake president. In 2002 he was called to the Second **Quorum** of the **Seventy**. He and his wife, Retta, have seven children.

LYON, JOHN (1803–1889). Poet, missionary, drama critic. Born on 4 March 1803 in Glasgow, Scotland, John Lyon was raised by his mother after his father's death in 1811. He left home to become a weaver's apprentice and then a spinner's apprentice, but lost both positions when economic conditions became tight. Anxious for self-improvement, he took classes in the local charity schools.

At 21, John moved to Kilmarnock, Scotland, and found work as a weaver. He married Janet Thomson. Twelve children were born, eight surviving to adulthood. He joined a local literary society and worked hard to master basic writing skills. To supplement his primary income, Lyon worked as a correspondent for several newspapers of the region, publishing sketches, news items, and poems.

In 1843 he heard a Mormon preacher. After reading the ***Book of Mormon*** and various tracts, Lyon was baptized in March 1844. Soon after, his wife and older children also joined the new religion. During the next five years he became presiding **elder** of the Mormon congregation in Kilmarnock. He wrote poetry on Mormon themes and published in the ***Millennial Star***.

From 1849 he served as a **missionary** in Worcester, England, baptizing at least 360 people. At the end of 1851 he moved to Glasgow as **president** of the missionary district. Along with preaching, baptizing, and traveling, Lyon also found time to write poetry and collect poems previously written. In early 1853 his collected poems were published as *Harp of Zion*, with all proceeds earmarked for the assistance of Mormon immigrants.

Emigrating with his family to Utah in 1853, the 50-year-old Lyon plunged into Church activity. Entering **polygamy**, he took a second wife in 1856. He was appointed president of the Endowment House, where **ordinances** of the **temples** were provided while awaiting the completion of the Salt Lake Temple, and for 30 years he officiated there regularly. Lyon also became official territorial librarian. In addition to publishing many poems in the newspapers, he wrote others that remained unpublished. As drama critic for the ***Deseret News*** he attended opening nights at the Salt Lake Theatre and gave his evaluations.

A biography by great-grandson T. Edgar Lyon Jr. acknowledges that much of the creative work of the self-taught John Lyon was undistinguished. Yet he often successfully communicated the values and aspirations of his fellow believers, and he was among those who sought to raise the standards of Mormon literary expression.

LYON, T. EDGAR (1903–1978). Educator, **missionary**, historian. Born in Salt Lake City, Utah, in 1903, T. Edgar Lyon was the son of David and Mary Cairns Lyon and a grandson of poet **John Lyon**. He attended the University of Utah for two years and then was called as a missionary to the Netherlands. After his return, he married Hermana Forsberg; they went on to have six sons.

After graduating Lyon taught high school in Rigby, Idaho, and then became a **seminary** teacher. When summer seminars at **BYU** from **Sidney B. Sperry** piqued his interest, Lyon arranged a leave of absence and attended the University of Chicago, where he studied with Edgar Goodspeed and William W. Sweet and earned a master's degree.

Lyon was called at age 30 to be **president** of the Netherlands Mission, serving from 1933 to 1937. He concentrated on training local leadership, which turned out to be timely since World War II forced the evacuation of American missionaries.

Returning to Utah, Lyon was assigned to the new **institute of religion** at the University of Utah. For more than 30 years he taught classes in the **Bible**, ***Book of Mormon***, ***Doctrine and Covenants***, and Mormon history. His close associate was fellow teacher **Lowell L. Bennion**. Lyon entered the graduate program in history at the University of Utah and in 1962 was awarded the Ph.D. A prolific writer, he authored many articles and manuals.

In the 1960s, Lyon was named official historian for **NRI,** exerting his influence to encourage authenticity in the project and compiling extensive files on the **Illinois Period**. He became an early member of the **MHA** and in 1967 served as its president. He launched a major new one-volume history of Nauvoo and made methodical progress through its early stages. With Lyon's death, this project was inherited by historian Glen M. Leonard, who in 2002 published *Nauvoo: A Place of Peace, a People of Promise*.

– M –

MAESER, KARL G. (1828–1901). Educator, moralist. Born in Vorbrucke, Meissen, Germany, Maeser enjoyed a good education. Private tutoring instructed him in French, Italian, and Latin. He also learned the piano and organ and conducted choirs. Maeser studied at the Krenz Schule and graduated from the Friederichstadt Schullehrerseminar. He became a teacher for a while in Dresden, Germany, and then took employment as a private tutor in Bohemia. In 1854 he married Anna Meith.

In 1855 Maeser came in contact with Mormonism. An agnostic, he was impressed by the sincere **testimony** of the Mormon **missionaries**. After being baptized he was named **president** of the Dresden branch, leading this small group to America the next year. Out of money, he stopped in the eastern United States and worked as a music teacher until he could go on to Utah.

From 1860 on, except for a three-year mission back to Germany, Maeser was an educator. He headed the Union Academy and tutored **Brigham Young**'s children. In 1876 he was named principal of the new Brigham Young Academy in Provo. Young's instructions included, "I want you to remember that you ought not to teach even the alphabet or the multiplication tables without the Spirit of God" (Wilkinson and Skousen, *Brigham Young University: School of Destiny*, 67). His students long remembered him for his aphorisms and moral lessons.

Appointed general superintendent of Church schools, he was released from the Brigham Young Academy so that he could travel and supervise scattered academies. In 1894 he became a member of the superintendency of the **Sunday School**. Crusty but tender of heart, Maeser spoke with a slight accent. He expressed his philosophy of education in *School and Fireside* (1898). He died on 14 February 1901. *See also* BRIGHAM YOUNG UNIVERSITY.

MANIFESTO. Document issued by Church president **Wilford Woodruff** in 1890 that is often regarded as a dividing point in Mormon history in that it marked the end of **polygamy**. Actually, the facts are a little more complex.

The manifesto itself (***Doctrine and Covenants***, official declaration 1) falls short of an absolute prohibition. "My advice to the Latter-day Saints," said Woodruff, "is to refrain from contracting any marriage forbidden by the law of the land." Moreover, there was a distinction between the contracting of a new marriage and the continuation of an existing relationship. Even those willing to discontinue the former would find it difficult to end the latter.

Following the 1890 Manifesto, Mormon polygamy went into a sharp decline. Relatively few new plural marriages—compared to all marriages and to pre-1890 marriages—were performed, mostly outside of the United States. Meanwhile, those who had become polygamists prior to 1890 were steadily dying off. In 1904 a second manifesto was issued and much more rigidly enforced.

The 1890 Manifesto was an official statement of intent. Signaling the beginning of the end of polygamy, it prepared the way for Utah's admission to the union as a state. None of the **general authorities**, none of the **stake presidents**, none of the **bishops** or branch presidents is now a polygamist. The Church does not now advocate polygamy. Anyone found guilty of teaching or practicing it is subject to **excommunication**. *See also* FUNDAMENTALISTS.

MARRIAGE. Marriage is held in high esteem by Mormons. In fact, it is considered a vital part of progress toward eternal life. Although **polygamy** was urged upon the faithful for some 40 years, far more fundamental is marriage itself, the joining together of a man and a woman in the bonds of matrimony. Premarital and extramarital sex are condemned. Marriage provides the necessary structure of love and adult modeling for children. It also enhances the happiness and fulfillment of husband and wife. "Faithfulness to the marriage covenant," said Church **president Ezra Taft Benson**, "brings the fullest joy here and glorious rewards hereafter."

The highest form of marriage is eternal marriage as performed in the **temples**. By **priesthood** authority the officiator pronounces the partners sealed together "for time and all eternity." Because the two partners share the same religious faith and have made the same solemn commitments, temple marriages have a significantly lower **divorce** rate than other marriages.

In terms of actual behavior, of course, Mormon marriage practice falls short of the ideal. Through choice or circumstance, a number of adults remain single. Many marriages are not performed in the temple, although some of these are later sealed as eternal relationships. Despite the greater durability of temple marriages, many marriages end in divorce.

A **First Presidency** statement of 19 October 2004 favored defining marriage as a union between a man and a woman. In June 2006, **Russell M. Nelson**, representing the Church, met with 55 rabbis, archbishops, evangelical leaders, priests of the Greek Orthodox Church, and others to sign a letter and hold a press conference in support of a defense of marriage amendment to the U.S. Constitution. The amendment failed in the U.S. Senate, but proponents, fearful that activist judges would redefine the institution of marriage, promised they would return. The ideal of a stable marriage is repeatedly taught. Probably no other religion emphasizes the importance and eternal significance of marriage to the same degree. *See also* FAMILY; SEALING.

MARRIOTT, J. WILLARD (1900–1985). Businessman, Church leader. Born in Ogden, Utah, on 17 September 1900, J. Willard (or Bill) Marriott had the experience of working on farms, herding sheep and cattle. For two years, from 1919 to 1921, he was a **missionary** in New England. Paying his way with summer jobs, he graduated from Weber College and in 1927 from the University of Utah.

He opened a root beer stand in Washington, D.C., and returned to Utah to marry Alice Sheets. Another root beer stand was followed by a restaurant, the Hot Shoppe. Other restaurants followed: Hot Shoppe Number One, Number Two, and so on. Marriott weathered the Great Depression and expanded his chain of restaurants, as well as moving into airline catering and hotels. After the war he became president of the National Restaurant Association.

Marriott became a **counselor** in the **stake** presidency in 1946 and two years later stake **president** in Washington, D.C. His accomplishments include seeing the completion of the first Mormon chapel there, supervising the expansion of **membership** from one little branch to several stakes, and finally acquiring property and watching the completion of the Washington, D.C., Temple in 1976.

Active Republicans, both Marriott and his wife participated in party politics and supported the arts. He chaired the inauguration committees in 1969 and 1973. For several years he chaired the American Historical and Cultural Society, which sponsored Honor America concerts at the Kennedy Center.

Marriott was awarded an honorary degree by the University of Utah. In return for a substantial gift to the University of Utah, the J. Willard Marriott Library was named after him. A generous donation to **BYU** resulted in the Marriott Activities Center, which houses major athletic events.

MASON, JAMES O. (1930–). Physician, public health administrator, **general authority**. Born on 19 June 1930 in Salt Lake City, Utah, Mason served a full-time **mission** in Denmark. He received a bachelor's degree and then a medical degree from the University of Utah. From Harvard University he received a master's degree and doctorate of public health. He interned at the Johns Hopkins University Hospital in Baltimore, Maryland. He served in the military branch of the U.S. Public Health Service and became an epidemiologist.

Mason was director of the infectious diseases division at a Salt Lake City hospital before being named Church commissioner of health services. In 1978 he returned to the University of Utah School of Medicine as chairman of the Division of Community Medicine. Then he served for four years as executive director of the Utah Department of Health. In 1983 he was named director of the national Center for Disease Control and Prevention in Atlanta, Georgia, and in 1989 became assistant secretary for health and head of the U.S. Public Health Service.

In the Church, Mason served as **bishop, stake president**, and **regional representative**. In 1994 he was called to the Second **Quorum** of the **Seventy**. In 1996 he became president of the **Africa area** and in 1998 president of the Africa West area. In October 2000, he was honorably released from his **calling** as a general authority. He and his wife, Marie, are the parents of seven children.

MAXWELL, NEAL A. (1926–2004). Educator, political scientist, **general authority**. Born on 6 July 1926 in Salt Lake City, Utah, Maxwell graduated from the University of Utah with a degree in political science. For two years he was a **missionary** in eastern Canada. After serving as a legislative assistant to U.S. Senator Wallace F. Bennett, Maxwell accepted teaching and administrative positions at the University of Utah. In 1970 he became executive vice president of the university. He was commissioner of education for the Church Educational System from 1970 to 1976.

In the Church, Maxwell served as **bishop**, general board member for **Young Men**, member of the Adult **Correlation** Committee, and **regional representative**. In 1974, he was named an **assistant to the twelve**. Two years later he was one of the presidency of the First **Quorum** of the **Seventy**. In 1981, at the age of 55, Maxwell became a member of the Quorum of the **Twelve Apostles**.

Known for his eloquent preaching, Maxwell authored more than 30 books. In 1998, the Neal A. Maxwell Presidential Endowed Chair in political theory, public policy, and public service was established by private donors at the University of Utah. In 2006 the Neal A. Maxwell Institute for Religious Scholarship was established at **BYU**.

MCCONKIE, BRUCE REDD (1915–1985). Attorney, **missionary**, **general authority**. Born on 29 July 1915 in Ann Arbor, Michigan, McConkie was raised in Utah. After serving a mission in the Eastern States Mission from 1934 to 1936, he attended the University of Utah Law School, receiving his law degree in 1939. In 1937, while still a student, he married Amelia Smith, daughter of **Joseph Fielding Smith**. McConkie was assistant Salt Lake City attorney and city prosecutor until entering the U.S. Army as an intelligence officer in 1941. At the end of the war he was a lieutenant colonel.

At the relatively young age of 31, McConkie was called as one of the First Council of the **Seventy**. From 1946 he traveled to **stake conferences**, addressed **general conferences**, and for three years served as **president** of the Southern Australia Mission. In 1972 he became a member of the **Quorum** of the **Twelve Apostles**.

A diligent student of the **scriptures**, McConkie came to be acknowledged as a doctrinal authority. As a young man he started the systematic scriptural study that provided the basis for his later exposition. The publication of *Mormon Doctrine* (1958) made his name a household word throughout the Church. Also important was a three-volume commentary on the New Testament. McConkie's personal commitment to **Jesus Christ**, the subject of many of his sermons, led to a six-volume work on the life and mission of the Savior, a hymn entitled "I Believe in Christ," and a moving **testimony** in his final conference address in April 1985. Less than two weeks later he died of cancer.

MCKAY, DAVID O. (1873–1970). Educator, apostle, Church **president**. Born on 8 September 1873 in Huntsville, Utah, McKay lived his early life in a rural environment. He played football and was president of his student body in college. After graduating from the University of Utah in 1897, he was a **missionary** in Scotland. Upon his return he married Emma Ray Riggs and took a teaching job at Weber Academy in Ogden, Utah. He became its principal from 1902 to 1908.

In 1906 he was called to be a member of the **Quorum** of the **Twelve Apostles**. In addition, he became a leader in the general **Sunday School** organization and Church commissioner of education. In 1922–1924 he was president of the European Mission.

Tall and handsome with a head of wavy white hair, McKay was striking. Exuding confidence and good will, he was popular among his people. His sermons were often illustrated with quotations from Shakespeare or his favorite poet, Robert Burns. The McKay family seemed a model with seven children and obvious affection and respect between the parents. When he could find time, McKay returned to his rural Huntsville, where he could ride horses and breathe fresh air.

In 1934 he was called as a **counselor** to Church president **Heber J. Grant**. During the 1930s and '40s he and his colleagues shepherded the Church through the Great Depression and World War II. In 1951 David O. McKay became ninth president of the Church.

Membership had passed the million mark. In addition to continuing emphasis on the **family**, he highlighted missionary work. "Every member a missionary" was an oft-repeated saying of his. From 1951 to 1971, the number of missionaries rose from 2,000 to 13,000, the number of **stakes** from 184 to 500. McKay had an international outlook. During his administration, **temples** were constructed at Los Angeles and Oakland and also in Switzerland, New Zealand, and England.

MCMURRAY, W. GRANT (1947–). Historian, **RLDS** Church authority. Born on 12 June 1947 in Toronto, Canada, McMurray was raised in the RLDS Church. He received a B.A. in religious instruction from Graceland College in 1969 and in 1975 the master of divinity degree from St. Paul School of Theology in Kansas City, Missouri. Starting in 1971, he was employed by the RLDS Church, serving as assistant to the director of the Division of Program Planning (1971–1972), historical research assistant (1972–1973), church archivist (1973–1976), assistant commissioner of history (1976–1982), world Church secretary and executive assistant to the **First Presidency** (1982–1992), and member of the **Quorum** of the First Presidency (1992–1996).

Ordained **president** of the RLDS Church on 15 April 1996, he was the first president of that church not a direct descendant of **Joseph Smith**. For personal reasons, he resigned from his presidential office on 29 November 2004. "I have made some inappropriate choices," he said, "and the circumstances of my life are now such that I cannot continue to effectively lead the church." On 12 October 2005 he was named executive director of Missouri Impact. *See also* VEAZEY, STEPHEN M.

MELCHIZEDEK PRIESTHOOD. The higher **priesthood**, to which every **worthy** adult male in the Church is eligible. It is conferred by the laying on of hands by those who are in authority (**Articles of Faith**, no. 5). Offices within the Melchizedek Priesthood include **elder**, **high priest**, **patriarch**, **seventy**, and apostle. As an indispensable part of the **restoration** of the **gospel**, **Joseph Smith** and **Oliver Cowdery** received the Melchizedek Priesthood in 1829 or early 1830 when the ancient apostles Peter, James, and John appeared and conferred it upon them. At the same time they were ordained apostles and received the keys of the **dispensation** of the fullness of times.

Mormons understand priesthood to be eternal, going back to the pre-mortal existence. Defined as the authority to act in God's name, it has been held by various individuals during the history of the world. The **patriarch** Abraham received it from Melchizedek, a priest and king of Salem, after whom it is named in order to avoid the frequent use of God's name.

Although it is a lay organization with no professional **clergy**, priesthhod is regarded as anything but unimportant; to the contrary, priesthood authority is a prerequisite to the authorized preaching of the **gospel** and validly administering the **ordinances** of salvation. *See also* AARONIC PRIESTHOOD; PRIESTHOOD.

MEMBERSHIP. Technically one becomes a member of the Church upon **baptism** and **confirmation**. Since age eight, the "age of accountability," is the minimum age for baptism, younger children of Mormon families are considered "children of record." The membership figures here will include these.

Starting with the original six members on 6 April 1830, Church membership grew to 26,000 members by 1844, the year of **Joseph Smith**'s death. In 1877, the year of **Brigham Young**'s death, the total reached 115,000. At the turn of the century there were over 283,000 Mormons. In 1919 membership passed 500,000. In 1947, it was 1 million; in 1963, 2 million; in 1979, 4 million; and in 1991, 8 million. At the end of 2005, membership was officially reported as 12,560,869, and in June 2007, the Church reported that it had passed the 13-million member mark.

The growth has not been uniform geographically. In February 1996 a corner was turned, with more than half of members living outside the United States. At the end of 2005, **Central America and Mexico** accounted for more than 1.5 million members, **South America** more than 2.9 million, **Asia** and the South Pacific 1.3 million. The time when Mormonism was exclusively an American church (never completely the case, of course, except at the very beginning) was obviously over. Predictably, differing rates of growth in the different continents will produce a less Anglo-Saxon mix in the future.

To cope with the demands of a skyrocketing membership, Church leaders have sought simplification and coordination through the **correlation** program, divided administrative responsibilities into different world **areas**, and increased the number of **general authorities.**

MENTAL HEALTH RESOURCE FOUNDATION. A nonprofit support organization that follows Church principles to provide resources to assist individuals, health care professionals, social workers, **bishops**, **stake presidents**, or anyone else faced with mental and emotional illness. Books and pamphlets deal with such topics as addictions, aging, bipolar disorders, codependency, depression, eating disorders, and pornography. Sources utilized include the National Institute of Mental Health, Alcoholics Anonymous, and Church articles. An online library can be accessed at MentalHealthLibrary.info.

MERRILL, JOSEPH FRANCIS (1868–1952). Educator, **general authority**. Born to Marriner W. Merrill and Mariah Loenza Kingsbury in Richmond, Utah, Merrill attended local public schools and the University of Utah Normal School. He earned a bachelor of science at the University of Michigan in 1893 and studied at Cornell University and the University of Chicago before earning a Ph.D. at the Johns Hopkins University in physics and electrical engineering in 1899. He had received an appointment as assistant professor of chemistry at the University of Utah in 1893, and he returned to that position after completing the Ph.D. At the University of Utah he served as the director of the Utah state School of Mines and Engineering.

For the next 28 years Merrill's career was focused on Utah. In 1911, while a member of the Granite Stake presidency, he was instrumental in establishing the **LDS** Church's first **seminary** courses for high school students near Granite High School. Through his work, the Utah legislature passed bills that established the University of Utah's School of Mines, Utah Engineering Experiment Station, and the Department of Mining and Metallurgical Research.

In 1898 he married Annie Laura Hyde. She died in February 1917, and he married Emily L. Traub in 1918. In 1928, after 35 years of service to the University of Utah, Merrill left to become the LDS Church's commissioner of education. He brought with him extensive experience in the educational field. In 1931, he was called to be a member of the Council of **Twelve Apostles**. He served in this position until his death in 1952.

MERRILL, MARRINER WOOD (1832–1906). Businessman, **general authority**. Merrill was the son of Nathan Merrill and Sarah Ann Reynolds, the 10th of 13 children. He grew up in New Brunswick, Canada. His mother converted to the **LDS** Church in 1836, but Merrill did not learn of her conversion until he was converted in September 1852. In the spring of 1853, Merrill left his family and all relatives in New Brunswick and traveled to the Salt Lake Valley. Though poorly educated, he was committed to education and made arrangements for his children to receive good educations. In 1857 he freighted supplies during the Utah War.

During the winter of 1859–1860, while residing in Bountiful, Utah, Merrill was called to move to northern Utah and settle in Cache Valley where land was more plentiful and the prospects of financial stability were greater. Along with others he traveled north of Logan, Utah, to help found the settlement at Richmond. He was involved in building and establishing businesses such as railroads, irrigation canals, flour mills, and mercantile stores. In 1861 he was ordained **bishop** of the Richmond **ward** serving for 18 years. In 1879 he was called a **counselor** in the Cache **Stake** presidency where he served for 10 years. In 1884 he was called to serve as the first **president** of the Logan Temple where he served until his death in 1906. In 1889, Merrill was ordained an apostle. Instead of moving to Salt Lake City, he continued living in Richmond and traveled to Salt Lake City to meet with the other general authorities. Ten years later, while still serving in the **Quorum** of the **Twelve Apostles**, he was given the added responsibility of presiding over the Cache Stake, serving two years. Upon his release, the stake was divided into three stakes.

A committed **polygamist**, Merrill married Sarah Ann Atkinson, 10 November 1853; Cyrene Standly, 1856; Anna Sophia Angum, 1857; Jennie Jacobson, 1857; Martha Mary Cardon, 1878; and Eliza Lucina Shepherd, 1880. He entered his last marriage to Hulda Maria Erickson in 1901, one of a number of Mormons to marry after the **Manifesto** of 1890.

MEXICO. *See* CENTRAL AMERICA AND MEXICO.

MILLENNIAL STAR. Official publication of the British Mission from its founding in 1840 to its termination in 1970. The complete title was the *Latter-day Saints Millennial Star*. Its contents include editorials, poetry, sermons, **baptisms**, names of **missionaries** and their activities, immigration organization and departures, and letters from various locations in Great Britain as well as the distant **Zion** of Utah. Starting publication when **Joseph Smith** was still alive, it included some of the earliest documents and historical writings of the Church. Especially for the 19th century, it is a valuable primary source.

MILLENNIUM. Like some other Christians, Mormons believe in a future era of a thousand years when the earth will be renewed (**Articles of Faith**, no. 10). In a strict and narrow sense of the word, they are pre-millennialists, believing that the millennial reign will be ushered in by the Second Coming of **Jesus Christ**. However, the obligation to work for improvement in the present is an integral part of the belief. Moreover, during the Millennium life will not be one of simply basking in the sun. Among other activities carried on will be **missionary** work and service in the **temples**.

Many early Mormons thought the Second Coming and the Millennium were very near. As time has gone on, the expectation has faded but not disappeared. The term *latter-day* in the title of the Church designates the present age as the final **dispensation**. The official belief in a winding-up scene and Millennium is still intact. The standard works, or **scriptures**, all have passages pointing forward to such a final act in the drama of human existence. But Mormon leaders are not among the millennialists who count the days or sell off property in order to await the great event. They insist that no one knows the exact timetable. It is simply "near"—a relative term. Members are urged to be ready—that is, have their "house in order" by following the **commandments**.

MISSION, MISSIONARY, MISSIONARY PROGRAM. From its beginning the Church has been a missionary organization. **Members** were anxious to invite friends and relatives to share the joy they had found in the restored **gospel**. On their own or as called by their leaders, Mormon men departed on missionary preaching tours. Some degree of organization, with mission areas and missionaries organized into conferences, or districts, began to take shape.

By the last generation of the 19th century, the basic outline was established: formal call to missionary service from the first presidency, correspondence through the mail from the mission president or mission office, missionaries going two by two and being assigned to specific locations by their president, missionaries being periodically reassigned, and missionaries being formally released at the end of the mission. In the 20th century the following developments took place:

- Young women were called as missionaries.
- Training programs for newly called missionaries were developed.
- Systematic programs for presenting the gospel to **investigators** were developed to assure adequate instruction.
- The number of missions was increased as opportunity allowed.
- Married couples were called as missionaries, both as full-time missionaries and as "Church service" missionaries to assist in a variety of activities, including assisting patrons at **family history** libraries and serving as guides at **visitors centers**.

Those willing to serve as missionaries are interviewed by their **bishop**. **Worthiness** is ascertained and financial arrangements are discussed. People are not paid to go on missions. With the exception of mission presidents, missionaries support themselves from savings, donations from family, **ward** mission fund, a general mission fund, or some combination of these. When the official letter comes from Church headquarters calling one to be a missionary, the specific mission is indicated. The place of service is determined by need of the Church, although the desire of the prospective missionary may be considered.

In 2004, previous missionary plans were replaced by *"Preach My Gospel": A Guide to Missionary Service*. A series of lessons instructs the investigator on the message of the **restoration**, **plan of salvation**, **commandments**, laws and **ordinances** of the **gospel**. While passages of **scripture** are used in teaching, flexibility is allowed as the missionary recognizes individual needs and follows the inspiration of the Spirit.

Although young men are encouraged to prepare themselves for mission calls, less than a third of males between ages 19 and 21 actually serve missions. They must desire to serve, pass a test of **worthiness**, and be mentally and physically sound. Young women who express a desire to serve and similarly qualify may be called at age 21.

In December 2006, 53,164 full-time missionaries were serving. In June 2007, the church had 341 missions. In addition, more than 12,000 church service missionaries served from 8 to 32 hours a week as office assistants, hosts at visitors centers, medical doctors, and many other positions that assisted in fulfilling the **mission of the Church**.

MISSION OF THE CHURCH. Building upon scriptural passages and earlier statements by previous Church leaders, Presidents **Spencer W. Kimball** and **Ezra Taft Benson** brought the mission of the Church into sharp focus. It is to "invite all to come unto Christ and be perfected in him" (***Doctrine and Covenants*** 20:50; ***Book of Mormon***, Moroni 10:32).

This mission has three dimensions: (1) proclaim the **gospel** to every nation, kindred, tongue, and people; (2) perfect the **saints** by preparing them to receive the **ordinances** of the gospel and by caring for the poor and needy; and (3) redeem the dead by performing vicarious ordinances for them in the **temple**.

In other words, through the **missionary**, nonmembers were to be addressed; through the various programs of the Church, members were to receive the saving ordinances and experience development and opportunities for service; and through **genealogy** and temples, those who are dead would receive the blessings of the gospel.

MISSIONARY TRAINING CENTERS. From the 1830s, missionaries were advised to study the **scriptures** and prepare themselves to be effective representatives of the Church (***Doctrine and Covenants***, sections 14–19, 88). To assist them a school operated briefly at Kirtland, Ohio. During the **Utah Period**, at the end of the 19th century, several academies, including the one that became **BYU**, offered brief missionary training classes. For several decades in the early to mid-20th century a "mission home" in Salt Lake City, Utah, provided lodging for newly called **missionaries** as they followed a series of classes that lasted about one week before departing for different fields of labor. A more comprehensive program of instruction came in 1961 with the establishment of the Missionary Language Institute at Provo, Utah, renamed the Language Training Mission in 1963. After 1978, it was called the Missionary Training Center and all missionaries, even those not learning a foreign language, were required to attend.

Following a rigorous program, outgoing missionaries receive instruction in the **scriptures**, missionary techniques, and, where applicable, language. Intensive language instruction follows the "total immersion" approach earlier pioneered by the U.S. military. Some introduction to culture and customs is also included. The typical term for those learning a foreign language is eight weeks. To accommodate the expanding missionary force, missionary training centers have also been established in **South America**, **Europe**, **Asia**, and the **Pacific**. On 22 May 2002 in Ghana, the Church opened its 16th missionary training center throughout the world.

MISSOURI PERIOD. The first Mormons in Missouri were the **missionaries**—**Oliver Cowdery**, **Parley P. Pratt**, Peter Whitmer Jr., and Ziba Peterson—sent in mid-1830 by **Joseph Smith** on an assignment to preach to the Indians. After unusual success in Ohio these missionaries proceeded westward, reaching Missouri in January 1831, completing a journey from western New York of 1,500 miles. Preaching to the Indians was thwarted by the agent, but a foothold was established. Western Missouri was declared the site of the New Jerusalem (***Doctrine and Covenants***, section 28) with Independence to be "the center place" and site for a **temple** (*Doctrine and Covenants*, section 57). The Mormons from Colesville, New York, moved there. The **gathering** to Missouri had begun.

By 1832 several hundred Mormons had come to Missouri. A printing press was established, two newspapers began publication, and schools were started. The next year saw the publication—interrupted by violence but partially successful—of the ***Book of Commandments***, a compilation of Joseph Smith's **revelations**. Mormons were settling not only in Independence but also in nearby Kaw Township and three other small settlements.

Contrary to instructions, some of the new arrivals came with no visible means of support. Some Mormons made themselves obnoxious by boasting that they were going to take over Jackson County. But the problem of internal discipline might well have been solved had it not been for the outside opposition that finally burst forth into mob violence in 1833. Mobs destroyed the printing press and tarred and feathered two of the Mormon leaders. Several were killed. By November the Mormons were fleeing across the Missouri River northward to Clay County. In an effort to restore his people to their lawful property Joseph Smith came from Ohio at the head of a military force of untrained volunteers, but, recognizing the reality of the situation, disbanded them before any actual battle.

Still looking for a place in Missouri where they might live peaceably, the Mormons moved northward into Caldwell County, newly created in 1836. A center was established at Far West, to which Smith moved his headquarters in 1838. Another center was begun in Daviess County. With the collapse of Kirtland, hundreds came from there to the new Missouri settlements. Those who owned land and property in Jackson County hoped that through legal processes they might return.

But friction seemed unavoidable. The Mormons were not faultless. **Sidney Rigdon** spoke out against dissenters, threatening them with violence, and declared that if mobs attacked again there would be a war of extermination. A paramilitary group, the **Danites**, resorted to violence against Church enemies, justified as self-defense. The Mormons did not limit their settlements to Caldwell County, as many in the Missouri legislature had thought they would, but insisted on their right to settle anywhere.

There was an abundance of guilt on the other side as well. Rabid **anti-Mormons** were eager to drive their enemies out and seize their property. A riot occurred when Mormons tried to exercise their right to vote. Seventeen were killed in a massacre at Haun's Mill. Militias armed on both sides. In this setting Missouri's Governor Lilburn W. Boggs issued his "extermination order": Mormons must leave the state or suffer extermination. When Far West was besieged and tensions were high, Joseph Smith and a few of his colleagues attempted to meet with the other side and negotiate. Instead, they were seized and thrown into prison.

The stage was set for the exodus of the Mormons from Missouri, accomplished in late 1838 and early 1839 under the direction of leaders left at large including **Brigham Young**, Heber C. Kimball, and Edward Partridge. In the cold season of the year, carrying such few belongings as they could salvage, some 12,000 Mormons straggled—in companies, as families, even individually—eastward to seek refuge in Illinois. The **RLDS** Church (now **Community of Christ**) later made its headquarters in Independence.

On 25 June 1976 Governor Christopher S. Bond rescinded the infamous 1838 extermination order. In 1997 a temple was completed and dedicated in St. Louis. At the end of 2005, 59,377 Mormons lived in Missouri, divided into 14 **stakes** and 98 **wards**. *See also* ILLINOIS PERIOD; OHIO PERIOD; ZION'S CAMP.

MONSON, THOMAS SPENCER (1927–). Businessman, **general authority**, **counselor** in the **First Presidency**, Church **president**. Born on 21 August 1927 in Salt Lake City, Utah, Monson received his primary and secondary education there. He served in the U.S. Navy during World War II and subsequently graduated from the University of Utah with a degree in business management.

Monson became a **bishop** at the age of 22. He was employed by the Newspaper Agency Corporation as executive in the advertising division. For Deseret News Press he took the position of sales manager, later becoming general manager. He was president of Printing Industry of Utah and a member of the board of directors of Printing Industry of America. He became a counselor in the **stake** presidency. In 1959 he was called to be president of the Canadian Mission and lived at its headquarters in Toronto for three years.

At age 36, he was called to be a member of the **Quorum** of the **Twelve Apostles**. Chairman of the board of the Deseret News Publishing Company and a member of the board of Newspaper Agency Corporation, he also served on the National Executive Board of **Boy Scouts** of America, receiving both the Silver Beaver and Silver Buffalo awards. He belonged to the Utah Association of Sales Executives, the Salt Lake Advertising Club, and the Salt Lake Exchange Club. For many years he was a member of the State Board of Regents. In 1985, Monson became second counselor in the First Presidency, and in 1995 first counselor to President **Gordon B. Hinckley**. On 4 February 2008 he was called as president of the Church.

MORMON. (1) The proper name of a great ***Book of Mormon*** prophet who lived at the end of the fourth century. In addition to leading his people militarily, Mormon abridged previous records into the plates later used by **Joseph Smith** in translating the *Book of Mormon*. The book is thus named after a person.

(2) Nickname for members of the **Church of Jesus Christ of Latter-day Saints**. Because it suggests a primary loyalty to an individual prophet and leaves out the central figure of **Jesus Christ**, the term has long been discouraged or carefully placed within quotation marks. But because of the length of the official title of the Church the shorter nickname has proved irresistible. Even Church writers and journalists use it. Properly used, the term applies strictly to the Church of Jesus Christ of Latter-day Saints, not **fundamentalism** and not the **Community of Christ**.

MORMON BATTALION. A battalion of the U.S. Army during the Mexican War (1846–1847) recruited from the Mormon refugees encamped in Iowa after their forced departure from Nauvoo, Illinois.

The point of view of the U.S. government is revealed in an entry dated 2 July 1846 in the diary of President James K. Polk: "Col. Kearny was also authorized to receive into service as volunteers a few hundred of the Mormons who are now on their way to California, with a view to conciliate them, attach them to our country, & prevent them from taking part against us" (Polk, *The Diary of a President*). The Mormon leaders, on the other hand, saw this as a chance to gain help in their migration. Not only were the battalion members fed and clothed during their westward march, but also the pay they earned as soldiers was made available to help their families. Approximately 500 men signed up. Accompanying them were about 80 women, some working as laundresses, and a few children. Recruiter Captain James Allen (promoted to colonel) first led the battalion. When he died en route, after an interim arrangement, Colonel Philip St. George Cooke became commander.

The battalion proceeded overland to Santa Fe. One group of sick, including nearly all the women and children, after wintering at Pueblo, Colorado, went on to the Salt Lake Valley, where they arrived on 28 July 1847, just four days after **Brigham Young**. The rest of the battalion left Santa Fe, marched in a southwestward direction through New Mexico, across southern Arizona and Southern California, and arrived at San Diego in January 1847. Most of them were discharged at Los Angeles in July 1847.

During a pivotal year in the colonization of the West, the Mormon Battalion found itself involved in important events: the settling of San Diego, the gold discovery at Sutter's Mill that precipitated the great California gold rush, and the colonizing of the Salt Lake Valley. *See also* ILLINOIS PERIOD.

MORMON HISTORIC SITES FOUNDATION. An independent foundation dedicated to preserving and restoring sites important in Church history. Formed in 1992 as the Ensign Peak Foundation, the group subsequently adopted a name reflective of its many interests. It has assisted in many projects. The most ambitious of these was the restoration of historic Kirtland, Ohio. Its journal, *Mormon Historical Studies*, is published semiannually.

MORMON HISTORY ASSOCIATION (MHA). An organization formed in December 1965 to further the research and publication of Mormon history. Since its first meeting in 1966, the MHA has held annual meetings, organized adjunct sessions in connection with other professional associations, given awards, and published a newsletter and the *Journal of Mormon History*. *See also* JOHN WHITMER HISTORICAL ASSOCIATION.

MORMON TABERNACLE CHOIR. A celebrated singing group started in the 1860s. For many years its leader was **Evan Stephens**, who increased its size to more than 300 voices. The choir became more widely known with the beginning of weekly live radio broadcasts in 1929, later extended to television, which included also a brief "sermonette," the "spoken word," by **Richard L. Evans**. Its members, amateur in the sense that they are unpaid, are trained musicians, selected by audition, who rehearse every Thursday evening. From

1975 to 1999 its director was **Jerold D. Ottley**. He was succeeded by **Craig D. Jessop**. In 2008 Mac Wilberg, internationally famed choral arranger, succeeded Jessop.

The Mormon Tabernacle Choir has made recordings for CBS Masterworks Records, London-Decca, Argo, and Bonneville Records. It has performed major choral works with the Philadelphia Symphony, Utah Symphony, and Jerusalem Symphony Orchestras. Tours within the United States started under director Evan Stephens. In recent years the choir performed concerts in Japan, Korea, Brazil, Western Europe, Russia, and Israel.

In 2003 the choir was awarded the National Medal of Arts. In 2006 the choir won the Laureate of the Mother Teresa Award for edifying the world through inspirational choral performances and recordings.

MORMON YOUTH SYMPHONY AND CHORUS (MYSC). Two groups of musicians between ages 18 and 33 established in 1969. Like the **Mormon Tabernacle Choir,** MYSC was sponsored by the Church. Musicians with experience in other orchestras and choruses were selected by audition. In addition to performing at **general conferences**, the groups made commercial recordings. The conductor since 1974 was Robert C. Bowden, who also composed and arranged some of MYSC's music. He retired after 25 years of service.

On 1 June 1999 this organization was disbanded. The chorus, renamed the Temple Square Chorale, became a training choir for the Mormon Tabernacle Choir. The orchestra was renamed the Orchestra at **Temple Square**, with no age requirement for membership.

MORONI. Pronounced in English with the accent on the second syllable and a long final vowel: more-own-eye. (1) A prominent leader at the close of the ***Book of Mormon***. (2) A resurrected being, who appeared to **Joseph Smith** several times. (3) The statue on the top spire of many **temples**, mistakenly thought by many to be the angel Gabriel. Moroni is sometimes identified as fulfilling Revelation 14:6.

MORRISON, ALEXANDER (1930–). Pharmacist, public official, **general authority**. Born on 22 December 1930 in Edmonton, Alberta, Canada, Morrison joined the Church as a college student. He earned a Ph.D. from Cornell University in 1956 and nine years later a master's degree in pharmacology. He obtained a faculty appointment in public health at the University of Guelph and rose to become department chairman. With the Health Protection Branch of the Canadian government, Morrison promoted laws and regulations to control contaminants. For many years he worked with the World Health Organization, chairing the Scientific and Technical Advisory Committee to the Special Program for Research and Training in Tropical Diseases. In this capacity he made many trips to different nations of **Africa**.

In the Church, Morrison served as branch **president**, **bishop**, and **regional representative**. In 1987, he became a general authority as a member of the First **Quorum** of the **Seventy**, then as a member of the Second Quorum of the Seventy, and again as a member of the First Quorum of the Seventy. In October 2000, he was awarded emeritus status. He and his wife, Shirley, have eight children.

MOUNTAIN MEADOWS MASSACRE. Tragic incident in September 1857 in which virtually an entire wagon company, at least 120 people, was killed by Mormon militiamen and a few Paiute Indians as they were passing through southern Utah on their way to California. The incident must be explained by identifying specific factors that converged at Mountain Meadows in 1857, including war conditions, poor communications, and perhaps provocation.

The summer of 1857 brought the announcement that U.S. troops were on their way to install a new governor in Utah Territory. Some of the soldiers bragged that they intended to kill Mormons, especially Mormon leaders. On the grounds that he had not been notified of his replacement, **Brigham Young** announced that the U.S. troops would be treated as a hostile force. During the latter part of 1857 and early 1858 the Mormon militia was mobilized, preparations were made to evacuate Salt Lake City, Utah, and the supply trains of the advancing army were harassed and burned. Mormons hoped for assistance from Indian allies, who had no love for Americans in general.

The Baker-Fancher wagon train company was from Arkansas. As they moved southward through Utah, they required supplies. Since the Mormons were preparing for war, they generally refused to sell to the company. Rumors of conflicts appeared, but the precipitating events seem to have occurred in Cedar City, Utah, with the harassment of Barbara Morris (the wife of a member of the bishopric and the mother of a member of the **stake** presidency) and, in particular, a conflict over the charges for milling some grain. War hysteria intensified what otherwise might have been solvable conflicts. Stake **president** and militia major Isaac Haight sent militia major John D. Lee and others to Mountain Meadows, where the company had camped to recuperate. They initiated an attack on the company, and when their assault failed, Haight mobilized the militia to assist them in massacring the emigrants. Some Paiutes were involved in the attacks, but local militiamen committed most of the murders.

In initiating the attacks, Haight acted against the consensus of the stake presidency and **high council**, who voted to send a messenger, James Haslam, on horseback to Salt Lake City to obtain instructions from Brigham Young. Young sent a letter with Haslam telling Haight that the settlers "must not meddle with them [the emigrants]." Haslam reached Cedar City two days after the massacre.

The attacks occurred between September 7 and 10 and the massacre took place on September 11. The settlers took most of the emigrants' property. Seventeen children survived the massacre and were returned to Arkansas in 1859.

Although some violence had occurred elsewhere, with the conclusion of hostilities in 1858, investigation into the massacre began. In 1859, Brigham Young, then a private citizen but leader of the Mormon people, offered assistance in bringing the perpetrators to justice, but the federal judges and U.S. marshal refused to accept his offer. In 1876–1877 John D. Lee, Mormon Indian farmer and one of the participants in the massacre, was tried, convicted, and executed by firing squad. None of the other participants was ever tried, either because they turned states evidence, because the U.S. Attorney was unable to accumulate sufficient evidence to try them, or because they escaped U.S. marshals sent to apprehend them.

Juanita Brooks, who wrote the most thorough study of the subject to date, saw the massacre as being the result of a collective hysteria. She did not hold Brigham Young responsible but described the subsequent execution of Lee as an act of scapegoating in the sense that others on the local level had also been involved in the unfortunate decision. At the beginning of the 21st century, histories of the massacre—especially those by Will Bagley and Sally Denton—(and even novels and motion pictures) sought, without any direct evidence, to fasten responsibility on Brigham Young. In response, a number of prominent historians have challenged these allegations. As of this writing, Ronald Walker, Richard Turley Jr., and Glen Leonard have a manuscript in press with Oxford University Press that should correct the record.

Since the massacre, Mormon leaders have denounced the act. They do not consider it justified by the fact of their own **persecution**. **Anti-Mormons** have repeatedly used this incident as an excuse for Mormon bashing, although the general Church **membership** and the **general authorities** bear no responsibility, which must rest with members of the Iron County, Utah, militia, and especially Haight, who led in organizing the affair.

On 11 September 1999, the dedication of a monument at the site was attended by descendants of those in the wagon train and the Mormons who participated. Seeking emotional closure to a painful chapter of history, President **Gordon B. Hinckley** said, "I come as a peacemaker. This is not a time of recrimination or the assignment of blame. . . . It is time to leave the entire matter in the hands of God who deals justly in all things. His is a wisdom far beyond our own." Speaking for the descendants of the victims, the Reverend Stanton Cram of Springdale, Arkansas, said, "We are finding out that we are good people on both sides, decent people—people who want to do the right thing. . . . No one in this world today has any blame for that, and we don't have any right to hold this evil against the Mormon Church or the people here." In 2007, **Elder Henry B. Eyring**, then a member of the **Quorum** of the **Twelve Apostles**, offered an apology for the massacre, placing the blame squarely on the Iron County militia. *See also* JUANITA BROOKS.

MOVIES. As a form of public entertainment, movies became popular in the 20th century. Like other people, Mormons attend movies. The Church counsels its members to avoid NC-17- and R-rated movies.

In the early 20th century, when Mormons appeared in movies as subjects, which was not often, Church members were stereotyped as sinister and manipulative or as quaint and simple-minded. For example, *Trapped by the Mormons*, a silent film, shows a missionary in England who mesmerizes a fair damsel in order to abduct her and take her to a fate worse than death in Utah. An exception is *Brigham Young*, made with the Church's cooperation for the 1947 centennial of the **exodus**, which portrays a heroic leader.

At the beginning of the 21st century, a flurry of movies appeared made by Mormon producers, directors, and often actors. Richard Dutcher produced *God's Army*, *Brigham City*, and *States of Grace. Best Two Years* showed the difficulty of proselytizing in the Netherlands and the humanness of the young **missionaries**. *The Work and the Glory*, a successful historical novel in several volumes, was recreated on film by director Sterling Van Wagenen. *The Other Side of Heaven*, based on the missionary experiences of John A. Groberg in Tonga, was directed by Mitch Davis. Several comedies spoofed Mormon behaviors: *Singles Ward, Home Teachers*, *R.M.*, and *Mormons and Mobsters. Saints and Soldiers*, a well-reviewed movie about the adventures of a unit of soldiers behind enemy lines in World War II, includes one Mormon character, but his religious identity is never explicit.

The realities of the market have discouraged some. Accustomed to the raucous and irreverent, many moviegoers are not drawn to films that take religion seriously. Christians who long for the spiritual component in entertainment are often prejudiced against anything Mormon. With such predictable audience reaction, investors are reluctant to fund Mormon movies. Richard Dutcher's ambitious recreation of **Joseph Smith** languishes.

Yet the mere existence of competent young Mormons, trained in film schools and experienced from work on other projects, assures that Mormon movies will continue to appear. *See also* EXODUS.

MOYLE, HENRY D. (1889–1963). Attorney, **general authority**. Born on 22 April 1889 in Salt Lake City, Utah, he was the son of James H. Moyle, a prominent Utah Democrat. Henry enrolled at the University of Utah in 1905, receiving his B.S. degree in mining engineering. From 1909 to 1911, he served a full-time mission in the Swiss-German Mission and remained in **Europe** for one year to study at Freiberg University. Returning to the United States, he pursued a law degree at the University of Chicago and earned the J.D. degree in 1915.

Enlisting in the U.S. Army, Moyle became an officer but remained in the United States during World War I. After the war, he began his own law practice. Moyle invested in several businesses, including the Deseret Livestock Company, the Wasatch Oil Company, and a silver mining company. A lifelong Democrat, he served as Utah's Democratic Party chairman and unsuccessfully ran for governor in 1940.

After serving in **ward** and **stake** positions, he was called to the **Quorum** of the **Twelve Apostles** in 1947. Active in organizing and promoting the **welfare program**, he assisted the Church in legal and business affairs. In June 1959, he became second **counselor** in the **First Presidency** under President **David O. McKay**.

MUSEUM OF CHURCH HISTORY AND ART. Following a series of earlier museums that housed artifacts, the present building in Salt Lake City, Utah, adjacent to **Temple Square** was dedicated and opened in 1984. Staffed by curators, historians, and art historians, the museum's basic purpose is to preserve and exhibit significant material remains, crafts, and art from the Mormon past as well as work being produced at the present. A voluntary staff of docents assists in greeting, providing tours and explanations, and visiting schools.

An especially interesting part of the permanent exhibit consists of works by Mormon artists of the 19th century who studied in France and brought back the style of the French impressionists. A handsome volume entitled *Harvesting the Light* prepared by art historian Linda Gibbs was published by the museum. Portraits of Church leaders from the beginning are numerous. For each of the Church presidents a collection of artifacts has been assembled. Temporary exhibits are changed every few months. Periodic Church-wide competitions result in submissions in different artistic media from many countries. *See also* ART.

MUSIC. From the beginning of the Church, music has been part of Mormon worship. Although Mormon musicians have achieved success as composers or performers in the larger arena, here we shall consider music in the Church setting.

In 1830 **Emma Smith** received instructions (***Doctrine and Covenants***, section 25) to compile a hymnal, which she did, publishing her collection in 1835. Hymns from the **Protestant** tradition were included, adapted where necessary, as well as new works by Mormons. As opportunity allowed, this hymnal was revised and expanded in a series of later editions, with music being added to the text by the 1870s. The present official edition was published in 1985. Editions in Spanish, French, German, and other languages have versions of 100 or more of the English hymns but also add others from their respective traditions.

Congregational singing was supplemented by choirs, as for the dedication of the Kirtland Temple in 1836. During the **Illinois Period** singing instructors and the arrival of trained musicians among converts from England led to some ambitious public performances. During the **Utah Period** bands and orchestras were popular. Concerts featured local performers and touring instrumental and vocal virtuosi. An examination of the concert offerings in Salt Lake City, Utah, during the last quarter of the 19th century shows a provincial capital with about as much urbanity and refinement as other cities of the same size. The great Adelina Patti and Jenny Lind thrilled Utah audiences. Gilbert and Sullivan operettas were heard and enjoyed. Helping to raise the standards of music among Mormons were several immigrant converts, including C. J. Thomas, John Tullidge, and George Careless, who gave lessons, wrote criticism, and directed groups.

Many **wards** had choirs, their quality depending on the available voices and the talent of the director. The choir with the greatest prestige was the one that came to be known as the **Mormon Tabernacle Choir**. When **Evan Stephens** took over its direction, the choir's fame expanded through many tours in Utah and eventually outside as well. In 1893 it performed at the Chicago Columbian Exposition and won second prize. In the 20th century and up to the present, the Mormon Tabernacle Choir has continued to be the most public expression of Mormon musicianship, especially as it began its network radio broadcasts in 1929 (later extended to television).

Also in the **Tabernacle** was a great pipe organ. Constructed originally by Australian convert Joseph Ridges, the organ has been improved periodically. The most recent upgrading, completed in 1988, was described by organ historian Barbara Owen in *The Mormon Tabernacle Organ: An American Classic* (1990). Frank W. Asper and **Alexander Schreiner** were the two famed organists for many years. Tabernacle organists Robert Cundick, John Longhurst, and Clay Christiansen, along with assistant organists Bonnie Goodliffe, Linda Margetts, and Richard Elliott, have occupied the great console both as accompanists for the choir and in solo performances. Universities have contributed significantly in teaching composition and training instrumental and vocal performers. **BYU, BYU–Idaho,** and **BYU–Hawaii** sponsor choir and instrumental performances and train successive cohorts of musicians.

Mormon musical composition goes back to the 19th century. Evan Stephens was a prolific composer of hymns and anthems. In the 20th century B. Cecil Gates wrote many single numbers, cantatas, and oratorios. **Leroy Robertson,** a highly accomplished professor of composition, completed *Oratorio from the* ***Book of Mormon***. Crawford Gates, Robert Cundick, and Merrill Bradshaw are among those who have composed serious choral or operatic works. Tabernacle Choir director Mac Wilberg has achieved international acclaim for his choral arrangements. On a more popular level, the 1947 musical drama *Promised Valley*, composed by Crawford Gates, continued to be produced for many years. Lex d'Azevedo's *Saturday's Warrior*, a dramatic presentation of the **plan of salvation**, employed popular rhythms.

Choirs organized by **seminaries** and **institutes** have performed to large audiences. Especially important in furthering music have been the programs at BYU, BYU–Hawaii, and BYU–Idaho. They not only train music majors but also provide experience for many other students in different choral and instrumental performing groups. As young people with such training return to their home **wards** and **stakes**, they raise musical standards throughout the Church.

With the expansion into parts of the world outside the United States and Western Europe, two principles are in tension. Creativity and a rich diversity are consistent with the scriptural injunction to "prove all things; hold fast to that which is good" (1 Thess. 5:21). Mormonism does not insist on transforming everyone into a single mold. On the other hand, in the interest of unity, the Church desires to have some practices, including worship services, that are the same for its members everywhere. Allowing centrifugal forces to operate without restriction could create chaos.

Up to the present it is the unifying principle that has predominated, as when African Mormons were told that drums were not appropriate to **sacrament** meetings. Yet they have been allowed as part of weekday Church activities, and cultural evenings featuring national and indigenous music and dance have been a popular activity in different parts of the world. In whatever form their music takes, Mormons are still fond of the revealed declaration to Emma Smith in 1830: "The song of the righteous is a prayer unto me" (***Doctrine and Covenants***, section 25). *See also* MEMBERSHIP.

MYSTICISM. Belief in and practice of direct contact, or union, with God, found in both **Christian** and non-Christian traditions. In its classic formulation, as represented by Plotinus and St. John of the Cross, Mormons are not mystics. Their concepts of God and man are simply not conducive to the kind of absorption described by Plotinus as "the flight of the alone to the alone." According to a looser definition, emphasizing direct communication from God to humans, Mormons might qualify, although they do not use the term *mysticism*, preferring **revelation**, inspiration, Holy Ghost, and other terms.

The return to the presence of God that awaits the righteous after death is not a reabsorption into the ground of being. Individual identity is retained, although it operates in perfect harmony with God. For the faithful, such unity begins in this mortal life. Jesus prayed in Gethsemane that "they may be one, even as we are one" (John 17:22). *See also* PLAN OF SALVATION.

– N –

NATIVE AMERICANS. American Indians, or Amerindians. The relationship between white Mormons and Indians has been one of unusual interest. On the one hand, early Mormons, practically all of whom were of white American or European ethnicity, experienced the same conflicts with the native population as other westward-moving Americans. On the other hand, Indians were regarded as descendants of the **Lamanites** described in the ***Book of Mormon***. A glorious future was promised for them. Because of the large number of Indians and mestizos in Central and South America, the growth of the Church in those regions is also seen as fulfillment of the scriptural promise.

NAUVOO RESTORATION, INC. (NRI). A Church-founded nonprofit corporation that supervises the partial restoration of historic Nauvoo, Illinois, which was occupied by Mormons from 1839 to 1846. Called to assist at NRI were young **missionaries** and older couples, who could play the roles of such period figures as blacksmiths and act as guides for visitors. Restored Nauvoo has become a major attraction not only for tourists but also for school children on field trips. *See also* ILLINOIS PERIOD.

NEAL A. MAXWELL INSTITUTE FOR RELIGIOUS SCHOLARSHIP. Located at **BYU**, this institute serves as the umbrella organization for the Middle Eastern Text Initiative (METI), Center for the Preservation of Ancient Religious Texts (CPART), and the FARMS. The Maxwell Institute publishes the *Journal of* Book of Mormon *Studies* and the *FARMS Review*. Rather than let uninformed or agenda-driven writing about Mormons to go unchallenged, the *FARMS Review* solicits specific reviews and rebuttals, often lengthy. Whether agreeing with the critic of the Church or the apologist (defender), or perhaps accepting some assertions from both, interested readers have a good means of keeping up with ongoing research. Also affiliated with the Maxwell Institute since 2006 is ***Brigham Young University Studies***.

NELSON, RUSSELL M. (1924–). Physician, **general authority**. Born on 9 September 1924, Nelson grew up in Salt Lake City, Utah, and graduated from the University of Utah in 1945. His medical studies, also at the University of Utah, led to the M.D. degree in 1947. After a residency at Massachusetts General Hospital in Boston, he transferred to the University of Minnesota, earning a Ph.D. in 1954.

Nelson has been director of the Thoracic Surgery Residency at the University of Utah and chairman of the Thoracic Surgery division at **LDS** Hospital. Among other professional positions he has been president of the Society for Vascular Surgery, a director of the American Board of Thoracic Surgery, chairman of the Council on Cardiovascular Surgery for the American Heart Association, and president of the Utah State Medical Association.

Nelson has served extensively in the Church. After serving as a **stake president** for seven years, he became general president of the

Sunday School in 1971. Later he was a **regional representative**. In 1984 he became a member of the **Quorum** of the **Twelve Apostles**. Nelson has been especially effective in gaining recognition in **Europe** and **Asia**, thus promoting the international growth of the Church. He and his wife, Dantzel, are parents of 10 children. On 12 February 2005, Dantzel died of cancer. In 2006 he married Wendy Watson.

***THE NEW ERA*.** Monthly magazine for youth, which began publication in January 1971. It contains photographic essays, features on youth activities in different parts of the world, and inspirational articles and stories.

NEW YORK PERIOD. Initial period of the Church, from April to December 1830. Organized on 6 April 1830, the Church had its first home in western New York. The family of **Joseph Smith** lived just outside Palmyra. It was there that the **First Vision** occurred in 1820 and there that Smith gained his first followers during the translation of the ***Book of Mormon***, published there in the spring of 1830.

Some early sources identify the place of the meeting that formally organized the Church as Manchester, while others say Fayette. After comparing their memories, Mormon leaders determined that Fayette was where it happened, although it is not improbable that an important meeting took place in Manchester at about the same time. To satisfy legal requirements, six men—Joseph Smith, **Oliver Cowdery**, and four others—were listed as charter members. A group of perhaps 50 people, filling and overflowing the house, were in attendance. Immediately, of course, the Church grew larger with the addition of those already **baptized** and other converts.

The New York phase of the Church as an organization lasted from April through December 1830. Three centers were the foci of the fledgling organization: Fayette (the Whitmers), Manchester (the Smiths), and Colesville (the Knights). Conferences were held at Fayette in June and September.

During these months not all of the activity was confined to New York. **Missionaries** embarked on preaching journeys, including the important mission of Oliver Cowdery, **Parley P. Pratt**, Peter Whitmer Jr., and Ziba Peterson to Missouri via Ohio. As he had done the previous year, Joseph Smith sometimes stayed at the home of his wife's parents in Harmony, Pennsylvania, more than a hundred miles from Palmyra and just across the state boundary.

To judge how much of Mormonism was introduced during this initial phase, one must look at the *Book of Mormon*, which became the chief missionary tool and gave the new religion its nickname. Joseph Smith began work on his "inspired revision" of the **Bible**. Approximately the first 40 **revelations**, now published as sections of the ***Doctrine and Covenants***, emanate from the New York Period. Among the topics introduced were: **priesthood** authority, the obligation of missionary work, the **sacrament** prayers, the assignment of preparing a hymnal, description of the duties of different offices, and the **gathering**. Although the **twelve apostles** were not yet called, this future development was predicted. The proclamation of the **gospel** to the Indians was begun, and the place where **Zion** was to be built (Missouri) was specified. Apocalyptic and millennial, Mormonism already showed some of the characteristics it would retain throughout its history.

It also began to experience **persecution**. Ridicule had been the lot of Joseph Smith from the time of his First Vision. Twice he was taken before a local court and charged with being a disorderly person. The early Mormons were harassed, as on the occasion when a mob broke up the temporary dam placed in a stream in order to allow **baptisms**.

In December 1830 the New York Mormons were instructed to move to Ohio (*Doctrine and Covenants*, section 37), which most of them did in the first two or three months of 1831.

In the 20th century the Church developed monuments and historic sites in the vicinity of Palmyra, New York. Conversions produced a build-up of the Church in the state. At the end of 2005 New York State had 69,882 Mormons, including 15 **stakes**. **Temples** were dedicated in Palmyra (2000) and New York City (2005). *See also* MISSOURI PERIOD; NATIVE AMERICANS; OHIO PERIOD.

NEW ZEALAND. *See* PACIFIC; COWLEY, MATTHEW.

NIBLEY, HUGH W. (1910–2005). Professor of ancient history, linguist, scholarly defender of Mormonism. Born on 27 March 1910 in Portland, Oregon, Nibley early showed signs of precociousness in his avid reading. He served as a Swiss-German missionary. Upon his return he attended UCLA, graduating summa cum laude in 1934. His Berkeley doctorate of 1938 was awarded after completing a dissertation in ancient history titled "The Roman Games as the Survival of an Archaic Year-Cult."

During World War II Nibley was a noncommissioned intelligence officer, first in England and then in the battle of Normandy and on the continent. After the war he took a post at **BYU**, where for some 40 years he offered courses on ancient history, Greek literature, patristics, and the Mormon **scriptures**. Nibley read voraciously in Greek, Latin, Hebrew, Arabic, and numerous modern languages. He studied Egyptian at the Oriental Institute in Chicago and Coptic at Berkeley. He has poured out a stream of writings, some of them published in the learned journals, many of them in Church magazines. In 1990 a two-volume festschrift, *By Study and Also by Faith*, was published in his honor, containing contributions by former students and colleagues, both in and out of the Church.

His massive work on the ***Book of Mormon*** gives example after example of its congruity with the ancient world. His erudition enabled him to show striking parallels between the Book of Abraham and ancient Egypt, between Mormonism and early Christianity. To critics who say that such parallels fall short of proof, Nibley responded with the challenge to explain how, short of **revelation**, a relatively uneducated **Joseph Smith** could come up with such details. His voluminous writings—including such titles as *Lehi in the Desert*, *The World and the Prophets*, *The Ancient State*, and *Temple and Cosmos*—are published in *Collected Works of Hugh Nibley*. *See also PEARL OF GREAT PRICE.*

NORTH AMERICA. Organized in New York State in 1830, the Church has always had its main center in the United States. But its message was preached to "all the world" as opportunity allowed. It has always been a misunderstanding, at least partially, to describe it as "an American church," just as it would not be accurate to describe the Catholic Church as "an Italian church."

Nevertheless, throughout the 19th century 90 percent or more of its members lived in the United States. As converts joined, they responded to the doctrine of **gathering** and moved to headquarters.

Only gradually was that practice reversed, starting with recommendations to remain where they were around the turn of the 20th century, becoming much more emphatic after World War II.

At the end of 2005 **membership** remained strong in Utah (1,752,467), California (756,807), Idaho (385,131), Arizona (344,473), Washington (245,665), Nevada (167,822), Oregon (142,545), and Colorado (128,723). The 20th century, especially since World War II, witnessed a dispersion of membership into other parts of the United States. Every state now has Mormon **stakes** and **wards**. **Temples** have been constructed in California, Washington, Oregon, Idaho, Nevada, Colorado, Georgia, Texas, Illinois, Missouri, and other states. (See appendix 3.)

Early preaching expeditions into eastern Canada in the 1830s led to some conversions, but gathering and the successive **persecutions** and moves of the Church left no permanent membership there. At the end of the 19th century, as part of a continuing program of **colonization**, Mormons moved into Alberta, Canada, and established settlements at Cardston and elsewhere. A **stake** was organized there in 1895.

At the end of 2006 there were 71,205 members in Alberta, divided into 22 stakes and 170 wards. Just as there had been an outward, centrifugal tendency in the United States, so membership in Canada spread. As a result of births, proselytizing, and movement of people from other areas, Mormons could be found in all parts of the country: Ontario (44,330), British Columbia (28,492), Quebec (9,681), Saskatchewan (5,280), Nova Scotia (4,661), Manitoba (4,285), New Brunswick (3,046), Newfoundland (675), Prince Edward Island (353),Yukon Territory (278), and Northwest Territories (147). In addition to the Cardston Temple, constructed in 1923, temples were completed at Brampton, Ontario, in 1990; in 1999 at Halifax, Nova Scotia, and Regina, Saskatchewan; and in 2000 at Longieil, Quebec. *See also* CENTRAL AMERICA AND MEXICO.

– O –

OAKS, DALLIN H. (1932–). Lawyer, educator, **general authority**. Born in Provo, Utah, on 12 August 1932, Dallin Oaks was raised in Provo by Stella Harris Oaks, his accomplished, widowed mother. He attended **BYU**, from which he received a B.A. degree in accounting in 1954. After three years at the University of Chicago Law School, serving as editor of the law review his senior year, Oaks graduated with a J.D. degree in 1957.

After serving as a law clerk to Chief Justice Earl Warren of the U.S. Supreme Court, Oaks moved back to Chicago, where he specialized in corporate litigation for a law firm before accepting a faculty position at the University of Chicago. In addition to serving as associate dean of the law school, he became executive director of the American Bar Foundation. He authored many articles on legal and historical subjects. From 1971 to 1980 Oaks was president of BYU. From 1975 to 1978 he was president of the American Association of Presidents of Independent Colleges and Universities. In 1980 he left his university presidency and became a Utah Supreme Court justice for three and a half years. From 1980 to 1985 he was chairman of the board of directors of the Public Broadcasting Service (PBS).

His Church positions include serving as **stake** mission **president** in Chicago, member of the presidency of the Chicago South Stake, and **regional representative**. In 1984 he was called to be a member of the **Quorum** of the **Twelve Apostles**. Dallin Oaks and his wife, June (who died of cancer in 1998), are the parents of six children. In 2000 he married Kristen McMain.

OAKS, ROBERT C. (1936–). Military officer, **general authority**. Born on 14 February 1936 in Los Angeles, California, Oaks earned a bachelor's degree in military science from the Air Force Academy, received a master's degree in business administration at Ohio State University, and attended the Naval War College. He became senior vice president of operations at U.S. Airway. He retired from the U.S. Air Force as a four-star general. Oaks served as **bishop**'s **counselor**, **high councilor**, district **president**'s **counselor**, **mission** president's **counselor**, and **stake** president. In 2000 he became a member of the Second **Quorum** of the **Seventy** and a member of the presidency of the seventy in 2004. He and his wife, Gloria, have six children.

OHIO PERIOD. From early 1831 to 1838. During the same years, western Missouri was the second center of Mormon activity. A mission to the Indians of western Missouri by **Parley P. Pratt** and others stopped in the vicinity of Kirtland, Ohio, a suburb of modern Cleveland. Finding seekers, or restorationists there, the **missionaries** succeeded in converting more than a hundred of them, which immediately gave Ohio about as many members as lived in New York. Among these early Ohio converts was **Sidney Rigdon**, a preacher known for his eloquence and leadership ability.

Not long after **Joseph Smith** heard of these developments, Rigdon having traveled to New York, instructions were given that the New York Mormons should move to Ohio (***Doctrine and Covenants***, sections 37, 38). Smith moved to Kirtland in February with his family. Not long after, in the summer of 1831, he traveled to Missouri and designated Independence as a **gathering** place. For the next few years, Mormon converts flowed into either Ohio or Missouri, with Smith living for most of the time in or near Kirtland, Ohio.

An examination of the *Doctrine and Covenants* shows Ohio to be the scene of many important developments during the 1830s. It was there that the Church organization made important advances from its simple beginnings. The office of **bishop** was created and a **high council** was established. In 1835 the **Quorum** of the **Twelve Apostles** was formed along with the Quorum of the **Seventy**. A School of the Prophets provided instruction for missionaries and Church officers. Periodicals were published, providing an outlet for **revelations** received by Smith as well as other instructions. In 1835 many of these revelations, which had earlier circulated in handwritten form or appeared in the periodicals, were published as the *Doctrine and Covenants*.

Kirtland became a nerve center of missionary activity, with proselytizers traveling outward through Ohio and wider regions and then returning. As new converts arrived in the Kirtland vicinity, a boom town atmosphere was created. Many houses were constructed. In 1836 the Kirtland **Temple** was finished and dedicated. An impressive structure for a religion that had been in existence just six years and whose members were mostly poor, the temple was the scene of visions to Joseph Smith and Pentecostal experiences for many others.

Although even in the brief **New York Period** several basic characteristics of Mormonism took form, the few years in Ohio saw important developments not only in organization but in doctrine. The health code known as the **Word of Wisdom** was issued. The gradations of eternal salvation were described (*Doctrine and Covenants*, section 76). An economic program of consecration and stewardship was introduced (*Doctrine and Covenants*, section 42). Joseph Smith continued work on his inspired revision of the **Bible** and produced the Book of Abraham after acquiring Egyptian papyri.

The creativity of the Ohio Period both organizationally and doctrinally took place against a backdrop of obstacles and opposition. Simply providing for the incoming Mormons was an enormous economic challenge. Not surprisingly, the influx, which meant Mormon domination, led to opposition and **persecution** by others in the region. To provide capital for construction, a Mormon bank was established. In an era of largely unregulated banking, the failure of wildcat banks was not unusual, but when the Kirtland Anti-banking Society (renamed to circumvent a statute) collapsed, all who suffered losses were bitter, including not only outside investors but, more importantly, some of the Mormon leaders. Historian Milton Backman has estimated that as many as 10 to 15 percent of the membership withdrew from the Church. It was the tumult over these matters, with opposition from within and without, that led to the flight of Joseph Smith and the great majority of Mormons in 1838.

Kirtland rapidly waned as a Mormon center. A few members lingered there for the next several years, and some much longer, but for practical purposes it was abandoned in 1838 as a church settlement. The Kirtland Temple, later acquired by the **RLDS** Church, still stands. In the second half of the 20th century Mormonism enjoyed a resurgence in Ohio as some Church members from the West moved there and as convert **baptisms** increased their number. At the end of 2005 there were 55,128 members in the state, with 12 **stakes** and 86 **wards**. *See also* MISSOURI PERIOD; *PEARL OF GREAT PRICE*.

ORDINANCE. A ceremony or procedure by which special blessings of God are mediated to the recipient, roughly equivalent to the term *sacrament* as used in the general Christian tradition. While the form and words are important, an ordinance, to be valid, must be performed by authority of the **priesthood**. Essential to salvation are **baptism** and **confirmation**, although these may be performed vicariously for the deceased in the **temples**. Priesthood ordination and certain temple rites are considered prerequisites for salvation in the highest degree. Other ordinances include the naming of children and administering to the sick.

OSMOND, DONNY (1957–). Singer, actor. Born on 9 December 1957 in Ogden, Utah, Donny Osmond is the son of George and Olive Davis Osmond. At age five, he launched his career in music when he sang with his siblings on the Andy Williams Show. He became famous for his solo song "Puppy Love." By his early 20s, he had released 23 top-40 songs. In 1976, Donny and his sister Marie began their own television show on the ABC network, which lasted four seasons. During the 1990s he performed in Andrew Lloyd Weber's *Joseph and the Amazing Technicolor Dreamcoat*—more than 2,000 performances in five years. He hosted a TV game show from 2002 to 2004. Donny Osmond and his wife, Debra Glen, are the parents of five sons. His website donny.com gives his answers to questions about his Mormon religion.

OSMOND, MARIE (1959–). Singer, actress. Born 13 October 1959 in Ogden, Utah, Marie performed as a child with her siblings, the children of George and Olive Davis Osmond. By the time she was a teenager, Marie had appeared on the Andy Williams Show, recorded the hit record "Paper Roses," and performed with her brothers before a sold-out crowd at New York's Madison Square Garden. With her brother Donny she hosted a variety TV show in 1976–1979 and from 1998 to 2000 a daytime talk show. Marie has written several books, developed the Marie Osmond Fine Porcelain Collection dolls, and raised money for charitable foundations. After the birth of her third child she suffered from severe postpartum depression, later writing a book on her experience to increase public awareness of the condition. With her brother Donny she hosted the Miss America Pageant at Atlantic City in 1999. After a lapse of 20 years, Marie returned to public performance in 2006 with a 15-city Christmas tour. She and her husband, Brian Blosil, have raised eight children. In March 2007 it was announced that she and her husband were divorcing.

OTTLEY, JEROLD (1934–). Musician, director of **Mormon Tabernacle Choir**. Born in Salt Lake City, Utah, on 7 April 1934, Jerold Ottley received his primary and secondary education there. In 1951 he moved to New Zealand and served as a **missionary** there from 1953 to 1955. Returning from his mission, he married JoAnn South in 1956. They have two children. Ottley graduated from the University of Utah in 1961. His master's degree in music was awarded by **BYU**; the doctorate, the D.M.A., by the University of Oregon in 1972. He also studied at the Academy of Music in Cologne, Germany.

Named director of the Mormon Tabernacle Choir in 1975, Ottley raised the level of its performance to new heights by a scrupulous selection of voices through auditions and intensive rehearsal. His wife, JoAnn Ottley, a highly accomplished soprano, assisted the choir as vocal coach. Jerold Ottley was an adjunct professor of music at the University of Utah and from 2005 a visiting professor at **BYU–Hawaii.** *See also* MUSIC.

– P –

PACIFIC. In addition to the Philippines, other Pacific islands have experienced steady expansion of Church **membership** from the 19th century. The following membership figures are for the end of 2005:

Country	Members	Stakes	Temples
American Samoa	14,252	4	
Cook Islands	1,807		
Fiji	14,120	4	1
Guam	1,669		
Marshall Islands	4,296		
Micronesia	3,504		
Niue	230		
North Mariana Islands	811		
Papua New Guinea	14,850	1	
Tahiti	21,567	6	1
Tonga	52,421	16	1
Western Samoa	63,640	16	1

The state of Hawaii has 65,447 members in 15 **stakes**. A **temple** at Laie was the first constructed outside the continental United States. A temple at Kona was completed in 2000.

Somewhat different because of size are Australia and New Zealand, which administratively are in the Pacific area. The first preaching of Mormonism in Australia started as early as 1840, but it was in 1851 that a mission was established. In the 19th century progress was slow. Anti-Mormon speeches and newspaper articles discouraged converts, and the **gathering** policy led many of the strong members to emigrate. In 1904, the first meetinghouse in Australia was constructed at Wooloongabba. As elsewhere, the latter half of the 20th century saw greater progress. At the end of 2005, 111,098 Australian members were divided into 32 stakes and 190 **wards**. A temple was dedicated at Sydney in 1984; four other temples followed.

In New Zealand the trajectory was similar. **Missionaries** arriving in the 1850s were able to convert only a few. By 1880 there were only 133 members. Then the missionaries began preaching to the Maoris and enjoyed much greater success. One of the great missionaries to the Maoris was **Matthew Cowley**. Expansion also occurred among New Zealanders of European ancestry. In 1958 two institutions were completed and dedicated: the Church College of New Zealand and the New Zealand Temple, both at Hamilton, south of Auckland. By the end of 2005, 96,027 members were divided into 25 **stakes** and 148 **wards**. *See also* ASIA; BRIGHAM YOUNG UNIVERSITY–HAWAII; POLYNESIAN CULTURAL CENTER; POLYNESIANS.

PACKER, BOYD KENNETH (1924–). Educator, **general authority**. Born on 10 September 1924 in Brigham City, Utah, Packer also grew up there. He enlisted and became a bomber pilot during World War II, serving in the Pacific Theater. Upon his return he studied at Weber College and Utah State University, from which he received B.S. and M.S. degrees. Subsequently he earned a doctor of education degree at **BYU**.

After accepting a position with the Church Educational System, Packer became supervisor of **seminaries** and **institutes of religion**. Active in community affairs, he served as a city councilman. He was then called to serve as **president** of the New England Mission.

In 1961 Packer became one of the **assistants to the twelve** and in 1970, at the age of 45, a member of the **Quorum** of the **Twelve Apostles**. He traveled throughout the world, gave countless sermons, officiated in the formation of **stakes**, and published several books. Special areas of responsibility have included **correlation** and education. He has served on the Church Board of Education and the Board of Trustees of BYU. He married Donna Edith Smith in 1947. They have 10 children.

PAGEANTS. Dramatic presentations of historic or scriptural events, usually in an outdoor setting. Pageants have become a popular means of commemoration. Usually produced locally, they vary in quality. Large casts assure a theatrical experience for many who would not have it otherwise. Scheduled in the summer, they attract not only the local population but also tourists as audiences. The largest of the pageants is the Cumorah Pageant at Palmyra, New York. Another, in Cache Valley, Utah, portrays the life of **Martin Harris**.

PARKIN, BONNIE D. (1940–). After earning a bachelor's degree from Utah State University, Parkin taught elementary school, was a docent for the Utah Symphony, and served as a page for the Utah Senate. She was **ward Primary** president, ward **Relief Society** president, **stake Young Women** president, and a member of the Relief Society general board. She served with her husband when he was **mission** president in England. She became a **counselor** in the general presidency of Young Women and in 2002 general president of the Relief Society. She was released from her position in April 2007. She and her husband are parents of four sons.

PATRIARCH. A **priesthood** holder ordained to give **patriarchal blessings** to Church members. Until 1979 a general Church patriarch, a descendant of the Joseph Smith Sr. family, was counted among the **general authorities**. On the grounds that **stake** patriarchs performed the function adequately, the patriarch to the Church, Eldred G. Smith, was retired in 1979. In principle, there is at least one patriarch in each **stake**.

PATRIARCHAL BLESSINGS. After receiving a **recommend** from a **bishop**, a member of the Church may receive an individual blessing from a **patriarch**. By the laying on of hands, the patriarch pronounces the person's lineage, whether by blood or adoption, leading back to

Abraham. By inspiration, the patriarch gives additional promises and counsel for guidance in life. Blessings are recorded and transcribed. One copy is preserved in the Church archives. Another copy is retained by the individual receiving the blessing. Mormons look upon their patriarchal blessing as a source of comfort, inspiration, and guidance.

PATRIOTISM. Mormons have expressed their loyalty to governments in general from the beginning. Frustrated at the failure of state and federal government to protect them in Missouri and Illinois, Mormons insisted on their devotion to the country. They argued that although the Constitution of the United States was divinely inspired (***Doctrine and Covenants***, section 101), corrupt individuals were responsible for the problems. Despite being forced to flee to the West, Mormons enlisted in the **Mormon Battalion** during the Mexican War and some fought in the Civil War. During the anti-**polygamy** prosecutions of the 1870s and 1880s, enthusiasm for the country may have cooled, but this did not prevent a vigorous effort to obtain statehood for Utah, which was accomplished in 1896. During the Spanish-American War and subsequent military conflicts, Mormons have served in the military service. Those living in countries other than the United States were expected to be loyal to their rulers. Wherever they live, Mormons proclaim loyalty to their country. *See also* ARTICLES OF FAITH, no. 12; POLITICS.

PEARL OF GREAT PRICE. One of the four standard works of **scripture** along with the **Bible, *Book of Mormon*,** and ***Doctrine and Covenants***. First published in 1851 by Apostle Franklin D. Richards, the book is a compilation of five writings previously published in Church periodicals: (1) portions of the first eight chapters of the Genesis text that restored by **revelation** the writings of Moses; (2) the Book of Abraham, a translation from Egyptian papyri brought to **Joseph Smith** in 1835; (3) Matthew 24, a selection from **Joseph Smith**'s inspired revision of the Bible; (4) an autobiographical account of Joseph Smith's early life and visions, including the **First Vision**, as written in 1838; (5) and the **Articles of Faith**.

In 1967 eleven fragments of the papyri once in the possession of **Joseph Smith** were discovered. They turned out to be from an Egyptian religious work called *The Book of Breathings*, and the Book of Abraham is clearly not a direct translation of these papyri. Mormon defenders, especially **Hugh Nibley**, raised questions as to whether those particular fragments were the ones underlying the Book of Abraham, stated that we do not know what Smith meant by "translation," and pointed out many parallels between the Book of Abraham and ancient writings. Some other items once included in the *Pearl of Great Price* are no longer there; the most important of these are now placed in the *Doctrine and Covenants*. The *Pearl of Great Price* was accepted as a standard work of scripture by a vote of approval in **general conference** on 10 October 1880.

PERRY, L. TOM (1922–). Business administrator, **general authority**. Born in Logan, Utah, on 5 August 1922, L. Tom Perry served as a **missionary** in the northern states, after which he joined the U.S. Marines and served for two years in the Pacific.

After the war he married Virginia Lee (they had three children) and attended Utah State University, receiving a B.S. degree in finance in 1949 and doing some graduate work. He was employed as treasurer and vice president of retail business companies, living in Idaho, California, New York, and Massachusetts. He served in two bishoprics, on a **high council**, and in two **stake** presidencies. He was **president** of the Boston Stake.

Called to be an **assistant to the twelve** in 1972, Perry became a member of the **Quorum** of the **Twelve Apostles** in 1974. He served as a member of the Church Board of Education and the General Welfare Services Committee. In 2004–2005 he served as president of the Europe Central area. He headed the Church's participation in the bicentennial of the United States celebration. His wife Virginia died in 1974. Two years later he married Barbara Dayton.

PERSECUTION. Opposition or harassment, especially when motivated by religious or ethnic prejudice. Mormons were opposed from the beginning. The activities against them have included verbal denunciation, misrepresentation, ridicule, vexatious lawsuits, imprisonment, mob attacks, and murders. Violence against them included tarring and feathering, burning homes and barns, driving off cattle, raping, and killing. Opposition on the level of the anti-**polygamy** statutes led to fines, prison terms, denial of the right to vote, and finally confiscation of Church property. Even if legal, all such harassment was experienced by Mormons as persecution.

Joseph Smith described the reaction to his account of the **First Vision** as persecution. In their own self-image, Mormons believed the label identifed them with the New Testament **saints**, who were told by the Lord, "Blessed are ye when men shall revile you, and persecute you, and shall say all manner of evil against you falsely, for my sake" (Matt. 5:11).

From the point of view of their opponents, of course, the activity was perfectly justified. When mobs or individuals struck out against the Mormons, this was self-defense, consistent with the history of vigilantism in the 19th century. When it was the government that promoted the activity, as in the campaign against polygamy, they were not persecuting people for religious belief but prosecuting stubborn lawbreakers. Point of view was all important.

Contrary to popular impression, motivation for the opposition to Mormonism was not primarily because of disgust with polygamy. That stick was used to beat them with, especially from the end of the Civil War to the 1890 **Manifesto**. But denunciation and harassment started much earlier and continued to flare up after the abandonment of polygamy. Antagonism due to religious differences was exacerbated by fears of the Mormons as a political or economic power. *See also* EXODUS; ILLINOIS PERIOD; MISSOURI PERIOD; NEW YORK PERIOD; OHIO PERIOD; UTAH PERIOD.

PETERSON, LEVI S. (1933–). Fiction writer, biographer. Born in Snowflake, Arizona, he received a bachelor's and master's degree at **BYU** and a Ph.D. at the University of Utah in 1965. He taught English at Weber State University in Ogden, Utah, where he was director of the honors program. Peterson's short stories and novels almost always have Mormon characters, and a strong comic streak is present, most notably in *The Backslider*. The incongruities of the religious life in a secular world also produce tragic scenes. Two collections of short stories and a second novel, *Aspen Marooney*, have been well received. In 1988 Peterson published a biography of **Juanita Brooks**, which won the Evans Biography Award. He became editor of ***Dialogue: A Journal of Mormon Thought***.

PIONEER(S). (1) Anyone who clears the way or the original settlers of an area. (2) The specific company, known as "the pioneer company," led by **Brigham Young** to go ahead of the others and establish the place of settlement in 1847. (3) All early settlers in the West. Needing to have a cutoff date for membership qualification, the Daughters of Utah Pioneers and Sons of Utah Pioneers specified 1869, when the railroad reached Utah, as the year before which the settlers were "pioneers." (4) Those who went out in a process of continuing **colonization** to establish settlements in adjacent states, Mexico, and Canada in the last two or three decades of the 19th century. (5) People first converted to Mormonism in any state or country, who establish the foundation for Church growth there. In this sense there are 20th-century and 21st-century pioneers in different American states; in the Philippines, Korea, and Thailand; and in France, Russia, and Nigeria. *See also* EXODUS.

PIONEER DAY. July 24. It was on this date in 1847 that **Brigham Young** emerged from the mountains, beheld the Salt Lake Valley, and proclaimed it "the right place" for settlement. As early as 1849, Church members began celebrating the date as Pioneer Day. Like other commemorations celebrating past events, Pioneer Day has always included a parade as well as speeches, picnics, and various kinds of recreation. Since it is a state holiday in Utah, the long parade has been expanded to include many high school bands, civic groups, politicians, U.S. military units, and different denominations. A strong Mormon tone remains in that many floats are sponsored by **wards**, and the historical themes they commemorate have to do with Mormon history.

PLAN OF SALVATION. An explanation of the purpose of human life drawn from the standard works, especially the modern **scriptures**. All humans naturally confront the questions "Where do I come from? Why am I here? Where am I going?" Mormons answer these questions in the plan of salvation.

Essentially it consists of three acts, or phases, of existence, each of which can be subdivided. First, the preexistence, or pre-mortal, stage during which all humans existed as spirit children of God. In a great council in heaven the Heavenly Father put forth a plan by which the spirits would come to earth. His firstborn son, **Jesus Christ**, volunteered to come to earth to atone for the sins of the world and to be the first fruit of the **resurrection**. All human beings born on earth accepted this plan in their pre-mortal state.

Born on earth, a veil of forgetfulness preventing any recollection of the prior existence, human beings enter a state in which two purposes are achieved. First, they gain a physical body. It is this physical body that will be recovered at the time of resurrection; without it the spirit could never obtain a "fulness of joy." Earth life is also a time of probation, a time in which to demonstrate one's real character, ability to withstand temptation, and willingness to repent. In this setting we show the kind of person we really are.

At death one enters the post-mortal phase of existence. Death is in essence the separation of the spirit from the body. The physical body, a mere shell, is placed in the grave and deteriorates. The spirit never ceases to exist. It enters the spirit world, still conscious and aware of its self-identity. This is a time during which instruction, even **missionary** proselytizing, is provided for those who, through no fault of their own, never had the opportunity to hear the **gospel** during earth life. Then come the resurrection and final judgment. Resurrection is the reuniting of the physical body (or the reassembled component elements of that body) and the spirit. By the atonement of Jesus Christ it comes to all, regardless of goodness or badness of one's actions.

The judgment determines the ultimate reward or punishment. Rather than a simple division into heaven or hell, there are three kingdoms, or degrees, of glory, each with an unknown number of subdivisions (***Doctrine and Covenants***, sections 76, 88). The lowest was the telestial kingdom, followed by the terrestrial and celestial kingdoms. It is in the highest level of the celestial kingdom that the righteous regain the presence of God.

Eternal salvation is characterized by continued progression. Ultimately, in the eons to come, those who qualify at the highest level become co-heirs with Christ and, joining God the Father in a heavenly aristocracy of character, even have the capacity to create worlds. Such is the plan that explains the meaning of life, its trials and tribulations, and where it is all headed. The ***Book of Mormon*** calls it "the merciful plan of the great Creator."

PLURAL MARRIAGE. *See* POLYGAMY.

POLITICS. Mormons proclaim loyalty to nation and currently acknowledge the inappropriateness of direct Church involvement in political matters. This basic stance is emphasized when the Church seeks permission for its **missionaries** to proselytize in a country. It is a good-faith statement and not a subterfuge. Still, historically, there have been counter-tendencies.

During the **Illinois Period** and later in territorial Utah where Mormons were the great majority of the population, they often voted as a block to elect their own people to office. This led to charges of "theocracy." A standard answer at the time was that people who chose to be represented by individuals of their own faith were only exercising their rights. During Utah's territorial period, voters divided into the Liberal party and the People's party. The latter, representing the majority of the population, the Mormons, won most elections, but the Liberals promoted their own ticket and even won some local elections. The federal government appointed the governor, territorial secretary, district attorney, U.S. marshal, and federal judges. From 1857 until Charles S. Richards's appointment in 1893, the federal government appointed no Mormons to territory-wide office in Utah.

In the 1890s, the introduction of the national political parties, with Mormons and non-Mormons in both parties, reduced fear of ecclesiastical domination, and Utah became a state in 1896. A leading Church authority, polygamist B. H. Roberts, a Democrat, was elected to the House of Representatives in 1898. Committee hearings were held, and he was not allowed to take his seat. When monogamist Reed Smoot, an apostle, was elected U.S. senator in 1903, the Senate Committee on Privileges and Elections held another round of committee hearings that lasted until 1907. A vote in the Senate allowed him to retain his seat. For about 30 years Smoot served as a respected and influential senator. Other Mormons holding influential office have included James H. Moyle, assistant secretary of the treasury;

Edgar Brossard, member of the U.S. Tariff Commission; Elbert D. Thomas, U.S. senator; **Ezra Taft Benson**, secretary of agriculture; **David Kennedy**, secretary of the treasury; Stewart L. Udall, secretary of the interior; and Michael Leavitt, secretary of health and human services. In addition to Utah's senators and representatives, Mormons have also been elected to office in other states, as Governor George Romney of Michigan, Governor Mitt Romney of Massachusetts, U.S. Senators Gordon Smith of Oregon and Harry Reed of Nevada, and senators and members of Congress from several states. In 2007, Harry Reed became senate majority leader.

Candidates for public office who ridicule religion, the **family**, or traditional morality would probably not garner support from Mormon voters. But there is no edict from the Church dictating how one must vote. When Church **president Heber J. Grant** came out in opposition to repealing the Prohibition amendment, the majority of Church members voted for repeal. It is sometimes assumed that Mormons are Republicans, but, like other Americans, the majority of them voted for Democrat Franklin D. Roosevelt. If they seem to stand in the Republican camp at present, this is because Republicans have in some instances successfully tarred Democratic candidates as opponents of traditional values, especially in the "red" states in the South, Midwest, and Rocky Mountains. There is no signal from the Church president dictating how votes must be cast. Party alignment is always subject to change. Both Republicans and Democrats, not to speak of Libertarians and others, continue to enlist Mormons to their ranks.

In other countries as well as the United States, Church members are encouraged to participate in the public process. Some have served on local councils and even national legislatures. Such participation, along with different kinds of community service, is expected to continue.

Although as late as the 1960 election, the Church president publicly expressed his support for one of the candidates, the Church as such has not openly endorsed a presidential candidate since 1936. In official statements, the **First Presidency** has asserted its neutrality in political matters. In January 2007 the following official statement was issued: "Elected officials who are Latter-day Saints make their own decisions and may not necessarily be in agreement with one another or even with a publicly stated Church position. While the

Church may communicate its views to them, as it may to any other elected official, it recognizes that these officials still must make their own choices based on their best judgment and with consideration of the constituencies whom they were elected to represent."

Church leaders have, however, taken positions on issues that they consider moral, and as late as 1954 on issues that might be considered political, such as returning Weber State College to the Church and legislative apportionment. Moral questions on which the leadership has taken stands in recent years include liquor by the drink, Sunday closing, and pari-mutuel betting. The Church leadership also opposed the proposed Equal Rights Amendment, arguing that it would undermine traditional family values and legal protections for women.

POLYGAMY. The practice, known technically as polygyny, by which an individual husband takes more than one wife. Publicly announced in 1852, Mormon plural marriage was officially terminated when a **manifesto** was issued by Church **president Wilford Woodruff** in 1890. An average of perhaps 25 percent of the families lived in polygamy in the late 19th century, even when it was publicly advocated and defended. Considering the Church's spectacular growth in the late 20th century, it is clear that only a very small percentage of all the Mormons who have ever lived practiced polygamy. Yet the media and critics continue to associate polygamy with the Church, and many uninformed people continue to associate the practice with Mormonism. The work of scholars allows us to consider the subject in somewhat greater detail with respect to its origins, its extent, its success or failure, and its termination.

Origins. As the Church was organized in 1830, polygamy was not part of its practice. The **revelation** authorizing it is dated 12 July 1843, the year prior to **Joseph Smith**'s death (***Doctrine and Covenants***, section 132). There is some evidence that Smith considered the possibility as early as 1830–1831, and it is probable that he married Fanny Alger as a second wife in 1833 or 1835. Nevertheless, it was in Nauvoo, Illinois, after 1842 that polygamy was privately introduced to some people along with the new **temple ordinances**.

The original reaction was usually shock and rejection. But after personal struggle and prayer—on the part of **Joseph Smith** and his wife **Emma Smith; Hyrum Smith**, the **twelve apostles**, and their wives; and the women who became plural wives—a small number of Church leaders became polygamists. Since the practice was not publicly acknowledged, exact numbers are difficult to come by. As an educated guess, less than 100 began practicing polygamy before the departure of the Mormons from Nauvoo in early 1846.

Motives are difficult to determine with any confidence. Not surprisingly, critics of the practice assumed that lust was behind it. Clearly, however, Mormons saw it in a religious context. It was defended as a biblical practice that by specific divine authorization could again be allowed. It was part of "the restoration of all things."

Extent. How many Mormons were polygamous in the 19th century? As already indicated, practically none until 1843, after which a relatively small group of leaders were inducted into it. The practice was officially admitted and defended from 1852. Its formal termination, with the Manifesto of 1890, came 38 years later. At the end of the century, a figure sometimes heard was 2 percent of the population, but this estimate was disingenuous, for it included only polygamist males in the numerator, while the entire Church membership was included in the denominator.

Estimates for the late 19th century have varied between 25 and 35 percent of the families. The higher figure refers to certain settlements, or **wards**, and includes in the numerator all children whose mothers are married, or have been married, to a polygamist male. Changing the definition obviously changes the percentage, and critics, defenders, and historians of the practice have not always clearly spelled out their criteria for inclusion or exclusion. It cannot be far off to say that roughly 25 percent of the entire Church population during the **Utah Period** lived in polygamous households, with variations from place to place and from decade to decade.

Even if 30 percent of Mormons were in polygamy in some way, that is still a minority of the **membership**. Yet virtually all of the leadership—**general authorities, stake presidents**, **bishops**—were polygamists, and the practice loomed very large in the public perception of Mormons.

Success or failure. Contemporary charges of miserable failure, portraying plural wives as chattels and the children as neglected waifs, are inaccurate. Likewise, glowing descriptions by some defenders of polygamy are unreliable. The several hundred divorces granted to plural wives, and approved by **Brigham Young**, are sufficient evidence of some marital malfunction. The fact seems to be that the success of these marriages depended on the people involved. Anecdotal evidence and diary accounts indicate that there could be cooperation and mutual support between the wives. Allegations to the contrary notwithstanding, children of plural marriages tended to be healthy and intelligent. On the other hand, there is no evading the inherent limitations of time and financial resources; a polygamist father could not give the same time and attention to individual wives and children as could a monogamist. However, a simple examination of divorce ratios is sufficient to prove that monogamy as well as polygamy varies greatly across a spectrum ranging from beautiful harmony to disastrous breakdown, with most coming somewhere in between.

Termination. Succumbing to a prolonged, increasingly intensive anti-polygamy campaign, Church president **Wilford Woodruff** issued a manifesto in the fall of 1890. Often cited as the end of Mormon polygamy, the document itself did not claim so much. Its concluding words are "And I now publicly declare that my advice to the Latter-day Saints is to refrain from contracting any marriage forbidden by the law of the land." It was not possible to make a clean break that would suddenly cause the system to vanish. The following points seem worthy of consideration.

1. Many husbands continued to support, live with, and have children by plural wives married before the manifesto. While agreeing not to enter any new plural marriages, they could not abandon those they already had even if a strict reading of the law seemed to require it. By a gentleman's agreement these were not prosecuted. Continuing to support wives and families seemed fair, and in time, if there were no new plural marriages, the system would die out.
2. Some new plural marriages, perhaps 1 to 300, were secretly performed with the approval of some **general authorities** between 1890 and 1904. Some of these were performed outside the boundaries of the United States, even on the high seas, where it was reasoned no law of the land made them illegal. Others used different forms of casuistry to justify their action: the manifesto

had only "recommended"; promises made under coercion need not be observed; the manifesto was addressed "to whom it may concern" and it does not concern me. When the clandestine plural marriages following 1890 were uncovered during the hearings for the seating of Senator **Reed Smoot**, a second manifesto was issued by Church president **Joseph F. Smith** in 1904 with a greater determination to enforce it.

3. After 1904, only **fundamentalists** have continued to perform plural marriages. They are **excommunicated** when discovered and are not properly called Latter-day Saints, or Mormons.

The practice of polygamy continues by people who are not Church members, both in the United States and Canada as well as in other countries. Numbers are very hard to come by. Several groups, even while rejected and excommunicated by the Church, claim that they represent true Mormonism. In addition to breaking the laws of the state against being married to more than one person at the same time, polygamists in the present generation have been associated with welfare fraud and child abuse.

Not relishing the association of these activities with the Church in the public mind, the general authorities and their spokesmen repeatedly insist that it is a misnomer to call polygamists *Mormon* polygamists. To say that the Church teaches or advocates polygamy today is false. *See also* UTAH PERIOD.

POLYNESIAN CULTURAL CENTER. A theme park located in Laie, Hawaii, on the north shore of the island of Oahu. A nonprofit corporation that provides employment to hundreds of Polynesian students at the campus of **BYU–Hawaii**, the center preserves and displays different Polynesian cultural traditions through song, dance, and crafts. In April 2003 the Polynesian Cultural Center welcomed its 30 millionth visitor.

POLYNESIANS. Missionary proselytizing began as early as 1843 among some of the Polynesians and was resumed later in the century. Each of the Polynesian groups has its own history of **pioneer** conversions, **persecution**, and continuity. Although not clearly stated in the **scriptures**, the idea is often expressed that Polynesians are heirs of the Abrahamic covenant by their descent from ***Book of Mormon*** peoples. In addition to substantial numbers of Mormon Polynesians in New Zealand, Hawaii, Samoa, Tonga, Tahiti, and other islands, many have emigrated to other locations, such as Australia or the United States. At **BYU–Hawaii** approximately one third of the students are from the different island countries of the **Pacific**.

PRATT, ORSON (1811–1881). Mathematician, **missionary**, **general authority**. Born in Hartford, New York, on 19 September 1811, Pratt had little formal schooling but avidly pursued different subjects on his own. In 1830 his older brother **Parley P. Pratt** taught him the new religion of Mormonism and **baptized** him. As was common at the time, Orson immediately went on a preaching mission. He participated in many of the experiences at Kirtland, Ohio, was a member of **Zion's Camp**, and in 1835 at the age of 24 became one of the original members of the **Quorum** of the **Twelve Apostles**. In 1836 he married Sarah Marinda Bates.

Pratt was one of the legendary missionaries of early Mormonism, traveling through the eastern states, Canada, Scotland, and England. Returning from England in 1841, he found a crisis. His wife had been introduced to **polygamy** in his absence. During much of 1842 Pratt was in turmoil, refusing to support **Joseph Smith** and the other apostles on some matters. He and his wife were excommunicated in August. Before the year had ended they were rebaptized and Orson Pratt was again one of the twelve apostles.

After the Mormons were forced out of Nauvoo, Illinois, during the great **exodus** to the West, Pratt was in the **pioneer** company that led the way. One of a small group of advance scouts, he entered the Salt Lake Valley on 21 July 1847, three days before **Brigham Young**. He invented an odometer to measure the mileage during the trip and supervised the surveying of the new location after their arrival.

Somewhat of a philosopher and mathematician, Pratt did not work within the context of the major universities of the Victorian era. But audiences on the Mormon frontier were interested in his lectures on such subjects as light and causation. Sometimes his teachings were too abstruse for Brigham Young, who occasionally reprimanded him. In 1875 President Young declared that Pratt's position of seniority in the twelve apostles was determined not by his original ordination but his readmission in 1842—which had the practical effect of putting Orson behind **John Taylor** in seniority. Yet Young recognized Pratt's deep commitment to Mormonism and did not want to lose his services.

In addition to Sarah, Pratt married four other wives before the move to the West. Two others were added later. Eventually he was the father of 45 children. Such personal involvement in plural marriage made Pratt the ideal choice as its defender. When the practice of polygamy was publicly announced in 1852, Pratt preached the main sermon and immediately began publishing *The Seer*, a periodical in Washington, D.C., dedicated to defending the practice. In 1870, when the prominent minister John P. Newman attacked polygamy, Pratt faced him in a public debate, the text of which was published in newspapers and as a pamphlet. The topic was not whether polygamy was good or bad but whether the **Bible** sanctioned it. The Mormons thought Pratt was the clear winner. *See also* OHIO PERIOD.

PRATT, PARLEY PARKER (1807–1857). Poet, **missionary**, **general authority**. Born 12 April 1807 in Burlington, New York, Parley Pratt married Thankful Halsey in 1827 and moved to Ohio. Having been a Baptist, he became a follower of **Sidney Rigdon**'s brand of the Campbellites. In 1830 he sold out and with his wife traveled to New York. Leaving her on a canal boat to continue their intended journey, he suddenly left her, explaining that he felt strongly that there was some special work for him in that part of the country. There he first saw the ***Book of Mormon***. After reading it with enthusiasm, he traveled to the Palmyra, New York, area; met **Hyrum Smith**; and was soon baptized.

With **Oliver Cowdery** he was called on a mission to the Indians in Missouri (***Doctrine and Covenants***, section 32). During the journey, they stopped at Kirtland, Ohio, and introduced Mormonism to Sidney Rigdon and his congregation. The conversion of Rigdon and most of his congregation paved the way for the establishment of a new center for the Church. Continuing on to Missouri, Pratt and his travel companions made contact with the Indians and, more important historically, provided the information leading to the declaration of Missouri as the new **Zion**. During the remainder of the 1830s Parley Pratt and his family participated in the exciting and trying events of early

Mormon history. They were driven from Jackson County, Missouri, in 1833. In 1834 he served in **Zion's Camp**. In 1835 he was named one of the original members of the **Quorum** of the **Twelve Apostles**.

Pratt served on many missions, including one to Canada and in 1840 to England. There he edited the ***Millennial Star***. His literary skills were also employed in the writing of pamphlets like *Voice of Warning* (1837). Pratt's hymns were among the most popular in Mormon worship, including "An Angel from on High," "Jesus, Once of Humble Birth," and "The Morning Breaks, The Shadows Flee."

After the Mormons moved west to Utah, Pratt assisted in drafting a constitution. He served in the territorial legislature. Much of his time was taken in settling and providing for his families. His wife Thankful died in 1837, after which he married Mary Ann Frost. Starting in 1843 he took plural wives and eventually became the father of 30 children.

The last of his wives, Eleanor McComb McLean, had not been legally divorced from her husband, an alcoholic in San Francisco. McLean, the father, kept the children and took them to Arkansas. A nasty custody suit followed. Pratt was attempting to recover Eleanor's children when he was charged with alienation of affection and acquitted. He tried to return to Utah by joining an immigration company when McLean overtook him, stabbed him twice, and shot him in the neck. Pratt was unarmed.

Although just 50 years old at the time of his death in 1857, Parley P. Pratt made important contributions during Mormonism's first generation. His autobiography, assembled from his unpublished manuscripts, is considered a classic. *See also* OHIO PERIOD.

PRAYER. A faithful Mormon approaches God in prayer evening and morning as well as any other time there is a special need or desire. **Family** prayers are held daily. A prayer of blessing and thanks is uttered at mealtime. All Church meetings are started and ended with prayers, known respectively as invocations and benedictions. Except for the **ordinances** of **sacrament** and **baptism**, fixed or written prayers are not used. Standard usage includes addressing God at the beginning of the prayer and concluding "in the name of Jesus Christ." The prayer should otherwise come from the heart and be appropriate for the occasion.

PRESIDENT. A common title in the Church organization, referring to the person who stands at the head. Thus there is a president of a **stake**, of **priesthood quorums**, of such **auxiliary** organizations as **Primary**, **Sunday School**, **Young Men**, and **Young Women** on the **ward**, **stake**, and general level. Although the head of the ward is a **bishop**, a congregation not yet large enough to achieve ward status is led by a branch president. Each of the 347 missions is presided over by a mission president.

The president of the Church stands at the head of the whole Church on earth, although the real head is regarded as **Jesus Christ**. In addition to his title of president, the Church president is sustained as "**prophet**, seer, and revelator" and is often referred to as "the prophet." He is the presiding **high priest** of the Church and holds all the keys, or authority, for its functioning on earth. One characteristic of Mormon organization is that each of these presidents is assisted by two **counselors**, the three of them constituting a presidency. Clerks or secretaries as needed also assist. As a **form of address**, the term *president* is regularly used for the president of the Church and presidents of stakes and **missions**. Others holding the title are more commonly addressed as **brother** or **sister**.

PRESIDING BISHOP. One of the **general authorities** of the Church. The presiding bishop and his two **counselors** form the Presiding Bishopric. Unlike other bishoprics, with responsibility for a single **ward**, the Presiding Bishopric oversees the entire Church.

Under the direction of the president of the Church, the presiding bishop and his counselors exercise specific responsibility over receiving **tithing** and other income, helping the poor, planning and erecting buildings, and maintaining **membership** records. In addition the Presiding Bishopric has had responsibility for the **Aaronic Priesthood**, the young men from 12 to 18 years of age, and even for young women of the same age. In 1977 presiding bishops were officially assigned to the presidency of the **Young Men** and **Young Women**. The growth of Church membership led to some decentralization. Under the supervision of **area** presidencies, area directors for temporal affairs were established. The Presiding Bishopric provides training, planning, and technical support.

PRIEST. An office in the **Aaronic Priesthood**. Young men are eligible for ordination as priests at age 16. They acquire authority to perform not only the functions of **deacons** and **teachers**, but in addition, under the direction of their **bishop**, to **baptize**, administer the **sacrament**, and ordain other priests, **teachers**, and **deacons**. This is the highest office of the Aaronic Priesthood. The priests in a **ward** are organized in a **quorum** of 48 or fewer. Their president is the ward bishop, with two priests serving as **counselors**. They meet regularly on Sundays with an adult adviser for study and training. In principle they are preparing for the **Melchizedek Priesthood** and **missionary** service.

PRIESTHOOD. The power or authority of God granted to **worthy** male Church members to act in his holy name for the salvation of human beings. Priesthood must be specifically received by ordination from someone who holds it (**Articles of Faith**, no. 5). It is not, therefore, a right that one arrogates to himself and not the prerogative of every baptized believer.

For the **restoration** of the Church to be efficacious, the authority to act in God's name had to be restored, which **Joseph Smith** described as having occurred by means of heavenly messengers. A church without such authority, or where the founder simply decides to work on his own, is an empty shell. **Baptisms**, or any of the other **ordinances**, if performed without priesthood authority, lack the essential ingredient that makes them valid. Mormons do not connect priesthood with professional preparation in divinity school. It is widely distributed by the ordination of every worthy male 12 years of age and older.

The two major divisions are the **Aaronic Priesthood** and **Melchizedek Priesthood**. In the Aaronic Priesthood are three offices: **deacon**, for which one is eligible at age 12; **teacher**, at age 14; and **priest**, at age 16. Each of these priesthood offices has specific rights and prerogatives; for example, as a deacon one may pass the **sacrament** to the congregation, but not until becoming a priest may one perform baptisms. At age 18 a male is eligible to be ordained an **elder** in the Melchizedek Priesthood. All male **missionaries** are called elder, whatever their priesthood. Later, depending on responsibilities, a man may be ordained a **high priest**. The **seventy** was previously a local office, but now it is reserved for general and **area authorities**. In each **ward** during priesthood meetings there are separate classes for the different offices: deacon, teacher, priest, elder, high priest.

Two important qualifications limit priesthood claims by any individual. First, God will recognize those things done in His name only to the extent that they are done in righteousness. Priesthood must not be used as an excuse for intimidation or unkindness. Second, in practice one exercises priesthood authority under the direction of ecclesiastical superiors, who possess the keys, or authority, of administration. Thus before performing a baptism, one must have approval from one's file leader.

PRIMARY. Organization for children under the age of 12. The Primary Association was founded in 1878 when Aurelia Spencer Rogers received approval from Church leaders. Primary soon spread to other **wards** and settlements. A general presidency of three women began to supervise the different Primaries in the 1890s. In 1902 they began publication of *The Children's Friend*, a magazine containing lessons as well as stories and pictures to interest children. It was superseded by the *Friend* in 1971. A program of sequential classes—with manuals, goals, and badges for achievement—was organized for both boys and girls. In 1980 Primary meetings were moved from weekdays to Sunday. Through classes and discussion, by participation in prayer and singing, children learn principles that prepare them for **baptism** and, in the case of the boys, **priesthood** ordination at age twelve.

PROPHET. One who legitimately transmits the will of God to the human race. A prophet must have been designated by God and be the recipient of divine communications. The biblical prophets are the prototypes. Part of the **restoration** that was Mormonism was the reappearance of prophets.

In a general sense all have access to this heavenly gift, for "the testimony of Jesus is the spirit of prophecy" (Rev. 19:10). More specifically, however, the title is reserved to those who are God's designated spokespersons on earth. In Mormon usage, members of the **First Presidency** and all of the **twelve apostles** are "prophets, seers, and revelators," but it is the **president** of the Church who specifically holds the keys of authority during his administration. It is he who is sometimes called simply "the prophet." The word designates not his administrative role, that of president, but his closeness to God, his capability and responsibility to convey God's message to Church members and all mankind. Not only is he endowed with this authority by being specially set apart by the other apostles, but he is also **sustained** by the uplifted hand of members throughout the Church, who thus testify that they accept him in the prophetic role.

From the prophet **Joseph Smith** to the present, Mormon leaders have worn the prophetic mantle. The title does not imply divinity or sainthood in the traditional sense of the word. Prophets are human beings. They are not worshiped. But faithful Latter-day Saints listen to their counsel with great respect. A common injunction, expressed in a song for children, is "Follow the prophet."

PROTESTANTISM. Some consider Protestants to be all Christian churches that are not Roman **Catholic** or Orthodox. During the Protestant Reformation of the 16th century, mainstream, or magisterial, Protestants included Lutherans, Calvinists, and Anglicans, each with different subgroups. Common principles were said to include salvation by faith, the unique authority of the **Bible**, the priesthood of all believers, and the two sacraments of baptism and the eucharist. But even these main groups could not agree on everything; for example, Zwingli and Luther denounced each other's view of the eucharist.

More radical 16th-century Protestants, including the Anabaptists, were rejected and persecuted by Catholics and mainstream Protestants alike. New groups came into existence later, notably Baptists and Methodists. With new organizations and repeated division and subdivision, by the 20th and 21st century there were hundreds of churches. Mormons are not Protestants. They do not trace their origin to the Protestant Reformation. Sometimes they emphasize their belief in a **restoration** as opposed to a *reformation*, but this ignores the existence of Protestant restorationism. Each of the so-called Protestant principles—salvation by faith alone, the inerrancy and sufficiency of the Bible—would be found unacceptable by Mormons, but of course many Protestants now also find these slogans to be inadequate.

The major premise that all **Christianity** is divided between Catholics and Protestants, followed by the minor premise that Mormons are neither Catholic nor Protestant, leads inevitably to the conclusion that they are not part of Christianity. Mormons see themselves as neither Catholic nor Protestant but decidedly Christian, even uniquely faithful to the purity of original Christianity. Theological distinctions notwithstanding, Mormons have much in common with many Protestants and Catholics in worship, lifestyle, and social agenda. Mormon, Catholic, and Protestant congregations have occasionally been able to cooperate, help one another, and achieve mutual respect.

PUBLIC AFFAIRS. The department responsible for disseminating information about the Church to media. News releases are prepared about programs and events. Radio and television programs are also produced. In addition to the central office at Church headquarters, **area** offices with full-time directors have been established in such major cities as Washington, D.C., Toronto, and London. More than 3,500 local public affairs directors on the level of **stakes** and **missions** are coordinated from the central and regional offices.

PUBLICATIONS. *See DESERET NEWS*; *ENSIGN*; *THE FRIEND*; *IMPROVEMENT ERA*; INTERNATIONAL MAGAZINES; *JOURNAL OF DISCOURSES*; *MILLENNIAL STAR*; *THE NEW ERA*; *RELIEF SOCIETY MAGAZINE*; *TIMES AND SEASONS*. ***Dialogue*** and ***Sunstone*** are privately printed. Refer to “Periodicals and Yearbooks” in the bibliography.

– Q –

QUORUM. A unit of the **priesthood** in the Church organization; thus the Quorum of the **First Presidency**, the Quorum of the **Twelve Apostles**, the First Quorum of the **Seventy**. On the level of **wards** and **stakes**, when a male receives the **priesthood**, he enters a quorum for the particular office to which he is ordained: **deacon**, **teacher**, **priest**, **elder**, or **high priest**. Quorum meetings are held regularly.

QUORUM OF THE TWELVE APOSTLES. *See* TWELVE APOSTLES, QUORUM OF THE; GENERAL AUTHORITIES.

– R –

RASBAND, RONALD A. (1951–). General authority. Born 6 February 1951 in Salt Lake City, Utah, Rasband attended the University of Utah. From 1970 to 1972 he was a **missionary** in the Eastern States Mission. He became president and chief operations officer of the Huntsman Chemical Corporation and then a self-employed businessman. He served as **bishop**, **high councilor**, and from 1996 to 1999 president of the New York New York North Mission. In 2000 he became a member of the First **Quorum** of the **Seventy** and in 2005 entered its presidency. He and his wife, Melanie, are parents of five children.

RECOMMEND. A certificate of **worthiness** necessary for entrance into the **temples**. A searching interview by one's **bishop** determines one's faithfulness to commitments and attitude toward the Church and its leaders. A follow-up interview is conducted by a member of the **stake** presidency. A recommend is valid for two years. Then the interviews are repeated, offering opportunity for self-evaluation and updating. In 2007 because of apparent abuse of the recommend privilege including the reported sale of some recommends on Internet sites, recommends were marked with an electronic code unique to each individual. A determination of worthiness similar to a recommend, although not necessarily resulting in a signed certificate, is made prior to being called as a **missionary** or to fill different positions of responsibility.

REFERRAL. The name of a person who has shown an interest in the Church, which is turned over to the **missionaries**, who then offer to schedule meetings for teaching the **gospel** prior to conversion and **baptism**. Church members are encouraged to explore such a possibility with friends and family. Otherwise missionaries rely on random door knocking, street contacting, or other inefficient methods of finding people willing to investigate Mormonism. Growth of the Church has been most spectacular in areas where members have been diligent in making referrals.

REGION. A grouping of several **stakes**. Smaller than an **area**, the region is an intermediate level.

REGIONAL REPRESENTATIVES. Priesthood leaders called to provide supervision over **regions**. They trained local leaders and visited conferences in the region, but were not considered **general authorities**. In 1995, this position was discontinued and replaced with that of **area authority**.

REID, HARRY M. (1939–). Attorney, attorney general, U. S. senator from Nevada, senate majority leader. Born in Searchlight, Nevada, 2 December 1939, Reid earned an A.S. at Southern Utah University and a B.S. in history and political science in 1961 at Utah State University, where he and his wife converted to Mormonism. He moved to Washington, D.C., where he worked for the police force while earning a J.D. at George Washington University in 1964.

Reid returned to Nevada where he practiced law and entered politics. After serving in the state legislature, he was elected to the state assembly in 1967 and served as lieutenant governor from 1971 through 1974. Active in Democratic politics, in 1974 he unsuccessfully ran for senator against former governor Paul Laxalt. Reid served as Nevada gaming commissioner from 1977 to 1981 and served two terms in the U.S. House of Representatives from 1983 through 1987. Elected to the U.S. Senate in 1986, he won successive elections. After serving as minority whip and minority leader, he was elected majority leader in 2006. During his term as majority leader, Reid actively opposed the administration position on the war in Iraq. He also worked actively for immigration reform. Reid has served as an **elders quorum president**, **stake high counselor**, and **Sunday School** president. He is married to Landra Gould, and the two have five children.

RELIEF SOCIETY. Women's organization of the Church. Organized in Nauvoo, Illinois, in 1842, with **Emma Smith**, wife of **Joseph**

Smith, as first president, the Female Relief Society, as it was first called, performed charitable service and solicited contributions. Joseph Smith explained that it was essential to the completeness of the Church. By 1844 it had reached a membership of 1,341.

With the death of Joseph Smith in June 1844 and the subsequent turmoil and **exodus**, the Relief Society suspended official operations. Women worked and met together on occasion, but not until 1854 did **Brigham Young** reinitiate the Relief Society on the **ward** level. The organization carried out charitable work, and some of the societies made clothing for Indian women and children. In 1866 the Relief Society was reorganized on a general church level with **Eliza R. Snow** as president.

During the last generation of the 19th century the Relief Society raised silk worms in the effort to establish sericulture. A grain storage program was organized. Nurses, midwives, and female doctors were selected, and money was raised to assist in their training. The organization founded and operated a hospital. Relief Society women were outspoken in defending Mormonism and in agitating for female suffrage. A semimonthly publication, *Woman's Exponent*, provided instruction and inspiration. Two of the organization's prominent leaders were Eliza R. Snow and **Emmeline B. Wells**.

In the 20th century the Relief Society expanded its educational role. Through the ***Relief Society Magazine*** lesson materials were provided in theological, cultural, and homemaking areas. With some Relief Society leaders professionally trained as teachers, psychologists, and social workers, the organization enlarged its role in child placement, in cooperation with other agencies, and sponsored health clinics. As the **welfare program** got under way during the 1930s, Relief Society presidents throughout the Church worked in close cooperation with ward **bishops**.

For many years Relief Society women studied courses in literature and comparative cultures, but this has been superseded by greater emphasis on spiritual training. Homemaking, considered broadly, continues to be a central part of the society's program. The voluntary membership and dues requirement was replaced in 1971 by automatic membership for all Mormon women. One of the central features of the organization, whose origins go back to Nauvoo, continues to be the **visiting teaching**, with each adult female member of the Church—all of whom are members of the Relief Society—receiving regular visits, support, and compassionate service.

Although promoting the home as a primary area of woman's responsibility, the organization recognizes the diverse life situations and needs of its members. The increasingly complex life patterns of women in the United States combined with the growth of the Church abroad have combined to present major challenges. In 1992, the sesquicentennial year of its organization, the Relief Society announced that each ward unit would undertake a community service or literacy project.

Remembering the number of **stakes** (2,733) and wards (27,087) in the Church, one notes that thousands of women are receiving administrative, teaching, and service experience. Passivity or timidity have not been the characteristics of this dynamic organization. Its motto from the beginning has been "Charity never faileth."

RELIEF SOCIETY MAGAZINE. Monthly magazine published by the **Relief Society** from 1915 to 1970. Intended to reflect and serve the women of the Church, it included reports on activities, recipes, and addresses given at the annual Relief Society conference. Creativity was encouraged by the publication of poetry and short stories. Lessons were published on religion, art, social science, and literature. When it was terminated in 1970, the magazine had 301,000 subscribers.

REORGANIZED CHURCH OF JESUS CHRIST OF LATTER DAY SAINTS (RLDS). A church that came into existence after the middle of the 19th century as an alternative to the **Church of Jesus Christ of Latter-day Saints** then led by **Brigham Young.** In the aftermath of the death of **Joseph Smith** some fragmentation occurred as different groups put forth claims to **succession**. Most remained small and later disappeared. The RLDS Church continues and though small by comparison—circa 260,000 versus 12 million plus—expresses an alternative vision of the **restoration.**

The departure to the West of the main body of the Church after their expulsion from Nauvoo, Illinois, left a minority of scattered Mormons who needed more time to prepare, followed one or another rival claimant, or had not made up their minds what to do. By 1851–1852 Jason W. Briggs and Zenos H. Gurley Sr. were rallying followers in Wisconsin. In addition to rejecting the leadership of the **Quorum** of the **Twelve Apostles** and Brigham Young, Briggs and Gurley looked forward to the time when "young Joseph," the **prophet**'s son, could take the leadership. On 6 April 1860 Joseph Smith III traveled to Amboy, Illinois, and accepted the position of prophet and president of the RLDS Church.

From its beginning the RLDS Church disassociated itself from its larger rival. Not only was the practice of **polygamy** denied but even the fact that Joseph Smith had introduced it (now well established). Other practices characteristic of early Mormonism were abandoned, such as the **gathering**, and the **ordinances** of the **temples** were rejected. For many generations RLDS people looked forward to the construction of a temple in Independence, Missouri, as the founding prophet had foretold, but when a structure was completed in 1993 it became a place of worship and education "dedicated to the pursuit of peace" with no special temple rituals being practiced. In 1881 RLDS headquarters were established at Lamoni, Iowa, where in 1895 **Graceland University** (formerly Graceland College) was founded. When Joseph Smith III died in 1914, three of his sons in a row succeeded to the presidency, followed by a grandson. In 1996, with the presidency of **W. Grant McMurray**, the insistence on lineal family succession was abandoned.

Through most of its existence the RLDS Church tried to draw sharp distinctions between itself and the Church of Jesus Christ of Latter-day Saints, on the one hand, and **Protestantism**, on the other. However, beginning in the 1960s the RLDS Church began to identify itself more with mainstream **Christianity** in its liberal or progressive forms. This tendency required soul-searching and redefinition. A 1970 report entitled *Exploring the Faith* discussed many topics that would be readily subscribed to by other Christians while maintaining some of the original Mormon distinctiveness.

"Inspired declarations" from the RLDS Church president have been issued from time to time. On this basis blacks were ordained to the **priesthood** (1865), polygamists in **Asia** and **Africa** were allowed to join the Church if they would not take on more wives (1972), women were ordained to the priesthood (1984), and the temple at Independence was announced (1984) and subsequently completed. In April 2000, after many years of discussion, the RLDS Church adopted a new official name, **Community of Christ**. *See also* EXODUS.

REPENTANCE. One of the first principles of the **gospel** (**Articles of Faith**, no. 4). When the apostle Peter was asked by his listeners what they should do, he replied, "Repent, and be baptized every one of you in the name of Jesus Christ for the remission of sins, and ye shall receive the gift of the Holy Ghost" (Acts 2:38). Mormons do not **baptize** infants. For the change of direction in one's life required of faithful Church **members**, there is no prescribed ritual such as penance, but Mormon writers, echoing a centuries-old Christian description, have said that proper repentance includes recognition, remorse, confession to proper Church authorities, and restitution where possible. With most humans the need for repentance continues throughout life.

RESTORATION. The basic idea of bringing back something that was there before; in Christian religious thought, the bringing back of the beliefs and practices of original **Christianity**. Mormons are restorationists. **Joseph Smith** sought to bring back the organization of the primitive Christian church and the true doctrines that had been lost during the Great **Apostasy**. Unlike some other restorationists, Smith also brought back such Old Testament concepts and usages as **Zion**, **polygamy**, and **temples.** Of central importance to the restoration as Smith conceived it was the appearance of heavenly beings and the actual transmission of the keys of authority from previous dispensations to the present. It was not to be a scholarly enterprise but one infused with divine power.

All of Mormonism is not summed up by the idea of restoration. The reestablishment of **prophets**, who would be the recipients of continuing **revelation**, meant that a direct channel of communication existed between God and the human race.

RESURRECTION. The reuniting of the spirit with the physical body. The spirit of individual humans is indestructible. It could live forever, a disembodied presence, but as such it could never obtain a fullness of joy. It was **Jesus Christ** who broke the bonds of death by his own resurrection and then made possible the resurrection of the entire human race. Resurrection comes to all, good and evil, thanks to the atoning sacrifice of **Jesus Christ**. Without pretending to know the exact mechanism by which it is accomplished, Mormons believe in a physical and literal resurrection, first of Jesus, then of others, and ultimately of the entire human race.

REVELATION. Communication from God. While accepting the **Bible** as **scripture** and thus God's word to the human race, Mormons usually use the term *revelation* to describe not the written **scriptures** but additional heavenly manifestations.

The **First Vision** of **Joseph Smith** is an example of such revelation. Angelic messengers from God appeared to Smith on many occasions. Communications have sometimes come in dreams, as in the Bible. The most common form of divine revelation is by means of "the still small voice," the whisperings of the Holy Spirit. Rejecting the idea that such miraculous intervention was limited to biblical times, Mormons are strongly convinced of the importance of "continuing revelation" (**Articles of Faith**, no. 9).

Who is eligible to receive revelation from God? Here two principles must be kept in salutary tension. On the one hand, all may petition God for guidance. Especially after **baptism** and **confirmation**, Church **members**, if **worthy**, may enjoy the constant companionship of the Holy Ghost, which includes spiritual prompting to assist in decisions. Individuals may also receive more dramatic manifestations. Such revelation is available for one's personal needs or responsibility, as parent in a family, **bishop** over a congregation, and the like.

On the other hand, guidance for the entire Church comes through the **president** and other **general authorities**. The **First Presidency** and the **Quorum** of the **Twelve Apostles** are **sustained** by a vote of the membership as "**prophets**, seers, and revelators." The instruction that comes from these leaders, especially the current president, is considered to have the same status as the canonical scriptures. Church members are urged to read the conference addresses as they are published in the ***Ensign*** twice a year and apply them to their lives. Members are also to seek personal manifestation to confirm that these messages come from God and to show how they may be applied.

What might appear to be anarchic decentralization, with everyone having access to the divine source, is in fact qualified by a subsidiary principle. Divine guidance for the whole Church comes to the president. Guidance for a congregation may come to its bishop, guidance for a family to its mother or father.

RICHARDS, LEGRAND (1886–1983). Businessman, **general authority**. Born on 6 February 1886 in Farmington, Utah, Richards spent much of his early life in Tooele, Utah, where his father, George F. Richards, was **stake** president. George F. went on to become one of the **twelve apostles** in 1906.

Much of LeGrand's early years were spent in farming. He attended business college in Salt Lake City, Utah. In 1905 he departed on a **mission** to the Netherlands. Upon his return in 1908 he met Ina Ashton, whom he married the following year. After about a year of employment in Portland, Oregon, the young family returned to Salt Lake City, where he worked for a lumber company. Then he was called to be **president** of the Netherlands Mission, serving from 1913 to 1916.

Back in Salt Lake City, Richards founded a realty company. He became **bishop** of his Sugar House **Ward** during several years of the 1920s. After a short-term mission in the East, he moved his family to Glendale, California. After serving as bishop of the Glendale Ward he became president of the Hollywood Stake. In 1934 he was **called** to be president of the Southern States Mission.

Returning to Utah in 1937, Richards again established a real estate business, became bishop of the University Ward, and in 1938 was called to be the Church's **Presiding Bishop**. For the remainder of his life he was one of the general authorities of the Church. As presiding bishop he was responsible generally for "temporal affairs" but also for the young men of the **Aaronic Priesthood**. Procedures were modernized, record keeping improved, a major building program launched. In 1954 LeGrand became a member of the **Quorum** of the **Twelve Apostles**. In the many **stake conferences** he visited and twice a year in **general conferences** he addressed the people, urging them to live their religion, bearing testimony to their faith.

Perhaps the accomplishment that touched more people than any other was his book. As president in the Southern States Mission, LeGrand prepared a topical plan to assist his missionaries in teaching the **gospel**. Responding to requests, he expanded on his earlier plan and in 1950 published *A Marvelous Work and a Wonder*, a presentation of Mormonism on the introductory level, buttressed by scriptural passages that he had used from the time he was a young missionary in Holland. The book went through many editions, and its proceeds were consecrated to the missionary program.

RICKS COLLEGE. Formerly a two-year accredited college at Rexburg, Idaho, owned by the Church, now **BYU–Idaho**. Originally the Bannock Academy, one of several **stake** academies at the time, the institution was renamed after stake **president** Thomas E. Ricks in 1903. A relatively small school of less than 200 students, Ricks College expanded to 5,150 by 1971. After a brief experiment with a four-year program it returned to its junior college status.

Ricks College offered liberal arts training and programs in nursing, agriculture, and other technical areas. Many of its students went on to complete bachelor's degrees at four-year institutions. Enrollment continued to climb, pushing past the cap to reach about 9,000 students. In 2000 it was announced that the institution would become a four-year college. The following year Ricks College took the new name of BYU–Idaho.

RIGDON, SIDNEY (1793–1876). General authority. Born on 19 February 1793 near Pittsburgh, Pennsylvania, Sidney experienced a Christian conversion as a young man and became a Baptist preacher. He married Phebe Brooks. His popular preaching style made his First Baptist Church one of the largest in Pittsburgh.

Longing for the purity of early Christianity, Rigdon became connected with the Mahoning Baptist Association, which included among its leaders Alexander Campbell and Walter Scott, who would soon found the Disciples of Christ. Rigdon did not follow them, however, but instead pastored a congregation in Mentor, Ohio. Among his parishioners he formed a communal society called "the Family."

In October 1830 four Mormon missionaries came to Ohio, including **Parley P. Pratt**, whom Rigdon had converted to the Reformed Baptist faith. After hearing their message and reading the ***Book of Mormon***, Rigdon accepted **baptism**. About a hundred of his congregation followed him into Mormonism. He traveled to Fayette, New

York; met **Joseph Smith**; and soon was assisting the **prophet** as a scribe.

During the **Ohio Period**, **Missouri Period**, and **Illinois Period** of Mormon history, Rigdon was a prominent figure. He participated with Joseph Smith in the great **revelation** on the graded salvation of souls after death (***Doctrine and Covenants***, section 76). He became a **counselor** in the **First Presidency**. He taught classes in Kirtland, Ohio, and assisted in preparing a lecture series, "Lectures on Faith." In Illinois he served on the Nauvoo City Council and as postmaster. When Joseph Smith declared his candidacy for president of the United States, Rigdon became the vice presidential candidate.

Rigdon was not always stable. In 1832, when along with Smith he was seized by a mob and tarred and feathered, he suffered head injuries and perhaps never fully recovered. Whatever the reason, he could be an unsettling influence. In Missouri he gave two inflammatory sermons that exacerbated the ill will already present. Upon the death of Joseph Smith in June 1844, Rigdon rushed from Pittsburgh and offered himself as "guardian" of the Church. By this time, however, the steadier hand of **Brigham Young** had demonstrated itself, and the Church members voted in favor of Young and the **twelve apostles** over Rigdon.

Rigdon lived for 32 more years, but they were anti-climactic. He established a Church of Christ in Pennsylvania, but it soon fizzled. In 1863, living in Freedom, New York, he founded the Church of Jesus Christ of the Children of Zion, but it too proved short-lived. A common charge was that Rigdon was the real brains behind Mormonism—that he provided the theology and had written or at least transmitted to Joseph Smith the transcript that became the *Book of Mormon*. In fact, he did not meet Smith until after the Church had been organized. Rigdon made important contributions during the first 14 years of Mormonism and then went his separate way.

ROBERTS, BRIGHAM HENRY (1857–1933). Missionary, politician, **general authority**. Born in Warrington, England, on 13 March 1857, Roberts emigrated to Utah as a boy and worked on farms, in mines, and in a blacksmith shop. Possessed of a powerful drive for self-improvement, he read voraciously and graduated from the territorial University of Deseret. At age 21 he married Sarah Louisa Smith, six years later he took a second wife, and six years after that a third. Roberts' employment included working as a journalist. His Church assignments included serving as a missionary in the United States and Great Britain. From 1888 he was a general authority and a member of the First Council of the **Seventy.**

During the 1890s when national parties came to Utah, Roberts became a Democrat. He served in the convention that drafted a constitution for the new state. After losing a close race for the U.S. House of Representatives in 1895, he was elected in 1898, only to become the center of a storm of controversy as a national campaign was organized to oppose seating him. After committee hearings in Washington, D.C., Roberts was denied his seat on the grounds that he was a **polygamist.**

Roberts had a brilliant mind and a forceful prose style. Works of apologetics included defenses of the ***Book of Mormon*** and of **Brigham Young** as **Joseph Smith**'s lawful successor. As a historian he compiled a massive, multi-volume source collection (*History of the Church of Jesus Christ of Latter-day Saints*) and wrote a magisterial narrative history in six volumes (*Comprehensive History of the Church*) that, even with its flaws, retains its value.

Some notes on a half dozen problems that had been raised by critics about the claims of the *Book of Mormon*, with reflections and reactions by Roberts, were published as B. H. Roberts, *Studies of the* Book of Mormon. Some have seen these notes as proof that he had privately lost his faith in the Mormon **scripture**, about which he had earlier written eloquent defenses. But his continued willingness to accept Church **callings**, including the presidency of the Eastern States Mission, and his later fervent **testimony** of the *Book of Mormon* make it more likely that the unpublished notes were tentative, exploratory, or intended to provoke answers rather than his own definitive faith statement. *See also* POLYGAMY.

ROBERTSON, LEROY JASPER (1896–1971). Musician, composer. Born on 21 December 1896 in Fountain Green, Utah, Robertson grew up on a farm. He showed musical aptitude but had little opportunity for formal training. He was sent to Provo, Utah, to attend Brigham

Young High School, after which he attended the Boston Music Center, graduating in 1923.

In 1925, Robertson became a professor of music at **BYU**. While there he continued his own formal training, receiving his A.B. and M.A. in music. In 1948 he accepted the chairmanship of the music department at the University of Utah. He received the Ph.D. from the University of Southern California in 1954. He retired in 1964.

Robertson was a serious composer. Among his compositions an overture won first prize in a 1923 competition, a quintet for piano and string won first place in 1936, and *Trilogy* won the coveted Reichhold award in 1947. His compositions were performed by many symphony orchestras and chamber groups in both **Europe** and the United States. In 1952 he completed an oratorio based on the ***Book of Mormon***; its recording was pronounced by critic Lowell Durham to be the high point in serious music among the Mormons. Robertson also contributed several works to the Church hymnal.

ROCKWELL, ORRIN PORTER (1813–1878). Bodyguard, hotelier, deputy sheriff. A neighbor of the **Joseph Smith** family near Palmyra, New York, Rockwell joined the Church at age 17 or 18. He followed the Mormons to Ohio and Missouri and finally to Nauvoo, Illinois, where in 1840 he became one of Smith's bodyguards. In 1842 Rockwell was caught in Missouri and arrested for the attempted murder of Governor Lilburn Boggs, who had issued an extermination order against the Mormons. Unable to convict Rockwell, the Missouri court released him after eight months. After the murder of Joseph Smith and **Hyrum Smith**, Rockwell participated in the defense of Nauvoo. He shot and killed an **anti-Mormon** leader named Franklin Worrell. During the migration to the West, he was a guide and hunter.

In Utah he became a deputy sheriff. He established a Pony Express station and hotel and raised horses. For several years Rockwell refused to cut his hair, claiming a promise from Joseph Smith that no harm would befall him if he let his hair grow. Just how many men were victims of his weapons is difficult to determine, for he became a popular folk hero; rumors and unconfirmed stories circulated. Sometimes he was called "the Destroying Angel" of Mormonism. In 1877 he was arrested and charged with a murder that had taken place in 1858, but he died before the trial.

ROMNEY, GEORGE (1907–1995). Businessman, civic leader, Church leader. Born on 8 July 1907 in the Mormon colonies in Mexico, Romney was five when his parents moved to Los Angeles, California, in 1912 during the Mexican Revolution. The next year they moved to Oakley, Idaho, where his father began farming. Low prices forced abandonment of the farm, and the family moved to Rexburg, Idaho. In 1921 the family moved to Salt Lake City, Utah. In addition to construction work on his father's house-building projects, George attended high school and played football, baseball, and basketball. He also courted Lenore LaFount.

In 1926 Romney began two years of foreign **missionary** proselytizing in Scotland. Inspired by mission president **John A. Widtsoe**, George was transferred to London and gained administrative experience as a secretary in the mission office. Returning home in 1928, he entered the University of Utah and also took speedwriting classes at a business college. Anxious to be in Washington, D.C., where Lenore had moved and had graduated from George Washington University, George landed a job on the staff of Senator David I. Walsh, Democrat, of Massachusetts. In 1930 he accepted a job with Aluminum Company of America (Alcoa) and moved to California, where Lenore was pursuing a movie career. They finally married in 1931.

Moving back to Washington, D.C., the Romneys participated in different community activities. Then he took a job with the Automobile Manufacturers Association in Detroit. In 1941 he became managing director of the Automotive Council for War Production. After the war he went to work for Nash-Kelvinator. In 1954 he became CEO of American Motors, which enjoyed a rise in production and profits under his direction.

Romney headed a Citizens Advisory Committee on School Needs, became chairman of Citizens for Michigan, and in 1962 was elected governor of Michigan, serving three terms. A front-runner for the Republican presidential nomination in 1968, Romney lost out partly because he claimed, with perfect justification, that he had been "brainwashed" during a tour in Vietnam. He was appointed secretary of housing and urban development. In the Church, Romney served in many capacities, including several years as **stake** president in Detroit. After his retirement he continued to promote volunteerism throughout the country.

ROMNEY, MITT (1947–). Businessman, Massachusetts governor. Born 12 March 1947 in Detroit, Michigan, son of **GEORGE ROMNEY** and Lenore Romney. He attended Cranbrook School, Stanford University, and **BYU**, graduating as valedictorian. He earned an MBA at Harvard and in 1975 the J.D. at Harvard Law School. Romney was vice president of Bain and Company and in 1984 cofounded Bain Capital. In 1999 he was named president and CEO of the Salt Lake City Olympic Games, then facing a serious financial crisis. Through reorganizing, cutting expenses, and increasing revenue, the games ended with a profit.

In 1994 Romney ran as Republican candidate for U.S. Senate from Massachusetts, losing to Senator Ted Kennedy. In 2002 he was elected governor of Massachusetts. He became president of the Republican Governors Association. In 2006 he announced that he would not run for reelection. He was a contender for the Republican nomination as candidate for president of the United States. Both Republican and Democrat opponents often cited his religion as a reason they would not vote for him. He argued that there should be no religious test for public office and that his support of traditional values was what the majority of voters wanted. In 2007 he announced his candidacy for the presidency of the United States. He suspended his campaign on 7 February 2008 after falling behind John McCain in the primaries.

Always **active** in the Church, he served as **missionary** in France, **bishop**, and **stake president**. He and his wife, Ann, have five sons.

– S –

SABBATH DAY. From the beginning Mormons have sought to remember the Sabbath day and keep it holy. Like other Christians, they designated Sunday for this purpose, although in countries where this proves difficult, like Israel, they have readily shifted to the seventh day.

The central activity of the Sabbath is worship. At **sacrament** meeting Mormons pray, sing, listen to sermons, and most importantly partake of the emblems of the sacrament in remembrance of the sacrifice of Christ. Other meetings include **priesthood**, **Relief Society**, and

Sunday School. In 1980 these meetings were consolidated into a single time block, including **Young Women** and **Primary** meetings. For **bishops** and other leaders there is usually an additional preparation meeting.

During the remaining hours of the Sabbath, members are on their own, but they are urged to avoid regular work where possible as well as secular recreation. The hours of this day are to be dedicated to **prayer**, letter writing, visiting the sick and lonely, appropriate family activities, music, and **scripture** study. Somehow this day should be set apart from the rest of the week and provide nourishment for the spiritual side of human nature that is so easily neglected.

In a **revelation** in 1831 (***Doctrine and Covenants***, section 59) **Joseph Smith** announced, "And that thou mayest more fully keep thyself unspotted from the world, thou shalt go to the house of prayer and offer up thy sacraments upon my holy day; for verily this is a day appointed unto you to rest from your labors, and to pay thy devotions unto the Most High."

SACRAMENT. In Mormon usage the sacrament of the Lord's Supper repeated each week in sacrament meeting. Bread and wine (replaced by water after a **revelation** authorized it) are blessed by prayers specified in the ***Book of Mormon*** and ***Doctrine and Covenants***. Regarded as a solemn remembrance and acknowledgment of the sacrifice of **Jesus Christ**, the sacrament includes no claim of transubstantiation or real presence. The regular partaking of the emblems by Church **members** is also considered a renewal of covenants and a recommitment to observe the **commandments**. Sacraments in the broad sense are usually described by Mormons as **ordinances**. *See also* SABBATH.

SACRAMENT MEETING. The main meeting for worship held in **wards** and branches throughout the Church each **Sabbath**. Although somewhat informal when compared to the structured worship of liturgical traditions, sacrament meetings follow a standard format:

1. Hymn by congregation
2. Announcements
3. Opening prayer or invocation
4. Sacramental hymn

5. Blessing and distribution of the sacrament
6. Speakers
7. Musical selection
8. Closing hymn
9. Closing prayer or benediction

Those unfamiliar with Mormon practices sometimes find the sacrament meeting lacking due to the inclusion of small children in the congregation with some inevitable noise and the unprofessional quality of music and sermons. On the other hand, if one recalls that a lay organization, entirely volunteer, is putting on the meeting, it can be recognized that it performs its basic purpose entirely adequately. Certainly the personal growth that goes with participation is abundantly evident. Those who attend these meetings regularly attest to hearing excellent instruction and being inspired to live better lives.

One sacrament meeting each month, normally the first, is designated as a "fast and testimony meeting." Instead of the usual sermons, members of the congregation who wish to do so stand and "bear **testimony**," telling what their religious faith means to them. *See also* FASTING; TESTIMONY.

SACRED GROVE. In the spring of 1820 **Joseph Smith**, desiring to know which church he should join, retired to a grove of trees near his home in Palmyra, New York. The **First Vision** set in motion the events that led to the organization of the **LDS** Church on 6 April 1830. The grove of trees that Smith prayed in, or one that seems to fit the requirements, has been designated the Sacred Grove and is a popular tourist site.

SAINTS. Synonymous with "**members** of the Church." Following the New Testament usage according to which Paul wrote to "the saints" at Ephesus or Corinth or another city where there were Christians, Mormons do not assign any special sanctity to the term, although obviously members are expected to live a life dedicated to God. There is no canonization process. The venerable dead, the heroic figures of the past, are not the subject of any special cult or veneration. Prayers are not addressed to them.

SALVATION. *See* PLAN OF SALVATION.

SAMUELSON, CECIL O. (1941–). Physician, educator, **general authority**. Born on 1 August 1941 in Salt Lake City, Utah, Samuelson received his medical degree from the University of Utah, after which he served his residency at Duke University Medical Center. Returning to the University of Utah, he became successively professor of medicine, dean of the school of medicine, and vice president of health services. He became senior vice president of Intermountain Health Care. His interest in rheumatic and genetic diseases led to the publication of many articles as well as eight books or chapters of books.

Samuelson served as **stake high councilor**, stake **president**, and **regional representative**. In 1994 he became a member of the First **Quorum** of the **Seventy**. In 2003 Samuelson became the 12th president of **BYU**. He and his wife, Sharon, have five children.

SATAN. A spirit personage who leads the forces of evil and tries to defeat God's purposes. In the pre-mortal existence this spirit, a child of God, rebelled and took with him a portion of the host of heaven—that is, other spirits. Since then Satan has tried to frustrate the **plan of salvation**. Knowing human weaknesses, he tempts individuals to the path of destruction. But those who have faith and keep the **commandments** will be safe, for God is more powerful and will ultimately prevail.

SATANISM. Rituals and cultic practices that have included the worship of **Satan**. Found in different time periods and geographical locations, Satanism has appeared even in modern, relatively educated communities. Mormons are warned by their leaders to have nothing to do with such practices.

SCHISMS. Splinter groups that leave the main body on grounds of differing beliefs or rejection of authority. The phenomenon is not limited to Mormonism. With regard to the **LDS** Church, such groups began appearing in the 1830s. At the death of **Joseph Smith** rival claims to the **succession** were put forth. The most successful of these, the **RLDS** Church, became a significant denomination.

With the official end of **polygamy**, new schismatics appeared. The schismatic groups remained small. Many have disappeared.

Because it is impossible to give separate histories of each splinter group, the present reference work concentrates on the mainstream **Church of Jesus Christ of Latter-day Saints**, popularly called Mormons. A group of a few score or a few hundred people that does not claim to be part of the Church, whose members are **excommunicated** if discovered, cannot receive equal space in a work of this kind. Further information on the many different groups claiming a connection with the **restoration** may be found in Steven L. Shields, *The Latter Day Saint Churches: An Annoted Bibliography*, listed below in the bibliography. At the same time, it is recognized that **dissent** and schism occur. *See also* BICKERTONITES; COMMUNITY OF CHRIST; DISSENT; FUNDAMENTALISTS; MANIFESTO; REORGANIZED CHURCH OF JESUS CHRIST OF LATTER DAY SAINTS; RIGDON, SIDNEY; STRANG, JAMES J.; SUCCESSION; WIGHT, LYMAN.

SCHREINER, ALEXANDER (1901–1987). Musician, **Tabernacle** organist. Born in Nuernberg, Germany, on 31 July 1901, Schreiner attended the Melanchthon School. His parents were musical and gave him the opportunity to learn piano. At a very young age he began accompanying at the Mormon branch. In 1912 his family moved to Salt Lake City, Utah. Young Schreiner was placed in school and learned English by the "assimilation" method. He resumed piano study. Then he added organ study and earned money by playing as a theater organist. In 1922–1924 he served as a **missionary** in California.

Returning to Salt Lake City, he became one of the Tabernacle organists. On leave, he studied organ and theory in Paris with Henri Libert, Charles-Marie Widor, and Louis Vierne. He also received an appointment as University Organist at UCLA, where for nine years he taught classes and performed recitals. Anxious to pursue his education, Schreiner earned a B.A. from the University of Utah. Continuing on the graduate level in musical composition under **Leroy J. Robertson**, he earned a Ph.D. in 1954. For over 30 years he was on concert tour yearly. He composed many organ voluntaries as well as *Concerto for Full Orchestra and Organ*. Several Church hymns are set to music by Schreiner, including "God Loved Us, So He Sent His

Son." He was the recipient of several honorary degrees. He retired in 1977. Schreiner and his wife, Margaret, had four children.

SCIENCE. The basic attitude of Mormonism toward science has always been positive. Truth will not contradict truth. Especially in the 20th and 21st centuries many Mormons became scientists. Studies demonstrated that Utah had more scientists per capita than any other state. Examples of Mormon scientists are **Henry Eyring**, prominent chemist; Harvey Fletcher, physicist and inventor; and **Philo Farnsworth**, inventor of television.

Controversy over scientific issues has flared up from time to time, as Mormons with a literal interpretation of **scripture** have condemned those with a more flexible interpretation. In the early 21st century, when critics cited DNA analysis of native populations as evidence against the ***Book of Mormon***, several highly trained Mormon scientists responded by pointing out fallacies in the argument. The Mormon scientific community has faith in God's ultimate power while acknowledging that His will may be worked through a variety of means. *See also* CREATION.

SCOTT, RICHARD GORDON (1928–). Nuclear engineer, **general authority**. Born on 7 November 1928 in Pocatello, Idaho, Scott grew up in the Washington, D.C., area, where his father was employed by the Department of Agriculture. He graduated from George Washington University in mechanical engineering and, after serving as a **missionary** in Uruguay, returned to do postgraduate work in nuclear engineering at Oak Ridge, Tennessee. From 1953 to 1965 Scott served on the staff of Admiral Hyman Rickover. He directed research and application of the use of nuclear energy for military purposes and land-based power plants. Later he was a consultant for nuclear power companies.

In 1965 Scott was called to be president of the Argentina North Mission in Cordoba. After his return in 1969 he was a **regional representative** in Uruguay, Paraguay, and the eastern United States. In 1977 he became one of the First **Quorum** of the **Seventy** and in 1988 a member of the Quorum of the **Twelve Apostles**. He and his wife, Jeanene (who died in 1995), are the parents of seven children, five of them living.

SCRIPTURE. (1) The four “standard works”: the **Bible**, ***Book of Mormon***, ***Doctrine and Covenants***, and ***Pearl of Great Price***. Proclaiming of the *Book of Mormon* as scripture at the Church’s beginning in 1830 signaled a belief in an open, not closed, canon. The acceptance of both the *Doctrine and Covenants* and the *Pearl of Great Price* as standard works was made official by a **sustaining** vote of the members of the Church in **general conference**.

(2) Whatever is spoken by God’s representatives when they are divinely inspired (*Doctrine and Covenants*, section 68). Although in common parlance “scripture,” or “scriptures,” as used among Mormons refers to the four standard works, this broader meaning is a reminder that **revelation** continues, that the living **prophets** express God’s will to the current generation, and that God, the ultimate source of truth, is not to be constrained. *See also* PROPHETS; REVELATION.

SEALING. **Ordinance** performed in the **temples** joining husband and wife, parents and children, in a relationship that continues after death as well as during mortality. When a temple **marriage** establishes such a sealing between husband and wife, children born to that union are considered “born in the covenant” and do not have to be sealed in a separate ceremony, for the eternal **family** unit was created by the temple marriage. People who are married outside of the temple may, upon their conversion or a later decision to do so, go to the temple to have their marriage sealed. Any children they have may go with them and participate in the sealing ordinance. Participation in temple ordinances is dependent upon **worthiness**, which is determined by a **bishop**. Ultimate enjoyment of the eternal blessings is always contingent upon faithfulness.

SECT. *See* CULT.

SEMINARIES. Religious instruction for youth of high school age, roughly 14 to 18, provided on a released-time basis for one class period each day in buildings adjacent to or nearby the regular school. The first seminary of this type began in 1912 in Salt Lake City, Utah; the program then expanded through those western states with a sufficient population of Church members. Seminary classes are taught by individuals with the same training and credentials as teachers in the public schools. The four-year curriculum includes Old Testament, New Testament, ***Doctrine and Covenants***, and ***Book of Mormon***. Where the released-time arrangement has not been allowed, perhaps because of an insufficient population of Church members, seminaries are conducted in the early morning prior to the beginning of the school day. Alternatively, especially for scattered students where other arrangements are not feasible, correspondence or home-study courses are available. *See also* INSTITUTES OF RELIGION.

SENIOR CITIZENS. In the late 19th century, organized outings and celebrations for "old folks" at least gave some recognition to the most advanced age group. At present, their health enhanced by adherence to the **Word of Wisdom**, more and more Mormons, like everyone else, are living many years beyond retirement.

The inherent problems of old age—dependency, loneliness, pain, disorientation—are faced by Mormons like everyone else. The increased incidence of Alzheimer's disease has been a painful challenge for many families. On the other hand, for Mormon senior citizens the "golden years" are alleviated by following a program of **home teaching** and **visiting teaching** that, when it works, sees to it that each person has others assigned to provide friendship, assist when required, and report special needs; provide activity in the **temples**, which occupies many, giving them something to do, people to associate with, and a sense of usefulness; give opportunities for **missions**, with retired couples especially in demand, some of them serving one mission after another; and surround with strong families that continue to accept responsibility for the love and care of aging parents and grandparents. *See also* FAMILY.

SEVENTY. An office in the **priesthood**. First established during the **Ohio Period** in 1835, the seventies had primarily a **missionary** responsibility. They were to work under the direction of the **Quorum** of the **Twelve Apostles**. For most of its history the seventy were simply those holders of the **Melchizedek Priesthood** who were ordained to this office with special orientation toward proselytizing. The seven presidents were called the First Council of the Seventy and were regarded as **general authorities** of the Church.

In 1975, to meet the needs of the expanding membership, the First Quorum of the Seventy was organized. It included those who previously had been called **assistants to the twelve**. Its leadership was a presidency of seven. In 1986 **stake** quorums of seventies were discontinued. In 1989 a Second Quorum of the Seventy was organized, also under the direction of the same seven presidents, the Presidency of the Seventy. Membership in the second quorum was to last about five years.

Under the direction of the **First Presidency** and the Quorum of the Twelve Apostles, members of the First and Second Quorums of the Seventy supervise training of leaders, attend **stake conferences**, and especially serve as presidencies over the **areas** of the Church throughout the world. In 1997 three additional quorums were created—the Third, Fourth, and Fifth Quorums—made up of men called to serve for five or six years on a Church-service basis. That is, they were to continue their present employment and reside in their homes. Of the 134 men first called to this position, 128 had already been serving as area authorities and henceforth would be identified as **area authority seventies**.

SHIPP, ELLIS REYNOLDS (1847–1939). Physician, educator. Born in Iowa to William F. and Anna Hawley Reynolds, Ellis emigrated with her family to Utah shortly after they joined the church. After the death of her mother and until her father remarried a year later, Ellis shouldered the responsibility for her father's house and her four brothers and sisters. She attended school with **Brigham Young**'s children in the Beehive House. In 1866 she married Milford B. Shipp. They were the parents of 10 children, 5 of whom survived infancy.

Shipp attended the University of Deseret and the Woman's Medical College of Pennsylvania, graduating in 1878. She did postgraduate work at the University of Michigan Medical School. After she returned to Utah, she opened a School of Obstetrics and Nursing in Salt Lake City, teaching women physiology, obstetrical procedures, and basic health information. She served on the board of the Deseret Hospital. After World War I's outbreak, Shipp opened extension programs in Mormon communities in Blackfoot, Idaho; Vernal, Utah; and Colonia Juarez, Mexico. She also participated in the Utah

Reaper's Club and the Utah Woman's Press Club. She also published a volume of poetry. Just four years before her death, the Woman's Medical College awarded her an honorary degree and Utah inducted her into the Utah Hall of Fame.

SHUMWAY, ERIC B. (1939–). President, **BYU–Hawaii**. Raised in St. Johns, Arizona, Shumway served as a **missionary** in Tonga before graduating from **BYU** with bachelor's and master's degrees in English, in 1964 and 1966, respectively. His book *Intensive Course in Tongan* was published by the University of Hawaii Press in 1971. In 1973, he received his doctorate in English literature at the University of Virginia.

Shumway accepted a position as instructor of English at **BYU–Hawaii**, then called Church College of Hawaii. In 1975 he was named chair of the Communications and Language Arts Division and in 1980 vice president for academics.

President of the Tongan Mission from 1986 to 1989, Shumway returned to Hawaii as acting president of the **Polynesian Cultural Center.** In 1994 he became president of BYU–Hawaii. In 2007 he was called to be president of the Nuku'alofa (Tonga) Temple. He has served as **bishop, high councilor, stake** president, and **area authority seventy.** He and his wife, Carolyn, have seven children. In 1996–1997 Carolyn was named American National Mother of the Year.

SINGLES. Unmarried adults who are Mormons face the same economic and social challenges as other singles. In addition, they must find their way in a Church that includes **marriage** among the prerequisites for the highest salvation.

A variety of factors have increased the number of single adults: later marriage age, increased **divorce**, and acceptance of the single lifestyle in the larger society. One study showed that **LDS** single adults were divided into three groups: divorced or separated, 23 percent; widowed, 13 percent; never married, 63 percent. Among these singles there is consistently a gender disproportion, with more women than men.

The Church has responded to the needs of singles by providing recreational activities, appointing committees for single adults on the

ward and **stake** level, establishing wards or branches for singles where the demand is sufficient, and including material on singles in manuals and Church periodicals.

SMITH, BARBARA BRADSHAW (1922–). Relief Society president. Born in Salt Lake City, Utah, on 26 January 1922, Barbara Bradshaw attended the local schools. She married Douglas H. Smith, an insurance executive, who later became a **general authority** as a member of the Second **Quorum** of the **Seventy**. They have seven children. In the Relief Society she had experience as a teacher and as **ward** president. (Her mother and sister were presidents of their ward Relief Societies at exactly the same time.) Smith served on the Relief Society **stake** board and then on the general board.

From 1974 to 1984 she was general president of the Relief Society, a decade during which the movement for women's liberation became more assertive and women's issues assumed an unprecedented prominence. Employment, **birth control**, abortion, **divorce**, one-parent families—such issues could not be ignored. In the meantime, economic conditions created welfare needs, and the women leaders of the Relief Society participated on every level of Welfare Services.

An opponent of the Equal Rights Amendment, Barbara Smith found herself under attack from those on the other side. She explained her position: "I stand as a representative of an organization that is in favor of rights for women. However, we may differ with some people on the best way or ways to achieve these rights. In my opinion, the Equal Rights Amendment is not the way" (B. Smith, *A Fruitful Season*, 227). She appeared on Phil Donahue's television show to explain this position.

Attempting to meet the needs of a variety of Mormon women—old and young; different races, ethnic groups, and nationalities; married and single—the Relief Society under President Smith's leadership adapted its teaching materials and introduced new resources. To celebrate the achievements and contributions of women, the Monument to Women was created in Nauvoo, Illinois, and dedicated in June 1978. Upon her release as general president in 1984, Smith accompanied her husband to Hong Kong, where for three years he served in the presidency of the **area**.

SMITH, BATHSHEBA BIGLER (1822–1910). Suffragist, **Relief Society** general president. Born 3 May 1822 in Shinston, West Virginia, Bathsheba grew up in a well-to-do southern family, so she received a good education considering the time and place of her childhood. When she was 15, her family joined the Church and emigrated to Missouri just in time for the final expulsion of Mormons. Her family then moved to Nauvoo, Illinois, where in 1841 she married George A. Smith, then a member of the **Quorum** of the **Twelve Apostles** and later a member of the **First Presidency**. Early in her marriage Smith faced hardships, including the frequent absence of her **missionary** husband. Her husband also entered into plural marriage. As first wife, Smith often had to mediate problems between other wives. She was a charter member of the Relief Society at its organization in 1842 in Nauvoo.

After moving to Utah, Bathsheba taught her children and engaged in charitable work. As her children reached maturity, she traveled with her husband on his Church assignments. Following her husband's death in 1875, Smith worked in the **temple** and from 1888 to 1901 served as a **counselor** to the **LDS** Relief Society's general president, Zina Young. After Young's death, Smith was called as the general president. She served from 1901 until her death in 1910. During her tenure, Smith encouraged women to become self-sufficient by learning how to sew, weave, spin, knit, raise their own food, and better their homes. Smith also campaigned in the women's suffrage movement.

SMITH, EMMA HALE (1804–1879). Relief Society president. Born in Harmony, Pennsylvania, where she met **Joseph Smith**, then working as a laborer in her area. Denied the permission of her parents to marry Joseph, Emma eloped (she was 22) on 18 January 1827, after which the newlyweds moved to Manchester, New York. Joining the new Church in 1830, Emma experienced **persecution** and frequent moves along with her husband. Her first three children, including a set of twins, died soon after birth, as did two other infants and an adopted baby boy. Surviving sons were Joseph III, Frederick, Alexander Hale, and David Hyrum.

She was appointed to select hymns for the new Church (a compilation published in 1835). In Nauvoo, Illinois, Smith became president in 1842 of the new organization for women, the Relief Society. She was among the first women to experience the **ordinance** of endowment even prior to the completion of the Nauvoo Temple in 1846.

When **polygamy** was "unofficially" introduced about 1840, Emma consented to her husband's marriage to plural wives but soon had second thoughts. Torn between aversion to this practice and loyalty to her husband, she suffered great emotional stress. After Joseph's death in June 1844, she refused to accept the leadership of **Brigham Young**, quarreling with him over property claims.

During the remainder of her life, Emma remained in Nauvoo, denying that her late husband had introduced polygamy—a denial psychologically understandable but untrue to historical reality. She married Lewis Bidamon, who assisted in raising her remaining five children. In 1860 her oldest son, Joseph III, became president of the **RLDS** Church, which she joined.

Although tension continued to exist between her and the leaders of the **Church of Jesus Christ of Latter-day Saints** in the West, she treated Mormon visitors kindly. In time they preferred to overlook the closing phase of her life by emphasizing instead the courage, faith, and loyalty of her life up to the death of her husband in 1844. *See also* TEMPLES.

SMITH, GEORGE ALBERT (1870–1951). General authority, Church **president**. Born on 4 April 1870 in Salt Lake City, Utah, George was the son of John Henry Smith and grandson of George A. Smith, both of whom were in the **Quorum** of the **Twelve Apostles** and **counselors** in the **First Presidency**. He studied at Brigham Young Academy and the University of Utah. He married Lucy Emily Woodruff, a granddaughter of **Wilford Woodruff**.

From 1892 to 1894, he was a **missionary** in the Southern States Mission. Work for the Republican Party led to being appointed receiver for the Land Office in 1896 and again in 1902. In 1903, at the age of 33, Smith was called to the Quorum of the Twelve Apostles. He had a special interest in the YMMIA. He served on its general board and, from 1921 to 1935, as its general superintendent. An advocate of the **Boy Scout** organization, he promoted its inclusion in the Church youth program. For years of service in scouting he was awarded the Silver Beaver and the Silver Buffalo.

Although afflicted with poor eyesight and chronic debilitation (from lupus erythematosus), Smith kept busily involved. President of the European Mission from 1919 to 1921, he made a special effort to make friends with government leaders. In 1938 he visited the Church missions in Australia, New Zealand, and several **Pacific** islands.

Smith took a keen interest in Church history sites and trails. He attended the dedication of a monument to **Joseph Smith** at Sharon, Vermont, in 1905. He helped to found the Utah Pioneer Trails and Landmarks Association, which erected many monuments, including the **"This Is the Place" Monument**. By seniority he became **president** of the Quorum of Twelve Apostles in 1943. Upon the death of President **Heber J. Grant** in 1945, Smith became president of the Church. He was 75 years old.

For six years, from 1945 to 1951, Smith led the Church. Among the achievements of these postwar years were the dedication of the new Idaho Falls Temple in 1945, the construction of many meetinghouses, the expansion of a program for microfilming genealogical records, and the rapid growth of missionary activity. Under his direction the Church sent substantial relief supplies to **Europe**.

His personal creed, which he allowed to be published in 1932, was an inspiration to many. Among its 10 goals or ideals were "I would be a friend to the friendless and find joy in ministering to the needs of the poor" and "I would not be an enemy to any living soul" (Pusey, *Builders of the Kingdom*, 255).

SMITH, HYRUM (1800–1844). Patriarch, general authority. Older brother and close associate of **Joseph Smith**, Hyrum was associate president of the Church at the time of his death. Born on 9 February 1800 in Tunbridge, Vermont, where he received some primary schooling, Hyrum moved with family to Manchester, New York, about 1816. For the next several years he worked on the family farm and occasionally hired out. He married Jerusha Barden in 1826.

When his brother Joseph was working on the manuscript of the ***Book of Mormon***, Hyrum, a believer from the first, assisted. He was one of the eight **witnesses of the *Book of Mormon*** allowed to see and handle the metal plates. When the Church was organized in 1830, Hyrum was among the six original members. Immediately he began preaching, going on several **missions** in New York and later in Ohio and Missouri. Along with the rest of the Church, Hyrum experienced the **persecutions**, moved to Missouri, served several months in jail, and spent the closing years of his life in Illinois. After bearing six children, his wife Jerusha died. His second wife, Mary Fielding, bore two more children, including **Joseph F. Smith**.

In addition to being the companion and confidant of his brother, Hyrum held important positions in the Church: assistant president from 1834, **counselor** in the **First Presidency** from 1837, presiding patriarch, and associate president. In June 1844 he refused the opportunity to take his family to Cincinnati, instead staying by his brother Joseph during their imprisonment in Carthage Jail. There both of them were killed by a mob on 27 June 1844. Latter-day Saints regard the brothers as martyrs.

SMITH, JOSEPH (1805–1844). Founding **prophet** of the **Church of Jesus Christ of Latter-day Saints**, Church **president;** sometimes known as Joseph Smith Jr. to distinguish him from his father. The external life of Joseph Smith—his places of residence, his travels, his public statements—is easily enough recounted, although even on this level his life was not easily lived, for he had more than his share of pain and trial. The internal life, the religious experiences, the dimension of **revelation** or **prophecy**—these are, of course, understood differently by believers and nonbelievers. He recognized the ultimate ineffability of such matters in a famous statement made at the end of his life: "No man knows my history; I cannot tell it. I shall never undertake it. If I had not experienced what I have, I should not have believed it myself" (J. F. Smith, *Teachings of the Prophet Joseph Smith*, 361.) In the present brief sketch the emphasis will be on the external matters, with the religious experiences and contributions presented in the way Smith told them to others and the way they have been accepted by his followers.

Born in Sharon, Vermont, on 23 December 1805, Joseph was the third living son of Joseph Smith Sr. and Lucy Mack Smith. Poor but hard working, the Smith family—nine children, not counting stillbirths or infant deaths—moved from farm to farm. In 1816, like other New Englanders, they moved into New York State, settling on a farm near Palmyra. Broadly Christian, reading and believing the **Bible**, the Smiths became unsettled over the question of religion during revivals. In this context, young Joseph, still a teenager, prayed to God, asking what he should do. The result was the **First Vision**, during which the Lord instructed him to join none of the existing churches, for they had all gone astray.

During the 1820s, between the ages of 15 and 25, Joseph Smith grew to adulthood, worked on the family farm, and hired out as a laborer. Reputed to be able to find treasure through a seer stone, he was briefly employed to dig for buried Spanish gold, but the enterprise failed. The most important events of these years, as he later saw them, were the appearances of an angel, who told him where to find buried metal plates. He was not allowed to take them at first, for he coveted them for their monetary value, but in 1827, after four years of discipline and purifying his heart, Joseph was allowed to take possession of them for purposes of translation. The same year he married **Emma Hale Smith**.

During the next two and a half years, Joseph moved to Harmony, Pennsylvania, and with the assistance of scribes worked on translating the hieroglyphics from the plates into English. Although ridiculed by ministers and others, he had the confidence of his parents, his siblings, his wife, and a few friends who provided financial support. Some of these were selected as **witnesses of the *Book of Mormon***.

When the resurrected John the Baptist appeared to Smith and Cowdery and gave them **priesthood** authority, they **baptized** each other and began baptizing others. In the spring of 1830 the *Book of Mormon* was published and on 6 April the Church was organized with six men to satisfy the legal requirement. During the next 14 years, from age 24 to 38, Joseph Smith's life was anything but dull. The head of a church and a movement, he had to answer many specific questions. Revelations on matters ranging from instruction to individuals on their duty to administrative details to lofty theological principles were issued by the prophet one by one. Eventually these were compiled into a volume entitled ***Doctrine and Covenants***.

Smith led the fledgling **LDS** Church, with a hundred or so members, to a new location at Kirtland, Ohio. At the same time he announced that the new **Zion** was to be built in western Missouri. During most of the 1830s, therefore, Mormon converts converged on these two locations. Smith himself lived at Kirtland but led an expedition to assist his persecuted followers in Missouri and in 1837 moved there with his family.

Opposition to the new religion had started early. Harassment in New York, verbal denunciation, burning of houses and barns, tarring and feathering, beating, and lynching—the early Mormons experienced all of this as not only terrorism but as **persecution**, the expected fate of the Lord's disciples. Smith himself had his life threatened and was tarred and feathered in Ohio. In Missouri, where the Mormons were driven from the state, Joseph Smith and several of his associates were imprisoned for several months in a jail at Liberty, Missouri. In the depths of despair, he still managed to maintain the rightness of his position, to provide inspiration to his followers, and to produce some of his most sublime revelations (*Doctrine and Covenants*, sections 121–123).

After escaping his captors, Joseph joined the bedraggled Mormons in western Illinois and there on the banks of the Mississippi River established a new center at Commerce, renamed Nauvoo. Illinois was the setting for the final period of Smith's life. In addition to his position as president of the Church, Smith became mayor of the city and an officer its militia. Missouri officials demanded Smith's extradition. Efforts to obtain protection or relief from the federal government came to naught. In addition to the rising tide of **anti-Mormonism** in surrounding towns, a small number of **apostates** denounced Smith, and to some extent the two groups cooperated.

Matters came to a head with the publication of an opposition newspaper, *The Nauvoo Expositor*, and a decision by the city council, including Smith, to destroy the press. Outraged opponents decried the act as inimical to freedom of the press. Some of these enemies, in speeches and editorials, called for solving the Mormon problem by the violence of "powder and ball." Charged with riot for destroying the press and assured by the state's governor that he would be safe, Smith was arrested and placed in Carthage Jail. Accompanying him were his brother, **Hyrum Smith**, Apostle **John Taylor**, and others.

Whipped up by anti-Mormons, militia members transformed themselves into a lynch mob. On 27 June 1844, with blackened faces, they fired into the jail from the outside and, charging up the stairs, attacked from the inside with guns blazing. In a few moments Hyrum Smith and Joseph Smith were killed. John Taylor was wounded.

It is hard to be neutral about Joseph Smith. His enemies and detractors viewed him as an imposter, a con man who took advantage of a gullible people. Mormons remembered his kindness and humor and charismatic leadership. Mormons do not believe that he was perfect. They do not worship him. For them he was a human being but one chosen by God to be the prophet of the last **dispensation**. He brought back to earth **priesthood** authority; restored the Church; brought forth the *Book of Mormon*, *Doctrine and Covenants*, and ***Pearl of Great Price***; led his people through times of perilous persecution and displacement; founded a city; and revealed many important religious truths. When he died, he was 38 years old. *See also* APOSTASY; CHURCH OF JESUS CHRIST OF LATTER-DAY SAINTS; COWDERY, OLIVER; ZION'S CAMP.

SMITH, JOSEPH F. (1838–1918). General authority, Church **president**. Although Fielding is his middle name, he is traditionally known as Joseph F. to distinguish him from his son. Born to **Hyrum Smith** and Mary Fielding Smith in Far West, Missouri, on 13 November 1838, he was carried by his mother to refuge in Illinois. He was only five years old when his father and uncle, the **prophet Joseph Smith**, were killed. As his mother took charge of seven children during the flight from Nauvoo, Illinois, and the trek to the Salt Lake Valley, young Joseph F. drove his mother's wagon. He was nine when they arrived in Salt Lake City.

Joseph F. worked hard in the fields and tending cattle. He was only 13 when his mother died. Two years later, having had only minimal schooling, he was called as a **missionary** to Hawaii, where for the next four years he mastered the language and gained leadership experience. Soon after his return he married Levira Smith. With her permission he married as a plural wife Julina Lambson, who was later followed by four others. He eventually fathered 43 children.

From 1860 to 1863 Joseph F. was a **missionary** in Great Britain. He was elected to the Utah Territory legislature and the Salt Lake City council. In the Church he served on his stake **high council**, worked in the Historian's Office, and officiated in ceremonies in the Endowment House. In 1867 he was ordained a member of the Quorum of **Twelve Apostles**. In 1874–1875 and again in 1877 he was president of the European and British Missions. For a while he was president of the Davis County, Utah, **stake**. In 1880, at the age of 41, he became second **counselor** in the **First Presidency** of the Church.

When **John Taylor** died in 1887, Smith continued as one of the twelve apostles and became a counselor to new Church president **Wilford Woodruff**. With the coming of national political parties to Utah, Joseph F. became a Republican. He participated in the Church policy decisions of the 1890s, continuing as a counselor to **Lorenzo Snow** in 1898. When Snow died in 1901, Joseph F. Smith became **president** of the Church.

As president, he worked to bring Mormonism into the 20th century by emphasizing its American loyalty, first in the Spanish-American War and later during World War I. Although **anti-Mormonism** continued during the hearings for Senator-elect **Reed Smoot** and afterward, President Smith emphasized education, missionary expansion, the construction of needed Church buildings, and the acquisition of historic sites. Known for his sensible discussions of doctrinal matters, he gave many sermons and wrote articles, from which the book *Gospel Doctrine* was compiled in 1918. A **revelation**, "Vision of the Redemption of the Dead," was added to the ***Doctrine and Covenants*** in 1981. *See also* POLYGAMY.

SMITH, JOSEPH FIELDING (1876–1972). Historian, doctrinal authority, **general authority**, Church **president**. Born in Salt Lake City, Utah, on 19 July 1876, Joseph Fielding Smith was the son of **Joseph F. Smith** and Julina Lambson. Since his father was out of the country during much of the 1880s, the boy was supervised by his mother, a midwife. He milked cows and did other farm work. In 1898 at the age of 22 he married Louie Shurtliff and the next year was called as a **missionary** to England.

Returning in 1901, Smith took employment in the Church Historian's Office. When his father became president of the Church that same year, he became a confidant and assistant. In 1905 and again in 1907 he wrote pamphlets defending the Church's practices against critics. Louie gave birth to two daughters, but during her third pregnancy she had complications and died. After several months of loneliness, Joseph married Ethel Reynolds, who became the mother of five sons and four daughters.

In April 1910 he was called to the **Quorum** of the **Twelve Apostles**. **Temple** and genealogical work were themes he often stressed.

He edited the *Utah Genealogical and Historical Magazine*. For 20 years he was in the presidency of the Salt Lake Temple either as a **counselor** or as president. Church history also was a passion. From his initial appointment as assistant Church historian in 1906 Smith went on to become Church historian from 1921 to 1970.

In 1937 his wife Ethel died. The next year, at age 62, he married Jessie Evans, a well-known contralto. A loving companion for the remaining 34 years of his life, she had a keen sense of humor that made her a well-known character in her own right. From 1950 Joseph Fielding was president (or acting president) of the twelve apostles. In 1965 he was **called** to be a counselor to the **First Presidency**. In 1970, at age 94, he became president of the Church. He supervised the reorganization of some departments, the expansion of missionary work, and the dedication of two temples.

SMOOT, REED (1862–1941). U.S. senator from Utah, **general authority**. Although born on 10 January 1862 in Salt Lake City, Utah, Smoot was raised in Provo, Utah, where his father was mayor and **stake president**. Reed studied at the new Brigham Young Academy from 1876. As a young man of 22 he became superintendent of the Provo Woolen Mills and also married Alpha Eldredge. Except for about a year's absence as a **missionary** in England (1890–1891) his base of operations was Provo. Manager of Provo Commercial and Savings Bank, he was also vice president of Grant Central Mining and a director of Los Angeles and Salt Lake Railroad. From 1884 he was appointed a director of the Utah Territory Insane Asylum in Provo. In 1900 he became a member of the **Quorum** of the **Twelve Apostles**.

Elected U.S. senator from Utah in 1903, after clearing his candidacy with the Church presidency, Smoot was immediately challenged. Issues included the alleged continuation of **polygamy** among the Mormons and Smoot's status as a Church **general authority**. For two and a half years the Senate Committee on Privileges held hearings. Accusers testified. Church leaders were summoned and cross-examined. Although the committee voted against Smoot, the Senate itself allowed him to keep his seat. For about 30 years Reed Smoot was an apostle in the Church, a leader of Utah Republicans, and a highly regarded member of the U.S. Senate.

SNOW, ELIZA ROXCY (1804–1887). Poet, author of hymns, **Relief Society** president. Born in Massachusetts but raised in Ohio, Eliza learned of Mormonism and in 1835 with other family members joined the new faith. With other Latter-day Saints the Snows were forced to leave Ohio, then to leave Missouri, and then to seek refuge in Illinois. Eliza published poems defending and encouraging her people and became a school teacher.

In 1842 she participated in the founding of the **Relief Society**, serving as secretary. She also became a plural wife of **Joseph Smith**, following whose death in 1844 she became a plural wife of **Brigham Young**. With the other Mormons who were driven from Nauvoo, Snow made her way westward, arriving in the Salt Lake Valley in the fall of 1847. There she continued to write and publish poetry, participated in a study group known as the Polysophical Society, and after 1866 led the reorganized and revitalized Relief Society. She also helped found organizations for children and young women. Until her death in 1887 was looked upon as leader of the Church's women. She wrote several hymns, including "O My Father," which includes the idea of a pre-mortal existence prior to this life and of a Heavenly Mother.

SNOW, LORENZO (1814–1901). Missionary, general authority, president of the Church. Born on 3 April 1814 and raised on a farm in Ohio, Snow received not only a common school education but, unusual for the time, completed high school and one term at Oberlin College. Becoming acquainted with Mormonism when **Joseph Smith** briefly resided at nearby Hiram, Ohio, the Snow family, including Lorenzo's sister **Eliza R. Snow**, became converts, Lorenzo in 1836. During his 20s he gained experience through a series of missions, presided over congregations in London, and led a party of emigrants from England to Illinois.

Snow arrived in Salt Lake City, Utah, in 1848 and one year later was named to the **Quorum** of the **Twelve Apostles**. Another mission took him to Italy, Switzerland, and Malta. In the 1860s he went to the Hawaiian Islands for a brief time and helped impose discipline on a rebellious leader. When not away on such missions, Snow was a community leader in Utah. For 29 years he served in the territorial legislature. He led the settlement of Brigham City, which became a model of economic cooperation and later impressed the visitor and writer Edward Bellamy.

Snow married four wives before leaving Illinois. In 1886 he served a prison term for violating the Edmunds Act but was released in early 1887 when his conviction was partially overturned by the U.S. Supreme Court. By seniority he became president of the twelve apostles in 1889 and in 1893 president of the newly dedicated Salt Lake Temple. In 1898, although old and weak, Lorenzo Snow became president of the Church. During his three-year administration he extricated the Church from serious financial indebtedness by strongly urging members to pay **tithing** and issuing bonds, extended missionary proselytizing to Japan, and issued with his **counselors** an address to the world. *See also* POLYGAMY.

SOARES, ULISSES (1958–). General authority. Soares was born on 2 October 1958 in Sao Paulo, Brazil. His parents converted to the Church when he was a child, and he was baptized when eight years old. After serving as a full-time **missionary** in the Brazil Rio de Janeiro Mission, he resumed his education, earning a bachelor's degree in economics from Pontificia Catholic University and an MBA from National Institute of Post Graduate Study. Employed by Pirelli Tire Company, he changed course when offered employment by the Church, first as an auditor and then as Director of Temporal Affairs.

Soares's experience in Church **callings** has been extensive. He was **elders** quorum president, **counselor** in the bishopric, **stake** executive secretary, **high councilor,** and stake **president**. Then for three years he was president of the Portugal Porto Mission. In April 2005, he became a general authority as a member of the First **Quorum** of the **Seventy**. He and his wife, Rosana, are the parents of three children.

SORENSEN, DAVID E. (1933–). Businessman, entrepreneur, **general authority**. Born on 29 June 1933 in Aurora, Utah, Sorensen attended **BYU**, Utah State University, and the University of Utah. He was a **missionary** in the Central Atlantic State Mission. After military service in the U.S. Army he had a successful career as president of United Homes, Inc.; chief executive officer of North American Health Care; chairman of Cal-Utah Feeders; and board vice chairman of Nevada Community Bank. He was a **bishop**, **high**

councilor, **stake** president, and **president** of the Canada Halifax Mission. Called to the Second **Quorum** of the **Seventy** in 1992, Sorensen became a member of the First Quorum of the Seventy in 1995. He and his wife, Verla, are the parents of seven children.

SORENSON, JOHN L. (1924–). Anthropologist, expert on the ***Book of Mormon***. Born on 8 April 1924 in Smithfield, Utah, Sorenson received his early education there. After service as a first lieutenant in the U.S. military during World War II, being trained as a meteorologist, he served as a **missionary** in New Zealand and the Cook Islands, where he prepared a Raratongan grammar. From **BYU** he received a B.S. and M.A. degree in archaeology, after which he pursued a doctorate in anthropology at UCLA, receiving the Ph.D. in 1961.

Sorenson became director of Social Sciences for General Research Corporation, Santa Barbara, California, from 1964 to 1969. He headed his own research corporation before returning to BYU in 1971. For 15 years he taught courses in anthropology and served as consultant in applied social sciences, chairman of University Studies, and chairman of the Department of Anthropology. His doctoral dissertation explored the effects of Geneva Steel on two Utah communities. Unconventional warfare and insurgency, along with transportation policy, were the focus of his research in the 1960s. A cultural anthropologist in the broad sense, Sorenson has been interested in language, cultural networks, and group personality.

Throughout his adult life Sorenson has also been especially persevering as a student of the *Book of Mormon*, examining its text through the eyes of an anthropologist and exploring its possible Mesoamerican milieu. A participant in the University Archaeology Society and the New World Archaeological Foundation, he prepared reports and published papers on many specific topics. His early *The World of the* Book of Mormon (1955), based on a series of lectures, was followed by studies of such topics as brass plates, wheeled figurines, and the *Book of Mormon* as a Mesoamerican codex.

Sorenson's *An Ancient American Setting for the* Book of Mormon appeared in 1985, an unrivaled work in showing respect for the text and due regard for geographical reality and the present state of knowledge about ancient Mesoamerica. In 1990, with Martin H. Raish, he compiled a two-volume bibliography of pre-Columbian transoceanic contacts with America. In 1998, he published *Images of Ancient America: Visualizing* Book of Mormon *Life*, a massive photographic compilation of suggested parallels, and the same year he began editing *Journal of* Book of Mormon *Studies*.

Among the founders of **FARMS**, Sorenson has been highly effective in organizing team research, facilitating publication of information as it becomes available, and encouraging younger scholars. In addition to his service as a missionary, Sorenson has at different times been a **bishop** and **high councilor**. He retired from his university duties as an emeritus professor in 1986 but has continued his scholarly interests.

SORENSON, VIRGINIA (1912–1991). Novelist. Born on 17 February 1912 in Provo, Utah, Virginia Eggertson also lived in Manti and American Fork, Utah, during her childhood. In the early 1930s she was a student at **BYU**. After marrying Frederick Sorenson, an English professor, she moved to California. Two children were born. Later, after a divorce, she married the novelist Alec Waugh, with whom she lived in Tangier. In 1981 they returned to the United States. She died in North Carolina in 1991.

Sorenson's writings included such children's books as *Miracles on Maple Hill* (1957), for which she won the Newbery Award. Her Mormon people and culture provided the subject matter for most of her fiction, including *A Little Lower Than the Angels* (1942), *On This Star* (1946), *The Neighbors* (1947), *The Evening and the Morning* (1949), *Many Heavens* (1954), and *Kingdom Come* (1960). A series of semi-fictional pieces first appearing in the *New Yorker* was published as *Where Nothing Is Long Ago* (1963).

SOUTH AMERICA. Parley P. Pratt attempted to proselytize in Chile in 1851–1852, but had practically no success. In 1925 the South American continent was dedicated for the preaching of Mormonism. At first conversions were limited to a few German immigrants.

After World War II **missionaries** were sent to most countries of South America. Chapels were constructed. **Scriptures**, lesson materials, and other publications were translated into Spanish and Portuguese. By the 1960s the Church was experiencing spectacular growth. In Brazil the first **stake** was created in 1966, and by the end of 2005 there were 193 stakes; 1,247 **wards**; and 928,926 members. Two **general authorities** have been Brazilians—Helio da Rocha Camargo and Helvecio Martins, the first **black** general authority.

Other South American countries have seen the Church grow from small beginnings, in some cases from zero to impressive heights. At the end of 2005, the Mormon presence in South America stood as follows:

Country	Members	Stakes	Wards	Temples
Argentina	348,396	70	451	1
Bolivia	148,630	22	156	1
Brazil	897,091	187	1,212	4
Colombia	149,973	26	158	1
Ecuador	170,736	32	212	1
Paraguay	61,308	9	56	1
Uruguay	86,943	16	103	1
Venezuela	134,597	24	173	1

Missionary work had also begun in Guyana, Surinam, and French Guiana. South America was divided into six **areas**: South America North, South America South, South America West, Chile, Brazil North, and Brazil South. Much of the success of the Church in South America can be attributed to the build-up of local leadership. As much as one third or even one half of the missionary force in these countries is made up of indigenous young men and women. After completion of their missions, they form a pool of talent and leadership experience.

SPAFFORD, BELLE SMITH (1895–1982). President of the **Relief Society**. Born on 8 October 1895 in Salt Lake City, Utah, Belle was educated through the secondary school level and then spent two years at the University of Utah. Thirsty for education, she later took many additional courses. In 1921 she married Earl Spafford. Named general president of the **Relief Society** in 1945, Belle occupied a prominent leadership role for nearly 30 years. Her accomplishments included raising funds for the construction of a beautiful Relief Society building, encouraging women to do voluntary work in the community, and establishing a health **missionary** program. She also participated in national and international organizations, including the National Council of Women, of which she served as president in 1968–1970.

SPERRY, SIDNEY B. (1895–1977). Educator, linguist. In his honor, since 1971 an annual symposium, the Sidney B. Sperry Lecture Series, brings together at **BYU** scholars who present papers on selected topics from the **scriptures**.

SPORTS. From almost the beginning of the Church, members have participated in sports activities to some degree. We know, for example, that **Joseph Smith** enjoyed wrestling, pitching quoits, and even playing an early form of baseball or one-o-cat. It was really after the Mormons moved west that sports blossomed. Especially after the Civil War, Utah Territory Church members played cricket, baseball, bowling, boxing, wrestling, horse racing, and later football and basketball. Some of these activities took place at the Church academies and **BYU**.

In 1971, with a rapidly expanding **membership**, Church leaders ended the all-Church competitions but encouraged a continuation of sports activity on the local level. Anxious to provide wholesome activities for young people, local leaders of **Young Men** and **Young Women** included sports in their weekday programs. During winter months these often take place in **ward** cultural halls. Intercollegiate and intramural athletics are sponsored by BYU, and **BYU–Hawaii**. **BYU–Idaho** has an extensive program in intramural athletics. *See also* DANCE.

STAKE. A stake is an administrative subdivision of the Church comprising several **wards**. Depending on the number and size of the wards, stake **membership** ranges from 1,500 to 3,000 members. The term is derived from Isaiah 54:2–3.

Year	Stakes
1950	180
1960	319
1970	537

1980	1,218
1990	1,784
2000	2,581

By April 2007 there were 2,745 stakes worldwide.

STANDARD WORKS. *See* SCRIPTURE.

STEPHENS, EVAN (1854–1930). Director, **Mormon Tabernacle Choir**, 1890–1916. In addition to directing the **Mormon Tabernacle Choir**, Evan Stephens had private students and conducted special choruses of children and youth. For a period of time he headed the Stephens Opera Company.

STRANG, JAMES J. (1813–1856). Leader of a schismatic group. Strang's community encountered internal dissension and outside opposition. In 1856 Strang was assassinated. Before he expired, he refused to name a successor. The Strangites on Beaver Island were rounded up, put onto steamships, and taken to Chicago where they disembarked. Many of them gravitated to those who in 1860 would form the **RLDS** Church. Those who clung to their Strangite identity were led for several decades by a disciple of Strang, Wingfield Watson. The Strangites now number less than 100, mainly living in and around Burlington, Wisconsin, and Artesia, New Mexico. *See also* SUCCESSION.

SUCCESSION. When **Joseph Smith** was murdered in 1844, the Church faced a crisis of succession. Who was the lawful successor as **prophet** and **president**? Had this been provided for in the **revelations**? Or must there be a struggle between competing claimants?

At the death of every Church president since, it has been the president of the **twelve apostles** who became the next president. On two occasions, 1877–1880 and 1887–1889, some time lapsed before the new **First Presidency** was organized, the twelve apostles acting as presidency during the interim. During his presidency, **Wilford Woodruff** said that he believed that in the absence of direct revelation to the contrary, the senior member of the **Quorum** of Twelve Apostles should automatically become president and that the change should take place immediately. Since then, the transition has taken place shortly after the president's death. A **sustaining** by the **membership** of the Church in conference expresses acceptance of the new leader, but this is not an election.

SUNDAY SCHOOL. Church **auxiliary** organization founded in 1867, building on a local Sunday School started by **Richard Ballantyne** at Farmington, Utah, in 1849. The first general superintendent was **George Q. Cannon.** A general board was appointed, lesson materials were produced, and a periodical, *The Juvenile Instructor*, was started. Children under 12 attend **Primary**.

SUNSTONE. Independent magazine published by the Sunstone Foundation, a nonprofit corporation. Subtitled *Mormon Experience, Scholarship, Issues, and Art*, *Sunstone* states on its title page that it is interested in "feature- and column-length articles relevant to Mormonism from a variety of perspectives; news stories about Mormons and the **LDS** church, and poetry, psalms, and limericks." Short stories are published and an annual award given for the best fiction. Annually in Salt Lake City, Utah, and at irregular intervals in other cities, the Sunstone Foundation sponsors a symposium, including papers and panel discussions on Mormon-related issues.

SUSTAINING. When individuals receive a **calling** to positions in the Church, those in the same jurisdiction have the opportunity to express their "common consent" by vote. The person conducting the meeting says, "All those willing to sustain X as **bishop** of the **ward** may express it by raising the hand," or words to this effect. With rare exceptions the resulting votes are unanimous. The attitude expressed by the sustaining vote is that of willingness to follow the leadership and do what is in one's power to support and assist those called to specific responsibilities. In a lay organization, good will and support of others provide the necessary atmosphere for growth and service.

– T –

TABERNACLE. (1) Building in Salt Lake City used for **general conferences** and other large assemblies or concerts. Completed in 1867, the Tabernacle is 250 feet long and 150 feet wide. Its dome-shaped roof has the appearance of half an egg shell or, as some have suggested, the back of a turtle. Constructed before the railroad arrived, the structure was made with many wooden dowels and even rawhide was used to reinforce and strengthen the lattice trusses in the attic. (2) The word *tabernacle*, of Old Testament origin, was also used to describe buildings put up in some of the **stakes**, but that usage is now rare.

TALMAGE, JAMES E. (1862–1933). Educator, university president, **general authority**. During the 1920s and early 1930s Talmage was a central figure in attempting to explain the consistency of the Mormon religion with the findings of modern science. His view was that the means of creation were not known, or at least were not part of the Mormon religious understanding, but that the earth and the human race owed their existence to God. *See also* CREATION.

TANNER, NATHAN ELDON (1898–1982). Businessman, politician, **general authority**. Reflecting admiration for his many contributions, the Salt Lake Area Chamber of Commerce named Tanner "Giant in our City" in 1978. In 1980 **BYU** named him Executive of the Year and named the new Management School building after him. "President N. Eldon Tanner will go down in history as one of the greatest **counselors** ever to serve in the **First Presidency** of the Church," said Apostle **Marvin J. Ashton.** "He is a man of few words and much performance."

TANNER, SUSAN W. (1953–). General president of **Young Women** from 2002 to 2008. She and her husband, John, are parents of five children.

TAYLOR, JOHN (1808–1887). Missionary, apostle, Church **president**. His was a holding action. The Edmunds Act (1882) and Edmunds-Tucker Act (1877) brought intense pressure on the Mormons, which by 1890 would eventuate in the **manifesto** formally ending **polygamy**. But during his lifetime Taylor refused to yield. With other Mormon leaders he went into hiding, leading the Church from "the underground." There he died of heart failure on 25 July 1887.

TEACHER. In addition to its general meaning, an office in the **Aaronic Priesthood**. Having already served as a **deacon**, a young man may be advanced to teacher at 14. Then at age 16, assuming **worthiness**, he is advanced to the office of **priest**. Teachers are organized into a **quorum** of 24 or less and, like other holders of the **priesthood**, meet on Sundays for instruction. During weekdays they often have service projects and social activities.

TEMPLE SQUARE. A square block at the center of Salt Lake City, within which stand some of the Church's most sacred and historic buildings and monuments: the Salt Lake Temple, the **Tabernacle**, the Assembly Hall, two **visitors centers**, and several sculptural works, including a replica of Thorvaldsen's renowned *Christus*.

Even in pioneer times Temple Square attracted visitors. Guides were showing people around as early as 1875. For much of the 20th century guided tours were conducted by volunteers. In the 1990s, most tours were conducted by full-time **missionaries**, young women from different countries. Tours were available in French, German, Spanish, Japanese, Chinese, and other languages. During the holiday season each year the trees are illuminated with 750,000 lights. More than 5 million visitors come annually to Temple Square, making it one of the major tourist attractions in the nation. *See also* TEMPLES.

TEMPLE SQUARE CONCERT SERIES. Concerts performed almost every Friday and Saturday evening of the year in the Assembly Hall on **Temple Square**. Admission is free and open to everyone over eight years of age. Orchestras, choirs, ensembles, and instrumental and vocal soloists are included. Performers are selected by a volunteer committee on the basis of tapes submitted. The concerts are sometimes held more often, as, for example, the performances given in connection with the Gina Bachauer International Piano Competition.

TEMPLES. Temples are not for regular worship services but are places in which "worthy" Church **members** participate in sacred ceremonies, or **ordinances.** In a general sense Mormon temples are analogous not to a church meetinghouse or synagogue but to the ancient temples described in the **Bible**.

Faithful Mormons describe the temple experience as a noble, Christ-centered service, a spiritual high point in their lives. To participate in the temples one must be not only a member of the Church but the holder of a signed **recommend**, or certificate of **worthiness**, from one's **bishop** and **stake president**. That curious nonmembers are not allowed into the temples has to do not so much with their secretiveness as their sacredness. Observation by curious, perhaps whispering and finger-pointing tourists would be disruptive to the purpose of the buildings. Temples are scheduled for virtually constant use from early in the morning until late at night. Prior to its dedication, a new temple is open to the general public for viewing during a specified period of time.

TESTIMONY. The conviction or assurance of the truth of the **gospel**, or more specifically of **Jesus Christ** and the modern **prophets**. When this conviction is expressed in words, one "bears testimony." Such certitude, ultimately dependent on the Holy Ghost, is promised to and claimed by readers of the ***Book of Mormon***: "And when ye shall receive these things, I would exhort you that ye would ask God, the Eternal Father, in the name of Christ, if these things are not true; and if ye shall ask with a sincere heart, with real intent, having faith in Christ, he will manifest the truth of it unto you, by the power of the Holy Ghost" (Moroni 10:4–5).

One Sunday each month Mormon congregations have a "fast and testimony meeting," in which individuals who wish can stand and express their feelings, that is, bear their testimony, about the gospel. Testimonies are expressed by Mormons in other meetings as well, often in conjunction with a sermon or **missionary** instruction.

THEOLOGY. Both in the technical sense of a doctrine of God and in the larger sense of religious beliefs about life and its purpose, Mormons have a theology. Indeed, students of Mormonism describe their belief system as rather complex, requiring more than a little study in the **scriptures** and various Church publications to master. But in two related respects Mormonism fits uneasily into usual theological discourse. First, Mormonism proceeds from revealed truth with virtually no effort made to employ standard philosophical terminology. Second, there is no class of professionally trained Mormon theologians.

Although some individual Mormons have had advanced study in philosophy, theology, or religious studies, such training is not considered necessary.

"THIS IS THE PLACE" MONUMENT. Monument on the east bench overlooking the Salt Lake Valley, commemorating the arrival of the original **pioneers** in July 1847. According to later recollections, when **Brigham Young** first beheld the valley on 24 July 1847, he said, "This is the right place. Drive on." Abbreviated to "This is the place," the saying was often repeated as an indication of divine protection and selection. A smaller memorial was replaced in 1947, the centennial year, by an imposing monument designed and sculpted by Mahonri M. Young. *See also* EXODUS.

THREE WITNESSES. *See* WITNESSES OF THE *BOOK OF MORMON.*

TIMES AND SEASONS. (1) Mormon newspaper published in Nauvoo, Illinois, 1839–1846. Motto: "Truth Will Prevail." Editors included Ebeneezer Robinson, Don Carlos Smith, and Robert B. Thompson, as well as **Joseph Smith**, **Wilford Woodruff**, and **John Taylor**. (2) Unofficial website discussing Mormon issues.

TINGEY, EARL C. (1934–). Corporate lawyer, **general authority**. Born in Bountiful, Utah, on 11 June 1934, Tingey served as **missionary** in Australia and then graduated from the University of Utah Law School with a juris doctorate. At New York University he received a master of corporate law degree. For three years he was a captain in the U.S. Army with the Judge Advocate General Corps. Tingey was an attorney on Wall Street. He was **bishop** of the Manhattan **Ward**, **counselor** in the Eastern States Mission presidency, **president** of the Australia Sydney Mission, and **regional representative.** He was called to the First **Quorum** of the **Seventy** in 1990 and in 1996 became a member of its presidency. He and his wife, Joanne, have four children.

TITHING. One tenth of income, paid to the Church on a voluntary and confidential basis. At an individual interview with their **bishop** at the end of the year, **members** verify the amount of their contribution and state whether or not they consider it a full tithing. Tithing is not mandatory. Failure to pay does not result in **excommunication**. Tithing is nevertheless considered a **commandment** and is paid faithfully by fully committed members. Tithing funds are sent by the **bishop** to Church headquarters, where they are accounted for and dispensed for such purposes as building and maintaining meeting-houses and **temples**, support of missions, and church educational activity. *See also* AUDITORS.

TRIPLE COMBINATION. Three of the standard works of **scripture**—the ***Book of Mormon***, ***Doctrine and Covenants***, and ***Pearl of Great Price***—when published together as a single volume. These works are of course also published separately.

TWELVE APOSTLES, QUORUM OF THE. Group of **general authorities** who have been ordained to this office in the **Melchizedek Priesthood**. When selected, a new apostle is presented in **general conference** for the **sustaining** vote of the Church **membership**. He then receives an ordination by the laying on of the hands of the **First Presidency** and the other members of the **Quorum** of the Twelve Apostles.

Apostles hold their office for life. Special witnesses of **Jesus Christ**, possessing the keys or rights of presidency, as a **quorum** they have taken the helm of leadership at the death of every Church **president**. The president of the apostles, after sustaining by a vote in general conference, has then been ordained the new president of the Church. *See also* SUCCESSION.

– U –

UCHTDORF, DIETER F. (1940–). Airline pilot, **general authority**. Born in Ostrava, Czechoslovakia, on 6 November 1940, Uchtdorf grew up in Frankfurt, Germany, as a member of the Church. After service in the German Air Force he graduated from airline pilot school in Bremen, Germany, attended Business Administration

School in Cologne, Germany, and the International Management Institute in Lausanne, Switzerland. An airline captain, he headed pilot school for Lufthansa and became senior vice president for flight operations. He served as **Young Men** president in his **ward**, **stake high councilor**, and **stake** president. In 1994 he was called as a member of the Second **Quorum** of the **Seventy.** In October 2004 he became a member of the Quorum of the **Twelve Apostles**. In 2008 he was called as second counselor in the First Presidency. He and his wife, Harriet, have two children.

UNITED ORDER. A system of cooperation not currently in operation in which Church **members** would give all their property to the Church, receive back a portion of it as a stewardship, continue to donate surplus production, and generally live in a framework of mutual support and equality. Some of the spirit of consecration and the United Order remains in the tradition of dedicating one's life to God's work on earth, commitments made in the **temples**, financial donations such as **tithing** and **fast offering**, and the ideal of equality that allows lay leaders of different wealth and background to work together as **brother and sister**. In the **welfare program** also these lay leaders have banded together in the spirit of fellowship to provide for those in need.

UTAH PERIOD. Roughly the second half of the 19th century. Following its origins in New York and unsuccessful efforts to establish itself in Ohio, Missouri, and Illinois, the great majority of Church **members** moved westward in a great **exodus** and established themselves in the Great Basin of the Rocky Mountains, with the headquarters in the Salt Lake Valley.

Statehood for Utah was achieved in 1896. During the closing quarter of the century, the Church was already showing signs of being much more than a one-state Church. Outposts had been established in Colorado, Arizona, Nevada, New Mexico, Idaho, Wyoming, and even Canada and Mexico. **Missionaries** were having success in Samoa, Tonga, New Zealand, the southern states, and **Europe**, and many of the convert families were staying put rather than migrating. But for half a century at least, Utah was a place of refuge and consolidation as well as continued adaptation.

– V –

VEAZEY, STEPHEN M. (1957–). President, **Community of Christ**. In 1992 he was named to the Council of Twelve Apostles of the Community of Christ church and in April 2002 became president of the council. In March 2005 he was approved as president of the church by a vote of a special World Conference in Independence, Missouri. On 3 June 2005, Veazey was ordained president of the Community of Christ. He and his wife, Cathleen, have three children. *See also* MCMURRAY, W. GRANT.

VINAS, FRANCISCO J. (1946–). Educator, **general authority**. In 1996 Vinas was called to be a member of the Second **Quorum** of the **Seventy** and in 1998 the First Quorum of the **Seventy.** He and his wife, Cristina, have three children.

VISITING TEACHING. Program of the **Relief Society** by which each member of the organization—now including all adult female **members** of the Church—is visited regularly, at least quarterly with additional telephone contacts. Those assigned as visiting teachers normally go as a team of two. They bring a teaching message, an item of instruction or inspiration. Most importantly, they show a personal interest in the person being visited. Where personal or family problems exist, they render whatever help they can. If the situations are extreme or if financial troubles loom large, the visiting teachers report back to the **ward** Relief Society president, who is able to enlist the help of the ward **bishop** in providing an appropriate response. *See also* HOME TEACHING.

VISITORS CENTERS. Departments or bureaus, usually in separate buldings, at historic sites where visitors can ask questions and obtain literature. Visitors centers are staffed by Church **members**, some of them serving as full-time **missionaries**, others as part-time volunteers. The first such center was established in 1902 at **Temple Square** in Salt Lake City, Utah, following complaints about the misrepresentation being purveyed to tourists by **anti-Mormons** or uninformed cab drivers. Other visitors centers are located near Palmyra, New York; in Nauvoo, Illinois; in Independence, Missouri; and at several of the **temples.** *See also* HISTORIC SITES.

– W –

WARD. The Church's basic ecclesiastical unit, similar to a parish or congregation. Membership is ordinarily somewhere between 300 and 700.

Year	Wards
1951	1,666
1961	3,143
1971	5,135
1981	11,063
1991	15,511
2001	22,249

In April 2007, the official report claimed 27,475 wards and branches worldwide.

WELCH, JOHN W. (1946–). Lawyer, writer, editor, student of **scriptures**. He has been **Sunday School** teacher, **bishop**, **high councilor**, and **counselor** in the **stake** presidency.

WELFARE PROGRAM. A continuing program instituted by the Church during the 1930s when the Depression had produced high unemployment and hardship. People in need are expected to look first to the resources of their **family**. Any assistance from the Church is regarded as temporary. Moreover, there is an expectation of work; one should not expect a handout. The underlying objective is not a dependency class but self-reliant members.

WELLS, EMMELINE B. (1828–1921). Leader of Mormon women, editor, **Relief Society** president. In 1910 Wells became general president of the Relief Society and thus official leader of Mormon women. In the Utah State Capitol stands a marble bust from the women of Utah in honor of "A Fine Soul Who Served Us."

WHITMER, DAVID (1805–1888). Early follower of **Joseph Smith** and one of the special three witnesses, along with **Oliver Cowdery** and **Martin Harris**, who testified that an angel showed them the metal plates from which the ***Book of Mormon*** was translated. Whitmer moved to Richmond, Missouri, where for 50 years he ran a livery stable and became a respected citizen. Many thought that his complaints about Joseph Smith would lead him to disavow his testimony. But to the end of his life he consistently held to his sworn statement. *See also* WITNESSES OF THE *BOOK OF MORMON*.

WIDTSOE, JOHN ANDREAS (1872–1952). Scientist, educator, **general authority**. From 1900 he was director of the Utah State Agricultural Experiment Station. Extensive research and travel assisting the farmers of the state led to early publications on dry farming. In 1905 he transferred to **BYU**, where he organized a department of agriculture. Then in 1907 Widtsoe was appointed president of Utah State Agricultural College. He published *Dry Farming: A System of Agriculture for Countries under a Low Rainfall* in 1910 and in 1912 a book on irrigation. In 1916 Widtsoe was selected as president of the University of Utah in Salt Lake City.

While pursuing his professional life, Widtsoe continued to teach classes and serve in different Church assignments. He published *Joseph Smith as Scientist* in 1908 and in 1915 *A Rational Theology*. In 1921, he was called as a member of the **Quorum** of the **Twelve Apostles**. In 1927 he became **president** of the European and British Mission, living in London until 1933. He had direct responsibility for the *Improvement Era,* the official Church magazine, and published a monthly column, "Evidences and Reconciliations," in which he answered many historical and doctrinal questions.

WIDTSOE, LEAH DUNFORD (1874–1955). Home economist, granddaughter of **Brigham Young**. Leah D. Widtsoe was an accomplished instructor, specializing in nutrition. She studied, lectured, and wrote. She was an advocate and model of the educated Mormon woman, serving as president of the Salt Lake Federation of Women's

Clubs and on the board of the Salt Lake Council of Women. With her mother, **Susa Young Gates**, she wrote on Brigham Young. Collaborating with her husband, **John Widtsoe**, she wrote *The Word of Wisdom: A Modern Interpretation*. She had seven children, three of whom reached maturity.

WIGHT, LYMAN (1796–1858). General authority, schismatic. He was among those who looked to "young Joseph," Joseph Smith III, to become leader of the Church, but since Wight was faithful to such practices as **polygamy** and **temple** ceremonies, he would have been a stormy petrel had he lived to participate in the **RLDS** Church. He died in central Texas on 31 March 1858 while attempting to move his followers north to Missouri. The movement, sometimes called the Wightites, quickly dissolved.

WILKINSON, ERNEST L. (1899–1978). Attorney, educator, university president. Wilkinson left the **BYU** presidency to become Republican candidate for the U.S. Senate in 1964, but lost. He returned to the presidency of BYU the year after his loss. He served on the board of directors of many corporations and received many awards, including the George Washington Medal from the Freedom Foundation and the Distinguished Service Award from his alma mater.

WILSON, WILLIAM A. "BERT" (1933–). Folklorist, educator. Born on 23 September 1933 at Tremonton, Utah, Wilson received his B.A. and M.A. degrees from **BYU**. At Indiana University he earned a Ph.D. in folklore. After serving on the faculty of BYU, from 1978 to 1984 he served as director of the Folklore Program at Utah State University.

In 1985 he returned to BYU, serving as chair of the English Department, director of the Charles Redd Center for Western Studies, and director of the BYU Folklore Archives. He published over 35 articles and one book on Mormon folklore. He was named the Karl G. Maeser Distinguished Faculty Lecturer at BYU and received the Grace Arrington Award for Historical Excellence and the Utah Governor's Award in the Arts. Among other Church positions, Wilson has served as **bishop** and **high councilor**. He married Hanele Blomqvist in 1957. They are the parents of four children.

WIRTHLIN, JOSEPH B. (1917–). Businessman, **general authority**. Drawing upon his business and church experience, Wirthlin made significant contributions in many areas of activity. As supervisor or executive administrator he had responsibility for the Southeast United States and Caribbean Islands (1978–1982) and Brazil (1982–1984). He was **president** of the **Europe area** of the Church from 1984 to 1986.

WIRTHLIN, RICHARD B. (1931–). Economist, pollster, **general authority**. Church callings included service as **bishop**, **high councilor**, **counselor** in **stake** presidencies, and **regional representative**. He was called to the Second **Quorum** of the **Seventy** in 1996. He and his wife, Jeralie, are the parents of eight children.

WITNESSES OF THE *BOOK OF MORMON*. In each copy of the ***Book of Mormon*** is found a page containing "The Testimony of the Three Witnesses" and "The Testimony of the Eight Witnesses." Although many of these witnesses became disaffected from the Church, they did not repudiate their testimony. Their lives have been studied in depth by historian **Richard L. Anderson**.

WOMEN, ROLES OF. In a large sense, Mormon women have experienced the same understanding of gender roles as the rest of American or Western society. The assumption was that most women would be wives and mothers. The idealized notion of "true womanhood"—woman as the refined, cultured, and religious influence in the home—was readily accepted by 19th-century Mormons. By the late 20th century, Mormon women enjoyed increased education, a higher percentage remained unmarried, **divorce** became more common, and paid work outside the home attracted (through desire or necessity) more and more women.

By comparison with some activists of the women's movement, certainly with those who disparage the role of wife and mother, Mormon women generally appear conservative. Those who know them, however, will acknowledge that they are articulate and talented. In the Church they occupy positions of leadership in the **Relief Society**, **Young Women**, and **Primary** organizations; serve as teachers in those organizations and in **Sunday School** and Church schools; and in many cases serve as full-time **missionaries**. They take the pulpit and deliver sermons at **sacrament** meetings and equal or surpass Mormon men in publicly bearing **testimony**. *See also* FEMINISM; RELIEF SOCIETY.

WOODRUFF, WILFORD (1807–1898). Missionary, apostle, **president** of the Church. One of the monumental achievements of Woodruff's life was his diary. Begun at the time of his conversion in 1834, this detailed record preserves many sermons of **Joseph Smith** and other early leaders, describes spiritual manifestations experienced by its author, and graphically conveys an abundance of concrete detail.

WORD OF WISDOM. Code of health announced by **Joseph Smith** in 1833 (***Doctrine and Covenants***, section 89). Not good for human consumption were alcohol, tobacco, and "hot drinks" (soon defined by **Hyrum Smith** as tea and coffee). Meat was to be used sparingly. Wholesome grains and fruits were recommended. The Word of Wisdom is "a principle with a promise." Consistent with the principle of caring for one's physical health, the lifestyle of Mormons includes cleanliness, physical exercise, recreation, abstinence from mind-altering drugs, regular medical examinations, and avoidance of excesses.

WORLD CONFERENCE ON RECORDS. Sponsored by the Utah Genealogical Society, the first World Conference on Records was held in Salt Lake City in 1969 and attracted nearly 3,000 participants from different countries. Its theme, addressed by many speakers in concurrent sessions, was "Records Protection in an Uncertain World." A second such conference was held in Salt Lake City in 1980. Emphasizing the compilation of pedigree charts and **family** histories, it attracted 11,500 registrants from many different countries. *See also* GENEALOGY.

WORLD RELIGIONS. In 1930, when the Church celebrated its hundredth year, **B. H. Roberts** insisted that it was not a narrow sect but a world movement. In her interpretation that Mormonism has the same relationship to historic **Christianity** that Christianity has to Judaism, historian Jan Shipps also comes close to granting the status of an incipient world religion. Sociologist Rodney Stark has advanced the possibility, based on his analysis of growth statistics, that in Mormonism we are seeing the emergence of another major world religion right before our eyes. Critics who emphasize its lack of correspondence to Christian orthodoxy at certain points tend to label it a **cult**, sect, or new religious movement. Even the Mormon self-definition is ambivalent. On the one hand, Mormons see themselves as a subset of Christianity; on the other hand, their claim to exclusivity, to being the only true church, sets them apart.

The traditional world religions include Christianity, Judaism, Islam, Buddhism, Jainism, and others. A **First Presidency** statement of 1978 reads, "The great religious leaders of the world such as Mohammed, Confucius, and the Reformers, as well as philosophers including Socrates, Plato, and others, received a portion of God's light. Moral truths were given to them by God to enlighten whole nations and to bring a higher level of understanding to individuals" (Palmer, *Mormons and Muslims*, 208). Appropriate in a period when Mormon **missionaries** are in all the inhabited continents, this general attitude was also expressed by **Joseph Smith** and other early Church leaders. *See also* CATHOLICISM; CHRISTIANITY; MEMBERSHIP; PROTESTANTISM.

WORTHINESS. A condition or status of moral uprightness considered essential for those performing certain Church functions or responsibilities. A general sincerity, while important, is not sufficient. Performance is expected. Regular attendance at meetings, payment of **tithing** and fast offering, observance of the **Word of Wisdom**, moral strictness, honesty in dealing with others, **sustaining** the Church leadership—these are among the determinants of worthiness. Mormons are under no illusion that ultimate salvation is determined only by a simple check-list. The heart must be right. But for determining minimal requirements for service in the Church on the earthly level, the concept of worthiness serves a useful purpose.

– Y –

YOUNG, BRIGHAM (1801–1877). Missionary, apostle, colonizer of the American West, and **president** of the Church. Versatile and strong of character, Young was able to hold the Church together and lead it to a new stability during crucial years. He died on 29 August 1877.

YOUNG, STEVE (1961–). Professional football player. Young participates in a variety of charitable causes. During the off-season he returned to **BYU** and earned a law degree.

YOUNG MEN. Auxiliary organization of the Church with programs to assist young male members develop socially, physically, and especially spiritually; formerly known as YMMIA. From the 1960s on, the organization came under direction of the **priesthood**, with activities revolving around the **quorums**. In 1977 the name was changed to Young Men. By age groups the young men meet on Sundays for religious instruction and on one evening during the week for scouting, service projects, sports, or career education. Joint activities, including social dances and the production of theatrical plays and skits, are also held with the **Young Women**.

YOUNG WOMEN. Starting in 1869 with a small organization founded by **Brigham Young** for his daughters, a Retrenchment Association expanded to include young women in the different **wards** of Salt Lake City, Utah. It replaced the Young Women's Mutual Improvement Association, which had replaced the YLMIA in 1934. Avoiding the expense and pretense of worldly fashions was one goal, but spiritual development, the study of literature, instruction in public speaking, and social projects were quickly added. From the 1960s on, the Young Women began to meet on Sundays at the same time as **priesthood** meetings were held for the **Young Men**. A meeting during the week allowed opportunities for recreation and social development. Sensitive to the inroads of secularism and temptation, leaders emphasized spiritual values.

YOUTH. In all human societies some kind of "coming of age" occurs. In 21st-century America, the stresses during this time of life have included experimentation with alcohol and drugs, sexual activity, teenage pregnancy, confusion over gender identity, and violence.

– Z –

ZION. (1) The pure in heart (***Doctrine and Covenants*** 97:21). The expectations of an imminent **Millennium** explain the emphasis placed on definition 2 at the Church's beginning, while the doctrine of **gathering** explains the usage embodied in definition 4. The cessation of efforts to gather converts from foreign lands and the growth of the Church **membership** in all of the states and many foreign countries, especially emphatic in the latter half of the 20th century, help to explain the current emphasis on definitions 1 and 5.

ZION'S CAMP. An expedition of 1834 intending to come to the aid of persecuted Mormons in Missouri. Living in Ohio at the time, **Joseph Smith** responded to appeals from his Missouri followers by issuing a revelation (***Doctrine and Covenants***, section 103) commanding the organization of volunteers. Eventually about 200 men banded together, organized themselves into units, and trained as they made their way westward in May and June. After a journey of 600 or 700 miles, the army reached the trouble spot in western Missouri. Internal dissension, sickness, and the collapse of negotiations with the Missourians led to the disbanding of the expedition. Although it did not achieve its objective of restoring the Missouri Mormons to their property, Zion's Camp provided valuable experience in organization. Most of the **twelve apostles** named in 1835 had served in the expedition. **Brigham Young** and others later looked back upon it as a time of trial and seasoning. *See also* MISSOURI PERIOD.

Appendix 1

Church Presidents

Joseph Smith, 1832–1844
Brigham Young, 1847–1877
John Taylor, 1880–1887
Wilford Woodruff, 1889–1898
Lorenzo Snow, 1898–1901
Joseph F. Smith, 1901–1918
Heber J. Grant, 1918–1945
George Albert Smith, 1945–1951
David O. McKay, 1951–1970
Joseph Fielding Smith, 1970–1972
Harold B. Lee, 1972–1973
Spencer W. Kimball, 1973–1985
Ezra Taft Benson, 1985–1994
Howard W. Hunter, 1994–1995
Gordon B. Hinckley, 1995–2008
Thomas S. Monson, 2008–

Appendix 2

The Family: A Proclamation to the World

We, the First Presidency and the Council of the Twelve Apostles of the Church of Jesus Christ of Latter-day Saints, solemnly proclaim that marriage between a man and a woman is ordained of God and that the family is central to the Creator's plan for the eternal destiny of His children.

All human beings—male and female—are created in the image of God. Each is a beloved spirit son or daughter of heavenly parents, and, as such, each as a divine nature and destiny. Gender is an essential characteristic of individual pre-mortal, mortal, and eternal identity and purpose.

In the pre-mortal realm, spirit sons and daughters knew and worshiped God as their Eternal Father and accepted His plan by which His children could obtain a physical body and gain earthly experience to progress toward perfection and ultimately realize his or her divine destiny as an heir of eternal life. The divine plan of happiness enables family relationships to be perpetuated beyond the grave. Sacred ordinances and covenants available in holy temples make it possible for individuals to return to the presence of God and for families to be united eternally.

The first commandment that God gave to Adam and Eve pertained to their potential for parenthood as husband and wife. We declare that God's commandment for His children to multiply and replenish the earth remains in force. We further declare that God has commanded that the sacred powers of procreation are to be employed only between man and woman, lawfully wedded as husband and wife.

We declare the means by which mortal life is created to be divinely appointed. We affirm the sanctity of life and of its importance in God's eternal plan.

Husband and wife have a solemn responsibility to love and care for each other and for their children. "Children are an heritage of the Lord"

(Ps. 127:3). Parents have a sacred duty to rear their children in love and righteousness, to provide for their physical and spiritual needs, to teach them to love and serve one another, to observe the commandments of God and to be law-abiding citizens wherever they live. Husbands and wives—mothers and fathers—will be held accountable before God for the discharge of these obligations.

The family is ordained of God. Marriage between man and woman is essential to His eternal plan. Children are entitled to birth within the bonds of matrimony, and to be reared by a father and a mother who honor marital vows with complete fidelity. Happiness in family life is most likely to be achieved when founded upon the teachings of the Lord Jesus Christ. Successful marriages and families are established and maintained on principles of faith, prayer, repentance, forgiveness, respect, love, compassion, work, and wholesome recreational activities. By divine design, fathers are to preside over their families in love and righteousness and are responsible to provide the necessities of life and protection for their families. Mothers are primarily responsible for the nurture of their children. In these sacred responsibilities, fathers and mothers are obligated to help one another as equal partners. Disability, death, or other circumstances may necessitate individual adaptation. Extended families should lend support when needed.

We warn that individuals who violate covenants of chastity, who abuse spouse or offspring, or who fail to fulfill family responsibilities will one day stand accountable before God. Further, we warn that the disintegration of the family will bring upon individuals, communities, and nations the calamities foretold by ancient and modern prophets.

We call upon responsible citizens and officers of the government everywhere to promote those measures designed to maintain and strengthen the family as the fundamental unit of society.

—presented by President Gordon B. Hinckley at the
General Relief Society meeting, 23 September 1995

Appendix 3

Temples Dedicated through February 2008

Location	Dedication
Kirtland, Ohio	27 March 1836
Nauvoo, Illinois	30 April 1846
St. George, Utah	6 April 1877
Logan, Utah	17 May 1884
Manti, Utah	17 May 1884
Salt Lake City, Utah	6 April 1893
Laie, Oahu, Hawaii	27 November 1919
Cardston, Alberta, Canada	26 August 1923
Mesa, Arizona	23 October 1927
Idaho Falls, Idaho	23 September 1945
Zollikofen, Switzerland	11 September 1955
Los Angeles, California	11 March 1956
Hamilton, New Zealand	20 April 1958
Newchapel Surrey, England	7 September 1958
Oakland, California	17 November 1964
Ogden, Utah	18 January 1972
Provo, Utah	9 February 1972
Kensington, Maryland	19 November 1974
São Paulo, Brazil	30 October 1978
Tokyo, Japan	27 October 1980
Bellevue, Washington	17 November 1980
South Jordan, Utah	16 November 1981
Sandy Springs, Georgia	1 June 1983
Apia, Western Samoa	5 August 1983
Nuku'alofa, Tonga	9 August 1983
Santiago, Chile	15 September 1983
Pirae, Tahiti	17 October 1983
Mexico City, Mexico	2 December 1983

Boise Idaho	25 May 1984
Carlingford, Australia	20 September 1984
Quezon City, Philippines	25 September 1984
Dallas, Texas	19 October 1984
Taipei, Taiwan	17 November 1984
Guatemala City, Guatemala	14 December 1984
Freiberg, Germany	19 June 1985
Vasterhaninge, Sweden	1 July 1985
Glenview, Illinois	9 August 1985
Johannesburg, South Africa	24 August 1985
Seoul, Korea	14 December 1985
Lima, Peru	10 January 1986
Buenos Aires, Argentina	17 January 1986
Littleton, Colorado	24 October 1986
Friedrichsdorf, Germany	28 August 1987
Oswego, Oregon	19 August 1989
Las Vegas, Nevada	16 December 1989
Brampton, Ontario, Canada	25 August 1990
San Diego, California	25 April 1993
Orlando, Florida	9 October 1994
Bountiful, Utah	8 January 1995
Hong Kong	26 May 1996
American Fork, Utah	13 October 1996
St. Louis, Missouri	1 June 1997
Vernal, Utah	2 November 1997
Preston, England	7 June 1998
Monticello, Utah	26 July 1998
Anchorage, Alaska	9 January 1999
Colonia, Juarez, Chihuahua, Mexico	7 March 1999
Madrid, Spain	19 March 1999
Bogotá, Colombia	26 April 1999
Guayaquil, Ecuador	1 August 1999
Spokane, Washington	21 August 1999
Columbus, Ohio	4 September 1999
Bismarck, North Dakota	19 September 1999
Columbia, South Carolina	16 October 1999
Detroit, Michigan	23 October 1999
Halifax, Nova Scotia, Canada	14 November 1999

Regina, Saskatchewan, Canada	14 November 1999
Billings, Montana	20 November 1999
Edmonton, Alberta, Canada	11 December 1999
Raleigh, North Carolina	18 December 1999
St. Paul, Minnesota	9 January 2000
Kona, Hawaii	23 January 2000
Ciudad Juáraz, Mexico	26 February 2000
Hermosilla, Mexico	27 February 2000
Albuquerque, New Mexico	6 March 2000
Oaxaca, Mexico	11 March 2000
Tuxtla Gutiérrez, Mexico	12 March 2000
Louisville, Kentucky	19 March 2000
Palmyra, New York	6 April 2000
Fresno, California	9 April 2000
Medford, Oregon	16 April 2000
Memphis, Tennessee	23 April 2000
Reno, Nevada	23 April 2000
Cochabamba, Bolivia	30 April 2000
Tampico, Mexico	20 May 2000
Villahermosa, Mexico	21 May 2000
Nashville, Tennessee	21 May 2000
Montreal, Canada	4 June 2000
San José, Costa Rica	4 June 2000
Fukuoka, Japan	11 June 2000
Adelaide, Australia	15 June 2000
Melbourne, Australia	16 June 2000
Suva, Fiji	18 June 2000
Merida, Mexico	25 June 2000
Vera Cruz, Mexico	9 July 2000
Baton Rouge, Louisiana	16 July 2000
Yukon, Oklahoma	20 July 2000
Caracas, DC, Venezuela	20 August 2000
Klein, Texas	26 August 2000
Gardendale, Alabama	3 September 2000
Santo Domingo, Dominican Republic	17 September 2000
Belmont, Massachusetts	1 October 2000
Recife, Pernambuco, Brazil	15 December 2000
Porto Alegre, Rio Grande do Sul, Brazil	17 December 2000

Montevideo, Uruguay	18 March 2001
Winter Quarters, Nebraska	22 April 2001
Zapopan, Jalisco, Mexico	29 April 2001
Stirling, Western Australia	20 May 2001
Richland, Washington	18 November 2001
Snowflake, Arizona	3 March 2002
Lubbock, Texas	21 April 2002
Monterrey, Nuevo León, Mexico	28 April 2002
Campinas, Brazil	17 May 2002
Asunción, Paraguay	19 May 2002
Nauvoo, Illinois	27 June 2002
Zoetermeer, The Netherlands	8 September 2002
Kangaroo Point, Queensland, Australia	15 June 2003
Redlands, California	14 September 2003
Accra, Ghana	11 January 2004
Frederiksberg, Denmark	23 May 2004
New York City, New York	13 June 2004
San Antonio, Texas	22 May 2005
Aba, Abia, Nigeria	7 August 2005
Newport Beach, California	28 August 2005
Rancho Cordova, California	3 September 2006
Helsinki, Finland	22 October 2006
Rexburg, Idaho	10 February 2008

Appendix 4

The Living Christ: The Testimony of the Apostles of the Church of Jesus Christ of Latter-day Saints

As we commemorate the birth of Jesus Christ two millennia ago, we offer our testimony of the reality of His matchless life and the infinite virtue of His great atoning sacrifice. None other has had so profound an influence upon all who have lived and will yet live upon the earth.

He was the Great Jehovah of the Old Testament, the Messiah of the New. Under the direction of His Father, He was the creator of the earth. "All things were made by him; and without him was not any thing made that was made" (John 1:3). Though sinless, He was baptized to fulfill all righteousness. He "went about doing good" (Acts 10:38), yet was despised for it. His gospel was a message of peace and goodwill. He entreated all to follow His example. He walked the roads of Palestine, healing the sick, causing the blind to see, and raising the dead. He taught the truths of eternity, the reality of our premortal existence, the purpose of our life on earth, and the potential for the sons and daughters of God in the life to come.

He instituted the sacrament as a reminder of His great atoning sacrifice. He was arrested and condemned on spurious charges, convicted to satisfy a mob, and sentenced to die on Calvary's cross. He gave His life to atone for the sins of all mankind. His was a great vicarious gift in behalf of all who would ever live upon the earth.

We solemnly testify that His life, which is central to all human history, neither began in Bethlehem nor concluded on Calvary. He was the Firstborn of the Father, the Only Begotten Son in the flesh, the Redeemer of the world.

He rose from the grave to "become the firstfruits of them that slept" (1 Corinthians 15:20). As Risen Lord, He visited among those He had loved in life. He also ministered among His "other sheep" (John 10:16) in ancient America. In the modern world, He and His Father appeared to the boy Joseph Smith, ushering in the long-promised "dispensation of the fulness of times" (Ephesians 1:10). Of the Living Christ, the Prophet Joseph wrote:

> His eyes were as a flame of fire; the hair of his head was white like the pure snow; his countenance shone above the brightness of the sun; and his voice was as the sound of the rushing of great waters, even the voice of Jehovah, saying: "I am the first and the last; I am he who liveth, I am he who was slain; I am your advocate with the Father." (D&C 110:3–4)

Of Him the Prophet also declared:

> And now, after the many testimonies which have been given of him, this is the testimony, last of all, which we give of him: That he lives! For we saw him, even on the right hand of God; and we heard the voice bearing record that he is the Only Begotten of the Father—That by him, and through him, and of him, the worlds are and were created, and the inhabitants thereof are begotten sons and daughters unto God. (D&C 76:22–24)

We declare in words of solemnity that His priesthood and His Church have been restored upon the earth—"built upon the foundation of . . . apostles and prophets, Jesus Christ himself being the chief corner stone" (Ephesians 2:20).

We testify that He will someday return to earth. "And the glory of the Lord shall be revealed, and all flesh shall see it together" (Isaiah 40:5). He will rule as King of Kings and reign as Lord of Lords, and every knee shall bend and every tongue shall speak in worship before Him. Each of us will stand to be judged of Him according to our works and the desires of our hearts.

We bear testimony, as His duly ordained Apostles—that Jesus is the Living Christ, the immortal Son of God. He is the great King Immanuel, who stands today on the right hand of His Father. He is the light, the life, and the hope of the world. His way is the path that leads to happiness in this life and eternal life in the world to come. God be thanked for the matchless gift of His divine Son.

The First Presidency
The Quorum of the Twelve

Bibliography

INTRODUCTION

The selective list of titles offered here is sufficiently extensive to provide entry into the major phases of development and leading personalities of a religion that in some ways appears up to date, encouraging education and using the latest technology, while in other respects it may give the impression of stepping back into the past. Although 19th-century writings are used as source material by historians, they have been superseded by later scholarship. It was after the middle of the 20th century that historians and social scientists with professional training began to tackle the subject of Mormonism. Publications continue to proliferate. Mean-spirited attacks on one extreme and syrupy devotional literature on the other are excluded as not likely to satisfy the desire of the general reader for reliable information.

As an introduction to Mormonism and its history, readers will be well served by Leonard J. Arrington and Davis Bitton, *The Mormon Experience: A History of the Latter-day Saints* (1979, 2nd ed. 1992), and James B. Allen and Glen M. Leonard, *The Story of the Latter-day Saints* (1976, 2nd ed. 1992). A recent survey is Claudia L. Bushman and Richard L. Bushman, *Building the Kingdom: A History of Mormons in America* (2001). For an outsider's perspective, see Jan Shipps, *Mormonism: The Story of a New Religious Tradition* (1985), and Douglas J. Davies, *Introduction to Mormonism* (2005). With disarming frankness, Jana Rees and Christopher Kimball Bigelow convey much basic information in a sprightly way in *Mormonism for Dummies* (2005).

Biographies of founding prophet Joseph Smith range from the adoring George Q. Cannon, *Life of Joseph Smith the Prophet* (1889), to critical hatchet jobs and tortuous, speculative mind reading. Most accessible to non-Mormons since its appearance in 1945 has been Fawn Brodie, *No Man Knows My History*, whose naturalistic, psycho-biographical approach is persuasive to many readers. But she did not examine all the primary material available even at the time she wrote, and much has been uncovered in the past 50 years. A recent biographer following Brodie's basic approach, trying to patch together a convincing interpretation of Smith based on dreams and deductions from family relationships, is Dan Vogel, *Joseph Smith: The Making of a Prophet* (2004).

By all odds, the most important biography now available is Richard Bushman, *Joseph Smith: Rough Stone Rolling* (2005). Beautifully written and based on exhaustive research, it is a cultural biography that places its subject in the context of his time, noting parallels with contemporary figures but also important differences, not denying foibles and weaknesses but also demonstrating as no one has before the phenomenal achievement in doctrine and institution building of a young man who died before his 39th birthday.

The best introduction to the *Book of Mormon* and the different reactions to it, both attacks and defenses, is now Teryl Givens, *By the Hand of Mormon: The American Scripture That Launched a New World Religion* (2002).

For the dramatic expansion of Mormonism into England as well as insight into the extraordinary experiences of the twelve apostles, see James B. Allen, Ronald K. Esplin, and David J. Whittaker, *Men with a Mission, 1837–1841:*

The Quorum of the Twelve in the British Isles (1992). For the 19th century, especially the second half, the indispensable book is Leonard J. Arrington, *Great Basin Kingdom: An Economic History of the Latter-day Saints* (1958). Also recommended is Arrington's *Building the City of God* (1976), coauthored with Feramorz Y. Fox and Dean L. May, which treats cooperative programs and utopian communities among the Mormons.

For the epic story of crossing the plains as the Mormons sought a place of refuge in the West, Wallace Stegner, *The Gathering of Zion* (1981), is engagingly written and full of human interest. A more recent work is Richard Bennett, *We'll Find the Place: The Mormon Exodus, 1846–1848* (1997). The compelling saga of Scandinavian and British Latter-day Saints as they abandoned their homeland and traveled to their land of promise is told by William Mulder, *Homeward to Zion: The Mormon Migration from Scandinavia* (1957) and P. A. M. Taylor, *Expectations Westward: The Mormons and the Emigration of Their British Converts in the Nineteenth Century* (1965).

Richard S. Van Wagoner, *Mormon Polygamy: A History* (1989) lays out the essential facts about its subject. Greater depth and quantitative analysis can be found in Kathryn M. Daynes, *More Wives Than One: Transformation of the Mormon Marriage System, 1840–1910* (2001). Defenders of monogamy who worked tirelessly to bring a halt to the Mormon plural marriage practice are thoughtfully studied by Sarah Barringer Gordon, *The Mormon Question: Polygamy and Constitutional Conflict in Nineteenth Century America* (2002).

The completion of the transcontinental railroad ended the relative isolation of the Latter-day Saints in their mountain retreat. A fascinating study of the resulting tensions and a new schism is Ronald W. Walker, *Wayward Saints: The Godbeites and Brigham Young* (1998). In 1903, the election of monogamist Reed Smoot to the U. S. Senate led to drawn-out committee hearings in the nation's capital. Casting light on many details about the Church as it struggled to adjust to new conditions, these hearings have been thoughtfully studied by Kathleen Flake in *The Politics of American Religious Identity: The Seating of Senator Reed Smoot, Mormon Apostle* (2004).

With polygamy abandoned and the economic and political differences largely erased, Mormon history in the 20th century became less interesting to many people. Yet it was a century of important development and skyrocketing growth. Thomas G. Alexander, *Mormonism in Transition: A History of the Latter-day Saints, 1890–1930* (1986, 2nd ed. 1996), studies a wide range of issues, Mormon life, and institutional development early in the century.

A rewarding approach is through the biographies of leaders. Especially recommended are Gregory A. Prince and William Robert Wright, *David O. McKay and the Rise of Modern Mormonism* (2005); Edward L. Kimball and Andrew E. Kimball Jr., *Spencer W. Kimball* (1977); and Edward L. Kimball, *Lengthen*

Your Stride: The Presidency of Spencer W. Kimball (2005). Workmanlike studies that capture a good deal of human interest while giving a concrete sense of what was happening are Sheri L. Dew, *Ezra Taft Benson: A Biography* (1987); and Sheri L. Dew, *Go Forward with Faith: The Biography of Gordon B. Hinckley* (1996). Studies of earlier church leaders include Davis Bitton, *George Q. Cannon: A Biography* (1999), and Thomas G. Alexander, *Things in Heaven and Earth: The Life and Times of Wilford Woodruff, a Mormon Prophet* (1993).

Many different themes within Mormon history have been studied. Five book-length studies are recommended: Philip L. Barlow, *Mormons and the Bible* (1990); Edwin Brown Firmage and Richard Collin Mangrum, *Zion in the Courts: A Legal History of the Church of Jesus Christ of Latter-day Saints, 1830–1900* (1988); Lester E. Bush Jr., *Health and Medicine among the Latter-day Saints* (1993); Michael Hicks, *Mormonism and Music: A History* (1989); and Richard G. Oman and Robert O. Davis, *Images of Faith: Art of the Latter-day Saints* (1995).

Because of its smothering mass of detail, as well as a complex method of bunching citations that make evaluating its sources difficult, D. Michael Quinn, *The Mormon Hierarchy* in two volumes (1994, 1997), is probably not for general readers approaching the subject for the first time. Yet it contains a vast amount of data, and serious scholars will wish to consult it.

Collections

For the major collections of resources one starts, of course, with the Church's own library and archives in Salt Lake City, Utah. The Utah State Historical Society, the University of Utah library, and the Brigham Young University library preserve much source material. Utah State University already possessed some Mormon-related material when, in the 1990s, the S. George Ellsworth collection was donated there and subsequently the rich Leonard J. Arrington papers. Outside Utah the main collections are the Bancroft Library, Huntington Library, Community of Christ Archives, Princeton University, the Beinicke Library at Yale University, and the National Archives of the United States. A valuable survey of these and other collections, David J. Whittaker, ed., *Mormon Americana: A Guide to Sources and Collections in the United States* (1995), also includes bibliographical essays on published sources, material culture, emigration trails, folklore, literature, photoarchives, performing arts, visual arts, and others.

Chad Flake, *A Mormon Bibliography, 1830–1930* (1978), attempts to list all books about Mormons published between 1830 and 1930. Articles in newspapers and magazines as well as in scholarly journals are not included. Secondary studies, the historical and sociological scholarship, as well as a certain number of pieces that have some value as primary sources, are listed in James B. Allen,

Ronald W. Walker, and David J. Whittaker, *Studies in Mormon History, 1830–1997* (2000), also available online with updates. No one should pretend to be *au courant* on the state of scholarship without first examining this work.

Theology and Religion

This whole category of publications is often ignored by those interested primarily in history. The five-volume *Encyclopedia of Mormonism* (1992), available in many libraries, provides excellent introductions to theological, scriptural, and historical subjects. An illuminating discussion in a civil, respectful tone is Craig L. Blomberg and Stephen E. Robinson, *How Wide the Divide? A Mormon and an Evangelical in Conversation* (1997). Especially energetic in attempting to clarify the issues and develop amicable relations with other faiths has been Robert L. Millet, former dean of religious education at Brigham Young University. His works include *Mormon Faith: A New Look at Christianity* (1998), *Latter-day Christianity: Ten Basic Issues* (1998), *Getting at the Truth: Responding to Difficult Questions about LDS Beliefs* (2004), and *A Different Jesus? The Christ of the Latter-day Saints* (2005).

Websites

Of the hundreds of websites and blogs, varying widely in reliability, the following can be recommended:

lds.org. The official Church website is a portal to information on doctrine, history, and current programs. It allows examination of church magazines and conference addresses, thus providing direct access to what is being said and what is happening at present.

mormon.org. A site intended to assist nonmembers in answering their questions about the Church and its teachings under the headings Church, Families, Nature of God, Purpose of Life, Frequently Asked Questions.

cofchrist.org. Official site of the Community of Christ, previously known as the Reorganized Church of Jesus Christ of Latter Day Saints.

farms.byu.edu. Sponsored by the Neal A. Maxwell Institute for Religious Scholarship, this site allows access to research on the *Book of Mormon*, the *Pearl of Great Price*, and specific incidents in Church history. Its analytical book reviews show what criticisms are published and how Latter-day Saint scholars respond.

fairlds.org. Sponsored by the Foundation for Apologetic Information and Research, this site addresses literally hundreds of questions and provides links to other sites.

byustudies.byu.edu. Besides providing information about an important scholarly journal, this site contains a helpful FAQ (frequently asked questions) section. Under "Mormon Bibliography" users have access to the constantly expanding research on Mormon history.

jefflindsay.com. A private site maintained by an industrial scientist with wide interests in the world of Mormonism.

PERIODICALS AND YEARBOOKS

Brigham Young University Studies 1 (1959–).

Church News, 1943–. Weekly.

Conference Reports, 1880, 1897, 1899–.

Deseret News Church Almanac. Salt Lake City: Deseret News, 1973–

Deseret News, Church Section, 1931–1943.

Dialogue: A Journal of Mormon Thought 1 (1966–).

Ensign, 1971–. Monthly.

Exponent II, 1974–. Quarterly.

FARMS Review of Books 1 (1989–). Originally titled *Review of Books on the* Book of Mormon.

Improvement Era, 1897–1970. Monthly.

The John Whitmer Historical Association Journal 1 (1981–).

Journal of Book of Mormon Studies 1 (1992–).

Journal of Discourses 1–25 (1854–1884).

Relief Society Magazine 1–56 (1915–1970).

The Saints Herald 1 (1860–).

Sunstone 1 (1975–).

REFERENCE WORKS

Brown, S. Kent, Donald Q. Cannon, and Richard H. Jackson, eds. *Historical Atlas of Mormonism*. New York: Simon and Schuster, 1994.

Jenson, Andrew. *Church Chronology: A Record of Important Events*. 2nd ed. Salt Lake City: Deseret News Press, 1914.

———. *Encyclopedic History of the Church of Jesus Christ of Latter-day Saints*. Salt Lake City: Deseret News Press, 1941.

Ludlow, Daniel H., ed. *Encyclopedia of Mormonism*. 5 vols. New York: Macmillan, 1992.

Olpin, Robert S. *Dictionary of Utah Art*. Salt Lake City: Salt Lake Art Center, 1980.

Whittaker, David J. *Mormon Americana: A Guide to Sources and Collections in the United States*. Provo, UT: BYU Studies, 1995.

BIBLIOGRAPHIES

Alder, Douglas D. "Writing Southern Utah History: An Appraisal and a Bibliography." *Journal of Mormon History* 20 (Fall 1994): 156–78.

Alexander, Thomas G. "Historiography and the New Mormon History: A Historian's Perspective." *Dialogue: A Journal of Mormon Thought* 19 (Fall 1986): 25–49.

———. "Toward the New Mormon History: An Examination of the Literature on the Latter-day Saints in the Far West." In Michael P. Malone, ed., *Historians and the American West*. Lincoln: University of Nebraska Press, 1983.

Alexander, Thomas G., and James B. Allen, eds. "The Mormons in the Mountain West: A Selected Bibliography." *Arizona and the West* 9 (Winter 1967): 365–84.

Allen, James B., David J. Whittaker, and Ronald W. Walker. *Studies in Mormon History, 1830–1997: An Indexed Bibliography*. Urbana: University of Illinois Press, 2000.

Arrington, Leonard J. "Scholarly Studies of Mormonism in the Twentieth Century." *Dialogue: A Journal of Mormon Thought* 1 (Spring 1966): 15–32.

Baker, Sherry, and Daniel Stout. "Mormons and the Media, 1898–2003: A Selected, Annotated, and Indexed Bibliography." *Brigham Young University Studies* 42 (2003): 124–81.

Bitton, Davis. *Guide to Mormon Diaries and Autobiographies*. Provo, UT: Brigham Young University Press, 1977.

———. "Mormon Polygamy: A Review Article." *Journal of Mormon History* 4 (1977): 101–8.

Bringhurst, Newell G., and Lavina Fielding Anderson, eds. *Excavating Mormon Pasts: The New Historiography of the Last Half Century*. Salt Lake City: Greg Kofford Books, 2004.

Clement, Russell T. *Mormons in the Pacific: A Bibliography*. Laie, HI: Institute for Polynesian Studies, 1981.

Cowan, Richard O., and Frank A. Bruno. *Bibliography on Temples and Temple Work*. Provo, UT: Brigham Young University, 1982.

Crawley, Peter. "A Bibliography of the Church . . . in New York, Ohio, and Missouri." *Brigham Young University Studies* 12 (Summer 1972): 465–537.

———. *A Descriptive Bibliography of the Mormon Church*. Vol. 1, *1830–1847*. Provo, UT: Religious Studies Center, Brigham Young University, 1997.

Crawley, Peter, and David J. Whittaker. *Mormon Imprints in Great Britain and the Empire*. Provo, UT: Friends of the Brigham Young University Library, 1987.

Dennis, Ronald D. *Welsh Mormon Publications from 1844 to 1862: A Historical Bibliography*. Provo, UT: Religious Studies Center, Brigham Young University, 1988.

England, Eugene. "The Dawning of a Brighter Day: Mormon Literature after 150 Years." *Brigham Young University Studies* 22 (Spring 1982): 131–60.

Fales, Susan L. *An Addendum to Mormons and Mormonism in U.S. Government Documents: A Bibliography*. Provo, UT: N.p., 1989.

Fales, Susan L., and Chad J. Flake, comps. *Mormons and Mormonism in U.S. Government Documents: A Bibliography*. Salt Lake City: University of Utah Press, 1989.

Flake, Chad J., ed. *A Mormon Bibliography, 1830–1930*. Salt Lake City: University of Utah Press, 1978.

Flake, Chad J., and Larry Draper. *Supplement to* A Mormon Bibliography. Salt Lake City: University of Utah Press, 1989.

Frazier, Karen Purser. *Bibliography of Social Scientific, Historical, and Popular Writings about Mormon Women*. Provo, UT: Women's Research Institute, Brigham Young University, 1990.

Grover, Mark L. *The Mormon Church in Latin America: A Periodical Index, 1830–1976*. Provo, UT: Brigham Young University Press, 1977.

Hawkins, Chester Lee. "Selective Bibliography on African-Americans and Mormons, 1830–1890." *Dialogue: A Journal of Mormon Thought* 25 (Winter 1992): 113–31.

Hill, Marvin S. "The Historiography of Mormonism." *Church History* 28 (December 1959): 418–26.

Homer, Michael W. "The Church's Image in Italy from the 1840s to 1946: A Bibliographic Essay." *Brigham Young University Studies* 31 (Spring 1991): 83–114.

Laughlin, David L. "A Selective, Evaluative, and Annotated Bibliography on Mormonism." *Bulletin of Bibliography* 48 (June 1991): 75–101.

———. "It Began with a Book: A Didactically Annotated Bibliography on Mormonism." *Journal of Religious and Theological Information* 2 (1994): 45–94.

Launius, Roger D. "A Bibliographical Review of the Reorganized Church in the Nineteenth Century." *Mormon History Association Newsletter* 64 (January 1987): 5–8.

———. "A New Historiographical Frontier: The Reorganized Church in the Twentieth Century." *John Whitmer Historical Association Journal* 6 (1986): 53–63.

———. "The Reorganized Church in the Nineteenth Century: A Bibliographical Review." In Marjorie B. Troeh and Eileen M. Terril, eds., *Restoration Studies IV*, pp. 171–87. Independence, MO: Herald Publishing House, 1988.

Leonard, Glen M. "Recent Writing on Mormon Nauvoo." *Western Illinois Regional Studies* 11 (Fall 1988): 69–93.

Madsen, Carol Cornwall, and David J. Whittaker. "History's Sequel: A Source Essay on Women in Mormon History." *Journal of Mormon History* 6 (1979): 123–45.

Mauss, Armand L., and Jeffrey R. Franks. "Comprehensive Bibliography of Social Science Literature on the Mormons." *Review of Religious Research* 26 (September 1984): 73–115.

Paul, Rodman W. "The Mormons as a Theme in Western Historical Writing." *Journal of American History* 54 (December 1967): 511–23.

Poll, Richard D. "Nauvoo and the New Mormon History: A Bibliographical Survey." *Journal of Mormon History* 5 (1978): 105–23.

Saunders, Richard L. *Printing in Deseret: Mormons, Economy, Politics, and Utah's Incunabula, 1849–1851.* Salt Lake City: University of Utah Press, 2000.

Scott, Patricia Lyn. "Mormon Polygamy: A Bibliography, 1977–91." *Journal of Mormon History* 19 (Spring 1993): 133–55.

Shields, Steven L. *The Latter Day Saint Churches: An Annotated Bibliography.* New York/London: Garland Publishing, 1987.

Taylor, P. A. M. "Recent Writing on Utah and the Mormons." *Arizona and the West* 4 (Autumn 1962): 249–60.

Wahlquist, Wayne L. "A Review of Mormon Settlement Literature." *Utah Historical Quarterly* 45 (Winter 1977): 3–21.

Whittaker, David J. "Bibliography: LDS Missionary Work." *Mormon History Association Newsletter* 69 (July 1988): 5–8.

———. "History—Educational System of the LDS Church." *Mormon History Association Newsletter* 68 (April 1988): 2–5.

Whittaker, David J., ed. *Mormon Americana: A Guide to Sources and Collections in the United States.* Provo, UT: BYU Studies, 1995.

———. "Mormonism in Great Britain, 1837–1987." *Mormon History Association Newsletter* 66 (July 1987): 1–4.

———. "Mormons and Native Americans: A Historical and Bibliographical Introduction." *Dialogue: A Journal of Mormon Thought* 18 (Winter 1985): 33–64.

———. "Mormon Social History: A Selected Bibliography." *Mormon History Association Newsletter* 6 (April 1986): 2–5.

———. "Sources on Mormon Origins in New York and Pennsylvania." *Mormon History Association Newsletter* 43 (March 1980): 8–12.

Whittaker, David J., and Chris McClellan. *Mormon Missions and Missionaries: A Bibliographic Guide to Published and Manuscript Sources*. Provo, UT: Harold B. Lee Library, Brigham Young University, 1993.

Wilson, William A. "A Bibliography of Studies in Mormon Folklore." *Utah Historical Quarterly* 44 (Fall 1976): 389–94.

PUBLISHED PRIMARY SOURCES

Bagley, Will, ed. *Scoundrel's Tale: The Samuel Brannan Papers*. Vol. 3 of *Kingdom in the West: The Mormons and the American Frontier*. Spokane, WA: Arthur H. Clark Company, 1999.

Barney, Ronald O., ed. "Letters of a Missionary Apostle to His Wife: Brigham Young to Mary Ann Angell Young, 1839–1841." *Brigham Young University Studies* 38 (1999): 156–201.

Baugh, Alexander L. "Joseph Young's Affidavit of the Massacre at Haun's Mill." *Brigham Young University Studies* 38 (1999): 188–202.

Bigler, David L. *Fort Limhi: The Mormon Adventure in Oregon Territory, 1855–1858*. Vol. 6 of *Kingdom in the West: The Mormons and the American Frontier*. Spokane: WA: Arthur H. Clark Company, 2003.

The Book of Mormon. Salt Lake City: The Church of Jesus Christ of Latter-day Saints, 1981.

The Book of Mormon: A Reader's Edition. Ed. Grant Hardy. Urbana/Chicago: University of Illinois Press, 2003.

Buchanan, Frederick Stewart, ed. *A Good Time Coming: Mormon Letters to Scotland*. Salt Lake City: University of Utah Press, 1988.

Campbell, Eugene E., ed. *The Essential Brigham Young*. Salt Lake City: Signature Books, 1992.

Cannon, Donald Q., and Lyndon W. Cook, eds. *Far West Record: Minutes of the Church of Jesus Christ of Latter-day Saints, 1830–1844*. Salt Lake City: Deseret Book, 1983.

Clark, James R., ed. *Messages of the First Presidency of the Church of Jesus Christ of Latter-day Saints*. 6 vols. Salt Lake City: Bookcraft, 1971–1975.

Collier, Fred C., and William S. Hartwell, eds. *Kirtland Council Minute Book*. Salt Lake City: Collier's Publishing Co., 1996.

Cook, Lyndon W. "'Brother Joseph Is Truly a Wonderful Man, He Is All We Could Wish a Prophet to Be': Pre-1844 Letters of William Law." *Brigham Young University Studies* 20 (Winter 1980): 207–18.

Cook, Lyndon W., ed. *The Revelations of the Prophet Joseph Smith*. Provo, UT: Seventy's Mission Bookstore, 1981.

Cook, Lyndon W., and Milton V. Backman Jr., eds. *Kirtland Elders' Quorum Record, 1836–1841*. Provo, UT: Grandin Book Co., 1985.

Cook, Lyndon W., and Matthew K. Cook, eds. *David Whitmer Interviews: A Restoration Witness*. Orem, UT: Grandin Book Co., 1991.

Cracroft, Richard H., and Neal E. Lambert, eds. *A Believing People: Literature of the Latter-day Saints*. Provo, UT: Brigham Young University Press, 1974.

Crawley, Peter L., ed. *The Essential Parley P. Pratt*. Salt Lake City: Signature Books, 1990.

Dahl, Larry E., and Charles D. Tate Jr., eds. *The Lectures on Faith in Historical Perspective*. Provo, UT: Religious Studies Center, Brigham Young University, 1990.

Daughters of Utah Pioneers. *Chronicles of Courage*. 1– (1990–).

———. *An Enduring Legacy*. Vols. 1–12 (1978–1989).

———. *Heart Throbs of the West*. 12 vols. (1939–1951).

———. *Our Pioneer* Heritage. 20 vols. (1958–1977).

———. *Treasures of Pioneer History*. 6 vols. (1952–1957).

The Doctrine and Covenants. Salt Lake City: The Church of Jesus Christ of Latter-day Saints, 1981.

Durham, G. Homer, comp. *The Discourses of Wilford Woodruff*. Salt Lake City: Bookcraft, 1946.

Ehat, Andrew F., and Lyndon W. Cook, eds. *The Words of Joseph Smith*. Provo, UT: Religious Studies Center, Brigham Young University, 1980.

Ekins, Roger Robin, ed. *Defending Zion: George Q. Cannon and the California Mormon Newspaper Wars of 1856–1857*. Vol. 5 of *Kingdom in the West: The Mormons and the American Frontier*. Spokane, WA: Arthur H. Clark Co., 2002.

Ellsworth, Maria S., ed. *Mormon Odyssey: The Story of Ida Hunt Udall, Plural Wife*. Urbana: University of Illinois Press, 1992.

Ellsworth, S. George, ed. *Dear Ellen: Two Mormon Women and Their Letters*. Salt Lake City: Tanner Trust Fund, University of Utah Library, 1974.

Godfrey, Kenneth W., Audrey M. Godfrey, and Jill Mulvay Derr, eds. *Women's Voices: An Untold History of the Latter-day Saints*. Salt Lake City: Deseret Book, 1982.

Gospel Ideals: Selections from the Discourses of David O. McKay. Salt Lake City: Improvement Era, 1953.

Grant, Heber J. *Gospel Standards: Selections from the Sermons and Writings of Heber J. Grant*. Salt Lake City: Improvement Era, 1941.

Hansen, Jennifer Moulton, ed. *Letters of Catharine Cottam Romney, Plural Wife*. Urbana: University of Illinois Press, 1992.

Hardy, B. Carmon, ed. *Doing the Works of Abraham: Mormon Polygamy, Its Origin, Practice, and Demise*. Vol. 9 of *Kingdom in the West: The Mormons and the American Frontier*. Norman, OK: Arthur H. Clark Co., 2007.

Harris, James, ed. *The Essential James E. Talmage*. Salt Lake City: Signature Books, 1997.

Harwell, William S., ed. *Manuscript History of Brigham Young, 1847–1850.* Salt Lake City: Collier's Publishing Co., 1997. (See also Watson, Elden.)

Higbee, Marilyn. "'A Weary Traveler': The 1848–50 Diary of Zina D. H. Young." *Journal of Mormon History* 19 (Fall 1993): 86–125.

Hill, Marvin S., ed. *The Essential Joseph Smith.* Salt Lake City: Signature Books, 1995.

Holzapfel, Jeni Brobert, and Richad Neizel Holzapfel, eds. *A Woman's View: Helen Mar Whitney's Reminiscences of Early Church History*. Provo, UT: Religious Studies Center, Brigham Young University, 1997.

Homer, Michael W. *On the Way to Somewhere Else: European Sojourners in the Mormon West, 1834–1930*. Vol. 8 of *Kingdom in the West: Mormons and the American Frontier*. Spokane, WA: Arthur H. Clark, Co., 2006

Huntress, Keith C., ed. *Murder of an American Prophet*. San Francisco: Chandler Publishing Co., 1960.

Jessee, Dean C., ed. *Letters of Brigham Young to His Sons*. Salt Lake City: Deseret Book, 1974.

———. *The Papers of Joseph Smith.* Vols. 1–. Salt Lake City: Deseret Book Company, 1989–.

Johnson, Clark V., comp. *Mormon Redress Petitions: Documents of the 1833–1838 Missouri Conflict*. Religious Studies Center, Brigham Young University. Salt Lake City: Bookcraft, 1992.

Kimball, Edward L., ed. *The Teachings of Spencer W. Kimball*. Salt Lake City: Bookcraft, 1982.

Kirkham, Francis W. *A New Witness for Christ in America.* 2 vols. Independence, MO: Zion's Printing and Publishing, 1942, 1951.

Knight, Greg R., ed. *Thomas Bullock Nauvoo Journal.* Orem, UT: Grandin Book, 1994.

Larson, Stan. "A 'Meeting of the Brethren': The Discovery of Official Minutes of a 1902 Meeting of the First Presidency and Twelve Apostles." *Dialogue: A Journal of Mormon Thought* 31 (Summer 1998): 77–95.

———, ed. *Prisoner for Polygamy: The Memoirs and Letters of Rudger Clawson at the Utah Territorial Penitentiary, 1884–87*. Urbana: University of Illinois Press, 1993.

Lieber, Constance L. "'The Goose Hangs High': Excerpts from the Letters of Martha Hughes Cannon." *Utah Historical Quarterly* 48 (Winter 1980): 37–48.

Lieber, Constance L., and John Sillito, eds. *Letters from Exile: The Correspondence of Martha Hughes Cannon and Angus M. Cannon, 1886–1888*. Salt Lake City: Signature Books, 1989.

Madsen, Carol Cornwall. *In Their Own Words: Women and the Story of Nauvoo*. Salt Lake City: Deseret Book, 1994.

McKiernan, F. Mark, and Roger D. Launius, eds. *An Early Latter Day Saint History: The Book of John Whitmer*. Independence, MO: Herald Publishing House, 1980. (See also Westergren, Bruce.)

Millett, Robert L., ed. *Joseph Smith: Selected Sermons and Writings*. New York: Paulist Press, 1989.

Mulder, William, and A. Russell Mortensen, eds. *Among the Mormons: Historic Accounts by Contemporary Observers*. New York: Knopf, 1967.

Owens, Kenneth N. *Gold Rush Saints: California Mormons and the Great Rush for Riches*. Vol. 7 of *Kingdom in the West: The Mormons and the American Frontier*. Spokane, WA: Arthur H. Clark Co., 2004.

The Pearl of Great Price. Salt Lake City: The Church of Jesus Christ of Latter-day Saints, 1981.

Smith, Hyrum M., ed. *From Prophet to Son: Advice of Joseph F. Smith to His Missionary Sons*. Salt Lake City: Deseret Book, 1981.

Smith, Joseph. *History of the Church of Jesus Christ of Latter-day Saints*. 7 vols. Ed. B. H. Roberts. Salt Lake City: Deseret Book, 1902–1912.

Smith, Joseph F. *Gospel Doctrine*. 2nd ed. Salt Lake City: Deseret News, 1919.

Smith, Joseph Fielding, comp. *Teachings of the Prophet Joseph Smith*. Salt Lake City: Deseret Book, 1938.

Snow, Lorenzo. *The Teachings of Lorenzo Snow*. Comp. Clyde J. Williams. Salt Lake City: Bookcraft, 1984.

Taylor, John. *Gospel Kingdom: Selections from the Writings and Discourses of John Taylor*. Comp. G. Homer Durham. Salt Lake City: Bookcraft, 1943.

Van Orden, Bruce, ed. "Writing to Zion: The William W. Phelps Kirtland Letters (1835–1836)." *Brigham Young University Studies* 33 (1993): 542–93.

Vogel, Dan, ed. *Early Mormon Documents*. Vol. 1. Salt Lake City: Signature Books, 1995.

———. *Early Mormon Documents*. Vol. 2. Salt Lake City: Signature Books, 1998.

Watson, Elden J., ed. *Manuscript History of Brigham Young, 1846–1847*. Salt Lake City: Elden J. Watson, 1971. (See also Harwell, William.)

Welch, John W., ed. *Opening the Heavens: Accounts of Divine Manifestations, 1820–1844*. Provo, UT: Brigham Young University Press, and Salt Lake City: Deseret Book, 2005.

Westergren, Bruce N., and Julie J. Westergren, eds. *From Historian to Dissident: The Book of John Whitmer*. Salt Lake City: Signature Books, 1994. (See also McKiernan, Mark, above.)

Whittaker, David J., ed. *The Essential Orson Pratt*. Salt Lake City: Signature Books, 1991.

Woodruff, Wilford. *The Discourses of Wilford Woodruff*. Comp. G. Homer Durham. Salt Lake City: Bookcraft, 1946.

Young, Brigham. *Discourses of Brigham Young*. Comp. John A. Widtsoe. Salt Lake City: Deseret Book, 1925.

DIARIES AND AUTOBIOGRAPHIES

Allen, James B., and Thomas G. Alexander, eds. *Manchester Mormons: The Journal of William Clayton, 1840 to 1842*. Santa Barbara, CA/Salt Lake City: Peregrine Smith, 1974.

Anderson, Lavina Fielding, ed. *Lucy's Book: A Critical Edition of Lucy Mack Smith's Family Memoir*. Salt Lake City: Signature Books, 2000.

Archer, Patience Loader. *Recollections of Past Days: the Autobiography of Patience Loader Rozsa Archer*. Logan, UT: Utah State University Press, 2006.

Arrington, Leonard J. *Adventures of a Church Historian*. Urbana: University of Illinois Press, 1998.

———, ed. "Crusade against Theocracy: The Reminiscences of Judge Jacob Smith Boreman of Utah, 1872–1877." *Huntington Library Quarterly* 24 (November 1960): 1–45.

———, ed. "Oliver Cowdery's Kirtland, Ohio, 'Sketch Book.'" *Brigham Young University Studies* 12 (Summer 1972): 410–26.

Bagley, Will, ed. *Frontiersman: Abner Blackburn's Narrative*. Salt Lake City: University of Utah Press, 1992.

———. *The Pioneer Camp of the Saints: The 1846 and 1847 Mormon Trail Journals of Thomas Bullock*. Vol. 1 of *Kingdom in the West: The Mormons and the American Frontier*. Spokane, WA: Arthur H. Clark Co., 1997.

Barney, Ronald O., ed. *The Mormon Vanguard Brigade of 1847: Norton Jacob's Record*. Logan, UT: Utah State University Press, 2005.

Beecher, Maureen Ursenbach, ed. "'All Things Move in Order in the City': The Nauvoo Diary of Zina Diantha Huntington Jacobs." *Brigham Young University Studies* 19 (Spring 1979): 285–320.

———. "Eliza R. Snow's Nauvoo Journal." *Brigham Young University Studies* 15 (Summer 1975): 391–416.

———. "The Iowa Journal of Lorenzo Snow." *Brigham Young University Studies* 24 (Summer 1984): 261–73.

——. *The Personal Writings of Eliza Roxcy Snow*. Salt Lake City: University of Utah Press, 1995.

Bergera, Gary James, ed. *The Autobiography of B. H. Roberts*. Salt Lake City: Signature Books, 1990.

Bigler, David L., ed. *The Gold Discovery Journal of Azariah Smith*. Salt Lake City: University of Utah Press, 1990.

Bishop, William W., ed. *Mormonism Unveiled, or Life and Confession of John D. Lee*. Albuquerque, NM: Fierra Blanca, 2001

Brimhall, Sandra Dawn Allen, ed. *Journal of Isaiah Moses Coombs (1855–1856)*. Vol. 1. Salt Lake City: Privately published, 1993.

Brooks, Juanita, ed. *On the Mormon Frontier: The Diary of Hosea Stout, 1844–1861*. Salt Lake City: University of Utah Press, 1964.

——. *Quicksand and Cactus: A Memoir of the Southern Mormon Frontier*. Salt Lake City: Howe Brothers, 1982.

Buice, David. "'All Alone and None to Cheer Me': The Southern States Mission Diaries of J. Golden Kimball." *Dialogue: A Journal of Mormon Thought* 24 (Spring 1991): 35–54.

——. "Excerpts from the Diary of Teancum William Heward, Early Mormon Missionary to Georgia." *Georgia Historical Quarterly* 64 (Fall 1981): 317–25.

Bullock, Thomas. "Journal of Thomas Bullock, 31 August 1845 to 5 July 1846." *Brigham Young University Studies* 31 (Winter 1991): 15–75.

Busche, F. Enzio. *Yearning for the Living God: Reflections from the Life of F. Enzio Busche*. Salt Lake City: Deseret Book, 2004.

Cannon, M. Hamlin, ed. "The Prison Diary of a Mormon Apostle." *Pacific Historical Review* 16 (November 1947): 393–409.

Clayton, William. *William Clayton's Journal: A Daily Record of the Journey of the Original Company*. Salt Lake City: Clayton Family Association, 1921.

Cleland, Robert Glass, and Juanita Brooks, eds. *A Mormon Chronicle: The Diaries of John D. Lee*. 2 vols. San Marino, CA: Huntington Library, 1955.

Creer, Leland H., ed. "Journey to Zion: From the Journal of Erastus Snow." *Utah Humanities Review* 2 (April and July 1948): 107–28, 264–84.

Crookson, Douglas L. *Henry Ballard: The Story of a Courageous Pioneer*. N.p.: Privately published, 1994.

Egan, Howard R. *Pioneering the West, 1846–1878: Major Howard Egan's Diary*. Richmond, UT: Howard R. Egan Estate, 1917.

Ellsworth, Maria S., ed. *Mormon Odyssey: The Story of Ida Hunt Udall, Plural Wife*. Urbana/Chicago: University of Illinois Press, 1992.

Ellsworth, S. George, ed. *The History of Louisa Barnes Pratt: Being the Autobiography of a Mormon Missionary Widow and Pioneer*. Logan: Utah State University, 1998.

———. *The Journals of Addison Pratt*. Salt Lake City: University of Utah Press, 1990.

England, Eugene, ed. "George Laub's Nauvoo Journal." *Brigham Young University Studies* 18 (1978): 151–78.

Evans, Cleo H., comp. *Curtis Bolton: Pioneer Missionary*. N.p.: Privately published, 1968.

Firmage, Edwin Brown, ed. *An Abundant Life: The Memoirs of Hugh B. Brown*. Salt Lake City: Signature Books, 1988.

Garner, Hugh, ed. *A Mormon Rebel: The Life and Travels of Frederick Gardiner*. Salt Lake City: Signature Books, 1993.

Godfrey, Donald G., and Brigham Y. Card, eds. *The Diaries of Charles Ora Card: The Canadian Years, 1886–1903*. Salt Lake City: University of Utah Press, 1993.

Groberg, John H. *The Fire of Faith*. Salt Lake City: Bookcraft, 1996.

———. *In the Eye of the Storm*. Salt Lake City: Bookcraft, 1993.

Hart, Edward L. *Mormon in Motion: The Life and Journals of James H. Hart, 1825–1906*. Provo, UT: Windsor Books, 1978.

Hartley, William G. *My Best for the Kingdom: History and Autobiography of John Lowe Butler, a Mormon Frontiersman*. Salt Lake City: Aspen Books, 1993.

Hatch, Charles M., and Todd M. Compton, eds. *A Widow's Tale: The 1884–1896 Diary of Helen Mar Kimball Whitney*. Logan: Utah State University Press, 2003.

Heath, Harvard S., ed. *In the World: The Diaries of Reed Smoot*. Salt Lake City: Signature Books, 1994.

Holzapfel, Jeni Broberg, and Richard Neitzel Holzapfel. *A Woman"s View: Helen Mar Whitney's Reminiscences of Early Church History*. Provo, UT: Religious Studies Center, Brigham Young University, 1997.

Horne, Dennis B., ed. *An Apostle's Record: The Journals of Abraham H. Cannon*. Clearfield, UT: Gnolaum Books, 2004.

Jenson, Andrew. *Autobiography of Andrew Jenson, Assistant Historian of the Church*. Salt Lake City: Deseret News Press, 1938.

Jessee, Dean C., ed. "The John Taylor Nauvoo Journal." *Brigham Young University Studies* 23 (Summer 1983): 1–124.

———. "The Kirtland Diary of Wilford Woodruff." *Brigham Young University Studies* 12 (Summer 1972): 365–99.

Jessee, Dean C., et al., eds. "The Last Months of Mormonism in Missouri: The Albert Perry Rockwood Journal." *Brigham Young University Studies* 28 (1988): 5–41.

Johnson, Benjamin F. *My Life's Review: The Autobiography of Benjamin F. Johnson*. Provo, UT: Grandin Book Co., 1997.

Jones, Daniel W. *Forty Years among the Indians*. Salt Lake City: Juvenile Instructor Office, 1890.

Kenney, Scott G., ed. *Memories and Reflections: The Autobiography of E. E. Ericksen*. Salt Lake City: Signature Books, 1987.

———. *Wilford Woodruff's Journal*. 9 vols. Salt Lake City: Signature Books, 1983.

Kimball, Stanley B., ed. *On the Potter's Wheel: The Diaries of Heber C. Kimball*. Salt Lake City: Signature Books, 1987.

Krenkal, John H., ed. *The Life and Times of Joseph Fish, Mormon Pioneer*. Danville, IL: Interstate, 1970.

Landon, Michael N., ed. *The Journals of George Q. Cannon*. Vol 1, *To California in '49*. Salt Lake City: Deseret Book, 1999.

Larson, A. Karl, and Katherine Miles Larson, eds. *Diary of Charles Lowell Walker*. 2 vols. Logan: Utah State University Press, 1980.

Larson, Stan, ed. *A Ministry of Meetings: Diaries of Rudger Clawson*. Salt Lake City: Signature Books, 1993.

———. *Prisoner for Polygamy: The Memoirs and Letters of Rudger Clawson at the Utah Territorial Penitentiary, 1884–87*. Urbana/Chicago: University of Illinois Press, 1993.

Lee, George P. *Silent Courage, an Indian Story: The Autobiography of George P. Lee, a Navajo*. Salt Lake City: Deseret Book, 1987.

Lund, Anthon H. *Danish Apostle: The Diaries of Anthon H. Lund, 1890–1921*. Ed. John P. Hatch. Salt Lake City: Signature Books, 2006.

Madsen, Carol Cornwall, ed. *Journey to Zion: Voices from the Mormon Trail*. Salt Lake City: Deseret Book, 1997.

Martins, Helvecio. *The Autobiography of Elder Helvecio Martins*. Salt Lake City: Aspen Books, 1994.

McIntyre, Myron W., and Noel R. Barton, eds. *Christopher Layton: Colonizer, Statesman, Leader*. Salt Lake City: Christopher Layton Family Organization, 1966.

Neilsen, Reid L., ed. *The Japanese Missionary Journal of Elder Alma O. Taylor, 1901–10*. Provo, UT: BYU Studies, 2001.

Nixon, Loretta D. and L. Douglas Smoot. *Abraham Owen Smoot: A Testament of His Life*. Provo, UT: Brigham Young University Press, 1994.

Partridge, Scott H., ed. *Eliza Maria Partridge Journal*. Provo, UT: Grandin Book Co., 2003.

Pratt, Parley P., ed. *Autobiography of Parley Parker Pratt*. Salt Lake City: Deseret Book, 1961. (Orig. pub., 1874.)

Robertson, Frank C. *A Ram in the Thicket: The Story of a Roaming Homesteader Family on the Mormon Frontier*. Moscow, ID: University of Idaho Press, 1994.

Sessions, Gene A., ed. *Mormon Democrat: The Religious and Political Memoirs of James Henry Moyle.* Salt Lake City: James Moyle Genealogical and Historical Association, 1975.

Shipps, Jan. *Sojourner in the Promised Land: Forty Years among the Mormons.* Urbana/Chicago: University of Illinois Press, 2000.

Shipps, Jan, and John W. Welch, eds. *The Journals of William E. McLellan, 1831–1836.* Provo, UT: BYU Studies, and Urbana: University of Illinois Press, 1994.

Smart, Donna Toland, ed. *Exemplary Elder: The Life and Missionary Diaries of Perrigrine Sessions, 1814–1893.* Provo, UT: BYU Studies and Joseph Fielding Smith Institute for Latter-day Saint History, 2002.

———. *Mormon Midwife: The 1846–1888 Diaries of Patty Bartlett Sessions.* Vol. 2 of *Life Writings of Frontier Women.* Logan: Utah State University Press, 1997.

Smith, George D., ed. *An Intimate Chronicle: The Journals of William Clayton.* Salt Lake City: Signature Books, 1991.

Smith, Oliver R., ed. *Six Decades in the Early West: The Journal of Jesse Nathaniel Smith, 1834–1906.* Provo, UT: Jesse N. Smith Family Association, 1970.

Staker, Susan, ed. *Waiting for World's End: Diaries of Wilford Woodruff.* Salt Lake City: Signature Books, 1993.

Tanner, Annie Clark. *A Mormon Mother: An Autobiography.* Salt Lake City: Tanner Trust Fund, University of Utah Library, 1973.

Ward, Maurine Carr, ed. *Winter Quarters: The 1846–1848 Life Writings of Mary Haskin Parker Richards.* Logan: Utah State University Press, 1996.

Watson, Elden J., ed. *The Orson Pratt Journals.* Salt Lake City: Elden J. Watson, 1975.

Whitcomb, Elias W. "Reminiscences of a Pioneer: An Excerpt from the Diary of Elias W. Whitcomb." *Annals of Wyoming* 57 (Fall 1985): 21–32.

White, Jean Bickmore, ed. *Church, State, and Politics: The Diaries of John Henry Smith.* Salt Lake City: Signature Books, 1990.

BIOGRAPHIES

Alexander, Thomas G. *Things in Heaven and Earth: The Life and Times of Wilford Woodruff, a Mormon Prophet.* Salt Lake City: Signature Books, 1991.

Allen, James B. *Trials of Discipleship: The Story of William Clayton, a Mormon.* Urbana/Chicago: University of Illinois Press, 1987.

Anderson, Lavina Fielding. "A Ministry of Blessing: Nicholas Groesbeck Smith." *Dialogue: A Journal of Mormon Thought* 31 (Fall 1998): 59–78.

Anderson, Paul L. "William Henry Folsom: Pioneer Architect." *Utah Historical Quarterly* 43 (Summer 1975): 240–59.

Arrington, Harriet Horne. "Alice Merrill Horne, Art Promoter and Early Utah Legislator." *Utah Historical Quarterly* 58 (Summer 1990): 261–76.

Arrington, J. Earl. "William Weeks, Architect of the Nauvoo Temple." *Brigham Young University Studies* 19 (Spring 1979): 337–59.

Arrington, Leonard J. *Brigham Young: American Moses*. New York: Knopf, 1985.

———. *Charles C. Rich: Mormon General and Western Frontiersman*. Provo, UT: Brigham Young University Press, 1974.

———. *David Eccles: Pioneer Western Industrialist*. Logan: Utah State University Press, 1975.

———. *From Quaker to Latter-day Saint: Bishop Edwin D. Woolley*. Salt Lake City: Deseret Book, 1976.

———. *Harold F. Silver: Western Inventor, Businessman, and Civic Leader*. With John R. Alley Jr. Logan: Utah State University Press, 1992.

———. *Madelyn Cannon Stewart Silver: Poet, Teacher, Homemaker*. Salt Lake City, UT: Publishers Press, 1998.

———, ed. *The Presidents of the Church*. Salt Lake City: Deseret Book, 1986.

Arrington, Leonard J., and Davis Bitton. *Saints without Halos: The Human Side of Mormon History*. Salt Lake City: Signature Books, 1982.

Arrington, Leonard J., and Richard Jensen. "Pioneer Portraits: Lorenzo Hill Hatch." *Idaho Yesterdays* 17 (Summer 1973): 2–8.

Arrington, Leonard J., and Susan Arrington Madsen. *Mothers of the Prophets*. Salt Lake City: Deseret Book, 1987.

———. *Sunbonnet Sisters: The Stories of Mormon Women and Frontier Life*. Salt Lake City: Bookcraft, 1984.

Avery, Valeen Tippets. *From Mission to Madness: Last Son of the Mormon Prophet*. Urbana: University of Illinois Press, 1998.

———. "Sketches of the Sweet Singer: David Hyrum Smith, 1844–1904." *John Whitmer Historical Association Journal* 5 (1985): 3–15.

Avery, Valeen Tippetts, and Linda King Newell. "Lewis C. Bidamon, Stepchild of Mormondom." *Brigham Young University Studies* 19 (Spring 1979): 375–88.

———. "The Lion and the Lady: Brigham Young and Emma Smith." *Utah Historical Quarterly* 48 (Winter 1980): 81–97.

Backman, Milton V., Jr. *A Profile of Latter-day Saints of Kirtland, Ohio, and Members of Zion's Camp, 1830–1839*. Provo, UT: Brigham Young University Department of Church History and Doctrine, 1982.

Backus, Anna Jean. *Mountain Meadows Witness: The Life and Times of Bishop Philip Klingensmith*. Spokane, WA: Arthur H. Clark Co., 1995.

Barney, Ronald O. *One Side by Himself: The Life and Times of Lewis Barney, 1808–1894*. Logan: Utah State University Press, 2001.

Barron, Howard H. *Orson Hyde: Missionary, Apostle, Colonizer*. Bountiful, UT: Horizon, 1977.

Barton, Peggy Petersen. *Mark E. Petersen: A Biography*. Salt Lake City: Deseret Book, 1985.

Bates, Irene M. "Uncle John Smith, 1781–1854: Patriarchal Bridge." *Dialogue: A Journal of Mormon Thought* 20 (Fall 1987): 79–89.

Beecher, Maureen Ursenbach. "Each in Her Own Time: Four Zinas." *Dialogue: A Journal of Mormon Thought* 26 (Summer 1993): 119–35.

———. *Eliza and Her Sisters*. Salt Lake City: Aspen Books, 1991.

Bell, James P. *In the Strength of the Lord: The Life and Teachings of James E. Faust*. Salt Lake City: Deseret Book, 1999.

Bennion, Sherilyn Cox. "Lula Greene Richards: Utah's First Woman Editor." *Brigham Young University Studies* 21 (Spring 1981): 155–74.

Bergman, Ray L. *The Children Sang: The Life and Music of Evan Stephen*. Salt Lake City: Northwest Publishing, 1992.

Bishop, M. Guy. "After Sutter's Mill: The Life of Henry Bigler, 1848–1900." *Dialogue: A Journal of Mormon Thought* 20 (Spring 1987): 125–35.

———. "'A Great Little Saint': A Brief Look at the Life of Henry William Bigler." *Brigham Young University Studies* 30 (Fall 1990): 27–38.

———. *Henry William Bigler: Soldier, Gold Miner, Missionary, Chronicler, 1815–1900*. Logan: Utah State University Press, 1998.

Bitton, Davis. "Claude T. Barnes, Utah Naturalist." *Utah Historical Quarterly* 49 (Fall 1981): 316–30.

———. *George Q. Cannon: A Biography*. Salt Lake City: Deseret Book, 1999.

———. "'I'd Rather Have Some Roasting Ears': The Peregrinations of George Armstrong Hicks." *Utah Historical Quarterly* 68.3 (2000): 196–222.

———. *Images of the Prophet Joseph Smith*. Salt Lake City: Aspen Books, 1996.

———. *The Martyrdom Remembered*. Salt Lake City: Aspen Books, 1994.

———. *The Redoubtable John Pack*. Salt Lake City: Eden Hill, 1982.

Black, Susan Easton, and Larry C. Porter, eds. *Lion of the Lord: Essays on the Life and Service of Brigham Young*. Salt Lake City: Deseret Book, 1995.

Black, Susan Easton, and Charles D. Tate, Jr., eds. *Joseph Smith: The Prophet, the Man*. Provo, UT: Religious Studies Center, Brigham Young University, 1993.

Bradford, Mary Lythgoe. *Lowell L. Bennion: Teacher, Counselor, Humanitarian*. Salt Lake City: Dialogue Foundation, 1995.

Bradley, Martha Sonntag, and Mary Brown Firmage Woodward. *Four Zinas: A Story of Mothers and Daughters on the Mormon Frontier*. Salt Lake City: Signature Books, 2000.

Brady, Margaret K. *Mormon Healer and Folk Poet: Mary Susannah Fowler's Life of "Unselfish Usefulness."* Logan: Utah State University Press, 2000.

Bringhurst, Newell G. *Brigham Young and the Expanding American Frontier.* Boston: Little, Brown, 1986.

———. "The Private versus the Public David O. McKay: Profile of a Complex Personality." *Dialogue: A Journal of Mormon Thought* 31 (Fall 1998): 11–32.

Brodie, Fawn M. *No Man Knows My History: The Life of Joseph Smith, the Mormon Prophet.* New York: Knopf, 1945.

Brooks, Juanita. *Emma Lee.* Logan: Utah State University Press, 1984.

———. *Jacob Hamblin: Mormon Apostle to the Indians.* Salt Lake City: Westwater Press, 1980.

———. *John D. Lee: Zealot, Pioneer Builder, Scapegoat.* Rev. ed. Glendale, CA: Arthur H. Clark, 1972.

Buchanan, Frederick S. "Robert Lang Campbell: 'A Wise Scribe in Israel' and Schoolman to the Saints." *Brigham Young University Studies* 19 (Summer 1989): 5–27.

Burgess-Olson, Vicky D., ed. *Sister Saints.* Provo, UT: Brigham Young University Press, 1978.

Bush, Laura L. *Faithful Transgressions in the American West: Six Twentieth-Century Women's Autobiographical Acts.* Logan: Utah State University Press, 2004.

Bushman, Claudia, ed. *Mormon Sisters: Women in Early Utah.* 1st ed. Cambridge, MA, 1976. Rev. ed. Logan: Utah State University Press, 1997.

Bushman, Richard L. *Believing History: Latter-day Saint Essays.* New York: Columbia University Press, 2004.

———. *Joseph Smith and the Beginnings of Mormonism.* Urbana/Chicago: University of Illinois Press, 1984.

———. *Joseph Smith: Rough Stone Rolling.* New York: Knopf, 2005.

Campbell, Eugene E., and Poll, Richard D. *Hugh B. Brown: His Life and Thought.* Salt Lake City: Bookcraft, 1975.

Cannon, Kenneth L., II. "Brigham Bicknell Young, Musical Christian Scientist." *Utah Historical Quarterly* 50 (Spring 1982): 124–38.

Carmack, Noel A. "The Seven Ages of Thomas Lyne: A Tragedian among the Mormons." *John Whitmer Historical Association Journal* 14 (1994): 53–72.

Carmack, Noel A., and Karen Lynn Davidson, eds. *Out of the Black Patch: The Autobiography of Effie Marquess Carmack, Folk Musician, Artist, and Writer.* Logan: Utah State University Press.

Cheney, Thomas E. *The Golden Legacy: A Folk History of J. Golden Kimball.* Santa Barbara, CA/Salt Lake City: Peregrine Smith, 1974.

———. *Voices from the Bottom of the Bowl: A Folk History of Teton Valley, Idaho, 1823–1952.* Salt Lake City: University of Utah Press, 1991.

Christensen, Scott R. *Sagwitch: Shoshone Chieftain, Mormon Elder, 1822–1887.* Logan: Utah State University Press, 1999.

Condie, Spencer J. *Russell M. Nelson: Father, Surgeon, Apostle*. Salt Lake City: Deseret Book, 2003.

Cook, Lyndon W. "Isaac Galland—Mormon Benefactor." *Brigham Young University Studies* 19 (Spring 1979): 261–84.

———. *Joseph C. Kingsbury: A Biography*. Provo, UT: Grandin Book Co., 1985.

———. *William Law*. Orem, UT: Grandin Book Co., 1994.

———. "William Law, Nauvoo Dissenter." *Brigham Young University Studies* 22 (Winter 1982): 47–72.

Corbett, Pearson H. *Hyrum Smith, Patriarch*. Salt Lake City: Deseret Book, 1963.

Crawley, Peter. "Parley P. Pratt: Father of Mormon Pamphleteering." *Dialogue: A Journal of Mormon Thought* 15 (Autumn 1982): 13–26.

Davies, J. Kenneth. "Thomas Rhoads, Forgotten Mormon Pioneer of 1846." *Nebraska History* 64 (Spring 1983): 81–95.

Day, Kimberly. "Frederick Kesler, Utah Craftsman." *Utah Historical Quarterly* 56 (Winter 1988): 54–74.

Dew, Sheri L. *Ezra Taft Benson: A Biography*. Salt Lake City: Deseret Book, 1987.

———. *Go Forward with Faith: The Biography of Gordon B. Hinckley*. Salt Lake City: Deseret Book, 1996.

Durham, G. Homer. *N. Eldon Tanner: His Life and Service*. Salt Lake City: Deseret Book, 1982.

Edwards, Paul M. *The Chief: An Administrative Biography of Fred M. Smith*. Independence, MO: Herald Publishing House, 1988.

Ellsworth, S. George. *Samuel Claridge: Pioneering the Outposts of Zion*. Logan, UT: S. George Ellsworth, 1987.

England, Breck. *The Life and Thought of Orson Pratt*. Salt Lake City: University of Utah Press, 1985.

England, Eugene. *Brother Brigham*. Salt Lake City: Bookcraft, 1980.

Erekson, Arthur B. *A History of John Benbow*. Provo, UT: Author, 1987.

Erekson, Keith A., and Lloyd D. Newell, "The Conversion of Artemus Millet and His Call to Kirtland." *Brigham Young University Studies* 41 (2002): 76–115.

Euvrard, Christian. *Louis Auguste Bertrand (1808–1875): Journaliste Socialiste et Pionnier Mormon*. Paris: Privately published, 2005.

Evans, Richard L., Jr. *Richard L. Evans: The Man and the Message*. Salt Lake City: Bookcraft, 1973.

Flake, Lawrence R. *Mighty Men of Zion: General Authorities of the Last Dispensation*. Salt Lake City: Karl D. Butler, 1974.

Foster, Craig L. "From Temple Mormon to Anti-Mormon: The Ambivalent Odyssey of Increase Van Deusen." *Dialogue: A Journal of Mormon Thought* 27,3 (Fall 1994): 275–86.

Fox, Frank W. *J. Reuben Clark: The Public Years*. Provo, UT: Brigham Young University Press, 1980.

Gibbons, Francis M. *Brigham Young: Modern Moses, Prophet of God*. Salt Lake City: Deseret Book, 1981.

———. *George Albert Smith: Kind and Caring Christian, Prophet of God*. Salt Lake City: Deseret Book, 1990.

———. *Harold B. Lee: Man of Vision, Prophet of God*. Salt Lake City: Deseret Book, 1993.

———. *Heber J. Grant: Man of Steel, Prophet of God*. Salt Lake City: Deseret Book, 1979.

———. *John Taylor: Mormon Philosopher, Prophet of God*. Salt Lake City: Deseret Book, 1985.

———. *Joseph Smith: Martyr, Prophet of God*. Salt Lake City: Deseret Book, 1977.

———. *Joseph F. Smith: Patriarch and Preacher, Prophet of God*. Salt Lake City: Deseret Book, 1984.

———. *Lorenzo Snow: Spiritual Giant, Prophet of God*. Salt Lake City: Deseret Book, 1982.

———. *Spencer W. Kimball: Resolute Disciple, Prophet of God*. Salt Lake City: Deseret Book, 1995.

———. *Wilford Woodruff: Wondrous Worker, Prophet of God*. Salt Lake City: Deseret Book, 1988.

Goates, L. Brent. *Harold B. Lee: Prophet and Seer*. Salt Lake City: Bookcraft, 1985.

Godfrey, Donald G. "Zina Prescendia Young Williams Card: Brigham's Daughter, Cardston's First Lady." *Journal of Mormon History* 23 (Fall 1997): 107–27.

Godfrey, Kenneth W. "Charles S. Whitney: A Nineteenth-Century Salt Lake City Teenager's Life." *Journal of Mormon History* 27.2 (Fall 2001): 215–251.

Gregory, Thomas J. "Sidney Rigdon: Post Nauvoo." *Brigham Young University Studies* 21 (Winter 1981): 51–67.

Gunn, Stanley R. *Oliver Cowdery: Second Elder and Scribe*. Salt Lake City: Bookcraft, 1962.

Hafen, Bruce C. *A Disciple's Life: The Biography of Neal A. Maxwell*. Salt Lake City: Deseret Book, 2002.

Harris, Lynda W. "The Legend of Jessie Evans Smith." *Utah Historical Quarterly* 44 (Fall 1976): 351–64.

Hartley, William G. *Kindred Saints: The Mormon Immigrant Heritage of Alvin and Kathryne Christensen*. Salt Lake City: Eden Hill, 1982.

———. *My Best for the Kingdom: History and Biography of John Lowe Butler, Mormon Frontiersman*. Salt Lake City: Aspen Books, 1993.

———. *Stand by My Servant Joseph: The Story of the Joseph Knight Family and the Restoration*. Salt Lake City: Deseret Book, 2003.

———. *These Are My Friends: A History of the Joseph Knight Family, 1825–1850*. Provo, UT: Grandin Book Co., 1986.

Hatch, Jo Ann F. *Willing Hands: A Biography of Lorenzo Hill Hatch, 1826–1910*. Pinedale, AZ: Kymera Publishing Co., 1996.

Hefner, Loretta L. "From Apostle to Apostate: The Personal Struggle of Amasa Mason Lyman." *Dialogue: A Journal of Mormon Thought* 16 (Spring 1983): 90–104.

Hickman, Martin B. *David Matthew Kennedy: Banker, Statesman, Churchman*. Salt Lake City: Deseret Book, 1987.

Hiles, Norma Derry. *Gentle Monarch: The Presidency of Israel A. Smith*. Independence, MO: Herald Publishing House, 1991.

Hill, Donna. *Joseph Smith, the First Mormon*. New York: Doubleday, 1977.

Hinton, Wayne. "John D. T. McAllister: The Southern Utah Years, 1876–1910." *Journal of Mormon History* 29.2 (2003): 106–136.

Hoopes, David S., and Roy Hoopes. *The Making of a Mormon Apostle: The Story of Rudger Clawson*. Lanham, MD: Madison Books, 1990.

Howard, F. Burton. *Marion G. Romney: His Life and Faith*. Salt Lake City: Bookcraft, 1988.

Hunt, Larry E. *Fred M. Smith: Saint as Reformer*. Independence, MO: Herald Publishing House, 1982.

Hunter, Milton R. *Brigham Young the Colonizer*. 4th ed., rev. Santa Barbara, CA/Salt Lake City: Peregrine Smith, 1973.

Hyde, Myrtle Stevens. *Orson Hyde: The Olive Branch of Israel*. Salt Lake City: Agreka Books, 2000.

Hyde, Myrtle Stevens, and Everett L. Cooley. *The Life of Andrew Wood Cooley: A Story of Conviction*. Provo, UT: Andrew Wood Cooley Family Association, 1991.

Jenson, Andrew. *Latter-day Saint Biographical Encyclopedia*. 4 vols. Salt Lake City: Deseret News, 1901–1936.

Jessee, Dean C. "Brigham Young's Family: The Wilderness Years." *Brigham Young University Studies* 19 (Summer 1979): 474–500.

Johnson, Catherine M. "Emma Lucy Gates Bowen: Singer, Musician, Teacher." *Utah Historical Quarterly* 64 (Fall 1996): 344–55.

Johnson, Melvin C. *Polygamy on the Pedernales: Lyman Wight's Mormon Villages in Antebellum Texas, 1845 to 1858.* Logan: Utah State University Press, 2006.

Kimball, Edward L. *Lengthen Your Stride: The Presidency of Spencer W. Kimball.* Salt Lake City: Deseret Book, 2005.

Kimball, Edward L., and Andrew E. Kimball Jr. *Spencer W. Kimball.* Salt Lake City: Bookcraft, 1977.

———. *The Story of Spencer W. Kimball: A Short Man, a Long Stride.* Salt Lake City: Bookcraft, 1985.

Kimball, Edward L., and Caroline Eyring Miner. *Camilla: A Biography of Camilla Eyring Kimball.* Salt Lake City: Deseret Book, 1980.

Kimball, Stanley B. *Heber C. Kimball: Mormon Patriarch and Pioneer.* Urbana: University of Illinois Press, 1981.

Knowles, Eleanor. *Howard W. Hunter.* Salt Lake City: Deseret Book, 1994.

Larson, Andrew Karl. *Erastus Snow: The Life of a Missionary and Pioneer for the Early Mormon Church.* Salt Lake City: University of Utah Press, 1971.

Legg, Phillip R. *Oliver Cowdery: The Elusive Second Elder of the Restoration.* Independence, MO: Herald Publishing House, 1989.

Lund, Jennifer L. "Out of the Swan's Nest: The Ministry of Anthon H. Lund, Scandinavian Apostle." *Journal of Mormon History* 29.2 (Fall 2003): 77–105.

Lyman, Edward Leo. "The Alienation of an Apostle from His Quorum: The Moses Thatcher Case." *Dialogue: A Journal of Mormon Thought* 18 (Summer 1985): 67–91.

Lyon, T. Edgar, Jr. *John Lyon: The Life of a Pioneer Poet.* Provo, UT: Religious Studies Center, Brigham Young University, 1989.

———. *T. Edgar Lyon: A Teacher in Zion.* Provo, UT: Brigham Young University Press, 2002.

Macfarlane, L. W. *Yours Sincerely, John M. Macfarlane.* Salt Lake City: Privately published, 1980.

Madsen, Carol Cornwall. *An Advocate for Women: The Public Life of Emmeline B. Wells, 1870–1920.* Provo, UT: Brigham Young University Press and Salt Lake City: Deseret Book, 2006.

———. "Emmeline B. Wells: 'Am I Not a Woman and a Sister?'" *Brigham Young University Studies* 22 (Spring 1982): 161–78.

———. "Emmeline B. Wells: A Voice for Mormon Women." *John Whitmer Historical Association Journal* 2 (1982): 11–21.

Madsen, Truman G. *Defender of the Faith: The B. H. Roberts Story.* Salt Lake City: Bookcraft, 1980.

Maxwell, Bruce David. "George Careless, Pioneer Musician." *Utah Historical Quarterly* 53 (Spring 1985): 131–43.

McCloud, Susan Evans. *Not in Vain: The Inspiring Story of Ellis Shipp, Pioneer Woman Doctor*. Salt Lake City: Bookcraft, 1984.

McConkie, Joseph F. *The Bruce R. McConkie Story: Reflections of a Son.* Salt Lake City: Deseret Book, 2003.

———. *True and Faithful: The Life Story of Joseph Fielding Smith*. Salt Lake City: Bookcraft, 1971.

McConkie, Mark L., comp. *Remembering Joseph: Personal Recollections of Those Who Knew the Prophet Joseph Smith*. Salt Lake City: Deseret Book, 2003.

McKiernan, F. Mark. *The Voice of One Crying in the Wilderness: Sidney Rigdon, Religious Reformer, 1793–1876*. Lawrence, KS: Coronado Press, 1971.

Merrell, Kenneth W. *Scottish Shepherd: The Life and Times of John Murray Murdoch, Utah Pioneer.* Salt Lake City: University of Utah Press, 2006.

Merrill, Milton R. *Reed Smoot: Apostle in Politics*. Logan: Utah State University Press, 1990.

Milewski, Milessa Lambert, ed. *Before the Manifesto: The Life Writings of Mary Lois Walker Morris.* Logan: Utah State University Press, 2007.

Mortensen, Joann Follett. "King Follett: The Man behind the Discourse." *Journal of Mormon History* 32 (Summer 2005): 112–33.

Mullikin, Frances Hartman. *First Ladies of the Restoration*. Independence, MO: Herald Publishing House, 1985.

Newell, Linda King, and Valeen Tippetts Avery. *Mormon Enigma: Emma Hale Smith*. Garden City, NY: Doubleday, 1984.

Newton, Marjorie. *Hero or Traitor: A Biographical Study of Charles Wesley Wandell*. John Whitmer Association Monograph Series. Independence, MO: Independence Press, 1992.

Noord, Roger Van. *King of Beaver Island: The Life and Assassination of James Jesse Strang*. Urbana: University of Illinois Press, 1988.

O'Driscoll, Jefferey S. *Hyrum Smith: A Life of Integrity.* Salt Lake City: Deseret Book, 2003.

Olmstead, Jacob W., and Fred E. Woods. "'Give Me Any Situation Suitable': The Consecrated Life of the Multitalented Paul A. Schettler." *Brigham Young University Studies* 41 (2002): 108–26.

Oman, Richard G., and Richard L. Jensen. *C. C. A. Christensen, 1831–1912: Mormon Immigrant Artist*. Salt Lake City: Church of Jesus Christ of Latter-day Saints, 1984.

Parkinson, Benson Young. *S. Dilworth Young: General Authority, Scouter, Poet*. American Fork, UT: Covenant Publications, 1994.

Parrish, Alan K. *John A. Widtsoe: A Biography*. Salt Lake City: Deseret Book, 2003.

Petersen, Boyd Jay. *Hugh Nibley: A Consecrated Life.* Salt Lake City: Greg Kofford Books, 2002.

Peterson, Charles S. "'A Mighty Man Was Brother Lot': A Portrait of Lot Smith, Mormon Frontiersman." *Western Historical Quarterly* 1 (October 1970): 393–414.

Peterson, Janet, and LaRene Gaunt. *Elect Ladies: Presidents of the Relief Society.* Salt Lake City: Deseret Book, 1990.

———. *Keepers of the Flame: Presidents of the Young Women.* Salt Lake City: Deseret Book, 1993.

Peterson, Levi. *Juanita Brooks: Mormon Woman Historian.* Salt Lake City: University of Utah Press, 1988.

Peterson, Richard H. "Jesse Knight, Utah's Mormon Mining Mogul." *Utah Historical Quarterly* 57 (Summer 1989): 240–53.

Poll, Richard D. *Working the Divine Miracle: The Life of Apostle Henry D. Moyle.* Salt Lake City: Signature Books, 1999.

Porter, Larry C. "Reverend George Lane—Good 'Gifts,' Much 'Grace,' and Marked 'Usefulness.'" *Brigham Young University Studies* 9 (1970): 321–40.

Porter, Larry C., and Susan Easton Black, eds. *The Prophet Joseph: Essays on the Life and Meaning of Joseph Smith.* Salt Lake City: Deseret Book, 1988.

Pratt, Steven F. "Parley P. Pratt in Winter Quarters and the Trail West." *Brigham Young University Studies* 24 (Summer 1984): 373–88.

Prince, Gregory A., and William Robert Wright. *David O. McKay and the Rise of Modern Mormonism.* Salt Lake City: University of Utah Press, 2005.

Prince, Stephen L. "George Prince, Convert Out of Africa." *Journal of Mormon History* 28.2 (Fall 2002): 60–80.

Pusey, Merlo J. *Builders of the Kingdom: George A. Smith, John Henry Smith, George Albert Smith.* Provo, UT: Brigham Young University Press, 1981.

Quinn, D. Michael. *Elder Statesman: A Biography of J. Reuben Clark.* Salt Lake City: Signature Books, 2002.

———. "Jesse Gause: Joseph Smith's Little-Known Counselor." *Brigham Young University Studies* 17 (Summer 1984): 9–34.

———. *J. Reuben Clark: The Church Years.* Provo, UT: Brigham Young University Press, 1983.

Rollmann, Hans. "The Early Baptist Career of Sidney Rigdon in Warren, Ohio." *Brigham Young University Studies* 21 (Winter 1981): 37–50.

Romney, Thomas C. *Life Story of Miles Park Romney.* Salt Lake City: Zion's Printing and Publishing Co., 1948.

Rowley, Dennis. "Fishing on the Kennet: The Victorian Boyhood of James E. Talmage, 1862–1876." *Brigham Young University Studies* 33 (1993): 480–520.

Schindler, Harold. *Orrin Porter Rockwell: Man of God, Son of Thunder*. Salt Lake City: University of Utah Press, 1966.

Schlup, Leonard. "Utah Maverick: Frank J. Cannon and the Politics of Conscience in 1896." *Utah Historical Quarterly* 62.4 (Fall 1994): 335–48.

Schnibbe, Karl-Heinz. *The Price: The True Story of a Mormon Who Defied Hitler*. With Alan F. Keele and Douglas F. Tobler. Salt Lake City: Bookcraft, 1984.

Seegmiller, Janet Burton. *"Be Kind to the Poor": The Life Story of Robert Taylor Burton*. N.p.: Robert Taylor Burton Family Organization, 1988.

Seifrit, William C. "Charles Henry Wilcken: An Undervalued Saint." *Utah Historical Quarterly* 55 (Fall 1987): 308–21.

———. "The Prison Experience of Abraham H. Cannon." *Utah Historical Quarterly* 53 (Summer 1985): 223–36.

Sessions, Gene A. *Latter-day Patriots: Nine Mormon Families and Their Revolutionary War Heritage*. Salt Lake City: Deseret Book, 1975.

———, ed. *Mormon Democrat: The Religious and Political Memoirs of James Henry Moyle*. Salt Lake City: Signature Books, 1998.

———. *Mormon Thunder: A Documentary History of Jedediah Morgan Grant*. Urbana/Chicago: University of Illinois Press, 1982.

Smart, William B. "William H. Smart, Builder in the Basin." *Utah Historical Quarterly* 50 (Winter 1982): 59–67.

Smith, Andrew F. *The Saintly Scoundrel: The Life and Times of John C. Bennett*. Urbana: University of Illinois Press, 1997.

Smith, Henry A. *Matthew Cowley: Man of Faith*. Salt Lake City: Bookcraft, 1954.

Smith, Joseph Fielding. *Life of Joseph F. Smith*. Salt Lake City: Deseret Book, 1938.

Smith, Joseph Fielding, Jr., and John J. Stewart. *The Life of Joseph Fielding Smith, Tenth President of the Church*. Salt Lake City: Deseret Book, 1972.

Smith, Lucy Mack. *History of Joseph Smith by His Mother, Lucy Mack Smith*. Salt Lake City: Bookcraft, 1958. (Orig. pub., 1853.)

Sonne, Conway B. *Knight of the Kingdom: The Story of Richard Ballantyne*. Salt Lake City: Deseret Book, 1949.

———. *A Man Named Alma: The World of Alma Sonne*. Bountiful, UT: Horizon, 1988.

Speek, Vicky Cleverly. *"God Has Made Us a Kingdom": James J. Strang and the Midwest Mormons*. Salt Lake City: Signature Books, 2006.

Stott, G. St. John. "John Taylor's Religious Preparation." *Dialogue: A Journal of Mormon Thought* 19 (Spring 1986): 94–104.

Swetnam, Susan Hendricks. *Lives of the Saints in Southeast Idaho: An Introduction to Mormon Pioneer Life Story Writing*. Moscow, ID: University of Idaho Press, 1991.

Talmage, John R. *The Talmage Story: Life of James E. Talmage—Educator, Scientist, Apostle*. Salt Lake City: Bookcraft, 1972.

Tate, Lucile C. *Andrew B. Christenson: Mormon Educational Pioneer*. Provo, UT: Brigham Young University Press, 1981.

———. *David B. Haight: The Life of a Disciple*. Salt Lake City: Bookcraft, 1987.

———. *LeGrand Richards: Beloved Apostle*. Salt Lake City: Bookcraft, 1982.

Taylor, Samuel W. *The Kingdom or Nothing: The Life of John Taylor, Militant Mormon*. New York/London: Macmillan, 1976.

Taylor, Samuel W., and Raymond W. Taylor. *The John Taylor Papers: Records of the Last Utah Pioneer*. 2 vols. Redwood City, CA: Taylor Trust, 1984–1985.

Van Orden, Bruce A. *Prisoner for Conscience' Sake: The Life Story of George Reynolds*. Salt Lake City: Deseret Book, 1992.

Van Wagoner, Richard S. *Sidney Rigdon: A Portrait of Religious Excess*. Salt Lake City: Signature Books, 1994.

Van Wagoner, Richard S., and Mary C. Van Wagoner. "Orson Pratt, Jr.: Gifted Son of an Apostle and an Apostate." *Dialogue: A Journal of Mormon Thought* 21 (Spring 1988): 84–94.

Van Wagoner, Richard S., and Steven C. Walker. *A Book of Mormons*. Salt Lake City: Signature Books, 1982.

Vogel, Dan. *Joseph Smith: The Making of a Prophet.* Salt Lake City: Signature Books, 2004.

Walgren, Kent L. "James Adams: Early Springfield Mormon and Freemason." *Journal of the Illinois State Historical Society* 75 (Summer 1982): 121–36.

Walker, Ronald W. "Martin Harris: Mormonism's Early Convert." *Dialogue: A Journal of Mormon Thought* 19 (Winter 1986): 29–43.

———. "Mesquite and Sage: Spencer W. Kimball's Early Years." *Brigham Young University Studies* 25 (Fall 1985): 19–41.

———. *Qualities That Count: Heber J. Grant as Businessman, Missionary, and Apostle.* Provo, UT: Brigham Young University Press, 2004.

———. "Young 'Tony' Ivins: Dixie Frontiersman." *Brigham Young University Studies* 40 (2001): 105–31.

Ward, Margery W. *A Life Divided: The Biography of Joseph Marion Tanner, 1859–1927*. Salt Lake City: Publishers Press, 1980.

Welch, John W., ed. *The Worlds of Joseph Smith: A Bicentennial Conference at the Library of Congress. Brigham Young University Studies* 44.4 (2005). Special issue.

Welch, John W., and Larry E. Morris, eds. *Oliver Cowdery: Scribe, Elder, Witness*. Provo, UT: FARMS, 2006.

West, Franklin L. *Life of Franklin D. Richards*. Salt Lake City: Deseret News Press, 1924.

Whiting, Linda Shelley. *David W. Patten: Apostle and Martyr*. Springville, UT: Cedar Fort, 2003.

Widtsoe, John A. *Joseph Smith: Seeker after Truth, Prophet of God*. Salt Lake City: Deseret News Press, 1951.

Wight, Jermy Benton. *The Wild Ram of the Mountains: The Story of Lyman Wight*. Star Valley, WY: Afton Thrifty Print, 1996.

Williams, Frederick G., III. "Frederick Granger Williams of the First Presidency of the Church." *Brigham Young University Studies* 12 (Spring 1972): 243–61.

Wilson, Marian Robertson. *Leroy Robertson: Music Giant from the Rockies*. Salt Lake City, UT: Blue Ribbon Publications, 1996.

Winder, Michael K., comp. *Counselors to the Prophets*. Roy, UT: Eborn Books, 2001.

Winder, Michael K. *John R. Winder: Member of the First Presidency, Pioneer, Temple Builder, Dairyman*. Salt Lake City: Horizon, 1999.

Wixom, Hartt. *Edward Partridge: The First Bishop of the Church of Jesus Christ of Latter-day Saints*. Springville, UT: Cedar Fort, 1998.

Zobell, Albert L. *Sentinel in the East: A Biography of Thomas L. Kane*. Salt Lake City: Nicholas G. Morgan, 1965.

HISTORIES

General

Alexander, Thomas G., ed. *The Mormon People: Their Character and Traditions*. Provo, UT: Brigham Young University Press, 1980.

Alexander, Thomas G., and Jessie L. Embry, eds. *After 150 Years: The Latter-day Saints in Sesquicentennial Perspective*. Provo, UT: Charles Redd Center for Western Studies, 1983.

Allen, James B., and Jessie L. Embry. *Hearts Turned to the Fathers: A History of the Genealogical Society, 1894–1994*. Salt Lake City: Deseret Book, 1995.

Allen, James B., and Glen M. Leonard. *The Story of the Latter-day Saints*. 2nd ed., rev. Salt Lake City: Deseret Book, 1992.

Andrew, Laurel B. *The Early Temples of the Mormons*. Albany: State University of New York Press, 1978.

Arrington, Leonard J., and Bitton, Davis. *The Mormon Experience: A History of the Latter-day Saints*. New York: Knopf, 1979. 2nd ed., Urbana/Chicago: University of Illinois Press, 1992.

Barlow, Philip L. *Mormons and the Bible*. New York: Oxford University Press, 1990.

Barrett, Ivan J. *Joseph Smith and the Restoration: A History of the LDS Church to 1846*. Provo, UT: Brigham Young University Press, 1973.

Bartholomew, Rebecca. *Audacious Women: Early British Mormon Immigrants*. Salt Lake City: Signature Books, 1995.

Bates, Irene M., and E. Gary Smith. *Lost Legacy: The Mormon Office of Presiding Patriarch*. Urbana: University of Illinois Press, 1996.

Beecher, Maureen Ursenbach, and Lavina Fielding Anderson, eds. *Sisters in Spirit: Mormon Women in Historical and Cultural Perspective*. Urbana: University of Illinois Press, 1987.

Bergera, Gary James, and Ronald Priddis. *Brigham Young University: A House of Faith*. Salt Lake City: Signature Books, 1985.

Berrett, William E. *The Latter-day Saints: A Contemporary History of the Church of Jesus Christ of Latter-day Saints*. Salt Lake City: Deseret Book, 1985.

Bitton, Davis. *"The Ritualization of Mormon History," and Other Essays*. Urbana/Chicago: University of Illinois Press, 1994.

Bitton, Davis, and Leonard J. Arrington. *Mormons and Their Historians*. Salt Lake City: University of Utah Press, 1988.

Bitton, Davis, and Maureen Ursenbach Beecher, eds. *New Views of Mormon History: Essays in Honor of Leonard J. Arrington*. Salt Lake City: University of Utah Press, 1987.

Bradley, Martha Sonntag. "Seizing Sacred Space: Women's Engagement in Early Mormonism." *Dialogue: A Journal of Mormon Thought* 27 (Summer 1994): 57–70.

Bringhurst, Newell G. *Saints, Slaves, and Blacks: The Changing Place of Black People within Mormonism*. Westport, CT: Greenwood, 1981.

Britsch, R. Lanier. *Unto the Islands of the Sea: A History of the Latter-day Saints in the Pacific*. Salt Lake City: Deseret Book, 1986.

Brooke, John L. *The Refiner's Fire: The Making of Mormon Cosmology, 1644–1844*. Cambridge: Cambridge University Press, 1994.

Brunson, L. Madelon. *A History of the RLDS Women's Organizations, 1842–1983*. Independence, MO: Herald Publishing House, 1985.

Buerger, David John. *The Mysteries of Godliness: A History of Mormon Temple Worship*. Salt Lake City: Signature Books, 1994.

Bunker, Gary L., and Davis Bitton. *The Mormon Graphic Image, 1834–1914*. Salt Lake City: University of Utah Press, 1983.

Bush, Lester E., Jr. *Health and Medicine among the Latter-day Saints*. New York: Crossroad, 1993.

Bushman, Claudia L. *Contemporary Mormonism: The Latter-day Saints in Modern America.* Westport, CT: Praeger, 2006.

Bushman, Claudia L., and Richard L. Bushman. *Building the Kingdom: A History of the Mormons in America.* New York: Oxford University Press, 2001.

———. *Mormons in America.* New York: Oxford University Press, 1998.

Carter, Kate B. *Denominations That Base Their Beliefs on the Teachings of Joseph Smith.* Salt Lake City: Daughters of Utah Pioneers, 1969.

Cook, Lyndon W. *Joseph Smith and the Law of Consecration.* Provo, UT: Grandin Book Co., 1985.

Cooper, Rex Eugene. *Promises Made to the Fathers: Mormon Covenant Organization.* Salt Lake City: University of Utah Press, 1990.

Davies, Douglas J. *An Introduction to Mormonism.* Cambridge: Cambridge University Press, 2003.

Davis, David Brion. "The New England Origins of Mormonism." *New England Quarterly* 27 (June 1953): 148–53.

———. "Some Themes of Counter-Subversion: An Analysis of Anti-Masonic, Anti-Catholic, and Anti-Mormon Literature." *Mississippi Valley Historical Review* 47 (September 1970): 205–24.

De Pillis, Mario. "The Quest for Religious Authority and the Rise of Mormonism." *Dialogue: A Journal of Mormon Thought* 1 (Spring 1966): 68–88.

———. "The Social Forces of Mormonism." *Church History* 37 (March 1968): 50–79.

Derr, Jill Mulvay, Janath Russell Cannon, and Maureen Ursenbach Beecher. *Women of Covenant: The Story of Relief Society.* Salt Lake City: Deseret Book, 1992.

Divett, Robert J. *Medicine and the Mormons: An Introduction to the History of Latter-day Saint Health Care.* Bountiful, UT: Horizon Publishers, 1981.

Durham, Reed C., and Steven H. Heath. *Succession in the Church.* Salt Lake City: Bookcraft, 1970.

Edwards, Paul M. *Our Legacy of Faith: A Brief History of the Reorganized Church of Jesus Christ of Latter Day Saints.* Independence, MO: Herald Publishing House, 1991.

Embry, Jessie L. *Asian-American Mormons: Bridging Cultures.* Provo, UT: Charles Redd Center for Western Studies, 1999.

———. *Black Saints in a White Church: Contemporary African-American Mormons.* Salt Lake City: Signature Books, 1994.

———. *In His Own Language: Mormon Spanish-Speaking Congregations in the United States.* Provo, UT: Charles Redd Center for Western Studies, 1997.

Epperson, Steven. *Mormons and Jews: Early Mormon Theologies of Israel.* Salt Lake City: Signature Books, 1992.

Erickson, Dan. *As a Thief in the Night: The Mormon Quest for Millennial Deliverance*. Salt Lake City: Signature Books, 1998.

Firmage, Edwin Brown, and Mangrum, Richard Collin. *Zion in the Courts: A Legal History of the Church of Jesus Christ of Latter-day Saints, 1830–1900*. Urbana/Chicago: University of Illinois Press, 1988.

Foster, Lawrence. "New Paradigms for Understanding Mormonism and Mormon History." *Dialogue: A Journal of Mormon Thought* 27 (Spring 1994): 91–105.

———. *Religion and Sexuality: The Shakers, the Mormons, and the Oneida Community*. Urbana/Chicago: University of Illinois Press, 1984.

———. "Sex and Prophetic Power: A Comparison of John Humphrey Noyes, Founder of the Oneida Community, with Joseph Smith, the Mormon Prophet." *Dialogue: A Journal of Mormon Thought* 31 (Winter 1998): 65–83.

———. "Women and Utopia: Life among the Shakers, Oneidans, and Mormons." *Communities: Journal of Cooperative Living* 82 (Spring 1994): 53–56.

———. *Women, Family, and Utopia: Communal Experiments of the Shakers, the Oneida Community, and the Mormons*. Syracuse, NY: Syracuse University Press, 1992.

Givens, Terryl L. *The Viper on the Hearth: Mormons, Myths, and the Construction of Heresy*. New York: Oxford University Press, 1997.

Hansen, Klaus J. *Mormonism and the American Experience*. Chicago/London: University of Chicago Press, 1981.

———. *Quest for Empire: The Political Kingdom of God and the Council of Fifty in Mormon History*. East Lansing: Michigan State University Press, 1967.

Hardy, B. Carmon. *Solemn Covenant: The Mormon Polygamous Passage*. Urbana: University of Illinois Press, 1992.

Hicks, Michael. *Mormonism and Music: A History*. Urbana/Chicago: University of Illinois Press, 1989.

Hill, Marvin S. *Quest for Refuge: The Mormon Flight from American Pluralism*. Salt Lake City: Signature Books, 1989.

———. "The Shaping of the Mormon Mind in New England and New York." *Brigham Young University Studies* 9 (Spring 1969): 351–72

Hill, Marvin S., and James B. Allen, eds. *Mormonism and American Culture*. New York: Harper & Row, 1972.

Howard, Richard L. *The Church through the Years*. Vol. 1, *RLDS Beginnings to 1860*. Independence, MO: Herald Publishing House, 1992.

———. *The Church through the Years*. Vol. 2, *The Reorganization Comes of Age, 1860–1992*. Independence, MO: Herald Publishing House, 1993.

———. *Restoration Scriptures: A Study of Their Textual Development*. Independence, MO: Herald Publishing House, 1969.

Hughes, Dean. *The Mormon Church: A Basic History*. Salt Lake City: Deseret Book, 1986.

Launius, Roger D., and Linda Thatcher, eds. *Differing Visions: Dissenters in Mormon History*. Urbana/Chicago: University of Illinois Press, 1994.

Mangum, Garth L., and Bruce D. Blumell. *The Mormons' War on Poverty: A History of LDS Welfare, 1830–1990*. Salt Lake City: University of Utah Press, 1993.

Matthews, Robert J. *"A Plainer Translation": Joseph Smith's Translation of the Bible*. Provo, UT: Brigham Young University Press, 1975.

McKiernan, F. Mark, Alma Blair, and Paul M. Edwards, eds. *The Restoration Movement: Essays in Mormon History*. Lawrence, KS: Coronado Press, 1973.

Paul, Erich Robert. *Science, Religion, and Mormon Cosmology*. Urbana/Chicago: University of Illinois Press, 1992

Priddis, Ron, and Gary James Bergera. *The Lord's University: Inside BYU*. Salt Lake City: Signature Books, 1994.

Quinn, D. Michael. *Early Mormonism and the Magic World View*. Salt Lake City: Signature Books, 1987.

———. "LDS Church Finances from the 1830s to the 1990s." *Sunstone* 19 (June 1996): 17–29.

———. *The Mormon Hierarchy: Extensions of Power*. Salt Lake City: Signature Books, 1997.

———. *The Mormon Hierarchy: Origins of Power*. Salt Lake City: Signature Books, 1994.

———, ed. *The New Mormon History: Revisionist Essays on the Past*. Salt Lake City: Signature Books, 1992.

Riess, Jana, and Christopher Kimball Bigelow. *Mormonism for Dummies*. Hoboken, NJ: Wiley, 2005.

Roberts, B. H. *A Comprehensive History of the Church of Jesus Christ of Latter-day Saints*. 6 vols. Salt Lake City: The Church of Jesus Christ of Latter-day Saints, 1930.

Shepherd, Gordon, and Gary Shepherd. *A Kingdom Transformed: Themes in the Development of Mormonism*. Salt Lake City: University of Utah Press, 1984.

Shields, Steven L. *Divergent Paths of the Restoration: A History of the Latter-day Saint Movement*. Bountiful, UT: Restoration Research, 1982.

Shipps, Jan. *Mormonism: The Story of a New Religious Tradition*. Urbana/Chicago: University of Illinois Press, 1985.

Smith, George D., ed. *Faithful History: Essays in Writing Mormon History*. Salt Lake City: Signature Books, 1992.

Talbot, Wilburn D. *The Acts of the Modern Apostles*. Salt Lake City: Randall Books, 1985.

Tobler, Douglas F., and Nelson B. Wadsworth. *The History of the Mormons in Photographs and Text, 1830 to Present*. New York: Saint Martin's Press, 1987.

Todd, Jay M. *The Saga of the Book of Abraham*. Salt Lake City: Deseret Book, 1969.

Underwood, Grant. *The Millenarian World of Early Mormonism*. Urbana: University of Illinois Press, 1993.

Van Wagoner, Richard S. *Mormon Polygamy: A History*. Salt Lake City: Signature Books, 1989.

Walker, Ronald W. "Golden Memories: Remembering Life in a Mormon Village." *Brigham Young University Studies* 37 (1997–98): 191–218.

———. "Seeking the 'Remnant': The Native American during the Joseph Smith Period." *Journal of Mormon History*19 (Spring 1993): 1–33.

Wilcox, Pearl. *Roots of the Reorganized Latter Day Saints in Southern Iowa*. Independence, MO: n.p., 1989.

Wilkinson, Ernest L., ed. *Brigham Young University: The First One Hundred Years*. 4 vols. Provo, UT: Brigham Young University Press, 1976–1976.

Wilkinson, Ernest L., and W. Cleon Skousen. *Brigham Young University: A School of Destiny*. Provo, UT: Brigham Young University Press, 1976.

Winn, Kenneth H. *Exiles in a Land of Liberty: Mormons in America, 1830–1846*. Chapel Hill/London: University of North Carolina Press, 1989.

Yorgason, Laurence M. "Preview on a Study of the Social and Geographical Origins of Early Mormon Converts, 1830–1845." *Brigham Young University Studies* 10 (Spring 1970): 279–82.

New York Period

Anderson, Richard Lloyd. *Investigating the* Book of Mormon *Witnesses*. Salt Lake City: Deseret Book, 1980.

———. *Joseph Smith's New England Heritage: Influences of Grandfathers Solomon Mack and Asael Smith*. Salt Lake City: Deseret Book, 1971.

———. "The Mature Joseph Smith and Treasure Searching." *Brigham Young University Studies* 24 (Fall 1984): 489–560.

Arrington, Leonard J. "Mormonism: From Its New York Beginnings." *New York History* 61 (October 1980): 387–410.

Backman, Milton V., Jr. *American Religions and the Rise of Mormonism*. Rev. ed. Salt Lake City: Deseret Book, 1970.

———. *Eyewitness Accounts of the Restoration*. Salt Lake City: Deseret Book, 1986.

———. *Joseph Smith's First Vision: Confirming Evidences and Contemporary Accounts*. 2nd ed. Salt Lake City: Bookcraft, 1980.

Hill, Marvin S. "The Rise of Mormonism in the Burned-over District: Another View." *New York History* 61 (October 1980): 411–30.

Madsen, Gordon A. "Joseph Smith's 1826 Trial: The Legal Setting." *Brigham Young University Studies* 30 (Spring 1990): 91–108.

Marquadt, H. Michael, and Wesley P. Walters. *Inventing Mormonism: Tradition and the Historical Record*. Salt Lake City: Signature Books, 1994.

Morris, Larry E. "Oliver Cowdery's Vermont Years and the Origins of Mormonism." *Brigham Young University Studies* 39 (2000): 106–129.

Paul, Robert. "Joseph Smith and the Manchester Library." *Brigham Young University Studies* 22 (Summer 1982): 333–56.

Perciaccante, Marianne. "Backlash against Formalism: Early Mormonism's Appeal in Jefferson County." *Journal of Mormon History* 19 (Fall 1993): 35–63.

Prince, Gregory A. *Having Authority: The Origins and Development of Priesthood during the Ministry of Joseph Smith*. Independence, MO: Independence Press, 1993.

———. *Power from On High: The Development of Mormon Priesthood*. Salt Lake City: Signature Books, 1995.

Quinn, D. Michael. "The First Months of Mormonism: A Contemporary View by Rev. Diedrich Willers." *New York History* 54 (July 1973): 317–33.

Underwood, Grant. "Early Mormon Millenarianism: Another Look." *Church History* 54 (June 1985): 215–29.

———. *The Millenarian World of Early Mormonism*. Urbana: University of Illinois Press, 1993

Vogel, Dan. "The Locations of Joseph Smith's Early Treasure Quests." *Dialogue: A Journal of Mormon Thought* 27 (Fall 1994): 197–231.

Walker, Ronald W. "Joseph Smith: The Palmyra Seer." *Brigham Young University Studies* 24 (Fall 1984): 461–72.

Ohio Period

Adams, Dale W. "Chartering the Kirtland Bank." *Brigham Young University Studies* 23 (Fall 1983): 467–82.

Alexander, Thomas G. "Wilford Woodruff and Zion's Camp: Baptism by Fire and the Spiritual Confirmation of a Future Prophet." *Brigham Young University Studies* 39 (2000): 130–46.

Anderson, Karl R. *Joseph Smith's Kirtland: Eyewitness Accounts*. Salt Lake City: Deseret Book, 1989.

Backman, Milton V., Jr. *The Heavens Resound: A History of the Latter-day Saints in Ohio, 1830–1838*. Salt Lake City: Deseret Book, 1983.

———. "The Quest for a Restoration: The Birth of Mormonism in Ohio." *Brigham Young University Studies* 12 (Summer 1972): 346–64.

Bitton, Davis. "Kirtland as a Center of Missionary Activity, 1830–1838." *Brigham Young University Studies* 11 (Summer 1971): 497–516.

Grandstaff, Mark R., and Milton V. Backman Jr. "The Social Origins of the Kirtland Mormons." *Brigham Young University Studies* 30 (Spring 1990): 47–66.

Hill, Marvin S. "Cultural Crisis in the Mormon Kingdom: A Reconsideration of the Causes of Kirtland Dissent." *Church History* 49 (September 1980): 286–97.

Hill, Marvin S., C. Keith Rooker, and Larry T. Wimmer. *The Kirtland Economy Revisited*. Provo, UT: Brigham Young University Press, 1977.

Launius, Roger D. "The Dream Shattered: The Abandonment of the Kirtland Temple, 1837–1862." *Restoration Studies* 5 (April 1986): 13–19.

———. *The Kirtland Temple: A Historical Narrative*. Independence, MO: Herald Publishing House, 1986.

———. "The Latter Day Saints in Ohio: Writing the History of Mormonism's Middle Period." *John Whitmer Historical Association Journal* 16 (1996): 31–56.

Layton, Robert L. "Kirtland: A Perspective on Time and Place." *Brigham Young University Studies* 11 (Summer 1971): 423–38.

Matthews, Robert J. "The 'New Translation' of the Bible, 1830–33: Doctrinal Development during the Kirtland Era." *Brigham Young University Studies* 11 (Summer 1971): 400–423.

McKiernan, F. Mark. "The Conversion of Sidney Rigdon to Mormonism." *Dialogue: A Journal of Mormon Thought* 5 (Summer 1970): 71–78.

Newell, Linda King, and Valeen Tippetts Avery. "Sweet Counsel and Seas of Tribulation: The Religious Life of the Women in Kirtland." *Brigham Young University Studies* 20 (Winter 1980): 151–62.

Parkin, Max H. "Mormon Political Involvement in Ohio." *Brigham Young University Studies* 9 (Summer 1969): 484–502.

Radke, Andrea G. "We Also Marched: The Women and Children of Zion's Camp, 1834." *Brigham Young University Studies* 39 (2000): 147–65.

Robison, Elwin C. *The First Mormon Temple: Design, Construction, and Historic Context of the Kirtland Temple*. Provo, UT: Brigham Young University Press, 1997.

Missouri Period

Anderson, Richard Lloyd. "Atchison's Letters and the Causes of Mormon Expulsion from Missouri." *Brigham Young University Studies* 26 (Summer 1986): 3–47.

———. "Jackson County in Early Mormon Descriptions." *Missouri Historical* Review 65 (April 1971): 270–93.

Arrington, Leonard J. "Early Mormon Communitarianism: The Law of Consecration and Stewardship." *Western Humanities Review* 7 (Autumn 1953): 341–69.

Baugh, Alexander L. *A Call to Arms: The 1838 Mormon Defense of Northern Missouri.* Provo, UT: Joseph Fielding Smith Institute for Latter-day Saint History/BYU Studies, 2000.

———. "Missouri Governor Lilburn W. Boggs and the Mormons." *John Whitmer Historical Association Journal* 16 (1998): 111–132.

Blair, Alma. "The Haun's Mill Massacre." *Brigham Young University Studies* 13 (Autumn 1972): 62–67.

Bushman, Richard L. "Mormon Persecution in Missouri, 1833." *Brigham Young University Studies* 3 (Autumn 1960): 11–20.

Crawley, Peter, and Richard L. Anderson. "The Political and Social Realities of Zion's Camp." *Brigham Young University Studies* 14 (Summer 1974): 406–20.

Durham, Reed C., Jr. "The Election Day Battle at Gallatin." *Brigham Young University Studies* 13 (Autumn 1972): 36–61.

Gentry, Leland H. "The Danite Band of 1838." *Brigham Young University Studies* 14 (Summer 1974): 421–50.

Hartley, William G. "'Almost Too Intolerable a Burthen': The Winter Exodus from Missouri, 1838–39." *Journal of Mormon History* 18 (Fall 1992): 6–40.

Jennings, Warren A. "The Army of Israel Marches into Missouri." *Missouri Historical Review* 62 (January 1968): 107–35.

———. "The Expulsion of the Mormons from Jackson County, Missouri." *Missouri Historical Review* 64 (October 1969): 41–63.

———. "Factors in the Destruction of the Mormon Press in Missouri, 1833." *Utah Historical Quarterly* 35 (Winter 1967): 56–76.

Johnson, Clark V. "The Missouri Redress Petitions: A Reappraisal of Mormon Persecutions in Missouri." *Brigham Young University Studies* 26 (Spring 1986): 31–44.

Launius, Roger. *Zion's Camp: Expedition to Missouri, 1834*. Independence, MO: Herald Publishing House, 1984.

LeSueur, Stephen C. *The 1838 Mormon War in Missouri*. Columbia: University of Missouri Press, 1987.

———. "The Danites Reconsidered: Were They Vigilantes or Just the Mormons' Version of the Elks Club?" *John Whitmer Historical Association Journal* 14 (1994): 35–51.

———. "High Treason and Murder: The Examination of Mormon Prisoners at Richmond, Missouri, in November 1838." *Brigham Young University Studies* 26 (Spring 1986): 3–30.

Lyon, T. Edgar. "Independence, Missouri, and the Mormons, 1827–1833." *Brigham Young University Studies* 13 (Autumn 1972): 10–19.

Madsen, Gordon A. "Joseph Smith and the Missouri Court of Inquiry: Austin A. King's Quest for Hostages." *Brigham Young University Studies* 43 (2004): 92–136.

Maynard, Gregory. "Alexander Doniphan: Man of Justice." *Brigham Young University Studies* 13 (Summer 1973): 462–72.

McKiernan, F. Mark. "Sidney Rigdon's Missouri Speeches." *Brigham Young University Studies* 11 (Autumn 1970): 90–92.

McLaws, Monte B. "The Attempted Assassination of Missouri's Ex-Governor, Lilburn W. Boggs." *Missouri Historical Review* 60 (October 1965): 50–62.

Richards, Paul C. "Missouri Persecutions: Petitions for Redress." *Brigham Young University Studies* 13 (Summer 1973): 520–43.

Roberts, B. H. *The Missouri Persecutions.* Salt Lake City: Bookcraft, 1965.

Illinois Period

Allen, James B., Ronald K. Esplin, and David J. Whittaker. *Men with a Mission: The Quorum of the Twelve Apostles in the British Isles, 1837–1841.* Salt Lake City: Deseret Book, 1992.

Bishop, M. Guy, et al. "Death at Mormon Nauvoo, 1843–1845." *Western Illinois Regional Studies* 9 (Fall 1986): 70–83.

———. "Sex Roles, Marriage and Childrearing at Mormon Nauvoo." *Western Illinois Regional Studies* 11 (Fall 1988): 30–45.

———. "'What Has Become of Our Fathers?' Baptism for the Dead at Nauvoo." *Dialogue: A Journal of Mormon Thought* 23 (Summer 1990): 85–97.

Bitton, Davis. "The Martyrdom of Joseph Smith in Early Mormon Writings." *John Whitmer Historical Association Journal* 3 (1983): 29–39. Revised as a chapter in Bitton, *The Martyrdom Remembered* (1994).

Black, Susan Easton. "How Large Was the Population of Nauvoo?" *Brigham Young University Studies* 35 (1995): 91–94.

Cannon, Janath. *Nauvoo Panorama: Views of Nauvoo before, during, and after Its Rise, Fall, and Restoration.* Salt Lake City: Nauvoo Restoration, 1991.

Clark, David L. "The Mormons of the Wisconsin Territory, 1835–1848." *Brigham Young University Studies* 37 (1997–98): 57–85.

Compton, Todd. *In Sacred Loneliness: The Plural Wives of Joseph Smith.* Salt Lake City: Signature Books, 1997.

Daynes, Kathryn M. "Family Ties: Belief and Practice in Nauvoo." *John Whitmer Historical Association Journal* 8 (1988): 63–75.

Ehat, Andrew F. "'It Seems Like Heaven Began on Earth': Joseph Smith and the Constitution of the Kingdom of God." *Brigham Young University Studies* 20 (Spring 1980): 253–79.

Ellsworth, Paul. "Mobocracy and the Rule of Law: American Press Reaction to the Murder of Joseph Smith." *Brigham Young University Studies* 20 (Fall 1979): 71–82.

Flanders, Robert B. *Nauvoo: Kingdom on the Mississippi*. Urbana/Chicago: University of Illinois Press, 1965.

Gardner, Hamilton. "The Nauvoo Legion, 1840–1845: A Unique Military Organization." *Journal of the Illinois State Historical Society* 65 (Summer 1961): 181–97.

Gayler, George R. "The 'Expositor' Affair: Prelude to the Downfall of Joseph Smith." *Northwest Missouri State College Studies* 25 (February 1961): 3–15.

———. "Governor Ford and the Death of Joseph and Hyrum Smith." *Journal of the Illinois State Historical Society* 50 (Winter 1957): 391–411.

———. "The Mormons and Politics in Illinois: 1839–1844." *Journal of the Illinois State Historical Society* 49 (Spring 1956): 48–66.

Givens, George W. *Old Nauvoo: Everyday Life in the City of Joseph*. Salt Lake City: Deseret Book, 1990.

Godfrey, Kenneth W. "Crime and Punishment in Mormon Nauvoo, 1839–1846." *Brigham Young University Studies* 32 (Winter/Spring 1992): 195–227.

———. "Non-Mormon Views of the Martyrdom: A Look at Some Early Published Accounts." *John Whitmer Historical Association Journal* 7 (1987): 12–20.

Hallwas, John E., and Roger D. Launius. *Cultures in Conflict: A Documentary History of the Mormon War in Illinois*. Logan: Utah State University Press, 1999.

Hamilton, Marshall. "From Assassination to Expulsion: Two Years of Distrust, Hostility, and Violence." *Brigham Young University Studies* 32 (Winter/Spring 1992): 229–48.

Hampshire, Annette P. *Mormonism in Conflict: The Nauvoo Years*. New York: Edwin Mellen Press, 1985.

———. "The Triumph of Mobocracy in Hancock County, 1844–1845." *Western Illinois Regional Studies* 5 (Spring 1982): 17–37.

Harrington, Virginia S. *Rediscovery of the Nauvoo Temple*. Salt Lake City: Nauvoo Restoration, 1971.

Hartley, William G. "Nauvoo Stake, Priesthood Quorums, and the Church's First Wards." *Brigham Young University Studies* 32 (Winter/Spring 1992): 57–80.

Holzapfel, Richard Netzel, and Jeni Broberg Holzapfel. *Women of Nauvoo*. Salt Lake City: Bookcraft, 1992.

Homer, Michael W. "'Similarity of Priesthood in Masonry': The Relationship between Freemasonry and Mormonism." *Dialogue: A Journal of Mormon Thought* 27 (Fall 1994): 1–113.

Jeffress, Melinda Evans. "Mapping Historic Nauvoo." *Brigham Young University Studies* 32 (Winter/Spring 1992): 269–75.

Jensen, Richard L. "Transplanted Zion: The Impact of British Latter-day Saint Immigration upon Nauvoo." *Brigham Young University Studies* 31 (Winter 1991): 76–87.

Jolley, Jerry C. "The Sting of the Wasp: Early Nauvoo Newspaper—April 1842 to April 1843." *Brigham Young University Studies* 22 (Fall 1982): 487–96.

Jorgensen, Lynne Watkins, et al. "The Mantle of the Prophet Joseph Passes to Brother Brigham: A Collective Spiritual Witness." *Brigham Young University Studies* 36 (1996–97): 125–204.

Kimball, James L., Jr. "The Nauvoo Charter: A Reinterpretation." *Journal of the Illinois State Historical Society* 64 (Spring 1971): 66–78.

———. "A Wall to Defend Zion: The Nauvoo Charter." *Brigham Young University Studies* 15 (Summer 1975): 491–97.

Kimball, Stanley B. "Heber C. Kimball and Family: The Nauvoo Years." *Brigham Young University Studies* 15 (Summer 1975): 447–79.

———. "The Mormons in Illinois, 1838–1846: A Special Introduction." *Journal of the Illinois State Historical Society* 64 (Spring 1971): 4–21.

Launius, Roger D. "The Murders in Carthage: Non-Mormon Reports of the Assassination of the Smith Brothers." *John Whitmer Historical Association Journal* 15 (1995): 17–34.

Launius, Roger D., and John E. Hallwas, eds. *Kingdom on the Mississippi Revisited: Nauvoo in Mormon History*. Urbana/Chicago: University of Illinois Press, 1996.

LeBaron, E. Dale. "Benjamin Franklin Johnson in Nauvoo: Friend, Confidant, and Defender of the Prophet." *Brigham Young University Studies* 32 (Winter/Spring 1992): 175–94.

Leonard, Glen M. "Letters Home: The Immigrant View from Nauvoo." *Brigham Young University Studies* 31 (Winter 1991): 89–100.

———. *Nauvoo: A Place of Peace, a People of Promise*. Salt Lake City: Deseret Book, and Provo, UT: Brigham Young University Press, 2002.

———. "Picturing the Nauvoo Legion." *Brigham Young University Studies* 35 (1995): 95–135.

Lyon, T. Edgar. "Doctrinal Development of the Church during the Nauvoo Sojourn, 1839–1846." *Brigham Young University Studies* 15 (Summer 1975): 435–46.

Miller, David E., and Della S. Miller. *Nauvoo: The City of Joseph*. Santa Barbara, CA/Salt Lake City: Peregrine Smith, 1974.

Mulder, William. "Nauvoo Observed." *Brigham Young University Studies* 32 (Winter/Spring 1992): 95–118.

Oaks, Dallin H. "The Suppression of the Nauvoo Expositor." *Utah Law Review* 9 (Winter 1965): 862–903.

Oaks, Dallin H., and Marvin S. Hill. *Carthage Conspiracy: The Trial of the Accused Assassins of Joseph Smith*. Urbana/Chicago: University of Illinois Press, 1975.

Poll, Richard D. "Joseph Smith and the Presidency, 1844." *Dialogue: A Journal of Mormon Thought* 3 (Autumn 1968): 17–21.

Porter, Larry C., and Milton V. Backman Jr. "Doctrine and the Temple in Nauvoo." *Brigham Young University Studies* 32 (Winter/Spring 1992): 41–56.

Quinn, D. Michael. "The Council of Fifty and Its Members, 1844 to 1945." *Brigham Young University Studies* 20 (Winter 1980): 163–97.

Robertson, Margaret C. "The Campaign the Kingdom: The Activities of the Electioneers in Joseph Smith's Presidential Campaign." *Brigham Young University Studies* 39 (2000): 147–180.

Rowley, Dennis. "The Mormon Experience in the Wisconsin Pineries, 1841–1845." *Brigham Young University Studies* 32 (Winter/Spring 1992): 119–48.

Rugh, Susan Sessions. "Conflict in the Countryside: The Mormon Settlement at Macedonia, Illinois." *Brigham Young University Studies* 32 (Winter/Spring 1992): 149–74.

Saunders, Richard L. "Officers and Arms: The 1843 General Return of the Nauvoo Legion's Second Cohort." *Brigham Young University Studies* 35 (1995): 138–51.

Smith, George D. "Nauvoo Roots of Mormon Polygamy, 1841–46: A Preliminary Demographic Report." *Dialogue: A Journal of Mormon Thought* 27 (Spring 1994): 1–72.

Tanner, Terence A. "The Mormon Press in Nauvoo, 1839–1846." *Western Illinois Regional Studies* 11 (Fall 1988): 5–29.

Van Orden, Bruce A. "William W. Phelps' Service in Nauvoo as Joseph Smith's Political Clerk." *Brigham Young University Studies* 32 (Winter/Spring 1992): 81–94.

Van Wagoner, Richard S. "The Making of a Mormon Myth: The 1844 Transfiguration of Brigham Young." *Dialogue: A Journal of Mormon Thought* 28 (Winter 1995): 1–24.

The Exodus

Bashore, Melvin L. "On the Heels of the Handcart Tragedy: Mormondom's Forgotten 1856 Wagon Companies." *Annals of Wyoming* 68 (Summer 1996): 38–49.

Beecher, Maureen Ursenbach. "Women in Winter Quarters." *Sunstone* 8 (July–August 1983): 11–19.

Bennett, Richard E. "Cousin Laman in the Wilderness: The Beginnings of Brigham Young's Indian Policy." *Nebraska History* 67 (Spring 1986): 68–82.

———. "Eastward to Eden: The Nauvoo Rescue Missions." *Dialogue: A Journal of Mormon Thought* 19 (Winter 1986): 100–108.

———. "Lamanism, Lymanism, and Cornfields." *Journal of Mormon History* 13 (1986–1987): 45–59.

———. *Mormons at the Missouri, 1846–52: "And Should We Die."* Norman: University of Oklahoma Press, 1987.

———. *We'll Find the Place: The Mormon Exodus, 1846–1848*. Salt Lake City: Deseret Book, 1997.

Bigler, David L., and Will Bagley, eds. *Army of Israel: Mormon Battalion Narratives*. Vol. 4 of *Kingdom in the West: The Mormons and the American Frontier.* Spokane: WA: Arthur H. Clark Co., 2000.

Bitton, Davis. "Mormons in Texas: The Ill-fated Lyman Wight Colony, 1844–1858." *Arizona and the West* 11 (Spring 1969): 5–26.

Black, Susan Easton, and William G. Hartley, eds. *The Iowa Mormon Trail: Legacy of Faith and Courage*. Orem, UT: Helix, 1997.

Brown, Joseph E. *The Mormon Trek West: The Journey of American Exiles*. Garden City, NY: Doubleday, 1980.

Bryson, Conrey. *Winter Quarters*. Salt Lake City: Deseret Book, 1986.

Campbell, Eugene. "Authority Conflicts in the Mormon Battalion." *Brigham Young University Studies* 8 (Winter 1968): 127–42.

Carter, Lyndia. "The Mormon Handcart Companies." *Overland Journal* 13 (1995): 2–18.

Christian, Lewis Clark. "Mormon Foreknowledge of the West." *Brigham Young University Studies* 21 (Fall 1981): 403–15.

Coates, Lawrence. "Cultural Conflict: Mormons and Indians in Nebraska." *Brigham Young University Studies* 24 (Summer 1983): 275–300.

———. "Refugees Meet: The Mormons and Indians in Iowa." *Brigham Young University Studies* 21 (Fall 1981): 491–514.

Crockett, David R. *Saints in Exile: A Day-by-Day Pioneer Experience, Nauvoo to Council Bluffs*. Tucson, AZ: LDS-Gems Press, 1996.

Gardner, Hamilton. "The Command and Staff of the Mormon Battalion in the Mexican War." *Utah Historical Quarterly* 29 (October 1952): 331–52.

Homer, Michael W. "After Winter Quarters and Council Bluffs: The Mormons in Nebraska Territory, 1854–1867." *Nebraska History* 65 (Winter 1984): 467–83.

Kimball, Stanley B. *Historic Sites and Markers along the Mormon and Other Great Western Trails*. Urbana/Chicago: University of Illinois Press, 1988.

———. "Mormon Trail Network in Nebraska, 1846–1868." *Brigham Young University Studies* 24 (Summer 1984): 321–36.

Kimball, Stanley B., and Hal Knight. *111 Days to Zion*. Salt Lake City: Deseret News Press, 1978.

King, Robert R. "The Enduring Significance of the Mormon Trek." *Dialogue: A Journal of Mormon Thought* 13 (Summer 1980): 102–7.

Melville, J. Keith. *Conflict and Compromise: The Mormons in Mid Nineteenth-Century American Politics*. Provo, UT: Brigham Young University Press, 1975.

Powell, A. Kent. *Mormon Battalion Trail Guide*. Salt Lake City: Utah State Historical Society, 1972.

Ricketts, Norma Baldwin. *The Mormon Battalion: United States Army of the West, 1846–1848*. Logan: Utah State University Press, 1996.

Stegner, Wallace. *The Gathering of Zion: The Story of the Mormon Trail*. New York: McGraw Hill, 1964; Salt Lake City: Westwater Press, 1981.

Tyler, Daniel. *A Concise History of the Mormon Battalion in the Mexican War, 1846–47*. N.p., 1881. Reprint, Chicago: Rio Grande Press, 1964.

Utah Period

Alexander, Thomas G. "Charles S. Zane, Apostle of the New Era." *Utah Historical Quarterly* 34 (Fall 1966): 290–314.

———. "Cooperation, Conflict, and Compromise: Women, Men, and the Environment in Salt Lake City, 1890–1930." *Brigham Young University Studies* 35 (1995): 7–39.

———. "An Experiment in Progressive Legislation: The Granting of Woman Suffrage in Utah in 1870." *Utah Historical Quarterly* 38 (Winter 1970): 20–30.

———. "Federal Authority versus Polygamic Theocracy: James B. McKean and the Mormons, 1870–1875." *Dialogue: A Journal of Mormon Thought* 1 (Autumn 1966): 85–100.

———. "Some Meanings of Utah History." *Utah Historical Quarterly* 64 (Spring 1996): 155–67.

———. "Utah's Constitution: A Reflection of the Territorial Experience." *Utah Historical Quarterly* 64 (Summer 1996): 264–81.

———. *Utah: The Right Place*. Salt Lake City: Gibbs Smith, 1995.

———. "Wilford Woodruff, Intellectual Progress, and the Growth of an Amateur Scientific and Technological Tradition in Early Territorial Utah." *Utah Historical Quarterly* 59 (Spring 1991): 164–88.

Allen, James B. "'Good Guys' vs. 'Good Guys': Rudger Clawson, John Sharp, and Civil Disobedience in Nineteenth-Century Utah." *Utah Historical Quarterly* 48 (Spring 1980): 148–74.

Anderson, Nels. *Desert Saints: The Mormon Frontier in Utah*. Chicago: University of Chicago Press, 1942.

Arrington, Leonard J. *Great Basin Kingdom: An Economic History of the Latter-day Saints*. Cambridge, MA: Harvard University Press, 1958.

———. "Rural Life Among Nineteenth-Century Mormons: The Woman's Experience." *Agricultural History* 58 (July 1984): 239–46.

Arrington, Leonard J., and Dean May. "'A Different Mode of Life': Irrigation and Society in Nineteenth-Century Utah." *Agricultural History* 49 (January 1975): 3–20.

Arrington, Leonard J., and Linda Wilcox. "From Subsistence to Golden Age: Cache Valley Agriculture, 1859–1900." *Utah Historical Quarterly* 57 (Fall 1989): 340–69.

Arrington, Leonard J., Dean May, and Feramorz Fox. *Building the City of God: Community and Cooperation among the Mormons*. Salt Lake City: Deseret Book, 1976.

Ashton, Wendell J. *Voice in the West: Biography of a Pioneer Newspaper*. New York: Duell, Sloan, & Pearce, 1950.

Bagley, Will. *Blood of the Prophets: Brigham Young and the Massacre at Mountain Meadows*. Norman: University of Oklahoma Press, 2002

Beecher, Maureen Ursenbach. "Women's Work on the Mormon Frontier." *Utah Historical Quarterly* 49 (Summer 1981): 276–90.

Bergera, Gary James. *Conflict in the Quorum: Orson Pratt, Brigham Young, Joseph Smith.* Salt Lake City: Signature Books, 2002.

Bigler, David L. *Forgotten Kingdom: The Mormon Theocracy in the American West, 1847–1896*. Spokane, WA: Arthur H. Clark, Co., 1998.

Bitton, Davis. "B. H. Roberts at the World Parliament of Religions." *Sunstone* 7 (January–February 1982): 46–51.

———. "The B. H. Roberts Case of 1898–1900." *Utah Historical Quarterly* 25 (January 1957): 27–46. Revised and reprinted in Bitton, *"The Ritualization of Mormon History," and Other Essays* (1994).

———. "'Strange Ramblings': The Ideal and Practice of Sermons in Early Mormonism." *Brigham Young University Studies* 41 (2002): 4–28.

———. "Zion's Rowdies: Growing up on the Mormon Frontier." *Utah Historical Quarterly* 50 (Spring 1982): 182–95. Reprinted in Bitton, *The Ritualization of Mormon History and Other Essays* (1994).

Bitton, Davis, and Linda P. Wilcox. "The Transformation of Utah's Agriculture, 1847–1900." In Thomas G. Alexander and John F. Bluth, eds., *The Twentieth Century American West*, pp. 57–83. Provo, UT: Charles Redd Center for Western Studies, 1983.

Brooks, Juanita. *The Mountain Meadows Massacre*. Norman: University of Oklahoma Press, 1962.

Buchanan, Frederick S. "Education Among the Mormons: Brigham Young and the Schools of Utah." *History of Education Quarterly* 22 (Winter 1982): 435–59.
Campbell, Eugene E. *Establishing Zion: The Mormon Church in the American West, 1847–69*. Salt Lake City: Signature Books, 1988.
Cannon, Kenneth L., II. "After the Manifesto: Mormon Polygamy, 1890–1906." *Sunstone* 8 (January–April 1983): 27–35.
———. "Mountain Common Law: The Extralegal Punishment of Seducers in Early Utah." *Utah Historical Quarterly* 51 (Fall 1983): 308–27.
Clayton, James L. "The Supreme Court, Polygamy and the Enforcement of Morals in Nineteenth Century America: An Analysis of *Reynolds v. United States*." *Dialogue: A Journal of Mormon Thought* 12 (Winter 1979): 46–61.
Cornwall, J. Spencer. *A Century of Singing: The Salt Lake Mormon Tabernacle Choir*. Salt Lake City: Deseret Book, 1958.
Cornwall, Rebecca, and Leonard J. Arrington. *Rescue of the 1856 Handcart Companies*. Provo, UT: Charles H. Redd Monographs in Western History, 1981.
Cowan, Richard O. "The Mormon Battalion and the Gadsden Purchase." *Brigham Young University Studies* 37 (1997–1998): 48–64.
Davies, J. Kenneth. *Mormon Gold: The Story of California's Mormon Argonauts*. Salt Lake City: Olympus Publishing, 1984.
Daynes, Kathryn M. *More Wives Than One: Transformation of the Mormon Marriage System, 1840–1910*. Urbana: University of Illinois Press, 2001.
———. "Single Men in a Polygamous Society: Male Marriage Patterns in Manti, Utah." *Journal of Mormon History* 24 (Spring 1998): 89–111.
Dwyer, Robert Joseph. *The Gentile Comes to Utah: A Study in Religious and Social Conflict, 1862–1890*. 2nd ed., rev. Salt Lake City: Western Epics, 1971.
Ekins, Roger Robin, ed. *Defending Zion: George Q. Cannon and the California Mormon Newspaper Wars of 1856–1857*. Spokane, WA: Arthur H. Clark Co., 2002.
Embry, Jessie L. "Burden or Pleasure? A Profile of LDS Polygamous Husbands." *Dialogue: A Journal of Mormon Thought* 20 (Winter 1987): 158–66.
———. "Effects of Polygamy on Mormon Women." *Frontiers* 7 (No. 3, 1984): 56–61.
———. "Little Berlin: Swiss Saints of the Logan Tenth Ward." *Utah Historical Quarterly* 56 (Summer 1988): 222–35.
———. *Mormon Polygamous Families: Life in the Principle*. Salt Lake City: University of Utah Press, 1987.
———. "Mormon Polygamy: Unconventional Practice or Adaptation to American Values?" *Journal of Unconventional History* 3 (1992): 42–56.

Embry, Jessie L., and Martha S. Bradley. "Mothers and Daughters in Polygamy." *Dialogue: A Journal of Mormon Thought* 18 (Fall 1985): 99–107.

Flake, Kathleen. *The Politics of American Religious Identity: The Seating of Senator Reed Smoot, Mormon Apostle.* Chapel Hill: University of North Carolina Press, 2004.

Furniss, Norman. *The Mormon Conflict, 1850–1859.* New Haven, CT: Yale University Press, 1960.

Godfrey, Kenneth W. "Charles W. Penrose and His Contributions to Utah Statehood." *Utah Historical Quarterly* 64 (Fall 1996): 356–71.

———. "Moses Thatcher in the Dock: His Trials, the Aftermath and His Last Days." *Journal of Mormon History* 24 (Spring 1998): 54–88.

Gordon, Sarah Barringer. *The Mormon Question: Polygamy and Constitutional Conflict in Nineteenth Century America.* Chapel Hill/London: University of North Carolina Press, 2002.

Grow, Stewart L. *A Tabernacle in the Desert.* Salt Lake City: Deseret Book, 1958.

Hafen, LeRoy R., and Ann W. Hafen. "Handcarts to Utah, 1856–1860." *Utah Historical Quarterly* 24 (October 1956): 309–17.

———. *Handcarts to Zion: The Story of a Unique Western Migration, 1856–1860.* Glendale, CA: Arthur H. Clark Co., 1960.

Hartley, William G. "Brigham Young's Overland Trails Revolution: The Creation of the 'Down-and-Back' Wagon-Train System." *Journal of Mormon History* 28.1 (Spring 2002): 1–30.

———. "The Priesthood Reorganization of 1877: Brigham Young's Last Achievement." *Brigham Young University Studies* 20 (Fall 1979): 3–36.

———. "The Seventies in the 1880s: Revelations and Reorganizing." *Dialogue: A Journal of Mormon Thought* 16 (Spring 1983): 62–88.

Heinerman, Joseph. "The Old Folks Day: A Unique Utah Tradition." *Utah Historical Quarterly* 53 (Spring 1985): 157–69.

Homer, Michael W. "The Judiciary and the Common Law in Utah Territory, 1850–61." *Dialogue: A Journal of Mormon Thought* 21 (Spring 1988): 97–108.

Howard, Richard P. "The Changing RLDS Response to Mormon Polygamy: A Preliminary Analysis." *John Whitmer Historical Association Journal* 3 (1983): 14–29.

Iversen, Joan Smyth. "A Debate on the American Home: The Antipolygamy Controversy, 1880–1890." *Journal of the History of Sexuality* 1.4 (April 1991): 585–602.

Johnson, Jeffery Ogden. "Determining and Defining 'Wife': The Brigham Young Households." *Dialogue: A Journal of Mormon Thought* 20 (Fall 1987): 57–70.

Larson, Gustive O. *The "Americanization" of Utah for Statehood*. San Marino, CA: Huntington Library, 1971.
———. "The Mormon Reformation." *Utah Historical Quarterly* 26 (January 1958): 45–63.
———. *Prelude to the Kingdom: Mormon Desert Conquest, a Chapter in American Cooperative Experience*. Francestown, NY: Marshall Jones Co., 1947.
Leonard, Glen M. "The Mormon Boundary Question in the 1849–50 Statehood Debates." *Journal of Mormon History* 18 (Spring 1992): 114–36.
———. "William Allen's Clients: A Socioeconomic Inquiry." *Utah Historical Quarterly* 54 (Winter 1986): 74–87.
Logue, Larry. *A Sermon in the Desert: Belief and Behavior in Early St. George, Utah*. Urbana: University of Illinois Press, 1988.
———. "Tabernacles for Waiting Spirits: Monogamous and Polygamous Fertility in a Mormon Town." *Journal of Family History* 10 (Spring 1985): 60–74.
Long, E. B. *The Saints and the Union: Utah Territory during the Civil War*. Champaign, IL: University of Illinois Press, 1981.
Lyman, E. Leo. "The Political Background of the Woodruff Manifesto." *Dialogue: A Journal of Mormon Thought* 24 (Fall 1991): 21–39.
———. *Political Deliverance: The Mormon Quest for Utah Statehood*. Urbana/Chicago: University of Illinois Press, 1986.
Madsen, Carol Cornwall. "'At Their Peril': Utah Law and the Case of Plural Wives, 1850–1900." *Western Historical Quarterly* 21 (November 1990): 425–43.
———. "Mormon Women and the Struggle for Definition: The Nineteenth-Century Church." *Sunstone* 6 (November–December 1981): 7–11.
Madsen, Carol Cornwall, and Susan Staker Oman. *Sisters and Little Saints: One Hundred Years of Primary*. Salt Lake City: Deseret Book, 1979.
May, Dean L. "People on the Mormon Frontier: Kanab's Families of 1874." *Journal of Family History* 1 (December 1976): 169–92.
———. *Three Frontiers: Family, Land, and Society in the American West, 1850–1900*. New York: Cambridge University Press, 1994.
———. *Utah: A People's History*. Salt Lake City: University of Utah Press, 1987.
———. "Utah Writ Small: Challenge and Change in Kane County's Past." *Utah Historical Quarterly* 53 (Spring 1985): 170–83.
McLaws, Monte B. *Spokesman for the Kingdom: Early Mormon Journalism and the Deseret News, 1830–1898*. Provo, UT: Brigham Young University Press, 1977.
Mehr, Kahlile. "Women's Response to Plural Marriage." *Dialogue: A Journal of Mormon Thought* 18 (Fall 1985): 84–97.

Miller, David S. *Hole-in-the-Rock: An Epic in the Colonization of the Great American West*. Salt Lake City: University of Utah Press, 1959.

Miller, Jeremy M. "A Critique of the Reynolds Decision." *Western State University Law Review* 11 (Spring 1984): 165–98.

Moorman, Donald R., and Gene A. Sessions. *Camp Floyd and the Mormons: The Utah War*. Salt Lake City: University of Utah Press, 1992.

Nelson, Lowry. *The Mormon Village: A Pattern and Techniques of Land Settlement*. Salt Lake City: University of Utah Press, 1952.

Pace, D. Gene. "Changing Patterns of Mormon Financial Administration: Traveling Bishops, Regional Bishops, and Bishop's Agents, 1851–88." *Brigham Young University Studies* 23 (Spring 1983): 183–95.

Peterson, Charles S. "The Hopis and the Mormons, 1858–1873." *Utah Historical Quarterly* 39 (Spring 1971): 179–93.

———. "Jacob Hamblin, Apostle to the Lamanites, and the Indian Mission." *Journal of Mormon History* 2 (1975): 21–34.

Poll, Richard D. "The Mormon Question Enters National Politics, 1850–1856." *Utah Historical Quarterly* 25 (April 1957): 117–31.

———. "The Legislative Antipolygamy Campaign." *Brigham Young University Studies* 26 (Fall 1986): 107–21.

———. "The Move South." *Brigham Young University Studies* 29 (Fall 1989): 65–88.

———. *Quixotic Mediator: Thomas L. Kane and the Utah War*. Ogden, UT: Weber State College Press, 1985.

Poll, Richard D. and William P. MacKinnon. "Causes of the Utah War Reconsidered." *Journal of Mormon History* 20 (Fall 1994): 16–44.

Polson, D. Michol. "The Swedes in Grantsville, Utah, 1860–1900." *Utah Historical Quarterly* 56 (Summer 1988): 208–21.

Quinn, D. Michael. "LDS Church Authority and New Plural Marriages, 1890–1904." *Dialogue: A Journal of Mormon Thought* 18 (Spring 1985): 9–105.

Ricks, Joel E. *Forms and Methods of Early Mormon Settlement in Utah and Surrounding Regions, 1847 to 1877*. Logan: Utah State University Press, 1974.

Sherlock, Richard. "Mormon Migration and Settlement after 1875." *Journal of Mormon History* 2 (1975): 53–68.

Shirts, Morris A., and Kathryn H. Shirts. *A Trial Furnace: Southern Utah's Iron Mission*. Provo, UT: Brigham Young University Press, 2001.

Simmonds, A. J. *The Gentile Comes to Cache Valley: A Study of the Logan Apostasies of 1874 and the Establishment of Non-Mormon Churches in Cache Valley, 1873–1913*. Logan: Utah State University Press, 1976.

Smart, Donna T. "Over the Rim to Red Rock Country: The Parley P. Pratt Exploring Company of 1849." *Utah Historical Quarterly* 62 (Spring 1994): 171–90.

Smart, William B., and Donna T. Smart, eds. *Over the Rim: The Parley P. Pratt Exploring Expedition to Southern Utah, 1849–50*. Logan: Utah State University Press, 1999.

Smith, Craig S. "The Curious Meet the Mormons: Images from Travel Narratives, 1850s and 1860s." *Journal of Mormon History* 24 (Fall 1998): 155–81.

———. "Wyoming, Nebraska Territory: Joseph W. Young and the Mormon Emigration of 1864." *Brigham Young University Studies* 39 (2000): 30–51.

Smith, E. Gary. "The Office of Presiding Patriarch: The Primacy Problem." *Journal of Mormon History* 14 (1988): 35–48.

Snow, Edwina Jo. "British Travelers View the Saints." *Brigham Young University Studies* 31 (Spring 1991): 63–81.

Stott, Clifford L. *Search for Sanctuary: Brigham Young and the White Mountain Expedition*. Salt Lake City: University of Utah Press, 1984.

Van Wagenen, Lola. "In Their Behalf: The Politicization of Mormon Women and the 1870 Franchise." *Dialogue: A Journal of Mormon Thought* 24 (Winter 1991): 31–43.

Walker, Ronald W. "B. H. Roberts and the Woodruff Manifesto." *Brigham Young University Studies* 22 (Summer 1982): 363–66.

———. "Brigham Young on the Social Order." *Brigham Young University Studies* 28 (Summer 1988): 37–52.

———. "Growing Up in Early Utah: The Wasatch Literary Association, 1874–1878." *Sunstone* 6 (November–December 1981): 44–51.

———. "Toward a Reconstruction of Mormon and Indian Relations, 1847–1877." *Brigham Young University Studies* 19 (Fall 1989): 23–42.

———. *Wayward Saints: The Godbeites and Brigham Young*. Urbana: University of Illinois Press, 1998.

———. "When the Spirits Did Abound: Nineteenth-Century Utah's Encounter with Free-Thought Radicalism." *Utah Historical Quarterly* 50 (Fall 1982): 304–24.

West, Ray B. *Kingdom of the Saints: The Story of Brigham Young and the Mormons*. New York: Viking, 1957.

Whittaker, David J. "The Bone in the Throat: Orson Pratt and the Public Announcement of Plural Marriage." *Western Historical Quarterly* 18 (July 1987): 293–314.

Woods, Fred E. "East to West through North and South: Mormon Immigration during the Civil War." *Brigham Young University Studies* 39 (2000): 7–29.

Twentieth Century

Alexander, Thomas G. *Mormonism in Transition: A History of the Latter-day Saints, 1890–1930*. Urbana/Chicago: University of Illinois Press, 1986.

———. "The Reconstruction of Mormon Doctrine: From Joseph Smith to Progressive Theology." *Sunstone* 5 (July–August 1980): 24–33.

———. "Reed Smoot, the LDS Church, and Progressive Legislation, 1903–1933." *Dialogue: A Journal of Mormon Thought* 7 (Spring 1972): 47–56.

Allen, James B. "On Becoming a Universal Church: Some Historical Perspectives." *Dialogue: A Journal of Mormon Thought* 25 (March 1992): 13–36.

Allen, James B., Jessie L. Embry, and Kahlile B. Mehr. *Hearts Turned to the Fathers: A History of the Genealogical Society of Utah, 1894–1994*. Provo, UT: BYU Studies, 1995.

Anderson, Paul. "Heroic Nostalgia: Enshrining the Mormon Past." *Sunstone* 5 (July–August 1980): 47–55.

Arrington, Leonard J. "The Founding of the LDS Institutes of Religion." *Dialogue: A Journal of Mormon Thought* 2 (Summer 1967): 137–47.

———. "Origin of the Welfare Plan of the Church." *Brigham Young University Studies* 5 (Winter 1964): 67–85.

Bennion, Lowell C. "Ben," and Lawrence A. Young. "The Uncertain Dynamics of LDS Expansion, 1950–2020." *Dialogue: A Journal of Mormon Thought* 29 (Spring 1996): 8–32.

Calman, Charles Jeffrey, and Kaufman, William I. *The Mormon Tabernacle Choir*. New York: Harper & Row, 1979.

Cannon, Brian Q., and Jacob W. Olmstead. "Scandalous Film: The Campaign to Suppress Anti-Mormon Motion Pictures, 1911–1912," *Journal of Mormon History* 29 (Fall 2003): 42–76

———. "What a Power We Will Be in This Land: The LDS Church, the Church Security Program, and the New Deal." *Journal of the West* 43 (Fall 2004): 63–75.

Christianson, James R., and Richard Cowan. *The International Church*. Provo, UT: Brigham Young University Publications, 1982.

Cowan, Richard O. *The Church in the Twentieth Century*. Salt Lake City: Bookcraft, 1985.

———. *Temples to Dot the Earth*. Salt Lake City: Bookcraft, 1989.

De Pillis, Mario S. "The Persistence of Mormon Community into the 1990s." *Sunstone* 15.4 (September 1991): 28–49.

Driggs, Ken. "Twentieth-Century Polygamy and Fundamentalist Mormons in Southern Utah." *Dialogue: A Journal of Mormon Thought* 24 (Winter 1991): 44–58.

Hartley, William G. "The Priesthood Reform Movement, 1908–1922." *Brigham Young University Studies* 13 (Winter 1973): 137–56.

Holsinger, M. Paul. "For God and the American Home: The Attempt to Unseat Senator Reed Smoot, 1903–1907." *Pacific Northwest Quarterly* 60 (July 1969): 154–60.

Jacobson, Cardell K. "Black Mormons in the 1980s: Pioneers in a White Church." *Review of Religious Research* 33 (December 1991): 146–52.

Kimball, Richard Ian. *Sports in Zion: Mormon Recreation, 1890–1940.* Urbana: University of Illinois Press, 2003.

Mauss, Armand L. *The Angel and the Beehive: The Mormon Struggle with Assimilation.* Urbana: University of Illinois Press, 1994.

———. *All Abraham's Children: Changing Mormon Conceptions of Race and Lineage.* Urbana: University of Illinois Press, 2003.

Mehr, Kahlile. "Area Supervision: Administration of the Worldwide Church." *Journal of Mormon History* 27.1 (Spring 2001): 192–214.

Ostling, Richard N., and Joan K. Ostling. *Mormon America: The Power and the Promise.* San Francisco: HarperSanFrancisco, 1999.

Palmer, Spencer J., ed. *The Expanding Church.* Salt Lake City: Deseret Book, 1978.

———. *Mormons and Muslims.* Provo, UT: Brigham Young University Press, 1983.

Peterson, Charles S. "Life in a Village Society, 1877–1920." *Utah Historical Quarterly* 49 (Winter 1981): 78–96.

Petersen, Gerald A. *More Than Music: The Mormon Tabernacle Choir.* Provo, UT: Brigham Young University Press, 1979.

Taber, Susan Buhler. *Mormon Lives: A Year in the Elkton Ward.* Urbana: University of Illinois Press, 1993.

Takagi, Shinji. "The Eagle and the Scattered Flock: LDS Church Beginnings in Occupied Japan, 1945–49." *Journal of Mormon History* 28.2 (Fall 2002): 104–138.

———. "Riding on the Eagle's Wings: The Japanese Mission under American Occupation,1948–52." *Journal of Mormon History* 29.1 (Spring 2003): 200–232.

Thorp, Malcolm R. "The British Government and the Mormon Question, 1910–1922." *Journal of Church and State* 21 (Spring 1979): 305–23.

Tullis, F. Lamond. *Mormonism: A Faith for All Cultures.* Provo, UT: Brigham Young University Press, 1978.

Local and Regional United States

Anderson, Lavina Fielding, ed. *Chesterfield: Mormon Outpost in Idaho.* Bancroft, ID: The Chesterfield Foundation, 1982.

Arrington, Leonard J. "A Mormon Apostle Visits the Umatilla and Nez Perce in 1885." *Idaho Yesterdays* 31 (Spring/Summer 1987): 47–54.

———. "The Mormon Settlement of Cassia County, Idaho, 1873–1921." *Idaho Yesterdays* 23 (Summer 1979): 36–46.

———. *The Mormons in Nevada*. Las Vegas, NV: Las Vegas Sun, 1979.

———. "The Promise of Eagle Rock: Idaho Falls, Idaho, 1863–1980." *Rendezvous* 18 (Spring 1983): 2–17.

Bagley, Will. "'Every Thing Is Favourable! And God Is on Our Side': Samuel Brannan and the Conquest of California." *Journal of Mormon History* 23 (Fall 1997): 185–209.

Bitton, Davis. "Peopling the Upper Snake: The Second Wave of Mormon Settlement in Idaho." *Idaho Yesterdays* 23 (Summer 1979): 47–52.

Boyce, Ronald R. "The Mormon Invasion and Settlement of the Upper Snake River Plain in the 1880s: The Case of Lewisville, Idaho." *Pacific Northwest Quarterly* 78 (January–April 1987): 50–58.

Britsch, R. Lanier. *Moramona: The Mormons in Hawaii*. Laie, HI: Institute for Polynesian Studies, 1989.

Buice, David. "When the Saints Come Marching In: The Mormon Experience in Antebellum New Orleans, 1840–1855." *Louisiana History* 23 (Summer 1982): 221–37.

Coates, Lawrence G., Peter G. Boag, Ronald L. Hatzenbuehler, and Merwin R. Swanson. "The Mormon Settlement of Southeastern Idaho, 1845–1900." *Journal of Mormon History* 20 (Fall 1994): 45–62.

Cowan, Richard, and William E. Homer. *California Saints: A 150-year Legacy in the Golden State*. Provo, UT: Religious Studies Center, Brigham Young University, 1996.

Durham, Michael S. *Deseret between the Mountains: Mormons, Miners, Padres, Mountain Men, and the Opening of the Great Basin, 1772–1869*. New York: Henry Holt, 1997.

Ellsworth, S. George. *Mormon Settlement on the Muddy*. Ogden, UT: Weber State College Press, 1987.

Grattan-Aiello, Carolyn. "New St. Joseph, Nevada: The Muddy Mission Experience Revisited." *Nevada Historical Society Quarterly* 29 (Spring 1986): 31–52.

Hatch, William Whitridge. *There Is No Law: A History of Mormon Civil Relations in the Southern States, 1865–1905*. New York: Vantage Press, 1968.

Kimball, Monique E. "A Matter of Faith: A Study of the Muddy Mission." *Nevada Historical Society Quarterly* 30 (Winter 1987): 291–303.

Larson, Andrew Karl. *"I Was Called to Dixie": The Virgin River Basin, Unique Experiences in Mormon Pioneering*. Salt Lake City: Deseret News Press, 1961.

Logue, Larry M. *A Sermon in the Desert: Belief and Behavior in Early St. George, Utah*. Urbana/Chicago: University of Illinois Press, 1988.

Lyman, Edward Leo. *San Bernardino: The Rise and Fall of a California Community*. Salt Lake City: Signature Books, 1996.

May, Dean L. "Star Valley in the Context of Western Settlement." *Snake River Echoes* 14 (Autumn 1985): 103–10.

———. *Three Frontiers: Land, Family, and Society in the American West, 1850–1900*. New York: Cambridge University Press, 1994

Miller, Mark E. "St. Johns's Saints: Interethnic Conflict in Northeastern Arizona, 1880–85." *Journal of Mormon History* 23 (Spring 1997): 66–99.

O'Brien, Robert. *Hands Across the Water: The Story of the Polynesian Cultural Center*. Laie, HI: Institute for Polynesian Studies, 1983.

Orton, Chad M. *More Faith Than Fear: The Los Angeles Stake Story*. Salt Lake City: Bookcraft, 1987.

Peterson, Charles S. *Take Up Your Mission: Mormon Colonizing along the Little Colorado River, 1870–1900*. Tucson: University of Arizona Press, 1973.

Rich, Russell R. *Land of the Sky-Blue Water: A History of the LDS Settlement of the Bear Lake Valley*. Provo, UT: Brigham Young University Press, 1963.

Ricks, Joel E., ed. *The History of a Valley: Cache Valley, Utah-Idaho*. Logan, UT: Utah State University Press, 1956.

Simmonds, A.J. "Southeast Idaho as a Pioneer Mormon Safety Valve." *Idaho Yesterdays* 23 (Winter 1980): 20–30.

Tullis, F. LaMond. "California and Chile in 1851 as Experienced by the Mormon Apostle Parley P. Pratt." *Southern California Quarterly* 67 (Fall 1985): 291–307.

Vogt, Evan Z., and Ethel M. Albert, eds. *People of Rimrock: A Study of Values in Five Cultures*. Cambridge, MA: Harvard University Press, 1966.

Wells, Merle W. *Anti-Mormonism in Idaho, 1872–1892*. Provo, UT: Brigham Young University Press, 1978.

Countries Outside the United States and Immigration

Acevedo A., Rodolfo. *Los Mormones en Chile*. Santiago, Chile: Impresos y Publicaciones Cumora, 1990.

Arrington, Leonard J. "Mormon Women in Nineteenth-Century Britain." *Brigham Young University Studies* 27 (Winter 1987): 67–83.

Baldridge, Steven W., and Rona, Marilyn M. *Grafting In: A History of the Latter-day Saints in the Holy Land*. Murray, UT: Roylance Publishing, 1989.

Bartholomew, Rebecca. *Audacious Women: Early British Mormon Immigrants*. Salt Lake City: Signature Books, 1995.

Beecher, Dale F. "Rey L. Pratt and the Mexican Mission." *Brigham Young University Studies* 15 (Spring 1975): 293–307.

Biddulph, Howard L. *The Morning Breaks: Stories of Conversion and Faith in the Former Soviet Union*. Salt Lake City: Deseret Book, 1996.

Bloxham, V. Ben, James R. Moss, and Larry C. Porter, eds. *Truth Will Prevail: The Rise of the Church . . . in the British Isles, 1837–1987*. Solihull, England: The Church of Jesus Christ of Latter-day Saints, 1987.

Britsch, R. Lanier. "Church Beginnings in China." *Brigham Young University Studies* 10 (Winter 1970): 161–72.

———. "The Closing of the Early Japan Mission." *Brigham Young University Studies* 15 (Winter 1975): 171–90.

———. *From the East: The History of the Latter-day Saints in Asia, 1851–1996*. Salt Lake City: Deseret Book, 1998.

———. "The Latter-day Mission to India, 1851–1856." *Brigham Young University Studies* 12 (Spring 1972): 262–77.

———. *Unto the Islands of the Sea: A History of the Latter-day Saints in the Pacific*. Salt Lake City: Deseret Book, 1986.

Browning, Gary L. "Out of Obscurity: The Emergence of the Church of Jesus Christ of Latter-day Saints in 'That Vast Empire' of Russia." *Brigham Young University Studies* 33 (1993): 674–89.

———. *Russia and the Restored Gospel*. Salt Lake City: Deseret Book, 1997.

Buchanan, Frederick S. "The Ebb and Flow of Mormonism in Scotland, 1840–1900." *Brigham Young University Studies* 17 (Spring 1987): 27–52.

Cannon, Donald Q. "George Q. Cannon and the British Mission." *Brigham Young University Studies* 27 (Winter 1987): 97–112.

Card, Brigham Y. "The Canadian Mormon Settlements, 1886–1925: A North-American Perspective." *Canadian Ethnic Studies* 26 (1994): 19–38.

Card, Brigham Y., et al., eds. *The Mormon Presence in Canada*. Logan: Utah State University Press, 1990.

Conkling, J. Christopher. "Members without a Church: Japanese Mormons in Japan from 1924 to 1948." *Brigham Young University Studies* 15 (Winter 1975): 191–214.

Cuthbert, Derek A. "Church Growth in the British Isles, 1937–1987." *Brigham Young University Studies* 27 (Spring 1987): 13–26.

———. *The Second Century: The Latter-day Saints in Great Britain, 1937–1987*. Cambridge, England: Cambridge University Press, 1987.

Davies, Douglas J. *Mormon Spirituality: Latter-day Saints in Wales and Zion*. Nottingham, England: University of Nottingham, 1987.

Davis, Garold N., and Norma S. Davis. "Behind the Iron Curtain: Recollections of Latter-day Saints in East Germany, 1945–1989." *Brigham Young University Studies* 35 (1995): 47–79.

Dennis, Ronald D. *The Call of Zion: The Story of the First Welsh Mormon Emigration*. Provo, UT: Religious Studies Center, Brigham Young University, 1987.

Dixon, Joseph F. "Mormons in the Third Reich, 1933–1945." *Dialogue: A Journal of Mormon Thought* 7 (Autumn–Winter 1971): 70–78.

Ellsworth, S. George, and Kathleen C. Perrin. *Seasons of Faith and Courage: The Church of Jesus Christ of Latter-day Saints in French Polynesia, 1843–1993*. Sandy, UT: Yves Perrin, 1994.

Evans, Richard L. *A Century of Mormonism in Great Britain*. Salt Lake City: Deseret News Press, 1937.

Folsom, Marjorie Wall. *Golden Harvest in Ghana*. Bountiful, UT: Horizon Publishers, 1989.

Geddes, Ross. "Before Stakehood: The Mission Years in Brisbane, Australia." *Journal of Mormon History* 22 (Fall 1996): 92–119.

———. "'A Storm in the Camp of Brighamism': LDS-RLDS Relations in Brisbane, Australia, 1901–1918." *John Whitmer Historical Association Journal* 11 (1991): 47–59.

Grover, Mark L. "Migration, Social Change, and Mormonism in Portugal." *Journal of Mormon History* 21 (Spring 1995): 65–79.

Harris, Claudia W. "Mormons on the Warfront: The Protestant Mormons and Catholic Mormons of Northern Ireland." *Brigham Young University Studies* 30 (Fall 1990): 7–19.

Harris, Jan G. "Mormons in Victorian Manchester." *Brigham Young University Studies* 17 (Winter 1987): 46–56.

Haslam, Gerald M. *Clash of Cultures: The Norwegian Experience with Mormonism, 1842–1920*. New York: Peter Lang, 1984.

Hatch, Nelle Spillsbury. *Colonia Juarez*. Salt Lake City: Deseret Book, 1954.

Heaton, Tim B., et al. "The Making of British Saints in Historical Perspective." *Brigham Young University Studies* 27 (Spring 1987): 119–35.

Jensen, Richard L., and Malcolm R. Thorp, eds. *Mormons in Early Victorian Britain*. Salt Lake City: University of Utah Press, 1989.

Jenson, Andrew. *History of the Scandinavian Mission*. Salt Lake City: Deseret News Press, 1927.

Katanuma, Seiji. "The Church in Japan." *Brigham Young University Studies* 14 (Autumn 1973): 16–28.

Kissi, Emmanuel Abu. *Walking in the Sand: A History of the Church of Jesus Christ of Latter-day Saints in Ghana*. Provo, UT: Brigham Young University Press, 2004.

Knowlton, David Clark. "Mormonism in Latin America: Towards the Twenty-first Century." *Dialogue: A Journal of Mormon Thought* 29 (Spring 1996): 159–76.

LeBaron, Dale E. *All Are Alike unto God*. Salt Lake City: Bookcraft, 1990.
Lemblé, Jean. *Dieu et les Francais: Les saints des derniers jours francophones*. Paris: Editions Liahona, 1986.
Louder, Dean R. "Canadian Mormons in Their North American Context: A Portrait." *Social Compass* 40 (1993): 271–90.
Lozano, Agricol. *Historia de la iglesia en Mexico*. Mexico, D.F.:N.p., 1980.
Mabey, Rendell N., and Gordon T. Allred. *Brother to Brother: The Story of Latter-day Saint Missionaries Who Took the Gospel to Black Africa*. Salt Lake City: Bookcraft, 1984
Marsh, Don W., comp. *"The Light of the Sun": Japan and the Saints*. Tokyo, Japan: Japan Mission, 1968.
Mehr, Kahlile. "Enduring Believers: Czechoslovakia and the LDS Church, 1884–1990." *Journal of Mormon History* 18 (Fall 1992): 111–54.
———. "Keeping Promises: The LDS Church Enters Bulgaria, 1990–1994." *Brigham Young University Studies* 36 (1996–97): 69–106.
———. *Mormon Missionaries Enter Eastern Europe*. Provo, UT: Brigham Young University Press, and Salt Lake City: Deseret Book, 2002.
Morrison, Alexander B. *The Dawning of a Brighter Day: The Church in Black Africa*. Salt Lake City: Deseret Book, 1990.
Moss, James R., et al. *The International Church*. Provo, UT: Brigham Young University Press, 1982.
Mulder, William. *Homeward to Zion: The Mormon Migration from Scandinavia*. Minneapolis: University of Minnesota Press, 1957.
Neilson, Reid L. and Van C. Gessel, eds. *Taking the Gospel to the Japanese, 1901–2002*. Provo, UT: BYU Studies.
Newton, Marjorie. "The Gathering of the Australian Saints in the 1850s." *Brigham Young University Studies* 27 (Spring 1987): 67–78.
———. *Southern Cross Saints: The Mormons in Australia*. Laie, HI: Institute for Polynesian Studies, 1991.
Palmer, Spencer J. *The Church Encounters Asia*. Salt Lake City: Deseret Book, 1970
Palmer, Spencer J., and Shirley H. Palmer, eds. *The Korean Saints: Personal Stories of Trial and Triumph, 1950–1980*. Provo, UT: Religious Studies Center, Brigham Young University, 1995.
Phillips, Andrew. "Mormons in Essex, 1850–1870." *Essex Journal* 18 (Winter 1983–1984): 57–65.
Romney, Thomas C. *The Mormon Colonies in Mexico*. Salt Lake City: Deseret Book, 1938.
Scharffs, Gilbert W. *Mormonism in Germany*. Salt Lake City: Deseret Book, 1970.

Schiele, Melani, ed. *In Ostdeutschland auf Mission: Erinnerungen, Tagebuchaufzeichnungen und Zeugnisse ehemaliger Missionare.* Leipzig, Germany: N.p., 2004.

Sonne, Conway B. *Saints on the Seas*. Salt Lake City: University of Utah Press, 1983.

———. *Ships, Saints and Mariners: A Maritime Encyclopedia of Mormon Migraiton, 1830–1890*. Salt Lake City: University of Utah Press, 1987.

Sorenson, John L. "Mormon World View and American Culture." *Dialogue: A Journal of Mormon Thought* 8 (Summer 1973): 17–29.

Tagg, Melvin S. *A History of the Mormon Church in Canada.* Lethbridge, Alberta: Lethbridge Herald Co., 1968.

Taylor, P. A. M. *Expectations Westward: The Mormons and the Emigration of Their British Converts in the Nineteenth Century*. Edinburgh and London: Oliver & Boyd, 1965, and Ithaca, NY: Cornell University Press, 1966.

Thorp, Malcolm R. "Sectarian Violence in Early Victorian Britain: The Mormon Experience, 1837–1860." *Bulletin of the John Rylands University Library* 70 (Autumn 1988): 135–47.

Tullis, F. LaMond. "Early Mormon Exploration and Missionary Activities in Mexico." *Brigham Young University Studies* 22 (Summer 1982): 289–310.

———. *Mormons in Mexico: The Dynamics of Faith and Culture*. Logan: Utah State University Press, 1987.

———. "Reopening the Mexican Mission in 1901." *Brigham Young University Studies* 22 (Fall 1982): 441–53.

———. "Three Myths about Mormons in Latin America." *Dialogue: A Journal of Mormon Thought* 7 (Spring 1972): 79–87.

Van Orden, Bruce A. "The Decline in Convert Baptisms and Member Emigration from the British Mission after 1870." *Brigham Young University Studies* 27 (Spring 1987): 97–105.

Walker, Ronald W. "Cradling Mormonism: The Rise of the Gospel in Early Victorian England." *Brigham Young University Studies* 17 (Winter 1987): 25–36.

Williams, Frederick S., and Williams, Frederick G. *From Acorn to Oak Tree: A Personal History of the Establishment and First Quarter Development of the South American Missions*. Fullerton, CA: Etcetera, 1987.

Zobell, Albert L., Jr. *Under the Midnight Sun: Centennial History of the Scandinavian Missions*. Salt Lake City: Deseret Book, 1950.

SOCIAL SCIENCE

Albrecht, Stan L., and Tim B. Heaton. "Secularization, Higher Education, and Religiosity." *Review of Religious Research* 26 (September 1984): 43–58.

Alston, Jon P., and David Johnson. "A Cross-Cultural Analysis of Mormon Missionary Success." *Measuring Mormonism* 5 (Fall 1979): 1–17.

Bahr, Howard M., and Renata Tonks Forste. "Towards a Social Science of Contemporary Mormonism." *Brigham Young University Studies* 26 (1986): 73–121.

Bush, Lester E. "Birth Control among the Mormons: Introduction to an Insistent Question." *Dialogue: A Journal of Mormon Thought* 10 (Autumn 1976): 12–44.

Christensen, Harold T. "Mormon Sexuality in Cross-cultural Perspective." *Dialogue: A Journal of Mormon Thought* 10 (Autumn 1976): 62–75.

———. "The Persistence of Chastity: A Built-in Resistance within Mormon Culture to Secular Trends." *Sunstone* 7 (March–April 1982): 7–14.

Corcoran, Brent, ed. *Multiply and Replenish: Mormon Essays on Sex and Family*. Salt Lake City: Signature Books, 1994.

Cornwall, Marie, Tim B. Heaton, and Lawrence A. Young, eds. *Contemporary Mormonism: Social Science* Perspectives. Urbana: University of Illinois Press, 1994.

Leone, Mark P. *Roots of Modern Mormonism*. Cambridge, MA/London: Harvard University Press, 1979.

Mauss, Armand L. "The Mormon Struggle with Assimilation and Identity: Trends and Developments since Midcentury." *Dialogue: A Journal of Mormon Thought* 27 (Spring 1994): 129–49.

———. "Sociological Perspectives on the Mormon Subculture." *Annual Review of Sociology* 10 (1984): 437–60.

O'Dea, Thomas F. *The Mormons*. Chicago: University of Chicago Press, 1957.

Peck, Granger C. "The Religiosity of Mormon Academicians." *Measuring Mormonism* 5 (Fall 1979): 18–41.

Schow, Ron, Wayne Schow, and Marybeth Raines, eds. *Peculiar People: Mormons and Same-Sex Orientation*. Salt Lake City: Signature Books, 1995.

Shepherd, Gary, and Gordon Shepherd. *Mormon Passage: A Missionary Chronicle*. Urbana: University of Illinois Press, 1998.

Sorenson, John L. *Mormon Culture: Four Decades of Essays on Mormon Society and Personality*. Salt Lake City: New Sage Books, 1997.

Toney, Michael B., et al. "Mormon and Non-Mormon Migration in and out of Utah." *Review of Religious Research* 25 (December 1983): 114–26.

Vernon, Glenn M. *Research on Mormonism: A Collection of Readings*. Salt Lake City: Association for the Study of Religion, 1974.

———. *Sociology of Mormonism: A Preliminary Analysis*. Salt Lake City: Author, 1975.

Vernon, Glenn M., and Charles E. Waddell. "Dying as Social Behavior: Mormon Behavior through Half a Century." *Omega* 5 (Fall 1974): 199–206.

PHILOSOPHY

Edwards, Paul M. *Preface to Faith: A Philosophical Inquiry into RLDS Beliefs*. Midvale, UT: Signature Books, 1984.

McMurrin, Sterling M. *The Theological Foundations of the Mormon Religion*. Salt Lake City: University of Utah Press, 1965.

Ostler, Blake T. *Exploring Mormon Thought: The Attributes of God*. Salt Lake City: Kofford Books, 2001.

———. *Exploring Mormon Thought: The Problems of Theism and the Love of God*. Salt Lake City: Kofford Books, 2006.

FOLKLORE

Cheney, Thomas E., ed. *Lore of Faith and Folly*. Salt Lake City: University of Utah Press, 1971.

Eliason, Eric A. "Toward the Folkloristic Study of Latter-day Saint Conversion Narratives." *Brigham Young University Studies* 38 (1999): 137–50.

Fife, Austin, and Alta Fife. *Saints of Sage and Saddle: Folklore among the Mormons*. Bloomington: Indiana University Press, 1956.

Wilson, William A. "Mormon Folklore: Cut from the Marrow of Everyday Experience." *Brigham Young University Studies* 33 (1993): 521–40.

———. "Mormon Folklore: Faith or Folly?" *Brigham Young Magazine* 49 (May 1995): 47–54.

PERSONAL ESSAYS

Barlow, Philip L., ed. *A Thoughtful Faith: Essays on Belief by Mormon Scholars*. Centerville, UT: Canon Press, 1986.

Black, Susan Easton, ed. *Expressions of Faith: Testimonies of Latter-day Saint Scholars*. Salt Lake City: Deseret Book Company, and Provo, UT: FARMS, 1996.

Bradford, Mary Lythgoe, ed. *Mormon Women Speak: A Collection of Essays*. Salt Lake City: Olympus Publishing Co., 1982.

Christensen, Parley A. *All in a Teacher's Day: Essays of a Mormon Professor*. Salt Lake City: Author, 1948.

———. *Of a Number of Things*. Salt Lake City: University of Utah Press, 1962.

England, Eugene. *Dialogues with Myself: Personal Essays on Mormon Experience*. Salt Lake City: Orion Books, 1984.

———. *The Quality of Mercy: Personal Essays on Mormon Experience*. Salt Lake City: Bookcraft, 1992.

———. *Why the Church Is as True as the Gospel: Personal Essays on Mormon Experience*. Salt Lake City: Bookcraft, 1986.

Geary, Edward A. *Goodbye to Poplarhaven: Recollections of a Utah Boyhood*. Salt Lake City: University of Utah Press, 1985.

King, Arthur Henry. *The Abundance of the Heart*. Salt Lake City: Bookcraft, 1986. Revised, expanded edition entitled *Arm the Children: Faith's Response to a Violent World*. Provo, UT: Brigham Young University Press, 1998.

Newton, Marjorie. "My Family, My Friends, My Faith." *Brigham Young University Studies* 41 (2002): 141–46.

Poll, Richard D. *History and Faith: Reflections of a Mormon Historian*. Salt Lake City: Signature Books, 1989.

Rasmussen, Dennis. *The Lord's Question: Thoughts on the Life of Response*. Provo, UT: Keter Foundation, 1985.

DOCTRINAL AND APOLOGETIC

Alexander, Thomas G. "The Reconstruction of Mormon Doctrine: From Joseph Smith to Progressive Theology." *Sunstone* 5 (July–August 1980): 24–33.

———. "The Word of Wisdom: From Principle to Requirement." *Dialogue* 14 (Fall 1981): 78–88.

Bennion, Lowell L. *Religion and the Pursuit of Truth*. Salt Lake City: Deseret Book, 1968.

———. *The Religion of the Latter-day Saints*. Salt Lake City: LDS Department of Education, 1940.

Blomberg, Craig L., and Stephen E. Robinson. *How Wide the Divide? A Mormon and an Evangelical in Conversation*. Downers Grove, IL: InterVarsity Press, 1997.

Clark, David L., ed. *Of Heaven and Earth: Reconciling Scientific Thought with LDS Theology*. Salt Lake City: Deseret Book, 1998.

England, Eugene, ed. *Converted to Christ through the* Book of Mormon. Salt Lake City: Deseret Book, 1989.

Eyring, Henry. *The Faith of a Scientist*. Salt Lake City: Bookcraft, 1967.

Hafen, Bruce C. *The Believing Heart: Nourishing the Seed of Faith*. 2nd ed. Salt Lake City: Deseret Book, 1986.

———. *The Broken Heart: Applying the Atonement to Life's Experiences*. Salt Lake City: Deseret Book, 1989.

Jackson, Kent P., et al., eds. *Studies in Scripture*. 8 vols. Salt Lake City: Randall Book Co., 1984–1985, and Deseret Book, 1986–1989.

Keller, Roger R. *Reformed Christians and Mormon Christians: Let's Talk*. N.p.: Pryor Pettengill, 1986.

Lee, Rex E. *What Do Mormons Believe?* Salt Lake City: Deseret Book, 1992.

Ludlow, Victor L. *Principles and Practices of the Restored Gospel*. Salt Lake City: Deseret Book, 1992.

Madsen, Truman G., ed. *Reflections on Mormonism: Judaeo-Christian Parallels*. Provo, UT: Religious Studies Center, Brigham Young University, 1978.

Matthews, Robert J. *"A Plainer Translation": Joseph Smith's Translation of the Bible*. Provo, UT: Brigham Young University Press, 1975.

McConkie, Bruce R. *Mormon Doctrine*. 2nd ed. Salt Lake City: Bookcraft, 1966.

———. *A New Witness for the Articles of Faith*. Salt Lake City: Deseret Book, 1985.

McConkie, Mark L., ed. *Doctrines of the Restoration: Sermons and Writings of Bruce R. McConkie*. Salt Lake City: Bookcraft, 1989.

Millet, Robert L. *Alive in Christ: The Miracle of Spiritual Rebirth*. Salt Lake City: Deseret Book, 1997.

———. *By Grace Are We Saved*. Salt Lake City: Deseret Book, 1989.

———. *A Different Jesus: The Christ of the Latter-day Saints*. Grand Rapids, MI: Eerdmans, 2005.

———. *An Eye Single to the Glory of God*. Salt Lake City: Deseret Book, 1991.

———. *Getting at the Truth: Responding to Difficult Questions about LDS Beliefs*. Salt Lake City: Deseret Book, 2004.

———. *Latter-day Christianity: Ten Basic Issues*. Salt Lake City: Covenant Communications, 1998.

———. *The Mormon Faith: A New Look at Christianity*. Salt Lake City: Shadow Mountain, 1998.

Nibley, Hugh. *The Collected Works of Hugh Nibley*. 13 vols. Salt Lake City: Deseret Book, 1986–1992. (This multivolume work by Mormonism's most erudite defender of the late 20th century includes studies of the Old Testament, ancient history, the *Pearl of Great Price*, early Christianity, the *Book of Mormon*, and early Mormon history.)

Palmer, Spencer J., and Keller, Roger R. *Religions of the World: A Latter-day Saint View*. Provo, UT: Brigham Young University Press, 1989.

Peterson, Daniel C., and Stephen D. Ricks. *Offenders for a Word: How Anti-Mormons Play Word Games to Attack the Latter-day Saints*. Salt Lake City: Aspen Books, 1992.

Peterson, H. Donl. *The* Pearl of Great Price*: A History and Commentary*. Salt Lake City: Deseret Book, 1987.

Rector, Hartman, and Connie Rector. *No More Strangers*. 4 vols. Salt Lake City: Bookcraft, 1971–1990.

Reynolds, Noel, ed. Book of Mormon *Authorship Revisited: The Evidence for Ancient Origins*. Provo, UT: FARMS, 1997.

Richards, LeGrand. *A Marvelous Work and a Wonder*. Salt Lake City: Deseret Book, 1950.

Roberts, B. H. *The Falling Away*. Salt Lake City: Deseret Book, 1931.

———. *The Truth, the Way, the Life: An Elementary Treatise on Theology*. Ed. John W. Welch. Provo, UT: BYU Studies, 1994.

———. *The Truth, the Way, the Life: An Elementary Treatise on Theology: The Masterwork of B. H. Roberts*. Ed. Stan Larson. San Francisco: Smith Research Associates, 1994. (These two editions, published simultaneously, follow different but defensible editorial procedures. The former edition has the advantage of 12 essays by different scholars analyzing and evaluating different aspects of Roberts's work.)

Robinson, Stephen E. *Are Mormons Christians?* Salt Lake City: Bookcraft, 1991.

Sessions, Gene A., and Craig J. Oberg, eds. *The Search for Harmony: Essays on Science and Mormonism*. Salt Lake City: Signature Books, 1993.

Shipps, Jan. "Is Mormonism Christian? Reflections on a Complicated Question." *Brigham Young University Studies* 33 (1993): 438–65.

Sorenson, John L. *An Ancient American Setting for the Book of Mormon*. Salt Lake City: Deseret Book, 1985.

———. *Images of Ancient America: Visualizing Book of Mormon Life*. Provo, UT: Research Press, FARMS, 1998.

Sorenson, John L., and Thorne, Melvin J., eds. *Rediscovering the* Book of Mormon. Salt Lake City: Deseret Book, and Provo: FARMS, 1991.

A Sure Foundation: Answers to Difficult Gospel Questions. Salt Lake City: Deseret Book, 1988.

Talmage, James E. *The Articles of Faith*. Salt Lake City: Deseret News, 1899.

———. *The Great Apostasy*. Salt Lake City: Deseret News, 1909.

———. *The House of the Lord: A Study of Holy Sanctuaries, Ancient and Modern*. Salt Lake City: Deseret News, 1912.

———. *Jesus the Christ: A Study of the Messiah and His Mission According to Holy Scriptures Both Ancient and Modern*. Salt Lake City: Deseret Book, 1915.

Taylor, John. *The Mediation and Atonement of Our Lord and Savior Jesus Christ*. Salt Lake City: Deseret News, 1882.

Welch, John W., ed. *Reexploring the* Book of Mormon. Salt Lake City: Deseret Book, 1992.

———. *The Sermon at the Temple and the Sermon on the Mount*. Salt Lake City: Deseret Book, 1990.

Widtsoe, John A. *Evidences and Reconciliations*. Salt Lake City: Bookcraft, 1960.

———. *Priesthood and Church Government*. Rev. ed. Salt Lake City: Deseret Book, 1939.

———. *A Rational Theology*. Salt Lake City: General Priesthood Committee, 1915.

Widtsoe, John A., and Leah D. Widtsoe. *The Word of Wisdom: A Modern Interpretation*. Salt Lake City: Deseret Book, 1937.

LITERATURE AND ART

Anderson, Lavina Fielding, and Eugene England, eds. *Tending the Garden: Essays on Mormon Literature*. Salt Lake City: Signature Books, 1996.

Bell, Shane, ed. *Washed By a Wave of Wind: Science Fiction from the Corridor*. Salt Lake City: Signature Books, 1993.

Card, Orson Scott. *A Storyteller in Zion: Essays and Speeches*. Salt Lake City: Bookcraft, 1993.

England, Eugene, ed. *Bright Angels and Familiars: Contemporary Mormon Stories*. Salt Lake City: Signature Books, 1992.

Hamilton, C. Mark. *Nineteenth-Century Mormon Architecture and City Planning*. New York: Oxford University Press, 1995.

Howe, Susan Elizabeth, and Sheree Maxwell Bench, eds. *Discoveries: Two Centuries of Poems by Mormon Women*. Provo, UT: BYU Studies, 2004.

Jackson, Richard W. *Places of Worship: 150 Years of LDS Architecture*. Provo, UT: Religious Studies Center, Brigham Young University, 2003.

Mulder, William. "Telling It Slant: Aiming for Truth in Contemporary Mormon Literature." *Dialogue: A Journal of Mormon Thought* 26 (Summer 1993): 155–69.

Oman, Richard G., and Robert O. Davis. *Images of Faith: Art of the Latter-day Saints*. Salt Lake City: Deseret Book, 1995.

Swanson, Vern G., Robert S. Olpin, and William C. Seifrit. *Utah Painting and Sculpture*. Layton, UT: Gibbs Smith, 1997.

About the Authors

Davis Bitton was emeritus professor of history at the University of Utah. He received his B.A. degree from Brigham Young University and both his M.A. and Ph.D. from Princeton University. As a specialist in early modern European history, he published *The French Nobility in Crisis, 1560–1640.* He held faculty appointments at the University of Texas and the University of California at Santa Barbara. He had an interest in Mormon history for many years and was a charter member and past president of the Mormon History Association. He conducted oral history interviews with many participants in Mormon history at the end of the 20th century. His extensive publications include *Guide to Mormon Diaries and Autobiographies* (1977), *The Mormon Experience: A History of the Latter-day Saints* (1978), and *George Q. Cannon: A Biography* (1999).

Thomas G. Alexander is the Lemuel Hardison Redd Jr. professor emeritus of western American history at Brigham Young University. His B.S. and M.S. degrees are from Utah State University and he received the Ph.D. from the University of California at Berkeley. A specialist in U.S. history with an emphasis on the American West and American environmental history, he has authored, coauthored, edited, or coedited 24 books and monographs and more than 125 articles. Among his books are *A Clash of Interests: Interior Department and Mountain West, 1863–96* (1977), *Mormons and Gentiles: A History of Salt Lake City* (1984, with James B. Allen), *Mormonism in Transition: A History of the Latter-day Saints, 1890-1930* (1986, 2nd ed. 1996), *Things in Heaven and Earth: The Life and Times of Wilford Woodruff, a Mormon Prophet* (1991, 2nd ed. 1996), *Utah, the Right Place* (1995, rev. eds. 1996 and 2003), and *Grace and Grandeur: A History of Salt Lake City* (2002). He is one of the founders and a past president of the Mormon History Association.

Praise for the bestselling novels of Susan Mallery

"This poignant tale of family dynamics, the jarring impact of change, and eventual acceptance and healing is sure to please Mallery's many devoted fans."

—*Booklist* on *Already Home*

"Gritty and magical, angst-ridden and sweet, this coming-home story pulls no punches... Mallery adds layer upon layer to the women's history, while revealing the raw core of each with expert pacing guaranteed to keep a reader up way past bedtime to see how it all works out."

—*Publishers Weekly* on *Barefoot Season*

"*Barefoot Season* will appeal to book clubs (great discussion topics abound!) and fans of Barbara Delinsky and Jodi Picoult. Susan Mallery weaves a tale of broken friendship with enough twists and turns to keep even the most seasoned reader of commercial women's fiction guessing about where the story will lead."

—*Bookreporter*

"A character-driven tale of complex relationships, the costs of forgiveness, and the abiding security we can find, lose and rediscover within the complexity of feminine friendships... With strong characters, a vivid sense of place and intricate relational dynamics *Barefoot Season* will hold its own against best-selling women's fiction titles and please fans of mainstream romance as well."

—*USA TODAY* on *Barefoot Season*

"Susan Mallery gives us a candid, honest look into the turmoil of family life when tragedies and personal crises occur... Mallery never disappoints and *Three Sisters* is no exception. It's a winner and should be on everyone's short list of must-reads."

—*Fresh Fiction*

"Mallery has again created an engrossing tale of emotional growth and the healing power of friendship."

—*Library Journal* on *Three Sisters*

"Mallery pulls out all the stops in this highly enjoyable and insightful, funny, and poignant look at self-sacrifice and romantic entanglement."

—*Booklist* on *Evening Stars*, starred review

"Best-selling romance author Mallery...maintains her romantic charm and smooth voice yet embraces the freedom of a broader storyline with ease and a bit more depth."

—*Publishers Weekly* on *Evening Stars*

Also by Susan Mallery

Blackberry Island

Evening Stars
Three Sisters
Barefoot Season

Fool's Gold

Until We Touch
Before We Kiss
When We Met
Christmas on 4th Street
Three Little Words
Two of a Kind
Just One Kiss
A Fool's Gold Christmas
All Summer Long
Summer Nights
Summer Days
Only His
Only Yours
Only Mine
Finding Perfect
Almost Perfect
Chasing Perfect

To see more titles by Susan Mallery,
please visit SusanMallery.com.

Look for Susan Mallery's next Fool's Gold romance
Hold Me
available soon from HQN Books

SUSAN MALLERY

The Girls of Mischief Bay

Recycling programs for this product may not exist in your area.

ISBN-13: 978-0-7783-1774-6

The Girls of Mischief Bay

For questions and comments about the quality of this book, please contact us at CustomerService@Harlequin.com.

www.MIRABooks.com

Printed in U.S.A.

First printing: March 2015
10 9 8 7 6 5 4 3 2 1

The Girls of Mischief Bay

Dear Reader,

Welcome to Mischief Bay! This book is the first in what I hope will be a long-running series. I love creating a world that readers step into and experience fully. I'm hopeful it will be one you'll want to return to again and again.

While I love coming up with a fictitious place and discovering all the ways it can be as real as possible, there are challenges. One of the biggest ones is figuring out the types of businesses my characters will encounter and then naming them. Last year, when I was starting this book, I was suddenly and overwhelmingly stymied by the prospect of having to go through that. Realizing that sometimes it does indeed take a village to make a village, I turned to the people I adore most. My friends and readers at facebook.com/susanmallery. I asked for suggestions and you came through. I was amazed by the response, even though I really shouldn't be. You're always there for me.

So, with gratitude, I dedicate this book to those of you who took the time out of your busy lives to help a struggling author. I hope you love Mischief Bay as much as I do. Special thanks to these Mischief Makers:

Alicia H, Oklahoma City, OK; Andie B, Woodstock, ON; Ann L, Pittsburgh, PA; Cat J, Johnson City, TN; Cheryl H, Auburn, MA; Dale B, Ocala, FL; Jennie J, Monroe, TN; Joyce M, Orange, TX; Karen M, Exton, PA; Kelly M, Corvallis, OR; Kelly R, Oregon City, OR; Kimberly C, Corning, NY; Kriss B, Chassell, MI; Kristen P, Westfield, NJ; Krystle P, Smithfield, PA; Linda H, Glen Burnie, MD; Lindsey B, Nestleton Station, ON; Lisbeth G, Honesdale, PA; Lora P, Papillion, NE; Melanie O, Chico, CA; Melissa H, Versailles, KY; Patricia K, Ashdown, AR; Phyllis G, Holbrook, MA; Roberta R, Berne, NY; Sandy K, Tucson, AZ; Sherry S, Jane Lew, WV; Susan P, DeValls Bluff, AR; Susan W, Morganville, NJ; Suzanne V, Rockaway, NJ; Suzi H, Kansas City, MO; Tina M, Warner Robins, GA; Tracy A, Rochester, NY; Yvonne Y, Edmonton, AB.

Love,

Susan Mallery

One

"DID TYLER MAKE THAT FOR YOU?"

Nicole Lord turned to look at the picture she'd posted on the wall of Mischief in Motion, her Pilates studio. Three large red hearts covered a piece of pink construction paper. A handprint had been outlined over the hearts. The hearts were wobbly and highly stylized, but still recognizable. Not bad, considering the artist in question was not yet five. The handprint had been traced by one of his teachers.

"He did," Nicole said with a smile. "I promised him I would bring it to work and show everyone."

Her client, a thirtysomething fighting her way back from a forty-five-pound pregnancy weight gain, wiped sweat from her face and smiled. "He sounds adorable. I look forward to when my daughter can do more than eat, poop and keep me up all night."

"It gets better," Nicole promised.

"I hope so. I'd always assumed once I started having kids, I'd want six." The woman grimaced. "Now one is looking like more than enough." She waved and walked toward the exit. "See you next week."

“Have a good weekend.”

Nicole spoke without looking, her attention already back on her computer. She had her noon class, then a three-hour break before her late-afternoon classes. Which sounded nice until she thought about all she had to get done. Grocery shopping for sure—they were out of everything. Her car needed gas, there was dry cleaning to pick up and somewhere in the middle of all that, she should eat lunch.

She glanced at the clock, wondering if she should text Eric to remind him to pick up Tyler from day care at four. She reached for her phone, then shook her head and sagged back in her chair. No, she shouldn’t, she told herself. He’d only forgotten once and he’d felt awful about it. She had to trust him not to forget again.

Which she would, she told herself. Only these days he was forgetting a lot of things. And helping less around the house.

Marriage, she thought ruefully. It all sounded so romantic until you realized that hey, you not only had to live with someone else, but there would also be days when they actually thought you were wrong about things.

She was still trying to figure out in which order she was going to run her errands when the door to her studio opened and Pam Eiland strolled in.

“Hey, you,” Pam called cheerfully, an oversize tote hanging off one shoulder.

Anyone who didn’t know Pam would assume she had a clutter problem if she needed to haul around that much stuff in her bag. Those who did know Pam were privy to the fact that her actual handbag was fairly small and that most of the space in the tote was taken up by a soft blanket and a very weird-looking dog.

Right on cue, Lulu poked her head out of the tote and whined softly.

Nicole stood and approached them both. After giving Pam a hug, she reached for Lulu. The dog leaped into her arms and snuggled close.

"I see you're in pink today," she said, stroking Lulu's cheek, then rubbing the top of her head.

"We both felt it was a pink kind of day," Pam told her.

Lulu, a purebred Chinese crested, had white hair on the top of her head, by her ears and on her tail and lower legs. The rest of her spotted body was pretty much naked and an unexpected shade of grayish pink with brown spots. Her health issues were legendary and what with having no fur, she was chronically cold. Which meant Lulu had a collection of sweaters, jackets and T-shirts. Today's selection was a lightweight, sleeveless pink sweater trimmed with shiny gray ribbon. With money tight and her own clothes threadbare, Nicole found herself in the embarrassing situation of envying a dog's wardrobe.

Lulu gave her a quick puppy-kiss on the chin. Nicole held onto the warm dog for a few seconds more. Her relationship with Lulu was the least emotionally charged moment in her day thus far, and she was determined to enjoy it.

Pam, a pretty brunette with an easy smile, wore a loose short-sleeved dress over her leggings and workout tank. Unlike the other clients who came in for the noon class, Pam didn't walk over from an office. Nicole knew the other woman had held a job at her husband's company years ago. She understood how a small business worked and often gave Nicole sound advice. Aside from that, Pam seemed to have her days to herself. Right now that sounded like a dream come true.

"Who's coming today?" Pam asked as she pulled the blanket out of the tote and folded it before setting it in a corner of the room. Lulu obligingly curled up, with her long legs tucked gracefully under her body. Nicole knew the dog wouldn't budge until class was over. She supposed the sweet temperament and excellent manners made up for Lulu's odd and faintly sci-fi appearance.

"Just you and Shannon," Nicole said, clicking on her computer's scheduling program to confirm. She was actually relieved to have a smaller class. Lately she was so damned tired all the time. Pam and Shannon could have run the workout themselves, so there wouldn't be pressure to stay on top of every move.

Even better, all three dropouts had come in early that morning. The studio had a strict twenty-four-hour cancellation policy, which meant she was going to be paid for five students regardless. She accepted her momentary pleasure even though the thought made her a bad person, and vowed she would work on her character just as soon as she figured out how to fix what was going on with her marriage and got more than four hours of sleep on any given night.

Pam had slipped off her sandals in preparation for class. But instead of putting on her Pilates socks, she turned to Nicole and grinned.

"Want to go to lunch?"

Pam's smile was infectious. Her hazel-green eyes crinkled at the corners and her mouth curved up.

"Come on," Pam teased. "You know you want to."

"Want to what?" Shannon Rigg asked as she walked into the studio. "I've had a horrible morning dealing with a misogynistic idiot from the bank who insisted on continually asking to speak to my supervisor. When I explained I was the CFO of the company, I think he had a seizure." She paused, her blue eyes dancing with amusement. "I offered to send him a scanned copy of my business card, but he declined. Then I told him that if he didn't get his act together, I would be moving the company's four-hundred-million-dollar account to another bank." She paused for dramatic effect. "I think I made him cry."

Pam held out her arm, hand raised, for a high five. "You both constantly impress me. Nicole juggles her husband, her five-year-old son and her growing business. You're busy frightening men who really should know better. I, on the other hand, will pick out my dog's wardrobe for tomorrow and make biscuits from scratch. It's sad."

"I don't even know what you put in the bowl to make a biscuit," Shannon admitted as she gave her friend a high five, then turned to Nicole. "Do you?"

"Flour, water, something else."

Shannon laughed. "Yeah, that's where I would get lost, too. It's the something else that always gets you."

Nicole thought about how Pam had described her. Juggling sounded so perky and positive. Unfortunately most days she found herself cleaning up what had fallen and shattered rather than keeping her plates spinning in the air.

Okay, that was a confused and slightly depressing analogy. She really needed to think more positively. And maybe learn how to make biscuits.

Shannon had on a tailored sleeveless dress and three-inch pumps. Her legs were bare and tanned, her hair a glorious tumbling mass of auburn waves that fell past her shoulders. She wore expensive watches and elegant jewelry. She drove a BMW convertible. If Nicole could pick, she would want Pam for her mother and to be Shannon when she grew up.

Only at thirty, Nicole had a feeling she was about as grown-up as she was going to get.

"Wait," Pam said as Shannon headed for the small dressing room next to the restroom. "I thought we'd go to lunch instead of working out."

Shannon already had her exercise clothes out of her gym bag. She turned back to Pam. "Not exercise?"

"Sure. We're the only two today. It's Friday, my friend. Live a little. Have a glass of wine, mock your uninformed banking friend and unwind."

Shannon looked at Nicole and raised her eyebrows. "I'm in," she said. "What about you?"

Nicole thought about her to-do list and the fact that she was behind on the laundry and had a stack of bills to pay and a husband who had walked away from a successful career in computer software to write a screenplay. She thought of the spinning and falling plates and how she spent her life exhausted.

She pulled the tie from her blond ponytail, shook her hair loose, grabbed her keys and her handbag and stood. "Let's go."

McGrath's Pub had been around nearly as long as the Mischief Bay pier and boardwalk. Shannon remembered coming here when she'd been a teenager. The drive in from Riverside had taken about an hour, if there wasn't any traffic. She and her girlfriends had spent the whole time talking and laughing, imagining the cute boys they were going to meet. Boys who lived by the ocean and surfed and had sun-bleached hair. Boys not like those they knew in high school.

Because back then all it took to get her heart beating faster had been sun-bleached hair and a retro convertible.

She liked to think that in the past twenty-plus years she'd matured.

As she followed her friends into the pub, her gaze strayed to the sand and the ocean beyond. It was midday and low tide. No surfers out there now. As it was also a weekday in February, there weren't any people playing volleyball. Despite the fact that it was probably seventy degrees.

McGrath's was a three-story building with outdoor dining on the main level. Inside there was a big, open bar. Pam led the way directly to the stairs. They bypassed the second-floor dining room and went up to the top-floor eating area.

"By the window?" Pam asked, already heading in that direction.

The big windows offered a view of the Pacific. Today they were partially open, allowing in some fresh air. When temperatures dropped to anything below sixty-five they could be closed and in the summer, they were removed completely.

Shannon sat across from Nicole. Pam settled next to Nicole and put her tote on the floor next to her chair. The perfectly trained Lulu would stay hidden until they left.

The first time the three of them had played hooky and gone to lunch, Shannon had spent the entire time freaking out about Lulu. Now she saw the strange creature as the mascot for their friendship—odd, unexpected and over time, very comforting.

She turned her attention from thoughts of a Chinese crested to the restaurant location. The view should have captured their attention and left them speechless. Taupe-colored sand led the way to midnight blue water. A couple of sailboats leaned in to capture the light breeze, and in the distance container ships chugged toward the horizon and the exotic ports beyond.

But this was L.A. and amazing views existed around every turn. Whether it was a star sighting at a Whole Foods or the lapping waters of the Pacific. Instead of talking about the beauty of the moment, Pam passed out menus.

"There's a burger special," Pam said with a sigh. "Did you see it? If I get that, will someone eat some of my fries?"

"I will," Nicole told her. "I get the protein plate here."

Pam wrinkled her nose. "Of course you do."

Shannon knew the protein plate consisted of broiled fish and shrimp with a side of steamed vegetables. Healthy, sure, but the low calorie count was of more concern to the body-conscious, bikini-clad locals.

"I'll have a couple of fries, too," she said. They would nicely round out the salad she generally ordered.

Pam poked Nicole in the upper arm. "You're a stick. You should eat more."

"I eat plenty."

"Roots and grubs. Have a burger." Pam leaned back in her chair. "Enjoy your metabolism while you can. Because one day, it's all going to hell."

"You look great," Nicole said easily. "You're in terrific shape."

Pam's brows rose. "If you say 'for a woman my age' I'm pitching you out the window."

Nicole laughed. "I'd never say that. You're nowhere near a certain age. That's old."

So spoke the thirty-year-old, Shannon thought wryly. Time was going faster and faster every day. She couldn't believe she was only a few months away from turning forty, herself. She glanced at Pam and Nicole's hands and saw the wedding bands and diamond engagement rings winking back at her. Not for the first time, Shannon considered the fact that somewhere along the way she should have gotten married.

She'd meant to, had always thought she would. Only her career had been her first priority—a fact that the men she knew didn't like. The more successful she got, the harder it was to date. Or at least find a man who didn't resent her devotion to her career. Lately, finding someone interesting and appealing had started to seem nearly impossible.

She briefly toyed with the idea of mentioning that. All the articles she read said that she had to put herself out there if she wanted to meet a great guy. She had to be willing to tell all her friends that she was serious and looking. Of course, she had a sneaking suspicion that many articles in women's magazines were written by people who had no idea what they were talking about. Besides, she wasn't keen on pity. She was a successful, vital businesswoman. Hell, she was the chief financial officer of a company grossing more than a billion dollars a year. She didn't need a man in her life. Which wasn't to say she might not like having one around.

"How's my favorite young man?" Pam asked.

Nicole smiled. "Tyler is great. I can't believe he's turning five in a couple of months. It's going so fast. He'll be in kindergarten in September." She paused. "In a way, that will be nice. There'll be less day-care juggling."

As she finished speaking, her smile faded and a muscle twitched in her cheek. As if she were clenching her teeth.

Shannon hesitated, not sure if she should ask what was wrong. Because she already knew the answer. The three of them had been in the same exercise class for nearly two years. While she and Pam were faithful participants, the same couldn't be said for anyone else. For some reason, the Friday noon class tended to attract the flakier clients.

Which meant it had often been just the three of them. They'd talked between Pilates moves, had shared various ups and downs. Shannon knew that Brandon, Pam's youngest, had been a wild teenager—to the point of driving so drunk, he'd wrapped his car around a tree. Now he was a sober, determined student in medical school. She'd listened as Nicole had tried to explain her bewilderment that her stable, hard-working husband had quit his job to write a screenplay and surf. In turn, Shannon had shared the tribulations of her own personal life. Everything from the challenge of being the only female executive at a tech company to the difficulty finding a Mr. Right who supported her career goals.

While Shannon searched for a delicate way to ask if Nicole's comment meant Eric was still determined to conquer Hollywood, Pam plunged right in.

"He continues to be an idiot?" she asked.

Nicole wrinkled her nose. "He's not an idiot. He's..." She hesitated. "Confusing. I know it's been six months, so I should be over it, right? It's not that I didn't know."

Pam angled toward her friend. "Honey, everyone *says* they want to write a screenplay or be on *American Idol* or something, but no one takes them seriously. There are dreams and then there's real life. Eric has a wife and a son. He walked away from a great job to type and surf. Who does that?"

Nicole winced. "He's writing, not typing."

"Details. He's not contributing financially or in any other way."

"He helps," Nicole said, then sighed. "Sort of. I don't know what to do. You're right. Everyone says they want to be rich or famous, and that's great. But I don't know. When he walked in and told me he'd quit his job..." She raised her shoulders. "I still don't know what to say."

Shannon got that one. She had been just as shocked as her friend and she didn't have to live with Eric. She supposed a case could be made for everyone having the right to follow his or her dreams, but in a marriage, shouldn't both parties get a vote? That was what had been so stunning about Eric's decision. He hadn't mentioned it or negotiated or anything. He'd simply walked away from his job and told his wife after the fact.

"While I don't recommend this for every situation," Pam said slowly, "have you considered smothering him with a pillow?"

Nicole managed a soft laugh. "Not my style."

"Mine, either," Pam admitted. "I'm more direct. But it's an option."

Shannon grinned. "This from a woman who carefully dresses her dog so she won't be cold? You talk tough, but on the inside, you're a marshmallow."

"Don't tell," Pam said, glancing around, as if afraid they would be overheard. "I have a reputation to protect." She touched Nicole's hand. "All jokes aside, I know this is difficult for you. You want to shake some sense into him and right now you can't. Hang in there. You two love each other. That'll get you through."

"I hope so," Nicole said. "I know he's a good guy."

"He is. Marriage is like life. Just when you think you have it figured out, it changes. When I stopped working, I felt guilty that John was carrying the whole financial load.

But we talked about it and he finally convinced me he liked having me home. I take care of things there and he handles bringing in the money."

A world she couldn't imagine, Shannon admitted, if only to herself. It was as if Pam was from another planet. Or another era. Shannon knew there were plenty of stay-at-home moms. The difference was she didn't know any of them. Not as friends. The mothers she knew were like Nicole—always scrambling to keep up.

Although now that she thought about it, there were a couple of friends who had left their jobs and become stay-at-home mothers. Only once that had happened, Shannon had lost touch with them. Or maybe they'd lost touch with her.

"There are always rough patches," Pam said. "But if you remember why you're together, then you'll get through it."

Two

PAM WALKED THROUGH FROM THE GARAGE to the main house, Lulu keeping pace with her. In the mudroom they both paused. Pam fished her small handbag out of the tote, then hung the larger bag on a hook.

The open area served as a catchall for things that otherwise didn't have a home. There was a built-in storage unit with plenty of hooks, shelves and drawers. The latter were mostly filled with Lulu's various clothes.

Now Pam eyed the lightweight sweater her pet wore and decided it would keep the dog warm enough until bedtime. Like the rest of the family, Lulu wore pj's to bed. Pam didn't care if anyone laughed at her for that. She was the one Lulu cuddled next to under the covers and she wanted her dog wearing something soft when that happened.

They continued through the house to the kitchen. Pam pulled her cell out of her purse and stuck it on the side table by the hall, then checked on the Crock-Pot she'd left on that morning. A quick peek and stir confirmed the beef burgundy was coming along. She added the vegetables she'd already prepared and stirred again, then went out the front door to collect the mail.

The day had warmed up nicely. February in the rest of the country could mean snow and ice. In Southern California there was every chance it would be sunny and seventy. Today was no exception, although she would guess it was closer to sixty-five. Hardly reason to complain, she told herself as she pulled the mail out of the box and started back toward the house.

Mischief Bay was a coastal community. Tucked between Redondo Beach and Hermosa Beach, it had a small pier, plenty of restaurants, a boardwalk and lots of tourists. The ocean regulated the temperatures and the steady light breeze made sure there wasn't much in the way of smog.

She and John had bought their sprawling ranch-style home ages ago. Jennifer, their oldest, had been what? Three? Pam tried to remember. If Jennifer had been three, then Steven had been a year and she'd been pregnant with Brandon.

Oh, yeah. She *had* been pregnant all right. There'd been the charming moment when she'd thrown up in front of the movers. Brandon had been a difficult pregnancy and she'd been nauseous a lot. Something she brought up every so often—when her son needed a little humbling. As all children did, now and then.

She paused to wait for Lulu to do her business by the bushes and studied the front of the house. They'd redone much of both yards a few years ago, when they'd had the house painted. She liked the new plants that edged the circular drive. Her gaze rose to the roof. That had been replaced, as well. One of the advantages of having a husband in construction—he always knew the best people.

Lulu trotted back to her side.

"Ready to go in, sweet pea?" Pam asked.

Lulu wagged her feathered tail and led the way. Pam glanced down at the mail as she walked. Bills, a letter from an insurance agent she'd never heard of—no doubt an ad—along with two car magazines for John and a postcard from the local high school.

Pam frowned at the postcard and turned it over. What on earth could they...?

Lulu walked into the house. Pam followed and automatically closed the door. She stood in the spacious foyer, afternoon light spilling onto the tile floor.

But she didn't see any of that. She didn't see anything but the stark words printed on the postcard.

Class of 2005. Fellow Cougars—save the date!! Your 10-year high school reunion is this August.

There was more, but the letters got blurry as Pam tried to make sense of the notice. A ten-year high school reunion? Sure, Jennifer had graduated in 2005, but there was no way it had been ten years, had it? Because if Jen was attending her ten-year reunion, that meant Pam was the *mother* of a woman attending her ten-year high school reunion.

"When did I get old?" Pam asked, her voice a whisper.

Involuntarily, she turned to stare at the mirror over the entry table. The person staring back at her looked familiar and yet totally wrong. Sure the shoulder-length dark hair was fine and the irises were still hazel-green. But everything else was different. No, not different. Less...firm.

There were lines around her eyes and a distinct softness to her jaw. Her mouth wasn't as full as it had been. Ironically, just last November she'd turned fifty and had been so damned proud of herself for not freaking out. Because these days fifty was the new thirty-five. Big deal, right?

John had thrown a huge party. She'd laughed over the gag gifts and had prided herself for achieving the big 5-0 with grace and style. Not to mention a pretty decent ass, thanks to the three-times-a-week classes she took at Nicole's studio. She hadn't felt…old. But that was before she had a daughter who had just been invited to her ten-year high school reunion.

Sure, she'd had kids young. She'd married John at nineteen and had Jen when she'd turned twenty-two. But that was what she'd always wanted.

She and John had met at Mischief Bay High School. He'd been tall and sexy, a star player on the football team. His family had a local plumbing company. One that worked in new construction rather than fixing stopped-up toilets.

John's plans had been set. He was going to get his AA in business from Mischief Bay Community College, then work in the family firm full-time. He would start at the bottom, earn his way to the top and buy out his parents by the time he was forty.

Pam had liked how he'd known what he wanted and went after it. When he turned his blue eyes on her and decided she was the one to share the journey, well, she'd been all in.

Now as she studied her oddly familiar and unfamiliar reflection, she wondered how the time had gone by so quickly. One second she'd been an in-love teenager and now she was the mother of a twenty-eight-year-old.

"No," she said aloud, turning away from the mirror. She wasn't going to freak out over something as ridiculous as age. She had an amazing life. A wonderful husband and terrific kids and a strange little dog. They were all healthy—except for Lulu's ongoing issues—and successful and, best of all, happy. She'd been blessed a thousand times over. She was going to remember that and stay grateful. So what if she wasn't firm? Beauty only went skin deep. She had wisdom and that was worth more.

She headed into the kitchen and flipped on the wall-mounted TV. John got home between five fifteen and five thirty every day. They ate at six—a meal she'd made from scratch. Every Saturday night they either went out to dinner or had an evening with friends. Sunday afternoon the kids came over and they barbecued. On Memorial Day they held a big party, also a barbecue. It was LA. When in doubt, throw meat on a grill.

She automatically collected the ingredients for biscuits. Self-rising flour, shortening, sugar, buttermilk. She'd stopped using a recipe years ago for nearly everything. Because she knew what she was doing. John liked what she served and didn't want her to change. They had a routine. Everything was comfortable.

She measured the flour and told herself that comfortable wasn't the same as old. It was nice. Friendly. Routines meant things went smoothly.

She finished cutting in the shortening, then covered the bowl. That was the trick to her biscuits. To let them rest about twenty minutes.

Lulu sat patiently next to her bowl. As Pam approached, the dog wagged her fluffy tail and widened her eyes in a hopeful expression.

"Yes," Pam told her. "It *is* your dinnertime."

Lulu gave a bark, then followed her to the refrigerator, where the can waited.

Lulu's diet was an on-going challenge. She was small so didn't need all that much. She had allergies and skin conditions, not to mention a sensitive stomach. Which meant she ate prescription dog food, consisting of a "novel protein" diet. In her case, duck and sweet potato.

Pam stuck a quarter cup of water into the microwave and hit the start button. After measuring out the right amount of canned food, she swapped the plate for the measuring cup, then started the microwave again. Hot water was stirred into kibble. Lulu had delicate teeth and couldn't eat regular kibble. So hers was softened with hot water.

They went through this ritual every night, Pam thought as she held out the bowl. Lulu immediately sat, as she was supposed to, then lunged for the bowl and devoured her meal in less than eight seconds.

"You do remember you had breakfast this morning and a snack after lunch, right? You act like we feed you weekly."

Lulu was too busy licking her bowl to answer.

Pam rolled out the biscuits and put them on the cookie sheet. She covered them with a clean towel and started the oven. She'd barely finished setting the table when she heard the faint rumble of the garage door opener. Lulu took off running down the hall, barking and yipping in excitement.

A few minutes later John walked into the kitchen, their ridiculous dog in his arms. Pam smiled at him and turned her head for their evening kiss. As their lips touched, Lulu scrambled from his arms to hers, then swiped both their chins with her tongue.

"How was your day?" John asked.

"Good. Yours?"

"Not bad."

As he spoke he crossed to the bottle of wine she'd put on the counter in the butler's pantry off the kitchen. It was a Cab from a winery they'd visited a few years ago on a trip to Napa.

"Steven's working on a bid for that new hotel everyone's been talking about. It's right on the water. Upscale to the max. He said they were talking about the possibility of twenty-four-karat gold on the faucets in the penthouse. Can you believe it?"

"No. Who would do that? It's a hotel. Everything has to be scrubbed down daily. How do you clean gold?"

"I know." John opened the drawer to pull out the foil cutter. "It's a bathroom. They're idiots. But if the check clears, what do I care?"

As they spoke, she studied the man she'd been married to for thirty-one years. He was tall, just over six feet, with thick hair that had started going gray. The dark blond color meant the gray wasn't noticeable, but it was there. Being a man, it only made him look more appealing. A few months ago he'd asked why she wasn't going gray, too. When she'd reminded him of her visits every six weeks to her hair person, he'd been shocked. John was such a typical guy, it had never occurred to him she colored her hair. Because he thought she was naturally beautiful.

Silly man, she thought affectionately, as she watched him.

He had a few wrinkles around his eyes, but otherwise looked as he had when they'd first met. Those broad shoulders had always appealed to her. These days he claimed he needed to lose ten or fifteen pounds, but she thought he looked just fine.

He was handsome, in a rugged kind of way. He was a

good man. Kind and generous. He loved his wife and his kids and his routine. While he had his faults, they were minor and ones she could easily live with. In truth, she had no complaints about John. It was the her-getting-older thing she found faintly annoying.

He pulled out the cork and tested it with his thumbnail, then poured them each a glass of Cab. She slid the biscuits into the oven and set the timer.

"What are we having?" he asked as he handed her a glass.

"Beef burgundy and biscuits."

His mouth turned up in an easy smile. "I'm a lucky man."

"Even luckier. You'll be taking leftovers for lunch tomorrow."

"You know I love me some leftovers."

He wasn't kidding, she thought as she followed him through the kitchen. His idea of heaven was any kind of red meat with leftovers for lunch the following day. He was easy to please.

They went into the sunroom off the back of the house. In the cooler months, the glass room stayed warm. In the summer, they removed the glass and used the space for outdoor living.

Lulu followed them, then jumped up on the love seat where Pam always sat and settled next to her. Pam rubbed her dog's ears as John leaned back in his chair—a recliner with a matching mate in the family room—and sighed heavily.

"Hayley's pregnant again," he said. "She told me this morning. She's waiting until three months to make a public announcement."

Pam felt her mouth twist. "I don't know what to say," she admitted. "That poor girl."

"I hope this one takes," John said. "I don't know how much more of her suffering I can stand."

Hayley was John's secretary and desperate to have children, but she'd miscarried four times over the past three years. This would be try number five. Rob, Hayley's husband, wanted to look into adoption or a surrogate, but Hayley was obsessed with having a baby the old-fashioned way.

"I should send her a card," Pam said, then shook her head. "Maybe not." She took a sip of her wine. "I have no idea how to handle this."

"Don't look at me. You're in woman territory."

"Where if you stray too far, you'll grow breasts?"

"Damned straight."

"I'll write a note," she decided. "I can say we're rooting for her without a you're-having-a-baby message. Did the doctor say she would be okay if she could get to three months?"

Her husband forehead furrowed. "I don't know. She probably told me, but I barely want to know if she goes to the bathroom. Baby stuff is too intimate."

"You're not a complex man, are you?"

He raised his glass to her. "And that's why you love me."

He was right. She did love that he was dependable and predictable. Even if every now and then she wanted something different in their lives. A surprise trip to somewhere or a fancy bracelet. But that wasn't John's style. He would never plan a trip without talking to her and as for buying jewelry, he was more of a "go buy yourself something pretty" kind of man.

She didn't object. She'd seen too many of her friends endure surprises of the not-very-pleasant kind. Ones that involved other women or divorces. John wasn't looking for more than she had to offer. He liked his routine and knowing that gave her comfort.

"Jen got mail from the high school today," she said. "An invitation to her ten-year reunion."

"Okay."

"You don't think it's stunning that we have a daughter old enough to have been out of high school ten years?"

"She's twenty-eight. So the reunion is right on time."

Pam sipped her wine. "I was shocked. I'm not ready to have a daughter that old."

"Too late to send her back now. She's used."

Despite her earlier distress, Pam laughed. "Don't let her hear you say that."

"I won't." He smiled at her. "And you're not old, sweetheart. You're barely in your prime."

"Thanks." She heard the timer chime and stood. "That's our dinner."

He scooped up Lulu and followed Pam back to the kitchen. As Pam went about serving the meal, she reminded herself she was a very lucky woman. That a bit of sagging and a few lumps and bumps didn't change who she was as a person. Her life was a blessing. If there weren't any tingles anymore, well, that was to be expected. Wasn't she forever hearing that you couldn't have it all?

It's just drinks, Shannon told herself as she pushed open the door that led into Olives—the martini bar/restaurant where she was meeting her date. Her online date.

She wanted to pause and maybe bang her head against the wall. Why did she do this to herself? It never went well. Dating wasn't her strong suit. It just wasn't. She was a successful businesswoman. She earned mid six figures and fully funded her 401K every single year. She had friends, she had a beautiful condo with an ocean view. Okay, there had been a string of boyfriends over the years and she'd been engaged twice, for no more than fifteen minutes each time. But no marriage. Not for her.

The truth was, she didn't have good romantic relationships. Maybe it was her, maybe it was men, but she had to accept the truth that having it all simply wasn't going to happen. Not to her. So why was she back dealing with the nightmare that was dating? Worse—online dating.

The only saving grace was that ProfessionalLA.com was a halfway decent site that actually screened subscribers. So the guy was going to look like his profile picture and wouldn't have any felony convictions in his past. But the distance from that to happily-ever-after seemed insurmountable.

Still, she was here. She would go in and say hi. She would be pleasant and as soon as she was able to duck out without seeming wildly rude, she would run back to her office, get her car and head home. One glass of wine, she promised herself. She could survive that. Maybe what's-his-name would be great.

She paused for a second, as panic set in. What was his name? Crap. Double crap. She kept moving even as her brain hustled toward whatever synapses stored short-term memory. Andrew? *A* something. Adam? Right. Adam. Adam something she would never remember. He sold cars maybe. He was about her age, divorced and possibly blond?

She made a mental note to spend a little more time with the profiles, even as she scanned the people in the bar and hoped to find someone who looked vaguely familiar.

A man rose and smiled at her. He was about six feet, with dark hair and eyes and a crooked smile. He was tanned and fit, but not in a look-at-me kind of way. And he was staring at her as if she had a monkey on her head.

She did her best to appear casual as she glanced over her shoulder to make sure she wasn't being followed by Taylor Swift or someone else who would cause a grown man to simply stare. There wasn't anyone of note. So she kept moving toward him and hoped for the best.

"Shannon?" he asked as she got closer.

"Yes. Hi."

"I'm Adam." He held out his hand and they shook. "Thanks for meeting me."

He continued to look at her in a way that made her wonder if she'd forgotten to check her teeth or had grown a wart on her nose in the five minutes it had taken her to walk from the office to the bar. It couldn't be that she looked different from her picture. She'd used a business head shot. Nothing that would overpromise.

They sat down.

Olives was the kind of place that catered to locals and tourists alike. The bar was well lit, without a diner feel. Tables were spaced far enough apart that you didn't have to worry about everyone listening to your conversation. The restaurant was upscale-casual, with an eclectic menu. Except for a few paintings of olives and martini glasses on the walls, they hadn't gone crazy with the motif.

Shannon liked it for a first date because she came here just enough to be familiar with the staff and all the exits. If a first date went bad, she could easily call for help or bolt. It was also within walking distance of her office, which meant she didn't have to worry about a second drink before driving. If it was time to leave, but she wasn't ready to get behind the wheel, she simply returned to her office and did something mindless until she was ready to make the six-minute commute to her condo.

Adam's gaze was steady. Shannon couldn't stand it anymore.

"You're staring at me," she said, trying to keep her voice as friendly as possible. "Is something wrong?"

His eyes widened, then he glanced away before returning his attention to her. "No. Sorry. Jeez, I'm being an idiot. It's just…you. Wow. You sent a picture and it was so great, I figured there had to be a mistake. Then when I saw you just now and you were even more beautiful in person…" He verbally stumbled to a stop, then cleared his throat. "Can we start over or do you want to leave?"

His expression was both chagrined and hopeful. Shannon tried to remember the last time anyone had been so rattled by her looks. She knew she was pretty enough and when she made an effort, she could up her game, but she wasn't the kind of woman who left men tongue-tied. Or staring.

She smiled. "We can start over."

"Good. I'll do my best not to be scary." He smiled. "It's nice to meet you, Shannon."

"Apparently."

He chuckled and motioned to the server. "What can I get you to drink?"

She ordered a glass of the house red while he chose a Scotch. He added the fruit and cheese plate to the order. When they were alone again, she leaned back in her chair.

He was nice, she thought. A little awkward, which meant he didn't date a lot. At least he wasn't a player. She didn't need any more of them in her life. Divorced, if she remembered correctly.

"So, Adam," she said. "Tell me about yourself."

"What do you want to know?"

Everything that had been in his profile, she thought, wishing she'd paid just a little more attention. The thing was she didn't like online dating. She counted on the service to screen the men and then moved fairly quickly to a meeting. For her, emails and a couple of calls didn't provide any insight into how things would go in person.

"Do you live in the area?" she asked.

"Sure." The smile returned. "I was born and raised right here in Mischief Bay. Most of my family is still in the area, which means it's hard to get away with anything."

"Do you try to get away with things?"

The smile turned into a laugh. "I gave that up when I was a teenager. I'm a bad liar and if I cross the line, I get caught. So I don't bother with either anymore."

His smile faded. "You're not in to bad boys, are you?"

She had been, and had the heart scars to prove it. "Not anymore. They're great in theory, but life isn't about theories. It's about real people who take the time to show up."

"I agree."

They were on opposite sides of a small table. Adam leaned toward her. "You're in finance?"

"Yes. I'm a CFO for a software company."

She tried to speak normally, knowing that when she mentioned her job she tended to be both defensive and proud. An awkward combination at best.

The problem was some men resented her success and some men were intimidated by it. A few had seen her as a way to the easy life, but fortunately they weren't usually very subtle about their hopes of being kept. The ones who accepted that she'd done well and worked hard were often the keepers, albeit rare and therefore hard to find.

"Are you in line to be president next?" he asked.

She smiled. "No. I'm comfortable being the queen of the checkbook. I like the financial side of things." She shifted toward him and lowered her voice. "Software is not my thing. I'm better than most on a computer, but it's never been easy for me. You should see some of the college kids we hire every year. They're brilliant. What about you?"

"Not brilliant."

She laughed. "Thanks for the share. I meant, tell me about your work."

"Oh, that. My family's in construction. Large projects, mostly. Office buildings, hotels. I'm the foreman on a hotel we're dealing with now. It's just south of Marina del Rey. It's high-end, twenty stories."

Impressive, she thought. "Foreman sounds like a lot of responsibility."

Adam grinned. "I stand around and tell other people what to do. It beats a real job."

Their server arrived with their drinks and the cheese plate. Adam raised his glass.

"To unexpected surprises."

She touched her glass to his and thought he was certainly that and more. She'd had no expectations for their date, but here she was, having a nice time. So far Adam was funny and charming. There had even been hints of his being genuinely nice. She knew better than to get her hopes up, but the evening was turning out better than she'd anticipated.

"Tell me about the family that doesn't let you get away with anything," she said.

"I'm one of five kids and I could practically walk to four of their houses from here. Same with my parents." He shrugged. "My youngest brother is back east, but then he's always felt he had something to prove."

She stared at him. "You're one of five?"

"I know. I told my dad they figured out what causes pregnancy, but he said he and Mom always wanted a big family. I have to say it was a fun way to grow up."

"And loud," she murmured.

"Yeah, there was noise."

"How many boys and girls?"

"Three boys, two girls, and we alternate. I'm in the middle. My older brother was never interested in the family business. He's a graphic designer. Very talented. My older sister always wanted to be a veterinarian, so by the time I was six or seven, Dad was starting to get nervous that no one was going to go into the business. Fortunately my idea of a good time was building things. I got my first job at the company when I was fourteen."

He took a piece of cheese. "I know. Not very exciting."

"Exciting is highly overrated," she murmured. All this and stable, too. So what was the flaw? Emotional unavailability? A secret life as a serial killer? There had to be something, because to be honest, her luck simply wasn't that good.

"Where did you grow up?" he asked.

"Riverside. I'm an only child, so I can't relate to your noise. My house was always quiet."

"Were you the smartest girl in the class?"

"Sometimes. I liked math, which made me unacceptable to most groups. But I wasn't brilliant enough to major in it. Finance seemed like an interesting way to spend my days."

His brown eyes crinkled with amusement. "If I had a

nickel for every time I looked forward to spending time working on the company's financial records..."

"You wouldn't have a nickel?"

"Something like that."

She smiled. "Your profile said you're divorced?"

He nodded. "Nearly a year now. We were separated before that." He shrugged. "It wasn't anything dramatic. We were married young and over the past few years realized we didn't like spending time with each other."

There was something about the way he spoke that had her leaning forward. As if there was more to the story.

"That's no fun," she said quietly.

"Tell me about it." He looked at her, then swore softly. "Hell. Okay, she cheated. I don't like to say that because it makes me look like an idiot. I didn't know. She came to me one day and said she'd been having an affair and that she'd fallen in love with the guy. She didn't want to marry him or anything, but she'd realized that if she could be in love with someone else, she wasn't in love with me anymore."

He moved his glass back and forth on the table. Tension pulled at his mouth. "I was shocked and hurt and didn't know what to do. I grabbed some stuff and moved out that night. About a month later, when my pride and ego weren't so much in the way, I realized we'd been growing apart for a long time."

"That must have been hard," she said, thinking that if he was telling the truth, then she was liking him more by the second.

"It was. We have two kids. Charlotte is nearly nine and Oliver is six. We share them. One week on, one week off. Tabitha and I live about two blocks away from each other. Slightly awkward for us, but easy for the kids." Humor returned to his eyes. "Of course, my parents and three of my siblings live in the neighborhood, too, so I'm going to go out on a limb and say it's way more awkward for her than for me."

"As long as it works," Shannon told him.

"And you?" he prompted.

Yes, the inevitable questions. "No kids, no ex-husband. I was engaged twice, but never quite made it down the aisle."

"Who made the decision?"

"One time him, one time me."

She'd also had a long-term on-again, off-again relationship with a music producer, who'd been very bad for her, but there was no reason to mention him. At least not on the first date.

"What do you do for fun?" Adam asked.

"I love to travel. Take two or three weeks and go somewhere I've never been."

"Like?"

She smiled. "I've been on every continent except Antarctica. I was thinking of taking one of those ships there, but after one got stuck a couple of years ago and made headlines, I changed my mind."

"What's your next trip?"

She laughed. "You're going to be shocked."

"I doubt that."

"Okay. Machu Picchu."

His eyes widened slightly. "Remind me to listen to you next time. That's Peru, right?"

"Yes. I'm going with a girlfriend and it's going to be great. We'll be hiking the Inca Trail. The ruins are at seven thousand feet above sea level so I'm a little worried about my athletic ability. I'm—"

A familiar ringtone drifted from her purse. She reached for her bag.

"Sorry," she said as she pulled her phone out of its pocket and glanced at the screen. "It's work. I need to take this."

She was already standing and heading out of the restaurant. When she stepped onto the sidewalk, she pushed Talk.

"This is Shannon."

"Len Howard in the Seoul office. Sorry to bother you but we have a problem with the South Korean finance minister. He's insisting on speaking with you."

Shannon glanced back at the bar and saw Adam glancing her way. Adam, who appeared to be pretty darned close to perfect.

"Based on my other conversations with him, I'm guessing he wants me to phone him in the next few minutes."

"If possible."

Because he was a man of power and she needed his help with some banking regulations. Nolan, her boss, wanted their Asian headquarters in Seoul, which meant Shannon had to make nice with the finance minister.

"Please tell him I'll call him back in fifteen minutes," she said. "From my office."

"Will do."

She walked back into the restaurant. Adam rose as she approached the table.

"Everything all right?" he asked.

She shook her head. "I'm so sorry. I have to get back to work. There's a crisis in South Korea and I need to be on the phone in fifteen minutes."

"I'm sorry to hear that. I was hoping we could grab dinner. Should I wait?"

She wanted to say yes. He was an unexpected find. But

once she was done calming things down, she would have to call her boss and do paperwork.

"It's going to be a late night." She gave him a smile. "But I enjoyed meeting you."

She wanted to say more. She wanted to ask him not to be intimidated by what she did. She wanted to say it would be great if he mentioned he wanted to see her again. Instead, she reached for her wallet.

"No way," he told her. "I've got this. Go make your call."

"Thank you."

She waited a second, hoping he would say more. When he didn't, she smiled. "It was so nice to meet you."

"You, too."

She walked to the door and out into the cool evening. Her office was only a few blocks away. She would make it back in time with no problem.

Thoughts swirled and competed for her attention. If only, she thought, then pushed the words away. She'd wanted her career. She'd wanted to be successful and know that she could always take care of herself, no matter what. And she had that. There was no way she was going to feel bad about what she'd accomplished.

It was just that sometimes, she found herself wanting more.

Three

NICOLE TURNED ON THE COFFEEMAKER AND leaned against the counter to wait for it to work its magic. It was early still. Quiet. The time of day she liked best—except when she was exhausted, which was most of the time.

She told herself that eventually the situation would get better. That she would figure out a schedule that worked, that Tyler would get older and need her less, that Eric would get a real job and start helping support the family again.

The last thought made her feel both guilty and angry. Not a happy combination. Because as much as she loved her husband, there were times when she didn't like him very much.

No, she thought. She didn't like what he'd done. There was a difference.

Back before he'd quit his well-paying, very steady software development job to write a screenplay, things had seemed more balanced. She'd been comfortable in their roles. But lately...not so much.

She told herself she had to be fair. That he had the right to follow his dream. Only it wasn't the dream she minded as much as the fact that he hadn't asked her first. Instead, he'd announced what he was doing. And that announcement had come two days after he'd already resigned.

She closed her eyes against the memory, but it crowded into the kitchen, anyway. It had been a Friday morning. She'd been standing in the kitchen, just like she was now. Eric had walked in to the room, wearing shorts and T-shirt.

"Don't you have to get dressed for work?" she'd asked.

He'd taken her hand. "I have to tell you something. I've quit my job. I'm going to write a screenplay."

There had been more talk. She was sure of it. But she hadn't heard anything beyond the keen screaming of fear that had filled her head.

Quit? How could he quit? They had a mortgage and she was still paying back her old boss for buying out the exercise studio. They had a four-year-old and college to save for and nearly no savings. They'd put off having a second kid because they couldn't afford it.

The coffee flowed into the mug Nicole had left in place. She waited until it was nearly full, then expertly shifted the mug out of the way and the carafe into its spot without missing a drop. She inhaled the perfect earthy scent before taking her first sip of the day.

"Mommy?"

She took another quick sip, then turned as Tyler walked into the kitchen. He was tousled and still half-asleep. One hand held his battered, red stuffed toy, Brad the Dragon. The well-loved plush dragon was based on the popular series of children's books. The author must make a mint from all the merchandising, she thought as she put her mug on the counter, then bent down to scoop up her son.

She wrapped her arms around his waist. He settled his

around her neck, while hanging on with his legs. She pretended to stagger as she lifted him.

"You grew!"

He giggled at the familiar comment. "I can't grow *every* night," he told her.

"I think you can."

She kissed his cheek and breathed in the scent of his skin. Whatever else went wrong in her day, Tyler was always right.

"How did you sleep?"

"Good." He snuggled close. "Brad had bad dreams, but I said he was safe with me."

"That's very nice of you. I'm sure he appreciated having you to protect him."

She carried Tyler over to the table. He released her to stand on his chair. With a quick, graceful movement, he settled into a sitting position.

Based on how athletic he was and how well he did in preschool, Tyler seemed to have inherited the best from her and Eric. Nicole could only hope. She'd wanted to enroll him in a dance class, but Eric had nixed the idea. For a while he'd wanted his son to attend a computer camp. But that interest had faded when he'd started writing his screenplay last year. She supposed they could agree on drama camp or something. Assuming Eric didn't stop writing his screenplay to follow another surprise dream.

She walked over to the pantry. "Oatmeal and berries?" she asked.

Tyler looked at Brad the Dragon, then nodded. "We like that."

Because Brad was consulted on most decisions.

Nicole would have been worried about her son's constant

companion, except Brad stayed home when Tyler went to preschool or day care and from everything she'd read, his attachment was completely normal. She was sure having a couple more siblings would ease his dependence on the stuffed toy, but there was no way that was happening anytime soon. She was barely able to keep them financially afloat as it was. If she got pregnant… She didn't want to think about it.

Not that it was much of an issue. She barely saw Eric these days. They passed in the hall and their brief discussions were generally about logistics regarding Tyler. Sex wasn't happening.

As she measured out the oatmeal, she mentally paused to wonder if Eric was cheating on her. He was by himself every day. She didn't know how much time he spent writing. She wasn't here to see for herself and he didn't volunteer the information. Once he was done surfing for the day, he could be seeing anyone.

Her stomach tightened at the thought, then she turned her attention back to getting breakfast for her son. She had to get Tyler fed and dressed with one eye on the clock. Once she got him to preschool, she had a full day of classes to teach, payroll to run for her two part-time instructors, groceries to buy and life to deal with. Worrying about Eric's possible affairs was way down on her list.

As she carried the oatmeal over to Tyler, she thought maybe her lack of concern was the biggest problem of all. The question was: What, if anything, did she do about it?

Pam wrapped her towel around her body and reached for the tube of body lotion. While she stuck to a fairly faithful regimen for her face, when it came to body products, she liked to mix things up. Right now she was enjoying Philosophy's Fresh Cream—a vanilla-based scent that made her feel like she should have chocolate-dipped strawberries for breakfast.

But for once the thick lotion didn't make her smile. Probably because she was fully aware that while she was applying it, she was doing her best not to look in the mirror.

The shock of Jen's impending ten-year high school reunion hadn't gone away. It had faded, only to return. Telling herself age was a number and she was a lucky, happy woman wasn't helping, either. It seemed as if every time she turned around, there was yet another reminder that her days of being a hot thirtysomething were long over.

She put down the tube, braced herself for the horror and tossed the towel over the tub. Then she stared at her naked self in the very wide, very unforgiving mirror in the master bath.

She wasn't fat, she told herself. She'd gained the most weight with Jen when she'd thought pregnancy meant a license to eat. And she had. Yes, her daughter had been a robust eight pounds and the rest of the associated goo had some weight and volume, but it didn't excuse the seventy-five pounds she'd packed on.

Losing them had been a bitch, so with her next two pregnancies, she'd only gained a reasonable thirty. Still, her body bore the battle wounds—including stretch marks and a definite doughlike puddle where her once-flat tummy had been.

Her breasts were worse. More tube socks than mammary-shaped. She got by with a good, supportive bra. Of course at night, when she just had on a sleep shirt, they eased back into her armpits. On the plus side, getting a mammogram wasn't a problem. Her breasts oozed into place on the tray. Still, there'd been a time when they'd been full and round and damned sexy.

There were a handful of spider veins on her legs, a distinct lack of firmness to her jaw and—

"Kill me now," Pam muttered out loud, then reached for her panties. What was the point in all that self-assessment? It wasn't as if she was going to get any kind of plastic surgery. She worked out three days a week at Nicole's studio and walked on the treadmill at least two other days. She was fifty. She'd better get used to not being anything special. She had a feeling it was only downhill from here.

She finished dressing, then combed her hair off her face. At least it was still thick and had a nice wave. She kept the length just past her shoulders and layered, to take advantage of the waves. Color and a few highlights in summer meant no one had to know about the encroaching gray.

The thing was, she thought as she applied her anti-aging serum—the one that didn't seem to be doing its job as well as it had a couple of years ago—there wasn't any warning. Sure, everyone knew that old age was inevitable. It was that or death and she was willing to admit she was pretty happy to be alive.

But what about the rest of it? AARP had been chasing her for the past six or eight months. In addition to their chronic invitations to join, they should send a heartfelt letter that told the truth. Something along the lines of "enjoy it now—in ten years, you're going to look in the mirror and see your grandmother staring back at you."

Perhaps not the most effective marketing campaign, but at least it would be honest.

She patted the eye cream into place, then used her fingertips to pull at her skin. What about a face-lift?

She studied the results, liking how pulling her skin up and back gave her a nice taut look. She didn't want to be scary—one of those women who almost seemed plastic. But maybe a little nip and tuck wouldn't hurt.

She dropped her arms to her sides and watched her face return to its normal position. Who was she kidding? She wasn't ever going to have a face-lift. Surgery on her face for vanity? No way. She wasn't some megarich celebrity. She was a normal woman freaking out about the unkindness of time and gravity.

She leaned closer to the mirror. Although maybe she could get some kind of injection. A filler or BOTOX. Didn't everyone do BOTOX these days?

She left the bathroom and walked into the bedroom. Her morning chores awaited. John had left for the office nearly an hour before, but there was still plenty to do. Make the bed, throw in some laundry, clean up the kitchen dishes. She had a once-monthly cleaning service come in. Those hardworking women always made her feel guilty, but she still let them scrub her floors.

After preparing the marinade for the chicken pieces they would be barbecuing that night, Pam collected a light jacket for herself and a violet knit shirt for Lulu. She let the dog out for a quick potty break, then picked her up and tucked her under her arm. They had an appointment with the vet.

While Lulu was a sweet, loving, well-behaved little girl, she came with several expected Chinese crested issues. She had skin allergies and soft teeth, luxating patellas and tummy problems. They were lucky in that her eyes were fine. And her moving kneecap didn't seem to be a problem yet. John said it was because the dog never walked anywhere.

"You're cute," Pam told her pet as she carried her to her small SUV. "Of course people want to carry you."

Lulu was six years old and had a veterinary file so thick, it was broken up into two folders at the vet's office. Pam had a feeling that a lot of other families wouldn't have been able to afford her chronic medical costs, but she and John were blessed. For all his complaints that Lulu cost as much as sending any one of their kids to college, the truth was, he adored her.

Now Pam climbed into the driver's seat of her SUV. Lulu scrambled into her doggie car seat. Pam put her in her harness and made sure it was attached to the restraining leash, then confirmed the air bag was off.

"Ready to see Dr. Ingersoll?" she asked.

Lulu wagged her tail in agreement.

The drive was only about ten minutes. Come summer, it would take three times that long. Tourists loved Mischief Bay. Despite the fact that it was often warm and sunny all winter long, most visitors didn't bother their little community until Memorial Day weekend. Which made it nice for locals.

Pam drove along T Street and then turned right into the parking lot of Bayside Veterinary. Lulu whined until she was released from her harness, then jumped into Pam's arms for the short carry inside.

"Hi, everyone," Pam said as they walked into the foyer.

The two receptionists smiled at her. "Good to see you, Pam. How's our favorite girl?"

"Doing well on the new cream."

Pam set Lulu on the ground. The slightly pink dog with

the dark patches raced behind the counter and greeted the two women.

There was much skittering of nails on linoleum and yips of excitement as she was given her soft cookie. When Lulu finished munching, she returned to Pam and waited to be picked up.

Heidi, one of the techs in the office, appeared with Lulu's file. "He's just finishing up with another patient. Let's get her weighed and in a room."

Pam carried Lulu to the scale in the hallway. Lulu sat obligingly until she was told she could move.

"Exactly ten pounds," Heidi said, making a note. "Same as always. I wish I could maintain my weight as well."

"Me, too," Pam admitted.

"We're in room two."

Lulu jumped off the scale and led the way through the open doorway. Pam picked her up and put her on the examination table while Heidi went through the usual visit stats. Seconds later she left Pam alone and a few minutes after that, Dr. Fraser Ingersoll walked in.

"How's my best girl?" he asked with a smile.

Pam knew he was asking the question of Lulu, but every now and then she pretended it was addressed to her.

Dr. Ingersoll, a tall, slim, dark-haired man in his early forties, radiated sex appeal. Pam couldn't explain it, nor did she want to. It was one of those things best left undefined.

She was sure half his female pet parents had a mad crush on him, and she was comfortable adding herself to the ranks of the swooning. Vivid blue eyes stared out from behind adorable glasses. He always had an easy smile ready, along with a quick touch of reassurance. Sometimes, it seemed to her, that touch lingered.

While she loved John and would never do anything to screw up her marriage, every now and then she allowed herself a little daydream. One involved a request from Dr. Ingersoll to meet for coffee. She would reluctantly agree, he would suggest a place outside of Mischief Bay and she would pretend not to know why. Over lattes and muffins, he would confess his attraction to her and while she would be genuinely tempted, in the end, she would let him down as gently as she could. After all, she was a married woman. She might not have been a virgin on her wedding day, but John was the only man she'd ever been with. She wanted to *fantasize* about Dr. Ingersoll, not actually sleep with him.

Still, those little moments helped when her day was tedious or she was annoyed by always having to take care of everyone.

But now she was less sure of her crush. Did Dr. Ingersoll see her as a sexy, slightly older, vital woman? Or was she simply Lulu's old and wrinkled pet mom?

"How's the new skin cream working?" the vet asked. He stroked Lulu as he spoke.

"She's scratching less."

"Her skin looks clear."

Pam watched him pet her dog and noticed that while the backs of his hands were smooth and taut, she'd developed a few age spots on hers. She held in a sigh. She didn't like this, she admitted to herself. Not the questioning or the concerns. Not the self-absorption. She'd always considered her life to be one that was blessed. She was lucky. Lucky people didn't get old and wrinkly, did they? Which brought her back to what the AARP really should be doing for their future members—warning them about the coming apocalypse of old age.

Shannon finished the quarterly reports and hit the send button. She would meet with the CEO later to discuss the actual results, but she wasn't worried. The numbers looked good.

She'd recently revamped the timetables and discounts in accounts payable. Cash flow was better, which meant the company's expansion could be funded internally. When interest rates were low, taking out a loan made sense, but she had a feeling they were going to start climbing. Better to keep the money at home.

While a lot of finance people saw the products their companies produced as interchangeable "widgets," she didn't agree. Every company was different. The challenges to produce a physical good varied between industries and even within them. Cars were different from furniture and software was nothing like envelopes. Her attitude had been the key reason she'd been hired nearly five years before. Nolan could have hired any one of a dozen applicants, but he'd chosen her. She had a feeling her rant on the fact that manufacturing products shouldn't be reduced to the pejorative term "widget" was a part of the reason.

She glanced out the big window by her desk. The sun had set a while ago. There was no hint of light coming from the sky—not counting the bright lights from around the office building, of course. She'd been at the office since six thirty and except for taking a class at Mischief in Motion during her lunch break, she'd pretty much been chained to her desk.

She saved her files and began to shut down her computer.

She would stop for some Thai food on her way home and spend a quiet evening by herself.

Because she didn't have a date. Certainly not with Adam, who had yet to call after their single meeting.

She'd been hopeful, she thought as she watched her computer move from saving to shutting down. Hopeful that he was man enough to accept her success, her career demands, to respect them, even. But he hadn't and that meant he wasn't for her. But being logical didn't help the dull ache she'd learned to recognize as loneliness.

Sure there were friends she could call. With Eric so busy with his screenwriting, Nicole was often up for dinner out. Tyler came with her, which was fine with Shannon. She enjoyed hanging out with the charming, happy little boy. Or she could see if Pam and John wanted some company for an after-dinner glass of wine. No doubt there would be delicious leftovers for her to dine on.

But while she loved her friends, she wasn't lonely because of them. Every now and then, she wanted to find "the one." That ridiculous concept she'd been unable to shake, no matter how she tried. Sometimes Shannon worried that all the talk about pair bonding in humans just might be true.

She pulled open the bottom desk drawer and removed her handbag. She reached for her cell only to have it buzz with an incoming call.

The screen flashed with the icon she'd linked with the name. A skull and crossbones. Humorous, but also a warning. Because hearing from Quinn was never good.

She considered letting the call go to voice mail. Mostly because that was the safest action. He wouldn't leave a message. No doubt she wouldn't hear from him for weeks. But if she did answer…

She grabbed her phone and pushed the talk button.

"Hello?"

"Gorgeous."

That was all it took. A single word in that low, smoky voice. Her tension eased, her breathing slowed and between her legs she felt the telltale combination of hunger and dampness. She could talk all the successful-career, self-actualized crap she wanted, but at the end of the day, she was little more than Quinn's bitch.

"Hey," she murmured, even as she glanced at the clock on the wall and calculated how long it would take her to drive to Malibu at this time of the evening.

"Come over."

Quinn didn't ask. He instructed. He took charge. It was the same in bed, where he decided what they were going to do and who came first. She should have resented it, but she didn't. There was something to be said for a man who took charge. She relaxed around him because there was no point in fighting the tide.

"I can't stay," she said—a feeble attempt to take control. But she'd learned the hard truth. Better to get what she wanted and escape than spend the night.

"No problem."

There was a soft click. She knew the call had been disconnected.

She dropped her cell into her handbag, then crossed to the private bathroom that came with her C level title. After using the bathroom, she freshened her makeup and brushed her teeth. Then she left and headed for her car.

The drive to Malibu was simple. Head north on Pacific Coast Highway, which became Sepulveda and a half dozen other streets through Marina del Rey and Venice.

She picked it up again in Santa Monica, then followed the road until she reached Malibu.

When people thought of that town they pictured beachfront mansions and star sightings. Both were plentiful, but much of the community was also old and a little worn around the edges. Tiny restaurants favored by locals nestled against the larger, more famous attractions, like Gladstone's.

Shannon turned onto a small street. In one of those weird L.A. ironies, the most beautiful homes often had completely deceptive entrances. There was a garage, a secured gate and what looked like the beginning of a modest thousand-square-foot bungalow. All of which concealed eight or ten million dollars' worth of luxury living and incredible views.

Quinn's house was similar, although his gate kept anyone from pulling into the driveway. Shannon punched in the code. In that split second before the heavy iron gate swung open, she wondered if it would. Because she knew there would come a day when her code would no longer work. She often told herself that would be a good thing. Some days she even believed herself.

But it wasn't tonight, she thought as she drove into the open garage and parked next to his Maserati.

She got out and walked inside.

Quinn's house was built on the side of a cliff. The tri-level home was probably about five or six thousand square feet with an unobstructed view of the ocean from all three levels. During the day, the rooms were filled with light. At night, electric blinds protected the privacy from those who would try to capture a glimpse of how the beautiful people lived.

Shannon left her shoes in the foyer by the garage door and walked barefoot through the living room. Music played.

She didn't recognize the man singing, but she was sure he was one of Quinn's latest finds.

A couple of lamps had been left on to guide her, but she could have found her way blindfolded. She ignored the elegant furniture, the expensive artwork, the too casually arranged throw pillows and headed for the stairs.

Down a floor was the kitchen and another living room. This was where Quinn spent most of his time. The upper floor was for entertaining. A dumb waiter allowed whatever catering service he was using to deliver food quickly and easily.

Instead of elegance, this level was all about comfort. Oversize leather furniture and a giant TV on the wall dominated the room. The electronic equipment could probably intimidate a NASA scientist. Being a successful music producer paid well.

Shannon circled to the final staircase and took it down a floor. She passed a small guest room and walked into the master.

The glass doors were open. Cool night air and the sound of the ocean mingled with the scent of wood burning in the fireplace. There was a large, custom bed, a couple of chairs and a man. Her attention zeroed in on the latter.

Quinn had been reading. He put down his e-reader and rose as she approached. His blond hair was too long, his blue eyes slightly hooded. He was the kind of man who took what he wanted and he looked the part. Despite the loose cotton shirt and chinos, he was dangerous. Like a beautiful, yet venomous snake—the more appealing the appearance, the more you had to beware.

She dropped her bag onto the carpet. He removed his shirt by simply pulling it over his head and tossing it aside.

His pants followed. Being Quinn, he didn't bother with underwear.

Shannon studied the honed lines of his body. Defined muscles swooped and hollowed. The man was pushing forty and yet could have easily been hired as a butt double for stars half his age.

He was already aroused.

She hesitated. Just for a second. It was like being in the first week of a diet when cravings were insistent and tempers ran high, and someone offered you a brownie. Did you accept it and promise to start again tomorrow, or did you do the right thing, take the empowering step and walk away?

She knew she'd already made her decision. Answering the call had been the equivalent of picking up that brownie. Now all she had to do was take that first bite.

She walked over to him. Quinn drew her close and kissed her. With the stroke of his tongue, she surrendered to the inevitable and promised herself she would do better tomorrow.

Four

"AND HOLD," NICOLE SAID, HER TONE ENcouraging. "Five seconds more."

Pam stayed in the plank position. Every muscle in her body trembled with the effort, but she was determined to make it the entire minute. The image of her naked self still haunted her. The least she could do was give her all in exercise class.

"Time," Nicole called. "And you're done, ladies."

Pam collapsed onto the mat for a second to catch her breath. Her stomach muscles were still quivering. She would be sore well into tomorrow, which was kind of depressing considering she did three classes a week.

She rose and staggered over to the shelf that held the cleaner spray and the towels, and wiped down her mat and the equipment she'd used. The other students did the same. She kept her eye on Shannon, wanting to make sure they had a chance to talk. She figured of all the women she knew, Shannon was the one most likely to have a referral. Or at least be able to get one.

"She's trying to kill us," Pam said, moving next to the annoyingly firm redhead.

"I think that, too."

They collected their personal belongings from the cubbies by the waiting area. Lulu stood and stretched. Pam stuffed the blanket Lulu had been on into her tote, then walked toward the door. Lulu walked along with her.

When they were outside and heading for their cars, Pam scooped up the dog and wondered how exactly she was supposed to bring up such a personal topic.

"Do you have a second?" she asked.

Shannon stopped and faced her. "Sure. What's up?"

Pam took a second to admire the other woman's smooth face. No saggy jawline for her. And her skin was really bright. Pam had noticed a couple of dark spots on her cheek and forehead. All that time in the sun when she'd been a teenager was coming back to haunt her. Day by day her complexion was moving from human to dalmatian.

"I don't mean to imply anything," Pam began, wishing she'd planned this better. "Or be insulting. It's just…I don't know who else to ask."

Shannon's mouth curved into a smile. "I suddenly feel like you're going to ask me if I've had a sex change operation. The answer is no."

Pam tried to smile. "It's not that. I was thinking about maybe getting some BOTOX and wondered if you knew anyone who ever had or something."

"Oh, sure. That's easy. Of course I can give you a name. I have a person."

Pam frowned. "A person who does it?"

"Sure."

"Because you get it?"

"I have for about five years."

Pam's frown deepened as she studied her friend. "But your face is so smooth and natural looking."

"Which is kind of the point," Shannon told her. "I've been using it to prevent wrinkles."

"They can do that?"

"They can." Shannon moved her hair off her forehead. "I'm trying to scowl. Any movement?"

"Not much."

"So it works. I'll email the contact info for the place where I go. They're very good. The shots hurt—I won't lie. But after it's done, it's no big deal. Then about a week later, you have fewer wrinkles."

"That sounds easy," Pam murmured, even as she wondered if she'd left it too long. She was years past preventative care.

"I love it," Shannon told her. "But I will warn you, it's a slick road to more work. I'm flirting with the idea of injectable. Maybe a little filler in my lips, that kind of thing."

"Filler?" Pam's stomach got a little queasy. "I'm not sure I'm ready for that."

"So start with BOTOX. The rest will be waiting."

"Thanks."

They chatted for a few more minutes, then headed to their cars. As Pam strapped in Lulu, she sighed.

"I was kind of hoping she would tell me I didn't need anything done," she admitted.

Lulu wagged her tail.

"Be grateful," she told the dog. "You'll always be a natural beauty."

* * *

Nicole walked into the house at 6:28 p.m. Not a personal best, but pretty darned good, she thought. She ignored the ache in her back and her legs and how all she wanted to do was sleep for the next twenty-four hours. At least tonight was one of her early nights. Tuesdays and Thursdays she worked until eight.

"Mommy's home! Mommy's home!"

Tyler's happy voice and the clatter of his feet as he raced toward her made her smile. On Mondays, Wednesdays and Fridays she didn't get to see him in the morning. Her first class started at six, which meant she was up and out by five thirty.

She dropped her bag on the floor and held out her arms. Tyler raced around the corner and flung himself at her. She caught him and pulled him close.

"How's my best boy?"

"Good. I missed you. I practiced my reading today and Daddy made sketty for dinner."

"Spaghetti, huh? Sounds yummy."

"It was." He kissed her on the lips, then leaned his head against her cheek. "I love you, Mommy."

"I love you, too, little man."

She lowered him to the floor. Tyler headed back to the living room and she walked into the kitchen. There were dishes everywhere. The plastic container that had contained the "sketty" Tyler had enjoyed, along with everything from breakfast and lunch.

The pain in her legs moved up to her back. Frustration joined weariness. She walked into the bedroom and saw the laundry she'd sorted at five that morning still in piles. Hadn't he done anything?

Eric walked into the kitchen and smiled at her. "Hey, hon. How was your day?" As he spoke, he stepped close and kissed her. "I know you're going to say fine and that you're tired, but I gotta tell you, you look hot in workout clothes."

The compliment defused her annoyance for a second. "Thank you and my day was fine. Long, but good. How was yours?"

"Excellent. I rewrote a scene three times but now I have it right. At least I hope so. I'll find out at my critique group on Saturday. In the meantime, I have class tonight, so I'll see you later."

She stared at the man she'd married. He was so similar to the guy she remembered and yet so totally different. He still wore his hair a little too long and had hideous taste in loud Hawaiian shirts. But the old Eric had taken care of the details of their life, while this guy didn't seem to notice anything beyond his screenplay.

She told herself to breathe. That yelling never accomplished anything.

"I'd love to read the new scene," she told him.

"You will. When it's perfect."

The same answer she always received. Because he'd yet to let her read a word of his work. Which sometimes left her wondering if he was writing anything at all. Which made her feel guilty, which led to her wanting to bang her head against the wall in frustration.

"I gotta run." He kissed her again, then straightened. "Well, shit. I forgot to do the dishes. Leave them. I'll do them when I get home. Or in the morning. I promise."

"Okay," she murmured, knowing she would do them herself. Something inside of her made it impossible to relax with a sink full of dishes sitting around. "Any chance you got to the sheets today?"

His expression turned blank. "Did I say I would?"

"Yeah, you did."

"Oh, man. I'm sorry."

"I appreciate that, but Eric, we need to talk about this. You're excited about your screenplay and that's great, but lately it seems you're doing less and less around here."

"I'm not. I do the grocery shopping and take care of Tyler when he's not in day care. I forgot the dishes, but I'll do them. And the laundry." His expression tightened. "You have to understand. It's all about the writing for me. I've got to focus. That's my job. I know it's not paying anything right now, but it will. When I'm working, I'm as committed as you are at your job. I need you to respect my time."

"I do." Sort of, she thought grimly. "I need to be able to depend on you."

"You can. Trust me." He glanced at his watch. After picking up his backpack, he headed for the door. "Tomorrow. I swear. I'll get it all done. Gotta go. Bye."

And he was gone.

She stood alone in the kitchen and let various emotions wash over her. Annoyance, confusion, exhaustion, regret. They churned and heated until they formed a large knot in her belly.

Respect his time writing while she busted her ass to support them all? She closed her eyes. No, she told herself. That wasn't fair. He was working. At least she hoped he was.

The changes in her relationship with her husband had started so quietly, in such tiny increments, that she'd barely noticed. Excluding his decision to quit, of course.

At first he'd taken care of stuff around the house. The

laundry, the grocery shopping. But over time, that had changed. He forgot to get everything on the list. He put clothes in the washer, but not the dryer. He didn't pick up Tyler at day care. Now he wasn't cleaning up the kitchen as he'd promised.

She thought about going after him to talk about what was happening, then shook her head. He would be focused on getting to class. Soon, she promised herself. She would sit down with him and talk about what was wrong. She didn't want to have a roommate, she wanted a husband. Someone who was invested in their family, and not totally focused on his own dream.

Did he really think he was going to sell a screenplay? The odds against that were what? A billion to one? Talk about ridiculous. And yet there was a part of her that wondered if he would make it happen.

The knot in her stomach didn't ease. But that wasn't important right now. She picked up the empty laundry basket. Prioritize, she told herself. She could probably stay awake through two loads, so which were the most important?

Five minutes later their old washer was chugging away. She turned the radio on to an oldies station and danced with Tyler as they worked together to tidy the kitchen. Or rather she worked and he shimmied while "Help Me, Rhonda" played. By seven the dishes were in the dishwasher and the food put away. Tyler had had his bath the previous night so they had a whole hour before his bedtime.

She sank onto the floor in front of her son and smiled at him. "What would you like to do? We could play a game, or watch a show." She didn't offer to read a story, because that went without saying. Except for the two nights she worked late, she always read him a story. Usually some adventure about wily Brad the Dragon.

"A movie!"

"There's only an hour."

"Okay."

Tyler took off running toward the family room. His shows and movies were on a lower shelf where he could browse on his own. She walked to the refrigerator and opened the door. Nothing much inspired her, although she knew she had to eat. She picked a blueberry yogurt and an apple.

"This one," Tyler told her, holding out a familiar and battered DVD case.

Nicole studied the grainy picture on the front. It was sixteen years old. She'd been all of fourteen and this was a copy of her audition performance for The School of American Ballet in New York. For their summer session.

Not the actual audition. No one was allowed to watch, let alone record that. But she'd re-created the dance for her mother. On the same DVD were a half dozen other performances.

"Honey, you've seen that so many times," she reminded her son. "Don't you want to watch something else?"

He thrust out the DVD—his small face set in a stubborn expression she recognized.

"Okay, then. Dancing it is."

She put in the DVD, then settled on the sofa. Tyler cuddled up next to her. She offered him some of her yogurt, but he shook his head. On the TV, the picture flickered, then familiar music filled the room.

Nicole watched her much younger self perform. She was all legs, she thought, without the usual gangliness of adolescence. Probably because she'd been studying dance since she'd been Tyler's age.

She'd made it into the summer program only to be told at the end that she didn't have what it took to make it professionally in ballet. At the time she'd been both heartbroken and secretly relieved. Because her being a famous ballerina had been her mother's dream for her.

Nicole's mother had cried for two days, then come up with a new plan. There were many kinds of dance, she'd informed her only child. Nicole was going to conquer them all. There had also been acting classes and voice lessons. She'd barely managed to get the grades to graduate from high school because she was always attending some coaching session or another.

On the screen, the scene shifted to yet another performance. Nicole figured she'd been about seventeen. It was the year her mother had started complaining of headaches. By the time Nicole had received word of a full dance scholarship at Arizona State University, her mother had been diagnosed with an inoperable brain tumor. The funeral had been the Saturday before Labor Day. Nicole had already started at ASU.

So many choices made that weren't really choices at all, she thought, pleased she'd reached the point of only sadness. For a long time she'd tasted bitterness, too, when she'd thought about her past. Maybe watching the DVDs with Tyler helped. He only saw the beauty of the dance. There weren't any emotional judgments. No history fogged his vision.

Nicole hadn't been so lucky. Her mother had wanted her to be a star. The origin of the dream wasn't clear. Something from her own childhood perhaps. But they hadn't talked about that. Instead, their most intimate conversations had been about how Nicole could do better, be better. Always strive for more, her mother had told her. How disappointed she would be today.

Sometimes Nicole wondered if she was disappointed, too. How different things would have been if she'd been just a bit better. A hair more talented. Not that regrets helped, she reminded herself. They only wasted time and energy because regrets didn't change anything.

She stared at the screen and watched her younger self dance with a grace and confidence that seemed to be lacking these days. While she didn't regret not being famous, she knew that somewhere along the way she'd lost something important. All the elements of a happy life were there—a growing small business, a husband, a wonderful son, friends—but somehow they didn't come together the way they should. She accepted the exhaustion. That came with the territory. It was everything else—the sense of never having quite found what made her happy, the wondering if she'd made a mistake somewhere along the way. That was what kept her up nights.

Sunday morning Pam double-checked the contents of her refrigerator. The whole family was coming over for dinner later that afternoon and she needed to make sure she had all she needed.

Sunday dinners were an Eiland family tradition. When the kids had been younger, they were all required to be home by four, regardless of whatever fun they might be having somewhere else. Exceptions were made for travel, of course, and now, vacations. But otherwise, Sunday dinners were required.

During the summer, they were casual affairs, mostly outside with barbecued whatever as the entrée. Come September, there was usually a football game playing and when favorite rivalries were on the line, dinner became a buffet in the family room.

For today Pam had decided on prime rib. She'd ordered a large one so she and John could have plenty of leftovers. The rest of the menu was simple. Mashed potatoes and green beans. Steven, their middle child, had requested her jalapeño-corn biscuits. She'd made pies yesterday. Custard and chocolate. She liked to do as much in advance as possible so that when her kids arrived, she didn't have to spend all her time in the kitchen.

She wandered into the dining room and walked to the built-in hutch along the far wall. She opened the cabinet doors and studied the stacked dishes. There were three sets of them, all inherited from grandmothers. One was only used for special occasions. She looked at the other two and picked up a side plate with blue-and-green swirls. She put it on the table, along with a tablecloth and a stack of napkins. John would set the table later, using what she'd set out.

There would be six of them today. Jen and her husband, Kirk, Steven and Brandon. Steven used to be allowed to bring a date but he went through women like most people went through chewing gum. Pam had grown tired of liking girl after girl only to have them disappear. It was discouraging. Now Steven was under a very strict rule. No girlfriends allowed at family functions until they'd been together for at least six months. Which meant they hadn't met anyone he'd dated in the past three years.

She told herself he would grow out of it. He was only twenty-six. Which seemed young. How funny. John had only been twenty-two when they'd gotten married. But times were different now. People were different.

The doorbell rang and Lulu took off toward it, barking excitedly.

Pam followed her. "You know, I can hear it, too."

Lulu was unimpressed by the information and continued to bark until Pam scooped her up and opened the door.

Hayley Batchelor held out a plate of cookies. "Hi. I haven't seen you in forever. Is this a good time?"

"Sure."

Pam stepped back to let in her neighbor and John's secretary. Hayley set down the plate of cookies and held out her arms. Lulu made an easy jump from one cuddler to the other.

"How's my favorite girl?" Hayley asked.

Lulu snuggled close and gave a quick chin kiss.

"So sweet," Hayley murmured. "Why did your mom get you fixed? There could have been more Lulus in the world."

"Given her health issues, I don't think that's a good idea," Pam told her. "Come on. I have herbal tea in the kitchen."

"John told you," Hayley said.

"He did. Congratulations. You must be excited."

"I am. It's going to be different this time. It has to be."

Pam admired her determination and belief. Hayley had suffered a series of miscarriages in her quest to get pregnant. She'd been probed and tested and there didn't seem to be any specific reason for the problem. She wasn't allergic to her husband's sperm—or so she'd shared with Pam a year ago. Pam hadn't known such a thing could happen. Allergic to sperm? What were their bodies thinking?

The plumbing all worked and was in the right place, the hormone levels were good, she wasn't lacking in any vitamins or minerals. But Hayley was unable to carry a baby past twelve weeks.

With the last pregnancy, she'd gone straight to bed rest the second she'd found out she was pregnant and that hadn't helped, either.

Now Hayley sat in one of the stools at the bar-level counter while Pam put water on to boil. She pulled out her tea tray and chose her friend's favorite—a white tea with pear.

"How far along are you?" she asked.

"Seven weeks. Only five more to go."

"You feeling okay?"

"I feel great."

Pam nodded. So that wasn't different. Hayley always felt perfectly healthy right up until she started bleeding.

"I wish I could help," Pam told her. "Give you something."

"You offering to be my surrogate?" Hayley asked, her voice teasing.

"God, no."

Hayley laughed. "I figured." Her humor faded a little. "I appreciate what you're saying, though. I'd like some of whatever magic it is that so many other women get to take for granted."

Pam nodded. She'd been pregnant three times and had three healthy children to show for it. She'd suffered bad morning sickness with Brandon, but otherwise, the pregnancies had been uneventful. She'd never considered how many other women had to deal with so much more.

"How's Rob doing?" she asked.

Rob, Hayley's husband, worked two jobs to help pay for the various fertility treatments Hayley wanted them to try. He was a good guy and Pam knew he worried about his wife.

"Good," Hayley said brightly. "Excited I'm pregnant again."

Pam nodded without speaking. She would bet Rob was a whole lot more worried than excited. She knew he wanted Hayley to stop trying. To give her body a rest. Not that Hayley listened.

Pam poured boiling water into two mugs and passed one to Hayley, along with the tea bag and spoon. She dropped a bag of Earl Grey into her mug just as John strolled into the kitchen.

"Hey," he said as he walked around to Hayley and gave her a quick hug. "How's my favorite secretary?"

"Good."

"I see you brought cookies. I've always liked you. Remind me to give you a raise on Monday."

Hayley grinned. "I will."

John winked at Pam, took a couple of cookies from the plate and headed for the garage. Lulu, sensing the possibility of a snack, followed her dad.

"John is about the nicest man I know," Hayley said when the door had closed. "Everybody at work loves him."

"I was lucky to find him," Pam said, knowing that nice was more important than exciting and after thirty years anyone—even George Clooney—could seem less thrilling. It was simply how life worked.

Hayley mentioned something about the hotel project the company was working on. Pam mostly listened. The light had shifted and she noticed a subtle glow to her friend's skin.

Hayley was what? Thirty? Thirty-one. She had a firm jaw and no wrinkles at all. Her hands and arms were so smooth.

Pam drew in a breath as she realized that except for John, she was nearly always the oldest person in the room. And while she should probably be happy that so many young people wanted to hang out with her, she would rather it was because she was young, too.

She mentally gave herself a firm shake. She had to stop thinking about herself all the time. She was becoming obsessed and tedious.

She tuned back in to Hayley's conversation and laughed over a comment about a client.

"I should head home," Hayley said, coming to her feet. "Thanks for the tea and the company."

"When does Rob come back?" One of Rob's two jobs involved business travel.

"In a few days."

"If you need anything or get scared, just grab your pillow and come over," Pam told her. "You're always welcome. We have that guest room sitting empty."

Hayley nodded, then hugged her. "Thanks. It helps to know you're right across the street."

"And down two houses. You go across the street, you'll find yourself at the Logans' and they have those really mean cats."

Hayley laughed. "Good point."

Pam walked her out. When she turned to go back to the kitchen, she saw John and Lulu walking toward her.

"Everything okay with her?" he asked.

"So far." She drew in a breath. "I don't want to send a message to the universe or anything, but I have a bad feeling about this. Why can't the doctors figure out the problem? And when are they going to tell her that all these miscarriages are a bad idea?"

She'd bled a lot with the last one and Pam had ended up insisting she go to emergency.

John put his arm around her. "She really wants a baby."

"And I want her to have one. Just not like this."

Her husband squeezed, then released her. "Jen texted me. She and Kirk are coming over an hour early. They want to talk."

Pam pressed her lips together. "Why didn't she text me?"

"Probably because she knew you would ask questions."

"Didn't you? Is something wrong?" A thousand possibilities, all of them horrible, flashed through her mind. "You don't think one of them is sick, do you? Or maybe Kirk shot someone and is going to be indicted for murder." She pressed a hand to her chest as her breathing hitched. "Oh, God. What if they're getting a divorce?"

Her husband chuckled. "I have to admire your ability to see disaster in every situation. You think they'd tell us that together, before Sunday dinner?"

"Probably not."

"Then maybe stay calm until we hear what it's about. For all we know, they want to move in with us to save money."

Pam rolled her eyes. "Don't even joke about that." Her mind stopped swirling with disastrous possibilities and she tried to think of good ones. "I wonder if they're getting that puppy they've been talking about. Jen called me last week to ask about how long it took to house-train Lulu. A puppy would be nice."

"I'm sure they're getting a puppy."

"I don't know if that's a great idea. They both work, so they're gone all day."

John kissed the top of her head. "You are the queen of finding the cloud in every silver lining."

She smiled. "Okay. Point taken. I'm going to get the roast ready."

"Need any help?"

"No, thanks."

She returned to the kitchen, Lulu walking beside her. The dog curled up in her kitchen bed while Pam set the roast on the counter. She would let it warm up for about an hour before popping it in the oven. In the meantime she could peel the four hundred pounds of potatoes they would be eating tonight. Unlike a lot of their friends, she and John saw their grown kids a lot. They'd stayed close geographically and seemed to like hanging out with their parents.

So far they'd been blessed with their children. Jen, their oldest, had been sweet and funny. Steven had been a typical boy—always getting into trouble. But he had a good heart and lots of friends. Brandon, their youngest, had been more difficult. He'd been moody and attracted to trouble. High school had been hell. He'd skipped class, hung out with horrible kids and discovered he liked to party. The summer he turned seventeen, he'd wrapped his car around a tree.

Angels had been with him, Pam thought, as she peeled her potatoes. The crash should have killed him, yet he'd walked away with nothing more than some bruises and a broken arm.

She and John hadn't known what to do, so they'd erred on the side of tough love. They'd sent him to rehab for six weeks. Not one of those touchy-feely kinds with meetings where you shared and did crafts, but one with a boot-camp philosophy and lots of lectures from people in recovery. Brandon had quickly realized he was far from the biggest, baddest dog in the pack. He'd come home older, wiser and, most important, sober.

He'd completed his senior year with a 4.0 GPA and had made what had seemed like the impossible decision to be a doctor. But he'd stuck with it and was now in his second year of medical school.

"My son, the doctor," Pam murmured.

They were all in a good place right now. She would be grateful and not borrow trouble. Although she did think that Jen and Kirk might not be ready for a puppy.

Five

PAM SAT NEXT TO JOHN ON ONE SOFA WHILE Jen and Kirk sat on the other. Her daughter, a pretty brunette, smiled broadly.

It didn't *seem* like there was anything wrong. They both looked happy. Kirk was relaxed, which he probably wouldn't be if he'd shot someone in the line of duty and was going to prison. Plus, they would have seen it on the news.

Pam glanced at the clock. It was barely two—probably too early to make herself a Cosmo. Although she would like to point out that it was already five in New York and probably tomorrow in Australia.

She reached for John's hand. He gave her fingers a reassuring squeeze.

"All right, you two," he said. "You've kept us in suspense long enough. What's going on? Is it a puppy?"

They were moving, Pam thought, looking at their faces. Kirk had gotten promoted or something. No, that wouldn't work. He was on the Mischief Bay police force. It wasn't as if they were going to relocate him to San Francisco.

Jen glanced again at Kirk, then turned back to her parents. She drew in a breath and laughed.

"No puppy. We're pregnant!"

Pam felt her mouth drop open.

"What?" John stood and crossed to them. "Pregnant? How far along? Did you plan this? Pregnant!" He pulled his daughter into his arms. "My baby's going to be a mommy. That's great, honey. We're so happy for you."

Pam felt the room shift a little. As if one side of the house had suddenly dropped a couple of feet. She managed to stand and felt her face moving, so guessed she'd smiled. Kirk walked up to her and she hugged him because it was the obvious thing to do.

Jen pregnant. There was going to be a baby. She loved babies. Adored them. She couldn't be happier for her daughter and son-in-law. There was only one unbelievable catch.

She was going to be a grandmother.

The Farm Table was an upscale, organic, locally sourced restaurant. The kind of place completely at home in the beachy, LA-vibe quirkiness that was Mischief Bay. Everything in the restaurant was either sustainable or repurposed. The floors were bamboo, the tables and chairs rarely matched and the dishes were all old Lenox, Spode and Wedgwood patterns. But the odds of any one table getting two place settings that were the same were slim.

Eclectic didn't begin to describe the decor. A combination of elegant, shabby chic and country, with a rabid interest in recycling to the point that the restaurant kept a pig and two goats to eat any food leftovers that couldn't be given to a local organization that specialized in feeding the homeless. The food was extraordinary.

There was generally at least a three-week wait to get a reservation. Which meant getting a call from Adam inviting her to dinner was only half as shocking as hearing his suggestion as to where they would go. The man obviously had some pull, she thought as she stopped in front of the valet and handed over her keys.

She tucked her clutch under her arm, walked into the restaurant and glanced around. Adam was already there, standing in the foyer. He smiled when he saw her—a warm, welcoming smile that made her feel just a little bit giddy.

She was willing to admit she had been more than a little pleased to hear from him. She hadn't thought she would. Now, as she moved toward him, she saw his gaze drop to take in what she was wearing. The sudden widening of his eyes added to her sense of anticipation.

She'd put a lot more thought into what she would wear on this date, as opposed to the last one. Despite the fact that it was late February, this was still Southern California and evening temperatures weren't going to dip below fifty-eight. She'd been able to wear her favorite outfit and bring a pashmina as a wrap.

The dress was one of her rare clothing splurges. An Oscar de la Renta silk cloqué cocktail dress. The fabric—a textured silk—was simply tailored. A scooped-neck tank style, front and back, fitted to the waist, then flaring out. She'd left her red hair loose and wavy, and added diamond studs for her only jewelry. She'd left her legs bare, with only a hint of a shimmery lotion to add a glow, then finished off the outfit with a classic pair of black pumps.

Honestly, she'd been hoping for some kind of a reaction and Adam didn't disappoint. He crossed to her and took both her hands in his.

"I know this is going to get old, but wow."

She smiled. "Thank you. You're looking very handsome yourself."

Dress at The Farm Table was generally nice to fancy. Adam wore a suit and tie. Men had it easy, she thought. Give them some decent tailoring and they look great.

He excused himself and gave his name to the hostess, then returned to her side.

"It'll just be a few minutes."

"Thank you." She stared into his dark eyes. "I was surprised to hear from you."

His brows drew together. "Why?"

"I didn't think our first date went very well."

Genuine confusion tugged at his mouth. "Seriously? I thought it was good. We were getting to know each other. If you thought it went badly, why did you say yes to dinner?"

She touched his arm. "I meant I thought I wouldn't hear from you because I got called back to work. I'm not saying it happens all the time, but when it does, I have to take care of the problem."

There it was—her career out there. So far she liked Adam. He made her hope in a way she hadn't for a long time. But she wasn't going to pretend to be other than who she was for anyone and she wanted to make sure he got that.

He relaxed. "Oh, that. It's okay. You have a job with demands. I do, too. Would you have a problem if I had to cancel because of a crisis at the job site?"

"No."

"So we both get that we have responsibilities."

As easy as that? "It's my turn to say wow."

He chuckled. "If that impresses you, then I'm doing a

whole lot better than I thought. Makes me glad I called in all those favors to get the reservation here."

"I am impressed by you and the venue. So it's a win-win."

"I like that in a date."

His gaze dropped to her mouth for just a second longer than was polite.

Shannon knew it was silly to let the man's obvious attraction win her over. She had to be feeling it, too. But she had to admit it was pretty nice to be wanted.

A voice in her head pointed out that Quinn also wanted her. Only it was on his terms, his way, on his schedule. Theirs wasn't a relationship. It was some kind of twisted addiction. Adam just might be the right antidote.

The hostess led them to a small table by a window. They were tucked into a private alcove, a little bit away from the other diners.

"Have you dined here before?" she asked.

They both said they had.

"Then you know how our menu works. The chef has some very special dishes in store for you. Enjoy."

The Farm Table's menu was information, not a choice. The items changed every week and there were a few vegetarian options for main courses. Otherwise, you ate what was put in front of you. They were taking a stand and Shannon could respect that.

She glanced at the five-course menu and was grateful she hadn't put on Spanx. At least she would have some extra room for all the yummy food.

Adam picked up his menu. "What's a squash blossom and how do you put salmon in it?"

"It's a plant."

"You're guessing."

"No, I'm sure it's a plant-based thing that has an opening or can be stuffed or something."

He looked at her, his brows raised.

She sighed. "Fine. I have no idea what it is. I'm sure it's delicious. Do you know what sorrel tastes like? We have sorrel sauce in our third course."

"Not a clue."

"Then I guess we'll find out together."

He nodded and put down his menu. "Want to go with the wine suggestions?"

"Sure."

"Me, too." He leaned toward her. "I really was okay about the job thing."

"I get that now."

"I didn't call right away because I was away on business. The guy who's building the hotel insisted I fly to Denver to meet with him personally. He doesn't like email updates."

"Not a problem."

"I didn't want you to think I was flaky. Or not interested." He leaned back and smiled. "I see the biggest problem here is that you're too attractive. I'm not sure I can see you as a person."

"What would I be if not a person?"

"An object." The smile faded. "All joking aside, Shannon, I'm not in this to get laid. I'm not that guy. Don't get me wrong. Of course I want to sleep with you. I'm breathing, right? I guess what I'm trying to say is I'm a divorced father with two kids and the thought of playing the field exhausts me. I want to find somebody special. Somebody I can care about and share things with. A relationship, I guess."

He paused and grimaced. "That was sure more than you

needed to know. Sorry. Did I mention I'm not the greatest first date?"

"This is our second date."

"That, too."

He looked embarrassed, but she wasn't put off by what he'd said. It was honest, and lately it seemed honest men were hard to find.

He wasn't looking to play games or torment her or be totally in charge. He wanted to connect on a level that was meaningful.

"I appreciate what you've said," she told him. "And I get it." She did her best not to smile. "Especially the part about not wanting to sleep with me. Because every girl longs to hear that."

He groaned. "Of course I want to sleep with you. I said that. I made that really clear."

Their server appeared. If she'd overheard what they were saying, she didn't let on.

"Good evening and welcome to The Farm Table. I'll be taking care of you tonight."

Despite the fact that it was a set menu, it still took a good three or four minutes to perform the niceties and order the wine. After their server left, Shannon stretched out her hand, palm up.

"It's okay," she told Adam.

He put his hand on top of hers. "Yeah?"

"Yeah. I'm not going to sleep with you tonight."

He sighed. "Would you have before I said anything?"

"Not a chance."

He brightened. "Now we're getting somewhere."

"You are very strange."

"I've been told that before."

The server returned with their first glass of wine. When she left Adam raised his.

"To the most beautiful woman I've ever gone out with and the fact that she won't sleep with me."

"At least tonight," she added, before touching his glass with hers.

Adam cleared his throat. "Temptation. I like it."

She laughed and sipped her wine. "I'm going to have to time my tempting moments. You have children and shared custody. How does that work?"

"Friday is our exchange day. My week starts when they get out of school. I have the kids this weekend, but they're spending a night with my folks."

"So no curfew."

"Don't. You're only teasing."

"Yes, I am."

Conversation shifted to his work and the big hotel project. As he described it, Shannon felt as if she'd heard a conversation like this before.

"Do you know John Eiland?" she asked.

"John? Sure. His company is installing all the plumbing. Why?"

"I know them. Pam and I are friends and I hang out at their house every now and then. I've been to the big Memorial Day barbecue they have."

"No way. Was last year your first one, because it's the only one I've missed. I've been going since I was a kid and I would have remembered you."

She laughed. "It was my first. I met Pam at Mischief in Motion. It's an exercise studio. We take a class together three days a week."

He shook his head. "What I would pay to see you work out."

"Really?"

"Too much? Sorry. I'll get my mind back in the game. John's a great guy. And Pam's a sweetie. She reminds me of my mom."

"What are your thoughts on Lulu?" she asked. "Cutest dog ever or frightening genetic experiment?"

"A test. Okay, I'm good at these. Um, great personality, very well trained and the weirdest-looking dog, ever. What's up with the clothes?"

"She's naked. She gets cold." Shannon sipped her wine. "And I agree with you. I love Lulu, but the spots, the pink skin. It's not natural. Dogs should shed. It's nature's way of keeping us humble."

Their first course arrived. Caviar on some kind of leaf with three drizzled sauces. There were also tiny shaved white things—turnips, so they said.

Adam stared at the dish. "You first."

She grinned. "So you're not the wild adventurer type."

"I can be. But turnip and caviar? Who thought that up?"

"The famous chef in the back." She lifted the leaf and took a bite. The saltiness blended with the faint bitterness of the leaf, while the shaved turnip piece was surprisingly sweet.

"It's really good."

Adam looked doubtful but followed her lead. He chewed and swallowed. "I don't hate it."

"Then you need to write a review." She looked around the restaurant. "Pam and John came here for their last anniversary. They are such a great couple. I love watching them together. It makes me believe that true love is possible."

"Otherwise you don't believe?" he asked.

"Not exactly. I think it's hard for people to stay together. I've never gotten married. You're divorced. My friend Nicole, she's the owner of Mischief in Motion, is having trouble in her marriage right now."

"That's never easy," Adam said. "What's going on?"

"Her husband decided to write a screenplay. Only he didn't discuss it with her first. He just quit his job. He hasn't worked in nearly a year. They have an almost five-year-old and Eric barely helps out at all. I feel so badly for her, and I have no idea what to say. It's hard."

"You're a good friend."

"Thanks. I try. Now, tell me about your kids," she urged.

He smiled. "They're great. Char—Charlotte—is going to be nine in a couple of months. Sometimes I swear she's pushing thirty instead. She's bossy and she would draw blood to protect her little brother. She loves anything princess-related and can't wait to start wearing makeup. She's beautiful and I'm terrified to think about her starting to like boys."

He paused. "Oliver is my little man. He's all boy. He likes trucks, building things and breaking things. He's six. He'll be seven this summer."

She could hear the love and pride in his voice, which was very appealing. She'd dated plenty of guys who didn't seem that interested in the families they'd already created. "Do you like having them half the time?"

"I'd rather have them all the time, but I accept the compromise."

"Are you and your ex friendly?"

"We get along. I regret that my marriage failed, but I don't miss our relationship, if that makes sense."

"It does. I like that you don't call her names."

"Why would I? I married her and chose to have children with her. Calling her names means I'm the moron."

Their server appeared to remove their plates. Conversation flowed easily throughout the rest of the meal. It was after ten when she and Adam left the restaurant. He handed her ticket to the valet, then pulled her to the side of the waiting area.

"I had a great time tonight," he told her.

"Me, too."

"Next time maybe you'll let me pick you up. You know, like a real date."

She smiled. "Next time I will." She leaned in and lightly kissed him. His mouth was firm and warm. She drew back. "You have the kids this week, right? So we'll keep in touch by text?"

He looked startled. "You're okay with that?"

"Sure. It's way too soon for them to know about me."

"Thanks for understanding. Or to repeat myself...wow."

She laughed.

He put his arm on her waist and drew her against him. "About that sleeping together thing."

"Not a chance."

"You're amazing."

"You are the only man I know who would say that after being told he *isn't* getting laid."

"I'm special."

"You are."

She had more to say but he kissed her and suddenly talking seemed highly overrated. His mouth lingered. Had they been anywhere else, she would have wanted a little more. But they were outside at a valet stand, waiting for their cars. This wasn't the time to get into tongue.

She heard a car engine and stepped back. "That's me," she said, pointing at her convertible. "I'll talk to you soon."

"Promise."

Shannon got in her car and drove away. As she headed for home, she thought about the tingles and the quivers. How just being with Adam made her feel good. This was so much better than the post sex-with-Quinn drive of shame. Something she had to remember.

Pam typed quickly on the laptop in Nicole's small office, while Nicole sat in the chair beside the desk and waited for the news.

When she'd first bought Mischief in Motion, she'd only been able to afford basic remodeling and had put every penny into the studio itself. Her small down payment had been supplemented by money from a business angel network called Moving Women Forward. They'd given her advice along with start-up funds.

With no money left over for something as frivolous as an office, she'd made do with what she had. Her six-by-eight work space was little more than a human cubby, with a desk, two chairs and an overly bright light fixture.

Not that it mattered much to her. She was in her office as little as possible. Technology allowed all her clients to sign up for classes online. Once they created an account, they could purchase sessions individually or in packages. She received a report every day, the money was automatically deposited in her account and, best of all, she didn't have to pay for a receptionist. That savings meant that she'd been able to hire a couple of part-time instructors and cut her work hours down to sixty instead of eighty.

About a year ago, she'd been struggling with her accounting software. She'd casually mentioned it and Pam had offered to help. Now her friend spent about an hour every couple of weeks going over the books and making sure Nicole stayed on top of things like taxes and the mortgage. Because she hadn't just bought the business, she'd also bought the building. An expense that sometimes had her lying awake at night, wondering if she was ever going to feel that they were financially stable.

"You're in great shape," Pam said as she looked up. "And I'm not just talking about your ass."

Nicole smiled. "You're sure?"

"Yes. I haven't had to correct any entries for at least a couple of months. With the automatic payment reminders in place, you're able to hold on to your money as long as possible and still get the bills paid on time. You, my dear, are turning into a tycoon."

"I think tycoons take home more than what I do."

"It's all a matter of perspective."

Nicole wished she had her friend's confidence in herself. Pam had worked in her husband's company for years so all this came easily to her. She'd also most likely paid attention in school. Nicole had grown up with the idea that an education was for other people and that she needed to focus on her *art*. All fine and good until the moment when art ended and the real world began.

Pam tilted her head. "Are you all right? You really are doing well. You're putting aside money for taxes and into savings every month. The monthly costs are fairly stable and the business is growing. So why aren't you smiling?"

"I'm smiling on the inside." Nicole shifted in her chair. "I'm sorry. I really appreciate the help and you're right. The news is great. I'm just tired."

Pam nodded, but didn't speak. She was good at that, Nicole thought. Knowing when to ask and when to keep quiet. Was it a mom thing? Would she develop the skill as Tyler got older?

The silence stretched on a few seconds more. Nicole gave in to the inevitable and sighed.

"Eric and I aren't seeing much of each other these days," she admitted. "I'm always heading to work and when I get home, he's going out to his critique group or his screen-writing class. It's hard."

What she didn't mention was that her husband was getting home later and later, often smelling of beer. She understood that a few people in class wanted to go out afterward, but Eric had a family to come home to. She didn't understand what was happening to him. To them. And the unknown scared her.

"I know it's hard," Pam told her, her tone caring and warm. "I don't know how you haven't killed him. I swear to you, if John came home and told me he was quitting his job to write a screenplay, I'd back the car over him."

"John would never do that. He's a responsible guy. Predictable."

Pam body tensed a little, then relaxed. "You're right. And most of the time, that's a good thing."

"When isn't it a good thing?"

Her friend shrugged. "After thirty years of marriage, a little unpredictability would be nice."

"Is everything okay?" Nicole asked. Because selfishly, she needed Pam's marriage to be better than her own. Somehow knowing Pam was okay gave her a safe place to be.

"We're fine," Pam assured her. "It's just..." She drew in a breath. "I'm fifty."

Nicole waited for the revelation. When Pam didn't say anything else, she searched for some kind of meaning. "I was at your birthday party last fall. You've been fifty for a while."

"I know, but I didn't feel it before." She waved her hand. "You're thirty and gorgeous and you won't understand, but trust me. One day you're going to look in the mirror and wonder what happened. It's not that I'm unhappy with my life. I get the blessings. My kids are still talking to us and coming over to dinner every Sunday. They're happy. John and I are healthy and I'm pleased to see him at the end of the day. It's just I didn't think it would happen so fast. Me getting old."

"Pam, you're not old. You're fantastic. You're one of my best students. You can keep up with anyone. You're in terrific shape."

"You haven't seen me naked," Pam muttered. "It's nothing like what it used to be."

Lulu wandered into the office. Pam bent down and picked her up, then petted her.

"All I can tell you is pay attention to what you're doing, because you're going to blink and it's going to have been twenty years."

Nicole wasn't exactly sure what she meant, but she nodded, anyway. "I can see that with Tyler. He's growing so fast. He still thinks watching my old performances is great fun. In a few years he'll pretend he doesn't know me."

"They do go through that stage." Pam cradled Lulu in her arms. "I'm glad you had all those tapes put onto DVD. You'll always have them."

"They're not all that great to watch."

"To you, maybe. I've only seen a couple, but they were beautiful. You're a talented dancer."

A few months ago talk during class had turned to her former dancing career, such as it was. Pam and Shannon had insisted on seeing proof of her claims to have danced professionally and she'd brought in a DVD.

After graduating from ASU, she'd done what every other self-respecting dancer did. She'd headed for New York. Armed with determination, a lifetime of her mother telling her that she had to be a star and recommendations and introductions from her instructors, she'd started the arduous process of going to auditions.

It had taken two brutal winters for her to realize that she simply wasn't Broadway material. Or off-Broadway. She managed to get hired for two different Rockette shows and had danced for free for a few small productions that no one had seen. But she hadn't had whatever it was that got dancers noticed. At the end of those two years she'd returned to LA, where at least she could be poor and hungry in a sixty-degree winter.

She'd been down to her never-to-be-touched emergency five hundred dollars. It was all that stood between her and finding a bed at a shelter. A sign outside of Mischief in Motion had said the owner was looking for someone to teach a dance-based exercise class. She'd been desperate enough to try.

Nicole had found that she liked the work. Over the next couple of years, she'd gotten certified in several kinds of fitness instruction, including Pilates. Now six years later, she owned the studio. So at least that part of her life was doing well. And she had Tyler. As for her marriage, well, maybe that was a problem for another day.

"I like what I do now," Nicole said, knowing that she had been luckier than most. "I just need to get better at juggling."

"Balance is never easy. I'm not sure it's possible." Pam rose, Lulu still in her arms. "Trust me. I think it's like those fake holidays created by the greeting card industry. We pay attention to different things at different times in our lives. Sometimes we get it right and sometimes we don't."

"Always with the wisdom," Nicole teased. "Can I be you when I grow up?"

Pam smiled. "You're already grown-up. See? Everything happens when we're not paying attention."

Six

"I NEVER GET TIRED OF THAT DVD," JOHN said as he turned off the TV.

"It's a good one," Pam agreed.

They'd just watched *The Bourne Identity* for maybe the four hundredth time. She didn't mind the movie repeats. It gave her a chance to catch up on her magazine browsing. John didn't require her to pay attention so much as he liked her to be in the room.

She set her unread magazine back in the basket by her side of the sofa. The ones she'd gotten through would go into recycling. Lulu, curled up in her bed on the other end of the sofa, raised her head, as if asking if it was time.

"Ten o'clock, baby girl."

Lulu stood and stretched. Ten o'clock was the phrase that meant "last time to pee before morning" or however the dog translated it in her head.

John got out of his recliner—because yes, they were that couple. The ones with a recliner in the family room. At least they weren't at the stage of having two recliners. John had suggested it, but Pam knew she wasn't ready. She was sure the time would come, but not today.

"You going to take her out?" he asked, which he did every night.

Pam wanted to ask when he let the dog out. Not that he wouldn't if she asked. But the routine was him asking and her doing it.

How did things like that happen? she wondered. How did people get stuck in ruts? It must be part of the human condition—a need to not think about everything, maybe. So the brain found routines and being in a routine was oddly comfortable. Until it became a rut, at which point it wasn't comfortable anymore.

Pam smiled at her husband. It wasn't his fault she was thinking too much these days. "I'll take her out."

John nodded and walked past her. As he did, he paused to lightly pat her butt.

She would guess he didn't even know he was doing it. That if she mentioned it, he would look at her blankly. Which was so like him, and mostly endearing. It was yet another routine. A signal that the outside observer would never catch, but that a wife of thirty years knew intimately.

Later, when he finished in the bathroom, he would look at her expectantly. The question would hang in the air until she nodded and said something along the lines of "I'd like to." Because the butt pat was John's signal that he was interested in sex that night.

Pam and Lulu walked to the back door. She opened it for her little dog, then waited while Lulu took care of business. They walked back to the bedroom.

When Steven had moved out, they'd done a remodel of the rear of the house. They'd expanded the master and added a second bathroom, while redoing the first. They'd also enlarged the closet. Pam didn't mind sharing any part of her life, but she'd always wanted a completely girly bathroom and a few years ago, she'd gotten it.

There was a huge shower with a built-in bench so she could shave her legs easily. She had an oversize tub, a single sink with long countertops on both sides and as much storage as the makeup department at Macy's.

John's bathroom suited his needs, as well. There was a TV so he wouldn't miss any part of a game if he had to pee, a steam shower and a vanity that was several inches higher than usual.

Now she went into the closet and pulled out the drawer designated for Lulu's pj stash. The little dog had already gone over to the bed and used the pet stairs to make it onto the high mattress. Pam selected a soft T-shirt—pink, of course.

"All right, little girl," she said softly as she sat on the bed.

Lulu dropped her head as Pam removed the light sweater. The garment slid off easily. Then Pam held out the T-shirt. Lulu stuck her head through the opening and raised her left front leg to step into the arm hole. She always tried to do the right one, too, but usually missed. Pam got her shirt on. Lulu went up to the decorative pillows on the bed and burrowed in behind them, where she would stay until the humans got into bed.

Pam retreated to her bathroom where she removed her makeup, applied three kinds of serums and creams, then brushed her teeth. As she performed the familiar rituals, she tried to think sexy thoughts to get herself into the mood. But she couldn't seem to summon any energy about it.

Sex with John was fine, but it wasn't exciting anymore. She remembered how it had been at the beginning. The thrill of seeing him naked. The constant need to make love. How every touch had been arousing. Time and familiarity made that difficult to maintain. Add to that three kids and busy lives and it just wasn't the same.

But she loved him and wanted him to know that. While the words were always welcome, he also needed her to desire him. Something she'd figured out the second decade of their marriage when she'd been caught up in the exhaustion that came from having three active kids in the house.

She slipped on her nightgown and returned to the bedroom.

John was already there, sitting up, reading. He wore reading glasses—something that he'd resisted until any kind of printed material had become impossible. Lulu was on his lap. When she spotted Pam, she jumped up and came over to her side.

She put the dog in her bed in the corner. John put down his glasses and e-reader, then flipped back the covers and patted the mattress invitingly.

She climbed in next to him and studied his familiar face. She knew everything about this man, she thought. How he talked and laughed and thought. She knew his scent. When he put his arm around her waist and drew her close, she knew how their bodies would go together.

They kissed as they always did. She tried to ignore the thoughts whipping through her brain, but they were insistent. Somewhere in the back of her mind a bored voice announced the next step in the process. *Three tongue kisses, two nibbles on her neck. Right breast, left breast, then down to the promised land.*

Pam moved against him, searching for a spark to focus on. But she was thinking too much, and for her that was always trouble. She could feel what he was doing, but couldn't find the sex in it. After a moment she felt his erection pressing into her thigh.

When he was done, he rolled off her and cleaned up, pulled on his briefs and then returned to her side.

"What about you?" he asked, sliding his hand along her thigh. "Want to do it the old-fashioned way?"

Because he always knew if she'd had an orgasm or not. And her pleasure was important to him. Yet another excellent quality when it came to a husband, she thought. If she asked, he would touch her until she found her release. He knew how—they'd done it a thousand times before. Or maybe ten thousand.

"I'm in my head tonight," she admitted.

"You sure?" he asked, even as he withdrew his hand.

"I am."

"All right. I love you." He kissed her, then stretched out on his side.

Pam pulled on her nightgown and retreated to the bathroom to wash up. As she closed the bathroom door she wondered when he'd stopped pressing her to try a little before giving up. A year ago? Five?

She wasn't complaining, but she was curious. Was she really "in her head" so much that he'd given up convincing her otherwise? That wasn't good.

She finished and returned to the bedroom. John was already asleep. The sound of his steady breathing calmed her, as did his solid presence.

She collected Lulu from her dog bed and carried her into the people bed. Lulu dove under the covers and waited until Pam lay on her back, then curled up next to her.

The tiny ball of warm life was familiar. Just like John

and her routine and their lovemaking. Familiar and comfortable and safe and boring. No, she thought. Boring was too harsh. It was something else.

Dusty, she thought as she stared into the darkness. Her life was dusty. She'd been given so much, so if she wasn't happy, then she was the problem.

"So you like him," Nicole said late Saturday morning.

Shannon tried to play it cool, but she couldn't help smiling. "I do. Adam's really nice. We've been out three times since our first date."

All three evenings had gone well. The last one had been the previous weekend when they'd gone sailing on a friend's boat and then had eaten at Gary's Café. He'd driven her home and they'd ended up making out in his car like teenagers.

She'd been tempted to invite him in for something more adult, only a part of her was enjoying the anticipation.

"And he's with his kids this weekend?" Nicole asked.

"Uh-huh. Last night until next Friday morning."

They stood by the carousel at the base of the Mischief Bay pier, otherwise known as Pacific Ocean Park. The original "POP" had been built in Santa Monica in the fifties and torn down in the 1970s. When Mischief Bay had rebuilt the pier, they'd named it the POP, to continue the tradition.

The town was big on old things. Several of the city's outdoor sculptures had been purchased from other places and relocated here. The carousel itself had been rescued from an east coast boardwalk that had wanted to put in more modern rides. Residents had formed a joint task force with city officials to raise money and bring the hundred-year-old carousel to the pier. It had been restored and put into use.

Nicole waved as Tyler rode around on a black horse. A leather strap held him securely in place. He was a cute kid, blond, with his mother's eyes. He was friendly and sweet. Being around him made Shannon wonder what it would be like to have a child of her own. And when that happened she would remind herself that she'd always wanted to go the traditional route. Husband, then kids. Which hadn't seemed possible.

Only now that she'd met Adam, she was starting to wonder if maybe it was. If maybe now she *could* have it all. While she knew it was way too soon to be thinking that, the thoughts wouldn't go away.

"It wasn't that long ago that Tyler still wanted you to stay with him," Shannon said, mostly to distract herself.

"I know. He's growing up so fast."

"Soon he'll be wanting to borrow the car," she teased.

"Don't even go there. I can't stand to think about it." Nicole pulled her cell phone out of her pocket and pointed it toward the carousel. "I'm still trying to accept the fact that he's going to be five."

Tyler circled into view again. Nicole snapped his picture and Shannon waved.

"Speaking of his birthday," Shannon said, "you'll never guess what I saw the other day."

Nicole groaned. "If you say Brad the Dragon supplies, I'm going to slit my wrists."

"Not something any of us wants."

Shannon waited while Nicole put her phone away. The other woman squared her shoulders, as if gathering strength. Nicole then tossed her blond hair over her shoulder and nodded.

"Give it to me straight."

Shannon laughed. "What do you have against Brad the Dragon? He's a pretty low-key guy." She knew. She'd read several of the books to Tyler the few times she'd babysat. "Doesn't he grow from a toddler to a young dragon in school?"

"Yes, which means I can never escape him. I have no idea why he bugs me, but he does. So what did you find?"

"There's a gift store in Hermosa. They have an entire selection of Brad the Dragon party supplies. Plates, napkins, goodie bags and a few games. There's a Brad the Dragon bean bag toss, Brad the Dragon pin the tail on the...dragon, I guess."

"Kill me now," Nicole murmured.

"You're not going to check them out?" Shannon found herself a little disappointed. She figured Nicole would ask her to help with the party and to be honest, she was looking forward to a Brad the Dragon birthday celebration.

Her friend groaned. "Of course I am. And then I'll buy them and Tyler will be the happiest little boy there is. Which is what I want. After all, it's his birthday. Dear God. Brad the Dragon. I swear, if I ever meet that author, I'm going to strangle him with a Brad the Dragon stuffed animal, wrap him in a Brad the Dragon blanket and throw his body out to sea."

"Someone needs to scale back on the caffeine," Shannon murmured.

Nicole laughed.

The ride came to an end. Nicole stepped on to talk to Tyler, because there was every chance he wanted to go again. This was only his second time and he was usually good for three or four sessions.

Shannon watched how mother and child interacted, their

blond heads nearly touching as they laughed together. They were so close, she thought wistfully. So happy with each other. She wanted that. Not that she was all that sure she would be very good at it. When she'd been growing up, her mother hadn't ever given her a birthday party. Not with friends invited. There was a special dinner at home and a couple of presents, but nothing to compare with a Brad the Dragon extravaganza.

Different styles, she told herself, even though she knew in her gut that the real problem had leaned a lot more toward indifference.

The ride started up again.

"Hello, Shannon."

She turned and was startled to find Adam walking toward her. He had two children with him. A dark-haired daughter with ribbons in her curls and a younger, light-haired boy.

Thoughts crowded in her brain. Obviously these were his children and they'd both agreed it was too soon for them to meet her. So what was he doing? Thinking?

"Hi," she said, feeling both children staring at her.

"This is my friend Shannon. Shannon, these are my kids. Charlotte and Oliver."

She smiled at them. "Nice to meet you both. And this is my friend, Nicole. Her son is Tyler and he's riding the carousel."

Nicole shook hands with Adam.

"We love the pier," Charlotte said, her dark eyes the same as her father's. She was a pretty girl. Almost nine if Shannon remembered correctly. "Daddy, can we ride the carousel, too?"

"Sure. Let's go get tickets." He glanced at Shannon. "I'll be right back. Don't go anywhere."

"He's cute," Nicole whispered when he reached the ticket booth. "Cute kids, too."

"I don't understand. He said it was too soon. I said it was too soon. Why did he introduce me to his kids? Is this weird?"

"No. Come on. He saw you at the pier. You're a friend. It's not like they walked in on you two doing it." Nicole grinned. "Have you done it?"

"Not yet."

"Do you want to?"

Shannon watched him lead both children up to the carousel. Charlotte chose a white unicorn with painted flowers in her mane, while Oliver took the black horse next to Tyler. Adam pointed to him and Nicole waved.

"That one's mine," she confirmed, before turning back to Shannon. "Do you?"

"Yes," Shannon hissed. "I want to sleep with him. Are you happy?"

"Not as happy as you're going to be. Look. Here he comes. Act natural."

Great advice except she didn't feel she was acting unnaturally.

"Hey," Adam said as he approached. "You okay with this?"

"Meeting your kids? Sure. But I thought we'd agreed on the timing."

"We had, but then I saw you with your friend and figured I'd introduce you as someone I know. The pier isn't that big. You were bound to see us and I didn't want you feeling like you had to avoid me."

She had to admit that would have been awkward and potentially comical. "Can I be someone you know through work?" she asked.

"Sure."

Nicole laughed. "I'd forgotten all the intrigue that goes into dating. I'm both envious and relieved I'm not dealing with it."

"Kids add a layer of complication," Adam admitted. "We were going to get lunch after this. Want to join us?" He nodded at Nicole. "Oliver and Tyler seem to be getting along."

Shannon glanced at the carousel and saw the two boys were talking and laughing.

"Sure," Nicole said. "We'll be your beard. Or is it your shill?"

"I think it's beard," Shannon told her.

After two more rides on the carousel even Tyler was ready for lunch. The six of them made their way to The Slice Is Right, where Shannon and Nicole claimed a table while Adam and the kids went to order the pizzas.

"He's nice," Nicole murmured as they sat down. "And cute."

"You already said he was cute. You're pressuring me."

"I know. I can't help it. I can feel the sexual tension radiating between you. It sizzles. Now I know what Pam says when she complains about feeling old."

"You're younger than me by years."

"But I'm married. There's a lot less sexual tension now."

Shannon watched her friend as she spoke and saw something in her eyes. Before she could ask what was going on, Charlotte walked over.

"Daddy's ordering three pizzas," she informed them.

"Cheese, pepperoni and one with vegetables." She shuddered visibly. "He wants to know if that's okay and what you'd like to drink."

"The pizzas are great," Shannon said as Nicole nodded. "Iced tea for me."

"Me, too."

Shannon touched Charlotte's arm. "Thank you for taking our orders."

The girl beamed. "You're welcome. I'm the oldest, so I'm responsible."

"Apparently so."

She walked back to join her father.

"Adorable," Nicole whispered. "Don't you just want to hug her?"

Shannon nodded. Sure it was early hours, but she had to admit she liked what she'd seen so far. Not to be one of those scary it's-been-one-date-can-I-see-myself-married-to-you? women, but maybe being a stepmother wasn't as bad as a lot of her friends claimed. Some of the pain and suffering was determined by the personalities of the children.

Adam collected a tray of drinks and led the three kids back to the table.

"I hope it's okay," he told Nicole as he approached. "Tyler said he was allowed chocolate milk when he ate out."

"He's right and he is," she said, scooting over to make room for her son.

Adam settled next to Shannon. They were just close enough that she could feel the heat of his body and there was no impediment to her sliding close to get her touching fix. Not counting his two children, her friend and Tyler, of course. Suddenly, it seemed her life had gotten, as Adam had described the situation earlier, complicated.

Nicole turned to Charlotte. "You're in the third grade?" she asked.

"Yes."

"Do you like school?"

"Uh-huh. My teacher's nice and I'm reading above my grade level so she gets me extra books from the library." Charlotte snapped her attention back to Shannon. "Are you married?"

"No. I'm not."

"Do you have children?"

"No."

She opened her mouth as if she was going to ask another question, but Shannon got there first.

"I like the ribbons in your hair."

"My mom put them in yesterday." Charlotte gave an exaggerated sigh. "My dad's not good with girl stuff, but he tries."

"I do try," Adam added.

"Dad can do stuff Mommy can't," Oliver said loyally.

Adam put his arm around the boy. "Thank you for defending my honor."

"What's honor?"

"My mommy bakes cookies and reads to us every night," Charlotte added. "Even if she's busy."

Shannon tried to wrap her mind around the subtext. She had no way of knowing how the divorce had played out at home. Given how cautious Adam was with his kids, she wondered if they'd ever seen him with another woman. So even though no one had said anything about her and Adam dating, she might still be a potential threat.

She kept her smile easy and her expression friendly.

"She sounds great. You're lucky to have such a caring mom. Nicole is like that, too. Moms are the best."

Charlotte studied her for a second, then seemed to relax. Adam watched his daughter, but under the table Shannon felt his knee bump into hers. He kept it there for a second before moving it away.

She told herself not to read too much into the gesture or the conversation. One friendly disarmament did not a relationship make. But maybe a little smugness was allowed.

Seven

TUESDAY EVENING NICOLE TOLD HERSELF not to panic as she pulled into the garage. The fact that Eric's car wasn't there didn't mean he'd forgotten Tyler. If that had happened, she would have gotten a phone call from the day care. They wouldn't close and simply leave her son there alone.

Maybe they'd gone to the store. Or Eric had thought this was a late night for her and had taken their son out to dinner. Although these days he didn't seem interested in anything but surfing and his screenplay. While she couldn't imagine him taking Tyler out, that didn't mean it hadn't happened. Because the alternative…

She grabbed her bag and raced into the house.

"Tyler? Tyler!"

"Mommy."

Her little boy came running to greet her. She dropped her bag and fell to her knees, her arms open wide. He thundered into her. She held him so tight, she was afraid he couldn't breathe, but for that second, she simply couldn't let go.

"Hey, you," she said as she relaxed her grip and smiled at him. "How are you?"

"Good. I like Ce."

"See what?"

Tyler giggled. "That's funny."

"He means Cecilia. The name seemed to be causing him trouble so I told him he could call me Ce."

Nicole looked at the petite, curly-headed teenager standing in her kitchen. While she looked harmless enough, Nicole had never seen her before.

She resisted the urge to lunge for a knife from the block, then stood and carefully positioned Tyler behind her. "Hi. Who are you?"

Cecilia pointed to the refrigerator. "Eric left a note. He knows my brother. They're in a screenwriting class together. From what I heard, the two of them got invited to some lecture by some screenwriter guy. My brother asked if I could emergency babysit. He promised Tyler, my man here, would be in bed by eight, and I could study as much as I wanted. So here I am."

Nicole scanned the note. It said basically the same thing and was in Eric's writing. Which should have relieved her, but didn't.

She forced a smile for the teen. "Thanks, Cecelia. I really appreciate you helping out like this. How much do I owe you?"

"I haven't been here very long." Cecelia waved her hand. "You know what? This one's on me. I'll leave you my number. If you want to do this again, I'll text you some references."

Because Nicole probably hadn't done a very good job of

concealing her horror on finding someone she didn't know with her son.

She waited while the teen collected her belongings. There really was a chemistry textbook and a notebook, along with an iPad and headphones. She and Tyler walked "Ce" to the door.

"I had fun," Tyler told her.

"Me, too," Cecelia said.

Nicole fished a twenty out of her jeans pocket. "Thanks so much for helping us out."

"You bet." She stared at the money, then shrugged. "I won't say no. I have expenses."

Nicole grinned. "I'm sure you do."

She waited until Cecelia got into her battered Corolla before closing the door.

"That was fun," she lied. "Did you get dinner?"

"Daddy and me went to McDonald's. I had a burger and fries."

"The dinner of champions," she murmured, making a mental note to make the fruit and veggie smoothie he liked for breakfast in the morning. She wasn't sure if that was going to be before or after she killed her husband, though. She would have to play the timing by ear.

In the hour before Tyler's bedtime, she vacuumed, then they played the tickle game. She also got through the first load of laundry. After reading him not one, not two, but six different Brad the Dragon books, she was able to attack the kitchen. She scrubbed the stove and sink until they gleamed, sorted through the crap mail that always collected on the island and wiped down the table.

Next she used her bubbling anger to fuel cleaning both bathrooms, including taking a stiff brush to the tiles in the shower in the three-quarter bath. By the time she heard the garage door open, it was nearly midnight. The house smelled of lemon and verbena. The laundry was done and put away and she was more than ready for a fight.

She positioned herself in the center of the sofa, which would force Eric to the lower, less comfortable club chairs, and waited.

He walked in, humming under his breath. When he saw her, he jumped in an almost comical exaggeration. She might have laughed if he'd tripped and hit his head, but no such luck.

"Nicole, jeez, you startled me. I didn't think you'd still be up. It's after midnight. Don't you have an early morning?"

"No, that was today. I was home by six thirty."

"Oh, I guess I got the days mixed up. Why are you still up?"

For a second she only looked at him. Looked at the man she'd married and had a child with. Eighteen months ago, she would have said she knew everything about him. That he was a nice guy. Friendly, funny, smart, dependable. She would have said he was a good father and provider. She would have said they were a team.

Their marriage hadn't been perfect. Sure, there were times when they looked at each other as if there was nothing left to talk about, but so what? Every marriage had its issues.

She would have said no matter what, Eric would be there for her, just like she would be there for him. But she never, ever would have guessed or believed he was capable of quitting his job to write some goddamn screenplay and then leave their child with a stranger!

"I met Cecelia."

She'd expected a little panic, or maybe some shame. Instead, he grinned. "I know, isn't she great? I took her information so we can use her again. Tyler really seemed to like her."

"You left him with someone I don't know," she said between gritted teeth. "You left him with someone *you* don't know."

"It's not like that. She's Ben's little sister. I've known Ben for over a year. He's a good guy. The family is cool."

"I don't care about the family. I care about my child and the fact that you didn't call me or text me. I came home to find your car gone and Tyler being looked after by someone I don't know from a rock. What the hell is wrong with you?"

He dropped his backpack onto the chair and narrowed his gaze. "Nothing. I had a chance to attend a lecture at the Writers Guild. A private lecture. Do you know how rare that kind of invitation is? Do you know who I got to meet? You were working. I would have called, but you get pissed when I interrupt one of your classes."

"Then text me. Do something."

"I left a note," he yelled, his brown eyes bright with anger. "I left a fucking note. What do you want from me?"

"I want you to think about someone other than yourself. I want you to do something around here other than eat food and sleep and work on your screenplay."

He rolled his eyes. "Okay, here we go." He folded his arms across his chest, then used his right hand to motion her forward. "Come on. Let's hear it. You've got a whole list of things you want to complain about. Let's get to it."

His complete dismissal of her before she'd said anything made her want to throw something. Or him.

She stood and glared at him. "You're an asshole, you

know that? You can pretend this is me being me, but you're wrong. Completely wrong. You're rarely here anymore. We don't ever see each other. You make promises you don't keep—like helping around the house or buying groceries. You do nothing to keep this household going. I work, I bring in all the money and I have to do almost everything around here."

She sucked in a breath. "Sometimes you won't even help with Tyler. He's your son, Eric. Your child. Why won't you be there for him?"

Eric stared at her for a long time. She watched anxiously, hoping for something that wasn't anger. His jaw twitched, his mouth twisted. Remorse? Could she possibly have gotten through to him?

"This is all your fault," he said quietly.

She blinked. "What?"

"You did this. You made this happen."

Her mouth dropped open. "What are you talking about?"

He waved his hand at the room. "All of this. If you're unhappy, then you only have yourself to blame. I took it, Nicole. For as long as I could. What about me? What about what I want? But none of that matters to you. You don't care that I was unhappy with my life. You don't care that I wanted more than what we had."

She couldn't have been more surprised if he'd sprouted a second head and started breathing fire.

"Are you drunk?"

"No. I'm completely sober and I know exactly what I'm saying." He took a step toward her. "Before you and I met, I'd been saving every penny I had so that I could quit my job and write a screenplay. It was something I'd always wanted to do."

"What? That's not true. You talked about it maybe twice the whole time we were dating. You never said anything more until the day you quit your job."

"That's because I knew you'd mock me. I knew you wouldn't be supportive. Or believe in me."

She opened her mouth, then closed it. What was she supposed to say to that? Realistically, the odds of him actually selling a screenplay were tiny. But if she pointed that out, she fell into the unsupportive camp. Because Eric had a dream and nothing else mattered.

"I'm sorry you think that," she said instead. "Eric, I want you to be happy, but I also need you to be a part of our marriage. Our family. I feel like we're living separate lives."

"I have to do what I'm doing," he told her stubbornly. "This my time. My dream. You lost yours. You couldn't make it, but at least you had the chance to try. It's like you don't want me to have my shot. Because what if I'm talented? You'd hate that."

It took her a second to figure out what he was talking about. "My dancing? I let that go years ago."

"Because you had to. I don't. And you resent that."

"My God, do you really think that about me?" Pain sliced through her. Could it be that they'd never really known each other at all?

"You've never once asked to read my screenplay."

"No," she said firmly. "That is not true. I've asked and asked. You keep saying it's not ready. You won't let me read it until it's perfect. We just had that conversation a couple of weeks ago."

He shifted and looked away. "All right. I guess that's true."

"You know it is. Just like you know you never really

told me how much you wanted to write until the day you quit. You didn't ask, you didn't negotiate. You just did it."

"I knew you'd say no."

"Neither of us know what I would have said. What happened to negotiating? To writing on the weekends."

"I wanted to just go for it."

"And damn the rest of us? Where does that leave us?"

"Nowhere." He spoke flatly, as if he didn't care what he was saying.

She didn't know what to say or do. They had the same argument about him quitting at least once a month and here they were again. Back where they'd started.

"You might be nowhere," she said with a sigh, "but I've got a thousand places to be and a to-do list that goes on for miles."

She was about to say that she wanted them to work as a team, to be in a marriage again, when he turned suddenly and stalked out.

"Then I'll leave you to it," he said, before he stepped into his office and closed the door behind him.

Nicole sank back on the sofa and covered her face with her hands. She waited for the tears, but there weren't any. Just a knot the size of Ecuador and the heaviness that came with a strong sense of foreboding.

Pam lay on the padded mat and waited for her insides to stop quivering.

"I think that was a personal best," she gasped, barely able to raise her head to stare at Nicole.

"I second that," Shannon called from two mats away. "I'd raise my arm in solidarity, but I don't think I can."

The two other women in the class simply groaned.

"Too much?" Nicole asked anxiously. "Sorry. I didn't mean to…"

Pam heard something in her voice and forced herself to sit up. Her stomach muscles screamed in protest. Pam knew that they wouldn't be all that was screaming come morning. She wondered if she could get in for a massage.

"What?" she asked when she was upright.

Nicole gave her a slightly off-center smile. "Nothing. I'm fine."

Uh-huh. A likely story. The truth was she probably didn't want to mention it in front of her other clients.

Pam shifted to her knees, braced herself and stood. Her thigh muscles actually trembled. For a second she wasn't sure she could stay standing.

"Lulu," she called.

Her little dog got up from the blanket and obediently trotted over.

Pam pointed to Nicole. "Go say hi." She looked at her friend. "Pick her up, please, and hold her."

Nicole did as she requested. Lulu cuddled close, then reached up and licked the bottom of her chin.

Pam started for the water dispenser. Nicole trailed after her.

"Why am I holding Lulu?"

"So you'll feel better. You obviously need a hug. Until the other clients leave, it's the best I can offer."

Nicole's eyes filled with tears. "Thank you. Can you stay a few minutes? I would like to talk."

"No problem."

Pam got a glass of water and sipped it slowly. She was gratified to see the other clients walked just as gingerly.

One of them pressed an arm into her stomach, as if trying to support the muscles.

Shannon walked over. “That was a killer workout.”

Pam eyed her. “Uh-huh. You obviously don’t care. How’s the new boyfriend?”

“Adam? He’s great.” She ducked her head. “He sent me flowers. Because of how things went this past weekend. With his kids.”

Pam nodded. On Monday Shannon had told her all about the random meeting on the pier. She’d practically glowed as she talked. Which was nice. Shannon didn’t tend to glow that much when she talked about her various boyfriends.

She was nearly forty and still single, Pam thought. A concept that was so foreign to her. No husband, no kids. She did what she wanted, went where she wanted, answered to no one.

Pam supposed a case could be made for how appealing that was, just not to her. She *liked* knowing John was coming home every evening. She *liked* her kids. While she complained from time to time and whined more than was probably funny, the truth was, she liked her life. Even the impending doom that was being a grandmother came with a really cool perk. Namely a baby.

“Did I tell you I know him?” she asked.

“Adam? He’s worked with John, right?”

“Yes. They’re building that hotel. It’s going to be beautiful when it’s done, but getting there is a mess. Anyway, we know Adam and his brothers and sisters, along with his parents. They’re great people. Very friendly.”

Pam nearly pointed out that Adam’s parents were much older than her and John, but figured there was no point. Her demons wouldn’t make sense to anyone else.

"I'm glad about the flowers," she added. "He's a good guy."

"I'm getting that." Shannon glanced at the clock. "I need to get back to work." She turned to Nicole. "You made me sweat today. You know how I feel about that!"

Nicole faked a smile back.

By the time Shannon collected her things and left, the other clients were gone, too. Nicole sank down on one of the mats, forcing Pam to do the same. She tried not to wince as she wondered how on earth she was going to get up again.

Lulu immediately crossed from Nicole to Pam and climbed onto her lap.

"Tell me," Pam said gently.

Nicole nodded, then started to cry. She covered her face with her hands and her shoulders shook with her sobs.

Pam waited, stroking Lulu and breathing slowly. Three kids and a combined total of twenty-one teenage years had taught her that if she stayed calm, the other person tended to stay calm. It was all about controlling the energy in the room.

Nicole hiccupped a couple of times, then sniffed and raised her head.

"It's Eric."

"I guessed it was him." The little pinhead.

"We had a big fight. I came home to find he'd left our son with a teenager I'd never met."

"Are you kidding? How could he do that?"

"I don't know. She's the sister of one of his writing friends. She seemed nice enough..." Her voice trailed off.

"It's not about her being nice," Pam pointed out. "It's about not talking to you first. It's about being a parent and a husband. I swear, I want to slap him."

Nicole brightened. "Me, too." Her shoulders slumped again. "It's just hard right now."

Pam couldn't begin to imagine. While she was sure there were two sides to what was going on in their marriage, there was no excuse for acting the way he was. He had responsibilities and it was time for him to deal with them.

None of which would be news to Nicole, or the least bit helpful.

"I'm going to take Tyler," Pam announced suddenly.

"What?"

"For a couple of days. He and I get along great. Lulu loves him, as does John. Honey, you need a break."

"Pam, that's too much."

"I've had him before. Overnight."

"Once and I couldn't ask."

"You're not. I'm offering. Seriously. I'll take him for two nights. If he gets upset, I'll call, but I think he'll be fine."

Nicole's eyes filled with tears. "You're so good to me."

"I know. And later, you can walk in front of me while throwing rose petals at my feet."

Nicole chuckled. "That would be very strange."

"Yeah, but I like it when I make people talk." She staggered to her feet and rubbed the front of her thighs where the burn was the worst. "Just tell me what time to be at your place."

"I'll bring him to you. It's the least I can do."

Nicole stood and hugged her. Pam returned the embrace and realized except for the angry muscles, she was feeling pretty good. This was what she needed, she told herself. To think about someone else. It was good for her.

Eight

FRIDAY AFTERNOON SHANNON LEFT WORK at four. Her assistant tried not to show her surprise and failed miserably.

"You can head out, too," Shannon told her. "Start the weekend early."

"Thank you."

Shannon told herself that her good mood came from her satisfaction with work and the blue sky and a bunch of other crap she didn't believe. Because she knew the truth. She was happy and bouncy and okay, giddy, because she had a date with Adam that night.

She tried to remember the last time she'd been so excited to see a guy. Nothing came to mind. Maybe it was because they were taking things slow. They hadn't done more than kiss, which she kind of liked. Not that she wasn't interested in taking things to the next level. She was. Very much. But anticipation had its place.

She was home by four fifteen and rode the elevator up to her condo. The space was considered a one-bedroom, plus. There was an alcove off the living room that she used as her home office.

Sunlight spilled into the living room as she stepped inside. She was on the fifth floor of the six-story building, with a northwest-facing unit. She had a view of the Pacific to her west and the pier and beach beyond to her north. The wide balcony wrapped around from the living room to the bedroom. There was lots of storage, a huge closet in the master and a laundry room big enough for her washer and dryer to sit next to each other rather than stack.

When she'd bought the place four years ago, she'd worried about paying the mortgage. But the lifestyle Mischief Bay offered had made it worth the gamble. Two raises later, she was paying down her mortgage with a little extra every month and still having some left over for savings and retirement. Life was very, very good.

She stepped out of her shoes as she entered the bedroom. She was going to shower and redo her makeup and revel in her anticipation.

She set her phone in the docking station by her bed and selected a playlist. While easy jazz filled the bedroom, she walked to the kitchen and poured herself a glass of wine, then returned to the bathroom.

After her shower, she dried her hair, then set it with hot rollers. She wanted lots of girly waves for tonight. Her wardrobe would take a little more thought. Sexy, but not obvious, she thought. Adam was taking her out to dinner. What were her options?

One hour later, she opened her door to let in Adam. She'd chosen a simple strapless empire waist dress that skimmed her curves. It wasn't fancy, it wasn't supersexy, but the color brought out the blue of her eyes and the only thing holding it up was one long, easy zipper. She wasn't sure Adam would notice that fact and be distracted by it, but a girl could dream.

He wore jeans and a long-sleeved shirt. Simple. Easy. And he still got her heart to fluttering just a little.

"Hey," she murmured, stepping back to let him in.

"Hey, yourself."

He looked her over, then shook his head. "How'd I get so lucky? You're gorgeous, smart and funny. There's got to be a catch."

"I used to be a spy, so I know fifty ways to kill you."

He chuckled, then pulled her close.

She stepped easily into his embrace. She wrapped her arms around his neck and let her eyes drift closed. He kissed her. Softly at first, but then with growing intensity. She parted her lips and felt the first stroke of his tongue.

Heat poured through her. Wanting followed, leaving tingles and aches in all the most interesting places. Before she could decide if she wanted to take things further, he stepped back and sucked in a breath.

"Have I said *wow* yet today, because I should."

She laughed. "You're really sweet to me."

"I'm trying to be a good guy. You make it tough."

His compliments were handed out so easily, she thought, amazed by the lack of game-playing. Adam thought she was pretty and sexy and he told her. There was no payment for the information, no expectation. She couldn't remember the last time she'd experienced that. Maybe never.

"You're nice to say that, but I have plenty of flaws."

"Not that I can see. Why aren't you dating George Clooney?"

She laughed. "Because he's too old for me." She stepped

close to Adam again. "You know what I would really like for dinner?"

"What?"

"Pizza. We could have it delivered and just stay in."

"I'd like that, too."

"Good." She put her hands on his chest and stared into his eyes. "I'm thinking we can order in about an hour."

Confusion drew his eyebrows together. But before he could ask what they were going to do in that time, she very deliberately stepped out of her shoes and then raised herself up on tiptoe to kiss him.

He responded in kind, moving his mouth against hers. She stepped closer still, pressing her body against his and felt the exact moment he figured out what she was offering. His arms came around her, his kiss deepened and she felt his fingers reach for the zipper at the back of her dress.

Friday Nicole arrived home at her usual time. She was surprised that Eric's car was in the driveway. He hadn't been around much since their fight, and when he was, he tended to avoid her. He'd been sleeping on the futon in his office and heading out long before she was up. Quite the trick considering when she had to get up for her early classes.

But she hadn't said anything or even left a note. Probably because she was as reluctant to talk to him as he was to talk to her.

Their fight had rocked her. Mostly because he seemed to want to assume the worst about her. Like his claim that she didn't want to read his screenplay and his assumption that she wouldn't be supportive. That hurt her and left her not sure what to do next.

Now she carried her tote and gym bag into the house.

"Hi," she called.

"Mommy!" Tyler came running down the hall. "You're home! You're home."

She dropped everything on the floor and kneeled down to catch him when he flung himself at her. Love washed through her, reminding her what was really important. Whatever she and Eric had going on, they had to protect Tyler. He had to come first.

She stood and collected her bags, then walked into the kitchen. Eric sat at the table. His gaze was wary, as if he expected her to start yelling at him. Instead, she offered a calm hello.

"I'm going to put my things away, then start dinner. Are you eating with us tonight?" she asked. Because lately he'd been gone for most evenings.

"My critique group doesn't meet until eight tonight," he said. "I can stay."

"Good."

She noticed there were a lot fewer dishes in the sink than there had been that morning and that the dishwasher indicator showed the load was clean. But because of their recent fight, she wasn't sure if she should say anything or not.

She started the oven. A few months ago she'd turned to the most likely candidate for domestic goddess that she knew and had asked for help. She'd explained how she was always tired and running from place to place and never sure what to do about dinner.

Pam had told her to set aside an afternoon to cook for the week. She'd also offered a few easy recipes for casseroles and the Crock-Pot.

Nicole had taken her advice to heart. But rather than give up an afternoon every week, she tried to do two or three weeks of food at a time. She doubled and tripled their favorite recipes. She'd bought smaller casserole dishes that suited the size of their family. Instead of one time consuming lasagna, she made four smaller ones—two meat, two vegetable. They were big enough for dinner and for her to have for lunch the next day. Eric didn't do leftovers and something like that was too hard for Tyler to have at preschool.

She made chili and dozens of chicken recipes. She also made it a habit to steam double amounts of vegetables and freeze the extras. They either had them later or she used them in soup.

After she'd put her things away, she pulled a casserole out of the refrigerator and popped it in the oven.

"Dinner's in thirty minutes," she said. "I'm going to take a shower."

Before she headed for the bathroom, she tossed in a load of laundry. To her surprise, she saw that there were towels in the dryer. So he'd done a load today. That was an improvement.

She hurried through her shower. When she was dressed again, she combed her wet hair, then pulled it back in a braid.

When she returned to the kitchen, Tyler was gone.

"He's watching one of his shows," Eric said as he set the table. "I thought we should talk."

"Okay."

He set down the last fork, then faced her. "This is important to me, Nicole. What I'm doing. The screenplay. I think it's really good. But it's not just me. It's my critique group and a couple of other people who have read it. I'm making contacts all the time. Networking. I can do this. I need you to believe in me."

All of which would have been nice to hear during one of their fifty thousand fights, she thought grimly. Not that it would have changed much.

She wanted to say it wasn't fair. That he was basically holding her hostage. That she'd never been given a choice. But her head told her this was one of those times when she had to suck it up and do what was best for them rather than what was best for her.

If only they could be the same thing. But they weren't. So far, she'd rarely found a time when they were.

"I do believe in you," she told him. "And I have asked to read your screenplay. A lot."

"I know. I was wrong to say that. I'm sorry." He looked at her. "I need to do this. I need to have my shot. I should have explained all this before, I guess. That one day my boss was talking to me about a new project and I realized this was my life. This was all it was ever going to be. Work I wasn't sure I liked, let alone loved. I couldn't do it. So I quit."

Without warning. No, she told herself. She'd said that too many times already. They were here, now. They had to deal with this current reality.

"Okay," she said slowly.

"All my energy is going into creating this right now. I'm sorry I don't have enough left over for you and Tyler, but it's an all-or-nothing thing for me. This is my shot. I can feel it. I have to put a hundred percent of what I have into the screenplay."

"Except for surfing."

The words burst out before she could stop them.

She waited for him to get mad, but he only shrugged. "The surfing helps. It clears my head. So it's kind of part of my process."

Seriously? "I'm guessing housework doesn't clear your head?"

One corner of his mouth twitched. "Okay, good point. I'm trying to help out more."

"I appreciate the laundry you did and running the dishwasher."

He nodded. "Thanks. I know it shouldn't all be you."

The timer dinged.

"I'll go get Tyler," he said and walked out of the kitchen.

Nicole stared after him. She had thanked him for pushing a couple of buttons on the dishwasher and throwing in a load of towels. When did she get thanked for everything she did, including supporting their damned family? When did she get to go surfing to clear her head? How come she had to be the only grown-up?

She shook her head and reminded herself she had to focus on what was important. Eric wanted to try. That was something. But what she didn't know was if it was enough.

"You are such a girl," Adam said, his tone teasing.

Shannon sat on the sofa, her wineglass in her hand. She felt good. Satisfied and happy and full. It was a nice combination. She tucked her feet under her. The action caused her robe to fall open a little. But she decided showing a little of the girls wasn't a bad thing. Adam had certainly appreciated them earlier.

The lovemaking had been good. Hot and fast the first time, then slow and sensuous the second. He'd explored her body with a combination of skill and enthusiasm, and expressed his appreciation of every inch of her. Afterward, they'd ordered pizza and opened a bottle of wine.

She watched him peruse her movie collection and realized

the piece that seemed to be missing. Drama and pain. She didn't worry that he was going to try to push her away by being mean, or want to point out that despite what they'd done, she didn't matter to him. He wasn't self-absorbed or difficult.

Bad boys played well in fiction but in real life they were what the name implied. A sucker bet she always lost.

"I thought my being a girl was something you really liked," she murmured.

He winked at her. "It is. But this movie collection. It's sad."

"Too many chick flicks?"

"Way too many. Where are the action movies? Men with guns driving fast cars?"

"Oh, right. Well, now you've found a flaw."

He returned to the sofa and sat next to her. He took the wineglass from her hand and set it on the table then leaned in and kissed her. At the same time he slipped his hand under her robe and cupped her breast. Tendrils of desire curled through her.

"It's an easy flaw to live with," he whispered, then kissed his way down her neck.

She pulled her robe open and shifted so she was lying beneath him.

He didn't need to be invited twice. They went from playing to serious in less than a minute. When he entered her, she arched against him, wanting all of him. Her still-tingling body was coming by the third thrust.

Later, when they were semiclothed again, she leaned against him. He had his arm around her and kissed the top of her head.

"You're amazing," he told her. "Why aren't you married?"

She looked up at him. While this wasn't the first time she'd been asked the question, she generally deflected it. "You mean why hasn't George Clooney snapped me up?"

"I know about your thing against George. He looks good, though."

"He does." She stretched her legs across his lap and decided she was okay having this conversation with Adam. A testament to how different he really was from her usual fare. Or Quinn. Talk about a disaster relationship.

"I'm not married because I've never found anyone who could get past my commitment to my career." She waved her hand. "I'm talking about the past ten years. Not when I was younger. From what I've found, men say they're fine with it until I have to cancel a date or a weekend and then it becomes a problem."

"Then they're idiots. What about kids? Do you like them?"

"Sure. I've always liked kids." She thought about mentioning how she was shocked to find herself turning forty and not yet a mother, but that might sound weird. Or like she was pressuring him.

"I would still like to have children in my life," she continued. "In the meantime, I make do with my friends' kids. Like Tyler. He's great."

"Oliver liked him a lot."

"I'm glad. Tyler has this thing for Brad the Dragon."

"I'm familiar with the character."

Shannon laughed. "You have that same tight voice Nicole gets when she talks about him."

"There's a cultlike quality to the series," Adam admitted. "I can't figure out how the author does it, but kids get obsessed."

"I know. Tyler's going to be turning five soon. I'm helping Nicole with his party. I found a store that carries Brad the Dragon everything. She can't decide if she's going to go for it or not."

He pretended to shudder. "I share her pain."

"You should. I think Nicole is going to invite Oliver to the party. Which means if she goes all Brad the Dragon, you're in trouble."

He grinned. "So you have a dark side."

"You know it."

He drew her against him and kissed her.

Adam stayed until about two in the morning. Shannon thought about inviting him to spend the night, but decided she needed the space. Maybe next time. For now, the physical intimacy had been enough.

He'd been gone all of ten minutes when her phone buzzed with a text message.

"You're such a romantic," she said as she reached for the phone.

But it wasn't Adam. Instead, the message was from Quinn.

Whatsup?

The single word was his way of asking her to a booty call.

She dropped her phone onto the sofa and walked into the bedroom without looking back. As she got ready for bed, she reminded herself that she couldn't take credit for being a stellar person. It wasn't as if she'd grown in the character department and decided to end a relationship that was totally bad for her. Instead, she'd had a great night with Adam. There was a difference.

Still, she should accept the victory, regardless of its cause. Maybe romance *was* all it was cracked up to be.

Nine

"WE'RE GOING TO TAKE A PICTURE OF THE left side of your face," the woman in the white coat said. Her name—Anne—was stenciled on her coat.

She was tall, thin and looked maybe thirty, which was intensely annoying.

"We do the left side," Anne informed her with what Pam was pretty sure was a smug smile, "because that's the side that gets all the damage when we drive. Unless you've always used sunscreen."

Another smug smile that told everyone that Anne knew for a fact Pam *hadn't* used much sunscreen.

Pam had been asked to show up at her consult/BOTOX appointment without any makeup. Being seen in daylight bare-faced should be enough of a punishment. She was committed to have a lethal neurotoxin injected into her face. Wasn't that enough on the pain and suffering scale? Anne of the white coat didn't seem to think so.

The medi-spa was tucked into a corner of an actual medical building. There were plenty of dentists and internists and even a practice devoted to cardiac care. So this place must be okay. It was the one Shannon had recommended. That had to matter more than Anne's attitude.

"All right," Anne said, positioning her in front of a white cone. "Keep very still."

Pam did as she was instructed, then was left to wait for a few minutes. She had a feeling the images were instantly available. They were digital after all. No doubt the extra time was for her to fully embrace her lack of sunscreen shame.

Anne returned and sat in front of her computer. She typed a few keys and an awful purple-and-green-spotted picture of the side of Pam's face appeared on the large television mounted on the wall.

The side of her nose was covered in massive craters and dark blotches. Her cheeks looked as if they were as uneven as the surface of Mars. Her forehead was a battleground. She nearly ran for the nearest exit.

Anne, her power firmly restored, gave her a sympathetic smile. "It's not as bad as it looks."

"Oh, good."

"You have significant sun damage. Here, here and here." She pointed as she spoke, touching the screen on the picture's nose, cheeks and forehead. "Your number is forty-five."

That wasn't so bad, Pam thought. "So I have the skin of a forty-five-year-old?"

"No. The scale takes a hundred women your age and tells you how many have better skin and worse skin."

"Oh. Which is better? A hundred or one?"

The sympathetic look appeared again. "Your sun damage is less than forty-four of the women."

Rats. "So higher is better."

"Yes. Now on to inflammation."

Thirty minutes and a half-dozen pictures later, Pam thought seriously about simply slitting her wrists. It would be faster and cheaper. And maybe embalming would make her look fabulous.

"I'm mostly interested in BOTOX," she told Anne.

"Of course. You mentioned that when you made your appointment. I agree."

"You do? You don't want to talk me in to some injections?"

Anne studied her face for a second, then shook her head. "No. BOTOX will smooth out your forehead. We'll do the bunny lines, as well."

"Bunny lines?"

Anne pointed to the mirror. "Wrinkle your nose."

Pam did as she was asked. Her brow lowered and horizontal lines appeared on the bridge of her nose.

Anne pointed. "Bunny lines."

"Right. Like a rabbit."

"Yes. As for the rest of it, injectable will get expensive and won't give you the results you want."

Pam didn't like the sound of that. "What would?" she asked before she could stop herself.

Anne rose. "A face-lift. Now if you'll come with me, I'll introduce you to Reveka. That is who you requested."

Pam followed automatically. Reveka was who Shannon had recommended. She entered a treatment room with an adjustable chair and some scary looking lasers. But none of that registered. She was too busy trying to keep breathing after hearing the dreaded *F* word.

★★★

Pam arrived home in one piece. She was extra grateful not to have been in an accident. Not only had the BOTOX hurt like hell—not just needles piercing her face, but the actual stuff burned as it oozed into her muscles—but Reveka had also told her not to lie down for at least four hours. All Pam could think after that was if she was in a car accident, she was going to have to tell the paramedics to simply leave her in place until her BOTOX had set.

She greeted Lulu and let her out, then walked into the kitchen. Her face still hurt a little. One of the injections had hit a capillary, which Reveka had said wasn't uncommon. The downside for Pam was she would have a little bruise.

She thought longingly of a glass of wine or a very large vodka tonic, only she wasn't supposed to drink for twenty-four hours. What on earth had she been thinking?

Lulu walked back inside and raced over. She assumed her pick-me-up position. Pam squatted, rather than bending over, and was careful to keep her body lower than her head. After straightening, she cuddled her dog and tried to take comfort in Lulu's familiar warmth.

Her phone buzzed. She fished it out of her bag and glanced at the screen. Brandon, her youngest, had texted to say hi.

She stared at the phone for a second. Her twenty-four-year-old son in medical school had taken the time to text her to say hi. Steven was thriving working with his father. Jen and Kirk were having their first baby.

She was married to a wonderful man who loved her, took care of her and who had never once been unfaithful. She had a beautiful house, great friends. In truth, she'd been blessed in every way possible. Why was she suddenly so obsessed with how she looked? So she was fifty. It was just a number. A meaningless number that only had the value she gave it. By itself it was powerless.

She walked into her small office and booted her computer. When it was ready, she sat down and settled Lulu in her lap, then raised her hands to type. Then she paused.

What was she looking for? What did she want? Not counseling. Not really. She wanted…

She wanted to be excited about marriage again, she decided. She wanted to feel like she had even twenty years ago. When they'd been a young family. Or like when they'd first started dating. That would be fun. Like she'd thought to herself the other night, their marriage wasn't broken but it sure was dusty.

She typed into the search engine. The first few tries got her nowhere, but eventually she stumbled onto several sites that promised to refresh a strong marriage.

Are you looking to put passion back in the bedroom?

Pam clicked on the link and stared at the picture of a nice resort in Palm Desert. The information on the site promised small classes where "laughter and passion are the keys to renewing the bonds of love."

As long as it's not stand-up and bondage, Pam thought. She glanced at the date and saw it was the following weekend. "What's the worst that could happen?"

She clicked on the registration link and saw there were still spaces available.

"If nothing else, we'll have a weekend away." She quickly filled out the form and typed in her credit card number. As soon as she got the confirmation, she called her daughter to see if she could take Lulu.

"It's just a weekend in Palm Desert," Pam said. "Your dad and I haven't been away together for a while."

"I think it's great," Jen told her. "We're happy to take her. She's such an easy dog. Maybe I can practice my diapering skills on her."

"Or maybe not," Pam said. "Thanks, honey." The phone beeped. "Jen, it's your dad. I'll talk to you later, okay?"

"Sure, Mom. Bye."

Pam toggled to the second call. "Hi. Guess what I just did."

"Pam." John's voice was heavy and sad.

She caught her breath and put her free hand on Lulu's warm back. "Oh, God. What?"

"It's Hayley. She miscarried last night. She just got home. Rob called this morning to tell me what had happened and that she wouldn't be in to work. I asked him to let me know when she was back. I knew you'd want to go over."

"I do. Thanks for letting me know." She paused. "I feel so bad for her."

"I know. Me, too. I'm not sure how many times she can keep doing this."

"I know. Okay, I'll go see her right now. Thanks for letting me know."

"Sure thing. I love you."

"I love you, too."

She hung up and printed out their confirmation, then logged off her computer.

"Come on, pretty girl. We have to go help a friend."

She detoured to the laundry room, where there was a spare upright freezer. After checking what she had prepared, she chose a lasagna and a chicken broccoli dish she knew that Hayley liked.

She put them in a large tote, along with a couple of bottles of wine, then picked up her keys and cell phone and headed for the front door. Lulu trotted along with her.

Pam had the dog do her business before they crossed the street and walked down two houses. When she reached the front door, she knocked twice, then let herself in.

"Hey, it's me," she called.

"We're in here."

The voice, familiar, but not Hayley's, caused Pam to pause for a second. She told herself that it was nice for Hayley to have family around, even if that family was Hayley's slightly overbearing sister. Rob would have dropped off his wife and then returned to work. Because he had two jobs to deal with, thanks to his wife's determination to have a baby.

The logical side of Pam's brain understood that every woman had to figure out what would make her happy. But her heart ached for her friend and what she was putting herself and her wonderful husband through.

Pam closed the front door behind her. Lulu took off at a run, headed through the foyer and turned right into the family room. Pam detoured through the kitchen, where she left the chicken casserole on the counter to thaw faster and stuck the lasagna in the refrigerator. She wrote instructions for heating both on a Post-it and stuck the note on a cupboard door. Then she, too, headed for the family room.

Hayley sat curled up in a corner of the sofa. She had a blanket draped across her lap and a box of tissues by her side. Lulu had already curled up next to her, her brown doggie eyes watching anxiously.

Morgan, Hayley's sister, sat in one of the club chairs. She smiled brightly as Pam walked in.

"You're so sweet to come by. I appreciate it. I don't think

Hayley should be alone right now, but I have my kids to deal with. Amy has a cold and the other two are…" She trailed off. "It doesn't matter. The point is I'm superbusy."

She was picking up her purse as she spoke. "Hayley, hon, if you need anything, you know you only have to call, right? I can be here in ten minutes. I swear."

Hayley nodded.

"Good. I hope you feel better."

With that, Morgan waved and was gone. Pam waited until the front door closed before she walked over to Hayley and hugged her.

"I counted six *I*s in less than ten seconds," she said by way of greeting. "What number did you get?"

Hayley smiled. She started to laugh, then the humor turned into tears and she covered her face with her hands and cried. Pam scooped up Lulu and sat in her place, then set the dog on her friend's lap. The little dog trembled slightly, as if undone by all the emotion. She leaned in and licked the back of Hayley's hand.

Hayley raised her head and sniffed. She was pale and had dark circles under her eyes.

"I hate this," she admitted, stroking Lulu. "It's wrong and unfair."

"You know it. Why does Morgan get to pop out kids like she's a toaster and they're waffles? She's so annoying. You, on the other hand, are lovely and everything about this situation sucks."

Hayley continued to cry, but she was smiling, too. "You're my weirdest friend and I love you so much."

"I love you, too." Pam hugged her. "I'm so sorry you're going through this again."

Hayley pulled Lulu close and kissed the top of her fluffy

head. “Me, too. I was so sure this was the one. That I was going to be fine.” She sucked in a breath. “The doctor says I can’t keep doing this. You know last time I lost all that blood. This time was better, but she’s worried.”

“We’re all worried.”

Hayley shook her head. “I know. It’s just…I don’t want to spend the day crying. Please, please distract me.”

Pam grinned. “You know, I can do that. I can make you totally forget how sad you are.”

Hayley tilted her head. “That isn’t possible.”

“I had BOTOX today.”

“What?”

“I did.” She moved her bangs so her friend could see the puncture marks. “It takes about a week to work and I’m not supposed to lie down for four hours. So if I have a heart attack or stroke, keep me propped up until two.”

Hayley was wide-eyed. “I can’t believe you did that. Did it hurt?”

“Yes. A lot.”

“BOTOX. Wow. Impressive.”

“I know.” She patted Hayley’s hand. “Now let’s check out pay-per-view. There has to be some trashy movie we’re both dying to see.”

Ten

NICOLE WALKED INTO THE BEDROOM AND watched Eric pull on shorts and a T-shirt. It was still dark outside but the sun would be up soon, and with the sun, the waves.

"I have to leave at eight," she told him.

"I'll be back in time."

She nodded.

For a second they looked at each other. It seemed like there should be something to say—after all, they were married. But lately the words were few and far between.

Eric still slept in his office. So far Tyler hadn't figured it out. For the most part, Eric was up before his son and the boy was used to his dad taking naps on the futon. But still... She worried.

Not just for what Tyler might think but for what it said about their marriage. They hadn't been much of a couple for a while. Now they were roommates. She knew that his sleeping in the other room was a big part of it, yet she didn't want to be the one to invite him back into their bedroom. It felt too much like giving in. Yet wasn't a good relationship based on being willing to think more about the other person? Maybe that was what Eric was waiting for—a little give on her part.

Marriage should come with a manual, she thought as she walked to the kitchen and started coffee. Outside there was just enough light for her to see the backyard and the stone fence that was nearly as old as the house itself.

Their home was an old Spanish-style bungalow built in the 1930s. The walls were thick, the ceilings high and the rooms designed to maximize cool ocean breezes.

There had been a handful of owners. The last one—a guy in the movie industry—had redone the kitchen and a bathroom before losing everything in a film he'd backed that had flopped. He'd listed the house at 1.2 million. While it only had three bedrooms, a tiny office and two bathrooms, it was still four blocks from the beach and in Mischief Bay.

Nicole had seen it at the first open house. She'd fallen in love with the tidy little backyard, the lemon tree that provided shade and the original touches, including beamed ceilings and arched windows. But with its price tag, it might as well have been a hundred million dollars. There was simply no way.

Within a few weeks, there had been a couple of offers, a home inspection, then the revelation of the equivalent of suburban black plague: mold. Mold was found in one of the closets. The deal had fallen through and the house had been abandoned for months.

She'd watched the price drop and drop. Jokingly she'd told the real estate agent when it hit the mid-threes, she would risk it, mold and all. One day she got a call.

Armed with an experienced mold-eradicating guy, she'd faced down the enemy. He'd scraped and tested and sent samples to a lab back east. The results had stunned her. It wasn't mold. The black growing mess was instead decomposing wallpaper from the 1930s. Suddenly she had a bargain on her hands.

Using every penny she'd saved and some very creative financing, she'd bought the house. About a month after she closed escrow, the economy collapsed and the housing bubble with it. Nicole knew she never would have qualified without the loan she'd received, but she didn't care. She had the house and thanks to the faux mold, she wasn't even close to underwater on it.

She'd met Eric a few months later and the rest was history.

She turned her attention back to the kitchen and with it, her life as it was today. She would try harder, she vowed. Would reach out to her husband. His writing the screenplay was a given. But that didn't mean they couldn't be happy together. She just had to find a way to make that happen.

"You sure about this?" John asked.

Pam leaned back in her seat and watched as they drove east toward Palm Desert. "Not really, but it seemed like a good idea at the time. At least the hotel is nice."

Now that they were going to their relationship-find-the-passion-weekend, she was having some serious second thoughts. What a ridiculous idea. Yet, she was reluctant to say they should turn back. Because they needed something to add a little zing to their lives. Everything was so routine.

"I went and saw Hayley this morning," she said. "She's doing better and she'll be back at work on Monday."

"Poor kid."

"I know. It's so hard to watch her go through this."

Harder still for Hayley and her husband to have to deal with it, she thought.

John reached across the console and patted her leg. "We were lucky with our kids."

"We were. Lingering morning sickness and me getting fat. That was it."

"You were never fat."

"I was a porker with Jen."

"Never. You were beautiful. Still are."

He spoke without looking at her, his attention on the road. But she had a feeling he wasn't teasing or being polite. In his mind, she *had* been beautiful. Silly man—although as far as flaws went, it was a really good one.

"I told you my friend Shannon is dating Adam Lewis."

"Did you?" He glanced at her. "I don't think I knew that. Good for her. Adam's a great guy."

"I know. I hope it works out. Shannon doesn't say much, but I get the feeling she wants to be in a serious relationship. She looks amazing, but she's close to forty and she's never been married. I know she likes kids. But to be starting at that age..."

He grimaced. "I agree. If we'd done that, Brandon would only be what? Four? To think we had all of that ahead of us."

"I wouldn't have the energy," Pam admitted. "Plus I'd worry more. When I was in my twenties, I did the best I could, but I didn't know that much."

"With years comes experience," he said. "I'm glad Jen and Kirk are starting their family now."

"Me, too. Kirk can't go with her to her first doctor's appointment, so she wants me to go with her."

"I'm glad you can be there for her."

"Me, too."

She looked at him. He was so steady, she thought. So concerned about others. A genuinely nice man. He liked sports and loved his country and his family. He was honest in business. She'd been lucky to find him, she realized, thinking of Shannon and even Nicole, who was going through hell with Eric.

"I want you to know I appreciate all you've given me," she blurted.

Her husband turned to her. "What are you talking about?" he asked before returning his attention to the road. "What have I given you?"

"A wonderful life. Three great kids. A beautiful home. Lulu."

"I didn't give you those things, Pam. We're a partnership. You've got my back and I've got yours." He reached across the console again, this time taking her hand in his. "I'm a lucky man."

"I'm lucky, too."

Palm Desert was a lush and green oasis in the middle of brown desert. Golf courses surrounded upscale communities. The shopping was elegant, the dining fine and the hotel where the retreat was being held looked like some billionaire's idea of a rustic castle.

Pam had booked them into a suite. There was a living room with a deep sofa and large fireplace. The master had a huge bed, views of the mountains and a stunning marble bath. The tub was big enough for five. Maybe using it would be one of their homework assignments, Pam thought as she stared at it. She couldn't remember the last time she and John had taken a bath together.

They unpacked, then headed down for the evening's

meet-and-mingle with their fellow attendees. Signs led them to a cozy room with French doors that led onto a patio lit by glowing tiki lamps. There was a bar on one side and a light buffet on the other.

Pam held on to John's hand as they entered. Her first impression was that everyone was gorgeous. The second and more startling was that no one looked to be over thirty-five.

She turned to her husband. "Oh, no. We're the oldest people in the room."

John glanced around and then started to laugh. He tugged her close and wrapped his arm around her waist. "Then good for us."

While she applauded his attitude, she wasn't sure she could be so casual about the very obvious fact. Were the younger women looking at her? Judging her? Imagining that no man would ever want to see her naked? Except John, of course. But he loved her so did that count?

They crossed to the bar. She got a vodka tonic while he chose a Scotch. Conversation was quiet. Most of the couples were standing around awkwardly, with only a few actually mingling. About twenty minutes later, a couple in their late thirties walked in. Pam recognized them from the website.

"That's them," she whispered to John. "The ones leading the weekend."

"Hi, everyone," the woman said. "I'm Vivian and this is my husband, David. Welcome to our seminar weekend."

There were a few murmured greetings, but nothing too enthusiastic.

They were attractive. Both blond, fit and tanned. He was in jeans and a button-down shirt, while she had on a pretty summer dress.

David smiled at them. "We want this to be a safe place

for you and your partner. There are no judgments, no criticisms. Just information and suggestions. We want you to have fun and we want you to learn something. And to answer the question you've all been wondering but didn't want to ask—no. You will not be performing in front of the group."

Several people chuckled.

Pam felt her mouth drop open. That question had never occurred to her. If it had, she wouldn't have signed them up in the first place. This had been a mistake, she thought as she looked around. A really stupid mistake.

"We're going to start with an easy game," Vivian said. "We'll go around the room and everyone will say their name and share one sexual fantasy."

"Just one?" one guy yelled.

Vivian grinned. "If we have time, we'll come back to you for a second one."

John leaned down and pressed his mouth to her ear. "This is going to be fun," he whispered.

Fun? This was his idea of fun? She didn't want to share a sexual fantasy with the group. She hadn't ever shared one with her husband. Did she even have any?

Her traitorous mind immediately went to Lulu's vet. No, she couldn't mention him or his dreamy eyes. Besides, her crush on Dr. Ingersoll was more mental than physical. She'd never imagined them having sex.

Vivian pointed to the couple closest. "Why don't you start?"

The woman giggled and blushed. "I'm Amanda. My fantasy is making love with two guys."

Her partner, an equally young, equally buff man, put his arm around her. "I'm Jeff and my fantasy is two girls."

"I see we're going to have some work here," David said easily. "Nice to meet you both. Next?"

Pam tried to pay attention to the names, but was too busy frantically searching her brain for a fantasy. When it was her turn, she went totally blank.

"Um, I'm Pam and my fantasy is to, ah, make love on a beach."

Lame, she thought grimly. Totally lame. Talk about sounding like everyone's grandmother.

"I'm John and I'm happy to know my wife's fantasy wasn't about spanking."

Several people laughed.

"Because you want that for yourself?" Vivian asked with a wink.

"No. My fantasy is to do it as much as I want for a whole week."

Several of the guys clapped. David pointed to the next couple. Pam stood where she was, her drink in her hand and guilt settling over her like a thick, heavy weight.

Was that really his fantasy? It was such a small thing, she thought sadly. Because she knew what he meant. He didn't just want access, so to speak. He wanted an eager, willing partner. One who wasn't always "in her head." He wanted his wife to be excited about him, about them. Maybe this weekend would help her give him everything he wanted, in more ways than one.

Dinner at the resort was a quiet affair. Pam was relieved to discover they were going to dine as couples, rather than as a group. After she and John had eaten their fill of steak and red wine, they returned to their room. John settled in front of the TV and picked up the remote.

While he clicked channels, Pam checked her phone. Jen had texted a picture of Lulu curled up on Kirk's lap. Man and dog both looked happy.

"Pam?"

She turned and saw John staring at the TV with the strangest expression on his face. Not shock, exactly. More bewilderment.

"What is it?" she asked.

He pointed to the TV. She walked over and stared.

As her eyes focused, he turned up the sound.

A naked woman lay on a bed, while an equally naked man lay next to her, on his side. She was shaved completely bare and the camera angle gave them a clear view of her privates.

The man put his hand on the woman's thigh. The voice-over, a soft-spoken British man, continued.

"Explore your partner's genitals slowly and gently. Start at the top and go down one side, before making the return journey. Men, it is your nature to go directly for the clitoris, but women often prefer a more circuitous route.

"If your partner isn't yet swollen and wet, a lubricant can be used."

"It's not porn," Pam murmured. They'd watched porn a couple of times and while it was sort of interesting, it had never been their thing.

"Oh, there's porn."

He changed the channel and they were immediately assaulted by a shot of an incredibly huge penis sliding in and out of another man's anus.

"There's girl-on-girl and heterosexual couples," he added.

"Something for everyone." She cleared her throat. "Is there regular TV?"

"Not that I can find."

Someone knocked on their suite door. John and Pam looked at each other. John quickly turned off the TV and tossed the remote on the coffee table. He looked as guilty as a teenager caught reading *Playboy* at his grandmother's house.

She was still smiling when she opened the door to find perky Vivian standing there.

"Hi," their instructor said. "This is for you." Vivian handed over a large gift basket. "And just a reminder, there's no TV for the whole weekend. If you're looking for entertainment or inspiration, we're running several instructional videos, along with different kinds of erotic movies."

"Is that what we're calling it?" Pam asked before she could stop herself.

Vivian grinned. "Try a couple. You might surprise yourself."

"Thanks." Pam closed the door, then carried the basket over to the small dining table. "We have a gift."

John got up and walked over. "No TV?"

"I know, honey. You'll have to stream CNN on your iPad."

She untied the ribbon holding the crinkly wrap over the basket. The opaque paper fell away.

"This we can use," John said as he picked up a bottle of champagne. "I'm getting the glasses."

Pam nodded without speaking. She picked up a bottle of what she thought was some kind of ice cream topping. Only the label showed breasts and promised a delicious, licking treat. There were also masks, blindfolds, velvet-covered handcuffs and the biggest dildo she'd ever seen in her life. Not that she'd seen very many, but still.

There were rings and balls and other things that were just plain confusing. Where did they go and what did they do when they got there?

She picked up what was obviously a vibrator. It was bright pink, in the form of a small beaver next to a large tree.

"What on earth is this?" she asked.

John handed her a glass of champagne. "Are there instructions?"

"For some things, not this."

He took it from her and turned the base. Immediately the tree began to vibrate while the beaver head moved in a circular motion. John's smile widened.

"We are so taking this for a test drive."

Eleven

"THAT SHOULD DO IT," NOLAN SAID. "THANK you all for your hard work."

Shannon gathered her notes. The monthly senior staff meetings were always grueling. Four or five hours of every department reporting what was going on. Results were compared to benchmarks and then conversation ensued.

She minded the long meetings less than most. Her department had been in such disarray when she'd first been hired that there hadn't been anywhere to go but up. Nolan, her boss and the owner of the company, had given her free rein in hiring and firing. She'd taken advantage of both. Over the past five years, she'd cleaned out the people who couldn't or wouldn't do the job the way she wanted and brought in bright, motivated staff. The finance side of things was now a well-oiled, money-handling machine.

The receivables cycle had been reduced from over ninety days to an average of thirty-two. Loans were consolidated, interest rates negotiated down and she'd played hardball with their bank until she'd gotten the terms she wanted for all their business.

"Shannon, would you stay a second?" Nolan asked, pushing up his glasses as he spoke.

"Sure."

She smiled at her colleagues as they left. A couple gave her sympathetic glances, but she wasn't worried. She and Nolan had a good working relationship. He was brilliant when it came to software and an idiot everywhere else. The difference between him and most almost-successful entrepreneurs was that he understood that his skill set was limited. He was willing to find the best and brightest to handle the rest of the business, freeing him to do what he did best.

She knew that wasn't always the case. When she'd still worked for a large bank, she'd seen dozens of brilliant businesspeople fail because they couldn't let go of control. Every small business had potential, but to get to the tipping point of making millions, there had to be a plan. And one person couldn't do it all.

Nolan had been different. He'd started out as a client, then they'd become friends. She'd helped him write a business plan to take his company to the next level and the one after that. When he'd offered her the job as CFO, she'd taken about ten minutes to make up her mind.

Now he looked at her and grimaced. "I'm going to have to fire Ted," he grumbled.

Ted, the head of operations, had missed every target for the quarter.

"You are," she said gently. "I know it's not going to be easy."

"He's my best friend."

She nodded.

"We dropped out of college together and lived in a garage apartment while we figured out what we were going to do. I owe him."

Nolan was a good guy. A little geeky—which came with the software brilliance. He was loyal and sweet. With his millions, he could have dated a string of starlets who wouldn't care about his thick glasses and wrinkled shirts. They would have their gazes fixed on his bank account. But instead of taking advantage of the local access to those beauties, he'd married his high school sweetheart and, to the best of Shannon's knowledge, had never once looked at another woman.

"You don't have to fire him," she pointed out. "Move him laterally."

"He'll know what I'm doing."

"Yes, but then staying is his decision, not yours. He's simply in over his head right now."

Nolan sighed heavily. "You want to run operations?"

She laughed. "Thanks, but no. I would do a terrible job. I know what I'm a good at and it's not program management. I know some headhunters that can help replace him, if you want me to set up a meeting."

"Yeah, let's do that. But quietly, you know?"

"Sure. We'll do a lunch away from here. No one will need to know."

"Thanks." He gave her a smile. "You're making me feel better about all this."

"Good."

They rose and walked out of the conference room.

Shannon returned to her office. Her assistant handed her a stack of messages. Shannon took care of them, then checked her email before reviewing the latest sales projections.

She was in the middle of studying a forecast when her

stomach gurgled and cramped. She ignored both and kept looking at the report. About thirty seconds later, the cramp grew, zipped through her entire intestinal track and had her running for her bathroom.

Twenty minutes later, she splashed water on her face and wondered if it was wrong to wish herself dead. The opening salvo of food poisoning was never happy news. She tried to review what she'd eaten in the past couple of days, but thinking about food wasn't a good idea. Through the closed door of her office, she heard her cell ring.

She managed to walk to her desk and grab it.

"Hello?"

"Hey," Adam said. "Are you okay?"

She pressed her hand against her stomach. "I'm not feeling that great."

"What's wrong?"

She thought about what had just happened in the bathroom. "Trust me. You don't want to know."

"I'm sorry to hear that. I was calling to see if you wanted to get dinner tonight. I'm guessing that's a no."

"I can't. I'm sorry. Rain check?"

"Absolutely. I'll touch base in a couple of days."

"That would be great." Her intestines twisted. "I gotta go."

She pushed End and dove for the bathroom.

Pam stepped into her panties, then reached for her bra. Twinges of pain rippled through her thighs as she moved. When she slipped her arms behind her back, there was a pulling sensation in her side. She laughed softly.

"What's so funny?" John asked as he walked into the bedroom.

"I hurt everywhere."

Her husband crossed to her, his eyebrows raised. "Yeah?" he asked, before pulling her close and kissing her. Not on the cheek, or casually, but on the mouth. With plenty of tongue.

She leaned into him, liking the feel of his body next to hers. His hands unfastened her bra, then slid around to her breasts. He cupped them as he deepened the kiss.

"You have to be at work in a few minutes," she murmured, even as he was backing her up toward the bed.

"I know." He was already pulling his shirttails out of his jeans. "What on earth will I use as an excuse?"

Twenty minutes later, she did her best to catch her breath. "We can't keep doing it like this," she gasped.

He rolled toward her and grinned. "How would you like to do it?"

Sunlight poured into the bedroom. It was nearly nine and any second now Steven would be calling to find out why his father was so late getting to the office. They both had a thousand things to do and she didn't care.

"I love you," she whispered, feeling the warmth deep inside.

"I love you, too, my beautiful bride."

It had been like this since the weekend, she thought happily. Between the way-too-explicit seminars, the porn and the basket of toys, she and her husband of thirty-one years had found their way back to each other.

They'd laughed, they'd tried everything in that basket and they'd made love more times in the past five days than in the previous five months.

She couldn't explain exactly what the shift was. Before she'd looked at John and felt that she loved him and liked him. But there hadn't been that old thrill. Now she got tingly. Yesterday, he'd snuck home for lunch and they'd gone at it on the kitchen table like teenagers. She was sore and ready to do it again at the same time.

Maybe the seminar had triggered some sexual hormone surge. Maybe the change of scene and a bit of education were all they'd needed to reignite their marital spark. Whatever it was, she was grateful. And very happy.

John stood. "I have to go earn a living. But be thinking about me."

"You know I will."

He winked. "We could try phone sex."

"I think I'd rather have you in person."

He laughed. "Which is exactly why I married you."

They both dressed. He kissed her once before he left. She made the bed for the second time that morning and hummed to herself as she worked around the house. About ten thirty, her cell phone rang.

"Hello?"

"Tell me morning sickness passes," Jen said, sounding miserable. "I feel awful."

"It passes. Are you throwing up?"

"No. I just feel like I'm going to every second. All I can get down is crackers."

"It will get better. I promise. In the meantime, eat what you can. You're not going to get malnourished."

"I have to eat right for the baby."

"You have stored vitamins. Do you feel better in the afternoon?"

"By about two, I'm okay."

"Then eat better then. Your stomach will settle when the hormones do. You're doing great."

"Thanks, Mom. I'm sorry to whine."

"It's okay. All this is new."

"I can't believe you went through this three times."

"It gets easier."

Jen sighed. "I have to run. Thanks for being there."

"I always will be. Love you."

"Love you, too."

Pam hung up and looked at Lulu. "I'm going to be a grandmother."

The dog gave a tentative tail wag, as if asking if that was good or bad.

"Good," Pam told her firmly. "It wasn't before, but it is now. I just remembered I'm pretty hot, for an old lady. So I'll be a hot grandmother."

She took Lulu and they went out to run all the errands. By three she was back and putting away groceries. The weather was already warming up, even though it was only early March. Life was funny, she thought as she set out steak on the counter. The east coast was knee-deep in snow and she and John would be barbecuing for dinner.

Just thinking about her husband made her body hum. She wondered if they would make love again that night. She wanted to. Very much. She wanted the rush of desire, the thrill of having him touch her. Maybe they'd take that ridiculous beaver-tree vibrator out of the drawer and play with it again. Adult toys, it turned out, could make things really interesting.

At five, John walked into the house. After greeting Lulu, he wandered into the kitchen and smiled at Pam.

"Prepare to be amazed," he told her.

She laughed. "I already am."

He pulled a folder from behind his back. "I'm taking you on a cruise. To the Caribbean."

"What? Really? When?"

"In May. We have a spectacular cabin with a big bed and a balcony. We're visiting several islands, including Grand Cayman. I know how you want to see those turtles."

She flung herself at him. "Really? You booked it?"

He set Lulu on the floor, then cupped Pam's face in his hands. "I booked it," he told her, staring into her eyes. "I'm sorry, Pam. You've mentioned those turtles and that island to me for years. I should have listened. I should have taken you sooner."

Tears filled her eyes. "It's okay. I'm so excited we're going on a cruise. We've never been."

"I know. Think how it's going to be when we do it to the rhythm of the ocean." He wiped the tears from her cheek. "I love you."

"I love you, too."

She held on to him. Her heart was so full, she wondered how there could be a moment more perfect than this. A man more wonderful. She'd been blessed, she thought with gratitude. So very, very blessed.

Nicole stared at her list and hoped she had it all. Shannon was still swearing she wanted to help, which was going to be great. Nicole had felt obligated to point out that seven five-year-old boys were going to be loud, but her friend had only laughed and said, "That's what birthday parties are supposed to be."

They were having Tyler's party in the backyard. The rain had ended for the season and the long-range forecast was for sunny, warm weather. Pam was loaning her two folding tables, along with eight chairs.

The food was simple enough. Hot dogs and chips with cut-up fruit and birthday cupcakes. She would be decorating with all things Brad the Dragon. As he was red, that made the frosting colors easy enough.

After waffling for a couple of days, she'd sucked it up and had gone to the party store Shannon had found. Now Nicole had a trunk full of Brad the Dragon party gear.

There were the usual paper plates and napkins. She'd bought sturdy tumblers that would double as part of the goodie bag. She'd added two centerpieces, tablecloths, a custom banner and assorted B the D, as she was now calling him in her head, toys, balls and games. She'd also rented a portable fort that came with slides and other outdoor activities. Her goal was to send her guests home happy and tired.

She heard Eric's car in the driveway and looked up from her lists. Things had been okay between them over the past few days. More friendly, which she liked. She had decided to tell him she wanted him to move back into their bedroom. In fact, she would be doing that tonight.

He walked into the house and saw her in the living room.

"You're up late," he said by way of greeting.

"I'm working on Tyler's birthday party. It's coming up quick. He's growing up so fast." She held out her list. "Want to see what I have planned?"

"Sure."

He crossed to the sofa and sat down. He wasn't next to her—there was a sofa cushion between them. Still it was the closest they'd been physically in weeks.

"How many boys?"

"Seven, counting him. All the toys and plates and stuff

come in packs of eight. That gives us one extra for breakage." She looked at him. "You've got the date on your calendar, right? It's on Saturday afternoon."

Eric handed her back the list. His mouth pulled into a straight line. "Why do you do that? Why do you set me up?"

Because he went to one of his critique groups on Saturday afternoons, she thought grimly. Right after she got home from her morning classes.

"It's his birthday, Eric. I'm not trying to be difficult. That is simply the day it is. I don't feel it's right to tell Tyler he can't have his party that day because you have critique group."

"And you expect me to be there?"

The question left her gaping at him. "Is that a real question?"

"You have friends," he said defensively. "I thought you said one of them was helping you with the party. A couple of the moms will probably stay. You don't need me."

It was as if he'd socked her in the stomach. All the air rushed out and she was left stunned.

"Never mind," he muttered. "You're always so dramatic."

"I didn't say anything," she snapped.

"You didn't have to. You looked at me like I'm an ax murderer. It's just a birthday party."

"Right. It's just your son turning five. Why would you want to be there?"

He stood up and faced her, his gaze accusing. "It's not like I wouldn't see him. I'll be here in the morning. I'll be here that night. I just wouldn't be here for the stupid party."

She rose and faced her son's father. "It's not stupid to him." When had this happened? When had he changed so much?

This man in front of her looked the same. Maybe his hair was a little longer, but it was still the same dark brown color. He looked the same on the outside, but on the inside, he was a stranger to her.

Every time she dared to hope they were making progress, she discovered they weren't. That he wasn't the least bit interested in being a part of their lives at all. She was starting to think the only reason he stayed was so that he didn't have to get a job to support himself. That if he ever sold that damned screenplay, he would leave.

She turned the idea over in her head and realized she wasn't sure how she felt about that. Which was incredibly sad. Shouldn't she be devastated? Broken? Begging him to—

"Earth to Nicole."

She blinked. "I'm listening."

"I said I would cancel critique group. I'll be here for the party."

"No," she told him. "Don't. Just go."

"You're not going to let me win on this, are you? So now I have to beg to attend my son's birthday party?"

"No, Eric. You don't have to beg."

"Then what do you want?"

"I want you to *want* to be there. He's your only child and he's turning five. I want you to think that sharing his birthday party is the best thing you could do with your time. I want you to be the kind of dad who wouldn't try to get out of coming." She turned away. "He'll be with his friends. I'm sure he won't notice that you're somewhere else."

He swore. "You don't have to make this so hard, you know. You could try to see things from my point of view."

"Right now I'm more interested in Tyler's point of view. You can take care of yourself."

"Because you're the wonderful mother and I'm just the asshole father. Is that it?"

She walked out of the living room and into the master bedroom. A few seconds later, she heard Eric enter his office and bang the door shut. She waited until she was sure he wasn't coming out, then crept into her son's room.

Tyler slept on his side. His breathing was slow and steady. She smoothed the covers and lightly kissed his cheek before returning to what had become *her* room. As she sat on the bed, she wondered what was happening in her marriage. How had they gotten to where they were and how on earth were they supposed to find their way back?

Twelve

SHANNON SUFFERED WITH FOOD POISONING for an ugly twenty-four hours, then spent the next day recovering. She'd had her first real food—a piece of dry toast—around noon and was now thinking she would make another attempt to keep something in her stomach.

She lay on her sofa, her midsection still sore from all the vomiting and other things that had happened. She'd also discovered that the grout around her toilet and on the edges of her bathroom floor was in excellent shape.

Beside her, on the coffee table, was an assortment of liquids. Some carbonated, some flat. All there to entice her into hydrating. Soup would be very nice, she thought. If she had any. But she didn't.

Someone knocked on her door. She sat up, then groaned as her stomach muscles protested. She was wearing jeans and a T-shirt, which were presentable enough, she thought as she stood and walked slowly to the door. She pulled it open and stared.

"Adam?"

She blinked at the man standing in front of her. The

man who looked all tidy in a long-sleeved white shirt and worn jeans.

She knew the clothes meant he'd come directly from work. Despite the fact that he'd put in a long day on a construction site, he looked good enough to model underwear. Or vodka.

She ran her palm across her hair, hoping to smooth out any sticking-up bits, and wondered how pale she was and how sick she looked.

"Hi," he said as he stepped into her condo and gave her a kiss on the cheek. "I called your office about an hour ago and your assistant said you were still out sick."

He held up two shopping bags and a take-out drink container. "Two kinds of soup, crackers, Sprite and ice cream. Because once you start to feel better, you're going to need ice cream. Oh, and a couple of chick flicks I don't think you have. Don't worry. I'm not staying. I just wanted to check on you."

He stared at her earnestly, obviously concerned he'd overstepped his bounds.

But more important to her was the fact that he'd cared enough to show up. He'd bought her food and movies. He was such a good guy.

She took the bags from him and put them on her side table, then raised herself on tiptoe and wrapped her arms around him.

"Thank you," she said, holding on tight. "You've really made me feel better."

"You sure? You're not mad?"

"Why would I be mad? You went to all this trouble. You're very sweet and I'm overwhelmed."

He hugged her, then kissed her lightly. "Good, because

you being overwhelmed does it for me." He stroked her hair. "How are you feeling?"

"Better. It was food poisoning and the worst of it is over. Now I just have to wait until I'm back to normal." She released him and reached for the bags. "Soup is exactly what I was thinking I wanted tonight. So you're not just a great guy, you're a mind reader."

"I appreciate the credit, however undeserved."

"Want to stay?"

The words were out before she could think things through. Adam probably had a million things to do. Not to mention she looked like crap. Weren't things too new for them to be sharing her being sick?

But he only smiled and said, "I'd love to."

Twenty minutes later, they were sitting at her table. He'd found a frozen dinner he liked in her freezer and heated it in the microwave while she warmed her soup on the stove. He had a beer while she sipped on Sprite. It was all very domesticated, she thought. And she liked it.

"Thank you for coming by," she said. "I appreciate you taking care of me."

"Happy to do it."

She looked at him and he met her gaze. "What?" he asked.

"It's a married thing. Men who have been married are better at dealing with things like a woman getting sick or hurt."

"Are we?"

"Yes. I assume it's the practice." If Quinn had found out she'd been sick, he would have avoided her for weeks. Adam had simply shown up.

"There were a lot of things I liked about being married," he admitted. "Things that I miss."

"Do you miss her?" A risky question, but one that needed to be answered, she thought.

"No. It's over. Long over." He hesitated. "I told you she cheated, but the end of our marriage wasn't that simple. When Tabitha and I were first married, everything was fine between us. We had our fights, but we mostly got along. Then a bunch of things happened at once. We had Char and moved and my dad started talking about taking early retirement. Over the next three years we had Oliver and I was responsible for a multimillion-dollar company and sixty employees."

He reached for her hand as he spoke. As if he wanted a physical connection as he told the story.

"I always knew I'd take over the company, but I thought I'd have a couple of decades to learn to be the boss. I was scrambling to learn everything and not screw up. Work was my priority."

"Something Tabitha didn't take well?"

"No. She was pissed. She tried talking to me and when that didn't work, she threatened me. She said if I wasn't around, she was going to find someone who would be. I didn't listen and I should have."

"That's when she cheated?"

He nodded. "By the time she came clean, things were better at work. I was ready to be a part of the family again. But it was too late. I'm not saying it's my fault she cheated. She made that decision on her own. And obviously there were problems in the marriage in the first place. We were both wrong, but I take a lot of the responsibility. I wasn't there. I didn't show up."

He stared into her eyes. “I learned from my mistakes. That’s why I make it a priority to be where I say I’m going to be. I call when I say I’m going to call. I’m on time to pick up my kids. I don’t ever want to make anyone feel the way I made Tabitha feel. I was wrong.”

No, she thought with wonder. He was perfect. Okay, not perfect, exactly, but close. Oh, so close.

She moved forward the last few inches separating them and pressed her mouth to his. “You’re a good man.”

“Thank you. I consider myself a work in progress, but I appreciate the compliment.”

He released her hand and picked up his fork. Conversation shifted to the movie filming by the pier and the subsequent traffic nightmare.

Later, when they were curled up together on her sofa watching one of the movies he’d brought her, she allowed herself to admit the obvious. That there was nothing about Adam she didn’t like. That if she were to make her fantasy list of what she wanted in a man, he would be it. All of it. So the odds of her not getting in too deep with him seemed pretty slim.

Which should have terrified her. Only this was Adam. Whatever happened, she trusted him to catch her when she fell.

“Don’t be nervous,” Pam said.

Her daughter looked at her and tried to smile. “I’m not sure saying it is going to help. What if I’m carrying an alien instead of a human baby? What if it has a lizard tail?”

“Did you have sex with a lizard alien?”

Jen rolled her eyes. “Of course not.”

"Then unless Kirk has some very unusual relatives, you can let the lizard fears go." She patted Jen's hand. "But I get that you're scared. Every mother goes through this. Once you have your ultrasound, you'll feel much better."

"I know. I'm sorry to be a freak."

"You're not a freak. You're my pregnant daughter. That makes you spectacular."

Jen smiled, then sucked in a breath. "No offense, but I wish Kirk was here."

"None taken." Unfortunately Kirk hadn't been able to get the afternoon off work. He was part of a joint task force with the Los Angeles Police Department and they'd had a training exercise he couldn't get out of.

"He'll be here for the later appointments," Pam assured her. "And when you have the baby. If there's a crisis, you always have me."

Jen leaned against her. "Mom, I couldn't do this without you. You're always so calm. The voice of reason."

"I try. Besides, this is an exciting appointment. They're going to date your pregnancy so we'll get to know when I'm going to be a grandmother."

"Because it's all about you?"

"You know it."

Jen laughed, then started to cry. Pam put her arm around her and rode out the emotions. Some of it was the stress of not knowing how things were going with the baby. Once Jen heard everything was normal, she would feel much better. The hormones didn't help, either.

"I used to cry every time I peeled potatoes," she admitted. "Holding them, I thought about the earth and that morphed into Mother Earth, then all mothers, then babies. Your father insisted we eat rice for the rest of my pregnancy."

Jen hung on to her, both laughing and crying. "I'm a mess."

"Kind of, but I love you so I'm not overly embarrassed. Plus, Kirk's not here. That's hard."

Her daughter wiped her face. "I thought you'd tell me to suck it up and be a grown-up."

"That doesn't seem like it would be helpful. He's your husband. This is your first child. While we both understand that he feels horrible not to share this with you, it's not because he doesn't care."

"He does care. He loves me."

The tears flowed again. The receptionist gave her a sympathetic smile. Pam had a feeling the staff was well used to the rush of emotion that came with pregnancy.

"You're going to be the best grandmother," Jen told her.

"Probably."

They both laughed.

Pam continued to hold her daughter. This was what she wanted, she thought happily. A connection with her children. For the life of her, she couldn't remember why she'd been so upset when Jen had told her about the pregnancy. So she was a grandmother? Age was just a number. She had a wonderful family and a new grandbaby on the way. She was also having more sex than was probably legal for a woman her age. She and John were still going at it like rabbits. Since their sex weekend getaway, the longest they'd gone without making love had been two days. Last night they'd joked that if they were paying for condoms, they'd have to take a mortgage out on the house.

Jen grabbed her hand and held on. "Mom, I want Kirk and me to be just like you and Dad when we're your age."

Pam grinned. "I want that, too, honey. I'm just not sure you could handle it."

Nicole used her straw to stir her iced tea. Not that the drink needed stirring, but she wanted something to do with her hands. Otherwise they would flap all over and betray her nervousness.

"So we have an approximate due date," Pam was saying. "Jen feels so much better now that she's had her first ultrasound. You remember what that was like."

"Scary," Nicole admitted. "You want to know everything is okay."

"Exactly." Pam sighed happily. "I'm going to be a grandmother. I can say that and be proud."

"I would expect no less," Nicole told her, knowing it was the truth. Pam was so warm and loving. She would be a great grandmother. Nicole wouldn't have minded her as her own mother. At least then she wouldn't have been pushed to be famous. Not that she hadn't loved dancing, but she would also have liked to have the time to be a normal teen.

Which wasn't what she wanted to talk about. But her mind was swirling and she couldn't seem to figure out how to ask her friend for marital advice.

They were at Let's Do Tea, in the upstairs dining room. The original structure had been a private residence built in the 1920s. Over the years, the neighborhood had become more business than residential and eventually someone had converted the house into a restaurant. About ten years ago, it had changed hands and become Let's Do Tea.

On the first floor was a retail store that sold all things tea with a small section of imported British food. There was also a take-out counter for sandwiches and scones to go. Upstairs was the actual restaurant with a menu that offered everything from high tea to ploughman's lunches. It wasn't unusual to see mothers with their ten-year-old daughters dressed in hats and lace next to a table of businessmen. Let's Do Tea had the best shepherd's pie in the state and petits fours that had been known to save more than one troubled marriage.

Nicole wondered if she should take a box home with her and see if they would help.

They placed their order, both getting the high tea with coronation chicken sandwiches and the scones of the day. When their server left, Pam glanced over her shoulder, as if making sure they were alone.

"Okay, so you can't tell *anyone* what I'm about to say."

Nicole held up one hand. "I promise. What?"

She wasn't worried—not exactly. Pam was looking too happy for the news to be bad.

"John and I went away for the weekend a few weeks ago," she said quietly.

"Right. To Palm Desert. You told me."

"What I didn't tell you was that we didn't just go to a hotel. It was like a sex camp." Pam flushed, even as she grinned. "It was the strangest thing. How-to classes and toys and lots of porn. But it turned out to be exactly what we needed."

She looked around again, then turned back to Nicole. "We're not like you and Eric. We've been married over thirty years. I can tell you the thrill really does fade. But now, it's all new again. We're like teenagers and it's so fun."

"I'm happy for you," Nicole told her honestly. "And only a little jealous."

"Oh, please. You two are probably still doing it twice a day."

If only, Nicole thought grimly. To be honest, she couldn't remember the last time she and Eric had hugged, let alone had sex.

"Uh-oh." Pam's humor faded. "That's not a happy face. What's going on?"

"Nothing's new, if that's what you're asking," Nicole admitted. "I'm genuinely at a loss. I don't know what to say to him. We barely speak. He's doing more around the house, but the other day we had a big fight about Tyler's birthday party."

"Didn't he like the party theme you'd chosen?"

She grimaced. "He has no idea what it is. It's not that he disapproves of what I'm doing with the party. It's that he's pissed he has to be there at all. It's one of his critique group afternoons and coming to his son's fifth birthday party will cut into that."

Pam's eyes widened. "Oh, hon, I'm so sorry."

"Me, too. Okay, he has a dream. I get that. I want him to be happy and if writing a screenplay fulfills him, then go team. But what about us? We're his family. Tyler is his only son. Shouldn't he be excited about his kid's birthday?"

The server returned with their pot of lavender Earl Grey. Nicole waited until she left before continuing.

"He's gone all the time. Do you think he's having an affair?"

"Do you?"

"I don't know." Nicole watched Pam pour them each tea. She stirred in milk, then held the beautiful rose-covered china cup. "If I had to answer that question right now, I'd say no. I don't think so. It just doesn't feel like that. Wouldn't he have all this sexual energy? I mean look at you. You're glowing."

"It's the BOTOX. I look younger." Pam sipped her tea. "You would have a sense of him cheating. I really believe that. Plus, he'd feel guilty and be a lot nicer."

Nicole sat up straighter. "You're right. That makes me feel better. Now I don't have to worry about hating another woman."

"Have you read his screenplay?"

"No. That's the other thing. I've asked and asked about it. And he kept saying it wasn't ready. So I stopped begging. Then a few weeks ago, he accused me of not being interested. How is that fair? I just don't get him. He's so different from the man I married. It's like he's a stranger. Aliens have sucked out his brain and replaced it with someone else's."

"What is it with you young people and aliens? Jen went on about being afraid she was having a lizard baby. I get sweating the fingers and toes, but a lizard baby? Is it a generational thing?"

Pam asked the question so earnestly, Nicole couldn't help laughing. She put down her tea and let the tension flow out of her body. When she finally caught her breath, she inhaled and felt significantly lighter.

"I love you so much," she said easily. "You're the best."

"That's so sweet, but you didn't answer my question."

"No, I don't think lizard babies are generational."

"I don't want to seem out of step."

Nicole grinned. "You can let go of your lizard baby concerns." She picked up her tea. "I welcome any marital insights you might have."

Pam shook her head. "Eric confuses me. I'm with you on the affair. I trust your gut and I go back to the he'd feel guilty and be nicer statement I made earlier. He's obviously obsessed with that ridiculous screenplay. I don't like that he won't let you read it. I don't suppose you want to snoop on his computer?"

"Not really."

"I wouldn't, either. What if it's horrible? Of course, it could be brilliant and that would be gratifying."

"I'm not sure I'd be able to tell the difference. I've never read a screenplay before."

"Good point." Pam paused for a moment. "Have you thought about negotiating with him? Maybe he's been secretive because he's convinced you simply want him to abandon his dream. If he knew that you were on board with him writing for a certain period of time, he might relax about it. So suggest he has six months to finish it and then he has to start bringing in money again."

"Maybe," Nicole said slowly, wondering if any kind of compromise was possible. "I'm not sure he wants to return to his regular life, but maybe we should talk about it."

"Knowing there's an end in sight would certainly help you."

"What if there isn't? What if he wants to go on like this forever?"

"Then you have to decide what you want," Pam said gently. "How long can you keep doing what you're doing?"

Their server arrived with their plates of sandwiches. There was a handful of chips on each, along with a small fruit cup.

A timely interruption, she thought ruefully. Because she didn't have an answer to her friend's question.

Thirteen

LULU TREMBLED AS SHE CUDDLED CLOSE TO Pam.

"I know," Pam murmured as she stroked her dog, careful to avoid the angry red blotches from her latest rash. "I know, sweet girl."

The dog had started scratching the day before and this morning she'd woken up with the painful rash on her side and down one leg.

"You are a delicate flower."

Lulu licked her chin, then huddled next to her. Pam knew she was cold, but she hadn't wanted to put on a T-shirt until they had the rash checked out by Dr. Ingersoll.

"Let's go back," Heidi said, holding open the door to the examination rooms.

Instead of jumping down and leading the way, Lulu stayed on Pam's lap.

"All right, pretty girl," Pam murmured as she picked up her pet. "I'll carry you."

They went through the usual steps of weight, temperature and heart rate before Heidi studied the rash on the dog's side.

"I already know the answer," she said with a sigh. "But I have to ask. Any changes in her diet or laundry soap or bath products?"

"No. It's all the same."

Lulu tried to scramble from the table into Pam's arms. Pam held her, trying to avoid the painful rash.

"That dog," Heidi murmured sympathetically. "Okay, he'll be right in."

Less than a minute later, Dr. Ingersoll entered the examination room. He smiled at Pam.

"We had a good run this time. All right. Let's see what our girl has gotten herself into."

Lulu fearlessly jumped from Pam's arms to his. For a second Pam's hands got tangled up with the good doctor's. Personal contact, she thought with amusement and waited for her crush quiver to activate.

Only there was…nothing. Not a hint, not even a whisper. She glanced away so he wouldn't see the amusement in her gaze. She was cured. Falling madly and sexually back in love with her husband had done the trick. Knowing what she knew now, she would have tried it ten years ago.

Dr. Ingersoll examined Lulu's rash. "That looks painful," he said. "I want to use a cream that combines a painkiller and numbing agent. You didn't dress her this morning?"

"No. She whimpered when I touched her, so I didn't want to put on clothes. It's tough because I know she's cold. I gave her Benadryl."

"Good. That should help a little. You're not feeding her any table food, are you?"

Pam cleared her throat. "Maybe a little."

"You know she's delicate. She might be having a reaction to something she ate."

"It's those big eyes. They're tough to resist."

"Try harder. We'll get her back on her steroids until this calms down."

He gave Lulu a couple of shots to get things started, then filled the prescriptions Pam would need for her. After he applied the cream, he got Lulu into her T-shirt.

"Leave the same shirt after applying the cream," he said. "She's not in fashion. She doesn't have to look perfect all the time."

Pam nodded. "We can go a couple of weeks looking casual."

"Good. Any other questions?"

She looked at him and thought about how he was nice and caring and very sexy. "I have a lot of friends with age-appropriate single daughters. Are you in a relationship?"

Dr. Ingersoll stared at her for a second. He had the most peculiar look on his face. Not surprise, exactly. Chagrin? Curiosity? Confusion? She just couldn't tell.

"I am in a relationship," he told her, at last with a smile. "A committed one. And I'm gay."

Something she hadn't expected him to say, she thought, careful to keep her mouth closed. "If that changes..." she said. "The committed relationship part, I mean. I like fixing up people."

"I'll keep that in mind." He petted Lulu. "You feel better."

After paying the bill, Pam carried Lulu and the meds to the car. She got them both inside and settled behind the steering wheel. Only then did she allow herself to think about her mad crush on Dr. Ingersoll and the fact that the whole time she'd been wondering if he was in any way attracted to her, he'd been gay.

Her mouth twitched. Then she started to laugh. She was still laughing and laughing as she backed out of her parking space and drove onto the street. Life, it seemed, had quite the sense of humor.

"Okay," Shannon said, watching seven boys wait eagerly to have their turn on the fort-swing-jumpy thing Nicole had rented for Tyler's birthday party. "Best entertainment ever. They love it and they're going to be exhausted."

"Right?" Nicole studied the table they were setting. "It's the perfect twofer. Because sending your kid home exhausted is kind of expected after one of these things. Okay—the food is ready. We'll get it out in about half an hour. Then presents, then cupcakes. Does that sound right?"

Shannon touched her arm. "Relax. You did a great job of planning. You even conquered your irrational fear of Brad the Dragon."

Nicole rolled her eyes. "I don't fear him. I hate him. Well, not him, of course. His creator. If I ever meet the guy who created Brad the Dragon, I swear I'm going to back the car over him. What a money machine. He's not in it for the stories. I'll bet he's making millions off the merchandising. Selfish you-know-what."

Shannon actually didn't know what, but with so many kids within earshot, she also wasn't going to ask. Nicole was certainly carrying around a lot of energy when it came to a fictional character. Only Brad wasn't the problem. Eric was. Because while the party had started thirty minutes ago, Tyler's father was nowhere to be seen.

Nicole hadn't said anything, but Shannon had watched her grow more and more tense. She had to be upset, maybe embarrassed. Shannon thought about what Adam had talked about a few days before. How he'd been more concerned about work than his family for several years. Now he regretted what he'd lost. Maybe not his marriage to Tabitha, but the time with his kids. She wondered if Eric would feel the same way when Tyler was older. If he would look back and have regrets. She hoped so. Although having him here in the first place would be a better solution all around.

"Hey, I was here first!"

Nicole looked over to where a couple of boys were starting to push each other. "That's not good."

She hurried over. Shannon went with her. She crouched down by one of the boys.

"I can't remember. Did you say you did want a cupcake after lunch or you didn't?"

The boy, a grinning, skinny redhead, looked at her as if she was an idiot. "I want a cupcake."

"You're sure."

"Yeah."

"Good to know." She straightened and pointed to the swing. "Oh, look. There's no line."

He made a beeline for the swing. Nicole moved next to her.

"Crisis averted," her friend said. "I'm feeling the pressure. None of the other mothers stayed. It's up to us to keep things running smoothly."

"We'll be fine. I'm not above using food as a bribe." She held up both hands. "I know. It's bad, but hey. They're not my kids and it's not like the other mothers left instructions not to."

Nicole laughed. "I like your style." Then her smile faded as she glanced toward the house.

Hurry up, Eric, Shannon thought, resisting the need to look and see if the father of the birthday boy had gotten here yet. Tyler was having too much fun to miss his dad right now, but that wasn't the point.

She wished Adam was here with Oliver, but they'd had a family thing they couldn't get out of.

The back gate opened.

"Thank God," Nicole said, and stared across the backyard, only to come to a stop when Pam walked in with a large, life-size Brad the Dragon behind her. Or rather someone in a Brad the Dragon costume.

"Hi," Pam said with a wave. "I know, I should have asked, but I was afraid you'd say it was too extravagant." She lowered her voice. "He does balloon animals. Who doesn't love a balloon animal?"

Tyler looked up and his mouth dropped open. "Mommy?" he asked, his voice squeaking with excitement. "Is that for me?"

Nicole held out her hands in a gesture of surrender. "Yes, it is. You're going to have to thank Aunt Pam, though."

Tyler flew across the grass and launched himself at Pam. "You're the best."

Pam held onto him for a second, then pushed him toward the life-size character. "I think Brad here wants to wish you happy birthday, young man."

Tyler skipped over to Brad. "Hi. I'm Tyler. It's my birthday."

Pam moved toward Nicole. Shannon joined them, thinking that the extravagant gesture was pure Pam.

"I remember my boys' fifth birthdays," she was saying quietly. "It's when the other mothers stopped staying. Something about the kids being old enough for school and the moms wanting some quiet time to themselves. I got the recommendation from a neighbor's sister. Evil woman, but she gives a great kid's party. You mad?"

Shannon wanted to give Nicole a little shake in the hopes she wouldn't get upset. Sure Pam hadn't asked, but wasn't it worth it? No way Tyler would be missing his father now.

The sudden realization had her studying Pam more closely. Had the other woman guessed that Eric would resist giving up his writing group to attend his son's birthday party? She'd been married for years—she probably knew all the pitfalls. Talk about a good person to have your back.

Nicole hugged her friend. "I will owe you forever."

"You don't owe me anything. I love you both. Now watch this guy make a dragon balloon animal. It's impressive."

The party continued without incident. The boys loved the balloon animals and the fort. Shannon and Pam took charge of serving lunch so Nicole could supervise all seven boys and somewhere around the time they were going to put out the cupcakes, Eric showed up.

As soon as he stepped out of the backyard, he called for Tyler and held out his arms. His son smiled and waved, but stayed with his friends. Shannon told herself it was petty to be pleased, then decided she could live with the character flaw. Pam hid a smirk.

"Serves him right," she murmured to Shannon. "I'm going to get the ice cream."

While the boys played games with Brad, Shannon cleared the tables, dumping the paper plates into the recycling bin. She did her best not to listen to the heated conversation happening by the fence.

"Why are you pissed?" Eric demanded. "I'm here, aren't I?"

"An hour and a half late," Nicole told him. "Never mind. I don't want to talk about it now."

"Well, I'm not talking about it later."

Shannon stepped inside to help Pam.

As she walked into the house, she thought about Adam. He'd already figured out what mattered to him. He was an ordinary guy with a steady job who loved his family. He wasn't a movie star or a record producer. On the surface, he wasn't flashy. And maybe that was the best news of all.

"I honestly don't know where to put my anger," Nicole admitted from her corner of the sofa.

Pam, who sat at the other end of the couch, nodded. "I get that. I really do."

"Throw him out."

That last bit of advice was offered by Shannon, who sat on the floor, stretching out her hamstrings. She looked up and shrugged. "He deserves to sleep in the street."

"I have to admit, the idea of it makes me all tingly inside," Nicole murmured. The picture of Eric shivering and cold was more gratifying than it should have been.

The three of them had had dinner with Tyler, then his two favorite "aunties" had read him bedtime stories until he fell asleep. Talk about a five-year-old boy's idea of bliss. Now Nicole and her friends were in the living room, drinking wine and talking trash.

Pam sipped her wine. "I know it sounds good to change the locks, but it's not that easy. You're married."

Shannon straightened. "The voice of reason speaks. I get that there are complications. Yes, they're married, but how does she get through to Eric? How does she get him to see he's ignoring what's most important in his life? He's going to have regrets later. All that's lost now can't ever be made up."

"You're assuming he *is* going to care someday," Nicole said, wondering if she sounded as bitter as she felt.

"Exactly." Shannon reached for her wine. "And here's another question for our longtime married friend. Why is where we are now the starting place? Why is the assumption that this is the situation we have and we're dealing? Why can't Nicole tell him she wants things exactly as they were and *that's* the starting point for negotiations?" Shannon glanced at Nicole. "I hope it's okay that I'm speaking for you."

"Please. You're doing a great job. I should have you around when I fight with Eric. I'd do much better."

"You would have been an excellent lawyer," Pam admitted.

Shannon wrinkled her nose. "I hear what you're thinking. But not so great at relationships."

"You're wonderful at relationships," Pam corrected. "But not so much on the yielding. There are stages of life. Sometimes we know exactly what we're doing and sometimes we're starting over, even in a familiar situation. Like my daughter, Jen. She and her husband have great jobs and a good marriage. Now Jen is pregnant and everything will be new again."

Nicole nodded slowly. "It's like learning anything. You have to start in the beginners class." She considered Pam's words. "You're saying Eric and I are in a new stage and the old rules don't apply."

"You know this kind of talk makes me crazy, right?" Shannon muttered.

Pam smiled at her. "I know. And you have an excellent point."

"I didn't make one."

"You were about to."

Shannon laughed. "Okay, Miss Smarty-pants. What was it?"

"That if Nicole accepts the premise that she's starting over in her marriage, that doesn't mean she should accept disrespect or allow Eric to treat her or Tyler badly."

Shannon sighed. "Damn, you're good."

Nicole pulled her legs up and tucked her feet under her. "So I let the past go and start with where we are," she said slowly. "But with the expectation that Eric still has to be a participating member of the family and a decent husband."

Was that the answer? To begin fresh?

"I'm still mad at him," she admitted.

"You should be," Pam told her. "There's no excuse for what he did. But that's different than dwelling on what was. You are where you are."

Nicole looked at Shannon. "You still think I should kick him out?"

"I think you should do what feels right for you and Tyler. I'll love you no matter what you decide."

"Me, too," Pam agreed.

Nicole smiled at them both. Love and support, she told herself. Always welcome and right there when she needed it.

Her friends stayed a couple more hours. When they left, she headed for the bedroom, but when she got there, she realized she wasn't tired. An odd restlessness filled her. She'd already cleaned up after dinner. She could watch TV or read, but she was too restless for either. She needed to be doing something, but what?

Without thinking, she headed for Eric's office, then pushed open the door. The futon was flat, with pillows, sheets and blankets at one end. Because this was where Eric slept now. For a while she'd worried that he wasn't coming back to their bed. Now she was more sure than ever. How could she make love with a man she didn't trust, didn't know? They weren't husband and wife anymore. They were roommates who had a kid together, and barely that.

She crossed to his desk and turned on the floor lamp, then sat down. His laptop sat in the center. There were papers in stacks. Printouts of his screenplay with notes in the margin. Some were handwritten and some were from track changes in his word processing program.

She looked at the desk. It had been hers before she'd married Eric. This had been her home office. But slowly, after their marriage, he'd taken it over and she'd moved her things to her small office at the studio.

Now she opened drawers and sorted through the contents. She had no idea what she was looking for. Proof of a secret life, maybe. Receipts or phone numbers. Ridiculous. Eric would keep phone numbers on his cell. As for receipts, she paid all the bills and there hadn't ever been anything unexpected.

He went out for drinks a couple of times a week with his writing buddies, but his bills weren't extravagant. He had lunches out, but they were rarely over twenty-five dollars. If he was seeing someone else, she had modest needs. With Eric not working, it wasn't like he had extra cash to flash around. So what exactly was she looking for?

Nicole hesitated, then pushed the power button on his laptop and waited. The machine cycled through the booting process, then the main screen appeared. Her heart sank.

The last time she'd seen the wallpaper on Eric's computer it had been a picture of her and Tyler. Now she stared at pictures that had been altered with Photoshop to portray Eric holding various awards. He'd dropped himself into several pictures with famous writers and actors. They flashed across the screen in a slideshow that made her desperately uncomfortable.

She understood the power of visualization. She'd been a dancer for years and knew that seeing the performance as she wanted it to be was vital to making it happen. But this seemed different. Or maybe she was simply being critical.

She clicked the icon for his browser, then tried to log on to his email account. She was surprised when his old password still worked.

His pending emails came up. She scanned the names of who had sent them and saw a lot of names she recognized. Names of people Eric had mentioned from his classes and critique groups. She opened a couple at random and they were all about writing. Comments about revisions he'd made or changes they were making in their own work.

Relief mingled with confusion. So he wasn't cheating. Or if he was, he was doing it brilliantly. So what exactly *was* going on?

She closed the email and opened his Facebook page. The news feed loaded automatically—the password saved by the program. Which meant he wasn't hiding anything there, either.

Nicole didn't bother scanning the posts or comments. She had access to them from her own account. Not that she spent much time on Facebook these days. She was too swamped with work.

She logged out of everything. The computer returned to

the main screen. She leaned back in the chair and stared at the pictures rotating through on the computer screen. Eric laughing between Cameron Diaz and Robert DeNiro. Eric with Steven Spielberg. Ridiculous images, yet ultimately harmless. And if they helped him focus on what he wanted most in life, then who was she to say anything?

She logged off his computer without bothering to open the file for his screenplay. She'd offered to read it and he'd always said no. She wasn't going to look at it behind his back. Which was a fascinating moral line to draw in the sand considering she'd just gone snooping on his computer.

When the computer screen was dark, she stood and walked to the door, then turned and glanced back at the office itself. Sadness tightened her chest, even as resolve straightened her spine.

Slowly but surely, they were drifting apart. The marriage she'd wanted was no more. As for this new version, she couldn't say where it was going or even if they were on the journey together. She only knew that she hadn't been the one to chart the course.

Latte-Da, a local coffee place by the Pacific Ocean Park, or POP, celebrated the arrival of spring with a big poster announcing they were now serving their homemade ice cream. It was the first Saturday after that illustrious event—the ice cream, not the changing of the season—and Shannon stood in line with Adam and his two kids.

Adam frowned. "I don't know, guys. It's going to be a long wait. Maybe it's not worth it."

Char—not Charlotte—as Shannon had been informed that morning, sighed. "Dad, it's totally worth it. You always do this, and then you taste the ice cream and you get it."

"I want ice cream," Oliver added.

The adorable six-year-old leaned against Shannon and smiled winningly up at her. His small, pudgy hand was in hers. Shannon knew it was exceedingly shallow of her to have a favorite, but she couldn't help it. Oliver was like a puppy. He couldn't begin to hide his emotions and when it came to Shannon, he was smitten. Char, on the other hand, was a little wary. She was still friendly enough, but there was always a distance between them.

No doubt the eight-year-old was protective of her mother and cautious about sharing her dad with another woman. Shannon could both understand and respect that. She wished she could simply take the girl aside and tell her she had no ill intentions. That she would never try to replace her mother. But assuming she could figure out how to say that, would Char even believe her?

They moved up in line.

Char looked up at her dad. "Did you talk to Mom about my birthday party?"

"I did."

"And?"

Instead of answering, he turned to Shannon. "My daughter is turning nine. She wants a..." He glanced down. "What is it called?"

"A spa party." Char's face brightened with excitement. "It's going to be at Epic. All my friends are having spa parties. They do mani-pedis." She pressed her palms together and locked her fingers. "And there's a new service called the skin care facial. We get a facial and they talk to us about how to take care of our skin. I'm dying for that."

Shannon thought about Tyler's party with the bouncy

fort and balloon animals. Boys, it seemed, were a little easier to entertain.

"Do you even know what a mani-pedi is?" Adam asked, his tone rueful.

"A manicure and pedicure," his daughter informed him. "Everybody knows that."

"Do they." He ruffled her hair. "You're growing up too fast."

Char's impatient look said it was all happening too slowly. Shannon wished there was a way to explain that she really needed to enjoy being a kid while she could. That once adulthood was reached, there was no going back.

"Are you going to talk to Mom?" Char asked.

"I will." He looked at Shannon. "I have Char for her birthday weekend this year, so I'm in charge of the party. There will be ten girls and a day to fill."

"I know the spa she's talking about," Shannon told him. "It's not too far from my office. Want me to check it out this week?"

"You wouldn't mind?" he asked.

"That would be so great!" Char said, interrupting them. "Two of my friends have had parties there but not the skin care facial. Can you ask about that, please? It would be the best."

Shannon nodded. "I don't mind. I've seen the, ah, parties they do." She had almost added the word *kids* to the sentence. Fortunately she'd stopped herself. She had a feeling Char didn't see herself as being a child. "There's usually food and cupcakes. It might be one-stop shopping, on the party front."

"And you wouldn't have to be there," Char added, beaming at her father.

"But it's your birthday. I want to be there."

Char's brown eyes widened in horror. "Da-ad."

"I want to go, too," Oliver said, smiling at Shannon. "Are you going to be there?"

Adam's phone chirped. He grabbed it. "This may be work."

Shannon tried not to smile at the pleading tone in his voice. She had a feeling he was hoping for some kind of emergency so he could have something other than Char's party to talk about.

"It's Grandma," he said as he glanced at his screen. "We're still on for dinner tonight and..." He looked at Shannon, then away. "Some other stuff."

"Is everything okay?" she asked.

"Sure."

The word sounded right, but Adam didn't look at her as he put his phone back in his pocket.

The line moved again and they were nearly at the front.

"What kind of ice cream do you like?" Oliver asked her.

"I like the fresh strawberry. What about you?"

"Chocolate. You can share mine."

"That's so sweet. Thank you."

His hand in hers was reassuring, even if everyone else in the family was acting weird.

They got to the front of the line and placed their orders. Adam asked for two empty cups to go with their cones, then they found an empty picnic table by the carousel. Shannon quickly discovered that Oliver could make a mess faster than she thought possible. In about three licks, he had ice cream all over his face. Thirty seconds later, the scoop was tottering precariously. Adam moved the empty cup into place and caught the scoop as it fell.

"You've done this before," she said with a laugh.

"I have." He whipped a spoon out of his front shirt pocket and handed it to his son.

As she studied father and son together, she felt a twinge of something in her chest. Longing, she thought. Need. Not so much her biological clock as a sense of possibility. For so long she'd told herself she couldn't have it all. That the men she met were intimidated by her career, or if they weren't, they also weren't anything close to father material.

But Adam was different. He admired her success, thought she was beautiful and sexy, and he was the kind of man she would want to have kids with. When she was with him, she dared to hope that this could be real. That finally she'd found *the one*.

"I don't need a cup," Char said proudly.

"You obviously don't." Shannon put her hand on Oliver's shoulder. It couldn't have been easy to be Char's baby brother, she thought. But he seemed to be handling it well.

After finishing the ice cream, Adam suggested the kids ride the carousel before they all walked over to the aquarium. When they were both in place and the music had started, he stepped back to stand next to Shannon.

"My mother texted me," he began, his gaze locked on Oliver.

"You mentioned that."

"Easter's coming up. It's a big thing in my family. I don't have the kids. Tabitha's taking them over spring break to visit her folks in Arizona. It's her week, so that works."

She couldn't figure out what the problem was. He still wouldn't look at her and he seemed to be shifting from foot to foot.

"It's okay to tell me you're going to be with your family for Easter," she murmured.

He swung around to face her. "My mom would like you to be there, too."

"Oh." Talk about unexpected.

"It's the fifth," he added, speaking quickly. "We have a big dinner and everyone is there. Siblings, in-laws, grandkids. It's big and loud and you'll be asked a lot of questions. Personal questions. Members of my family don't always filter well."

Understanding dawned. She tucked her arm around the crook of his elbow. "I get it. You're afraid they'll scare me off."

"No. I'm terrified. My family can be overwhelming. The more they like you, the less they worry about being strange. And trust me, they're going to like you a lot." He closed his eyes and winced. "My dad is going to want to talk about how good you look, while my mom will be so impressed by your job. It's going to be one long, humiliating lovefest."

"Sounds like fun. The only thing I can't figure out is if you want me to be there or if you don't."

"Oh, I want you to be there. I'm also concerned about the consequences."

She grinned. "What if I promise that no matter what happens, I'll see you at least one more time?"

He wasn't smiling as he looked at her. "I need you to swear that whatever happens, you won't break up with me. I like you, Shannon. A lot. I don't want that to change because of my family."

His words warmed her in places that hadn't been warm in a very long time. This wasn't about sex, it was about connecting. It was about caring and wanting to be with her.

Adam was a conventional man. Taking a woman home to meet his family was an important step. And not one he would take lightly.

She stepped in front of him and took both his hands in hers. "Whatever happens with your family, I will still like you," she promised. "I swear."

"I don't want to lose you."

"You won't."

He lightly kissed her mouth. "Okay, then. It's a date."

Fourteen

PAM PARKED IN THE LOT FOR THE ORIGINAL Seafood Restaurant. She felt vaguely guilty as she got out of her SUV. She and John never ate here. They were firmly Team Pescadores.

There were dozens of restaurant choices in town, but only two upscale seafood restaurants. The Original Seafood Restaurant and Pescadores. The story went that back in the day, The Original Seafood Restaurant had been started by two friends who had known each other from birth. Their fathers had been fishermen together, they lived on the same block and they'd always known they wanted to go into business together. And they had—opening their restaurant nearly twenty-five years ago.

Everything had been fine. They'd been an overnight success, had married and started their families. Then something had happened. No one knew what, although there were whispers of an affair. One day the restaurant had been open, the next it was closed—the partnership dissolved.

Everyone thought that was the end of it. The building had stood empty for months. Then one day, just down the street, Pescadores had opened. Nearly the same menu, certainly the same excellent quality. Locals had been thrilled and had flocked to the place. Six months later, The Original Seafood Restaurant had been back in business.

Residents had been torn. Who to support? Could you go to both? Discussions were heated. Some families were torn apart by the tussle. For Pam, the decision had been easy. John was friends with the owner of Pescadores, so that was where they ate. She couldn't remember being inside the rival restaurant even once in the past fifteen years.

That was all about to change.

She walked into the building and found two forty-something women waiting in the open foyer.

"Hello, Pam," Bea Gentry said warmly and shook her hand. She was a petite woman with graying hair and warm, blue eyes. "Thank you so much for coming today. This is my friend Violet."

Violet was a tall, willowy blonde. Pam shook hands with the other woman, all the while wondering what on earth they could want with her. She'd known Bea back in the day, through various sports events at the high school. Brandon, her youngest, had been friends with Bea's oldest. The two women had spent long hours on hard benches watching baseball games. But they hadn't spoken in several years. The invitation to lunch had come out of the blue.

They wore pants, shirts and jackets. Business casual in Mischief Bay. Pam had been nervous enough to eschew her usual jeans or cropped pants in favor of a simple green dress with a black blazer and low-heeled pumps. Looking at the well-groomed women as they walked to their table, she was grateful she'd taken a little extra time with her makeup.

After they were seated, there was plenty of friendly chitchat. Violet mentioned the annual wheelbarrow auctions were coming up.

Back in the late 1800s, when the town had been founded, the police had often transported drunks and criminals to jail in wheelbarrows. Over the years, several of the old pieces had been found and saved. They'd become something of a point of pride in the town. Now new and restored wheelbarrows were placed all around—in front of businesses, in parks. They were decorated. Some were used as planters, others had been converted into outdoor seating.

While the wheelbarrows were owned by the city, every year the rights to them—to decorate, name or brag about—were auctioned off. Proceeds went to everything from refurbishing older buildings to bringing the carousel to the POP. Pam and John had "bought" a wheelbarrow a few times.

"The proceeds this year are going to spruce up The Barkwalk," Violet was saying. "There are a couple of lots coming available on the east side. If they can raise the money, they want to buy the lots, tear down the houses and expand the park."

The Barkwalk was the town's dog park. The space was long and skinny—it started on the beach, then headed inland. "I'd heard that, too," Pam said. "They want to put in an area for smaller dogs and puppies."

"A worthy cause." Bea smiled at Pam. "But not why we asked you out to lunch. You must be wondering."

"I am," she admitted.

"Then let me explain it all to you." She smiled at her friend, then turned her attention back to Pam. "Violet and I are part of a group called Moving Women Forward. We're based here in town. Our group is an angel network."

"In the business sense, I assume," Pam murmured.

They both smiled. "Exactly."

Pam knew about different kinds of funding for startups. An entrepreneur could have his or her own funding, get it from family and friends, get a small business loan or even approach a bank. There were also angel funds. Often they were grants or small loans given when the entrepreneur needed them most. An angel fund helped a company get to the next level.

Bea smiled. "We work with women who are starting businesses or have one that's a couple of years old. We provide funding but also mentoring. We're careful about who we take on, but once we've made a commitment to a business, we're all in. We'll discuss anything from a business plan to marketing ideas to how to hire and fire. We become a silent partner, in a way. Our success rate is impressive. We've made a difference and we want to keep on doing that."

Pam glanced between them. "I don't have a business."

"We know. We want you to join us as an angel."

Pam couldn't have been more surprised. "What? I don't have any experience. I don't know how to write a business plan." She held up her hand. "I never went to college. Not seriously. I took a few classes here and there, but I never got my degree. I'm in no way qualified."

"You're exactly who we need," Bea told her. "You worked with John for over a decade. You juggled children and helped your husband grow his business."

"I was involved," Pam admitted. "But that was a long time ago."

"You're smart, capable and you have good instincts," Violet added.

Pam shook her head. "No offense, but you've just met me."

Violet's smile returned. "We've done our research. We've asked around. We talked to several people who know you, including Steven."

"He never said anything. Neither did John."

"We didn't tell John," Bea admitted. "He adores you. He couldn't possibly be expected to keep a secret. Your son is very impressed with you, by the way. He thinks you'd be terrific."

Pam couldn't take it all in. "I'm really not qualified," she repeated.

"Some of what we do falls outside of the sphere of traditional business," Violet explained. "We offer counseling on whatever topic the women need most. You have led an extraordinarily successful life, Pam. You bring a wealth of knowledge. Don't worry that you are unfamiliar with the specifics like writing a business plan. We have a team that helps with that. Your job would be to be the point of contact. To find out what the women really need, then deliver the resources."

Violet glanced at Bea, who nodded, then back at Pam. "The work is unpaid, in the traditional sense. We don't take a salary. We do have the satisfaction of what we accomplish, of course. For some people, that's not enough. We're also asking that you contribute to the angel fund. So far all our loans have been paid back. We want to be able to do more. If you're interested in joining us, we'd ask you to put in what we did."

"How much was that?" she asked.

"Fifty thousand dollars."

Pam felt her mouth drop open. "Fifty thousand dollars?"

"You could do it over time," Bea said. "We understand there are implications when taking that much out of your investments. So ten thousand a month for five months would be fine."

Pam's breath caught in her chest. "How generous," she murmured. They expected her to give fifty thousand dollars, work with businesses *and* not get paid? Seriously?

"Think about it," Bea urged. "At least for a little while. Talk it over with John. We're making a difference, Pam. We're helping the next generation of women entrepreneurs. We could do so much more with you on board. We'd like to have both of you come down to the office and meet some of the women we've worked with. Hear their stories. It's an amazing opportunity."

She nodded because speaking was impossible. But in her head, she knew she was going to refuse them. What a ridiculous idea. And amount. She and John were comfortable, but that kind of money! It was impossible to consider. Ridiculous.

She would do what they'd requested. She would think about it and then she would tell them there was no way on this planet she would ever agree to do such a thing.

The Lewis family lived in a big house not too far from Pam's. It was two stories and sprawling. Of course, there had been five kids living there at one time, Shannon thought as Adam pulled into the driveway. Now his parents lived there alone.

On the drive from her condo, Adam had explained some things about his family. How there were lots of grandchildren and that his parents complained the house was too big for just the two of them, but never could find a place where they wanted to move. All really good information that would have made sense if she wasn't so nervous.

She couldn't remember the last time a guy had taken her home to meet his family. High school, maybe. Certainly not since college. Except for one of her brief engagements, and that had only been one or two very awkward meetings. It wasn't the kind of thing she usually had to face.

She'd spent more time worrying about what to wear for this family Easter dinner than any other event in the past two years. A dress, she'd thought. Nothing too sexy, but she also didn't want to look frumpy.

She'd settled on a sleeveless faux wrap dress in mint green. The front wasn't too low and the hem was only a couple of inches above her knee. She'd added nude colored pumps and a simple straw bag.

Adam parked the car, then turned toward her and took her hand in his.

"It's okay," he told her.

"What?"

"You're nervous. I get it. My family is big and loud and sometimes I have trouble dealing with them."

"If you're trying to make me feel better, you need a different strategy."

He smiled, then moved toward her and lightly kissed her. "I think you're amazing, Shannon. Just for this conversation we'll ignore how beautiful you are and how you blow me away every time you walk into a room."

She stared into his brown eyes and smiled. "Oh, I don't know. I think we could talk about that for a little while."

"And we will. But right now I want you know how proud I am to be with you. Not just for how you look, but for how you are." A muscle twitched in his jaw. "I know this isn't the best timing, but I want you to know that I love you."

Her eyes widened and her mouth went dry. Those words.

Some men spoke them lightly, but not Adam. He would only say them if he meant them.

"I love you, too," she whispered, feeling desperately shy and totally elated at the same moment.

"Yeah?"

She nodded.

His mouth curved into a huge smile. "Wow. That's so great. And you're hot, too."

She started to laugh.

He kissed her, gently at first, then lingeringly. She relaxed into his embrace, only to have the moment interrupted by a car honking. Behind them, a door slammed.

"Get a room," a low male voice called.

Adam drew back. "My brother," he said. "You braced?"

"I am now."

Because he loved her. She held the most delicious secret in her hands. One she would hold close and take out when she needed.

He got out of the car and walked around to her side, then opened the door. She stepped out into the sunny afternoon. From the backseat he pulled a couple of bottles of wine and the brownies she'd made that morning. They were still warm.

She might not be a whiz in the kitchen, but years ago she'd decided she needed a go-to dish she could take anywhere. She'd chosen brownies and had spent the better part of two months finding the perfect recipe. Countless attempts and five pounds later, she had found one that worked for her.

They walked in the house. The large foyer was two stories tall, with plenty of light. From there she could see into a formal living room that was empty, and the big dining room set for dinner.

Loud conversation and music and what sounded like a baseball game drifted in from various parts of the house. The scent of ham mingled with the sweetness of lilies.

"Kitchen first," he told her. "Once you meet Mom, you'll relax."

She wanted to say she already was, only the "I love you" charm didn't seem to be working as well as she would have hoped. The nerves returned and with it the hope she would measure up.

Adam led the way to a big, open kitchen. The cabinets were white, the accent colors blue and green. There was a massive island and a six-burner stove. But she focused on all the people milling around.

Mostly women, she thought, spotting the sixtysomething woman who must be his mother. There were also a few other women who were younger, a couple of kids and one brother or brother-in-law.

"Adam!" The older woman smiled when she spotted her son. "You're here." She crossed to him and cupped his face in her hands. "You look good."

"Thanks, Mom." He kissed her on the cheek. "Mom, this is Shannon. Shannon, my mother, Marie."

Marie was of average height. Attractive and trim. Shannon saw he got his eyes and his smile from her. As her hair was blond, he must have inherited his coloring from his father.

Marie turned to her. "So nice to meet you, Shannon. Thank you for joining us today. The whole family is here, so you're going to see us all at once. Don't worry about remembering names. I'm the important one to get to know."

Everyone laughed. Shannon felt herself relaxing.

"Thank you for inviting me," she said. "It's a pleasure to meet you."

"She made brownies," Adam told his mother.

Marie raised her eyebrows. "Did you? Impressive. Tabitha never baked."

"Mom." His voice held a warning tone. "Don't start."

"Me? I didn't say a word." Marie linked arms with Shannon and drew her close. "She cheated. Did he tell you that? A woman with two babies at home. If you're unhappy, get a divorce or take a hammer to his car. But don't cheat. It's so tacky."

Adam flushed. "Mom, I'm begging you. Stop."

Shannon held in a smile.

"I'm just being friendly, that's all. Can I help it if Tabitha didn't bake? It's not like I told her she couldn't. Not that she ever would have listened to me. All right, who haven't you met?"

The next ten minutes passed in a whirlwind of names and faces. Marie kept a firm grip on Shannon's arm as she led her through the kitchen, then into the stadium-size family room. Shannon shook hands with and smiled at all the adults. She did her best to remember which child went with which sibling.

Adam appeared at her side. He held a glass of red wine in one hand.

"Mom, Erin says the ham smells funny."

Marie went white. "What? Excuse me. I'm needed in the kitchen."

"Is everything okay?" Shannon asked anxiously.

"Sure. The ham is fine. Erin gave me a way to help you escape."

"I don't need to escape." She took the wine. "I adore your mother."

"Really?"

"Sure. She loves her family and keeps you all in line. I totally respect that."

"You do realize one day all that laser attention will be focused on you, right?"

"I should be so lucky," she said, wondering what he meant by that comment. Was he hinting at a future together? Something else she could hope for because it seemed to her that belonging to a family like this one would be a very good thing.

"I was afraid she'd scare you off."

"I'm stronger than you think."

"All right you two. Break it up."

Shannon turned and saw a pretty blonde walking toward them. "Sister," she said. "Younger and your name is something exotic and beautiful that I can't remember."

"Gabriella," she said with a laugh. "Everyone calls me Gabby. I am his younger sister." Gabby smiled at Adam. "I'm going to tell her I'm an immigration attorney. Don't correct me."

"You *are* an immigration attorney," Adam pointed out.

Gabby sighed. "If only. I'm currently the stay-at-home mom of twins. But one day they will be in school and then I'm going back to work. Not that I don't love my children, but I can't tell you how I long for adult conversation and time in an office." She looked at Shannon. "You're in business, right?"

"Yes."

"Then you know what I mean. You can go into the bathroom by yourself. No one follows you. You get to close the door and everything."

Shannon lightly touched Gabby's arm. "You have my deepest sympathy and yes, you can pee alone when you go back to work. Are you counting the days?"

"Pretty much."

More family members joined the conversation. There was plenty of teasing and laughter. Shannon had the sense that they were a very loving, close-knit family. She liked all the noise, the bustle as people moved around. There were children running everywhere. A contrast to her parents' quiet, orderly house, she thought. A place where fitting in was the ultimate goal and achieving enough to stand out was frowned upon.

Adam slipped his arm around her. She relaxed into his embrace. He loved her. He'd told her and Adam wasn't the kind of man to play with words that powerful. She could trust them, and him.

Fifteen

THE STUDIO WAS QUIET—A WELCOME RELIEF, Nicole thought. While she adored all her clients and knew that without them, she would be lost, emotionally and financially, every now and then she just wanted quiet.

She was tired of fighting, she thought sadly. She was tired of not understanding Eric, of being disappointed by him. She would guess he was equally weary of their lack of connection and her refusal to be as excited by his dream as he was.

Sometimes she thought that divorce was the only option. She whispered the word in her head and turned it over in her mind. Still, she couldn't imagine saying it out loud. She and Eric were *married*.

But what were the alternatives? Really splitting up? When she considered the logistics, the reality of being a single mom, of possibly having to pay alimony to Eric so he could keep writing his stupid screenplay, she got so angry and so afraid, she couldn't breathe. The thought of going through that, of tearing apart their lives—it was awful. And worse, truly much, much worse, was what a divorce would do to

Tyler. While he wasn't as close to his dad as she would like, Eric was his father. She couldn't separate them. Couldn't force her son to travel from home to home, spending weekends with one and weekdays with the other. How could they make that work?

She looked at the names on the paper in her hand. Two were for therapists and one was for an attorney. The first two came from Pam and the latter from Shannon. It had been Shannon who had explained the grim reality of community property.

The house wasn't an issue. It was in Nicole's name and she'd never added Eric to the deed. He'd never asked, which only helped her case. Even more important, over the past year or so, she'd been the only one bringing in money. So whatever happened, she would keep her home.

But the business was more complicated. While it was in her name, they'd bought it with joint assets. So he had a claim there. Shannon had started to explain about business valuation, but Nicole's eyes had glazed over. She wasn't ready to know that much. She wasn't ready to go there.

Nicole fingered the paper. She knew she had to make a choice, one way or the other. Which was it to be?

She drew in a breath and picked up her cell phone, then dialed the first number. Therapy, she thought as the call connected. She went right to voice mail, as Pam had told her she would. The psychologist would call her back and set up an appointment.

Pam had explained how she and John had seen the woman while they were dealing with Brandon's difficult stage. There had been family counseling, of course, but she and John had wanted to see someone different. Someone who was in it for them and their marriage.

"Every marriage has its ups and downs," Pam had told her. "Dealing with Brandon's drinking and drug use had been so awful. John and I had ended up fighting all the time. Seeing the therapist helped us see that we were taking our fear out on each other instead of using each other for support. She's great. You'll love her."

Pam had also provided the name of a male therapist in case Nicole talked Eric into couples counseling. Most guys were more comfortable with a man, she'd said. Wise advice, but then Pam was always ready with the upbeat and practical suggestion.

Nicole left her name and number and mentioned Pam as the person who referred her, then hung up. She drew in a breath and noticed she wasn't as tense as she'd been. The knot in her stomach was a little smaller and her breath came easier.

"Okay," she whispered to herself. "I made the right choice. Therapy."

She had no idea how she was going to pay for it, but that was a problem for later. This was good—she had a direction. She would fix things with Eric. They would be a family.

A direction chosen and some small amount of faith restored, she turned her attention back to her computer. There were monthly bills to be paid.

She got out her business checkbook, then went on to her bank's website and used the bill-pay function. For a small fee they would even produce paychecks for her employees—a real gift. Because payroll for those not blessed with the accounting gene was a nightmare.

After paying the bills and generating the paychecks, she updated her balance. Talk about a virtuous hour, she thought. She had another hour until her next class. She could go get a coffee or she could stretch and do a mini-workout for herself. That would feel good.

She rose and started for the mats against the wall. As she walked toward them, someone knocked on her locked front door.

She changed direction, then slowed when she saw Eric. She couldn't remember the last time he'd come to the office. The knot returned when she got closer and saw his face.

He was wide-eyed and flushed. Everything about his body language told her something had happened. Her heart felt as though it actually stopped as she fumbled with the lock.

"Is it Tyler?" she demanded the second the door was open.

"What? No. He's fine. He's at day care. Why would you think something was wrong with him?"

"Because something's happened."

Eric surprised her by laughing, then he grabbed her hands. "I forget that you know me. Of course you'd guess." He spun her around. "Nicole, you're not going to believe it. I can't believe it. I did it. I swear to God, I did it."

"Did what?"

"I sold the screenplay. I have an offer and it's incredible." He kissed her on the mouth, then stepped back, as if he couldn't possibly stay still.

"You know I've been in meetings, right?" He walked to the door, then turned and moved toward her. "I can't believe it."

She was stunned. More than stunned. A little chagrined. She hadn't known he'd finished the screenplay. Not that he ever told her much lately, but still. Sold. He'd done it.

"I'm really proud of you," she told him. "You had a dream and you made it happen."

"I know. I'm still trying to figure it all out." He laughed again. "The money. Want to know how much they offered?"

"Sure."

"Guess how much."

"I have no way of knowing. Honey, it's not about the money. You sold a screenplay. No matter what, you'll have that for the rest of your life. It's incredible."

"A million dollars."

The room seemed to tilt a little. She shook her head, confident she hadn't heard right. "What?"

He threw back his head and yelled, "I sold my screenplay for a million dollars." He raced toward her, caught her in his arms and spun her around. "One million dollars. My agent's negotiating for more, but screw that. It's fantastic. Do you know what this means? I'll be helping again. Paying the bills, buying food. You want a new car, because you can have one. A Mercedes."

He put her down and kissed her. "I gotta go. I have to meet with my agent and then the studio wants to talk to me." He was beaming. He kissed her again. "I couldn't have done it without you, Nicole. I hope you know that. You're the best. I'll be late tonight because my critique group's taking me out. But you and I will celebrate soon. This weekend. I promise. I love you."

And then he was gone.

She stood alone in the quiet of her studio and didn't know what to feel. What to think. Eric had sold his screenplay for a million dollars?

She sank onto the floor and drew in a steadying breath.

When had that happened? How? And why hadn't she known it was possible? Of course the news was wonderful. Amazing and good for him. Of course she appreciated that money wouldn't be tight now. And he'd said he loved her. She hadn't heard those words in months. It was all wonderful and exciting.

But it wasn't anything they were doing together. Once again he was gone and she had no idea when she would see him again.

No, she told herself. Everything would be fine. He needed time to celebrate. He'd earned it. Good for him. And later, they would figure it all out together.

"It's ridiculous," Pam said firmly. "And I'm done having this conversation."

"You wouldn't say that if they'd come to me," Steven told her.

"It's a group that supports women," she pointed out, trying not to let her annoyance bleed into her voice. Why on earth her family couldn't let this go was beyond her. "They wouldn't have come to you."

"I can be very supportive of women."

Pam rolled her eyes. "Are you really going to go there? Because we can talk about how I took care of you after you were circumcised."

Her twenty-six-year-old son held up both hands in a gesture of surrender. "Sorry, Mom. I'll do anything if you don't talk about my penis."

She relaxed. Order was restored, she thought happily. "As long as you remember, I have ultimate power."

"Always and forever. You are the queen of this family and we worship at your feet."

"That's going a little far, but I accept your fealty."

They were in the kitchen, where all important conversations took place. It had been a couple of weeks since her meeting with Bea and Violet and for reasons she couldn't understand, no one in the family was letting it go.

She'd told John, expecting him to be as shocked and outraged as she had been, but he'd told her they could afford it and she should consider it. Forty-eight hours later, she'd still been openmouthed.

"It's fifty thousand dollars," she reminded Steven as she got up to get more coffee.

"You have the money. Besides, you're not blowing it. You're paying it forward in a really cool way. Come on, Mom, you could make a big difference. You know how you love taking care of all of us. Imagine what you could do in the real world."

"I don't have the business experience."

"You're selling yourself short."

Just what John had said, she thought, both pleased and frustrated by her family's faith in her. Of course, Steven was just like his dad. They were both over six feet, with dark blond hair and blue eyes. Strong men with good heads and gentle hearts. The difference being John had married young and settled down and Steven's idea of a long-term relationship was six weeks.

"Are you seeing anyone special?" she asked as she returned to the table and handed him his coffee.

"You know we don't talk about my love life."

"We don't talk about your sex life. There's a difference. Don't you want to fall in love?"

"Sure. One day. But for now, variety is the spice of life."

Part of the problem was Steven had it easy with women,

she thought with both pride and concern. He was handsome and charming.

She held her mug in both hands. “If you’re worried about it getting boring with just one person, it doesn’t have to. Sure there are times when things get routine, but there are also ways to break out of that. Your father and I still find each other exciting.”

Her son froze, his mug raised halfway to his mouth. The color left his face and his eyes widened. “Mom, I beg you. Stop. Honest to God, I would rather talk about my penis than this.”

Pam’s mouth twitched. “I’m just trying to reassure you.”

“I know and it’s great that you and Dad still do that kind of stuff. But I don’t want to know. Seriously. Don’t take this wrong, but it’s gross.”

“All right. We’ll talk about your penis instead.”

The mug slammed onto the table and coffee spilled over the edge. Steven sprang to his feet.

“Okay, that’s it. I’m out of here.”

He circled the table, kissed her cheek and called out a goodbye to Lulu.

“We’re still doing it like rabbits,” Pam called after him.

“I can’t hear you.”

The front door slammed shut.

She chuckled as she cleaned up the mess and put his mug in the dishwasher. Sometimes her kids were so easy to rattle. It almost wasn’t a sport.

She glanced at the clock, then pulled out the ingredients for meat loaf. She could prepare it now and still give Lulu a bath before John got home.

She was looking forward to seeing her husband more than usual. Not just because thinking about him still gave her a little thrill, but because of what Nicole had said when she'd called earlier. Eric had sold his screenplay for a million dollars.

Nicole was still in shock, which made sense to Pam. Who knew he was that talented? That he was making that much progress? Good for him and the family, but still, very strange.

The rest of the afternoon passed quickly. Pam finished her chores and popped the meat loaf in the oven. Lulu strutted around in her pink T-shirt, all fresh and happy after her bath. Her rash was better, so she wasn't quite so uncomfortable.

Pam got out the bag of potatoes and put a couple in a bowl. She had just reached for the peeler when she heard the garage door open.

Lulu barked and headed for the side door. Pam's stomach gave a little *ping* of excitement. Oh, yeah, it was good to be her.

"How's my best little girl?" John asked as he walked into the house. Lulu yipped with happiness as the pack was restored to its full glory.

"And how's my best big girl?" he asked as he came into the kitchen. He smiled at her, the dog still in his hands. "Meat loaf," he said just before he kissed her. "My favorite. You spoil me."

"Always." She stepped into his embrace.

Lulu was caught between them. The dog alternated who got puppy kisses while Pam and John did some adult kissing of their own. When they came up for air, he patted her butt.

"How was your day?" he asked.

"Good. Yours?"

"Not bad."

She took the dog and gave him a little push toward the family room. "Go. I know very well there's a Dodger game on even as we speak. Go and watch it. I'll call you when dinner's ready."

He paused to drop another kiss on her cheek. "Have I told you how lucky I am?"

"You have and you're going to get even luckier later tonight."

He chuckled, then walked toward the family room.

Pam set Lulu on the floor. The dog trotted away to join John. Not that she was all that interested in baseball, but she did enjoy a snooze on a warm lap.

Pam continued her preparations for dinner. She set the table while the potatoes and carrots cooked, then opened a bottle of wine. Lulu trotted back into the kitchen and stared at her.

"What?" Pam asked. "You've already eaten, remember?"

Lulu stared at her for a second, then barked.

"What?"

The dog looked toward the family room.

"John? Is everything okay?"

There was no answer.

Pam followed Lulu through the doorway. John was stretched out on his recliner, his eyes closed. The game played softly in the background.

"He's sleeping," she told the dog. "Silly girl. John, honey, it's nearly time for dinner."

John didn't stir.

Pam walked close and shook his arm. "John? John? Wake up. John!"

Sixteen

THE EILAND HOUSE WAS FULL OF PEOPLE Shannon didn't know. Somber strangers who were mostly dressed in black, murmuring about how unexpected it had been. How shocking. Poor Pam. The kids were mentioned by name. No one had seen it coming. He'd been so strong, so healthy. How would she survive?

All great questions, Shannon thought as she walked through the formal living room and picked up abandoned plates and cups. She carried them to the kitchen, where Nicole and a woman named Hayley were loading the dishwasher.

The caterer had offered to arrange for staff to assist with cleanup and putting out the food, but Shannon and Nicole had said they would handle it. Because somehow it felt like helping in a time when there was genuinely nothing to do. Hayley, who had introduced herself as John's secretary, obviously felt the same way. Every fifteen minutes she carried a coffeepot throughout the room of mourners, offering refills.

"Hey," Adam said as he came up and put his arm around her. "How are you holding up?"

"Okay. I was just thinking how we all get caught up in ridiculous tasks at a time like this. I can't stop cleaning up after people. Hayley's obsessed with the coffee and Nicole keeps topping up all the buffet items."

He squeezed her close. "No one saw this coming. We're all in shock. John was a great guy. From what my dad told me, there was no evidence of any heart trouble. His blood pressure was low and he was plenty active on the job. It was just one of those things."

Shannon knew what he meant but doubted Pam saw it that way.

She visually searched the room until she spotted Pam standing surrounded by her kids and a few friends. She was pale and seemed to have lost weight. Impossible considering it had only been three days, and yet she looked gaunt and drawn.

Shannon saw that everyone else was talking, except Pam. She stood in the middle of the group and yet entirely alone. Her hands shook as she balanced a plate of uneaten food. The half sandwich and scoop of mac and cheese trembled.

Jen, Pam's oldest, started to cry. Her husband led her to the largest sofa. Several guests moved to make room.

Jen was pregnant, Shannon thought, remembering when Pam had told her the news. The stress couldn't be good for her or the baby. Nor was the realization that her child would never know his or her grandfather. Was Pam thinking that? Was she aware she was going to be a grandmother alone?

Shannon couldn't grasp what it must feel like to have been with someone for over thirty years, yet imagining the loss was somehow easier. Maybe because pain was universal. Whatever the cause, everyone had felt it in some form or another.

She wanted to say something to her friend, to offer comfort. A ridiculous need. Because there was no comfort to offer. Pam had been married longer than Nicole had been alive. She'd just lost her husband. She had defined herself, lived her life, planned her day, raised her kids, all of it as John's wife. He was the rhythm of her days. And now he was gone and she was expected to go on? Impossible.

"I feel so bad for her," she said, not sure how to articulate any of it.

"Me, too. It's horrible."

She touched his arm, then stepped away. "I need to get back to my compulsive cleaning."

"Sure. I'll call you later tonight."

She nodded and allowed herself a moment to savor the fact that he would call. That she could depend on him. That at the end of every call, every date now, he told her he loved her. He said it clearly, looking into her eyes, with an intensity that chased away any doubts.

She walked through the family room and picked up a few plates and cups, then returned to the kitchen.

Nicole was alone, leaning against the counter. Shannon walked up to her and they hugged.

"It's so awful," Nicole said. "I feel sick to my stomach. I never told Pam, but sometimes I would pretend they were my parents. When things were bad, it was nice to think I wasn't alone, you know? So in a way, it's like I lost a part of my family. Not that I would tell her that. Am I making sense?"

"You are. We're all rattled. It's horrible for everyone."

"Especially Pam," Nicole said with a sigh. "She must be terrified."

"I think she's still in shock."

"I would be and I'm used to Eric being gone a lot. John was home every night, though. She's not used to that."

Shannon nodded without commenting on Eric. He'd been at the funeral, but then had left. Nicole had ridden back to Pam's in Shannon's car. Nicole had said something about him taking a meeting.

They watched the people move through the buffet line. There were several hot dishes, along with sandwiches and salads. On the island were the coffeemaker, pitchers with different kinds of juice and a plastic container filled with ice and sodas in cans. Open bottles of wine stood next to long-stemmed glasses. Cupcakes, cookies and brownies were on a smaller table by the door to the family room.

"Jen and her husband are staying with Pam tonight," Shannon said. "Steven mentioned he would be moving in for a week or so."

Nicole nodded. "That's nice of him, but then what? She has to figure out how everything is going to be different."

"I know. I was thinking we'd back off for the next couple of weeks. She'll have plenty of friends and family around. What if you and I agree to hang out with her after that? Through the time when everyone returns to their regular lives and she's still in shock."

Nicole nodded as tears filled her eyes. "That's perfect. I want to do that with you. We'll make a schedule or something. Because Pam's always been there for me."

"Yes," Nicole said firmly so the woman on the other end of the phone wouldn't know she was nervous. "I'm confirming my account balance."

Because Eric had received payment on his screenplay

and she couldn't quite grasp that much money was sitting in their checking account.

She waited while the woman typed.

"You have five hundred and fifty-one thousand dollars in your account."

Nicole exhaled slowly. "Okay. Great. Thank you."

She hung up, then tossed her cell phone onto the sofa. Hysterical laughter and tears both threatened. It was real. Totally and completely real. The contract had been signed and Eric had been paid. Fifteen percent had gone to his agent and he'd told her he was going to send off thirty percent to the government, so they wouldn't have to worry about that. Talk about being responsible. Just as startling, he'd put the balance of the money into their joint account.

Until this second, until she'd known for sure he would, she'd been half expecting him to take the money and run. Shannon's talk about community property be damned.

But he hadn't and now Nicole was left feeling pretty crummy about herself. Sure, Eric was busy a lot and he could be difficult and he wasn't always there for her and Tyler. But he obviously hadn't been secretly waiting to disappear from their marriage.

That was good, right?

Despicable Me 2 played on as Tyler cuddled next to her. In the distance the sound of the shower continued. She closed her eyes and told herself it *was* good. She had to look on the bright side and a few other clichés. Because as far as she could tell, selling the screenplay might have put money in their checking account but it hadn't changed anything else.

Eric was still gone all the time. He had meetings. Actually he was *taking* meetings. He had a rewrite due and was working on that. He was still surfing most mornings.

The sound of the shower turned off and she opened her eyes. For a second she wanted to hide her cell phone, which was ridiculous. Why would Eric care that she'd called the bank? He would probably think it was funny. It wasn't like he knew she'd been worried he would simply disappear with his windfall.

"Are we going to the park tomorrow, Mommy?" Tyler asked.

"We are. I get home at noon, then we're going to have lunch and go out all afternoon."

Her son smiled up at her. "I like the park."

"Me, too. After we're done with the park I thought we'd go see Auntie Pam and Lulu." Because she and Shannon were starting their plan of visiting their friend regularly.

So far Pam hadn't returned to class. She also wasn't very talkative whenever Nicole phoned to check in on her. Not a surprise— How could you get over losing a husband of over thirty years? Nicole was sure Pam couldn't remember what life was like without him.

Eric walked into the living room. He'd dressed casually— new jeans and a shirt she didn't remember seeing. Both looked expensive. Not that she was going to ask.

"What's the meeting tonight?" she asked.

"Jacob."

She nodded, although she had no idea who Jacob was. There were too many new people in her husband's life these days.

"I shouldn't be late," he added, then smiled at Tyler before returning his attention to her. "Can we talk in the kitchen for a second?"

"Sure." She kissed Tyler's forehead. "I'll be right back."

He nodded as he watched the minions having fun on what looked like a tropical island.

Nicole followed Eric into their small kitchen.

It was clean for once, mostly because she'd spent an hour after dinner scrubbing it. Since selling his screenplay Eric hadn't bothered with any of the household chores. Something she was going to have to discuss with him. But she saw him so rarely these days and fighting about chores seemed…

She couldn't say what. Uncomfortable wasn't right. She had a bad feeling that because he'd scored such a huge paycheck, she felt she didn't have the right to bug him about stuff around the house. A ridiculous concept that suggested contribution was only valued if it was monetary. Applying that theory, then before he'd sold the screenplay, he should have been doing everything. And he hadn't. Nor had she expected him to.

"About Tyler," he began, then checked his watch. It was gold and she couldn't remember seeing it before. "I'm going to be busy with my rewrites and meetings. There's no way I can be taking him to day care and picking him up."

She opened her mouth to protest, but he shook his head. "Let me finish."

"All right." She folded her arms across her chest and told herself she wasn't going to give in to anger. That the pissy feeling would pass.

"I want us to get some help around here. Like I said, I'm going to be busy and you have responsibilities with your business. Now that we have the money, it's ridiculous not to use it to make things easier. I think we should get a nanny to pick up Tyler and a cleaning service to come in once a week."

Talk about reasonable, she thought, oddly resentful and not sure why. "That would help a lot."

"Good. Do you want me to ask around for suggestions? Maybe we could get a housekeeper who is also a nanny. It would be nice if you didn't have to always be scrambling to cook dinner."

"I, ah, okay. I wouldn't know where to start with something like that," she admitted. A part-time housekeeper-slash-nanny-slash-cook? In her world? Was this really happening?

"I'll get some names and you can interview them."

"Thank you." She drew in a breath. "Eric, I appreciate that you're concerned about the logistics of our life. Thanks for that. But what about us?"

He stared at her blankly. "What do you mean?"

"You're gone a lot, which is fine. You have to be right now. We both have responsibilities. But you and I never spend any time together. We never talk. I'm worried about us."

Several emotions chased across his face. They were too quick for her to catch and read, so she was left wondering what he was thinking.

"I know," he said. "You're right. We need to find some time. And we will." He kissed her. "I gotta run. I'll see you later."

And with that, he was gone. Nicole stood in her kitchen and hoped he meant what he said. That he was paying more than lip service to the cracked vessel that was their marriage. Because if they weren't careful, it was going to shatter and fall apart completely.

* * *

Pam wasn't sure when the house had become the enemy. She would have said she knew every inch of it. She'd lived through remodels, understood the idiosyncrasies of the various systems. She was at peace in her house. Or she had been.

Now it was a torture chamber, a prison filled with memories. A mocking, living creature that held her captive with the simple reality that she had nowhere else to go.

John had lived in this house. John had talked and laughed and slept and made love and ultimately died in this house. She wandered from room to room, searching for something. Him, most likely, because even though her head knew the truth, her heart was still waiting to hear his footsteps, his voice. Her body longed to be held, to be comforted. Because only he could understand how she grieved.

The phone rang. Pam ignored it. She didn't want to take any calls, didn't want to hear the platitudes. Time did not heal. The gray skies were not going to turn blue. She wouldn't find closure. What the hell was closure? How could there be closure? She wasn't recovering from something small. Something simple. Every time she woke up, she remembered that the very essence of her being had been ripped from her. She was like one of those people who accidentally survived a horrific accident. She was parts, not a person, and she should have been left by the side of the road to die.

But no matter how she wished that to be true, she lived. She breathed, she walked through her house and knew that nothing was ever going to be the same again.

She stood in the center of her kitchen and shivered. Not from cold, but from a lack of warmth. A lack of comfort. She shivered with the realization that there was no deal to be made, there was nothing she could sell or offer. No authority would listen to her begging and respond with compassion. John was dead. He was never coming back.

She heard the click of Lulu's nails as her dog circled her anxiously. She reached down and gathered the small animal in her arms. For the past three weeks Lulu had been her silent companion. Except for the funeral, Pam hadn't left the house and Lulu hadn't left her side. At night, when Pam curled up in John's old recliner, Lulu curled up with her.

Her cell phone rang. Strains of "Footloose" filled the kitchen, which meant she could ignore the call. When her kids called, the phone ringtone was Michael Jackson's "Thriller." Not that she loved the song so much, but they all claimed it made them crazy, so it was a family joke that she'd chosen it.

She'd been careful to always take their calls so they wouldn't worry. She was able to do that much, at least. Let her children believe that she was healing. A ridiculous thought, but one they seemed to think was important.

John would have wanted that, she thought, still holding Lulu close and letting the dog's small body warm her. They would have discussed how well Brandon was doing in medical school and how he didn't need more to worry about. That Steven was struggling to fill his father's shoes at the business. And Jen had to stay calm because of the baby. So many reasons that none of her children could know how she woke every morning only to watch her heart bleed out yet again.

Her stomach rumbled. She looked at the clock. It was nearly four in the afternoon. She wasn't sure of the day. Time had started blurring. She knew at some point she had to eat, but the thought of food made her want to vomit.

It didn't matter how hungry she was, she simply couldn't stand to chew and swallow. Every few days she threw out the casseroles that were in the refrigerator and pulled a few more out of the freezer. She fed Lulu when the dog told her it was time. She let her out in the yard, collected the mail every day, paid the bills that arrived and when she thought she might have been in the same clothes for several days, she showered and changed them.

The first week had been different. People had been with her all the time. They had guided the rhythm of her now broken life. But one by one they'd left. There were other things to be tended to, other places to be. Jen had stayed the longest, but after four or five days,. she, too, had returned home.

Pam didn't mind the solitude. She bled whether someone was here or not. The nights didn't bother her, mostly because there was little sleep to be had. When she was alone, she could cry or scream or simply stand in the middle of the room and do nothing.

The doorbell rang. Lulu barked and struggled to get down. Pam put her on the floor and the little dog took off to announce that someone had arrived.

Pam followed more slowly. She wasn't completely sure of the day, so didn't know if her visitor was as simple as the UPS man or as complicated as anyone else.

She opened the door and saw Shannon standing there. Nicole and Tyler were beside her.

"You're not answering your phone," Shannon said by way of greeting. "That's going to get people to worrying."

"I don't want to talk to anyone," Pam admitted, trying to remember if she'd invited the three of them over. She didn't think so. "Why are you here?"

"Because we love you. Now let us in."

Pam stepped aside because it was easier. Tyler rushed toward her and Pam instinctively bent down to hug the small boy. For that brief second when she held him, she could breathe. Then she straightened and the hell returned.

Nicole smiled sympathetically. "Hey," she said softly. "We're all here for you."

Pam nodded, knowing she meant well, but that no company, no words, could possibly help. Shannon walked in, a large pizza box in her hand. The smell of cheese and tomato sauce made her stomach growl again. This time it cramped, as well, and she swayed a little on her feet.

"Are you okay?" Shannon asked. She closed the door behind herself and set the pizza box on the foyer table. After hanging her purse and jacket, she scooped up Lulu. "Hey, pretty girl. How's your mom?"

"I'm all right." Pam spoke deliberately, thinking about each word. Planning them so they came out in the right sequence. Normal conversation seemed impossible right now. How did people know what to say next?

"I'm going to get Tyler settled in the family room," Nicole said. "We brought movies."

Tyler went with her obediently. Because he was still at an age when being around Mom and Dad was the best part of the day. Pam remembered what that had been like—when all three kids had competed for her attention. That had been nice. Of course, John had still been with her.

Shannon put down the dog and picked up the box. "Come on. Let's eat. I'm starving. I missed lunch. Usually my department is a well-oiled machine but every now and then we screw up as much as everyone else. It's so discouraging. All is well now. I've chastised the ones who made the mistake and they are suitably afraid of me once again. Order is restored."

Pam listened to the words and wondered if any of them were funny. Should she laugh? Was that the right thing to do? She wasn't sure about anything anymore.

Following Shannon seemed like the easiest course of action, so she did. Once in the kitchen, her friend set the box from The Slice Is Right on the kitchen table and got out four plates.

"Have you been eating at all?" Shannon asked as she moved around the kitchen.

Pam thought about lying, but what was the point? Did it matter if anyone other than her children knew the truth? "No."

"I didn't think so. You've lost weight. Come on. Have a seat."

Pam walked over to the chair Shannon had pulled out and sat down. Her friend put a slice of mushroom and green pepper pizza—Pam's favorite—on a plate.

"What about Lulu?"

Pam stared at the melted cheese, the roasted vegetables, and her mouth watered. In that moment, she could see herself biting, chewing, then swallowing. In that moment, there wasn't the knowledge that her throat had sealed so tight she could never eat anything again.

"I feed her when she says it's time."

"I'll take care of her dinner," Shannon said. "Just take a bite. It's delicious."

Nicole walked into the kitchen. "Tyler says the cheese side only, please."

"I've already put his slice on a plate." Shannon pointed to a plate on the counter.

They continued to talk. Pam listened, but much of the time, their words didn't make sense. They came from far away—almost as if from under water.

She reached for her own pizza slice. It was heavy. Substantial. She took a small bite. It was still hot, but not burning. Flavors exploded on her tongue. The slight bite of the sauce, the hint of sweetness in the dough, the smooth, creamy tang of the cheese. The grilled vegetables offered a subtle counterpoint of tastes, with the peppers adding crunch.

Shannon set down a glass of orange juice. The small TV in the corner clicked on and channels switched. The sound of a shopping show chased away the quiet of the afternoon.

Pam chewed carefully and swallowed. She waited for her body to revolt, as it had every time she'd tried to eat since…

Her mind shied away from the ugliness, so she thought only of the pizza. She took another bite as carefully as she had the first, chewed and swallowed.

Behind her came the sound of Shannon feeding Lulu and Nicole's quiet conversation. Pam didn't bother to turn around or participate. She focused only on the food and her careful, deliberate eating.

Every time she swallowed, her stomach ached a little less. Her head cleared and she wasn't quite so cold. She tried the juice and was surprised at how good it tasted. She finished the glass, then got up to get more. She was surprised to find herself alone in the kitchen. Had her friends left?

Lulu had finished her canned food and now chomped on her special extrasoft kibble. She looked up at Pam and wagged her tail. Pam's face pulled in way that made her uncomfortable. She touched her cheek and realized she'd smiled.

Horror washed through her. She clutched her stomach

and waited to throw up all she'd eaten. Only she didn't. Her stomach grumbled for more food while her parched throat begged for juice.

She'd smiled! How could she have done that? She was never going to smile again. Never laugh, never not ache. It wasn't right. It wasn't allowed.

The room dipped and swayed as she struggled to breathe, to understand what was happening to her. The phone began to ring.

She wanted to ignore it, the way she always did. But with friends in the house—and where had the women gone?—she couldn't. She picked up the receiver.

"Hello?"

"Mrs. Eiland?"

"Yes."

"This is Dr. Altman's office. I'm calling to confirm your consultation tomorrow at three thirty."

Pam shook her head. "What? I'm sorry. I have no idea what you're talking about."

"Your consultation. For your face-lift."

The cold returned. A face-lift? "No," Pam said clearly. "I'm not getting a face-lift. My husband died. John is dead and who cares if I look old or not? How ridiculous." She started to cry. "How could it matter now?"

"I've got it," Nicole said gently, taking the phone from her. "Hello? I'm Pam's friend. Yes, it's all right. You had no way of knowing. It was sudden. Just a few weeks ago. Please cancel the appointment. Thank you."

Pam leaned against the island as tears poured down her cheeks. She wanted to vomit, to empty herself of anything that would sustain life, but her body refused to cooperate. Nicole put the phone on the counter, then returned to her side.

"Hey," she said gently. "Come here."

Warm arms held on tight. Pam clung to her, but it wasn't the same. It wasn't John. It would never be John.

She wasn't sure how long she cried. Eventually she straightened and reached for the box of tissue. She wiped her eyes and blew her nose.

"I'm sorry," she managed to say, even though she wasn't.

"It's okay. That's why we came by. To be with you." Nicole led her back to the table. "Try to eat a little more. I've got a load of laundry in and Shannon's changing the sheets."

"You don't have to do that."

"I know, but we want to." She sat across from her and squeezed her hand.

"You have lives, too."

Nicole shrugged. Her blond ponytail moved with the gesture. "Sure, but you're a part of that. I want to be here. I don't know how to help, but I do know how to do laundry. So that's what I'm going to do."

Pam nodded. Her friend rose, hugged her again, then headed out of the kitchen. Pam reached for the pizza box, then pulled her hands away. In the distance she heard the chugging sound of the washer. On the TV some woman explained why the blazer she was selling was perfect for spring. Pam rested her arms on the table and her head on her hands. Then she breathed in the pain that was missing John and let it fill her until there was nothing else.

"It was brutal," Shannon admitted, still stunned by Pam's grief. "Her pain is a living being. There's no escaping it. I'm not sure how she's getting through the day."

She sat on her sofa, her feet tucked under her. Adam was next to her, angled toward her. He held her hand in his.

"They were together a long time," he said. "That's really rough. My mom keeps talking about how she couldn't survive losing my dad. That she would never be as strong as Pam."

"That's how I feel, too. But I'm sure that's what Pam would have told everyone. We have no way of knowing what we'd do. I just wish I could help."

"You were there for her. That means a lot."

Shannon wasn't so sure. "Nicole and I did stuff, but does it really matter that she had clean sheets? There's still plenty of food. People brought it by and one of her friends arranged for groceries to be delivered for a few weeks." She wrinkled her nose. "I got rid of the last of the flowers. They'd reached the point where they just smelled awful. I don't know if she noticed, or if she didn't want to let go of the reminders of the funeral."

She didn't have a lot of experience with this kind of suffering. She'd never known anyone close who had died.

"You did a good thing," Adam pointed out. "Taking care of her. Your plan with Nicole is a good one. You'll be there for her and make sure she heals."

Shannon nodded. Assuming a person could heal from this sort of thing, she thought sadly. "She's so raw. I never expected that. I hate to admit this, but it's hard to be around her." She bit her lower lip.

Adam shifted closer. "Don't beat yourself up for being scared of all that emotion. It's hard to watch someone grieve. You stayed with her. That's what matters."

"I hope so. I just can't begin to imagine what it must be like." She'd been through breakups before, but nothing like this. She supposed that part of it was that she'd never loved anyone for that long. She'd been hurt, but never devastated. No one had ever been her world.

"Was it like that for you when your marriage broke up?" she asked him.

Adam shook his head. "No. We were living separate lives. I was angry and upset, but I wasn't grieving. Not the way she is. That's the difference. While I never would have chosen to get a divorce, I was part of the problem. Pam's the innocent party in what's happening to her."

She studied his face as he spoke, taking in the way his mouth moved and how he always looked at her when he talked. He was in the moment.

She'd seen him with his family. He was understanding with his parents and caring with his siblings. He adored his kids and did all he could to be the best dad possible. She loved him and for the first time in her life, she knew she could finally have it all. The dream—a career *and* a family. A man who loved her, kids, maybe even a dog.

"I'm turning forty soon," she said slowly, because talking about her birthday was so much easier than saying what was really on her mind.

He grinned. "I know. That's going to be some party."

"I hope so, but it's really not all that important. I have goals in my life. I've accomplished a lot of them. My career, where I live, the travel. But there's a lot more to being happy than a job and money."

His smile faded, as he nodded slowly. "You're right. There is. There's connecting with someone. Shannon, you're important to me. You know that, right?"

"Yes."

They both paused as the weight of the moment hit her. They were getting in deep, she thought, and she was both excited and terrified. This was the place she'd mostly avoided because she'd never seen it working out before. She'd never thought she wanted to grow old with someone. Except for Adam. She'd met his dad, had watched his parents interact, and she wanted that, too.

The thought of being a stepparent scared her. Oliver was easy, but Char was more of a challenge. Not that he was proposing, but what if he did? Did she want to say yes?

She cleared her throat. "You're important to me, too."

He gave her a rueful smile. "Now we're both dancing around the elephant in the room. It's too soon to take this to the next logical step, but I want you to know I'm thinking about it. A lot. You're so special to me. I love you and I respect you. I need you to tell me if you're thinking the same thing."

Something of a challenge, she thought as butterflies dive-bombed her stomach, considering they weren't saying what *it* was. They'd both said they loved each other, which meant the elephant was very possibly getting married.

"I hope we are," she murmured, shyness making her wanting to duck her head. She forced herself to keep meeting his gaze. "I want to be with you. I want us to be a family."

He leaned in and kissed her. "I want that, too. I'm glad you feel the same way."

In for a penny, she thought ruefully. "I want to have a baby."

Adam pulled back so quickly, she thought he might snap a bone. The warmth in his eyes faded and his mouth twisted into a not-happy expression. "You mean get pregnant?"

The question sounded a lot like an accusation. Shannon

quickly folded her arms across her chest and tucked herself more firmly into the corner of the sofa.

Something an awful lot like shame chilled her. She told herself she'd done nothing wrong. She was being honest and if Adam couldn't handle that, then maybe she was all wrong about him.

She raised her chin. "Getting pregnant is the traditional way to have a child, so yes."

"Shannon, I can't. I've had a vasectomy. I thought you knew."

Seventeen

PAM HUNG ON TO LULU AS IF THE SMALL DOG were the only thing keeping her safe in an otherwise not-to-be-trusted world. At Steven's insistence, she'd made her way to the office to meet with him and the company's lawyer. Not anything she wanted to deal with, but she'd recognized her son's stubborn tone. He'd said if it was too much for her to deal with, he and the lawyer would come to her. Which seemed like a generous offer, but it meant that Pam wasn't in control. If she went there, she got to decide when to leave.

But now that she was in the building that she and John had bought together so many years ago, now that she had to face the polite yet sad smiles of his employees, she knew it had been a mistake. There was no way she could get through whatever conversation Steven wanted to have without screaming. And if she started to scream, he would guess she wasn't as together as she pretended.

Maybe that wasn't a bad thing, she thought as Steven fussed with his fancy Keurig coffeemaker and brewed her a cup. Maybe someone should lock her up in a mental ward somewhere. As long as they drugged her, she wouldn't mind. Oblivion sounded really nice these days. She didn't want to have to think, didn't want to have to feel. Didn't want to deal with anything.

"I'd take you with me," she whispered to Lulu, not wanting the dog to think she was being left behind.

Steven handed her a tall mug with the company logo. Pam did her best to keep her fingers from trembling. She remembered when she and John had chosen the mugs. They had gotten so many samples, they'd ended up having a dessert and coffee party with their friends. Everyone had taken away a sample mug with them. There'd been a lot of trading between guests for colors and sizes. They'd had so much fun that night.

Her eyes burned with the familiar pressure of tears. She drew in a breath and reminded herself that when she got home later, she would be alone. She could curl up in John's chair and do nothing but breathe. There would be no expectations, no conversations.

Steven got his own coffee and sat down at his desk. She studied his face, taking in the shadows under his eyes and the tension in his shoulders. The physical manifestations of his grief reminded her she wasn't the only one suffering.

"How are you?" she asked.

"Okay. Tired. Sad." Steven cleared his throat. "It's hard to be here every day without him."

"Oh, honey, I'm sorry. Of course it is. I have my ghosts at the house, but you have as many here."

He nodded. "Everything is exactly the same and totally different." He glanced toward the closed office door and lowered his voice. "I called that counselor you mentioned.

The one you and Dad saw when Brandon was having his trouble."

She nodded. "I gave her name to a friend of mine, too. She's getting a lot of business from me these days. Did it help?"

"Yeah. I didn't think it would, but talking about what happened was good. I know it's going to take time to get that he's really gone. He was a good man."

Pam nodded and told herself they were talking about someone other than *her* John. If she could convince herself the conversation wasn't personal, she could survive this. She could fake her way through the meeting and then escape. That was what she had to focus on. Being not here.

"You remember Ashleigh from high school?" he asked.

Pam sipped her coffee and tried to recall the name. "She was your girlfriend. A sweet girl. You broke up with her because she wouldn't sleep with you."

"Mom!"

Pam shrugged. "Did I get it wrong?"

He flushed. "You weren't supposed to know that."

"I was your mother. You didn't have any secrets from me. I always respected her for not putting out. Why do you mention her?"

"We ran in to each other the other day. She's back in Mischief Bay. She's a nurse at the hospital. Pediatrics. She looked good. Still sweet, you know."

"You mean not your type?"

"Exactly."

He flashed her a grin that was so like John's. Pain sliced through her. She instinctively pressed her hand to her stomach to hold in whatever blood she could. Only there wasn't a visible wound. Just the kind that only mattered to her.

"We're going out this weekend. I don't know. It's just when I was talking to her I kept thinking how much Dad would have liked her."

Pam thought about pointing out that was a silly reason to date someone. But maybe losing his father would help Steven mature when it came to his romantic life. She thought about saying that, but exhaustion descended and the conversation would require more than she had.

"It's getting late," she said, putting her mug on the table. "I should go."

"Mom, we haven't talked about the money yet," her son said gently. "It's why I asked you to come by. Jason is going to meet us here in a few minutes."

She stared at him blankly.

"Jason is our lawyer," Steven added.

Because there were complications with the business. Finances. "Can't you handle it?" she asked. "Do I have to be here?"

"You do."

Someone knocked on the door, then opened it. Hayley smiled at her. "Hi, Pam."

Pam did her best to smile back.

"Jason's here," Hayley told Steven.

A tall man with blond hair and blue eyes walked into the office. Pam clutched Lulu and tried to remember if she'd met him before, then decided it wasn't worth the effort. So what if she had or hadn't?

He was probably in his forties. She vaguely recalled something about working with his father, before he retired.

Jason sat next to her. "I'm so sorry for your loss, Pam. John was a great man. I always admired him for his business sense and how he loved his family. I hope in time you'll find comfort in knowing how respected and admired he was in the community."

"Thank you," she murmured, telling herself than in ten minutes she was leaving, no matter what. Or she would start rocking and keening and they could lock her up and get the good drugs going in an IV.

"I'm not sure how familiar you are with the business structure of the company," Jason continued. "While you and John owned the majority of it, you also set up profit sharing and employee ownership."

Pam bit hard on her lower lip, trying to distract herself from her need to sob. Because sharing the good times with those who had worked for him for years had been important to John. He'd been so proud to be able to provide a way for his employees to have a stake in their own future.

"The corporation had something called a key man insurance policy," Jason continued. "In the event that something happened to John, the corporation received the proceeds from the policy. That money is to be used to buy you, Jennifer and Brandon out of the company."

"I don't understand," she admitted.

Steven cleared his throat. His eyes had a sheen, as if he, too, were holding back tears. "You know Dad always talked about leaving me the business."

She nodded. "Of course. You're the only one who was interested. Your father was so happy when you said you wanted to work with him."

"Yeah. I remember." Her son swallowed hard. "He, ah, wanted to make sure everyone was taken care of. The key man policy does that. Dad leaves me the company in his will and the insurance money buys everyone else out. Jen and Brandon have a chunk of cash to put away and you're taken care of for the rest of your life."

"And you're not saddled with a lot of debt as you run things here," Pam whispered, then gave in to the inevitable and let the tears free. They ran down her cheeks, almost certainly smudging the bit of makeup she'd managed to slap on.

Someone pushed a box of tissues into her hand. She grabbed a couple and wiped her face. No doubt she looked hideous, but who cared? Lulu licked her chin and watched her with worried eyes.

"He took care of everyone," she said, her voice thick with pain. "Even after he's gone, he's taking care of everyone. He was such a good man."

She clutched Lulu and let the shuddering sobs wash through her. She could feel the two men watching her, clearly worried about her emotional state, but she couldn't bring herself to care.

"He loved you so much, Mom. The way he talked about you. There was something in his voice."

She raised her head. "What are you talking about?"

Her normally totally cool son actually blushed. "I don't know," he said, avoiding her gaze. "It didn't matter what the subject was. When he said your name he got this tone. Love, I guess. I can't describe it but I heard it all the time. We all heard it. That's why I haven't been serious about anyone. I want to wait until I hear that in my voice, too. I want what you and Dad had. I want to be that in love after thirty years."

He got up and came around the desk, then crouched in front of her. His arm encircled her. For a second she wondered if she could pretend he was John, but there was no way. No one could fill in. No one could make up for what had been lost. What *she* had lost.

She knew the only way to get out of here was to survive the rest of the meeting. She gathered what little strength she had left and raised her head.

"Thank you for telling me that," she said and forced a smile. "It helps a lot."

"I'm glad."

He rose and returned to his seat.

Jason glanced between them. "Your share of the proceeds is substantial, Mrs. Eiland. Do you have a financial advisor?"

She nodded.

"I know who he is," Steven said. "I'll call him later today and let him know what's happening. If that's okay with you, Mom."

"Thank you. I don't want to deal with any of it right now. Just do what you have to. I won't make any rash decisions." Or any decisions at all, she thought.

Steven watched her carefully. "You know, Mom, he really wanted you to join that angel fund you were talking about. You still could."

She gathered her bag and Lulu and stood. The alternative was to blurt out the truth. The alternative was to tell him that there was no way she ever wanted to do anything again. She was barely hanging on. Couldn't anyone see that? Didn't they know how every moment, every breath, was an effort? That just living took everything she had? She barely had the strength to eat or shower, let alone leave the house.

"I need to go," she said, as both men came to their feet.

"Mom, we need to—"

She cut him off with a shake of her head. "No, we don't.

You've told me what you had to. I'm glad everyone is taken care of financially. Now if you'll excuse me."

She walked out into the hallway. Although she'd been to the office a million times, she suddenly couldn't remember which way to turn to find the exit. The walls seemed to be moving and the hallway got too narrow. She was trapped. Her chest tightened until breathing was impossible. Fear built up inside until the only thing left, the only possible way to escape was to scream and scream until—

"Pam?"

She turned and saw Hayley walking toward her. Instantly the hallway returned to normal and she could breathe again.

"All done with your meeting?"

"I am," Pam admitted. "They might not be."

"They'll survive. Do you have time for a cup of tea?"

The alternative was to go home and be in that house. Something Pam found comforting, only she'd always liked Hayley.

"Sure."

They went into the break room. It was big, with lots of windows that looked out onto a small walled garden. There were tables and chairs in both areas and when the weather was nice, the staff ate outside.

Hayley put a kettle on a burner of the small stove. There was also a microwave and refrigerator, along with several cupboards. Lockers lined the far wall. Pam remembered picking out the colors on the walls and all the appliances when the offices had been remodeled. Before that, she'd worked here, on and off, when she and John had first been married.

So many memories, she thought sadly. She kept expecting to see him walk in the door and smile at her. There was simply no way to escape. Not that she wanted to, she reminded herself. In the moments when the pain receded just enough that she could think, she knew that while she was devastated, she was totally connected to him. Healing wasn't an option. Healing was too much like letting him go.

Hayley sat across from her. Pam noticed the other woman's eyes were red, as if she, too, had been crying.

"I won't ask how you're feeling," Hayley said. "People always ask me that after a miscarriage and I just want to scream at them. I can't tell them how I really feel, which is like shit. As if my hopes and dreams have been ripped from me." She raised one shoulder. "I can't begin to imagine what you're dealing with."

Pam appreciated the understanding. "It's hard," she said, thinking that didn't begin to describe what she was feeling. "I thought it would get easier, but it doesn't. Ever."

The kettle whistled. Lulu perked up her ears, as if not sure what strange creature was invading her space. Hayley walked to the stove and pulled it off the burner.

"It's okay, baby girl," Pam told Lulu quietly. "It's okay."

Hayley fixed two mugs of tea and returned to the table. "I'm going to be working for Steven now. Linda, his assistant, has been toying with the idea of moving somewhere exotic. She got offered a job in Dubai and is going to take it."

"What? Dubai? Seriously?"

"I know." Hayley gave her a sad smile. "Steven and I get along, which is great. He reminds me a lot of his dad, which is both good and bad. I think he and I can do well."

"I know you can," Pam told her. "He's going to need a lot of help making the transition. He always knew he was going to take over, but not this soon."

Steven walked into the break room. "Mom, I know this may be a bad time, but several of the people here want to come by and offer condolences. Can you stand that?"

Pam shuddered. Listening to people she knew tell her how wonderful John had been to them was both heaven and hell. She was so tired, so lonely, so sad and so broken. There was almost nothing left of her. Where was she supposed to find the strength?

But this wasn't about her, she reminded herself. This was about John. They had loved him and while they couldn't say that to him anymore, they could say it to her.

"Of course," she said as she pushed away the tea and passed Lulu to Hayley. "That would be nice."

She stood and braced herself for the emotional dump. Soon she would be home, she told herself. Soon she could sit alone in the silence, cradled in John's old chair. Soon she could cry and scream and wait for the exhaustion to claim her. All so she could start it all again in the morning.

Shannon finished reviewing the report and typed in her initials on the margin. The good news was her hyperfocusing allowed her to sail through her work at a quicker than normal pace. The bad news was every time she surfaced, she had a split second of wondering what was wrong, followed by the dull thud of reality.

It had been two days since she'd seen Adam. He'd sent her a couple of texts, but they hadn't talked and she didn't know when they would.

Now she turned in her chair so she could stare out at the view from her office. She could see the businesses and houses of Mischief Bay, with the Pacific Ocean beyond. A killer view that she'd been so damned proud of back when

Nolan had hired her. She'd taken pictures and sent them to her friends. Not to her parents, of course. They wouldn't get the thrill and would instead focus on the fact that she was bragging. In the Rigg family, that wasn't allowed. You never talked about the good things, you never tried too hard, you never strived. And if you somehow, despite the goal of mediocrity, succeeded, you never mentioned that success to others.

Probably why she didn't spend all that much time visiting her parents, despite the fact that they were less than seventy miles away. Every time she went home, she counted the seconds until she could leave. She and her parents had nothing in common. Adding to that was the fact that she knew she was a disappointment to them. She'd never followed a traditional path. She'd majored in finance rather than studying something more acceptable—like teaching or nursing. She'd always wanted more and in her family, that was a cardinal sin.

She closed her eyes against the beauty outside her window. She knew that she was still feeling the effects of her last conversation with Adam. The shock of what he'd told her still had the power to make her second-guess the path she'd chosen. It seemed grossly unfair that she'd finally met a terrific man—a man she loved and trusted—and he'd chosen not to have more children.

She knew that for the average married guy with a couple of kids, getting a vasectomy was a no-brainer. It solved the birth control issue in a quick and permanent way. Why wouldn't he have done that? But from her position, it was a statement that went beyond that. It said he didn't want any more children.

The logical side of her brain pointed out that Adam had

acted responsibly and had assumed he wouldn't get a divorce, so why not? Her heart questioned why he hadn't guessed he could fall in love with her someday. Logic returned with the fact that he'd used a condom every time they'd had sex. Obviously that had been about protection from things other than pregnancy.

She was being idiotic, she told herself. And yet in the absence of other information, she was hard-pressed to not feel crappy about the whole thing. But what happened now? Was she expected to give up her dream of having a family? Was she simply to accept the possibility of being a stepmother and go no further?

Difficult questions, she thought. Ones without easy answers. She turned back to her computer, doing her best not to think about the fact that Adam wasn't overly eager to speak with her again. He hadn't set up another date and a couple of texts did not a relationship make.

Her office phone buzzed.

"Yes?"

"There's a gentleman here to see you," her assistant said. "He doesn't have an appointment but he seems pretty confident you'll see him."

Her heart melted as her doubts faded. Because Adam was here. Which was just like him. He wasn't the guy to ignore the problem or leave her in limbo. He would get things taken care of.

"He's right," she said. "Give me a second and I'll be out."

She hung up the phone, then stood and smoothed the front of her dress. She opened the small closet and checked her makeup in the mirror before walking out into her assistant's office only to come to a stop.

The man standing there was familiar enough, but he wasn't Adam.

Quinn smiled when he saw her. "Gorgeous."

Both a greeting and a compliment, she thought, stunned to see him. She and Quinn seldom saw each other outside of his place. Sometimes he came to hers, but rarely. As for being together in a nonbedroom situation…she couldn't remember the last time.

"What are you doing here?"

"I had a couple of meetings and remembered your office was nearby. I thought I'd take you to lunch." He winked at her assistant. "If you can spare her."

Molly, a happily married woman in her late fifties, practically swooned. "Of course. You don't have any appointments until later this afternoon."

"How convenient," Quinn murmured, moving toward her and kissing her cheek. "So lunch?"

She led him into her office. When they were out of earshot, she picked up her handbag and raised her eyebrows. "Are we actually talking lunch?"

"Sure. We can talk." He held up a hand. "We're capable of having a regular conversation."

"Without sex."

"Yes."

"I'm in. Do you know where you want to go?"

"Gary's Café. They have the best burger on the beach."

"I know several businesses that would disagree with you on that."

"Then they're just plain wrong."

They agreed to take his car with the understanding he would drop her off after lunch and go on to his next meeting. Today Quinn was driving a dark blue Maserati Gran-

Turismo. A ridiculous car that totally suited him. She had to admit it was nice to sit in, but she would rather have the money to pay down her mortgage. Not that anyone was offering her either choice.

They drove to Gary's Café and Quinn easily found parking in the lot. When they went inside, several heads turned. Shannon would like to think it was because she looked especially nice that day, but she knew the truth. Quinn might not be a rock star, but he still had that indefinable I'm-famous quality about him. People generally assumed he was "someone" and in his case, they were right.

They were seated in a booth by the front window. It was still early, not yet noon, and there were plenty of empty seats. A few old men sat in a row at the counter, and a couple of mothers with young children were in the back of the restaurant. The chalkboard on the wall detailed the special.

Quinn didn't bother with the menu. Shannon scanned hers and decided she was going to live large today, as well. Maybe it was wrong to medicate herself with food, but so what?

Their server—a young woman in her early twenties—walked over. She only had eyes for Quinn and tried a couple of ponytail tosses to get his attention.

"Hi," she said breathlessly. "I'm April. I'll be helping you today."

Quinn gave her his easy, sexy smile. "Great." He motioned to Shannon. "All right, love of my life, what are you having?"

April visibly deflated. She glanced at Shannon, then back at Quinn, and sighed heavily.

Shannon smiled. "I'll have the burger special, no cheese. And an iced tea."

"Same for me," Quinn said, then stretched out his arm across the booth and took her hand.

Their server glared at Shannon before flouncing off.

"Love of my life?" Shannon asked when they were alone. "Seriously?"

"I wanted to get the point across without hurting her feelings."

Something she could nearly believe. Quinn had many flaws but being cruel wasn't one of them.

"I haven't seen you in a while," he said. "You've been ignoring me."

There had been a couple of texts she hadn't answered. "A lot's going on. A friend of mine lost her husband."

"Not why you're avoiding me."

His voice was low. Quiet, but not suggestive. This was the Quinn she rarely saw. The regular guy who was her friend.

Funny how she wasn't sure which side of him was real and which was used simply because it worked for him. The smooth, handsome Quinn who charmed as easily as most people breathed was the one she had met. Sexy, slightly aggressive, thirty ways to please a woman Quinn was the man she had sex with. But they were rarely simply people sharing a normal conversation.

She wondered what part of her truth to share with him. He took the decision out of her hands by smiling and saying, "You're seeing someone."

"I am."

"And?"

"I'm in love with him."

One dark eyebrow rose. "As simple as that?"

"It's not simple. There are unexpected complications."

"He's gay?"

Shannon laughed. “You’d like that.”

“Ouch. Why would you say that?”

“Because then I’d want to continue having sex with you and never press you for more.”

“You don’t press me for more.”

Their server returned with their drinks and stalked away. Shannon busied herself with the wrapping on her straw.

“Good point,” she murmured. “Why is that?”

“You don’t want more,” he said simply.

“Not true. I want what everyone else has. A husband and a family.”

“I don’t have a husband and a family.”

“You know what I mean. I want a traditional happy relationship. I want something I can count on.”

“Which you could never have with me,” he pointed out.

“You don’t want that?” she asked. “Not ever?”

One shoulder rose and fell. His too-long hair added to the appeal of the man, she thought, watching him. The hooded blue eyes both promised and withdrew. An irresistible combination.

They’d met at a party. She didn’t do a lot of Hollywood events, but a friend had asked her to tag along and Shannon had just been through yet another hideous day at the bank where her boss had made it clear because she didn’t have a penis, she couldn’t possibly have enough of a brain to get where she wanted to at the firm. Not that he was above taking credit for her work.

She’d dressed to kill in the skimpiest LBD she owned and then had proceeded to ignore every man who had tried to come on to her. All the while she’d been aware of Quinn, who simply watched.

At the time she’d had no idea who he was. She’d kept

track of him, watched the people who moved in and out of his orbit. Those he'd spoken to and those he'd ignored. She'd wondered about him, but told herself she didn't care enough to speak to him.

After one too many cocktails, she'd gone out on the patio of the excessively large Bel Air mansion. The cool night had helped her catch her breath. Quinn had joined her then.

"What has your panties in a bunch?"

The unexpected question had gotten through far more than any of the compliments.

"Why do men assume being a woman is the same as being stupid?" she'd asked.

"Because they're threatened. Work issue?"

"My boss."

"He knows you're going to be *his* boss in less than three years and that scares the hell out of him."

"Yeah, right. I can't get anywhere with him in the way."

"Then force him out or leave."

Until that second, she'd never thought about leaving the bank. Getting through college and getting a job with upward mobility had violated every rule she'd been raised with. She had been so proud of herself, so smug. But she'd never once thought she should leave the bank and go find something better. Which was ridiculous.

"Understanding dawns," Quinn murmured.

She glared at him. "Who are you?"

"I'm crushed you don't already know." He took her drink from her and set it on a patio table, then took her hand in his and pulled her back inside. "Come on. We'll find your friend and you'll explain you're coming home with me."

"What? No way. I don't even know your name."

"You're not interested in my name. You're pissed and a

little drunk and you can't screw the boss the way you want, but you can screw me however you'd like."

Shannon let herself be pulled along. She hadn't decided what she was going to do, but going home with the stranger was getting more intriguing by the second. She'd been so good for so long. Didn't she deserve a single night of being irresponsible?

"There's your friend," he said as he pointed. "It's Quinn, by the way."

"Shannon."

"I already know that."

She'd gone home with him that night. It had been the first of many times she'd visited his house in Malibu. She hadn't tried to fool herself into thinking they were anything but part-time lovers. Sometimes she contacted him but mostly he got in touch with her. If she was available and in the mood, she went over.

They talked music. He gave her CDs and MP3 files from new artists he'd found. She'd steered him toward a couple of excellent investment bankers she knew. But their relationship never went beyond that.

"Why wasn't there more between us?" she asked as she pulled her glass of iced tea toward her.

"You only play at relationships."

Harsh but possibly true, she thought. "Now that you've identified my flaw, what's wrong with you?"

"I'm afraid to fall in love."

"As easy as that?"

"It's not easy. It's hell. The pleasure isn't worth the potential pain. How do you do that? How do you simply hand over your heart knowing there's a better than even chance it's going to be returned to you in smaller slices than coleslaw?"

"One day you're going to have to take that leap of faith."

"Why? I'm perfectly happy."

She wondered if that were true. Or even possible. Pam and John would have been the closest she'd known and look what had happened there.

"Is he a good guy?" Quinn asked. "The one you're in love with?"

"He is."

"Then what's the problem?"

"I want children and he had a vasectomy."

"So adopt."

"The conversation didn't get that far. He left. We haven't spoken much since."

Quinn studied her. "You're breaking up with me regardless."

A statement or a question? And then she knew. "I am." Because whether or not things worked out with Adam, Quinn was no longer good for her.

"We still going to have lunch? Because I've had a hankering for this burger for weeks."

She smiled. "I would never deprive you of a burger, my friend."

"Good to know."

Eighteen

PAM SAT IN THE RECLINER. IT WAS EARLY still. Light barely crept into the house. Lulu was curled up on her lap, asleep. Her baby girl had been faithful, she thought, careful not to move so she wouldn't disturb the canine's sleep. Lulu had stayed with her every second of every day. Night after night, the little dog had been her only source of warmth. A gentle beating heart to keep her going until dawn.

Pam looked at the bottle of wine on the table next to her. It was nearly finished. She'd taken to having a glass or three late in the evening. It helped her get sleepy. Nothing helped her stay asleep. She woke up every couple of hours to find herself crying. The fiery ache of missing John never faded, never wavered. It was as constant as the rotation of the earth.

This past night had been better than most. Not because she'd slept, but because she'd been alone. She hadn't had to pretend.

Shannon and Nicole had made good on their promise to keep her company. They dropped by after work, stayed for dinner and sometimes spent the night. She knew they had her best interests at heart, but most of the time she simply wanted them to go away and leave her alone.

Lulu stirred and opened her eyes. When she saw Pam looking at her, she wagged her tail, then rolled onto her back to show her belly.

"Good morning, sweet girl," Pam murmured. She stroked the bare skin of her stomach, then rubbed her chest. "How are you?"

Lulu scrambled to her feet, planted her front paws on Pam's chest, then lavished her with puppy kisses.

"Yes, it is a new day." Something that always made Lulu happy.

Pam lifted her to the floor, then stood herself. She felt stiff and creaky. Sleeping in the chair wasn't comfortable, but she couldn't possibly face her big bed. She took a step and groaned when her back and hips protested. Maybe she could try sleeping in the guest room, she thought. Maybe that would be better.

She made her way to the kitchen and let out the dog, then started her coffee. After collecting plates and ingredients for Lulu's breakfast, she let her girl back in, then prepared her food. By the time the coffee was done, so was Lulu. Together they went into the master bath.

Pam stared at her face. She looked old, she thought. Pale and lost. She hadn't been doing any of her usual skin care. There were flakes and dullness to prove it. She'd managed to put on makeup a few days before, but had never washed it off. Old mascara collected under her eyes. Not that it mattered. Who was there to impress?

She got through a shower and dried off. Lulu licked her damp feet, helping as best she could. Pam slipped on her robe and together they walked into the closet.

She stood and stared at the racks of clothes. The closet was divided between her things and John's. He'd taken about a third of the space, leaving her with the rest. She stared at the neatly hung shirts, the pants, the jeans. His shoes all in a row on a shelf.

She reached for one shirt, not sure what she was going to do with it. Roll it into a ball? Put it on? Regardless, it fell to the floor.

Lulu immediately jumped on it, thinking they were playing a game. Pam pulled another shirt off a hanger. It fell on the dog and she yipped with excitement.

Shirt after shirt was tossed. Pants and jeans followed, then ties and jackets. Lulu stood to the side and barked with excitement, then jumped on the giant pile. She started digging and soon was lost in the mass of clothing.

Pam quickly dressed. She changed Lulu into a light sweater, then opened the hatch of her small SUV and began carting the clothes to the back. She didn't fold them or organize them in any way. She simply stuffed them inside and when she was done, she got in her car and drove to the Goodwill.

She waited an hour for the donation center to open. A nice young man helped her take everything out, then offered her a receipt. She said that wasn't necessary.

She returned home to her quiet house and crawled into the recliner. Lulu curled up on her lap. Pam held the dog and waited for time to pass. Because that was all she had. The knowledge that time passed, however slowly.

By three Pam was shaking and by three thirty, she knew she couldn't manage any of this alone. She dug her cell phone out of her bag and scrolled through all the listings.

Not her kids. They were just getting back into their lives. They didn't need to know she was falling apart. Name after name flashed by and not one of them seemed right.

Nicole's name came up next and Pam felt the tension in her chest ease. She pushed the number to make the call.

"Hi," Nicole said. "I was just thinking about you. Tyler and I were thinking about coming by later. I talked to Shannon earlier and she'd like to stop by, too. Would that work?"

Pam closed her eyes and nodded in gratitude. "I'd like that."

"I'm bringing dinner. What are you in the mood for?"

"Anything."

"I'm on my way home now. Tyler and I will be there by five."

"Don't you have class at five?"

"Not anymore. I've hired another instructor. I'll tell you all about it when I get there."

"Thank you," Pam breathed.

"Of course. We miss you. See you soon."

Pam hung up. She patted Lulu. "You're going to have Tyler to play with."

Lulu wagged her tail.

Pam got up and studied the family room. There were plates with food on them, glasses and empty wine bottles everywhere. The kitchen was worse, she thought, remembering the partially eaten casseroles she'd left out, the stack of dirty dog food dishes.

"There's a mess," she told the dog. "I'd better get cleaning."

She moved slowly at first, carrying each dish individually back to the kitchen. But the more trips she made, the more she was able to carry. She loaded the dishwasher, then started the cycle. She took out the trash and saw the can was nearly full. Because Steven had stopped coming by to take out the can for her.

She stood there, breathing hard, knowing that there would be a million other moments like this. Moments when she would be forced to remember that she was alone. John was gone and he was never coming back.

"Stop it," she told herself. "Just stop it."

She had to learn to function. She had to start doing better. Or at least faking it better. Because healing was something she knew would never happen. The alternative was to fake enough not to frighten anyone. John would want that, at the very least.

She ignored the fact that he would also want her to keep moving forward, to have a life, to be happy. All impossible concepts when faced with a full trash barrel.

She tried to figure out what day it was and then remember when the trash came. It overwhelmed her, so she retreated to the house, where she at least knew what she was doing.

With the family room and kitchen looking reasonably presentable, she went into the master bath to do the same with herself. She washed her face and was shocked at how her skin was peeling like a snake. She quickly pulled out an exfoliating mask and used it, then slathered on moisturizer before applying light makeup. When she'd done all she could to be presentable, she let out Lulu for a potty run. While the dog was doing her thing, she collected three days' worth of mail before returning to the house.

She'd barely sorted the envelopes into piles—bills, condolence cards, crap—when the doorbell rang. Lulu barked with excitement and raced toward the front of the house. Pam followed, surprisingly eager for her company.

She opened the door and nearly started to cry again. Nicole stood with a take-out bag in one hand and a roller bag suitcase handle in the other. Tyler had a Brad the Dragon backpack over his shoulders.

"Hi," Nicole said. "We decided we wanted to spend the night. I hope that's okay."

Pam opened her arms. Nicole stepped into her embrace and hung on like she was never going to let go. Tyler grabbed Pam's leg and hugged tight, too. Pam breathed deeply for the first time in days and thought maybe, just maybe, this night was going to be easier.

Nicole sipped from her wineglass. "I miss you in class," she admitted, not sure if that was okay to say. Her decision to come visit her friend had been sudden. Driven as much by her need to get out of her house as to help Pam. But now that she was here, she wished she'd come by sooner.

The death of a husband had to be devastating, but even knowing that, she'd been unprepared for Pam's appearance. Her normally well-groomed, classy friend was disheveled at best. She'd lost weight and looked drawn. In the past month, she'd aged at least ten years.

Shannon had looked equally shocked when she'd arrived an hour later. She'd brought cupcakes and wine, along with her overnight tote. So far the two of them hadn't had a chance to go off together and compare impressions, but Nicole knew there was plenty to say. Pam wasn't doing well at all.

More upsetting than her friend's change in appearance was her lack of energy. It wasn't just how slowly she moved, it was the dullness in her eyes. The way she seemed to have difficulty following the conversation. She wasn't totally with it. Nicole hoped it was just grief and not something more troubling like pills or other drugs.

"Steven told me that you were invited to join Moving Women Forward," she said, then waited for Pam to catch up with the subject change. "Did I ever tell you that they helped me when I first bought the studio?"

"I didn't know that," Shannon said.

"I couldn't have gone into business for myself without their help. But I couldn't have stayed in business without your help and advice, Pam. I don't know what I would've done without you. You should really think about accepting their invitation."

"I need to get back into exercising," Pam admitted, missing the point but at least engaging in the conversation at last. "I'm so tired and sore all the time. I'm sure it would help."

"Whenever you're ready, we want you back," Shannon said. "It's not as fun without you. You're the glue that holds us all together."

"I'm not sure I'd be much fun now," Pam said. "Or glue-like. I can't remember the last time I laughed."

Nicole touched her arm. "We're not looking for a stand-up routine. Having you around would be enough."

They were in the large family room. In addition to John's recliner, there was a huge sectional sofa. Rather than separate into various bedrooms, they'd decided they were all going to sleep here. Tyler was already zonked out on the floor. He'd been thrilled with the chance to use his B the D sleeping bag. Nicole and Shannon would sleep on the sectional and Pam would settle in John's recliner.

Nicole wondered if that was where she slept now. To feel

closer to him, maybe. Or to avoid their bed. Because they'd spent the past thirty-plus years sharing a bed, she thought, aware that *her* husband still slept in his office. She was beginning to think he was never coming back into their bedroom.

Pam sipped her wine. "Enough about me and my troubles. How are you two doing?"

"I'm fine," Shannon said brightly. "Everything's great. Nicole, how are things with Eric? With the new screenplay?"

Nicole wasn't going to mention her romantic separation from her husband, but there was plenty of other news.

"It's been a whirlwind. He spends his days either doing rewrites or taking meetings."

"He's still the big-shot writer?" Pam asked.

"You know it. But I'm just as bad. Do you know I've actually been interviewing nannies? I can't believe it. But with him gone so much and all his strange hours, there's no way I can count on him to take Tyler to preschool or pick him up. And while I really like having another instructor, she's only part-time and that means I'm still the one mostly responsible for the classes. There's no way I can be running around with Tyler."

She didn't mention that she was also talking to the various women she'd interviewed about their willingness to do housework, laundry and cooking. Because Eric insisted they have a full-service nanny.

"Two months ago, we were struggling to pay the bills," she continued. "Now I'm interviewing nannies. It's surreal."

"Have you found anyone?" Shannon asked.

Nicole wrinkled her nose. "A woman named Greta. She's worked with two people Eric knows and they speak very highly of her. She's in her early fifties, she's never been married. She loves children and whenever I'm around her, I feel inadequate."

Pam smiled. "I doubt that."

"No, I do. She believes in a totally organic kitchen. She's a vegan but thinks meat is good for growing children. She bakes her own bread, does windows and looks at me like I'm an idiot. Should I hire someone who intimidates me?"

"What does Tyler think of her?" Shannon asked. "Because that matters the most."

"He adores her."

"We all make sacrifices for our children," Pam murmured.

"You think it's funny that she scares me."

"A little."

Nicole sighed. "I should probably just be grateful she comes so highly recommended." She shifted so she could sit cross-legged on the sofa. "Eric is turning into a total Hollywood type. He's reading *Variety* every day and quotes articles to me."

"More surreal moments?" Shannon asked.

"Daily. I'm trying to be supportive and at the same time, I'm completely uncomfortable."

Pam's expression turned sad. "Everything's different. You don't know where you are or how to find your balance. Life makes us start over again and again. Of course you feel different. Anyone would."

Nicole wanted to slap herself. She was supposed to be helping her friend, not making things worse. "I'm sorry," she murmured. "I'm not helping."

"You're wrong. Having you here is a great help. I really appreciate it." Pam turned to Shannon. "It's nice to have my friends with me."

"You sure?" Shannon asked.

"I swear." She managed a shaky smile. "And in the morning we'll have nonorganic calorie-filled pancakes and sausage for breakfast."

Nicole grinned. "You sure know how to show us a good time."

"I try."

The Goodwill store was big and bright, with high ceilings and more of a crowd than Pam would have expected on a Thursday morning. She pushed her cart through the aisles of clothing. She didn't have a plan, exactly. She was simply here to collect what was hers. Or more correctly, John's.

She'd tried to fill in the empty space in the closet by spreading out her things. She'd told herself it was for the better, that she had to start moving on. But the words didn't seem to help. She still felt she'd given away something precious and now she had to get it back.

What she hadn't expected was the sheer size of the men's department. There were dozens of racks of clothing, maybe hundreds. How was she supposed to find what had belonged to John? What if all the shirts looked the same and she couldn't tell which were his?

She reached the first rack of shirts and started flipping through it. The shirts were arranged first by color and then by size. She knew the brands he favored, so that would help. She also knew the collar size and sleeve length. But as she studied shirt after shirt after shirt, she began to wonder if she could know for sure she'd found one of his.

She turned and saw the jeans section was even bigger. White shirts seemed to go on for miles. The store was massive and there were so many people pawing through what could be her things.

The tightness in her chest began almost before she realized what was happening. Her breathing became labored and then the first cold claws of panic reached for her soft belly and ripped it open. She gasped and clutched her midsection just as the tears began to fall.

She gripped her cart, hoping to stay upright, but it was too much. All of it. The overhead lights, the chatter of conversation, the smell of fresh soap combined with the scent of guilt and fear. She gave in to it all and slowly sank to the ground.

Around her she heard a few murmurs as the nearest shoppers scattered. No doubt they were worried she was some crazy person who was going to brandish a knife or something.

"I just want to find John's things," she whispered.

"Ma'am? Are you all right?"

She raised her head and stared at the tall, thin, dark-haired woman standing by her cart.

"No," Pam admitted. "I'm not."

"What's wrong? Are you sick? Do you want me to call an ambulance?"

Pam sniffed. "You must really have to deal with a lot of things here. I'm not sick." She sniffed, then struggled to her feet. "I brought my husband's clothes in a few days ago. Now I'm trying to find them to buy them back."

"Did you have a fight?"

"No. He's gone. He died. I miss him so much." The tears started up again. "I don't know how to be without him." She noticed that two security guards were heading in her direction. "Are you going to ask me to leave the store?"

"No. Of course not. I'm going to help you find your husband's things. When did you make the donations?"

"Three days ago."

"Then they're probably not out yet. Come on back to the sorting area and we'll see what we can find."

Pam pushed her cart along and followed her through to the back of the store. "Thank you for being so nice."

"We all have to deal with something. I know that to be true. They say God never gives us more than we can handle, but I say sometimes He assumes we're stronger than we are. Life is a challenge."

She pushed through swinging doors. Pam left the cart in the store and went with her into a huge back room. There were dozens of people sorting through thousands of donations. There were televisions and furniture, household goods, pots, pans, dishes and clothes. Mountains of clothes.

The piles were higher than a basketball player's head. They were impossibly large. It was as if every single person in the Los Angeles metro area had donated the same day she had.

The woman at her side was talking, explaining about where the clothes would be, given when Pam had dropped them off. And then she knew the truth—that discovering a shirt or a jacket would in no way bring John back. He was gone.

There was no bargaining, no mourning, no begging that would bring him back. He was lost to her forever.

"Thank you for your help," she told the woman and started to leave.

"You don't want to look?"

Pam glanced back at her. "He's not there."

She walked to her car and got inside. As she leaned back

in her seat and closed her eyes, she remembered watching a movie with John. One he'd really liked—*The Shawshank Redemption*. Morgan Freeman's character had said something in the movie. That it was time to get busy living or get busy dying.

She probably had the line wrong, but that was the heart of it, she thought. Maybe her problem was she hadn't made a decision yet, and until she did, she was trapped in a world of pain and suffering with no possible way to escape.

Nineteen

THE FRIDAY NIGHT CROWD AT PESCADORES was loud and happy. Conversation flowed easily and there was plenty of laughter. In the bar, a baseball game played silently on several televisions. Shannon caught sight of the occasional play out of the corner of her eye. She'd never noticed the TVs before, but then she'd never felt the weight of silence when she'd been out with Adam before.

This was their first P-V-R date. P-V-R aka post vasectomy reveal. They'd gone from texting to a couple of quick calls, the last of which had been him inviting her out to dinner tonight at a place they generally enjoyed.

She'd accepted because she loved him and missed him, but also with a sense of dread. Because there was a part of her expecting this to be where he told her he was done with her. That she wanted impossible things, that his love wasn't the forever, I want children with you kind. That he'd been more interested in getting laid than happily ever after.

Even as she'd wrestled with her fears, she'd told herself she was being unfair. That Adam had been nothing but sweet and kind and open and attentive. That she shouldn't assume the worst about him or them. But she was scared. After years of thinking she could never "have it all," she'd finally found someone who saw who she was and still loved her. She'd allowed herself to hope and now this.

She'd had a late meeting so they'd met at the restaurant instead of him picking her up. Not as convenient, she thought, but if things went south, at least she would be able to get away without a hideously awkward ride home.

Not that the meal was going any better, she mused. Since being seated, they'd discussed the weather and how the Dodgers were off to a good start on the season but were likely to disappoint later in the summer.

They'd ordered wine and an appetizer and now were left on their own. Which was turning out not to be a good thing.

She glanced at him, liking the shape of his face and the kindness in his eyes. He was such a great guy, she thought wistfully. She'd known there were going to be issues they had to deal with but had assumed they would be about her getting involved with his kids or getting along with his ex-wife. For some reason, she'd never once thought they would be on different sides of the "I want kids" debate.

He reached across the table and touched the back of her hand. "We should talk about it."

She nodded. "We should. I'm sorry I sprang the topic of more kids on you without warning. It never occurred to me that you'd feel differently. Foolish, but there we are."

"My vasectomy doesn't meant I don't want kids," he began, then stopped himself. "At least, it..." Another pause.

She really wanted to pull her hand back, but that seemed hostile. In truth, she felt the need to protect herself rather than withdraw. She wanted to curl up in a ball or have some layer of armor between her and him. Not that all the steel in the world would be enough to protect her from what he was trying too hard not to say.

"I get it," she said quietly. "You had your family and you were happy with Oliver and Char. You didn't expect to get a divorce so why not? And even knowing you were going to be single again, you still had your complete family. I'm not there yet. I may not have made all the right decisions in the past, but that doesn't mean I'm willing to give up on being a mother."

"You shouldn't," he told her. "You'd be a great mom."

"That's yet to be proven."

He smiled and withdrew his hand. "I have faith in you."

She pressed her now-free arm against her stomach. "I wish I could say the same about myself. I guess I'll have to figure out that one later."

"I don't want to lose you," Adam told her. "The kid thing came up suddenly."

"I know. I didn't mean to scare you. We haven't been dating that long."

"Long enough. I love you, Shannon. I want this to work. Can we keep moving forward with the idea we'll be talking about our future and coming up with a plan that works for both of us?"

She nodded because it was the mature thing to do. But in her head, she was less agreeable. How were they supposed to fix the problem? Was it possible for him to get his vasectomy reversed? She understood there were other options but wasn't sure what he meant by coming up with a plan.

She opened her mouth to ask him to be more specific, then pressed her lips together. Their relationship was too new, she thought. There was too much going on too soon. They didn't have the history needed to get through it all.

They weren't going to make it, she thought suddenly. By bringing up children, she'd sent them down the road to the end. There was no fixing things now, she thought sadly. There was only getting through it all.

"We do need time," she said, doing her best to keep her mouth from trembling as she fought against the pain of the inevitable. She hadn't met anyone like Adam ever. She'd been so sure he was the one. Yet here they were.

"You won't give up on me?" he asked.

"No," she promised, knowing it was the truth. She wouldn't be giving up on him. But it was just a matter of time until he gave up on her.

"Come shopping with me," Eric said with a grin. "Come on, you've got time. Tyler's at preschool and Greta will pick him up when he's done. You don't have class until four. I'll get you back in time."

Nicole couldn't say what surprised her more. The invitation or the fact that Eric had shown up at her studio. He never came here. Sometimes she wondered if he remembered where it was.

She hadn't seen much of him in the past few weeks. He'd been busy starting his new life as a successful screenwriter. They'd hired the slightly scary Greta and she'd started on Monday. So far things seemed to be going fine. Tyler liked her and Nicole was determined not to be intimidated by her.

She thought about all the things she had to do, then told herself they could wait. She and Eric needed some time alone together.

"Shopping, it is," she said, grabbing her bag. "Where are we going?"

"Where else?"

"Not Beverly Hills," she said. "That's ridiculous. It's so expensive."

Eric opened the passenger side door of his new red BMW convertible. "Only the best for us. Only the best."

They headed toward the 405 freeway, then got on going north.

Traffic was light in the middle of the day. The temperature was warm and the sky a perfect California blue. Eric turned on the radio to a popular pop station, then surprised her by reaching across the console and taking her hand in his.

"I've finished the first round of revisions on my screenplay," he said. "There were a lot of notes. I'm expecting another go-round, but Jacob said with what I've done, he's ready to move forward."

"That's great."

She knew Jacob was the producer who had bought Eric's screenplay. He wanted to get it into production as quickly as possible. Nicole wasn't sure of all the steps involved, nor did she understand who the players were. From what she'd been able to piece together, Eric's sale had been something of a lightning strike. Instead of going through the usual channels and having it take forever, he'd gotten lucky.

A member of his critique group was neighbors with Jacob. While Jacob hadn't been interested in his buddy comedy, he'd been intrigued when told about Eric's techno-thriller. They'd had a meeting, Jacob had read the screenplay and had made the impossible offer.

Now they were moving forward with making a movie.

From what she heard, most screenplays got optioned first. Those that were bought generally languished and were never made. Talk about a roller coaster.

"You must be so proud of yourself," she said. "What you've done is impressive."

He smiled at her. "I couldn't have done it without your support."

"I don't think I was very supportive. I yelled a lot."

"I deserved it. I should have been more clear about what I wanted. I should have made you a part of things. I'm sorry about that. But it's going to be different now. You'll see."

A promise she wanted to believe. And while part of her was willing to accept that he was right, she couldn't be completely sure. Chasing dreams took time—she got that. But she still had the sense of being on the outside, looking in.

They exited the freeway and headed east into Beverly Hills. Eric talked about what it would take to get the movie into production, how they would be filming in Vancouver and London and who would be in the starring roles.

"Jacob and I have talked about an unknown for the female lead. Like a young Jennifer Lawrence."

Nicole laughed. "She's only what? Twenty-five. How young are you thinking?"

"Okay, not young, but undiscovered. The male lead would go to someone who can bring in the audience. There's a spot."

He pulled into a lot and parked. They got out and walked toward the sidewalk.

Nicole couldn't remember the last time she'd been in Beverly Hills. When she was little, her mother used to bring her here every few weeks. They would window-shop and study the rich women who strolled so casually.

"One day you'll be famous," her mother had promised. "You'll shop here. You'll buy the most expensive clothes and jewelry. Everyone will know who you are."

At first that dream had sounded fun but as Nicole had learned what it took to be successful as an actress or a dancer, she'd begun to wonder if it was worth all the effort. Of course, that had been before she'd discovered she didn't have the talent.

Now she lived what most would consider an ordinary life. She didn't have any regrets about how things had gone. Wouldn't it be funny if the whole dream her mother had for her was fulfilled by Eric?

"Here we are," Eric said, pointing to the front of a store.

She studied the big windows and the display mannequins in suits and more casual clothes. The styles were the right combination of trendy and timeless, with impeccable tailoring and beautiful fabrics. It took money to look that good, she thought, slightly startled and totally bemused.

Of course, she thought, doing her best not to laugh as they entered the European-based menswear store. Why would she have thought otherwise? Because when Eric had asked her to go shopping, she'd assumed it was for her. And she'd been completely wrong.

"Good afternoon," a middle-aged well-dressed salesman said as he approached. "How may I help you?"

"I'm looking for a few new looks," Eric told him. "Hollywood casual. Clothes I can wear to meetings and to parties." He turned to Nicole. "Maybe one suit and a tux. What do you think?"

"That sounds about right, although I'm not sure you need a tux right now. I'd wait until award season and get something then."

"Good point," Eric said, and kissed her cheek. He turned back to the salesman. "No tux."

"As you wish. I'm Phillip. And you are?"

Introductions were made all around.

"Why don't you come this way and we'll get started," Phillip said. "Would either of you like a glass of champagne?"

"We both would," Eric said easily, as if shopping with champagne was an everyday occurrence.

Nicole followed them to the back of the store. She was seated on a comfortable love seat. An assistant brought out two glasses of champagne on a silver tray while Phillip took Eric's measurements, then asked him a few questions about where he would need the clothing.

"You're in the business?" Phillip asked.

No need to clarify. There was only the one business in Los Angeles.

"Screenwriter."

Phillip's expression remained impassive. "You've sold it?"

"A seven-figure deal."

Phillip got a whole lot friendlier. "Excellent. Congratulations. We have everything you're going to need. You'll want to look fashionable, but without trying too hard. Casual but not sloppy. The focus is on you, not what you're wearing. One suit for now. Navy, I think. It will all be about the tailoring. Prada, perhaps. The Italians know what they're doing with a suit. Give me a few minutes to collect some samples. I'll be right back."

Two hours later, they left the store. They were each carrying bags. Eric had bought everything from socks to a leather bomber jacket. Most of the pants, along with the suit, required tailoring and he would pick them up later.

"I need to get you home," he said as he stored everything in the trunk. "Then get to my meeting." He walked around to the passenger side and held open her door. "You should take yourself shopping when you get a chance. Buy some new things."

She nodded as she got in. The message was clear. He wouldn't be going with her. After all, watching her shop wouldn't help his career. Perhaps a harsh judgment, she told herself. But was it inaccurate?

She'd long known that the Eric she'd married was gone. What about this new guy? Did they have anything in common? Because if they didn't, she didn't see how their marriage was ever going to work.

Riverside was less than ninety miles from Mischief Bay, but in terms of life, purpose and style, it was another galaxy in distance. Or maybe that was unfair, Shannon thought as she sat in her parents' backyard on a hot and sunny Saturday afternoon. Maybe the real distance was simply between her life and her parents'.

Her dad had gone golfing with a few of his friends. To the public course, he'd been careful to say before he left. Because he would never join a country club of any kind. She was pretty sure her parents could afford it and as much as her dad golfed these days, it made sense. But to do so was to cross that invisible line of being too much or having too much. You bought things because they were necessary. A golf club membership wasn't ever going to be necessary.

"It warmed up early this year," her mother said.

"It did. Your roses look beautiful."

"Sally's are much nicer, but I'm happy with how these came out. I've been working with them."

The backyard was a testament to her mother's love of and talent with all things plant-based. There were lush bushes, blooming flowers, artfully arranged and elegantly displayed. Shannon had never shared her mother's affection for the outdoors, but she'd still spent many happy hours on this small patio, reading while her mother gardened.

"Your father's thinking of retiring," her mother said.

"Good for him."

"He's sixty-six. It's past the retirement age."

Shannon understood that retiring could be mistaken for being lazy. Or not working hard enough. "He's earned this. What about you, Mom? Thinking about letting the kids teach themselves?"

Her mother, also a natural redhead whose only vanity was to color her hair ever four weeks, shook her head. "Shannon, I don't know where you get your strange ideas. Children can't teach themselves. I don't know how much longer I'll work. Your father and I have been thinking about buying an RV. A small one, of course. It's just the two of us. Used. We've been looking around and there are some bargains."

"That sounds like fun," Shannon said as she picked up her lemonade and sipped it. What she really wanted to say was "Go wild. Get a big one. Or even a medium-size one. And hey, look at a new one!"

But she wouldn't. Not only couldn't she possibly change their minds, but they would also be uncomfortable at what they perceived as waste.

Shannon told herself to respect their frugal natures. They'd been raised by depression-era parents who had taught them to squeeze every penny until it was reduced to its base elements. Saving was good for families and good for the economy. But, like anything worthy, it could be taken to the extreme.

And it wasn't the savings she took issue with, she thought. It was the attitude that went with it. The constant apology if something was new, or nice. That her mother couldn't simply accept a compliment about the roses—she had to say someone else's were nicer and that she'd worked hard to get them that way.

"I hope you and Dad get an RV," she said instead. "You've always wanted to travel."

"I have. And it's not like we're going to Europe. That would be so extravagant."

"It doesn't have to be," Shannon said gently. "There are discount trips..."

Her mother was already shaking her head. "We're not like you, Shannon. We don't believe in that sort of thing."

"Seeing the world?"

"Wasting money like that. You always wanted more. You were never content with what you had."

Shannon remembered being eight or nine. It had been close to Christmas and she'd seen a pair of red patent leather shoes in the store.

They had been the most beautiful shoes she'd ever seen in her life and she wanted them with a fiery desperation. Of course, her parents had told her no. That she already had her school shoes and her play shoes. If she needed something fancy, which was unlikely, she could borrow a pair from one of her friends. Come summer, she would get a pair of sandals and maybe they could be red.

She hadn't been appeased by the thought because she knew that come summer, she would get brown sandals. Brown was practical. Brown went with everything.

She'd tried begging, bargaining, and had even attempted to sell some of her toys to neighborhood kids. But no one would pay for her modest playthings. Christmas morning had come and gone. She'd gotten three presents, and no red patent leather shoes.

Years later, she'd started babysitting. She'd saved until she had enough and then she'd bought a pair of ridiculous high-heeled patent leather pumps. Her parents had been horrified. She was supposed to be saving for her future. She told them she'd been dreaming about red patent leather shoes for six years. She was past due.

Later she'd realized the pumps she'd bought were more suitable for someone who dabbled in prostitution than a high school sophomore. She'd only ever worn them a couple of times. But they'd represented something significant: she'd wanted them and she had bought them herself. Buying those shoes had represented possibilities and freedom.

Her mother would say they'd been her first step down the dark path and maybe they had been. But Shannon had decided then and there she was going to make enough money to buy whatever she wanted, whenever she wanted. No one was ever going to tell her no again.

"You do know I have a savings account, right?" she asked her mother. "And a 401K."

"I hope it's enough."

"Mom, I work in finance. I'm the CFO in a billion-dollar company. I know how to handle money."

Her mother glanced around, as if concerned someone would overhear them. "Keep your voice down. There's no reason to go bragging to the whole neighborhood. That sort of thing is private."

Right. Because aside from not spending money, her parents never talked about it, either. To this day she had no idea what either of them made. She could guess, but she didn't know. Of course they didn't know what she made either. She had a feeling they would faint with shock at her mid-six-figure salary.

"Maybe you could plan to go to Europe for your sixty-fifth birthday," she said. "That gives you a couple of years to save for it. It could be your present."

For a second her mother's expression turned wistful. "That would be nice," she admitted, before shaking her head. "Your father would never agree it was a good idea."

Shannon only nodded. No point in getting into it with her mom now. But later, she would drop a hint or two to her father. Maybe if she suggested it and offered to pay half as her gift to her mom, she could make it happen. Or maybe it would all blow up in her face with her father accusing her of bragging. It was difficult to know with them.

For the four hundred millionth time, she wished they could be different. An impossible request, of course, but she couldn't shake the feeling of sadness when she thought of her parents. They chose to live such small lives. They could afford to do more and wouldn't. If they didn't want to travel, then she could understand them choosing to stay home. Only they did. Or at least her mother did.

Shannon knew her love of exotic places came from the times when she and her mom would check out travel books from the library. They would pore over the color pictures and talk about going there…someday.

Shannon had learned that for her parents "someday" really meant never. Once she'd broken free and bought her red shoes, she'd also decided she was going to see the world. And she had. She supposed for her mother, the RV was enough.

Shannon wondered if the concept of enough should be one she embraced. But she wanted more—at least when it came to her personal life. A problem she and Adam had yet to resolve.

"Mom, why didn't you and Dad have more kids?"

Her mother picked up her drink and took a sip. "Are you sorry you're an only child?"

"It's all I know. I can try to imagine what it would have been like with siblings, but at this point, I'm not sure what difference it would make."

"We talked about having more children," her mother admitted. "But then it never happened."

The obvious question was why. Had there been problems getting pregnant? Problems in the marriage? Or had her parents simply made the sensible choice? The one to only have a single child so they wouldn't stretch their budget?

"I want to have a baby," Shannon confessed.

Her mother turned to her, her eyebrows raised, her mouth twisted in judgment. "Shannon, no. You can't. You're too old."

An unexpected slap, she thought, trying not to react, at least on the outside. "I'm going to be forty."

"I know how old you are. And you'd be close to sixty when your child graduated from high school. Are you sure you could even get pregnant at this age? Besides, you're not even married." Her mother's eyes widened. "You're not going to go adopt a foreign child on your own, are you?"

"I might." Because the stubborn kid in her thought defying her mother sounded pretty damned good right about now.

"I have no idea what your father would say about that."

Shannon wanted to find her way to the golf course and tell him that second. In front of his friends. Then she drew a breath and let the urge wash over her and away.

It was usually like this when she came home, she thought. She and her mother talked while her father disappeared somewhere. Conversation took a turn and she found herself on the teenaged side of parental disapproval.

She knew she was a disappointment. She hadn't followed the family rules. She wasn't modest enough or average enough or traditional enough. She'd been too driven, too flashy. Although her parents knew about her beachfront condo, they'd never seen it. No doubt their senior hearts couldn't stand the strain.

She told herself that love came in many forms. That she should be grateful she still had her parents and that while they couldn't be more different, if something bad happened, they would be there for her. She was only staying for a few more hours. She could afford to be gracious.

"You've raised some good points," she said gently. "I'm going to have to think about them. And I won't say anything to Dad."

Her mother relaxed. "He loves you very much. We both do. It's just sometimes..."

"I know, Mom. I don't make it easy."

Twenty

NICOLE STARED AT THE FOIL-COVERED GLASS casserole dish. The instructions were very clear. Thirty minutes in a 350-degree oven. Greta's writing was like the woman herself—precise and deliberate. Okay, and maybe just a little bit scary.

In addition to the prepared entrée, there was a salad for her and Eric, along with a weird blue smoothie drink in a child-size cup for Tyler. One he claimed to have had before and really liked. Nicole was sure all the ingredients were organic and locally sourced, wherever possible. That the meal couldn't be more healthy and that she would sleep better because of it.

All things to be grateful for, if only she could get over the weirdness of it all.

Two years ago, she'd been going along with her life. She had a husband and a son and a new business. All of which was still true, but somehow it all felt different. As if the traditional painting that was her life had been redone by Picasso. All that was missing were the flying goats.

Not that she was complaining. The changes had happened

gradually. But when she looked back at how much things had changed, she felt a little strange about it all.

She turned on the oven to preheat it. There wasn't much else for her to do. The laundry was done, the kitchen clean. Even the bathroom towels had a just-washed scent and softness. Tyler informed her that Greta had already given him a bath that afternoon *and* read him his favorite B the D book twice.

Nicole realized that she didn't have anything to do. Not cleaning, not getting dinner ready beyond the back-breaking task of turning on the oven, not anything. She was tired from a long day at work and she could simply relax with her son.

"Let's play while dinner's heating," she said.

Tyler shouted his pleasure and made a beeline for his room.

She followed and soon they were busy working on a puzzle. When the oven beeped it was hot enough, she put in the casserole, then returned to the fun. By six, they were sitting down to eat.

For once there was time to find a nice classical station on the radio and even pour a glass of wine. Tyler enjoyed his strange blue drink and didn't seem to notice the vegetables Greta had hidden in the casserole.

When they were done, they cleaned the kitchen together, then went into the living room to watch one of his movies. Movies that had been put away on their shelf…in alphabetical order.

The evening continued to pass smoothly. Nicole wasn't sure when Eric would be home, but that was true most nights. He was kept busy with his movie and starting a new screenplay. She only knew that last bit because she'd overheard him talking about it with Jacob. As for the current one, he still hadn't given it to her to read, despite her asking.

At eight, she put Tyler to bed and then wandered through her clean, organized house. She picked up a book she'd been wanting to read for at least two years and settled down to sink into the story. It was a weekend night and here she was—reading.

Somewhere around nine, Eric walked into the house.

"Hi," he said when he saw her. "How was your day?"

She looked up from her book. "Good. How was—" She stared at the man she'd married. The clothes were new, but then she'd been there when he'd bought them. But they weren't what startled her. She stared at his hair, taking in the blond ends of his new sticky-up style.

"Do you have highlights?" she asked, unable to grasp the possibility.

"Yeah. Do you like them?"

Sure, this was L.A. but highlights? Who did he think he was? Brad Pitt?

"Um, sure. They're, um, great." She closed her book. "Did you eat? There's a chicken casserole in the fridge. Greta outdid herself again."

"I ate, but thanks." He sat at the other end of the sofa. "We're getting serious about casting. That's been interesting. I'm learning a lot from Jacob."

"I'll bet. It's great that he's involving you in so much of the movie."

Eric leaned forward, his clasped hands dangling between his knees. "I know. We're becoming good friends. Most writers don't get to see all the magic happen. We've been brainstorming my next project. I'm going to have to take a few months to write it, but I want to stay with the movie as long as I can. Then I'll hole up and get the writing done. It's hectic, but fun."

She studied his face. He looked happy, she thought. Relaxed. The highlights would take some getting used to, but she could probably live with them.

"I'm glad it's all going so well." She paused, not sure what she wanted to tell him. "You're gone a lot."

"I know. It's tough, right? All this work. It comes with the business. I'm sure you can imagine. Jacob's going to be out of town for a few days. So the three of us can do something Sunday. Maybe go to the POP and hang out."

"Tyler would like that a lot. He misses you."

"I miss him, too." Eric rose. "I'm going to catch up on email."

"I miss you, too," she added.

Her husband nodded and gave her a kiss on the cheek. But instead of speaking, he headed for his office.

When she was alone again, she leaned back against the sofa. Had he noticed that he didn't say he missed her? They'd drifted so far apart. It had happened slowly at first, but now the chasm between them was wider and deeper every week.

She couldn't tell if he was excluding her deliberately or if it was simply happening through circumstance. While she was glad Eric was happy with his work, where did it leave their relationship?

What did he want from her and what did she want from him? And if they were rarely in the same room at the same time, how were they ever supposed to have that conversation?

Shannon hesitated only a second before walking into Latte-Da. It was ten in the morning on a Tuesday and there wasn't much of a crowd. She spotted Adam right away. He had two to-go cups in front of him and when he saw her, he stood and carried the cups over to her.

"Thanks for coming," he said, as he approached.

"You said it was important." She took one of the cups. "Thank you for my latte."

"You're welcome. Let's go outside and walk along the boardwalk."

Shannon held on to her coffee with both hands. Adam had called a half hour before and told her they had to talk. She knew he was right—they had things they needed to talk about. Her solution for dealing with the tough stuff had been to avoid him as much as possible. Not the mature response and not one she was proud of. So when he'd asked to get together, she'd cleared her calendar to meet with him.

She'd never been dumped by the POP, she thought as they walked across the street and stepped onto the cement path that stretched from Pacific Palisades to Santa Monica. And somehow she'd assumed that if her relationship with Adam ended, she would be the one saying goodbye.

But it hadn't happened that way. They'd reached an impasse. They wanted different things and there was no easy solution. Maybe if they'd been together longer, she thought sadly. Maybe they would have a chance.

She wasn't sure how she was going to deal with losing him. He was a great guy and she had fallen in love with him. Foolishly, she'd allowed herself to believe she was finally going to get to have it all. Marriage, kids and growing old with someone.

When she'd realized that wasn't going to happen, she'd put off the inevitable as long as possible. Now that it was here, she promised herself she would be reasonable. Even kind. She wouldn't cry. Not in front of him. When they were done, she would go back to her office and finish her day. But that night—all bets were off.

She wondered how long it would take to stop missing him. How long until she was able to think about seeing someone else. How long until thinking about him didn't cause a physical ache.

"You've been avoiding me," he said as they turned north.

"I have."

She wondered how they looked from the outside. A successful couple, she thought. Adam might be in jeans, a long-sleeved shirt and work boots, but he had an air of confidence about him. No one would be surprised to learn he ran an eight-figure construction project.

She had on one of her business suits. It was California-inspired—less structured than a traditional suit, but with all the pieces. Her high heels clicked on the cement path.

"If we don't talk, we can't fix the problem," he told her. "Something this big could get in the way of what we want." He pulled her to a stop and stared into her eyes. "Shannon, I love you. That hasn't changed. I don't want to lose you, but I don't know what you're thinking. Are you still in this with me or are you already gone?"

She stared into his eyes and read the truth there. He wasn't done with her. He wasn't breaking up with her. He was trying to fix things between them. He was acting like the grown-up in the room.

"I'm not gone," she whispered.

"Promise?"

She nodded.

He exhaled. "Thank you for saying that. I was really worried. Especially when you disappeared. I know this is hard. I'm working on it. Can you give me some time? I'm not talking years or even months, but I need a few weeks to get my head around things."

Because he took her seriously, she thought, amazed and grateful. Because he wanted her to be happy.

"Take as long as you need."

He smiled and touched her cheek. "I appreciate the offer. I want to work this out. I can't believe I found you. I don't want to blow it."

"Me, either."

"Then promise me you won't disappear on me again. If you're mad, say so. We can fight about it. We can search for solutions. I'm good at that. What I can't deal with is being shut out."

Something she hadn't thought about before, but now that she did, it made sense. Of course he didn't want to be excluded. He knew the price of doing that. It was one of the reasons he'd ended up divorced.

"I promise."

A skateboarder in shorts and a T-shirt whizzed past them. Adam ignored the guy as he leaned toward her and kissed her mouth.

"Thank you," he whispered. "For what it's worth, I'm not the only one who's missed you. The kids have been asking about you. Char keeps saying how she wants to make sure you're at her party."

Ah, the infamous birthday bash at Epic, Shannon thought. "Why do I know that's more about her fear that you're staying than her excitement at having me there?"

"Whatever works," he said with a smile.

She kissed him and felt the hardness in her heart crack.

"You're right. Whatever works. I don't want lose you, either. Thank you for not giving up on me."

"Never."

"I don't understand," Jen said, holding up a tiny onesie. "How can clothing be organic?"

"Maybe it's the cotton they use. Or the dying process." In today's world, Pam half expected to see a gluten-free sign over a bag of socks.

"I guess when Kirk and I register for the baby, we'll have to decide about organic fabrics."

Which would make them wildly popular with their friends, Pam thought. Not that she would say anything. Jen had invited her to lunch followed by an afternoon of wandering at South Bay Galleria. While Pam generally preferred the odd little stores in Mischief Bay, every now and then she enjoyed hanging out at the mall. These days having a reason to leave the house was good. She knew she was spending too much time on her own. While Lulu was a faithful companion, she wasn't much for conversation.

She knew it would be better if in addition to feeling she *needed* to get out, that she also *wanted* to get out. But that wasn't happening. Her days were still cold and empty, with the realization she would never be happy again. She still drank too much, didn't eat enough and had long given up ever feeling normal.

She knew down to the minute how long ago John had died. She resented him for dying and ached for him in equal measures. She was lost and alone and yet had apparently learned to fake it so well, no one bothered to ask her how she was doing in that worried tone she'd grown used to. Even Jen had barely mentioned John.

People moved on, she told herself. People healed. Not her, but then she had been his wife. Their relationship was different. No one else had marked the passage of time by his comings and goings.

"You don't have to decide anything now," Pam pointed out. "You have a lot of time until you need to register."

Jen nodded and linked arms with her. "You're right. Thanks. I'm not even showing. I'm still in all my regular pants." Jen wrinkled her nose. "Not the skinny day ones, but all the others."

Pam heard the impatience in her daughter's voice. Because like nearly every other expectant mother-to-be, she was ready to proclaim her baby to the world. She thought maternity clothes would be cool and fun.

Pam remembered her own excitement when she'd been pregnant. The thrill of knowing there was going to be a baby. The terror that she didn't know how to be a mother with the first one and the worry about exhaustion with the second and third.

"You'll be showing soon enough," she told her daughter. "Trust me, when it's finally time to have your baby, you'll be thrilled to get on the road to getting your body back."

"I guess."

"You sound doubtful. We'll have another conversation about this in seven months. I'll be the one saying 'I told you so.'"

Jen laughed. "You'd never say that."

They walked out of the store and headed for California Pizza Kitchen for lunch. Jen had suggested the place, admitting she was desperate for pizza. Pam had agreed because she generally liked their food and these days what did it matter?

She ate because she had to. Her stomach cramped and she felt light-headed if she didn't. But there was no pleasure in it.

They were seated at a booth. Jen eagerly opened the menu and studied the options. Pam looked at her daughter. Overhead light caught a few strands of Jen's sleek hair. Her skin looked firm and flush with good health.

At night, when she couldn't sleep, she thought about her children and wished them long and happy lives. If only she could spare them from future unhappiness, she thought. Because that was all she had to give them. Wishes and hopes. There wasn't much of anything else left. Not inside of her.

She knew that on the surface, she was doing fine. Quieter than usual, sure. But getting through the days. She'd figured out when the trash had to go out and was paying her bills. She answered the phone because if she didn't, people worried. Shannon and Nicole stopped by faithfully and she pretended to be excited to see them. But despite the physical actions, she wasn't fine. She was barely getting by.

Most nights, she couldn't sleep. She drank more than she should. She lost hours just sitting and thinking about John. Sometimes she would look up and be surprised to discover it was dark outside.

But those were *her* secrets. She protected her pain from outside scrutiny. She no longer thought she should be locked up, but she certainly wasn't ready to give up the daily grief that connected her so completely with John.

"Barbecue chicken pizza," her daughter said firmly as she closed the menu. "What about you, Mom?"

"I'm getting that soup I like."

"Dakota smashed pea and barley?"

"That's the one."

"Is it enough? Do you want a sandwich to go with that?"

"No, thanks." She pushed the menu aside. "I take it Kirk's working today."

"He is. He's been taking extra hours when he can. To pad our savings."

Pam thought about the sale of the business. "You'll be getting money from your father," she said. "Won't that be enough?"

Jen's easy smile faded. "We're saving that, Mom. For the kids' college. Our retirement. That's not money we'd spend."

Because her daughter was sensible, Pam thought with pride. "You're taking a long-term view. That's good."

"I can't help it. Somehow it seems wrong to spend it on a vacation or carpeting. I want it put away. There will be expenses later." She rested her elbows on the table. "Everything's different now that we're having a baby. Like we can't be frivolous. We're going to get a will, if you can believe it." Jen paused. "Is it okay I say that?"

"Of course." Pam forced a smile. "You're going to have a child of your own. Things change with that. When that happens, we're all forced to be the adult in the room. Harder for some than others. You've always made smart decisions."

"I wish that were true, but thanks for the compliment. I worry, though. About Kirk. He's in a dangerous line of work. What if something happened to him? I'm not like you, Mom. I couldn't be that strong."

Pam thought about the long nights, the crying, the way every single breath hurt. She wasn't nearly as strong as they all thought, but sharing that wouldn't help anyone.

"We all do what we have to," she said instead. "You'd get by because there isn't an alternative. But I suspect you and Kirk will be together for a long, long time."

Jen's eyes filled with tears. "Thanks for saying that. I hope you're right. I miss Daddy a lot."

Pam nodded. Her throat tightened and she found herself longing to be home. Lulu never brought up John. Pam was the one who decided what she could stand and what she couldn't.

"He's never going to see his first grandchild." Tears spilled down Jen's cheeks. "I think about that all the time. It's so unfair."

Pam wanted to shriek at her that Jen couldn't begin to understand what was unfair. That Pam's loss was greater. Harder. Sharper.

Parents were older. They were expected to die at some point. But not a husband. Not so soon. She hadn't been ready.

But she didn't say any of that. Instead, she pulled out the stash of tissues she kept with her and passed a couple across the table. Jen took one and wiped her eyes.

"Sorry."

"Don't be. I cry all the time. I try not to do it outside the house, but it's still happening."

Jen nodded and sniffed. "Mom, if you want to come stay with us, you know you can, right?"

For the first time in days, Pam smiled spontaneously. "I love you like you're my own daughter, but moving in with you and Kirk is my own version of hell."

Jen laughed. "I figured, but you're always welcome."

"Don't take it personally."

"I won't. You'd hate living with the boys even more."

"You got that right."

Jen squared her shoulders. "Enough of my emotions.

How are you doing? Really? Tell me the truth. Is it better than it was?"

Pam thought about the long nights, the hideously lonely days. She thought about how she wandered from room to room, waiting for someone who would never return. She thought about the pain, the tears, the bottles of wine she consumed. Then she looked into her daughter's beautiful face and knew lying offered the most kindness.

"It's better. Not great. But it's better."

Twenty-One

"WE SHOULD DO SOMETHING TODAY," ERIC said.

It was nine on Sunday morning. Nicole had yet to shower, let alone dress. She had been looking forward to a long day of doing nothing. With Greta taking care of things like grocery shopping and cleaning, Nicole's free time had taken a turn for the open and she was excited about that.

"What did you have in mind?" she asked as she thought about getting another cup of coffee. But that would mean getting up and walking across the kitchen. "I could look online. I'm sure the California Science Center has something fun going on."

It was also one place Tyler had a good time. He was still too young for the other museums. "Oh, there's also the La Brea Tar Pits. He'd like that."

"Not a museum," Eric told her. "I was thinking we'd have a party. Here."

"A party? Today?"

"Sure. Just a few people over. We'll grill burgers. It'll be great."

Nicole watched as her vision of a do-nothing day evaporated like mist. On the bright side, Eric hadn't been interested in socializing outside of his writer friends for months, which meant there were a lot of people she hadn't seen, either. Their friends were mostly couple friends. And with her and Eric not acting like a couple lately, they'd been turning down invitations regularly.

"You're right," she said firmly. She got up and walked to the coffeepot. "We should invite all our friends over. I'm sure some are busy, but we'll take who we can get. It'll be good for us to hang out with them."

Eric got a pad of paper and started making a list. It got up to twenty people pretty quickly, but Nicole figured they'd be lucky to get half that to attend. Once the list was made, they divided it and started texting people.

Within the hour they had seven yeses and a grocery list. Two of the couples would bring kids. So fourteen adults, two kids, plus them.

"That's nineteen people," Nicole said, double-checking her math.

"We'll get everything at Costco," Eric told her. "Burgers, buns, a couple of salads, beer and juice for the kids."

"It won't be organic," Nicole pointed out. "You don't think Greta will be able to smell it when she shows up tomorrow morning?"

Her husband laughed. "Leave Greta to me. I appreciate that she's looking out for Tyler, but sometimes you have to go with the flow and have a little fun."

"You say that now, but wait until she's staring you down."

"I can handle her."

Nicole savored the moment of happiness. This was the Eric she remembered, she thought with contentment. The fun, sweet man who wanted to spend time with his family and hang out with his friends. Maybe she'd been too judgmental about what he was doing and how things had changed. Maybe she should take his advice and go with the flow.

"While you deal with Costco, I'll take Tyler to Patty Cakes and get the cupcakes. We'll get home first, so I'll get out the folding tables and wash them down."

"This is going to be fun," he told her as he got up and circled around the table. He dropped a kiss on the top of her head.

"It is," she whispered when he'd left the kitchen.

"Oh, my God! I can't believe it." Julie clapped her hands together. "When we found out Eric had sold his screenplay, we were stunned. I mean we've known the two of you forever. And to think you're like a famous Hollywood couple now."

Nicole was careful to keep smiling as she put condiments on a tray to take outside. Smiling was important, she thought. Because the party was fun and these were her friends. Only things weren't going exactly the way she'd thought they would. Rather than spending time catching up, all anyone wanted to talk about was Eric's screenplay deal.

She was okay with him having the attention. He'd worked hard and he deserved to get credit for that. But she'd wanted to spend time with their friends, not have an event in celebration of him.

Julie sighed. "I wish Shane would do something like that. It would be so cool."

"You love Shane. He's a great guy."

Julie grinned. "I'd love him more if he was famous, that's for sure." She leaned in and lowered her voice. "I can't believe he's going to read part of it to us later. I'm so excited."

"What?"

Her friend nodded her head. "He told me he's going to read a couple of scenes. It's totally insider info. I can't wait."

Nicole did her best not to look as shocked as she felt. Reading part of his screenplay? Out loud? Wasn't that taking things a bit too far?

"What was your favorite part?" Julie asked. "You must be tired of it by now, so thanks for indulging the rest of us."

Nicole managed to keep smiling, even though she felt a little sick to her stomach. She didn't have a favorite part of Eric's screenplay because she hadn't read any of it. He'd never let her. Not once, no matter how many times she asked. But he was going to read a couple of scenes to their friends?

She handed Julie the condiments. "Would you take these out, please? I want to check on the drink supply. We want to make sure we have enough for everyone to toast Eric later."

"Oh, right. Sure."

Julie walked through the open back door and into the yard.

Nicole leaned against the counter. Everything was going to be fine, she told herself. At least she didn't have to worry about being bored during the reading. But as she stood alone in the kitchen, she wondered what was going on. Had Eric forgotten she hadn't read his screenplay? Was this a giant snub?

She told herself she would deal with it later. That right now there was a party and she wanted to have a good time.

She checked on the drinks, then took out a container of potato salad and carried it to the patio.

The three boys had already exhausted themselves running around and were now flopped down on a blanket in the shade of a tree playing with plastic dump trucks. Eric and a couple of the guys stood by the grill. Everyone else was either on folding chairs or on blankets on the grass. Music played from wireless speakers.

Bits of conversation drifted to her.

"No, really, have you met anyone famous?"

"I heard it was like a million dollars. I wonder if they'll move."

"They have a nanny now, you know. Must be nice."

Nicole looked at their guests and realized how long it had been since she'd seen any of them. Eric had chosen to bury himself in his screenplay, but what was her excuse? She'd let the friendships wither. Sure she'd been busy, but that was hardly a reason. If she wanted people in her life, she had to make time for them.

She put more potato salad into the bowl, then carried the empty container back into the kitchen.

Mark, a friend of Eric's at the software company where they had both worked, followed her inside.

"Everyone's talking about Eric's deal," he said.

"I heard."

"It's fun for all of us. Maybe you'll get to go to an award show and we can see you on TV."

"Maybe. I haven't seen you and Paige in forever. How are things going? Tell me everything."

Mark's gaze shifted away. "We're fine."

"What?" she demanded. "Is everything okay?"

Mark smiled. "Everything is great. Don't worry." He stepped toward her. "Can you keep a secret?"

"Sure. What?"

"Paige is pregnant. Three months. We were going to start telling people today, in fact, but then we got the text. This is about Eric and we don't want to steal the spotlight. But we're both really happy."

"Congratulations," Nicole told him. "That's wonderful. I wish you would tell everyone. It's wonderful, happy news."

"Next time," Mark said, then glanced back outside. "Oh, look. Eric's going to read from his screenplay. I don't want to miss that."

Nicole watched him walk away, then slowly followed. Shouldn't news of a baby trump a screenplay reading? What was going on here? Maybe it was her, she told herself. She was overly sensitive. She had a thing against fame and anything remotely entertainment-related because of how her mother had pushed her. But she couldn't shake the sense of being swept away by something she couldn't control and didn't completely understand.

"That's a lot of pink," Adam said.

"*Overwhelming* is the word you're looking for." Shannon stood next to him in the "party room" at Epic Salon and told herself that the paint wasn't really vibrating on the walls. It just seemed that way.

Whoever had designed the space had gone all out. While the front part of the salon was quiet and elegant, done in grays and lavenders, back here it was all pink, all the time. The walls, the tables, the chairs, the tablecloths, even the window coverings were shades of pink. Balloons in tones from palest rose to lipstick floated near the ceiling. Pink lemonade filled pitchers on tables. The cupcakes were iced in pink.

"Now I'm scared about the pizza," he admitted. "And woozy. Can too much of a color make you light-headed?"

"I think your testosterone is worried about being overwhelmed."

"Rightfully so." He looked around. "This isn't normal, right? I'm afraid for a reason?"

"You are, but you're going to have to deal. This is what you agreed to for your daughter's birthday party." Shannon patted his arm. "Don't worry. You're not staying and I doubt a few minutes in this hostile environment is going to be enough to turn you into a woman."

"You're mocking me."

"Right now you're kind of mockable."

Adam pulled her close and kissed her. "I can't tell you how glad I am you're here to save my butt."

"It's a nice butt and well worth saving."

He grinned. "You're irresistible and as soon as I return my children to their mother's I'm going to prove it five times over."

"Five times, huh? That's quite an offer."

"How about I throw in dinner, too?"

"Sold."

He released her and circled the room. "There's not much for me to do."

She nodded, guessing that was the point. Epic provided a full-service birthday party for the younger set. First the girls would have a mani-pedi, then they would adjourn to the back room for the actual party. Pizza, drinks and cupcakes were provided, along with the decorations. For a guy like Adam, it was a godsend. All he had to do was make the reservation and cough up the credit card. Pretty brilliant marketing, she thought.

"You're sure you're going to be okay?" he asked.

"I'll be fine," she assured him, thinking that a group of nine-year-old girls couldn't be that scary. And if she was wrong, she had a bottle of wine waiting back at her place.

"Because I can stay."

"You're adorable for offering, but I can see the fear in your eyes. It will be fine." She pushed him toward the door. "Go pay the nice lady for the party. The girls will be arriving soon."

Adam nodded and headed toward the front of the store. Shannon circled the room one more time, making sure everything was in place. There was a table for gifts, and another table with the small goodie bags prepared by the salon. Inside was a bottle of nail polish, several temporary tattoos and some plastic costume jewelry.

There was no present from her father at the party. He would be giving that to her tonight at dinner. Shannon had declined to attend. She had a feeling that a three-hour party was going to be more than enough family time for one day.

She walked up front to confirm that everything looked good and found Char in tears and Adam looking frustrated.

"She won't say what's wrong," he said. "Char, if you don't tell me, I can't help."

"It doesn't matter," his daughter told him. "Just go. I'm fine."

"I can't leave you like this. Your party starts in a few minutes. Tell me?"

Char sniffed. "Dad, I'm okay. I'm going to have a good party. I promise. Just go."

Adam hesitated, then looked at Shannon. "You'll call me if you need help?"

"In a heartbeat," she promised.

Char stepped close to her. "Shannon's here, Dad. I'm fine. You should go pick up Oliver."

Because her younger brother was at a friend's house.

Adam glanced at the door, then back. "Okay, but you know how to reach me." He kissed them both on the cheek, then left.

When he was gone, Shannon pointed to the chairs in the waiting area. "We have a few minutes before your guests arrive. Why don't you tell me what's wrong?"

Char sat and her eyes filled with tears again. "It's the party. I wanted the skin-care facial and my dad said no. That he wouldn't pay for it. But when Bree had her party here, we had the skin-care facial and everyone loved it. He says the party is already expensive. But all my friends are going to laugh at me."

Shannon felt the hit straight to her gut. She knew Adam had been against the facial from the beginning. She kind of saw his point. Char was only nine and a facial sounded pretty adult. But she hated seeing Char so upset right before her party.

"I'm sorry Char, but I can't help with something your dad specifically said he didn't want you to have," she said.

"I know." Char hung her head. "You can't go behind his back, even though it's my birthday."

Shannon recognized the attempt to guilt her. No way she was going to fall for it. But she still felt like crap.

"Is there something we could add to the mani-pedi package that would be different from the other parties?" she asked, confident she was both weak and being played, but unable to help herself.

Char brightened immediately. "Nail art. No one's had that." She pointed to the signs on the wall. "The glitter package."

Shannon saw that there was indeed a glitter package for the parties. The price made her wince, but it was too late to back out now.

She stood and walked to the receptionist. "Then let's get this party started."

Ninety minutes later, Shannon was fighting a killer headache. She'd had no idea ten nine-year-old girls could make so much noise. And at such a high pitch.

The party itself was brilliant. The salon partnered with a nearby beauty school. The technicians brought in for the event were students. Epic didn't tie up staff with clients who would not become regulars for at least another decade and the students had an opportunity to practice.

The glitter package had been a hit. Now, as they waited for their lunch of pizza to arrive, the girls ran around showing off their manicures and pedicures.

Shannon was kept busy circling the room and making sure everyone had drinks. She'd thought at least a couple of the mothers would stay, but they'd all taken off immediately. Leaving her as the only adult who wasn't hired by the salon. A fact that made it difficult for her to completely relax.

There were presents stacked on the table. They were to be opened after lunch but before the cupcakes, Char had informed her. And after the cupcakes, everyone went home. Hallelujah.

"We're out of soda," Char informed her. "Could you see about that?"

Shannon hesitated. While the pitchers were empty, there was something in the girl's tone that gave her pause. An imperiousness that was incredibly annoying.

"Sure," Shannon said, telling herself Char was simply running on adrenaline. It was her party, after all.

She went and mentioned they needed more soda to the party coordinator and returned to the back room in time to hear Adam's daughter say, "Oh, she's not my stepmother. She's just someone my dad's dating. I don't think they're even boyfriend and girlfriend."

"But you like her," one of the girls said. "She's really nice."

Char shrugged. "She's okay. We're not friends or anything. I would never hang out with her."

"At least your dad just dates one woman at a time. My dad doesn't. It's gross."

Shannon turned and walked out of the room. The party coordinator was hurrying toward her, a full pitcher in each hand.

"Oh, I'll help with that," Shannon said, and blindly took one. Because all she could do was keep moving. If she stopped, she would have to think about what Char had said. She would have to admit the truth. That while she'd been looking to get to know Adam's daughter, Char had only been interested in using her to get a better party.

Once back in the room, she poured soda into glasses and made sure she was smiling. She admired the glitter polish and told herself she would wallow in being a fool later. That she only had an hour or so left before she could make her escape.

A few minutes later the party coordinator walked in with

several pizza boxes from The Slice Is Right. Shannon helped her set out the food. The girls found seats.

Char sat at the head of the table. "I go first," she announced loudly, and studied the open pizza boxes. She pointed to the pepperoni pizza. "I want a slice of that. Shannon, would you get it for me?"

Every girl turned to look at her. Some seemed shocked by the request. A couple looked gleeful. As if this had been planned. Or maybe they were simply enjoying the opportunity to watch an adult squirm.

Shannon chuckled, as if Char was making a joke. "You're nine, not ninety. You can get your own pizza."

"But it's my birthday."

"Happy birthday to you." Shannon scanned the table. "We need more napkins. I'm going to get them."

She practically bolted from the room. Once outside, she leaned against the wall.

Had she handled that right? Should she have just handed her the pizza? She wished she knew the right thing to do. Maybe she was overreacting to what she'd heard—letting her own insecurities color her view of things.

"Here are extra napkins."

The party coordinator pressed them into her hand.

"Thanks."

Shannon sucked in a breath and then walked back into the party. The girls were deep in conversation and didn't seem to notice.

After the food, Char insisted everyone sit in a circle and pass her the presents, one by one. She opened them and thanked everyone, but also made a few digs about the choices. It was a side of her Shannon hadn't seen before.

She told herself to keep quiet and simply get through the

rest of the party. When the guests had left, she collected Adam's receipt along with her own and carried the presents to the car.

When the gifts were stacked in the backseat, Char fastened her seat belt and sighed.

"That was the best party ever!"

"I'm glad you enjoyed it."

Char looked at her. "What?" she demanded. "Why did you say it like that? Didn't you have fun?"

"I wasn't there as a guest," Shannon said. No, she'd been there as some girl her father was dating. Not that she was going to get into that. Simply get the kid home, she told herself. Don't fight about it. Walk away.

All good advice, except for one problem. She wasn't just someone Adam was dating. She was in love with him and they were talking about having a future together. If she let Char's behavior go, didn't that make her an accessory to it? Or at the very least, someone who condoned it?

She wasn't sure of her place in the situation. What was expected? What was allowed? No one had given her a manual or even basic instructions.

"I knew you'd be this way," Char said with a heavy sigh. "I knew you wouldn't be happy for me."

"What are you talking about?"

The girl glared at her. "You don't really like me. You're just doing stuff so my dad will think you do."

Shannon had no idea where the accusation was coming from. "Char, if I didn't like you, why would I have tried to make your party better? Your dad wasn't there. He doesn't know what I did. I did it for you." She angled toward her. "I have to say, I'm really disappointed by all this. I thought you and I were friends. I'm sorry I'm wrong."

Char turned away. "Why are you doing this? Why are you ruining my birthday? You wanted me to have a bad time. I know it."

"You're not making sense. You got everything you wanted. You wanted me to pay for the glitter package and I did."

Char swung back to face her. "You offered. That's not my fault. Besides, it's my birthday. I get to say. You wouldn't even hand me a slice of pizza. That was mean."

"No," Shannon told her. "What was mean was when you told Madison that her gift wasn't expensive enough and that you weren't sure you could be friends with her anymore."

Char flushed. "She bought me socks. That's a grandma gift."

"They were cute and in your favorite colors. You don't get to judge a gift, Char. That's the point. People want to show they care. By complaining about it, you're showing that you're the one who doesn't care. You embarrassed your friend in front of everyone. Whatever you remember from today, she's going to remember feeling sick to her stomach and wishing she could be anywhere but at your party. It's one thing to be the center of attention on your birthday. It's another to hurt people in the process."

Char's face went pale, then flushed again. Her mouth twisted as tears filled her eyes.

"I hate you," she breathed. "You ruined everything. I'm going to tell my dad what you did and he's never going to see you again."

"Very possibly," Shannon murmured. "Very possibly."

They drove back to Adam's place without talking. The only noise was the car engine and Char's choked sobs. When Shannon pulled into the driveway, Char bolted from the car and ran into the house. Shannon turned off the engine and rested her head on the steering wheel. She honestly didn't see a good outcome in her future.

She'd just loaded up with the presents when Adam burst out of the house.

"What the hell happened?" he demanded. "Char's shrieking that her party was ruined and that it's your fault."

"That's not exactly how it went. There were a few bumps in the road."

Adam expression hardened. "I need you to tell me exactly what happened. What did you say to upset her? Jesus, Shannon, it's my daughter's birthday. Why is she inside crying as if her heart is broken?"

She thrust the presents at him. "Well, for starters, she's mad because she didn't get her way. Oh, don't get me wrong. She played me like a pro. I paid for the glitter package for the mani-pedis. But that wasn't enough. She wanted to be the center of attention. Fine. It's her birthday. But I refused to serve her pizza and there was some other stuff."

He stared at her. "What are you talking about? This is because you didn't want to hand a nine-year-old a slice of pizza?"

"No. Not exactly. It's more than that. She was mean to some of her friends and—"

"She was mean to you? Shannon, she's a kid. You're the adult. Communication is your responsibility. I have to admit, I'm really disappointed by all of this. I thought it would go better. I thought I could trust you."

She felt the jab all the way down to her heart. Talk about a perfectly placed blow. Because there was nothing she could say in return. He had a crying birthday girl in the house and his girlfriend on the outside. When push came to shove, she knew exactly where his loyalties would lie.

"You're missing the point," she told him.

"Am I? This is why I'm usually so careful about introducing my children to anyone I'm dating. You don't have a family of your own, so you wouldn't understand. But it sucks. She's upset, I still don't know what happened and I'll be dealing with this all weekend. Then I have to explain to her mother how my girlfriend let this happen. All I wanted was to make sure my daughter had a good birthday."

She glared at him. "What makes you think I wanted anything different? You weren't there, Adam. Be careful with your accusations and assumptions. Because some things can't be unsaid."

He threw up his hands. "If you'll excuse me, I have to go fix things with Char."

He turned and walked back to the house. Shannon stood there and watched him go. She told herself to stay in the moment, to feel the feelings, to integrate that this was how it was going to be, should she and Adam stay together. That his children would always come first. That whatever the circumstances, they would be the ones he believed, while she was suspect.

She got in her car and told herself not to jump to conclusions. That he would figure out she wasn't the bad guy. That he would be sorry and they would get through this.

As she drove away, she wondered how long it would take for him to realize that Char wasn't the only person he had to fix things with. Or if he would realize it at all.

Twenty-Two

PAM SAT AT HER SMALL DESK IN THE STUDY and waited for her laptop to boot. She'd had a good night, sleeping for several hours in a row. This was the most rested she'd felt in weeks, which meant it was time to tackle one of the difficult tasks she'd been putting off: John's email.

Ever thoughtful, he'd kept a list of user names and passwords in his desk drawer. They had been there in case she needed to access something while he was at work, but had turned out to be helpful after his death.

The paperwork and logistics that went with a spouse's passing were ongoing and onerous. Steven and Jen had helped with some, but after the first couple of weeks, they'd returned to their lives. Pam had slowly been dealing with the rest.

There were bank accounts to change, investment accounts. Acquaintances to notify, subscriptions and memberships to cancel. Every time she turned around, there was something else she had to deal with. Some other forgotten element of his life that had to be tidied.

She carefully drew in a deep, calming breath before logging on to his email account, then shook her head when she saw well over a hundred emails waiting.

The spam was easy. She forwarded anything that needed answering to her own account. There were a few political notices, some ads from the car dealership he used and something from a cruise line.

Her gaze drifted to the subject line. She froze in her seat. Pain hit her hard, front and back, stealing her breath and making it impossible to fight back tears.

New information for Booking…

The actual number blurred, as did the email when she opened it. She sat there and let the tears flow down her cheeks.

The cruise. The cruise she and John had been so excited to go on. He'd made the reservations right after their sex-retreat weekend, when they were doing it like rabbits three times a day.

She covered her face with her hands. They'd talked about all the places they were going to have sex. How they would go visit the turtles in Grand Cayman and float down a river in Jamaica. They'd made plans and now he was gone.

Small paws touched her thigh. She looked down and saw Lulu standing on her back legs, looking up at Pam anxiously.

"I'm sorry, baby girl," she said as she picked up her dog and cradled her. Lulu licked her cheek.

"I know it's hard when I get like this," Pam murmured. "You hate to see me so sad. It's just I can't help it. I miss your dad so much."

Lulu's ears perked up. She struggled to get down. When Pam set her on the carpet, the little dog raced toward the garage door, barking as she went.

Sobs ripped through Pam. She'd said "Dad." Lulu thought John was finally coming home.

"He's not," she whispered, even though she knew Lulu couldn't hear her. "He's never coming home. We're never going to see him again."

She rested her elbows on the desk and covered her face with her hands again. This had to stop, she thought. She couldn't keep doing this to herself. Suffering day after day. Everyone said things would get easier with time, but they weren't. Everyone promised she would start to heal, but so far there had been nothing but the hell of knowing John was never coming home.

She dropped her hands to her lap and stared sightlessly at the computer screen. From deep in her chest came a primal scream of protest, and in the background, the steady beating of her heart.

Because while she might be falling apart emotionally, physically she was fine. She came from a long line of women who lived well into their eighties. She was facing the next thirty years without John and for the life of her, she couldn't figure out the point of that.

Lulu returned to the study. Her fluffy head hung in defeat. Her tail was tucked between her legs. Pam picked her up and held on tight.

"I know," she whispered. "It hurts so much."

She wiped her face and turned back to the computer screen. She was going to have to call the cruise company and cancel. Or maybe find out if she could send Jen and Kirk. Although they were both working and saving any extra time off for after the baby was born. No, she would cancel. It wasn't as if she was going to take a cruise by herself. That would be beyond depressing.

For a second she tried to imagine herself on the ship—a pathetic figure wandering aimlessly from place to place. She couldn't do it. Certainly didn't want to even try. The way she was feeling, she would end up throwing herself off the ship at some point.

Pam turned her attention back to the screen. There had to be a contact number somewhere. She started to scan the email, then realized what she'd thought just seconds before.

She could throw herself off the ship.

She set Lulu on the floor and placed her hands on the keyboard of her laptop. No, that was ridiculous. She wasn't going to kill herself. It was wrong and selfish.

People fell off ships all the time. She was forever hearing about it on the news. Lost at sea.

No, she couldn't do that to her children. Losing a parent unexpectedly was one thing, but to know that she had killed herself would be another. They would be devastated. They would think she didn't love them. And she did. Desperately. It was just they didn't understand how hard it was to be without John. They didn't know about the empty nights, the life that stretched before her.

Still, they were her children and she loved them. She would never hurt them.

What if they thought it was an accident?

Pam turned that idea over in her head. If it was an accident, then they would miss her, but there wouldn't be any sense of having been abandoned. Could she do that? Could she make them think she was fine and then simply jump off the ship?

She looked at the email again. In addition to the tickets, there was information on the itinerary and various shore excursions. She scanned the ports and saw that Friday was a day at sea.

The cruise started on Saturday. If she showed up at different activities, talking to people, pretended to be having a good time, no one would suspect. She could be memorable enough that when questioned, everyone would say she had been sad about her husband, but obviously healing. Then on Thursday night she would slip over the edge and never have to feel the loss of her husband again.

It was the perfect solution, she thought with more than a little surprise. And exactly what she needed to do.

She let the idea sit in her brain for a few seconds. There was no horror, no revulsion. Only a sense of rightness. She couldn't live without him, so she wouldn't.

She printed out the tickets. While the printer hummed away, she used the hotlink in the email to go look at the various excursions. It only took a few minutes to find the ones she wanted.

Her goal was to be visible and make friends. For the day in Jamaica she booked the Shaw Park Gardens, Dunn's River Falls and Beach trip. Her chest tightened a little when she went to look at trips in Grand Cayman. She'd wanted to see the turtle farm there for as long as she could remember. John had always teased her about it.

She squared her shoulders, then booked herself on the Turtle Farm, Hell, Tortuga Rum Cake and Scenic Drive tour. For the island of Cozumel, she chose the Tulum Mayan Ruins and Playa del Carmen trip.

Once it was all done, she printed out her confirmations, then turned off her computer and stood. Thousands of thoughts flitted in and out of her head. There was so much to do, she thought. She was filled with purpose in a way she hadn't been for weeks. A thousand details to manage. She wanted to get everything completely in order, down to the tiniest detail. She had a plan and she was determined to see it through.

"Sorry," Nicole said as she walked back in the living room. "I just wanted to make sure Tyler was asleep. Once he's out, he's gone until morning, but every now and then it can take him a bit to get to that point."

Shannon nodded. "I'm sure me showing up like this didn't help."

"He adores you." She sat across from her friend. "Want to talk about it?" she asked gently. It wasn't that she minded the company. Having Shannon stop by was great. It was just the sadness she saw in her eyes, not to mention the grocery bag with about five different flavors of Ben & Jerry's. There were a limited number of reasons for them to need that kind of emotional help.

Shannon pulled her knees to her chest and wrapped her arms around her shins. "It's Adam," she admitted. "We had a huge fight. I'm angry, he's angry. It was so awful."

She tucked her long red hair behind her ear and pressed her lips together. "It's the kid thing. Or rather the lack of kid thing. I don't have children. I get that. But why did he assume the worst about me? I'm not a bad person. I wanted Char to have a good time. But would he listen? Of course not. He played the parent card."

She held up one hand. "He's the parent. I know that. And I get that being a parent means having responsibilities. But I would never hurt Char or Oliver. She was horrible and he didn't want to listen. He simply assumed I'd done something awful and I was a bad person." Shannon shook her head. "I'm not a bad person."

Nicole did her best to sort through the information. "Okay, it would really help if I knew what happened with you and the kids. Was it Char's birthday party?"

"Yes. It was nowhere near as cool as Tyler's. Give me Brad the Dragon any day over a bunch of little girls at a spa."

Shannon explained about the glitter add-on and how Char had been rude and imperious.

"I wanted her birthday to be special," Shannon told her. "I wanted her to be happy and excited. But there was something else going on. It's like she had something to prove."

"Has she been like that before? Some kids are just obnoxious."

"I know what you're saying and I want to say that no, she's been more difficult than Oliver, but not in a bad way. I think she's really protective of her mom, and that's admirable. She's generally pleasant and normal. At the party, it's like she was possessed by some evil narcissist."

Shannon leaned her head against the back of the sofa. "I can't get over what Adam said to me. That he was disappointed. It was like he was scolding me. I really didn't like that at all. And why didn't he want to talk to me about what happened?"

Nicole raised her eyebrows. "You still haven't spoken to him?"

"No. I'm not calling and apparently he's not calling, either. What do you think?"

"That you're sweet and kind and he should find out the facts before assigning blame." Nicole thought about the people she knew who were divorced. No one in their inner circle of friends, she thought. A couple of clients had been through it.

"Being a single parent has to be hard," she admitted. "There's guilt and stress. But he should know you well enough to confirm what happened. I could forgive being upset in the moment, but not letting it go on for several days."

Shannon blinked several times, then stared at the ceiling, as if willing back tears. "Yeah," she said after clearing her throat. "That's what I thought, too. The longer I don't hear from him, the worse I think it is between us. He was so angry and he didn't want to hear my side. I love him, but I also know he's wrong about this. He should have talked to me."

Nicole thought maybe she was right. She couldn't imagine someone else telling Tyler what to do. He was hers. Hers and Eric's. But with Eric, it was different. As much as he was gone, she was confident he loved his son. But someone else in the mix would just be a mess.

"Dealing with stepkids can't be easy," Nicole admitted. "You get a lot of responsibility with little or no say in what happens. Talk about a minefield."

"They're not even my stepkids and I'm dealing with this," Shannon said glumly. "I thought he was the one. I thought we were going to work it out. But now I just don't know where we are. Does he even care that we're not talking? Is it over?"

"You could call him," Nicole said gently.

"And what should I say? Ask if he's ready to apologize?"

Nicole didn't have an answer. In her heart, she thought maybe reaching out was a good first step. Especially if Shannon wanted the relationship to work. But she got why her friend felt Adam should be the one to make the move. But if neither of them did anything, they would stay stuck.

Kind of like her and Eric. They were stuck—married but not actually a couple. Not for a long time now. The money problems had been solved, but nothing else was better. He was still gone a lot and moving in a direction that didn't seem to include them.

"I wish I had better advice," Nicole said.

"I don't think there's an answer right now. I think Adam and I both need time."

Nicole nodded. "Want some ice cream?"

"Yes."

"And tequila?"

Shannon smiled. "You sure know how to show a girl a good time."

Pam signed her name over and over. There were dozens of little stickers with an arrow on them, pointing to where she should sign her name. She went from page to page, feeling her sense of satisfaction grow with each signature.

"Excellent," Dan, her financial advisor, told her. "I'm impressed, Pam. At our first couple of meetings after you lost John, I was worried about you. But you're doing really well."

"Thank you," she murmured, careful to stare at the paperwork as she spoke. Dan was a friend of the family. She was afraid that if she actually looked him in the eye, he would quickly figure out something was up.

She wasn't doing well at all. It was impossible to draw a breath without wanting to scream for missing John. But her decision had given her energy. More important, she had a purpose. There were things to be done to prepare for her upcoming trip…and subsequent lack of return. She might not be willing to live with her grief, but she wasn't going to be a burden to her children in the process.

He took back the papers and flipped through them, checking to make sure all the signatures were in place. She waited patiently.

Several years ago she and John had put everything into a trust. It was the easiest way to transfer assets within the family without having to worry about sibling disagreements and huge tax bills. Since finding out about the key man policy and the buyout of her share of the business, she'd known she had to do something. Once she'd decided to kill herself, she'd been motivated to take the next financial step.

She'd divided the after-tax amount from the sale of the business into two equal halves. One had been put into her trust, the other half had been set aside for the children.

When she was declared lost at sea, aka dead, Dan would manage the trust for her estate. The kids would get their money with minimal hassle and waiting.

The house was also part of the trust. She thought it was possible that Jen and Kirk might want it. They would have enough to buy out Steven and Brandon. If no one wanted it, the house would be sold and the proceeds then split between the siblings.

She finished with Dan and then left his upscale office. Her next stop was to see Hayley. She and John's assistant were having lunch together.

She arrived at Gary's Café with five minutes to spare. When she got home, she would have to take Lulu for a long walk on the beach to make up for spending the morning alone. As she entered the restaurant, she thought that it would be hard to leave her little girl behind. Not just for the cruise. Lulu would miss her so much.

She briefly acknowledged that thinking about the dog was much easier than thinking about her children. That she truly *hadn't* thought about her children. About how all this would impact them. Losing two parents so close together would be devastating. She understood that. But she also knew she was making the right decision. She simply couldn't go on without John. People had to understand that.

She was seated in a booth and glanced at the chalkboard specials on the wall. Gary's Café had been established sometime in the 1950s and it hadn't changed much since. It had been refurbished several times but each new version looked exactly like the old one. There were red booths, Formica tables and a jukebox in the corner. The food wasn't fancy, but it was delicious and honest. Unlike the places that advertised no microwaves as a way to show the food was healthy, Gary's Café didn't use microwaves because they hadn't had them, back in the day.

Hayley walked in and spotted her. Pam stood and hugged the other woman, then slid back into the booth. Hayley settled across from her.

"How are you feeling?" Pam asked, studying her friend. The shadows under Hayley's eyes were gone. When she smiled, it reached all the way to her eyes. The air of sadness had faded. All signs that Hayley was healing from her latest miscarriage.

"I'm fine," the pretty blonde said. "And I should be asking that of you. How's it going?"

Pam brushed away the question. "I'm doing okay. It's hard, but I get through."

Hayley leaned toward her and smiled. "I'm so glad about you going on the trip. Getting away will help."

"I know. That's what I think, too. I love my house, but

it's impossible to escape there. I see John in every corner. I feel him with every breath. On the ship, I'll be scared and lonely, but I think it will be better. If that makes sense."

"It does. You'll make friends. Don't they have meet-and-greets with single people?" Hayley winced. "Sorry, I don't mean to make it sound like you'll be dating, but you know what I mean. You can meet other women traveling together. Make friends."

Which all sounded like a nightmare, Pam thought. But she wasn't going to get on with her life. She was going to end it. And part of her plan was to make enough friends that people remembered her.

"That's what I thought, too," she lied. "A change of scene will do me good."

Their waitress stopped by the table and took their drink orders. They both glanced at the menu.

"I'm still a few pounds underweight," Hayley said cheerfully. "I'm having a burger and fries."

"Me, too," Pam told her. Why not? It wasn't as if she had to worry about her cholesterol. People always said to live like you were dying. That it changed everything. She had to admit that they were right.

"I have the instructions for the last time I watched Lulu," Hayley said. "Is her food still the same?"

"It is. I have a new sunscreen we're using."

Hayley giggled. "I know it makes me weird, but I love that I have to put sunscreen on her." The humor faded. "Damn, it's because I see her as a baby. Which I can live with. She's sweet and having her cuddle with me is the best."

"What does Rob think about her?"

Hayley rolled her eyes. "He loves her more than me, if you can believe it. And you know Lulu dotes on him."

Her smile broadened. “I’ve already warned him that I’m your puppy guardian. If anything happens to you, we are so keeping Lulu.”

Information Pam had wanted to ask, but hadn’t been sure how. She and Hayley had discussed that point every time Pam had left Lulu with her. Jen had been her backup, but with a baby on the way, that wasn’t going to work.

Of course, Hayley could get pregnant, too. Pam remembered her friend’s miscarriages and knew she couldn’t mention anything about babies at this point. She would simply have to trust Hayley to handle Lulu and a child.

“There’s money for her medical care,” Pam said, careful to keep her voice sounding teasing. “It should last her whole life.”

The “take care of Lulu” clause had been in the will since she and John had brought the little dog home. There were also some individual bequests and a large amount to be given to her favorite charities.

Hayley shook her head. “I’m honestly not worried. Nothing’s going to happen to you. And if it does, I’ll be there for your little angel. I promise.”

Pam blinked against sudden tears. “You’re a good person. I appreciate all you’ve done for us over the years.”

“I haven’t done anything.”

“You took care of John. I always trusted you to do that.”

Hayley’s mouth twisted. “You’re going to get me crying. I loved John. He was a rock and the nicest man. Steven’s great. I like working for him, but I miss John every day.”

Pam nodded. “Me, too.”

Their waitress returned with their drinks and glanced between them. “You two okay?”

“We will be,” Pam told her. “After our burgers.”

"They do have magical powers," the server said. "You want fries with that?"

"Of course," Pam told her. "We're living large."

Shannon told herself that being the bigger person had value. That she could savor the moment of maturity, of being gracious. That, in karmic terms, she was taking care of her future. But it was all crap. The truth was she was hurt and frustrated and thinking that falling in love with Adam had been a huge mistake because he was nothing but a super butthead.

She walked up to the front door of Adam's house and knocked. Seconds later, he answered.

"Hi. Thanks for coming by."

He looked good and wasn't that just grossly unfair? A little rumpled, a lot tired and shaggy. Like he needed a haircut. Her fingers itched to sweep his hair off his forehead and then linger. Because touching Adam was always fun.

His dark gaze swept over her and in that moment, she could swear she heard his impressed "Wow!" like when they'd first met. Because whatever else might go wrong between them, he'd always thought she was the hottest thing that moved.

"You okay?" he asked.

"I don't know."

"You're still mad."

"Are you asking or telling?"

"Both."

"Quite the trick."

He stepped back. "Please come in."

When he'd called and asked to see her, she hadn't known if she wanted to. A week had gone by. A week of brief texts between them. His had been along the lines of "I need some time with this." And hers had been edited from "Go fuck yourself" to a more generous "Fine."

But as she stepped into his house, something inside of her shifted. She let herself remember how much she'd missed him, despite her attempts not to. She thought about how he made her laugh and how he was one of the most emotionally generous men she knew. Until the incident with Char, she would have said being with Adam always made her feel better about herself. And that was hard to find.

"You and I need to talk," he said. "But Char would like to speak to you, as well."

Char? Shannon came to a stop in the living room, then forced herself to keep walking. Saying she wanted nothing to do with his daughter wasn't an actual solution to their problem. If things were going to work out between the two of them, she had to figure out how to navigate the difficulties of dealing with his kids.

He had to do the same, but right now she was more concerned with her own reaction to hearing the girl's name.

They continued to the family room. Char sat on the edge of the oversize sectional. Her shoulders were slumped and she seemed smaller than Shannon remembered. As the girl raised her head, Shannon saw that she'd been crying.

She came to a stop and pulled Adam close. "Are you making her talk to me?"

"This is completely her idea." One corner of his mouth twisted. "Actually it's hers and her mother's, if you can believe it. She went home last night and today Tabitha called me to say Char wanted to talk to you."

Shannon glanced at the nine-year-old, who slowly stood.

Her lower lip trembled and a single tear slipped down her cheek.

If it was an act, it was a good one, Shannon thought, the wall around her heart cracking just a little.

"Thank you for talking to me," Char whispered.

"You're welcome."

Shannon crossed to the lounge side of the sectional and sat down. Char sat in the middle of the sofa part and faced her. Adam hovered, looking both hopeful and worried.

Char twisted her fingers together in front of her. She kept her head down and when she started to speak, Shannon could barely hear her.

"I'm sorry," the girl whispered. "About the party. I wanted it to be the best one and my friends wanted that, too. None of our parents would get the glitter package so we talked about how to make it happen at my party."

Shannon told herself not to react. While being played by several nine-year-old girls wasn't exactly a point of pride, she had been out of her element. And inexperienced. Which made Adam's comments about her not being their mother not only true, but also something she would have to consider later.

"You thought I'd be easy to manipulate?" she asked, careful to keep her tone neutral.

Char nodded. "I knew you liked my dad a lot and if you made me happy, he would like you more. Plus, a couple of my friends have divorced parents and they said that I needed to be careful with you. That I had to act a certain way so you would do what I said."

Shannon was about to ask her to explain that confusing statement more, when Adam spoke.

"What are you talking about?" he asked sharply. "How did you act?"

Char looked at her father. Tears ran down her cheeks. "Bratty. Like I was the boss of her and she had to do what I said. I made her get me stuff and I wasn't nice. I'm sorry, Daddy."

Adam shoved his hand through his hair. "Seriously?" He looked at Shannon and shook his head. "I had no idea."

She wanted to point out that was because he wouldn't listen, only she thought maybe this was a good time to be quiet.

Char seemed to physically shrink. "I didn't want to be mean. I didn't like it when I was doing it, but once I started, I couldn't stop myself. And everyone was having a good time at the party and I wanted it to go on."

She looked at Shannon. "I felt so bad when I talked to my dad, but I couldn't tell him the truth. So I waited until I saw my mom last night and I told her everything. She was really disappointed in me. For acting that way and for lying to my dad." Char turned to him. "I'm sorry, Daddy. I thought if you knew how bad I'd been, you'd punish me and you always punish way worse than Mom."

Adam muttered something under his breath.

Char bit her lower lip. "I was scared. Because of Shannon. I know you like her and if you believed her, you'd be so mad. But now I'm afraid you won't like me anymore and you'll go away and my dad will be sad and I'll miss you, too."

Shannon struggled to follow the logic. Her first thought was to wonder why Char would worry about her father leaving. Then she got the girl meant her.

The relief was instant. With an explanation in place, she

could understand how things had gotten out of hand. Kids made mistakes, right?

Adam circled around to the front of the sofa and sat down. He held out his arms. Char rushed into them and hung on. Her whole body shook with her sobs.

"Now Tabitha's comments make sense," he said over his daughter's head. "She wanted me to call later. She said that we needed to talk about getting Char into some different activities so she could make new friends." He stroked his daughter's back. "She also said we needed to come up with a punishment plan together, so the consequences for messing up were the same at both houses. Now I know why."

Char straightened and faced her. "I don't want you to go away," she admitted. "I don't want you to be mad at me. I'm sorry, Shannon. It's nice when you're here. Sometimes I get scared because I like you and you're not my mom."

Shannon's chest tightened a little. She was doing just fine until that last bit, she thought grimly.

"I like you, too," she told the girl.

Adam squeezed his daughter. "Okay, you've said what you wanted to. Now I'm going to take you back to your mom's."

Because it wasn't his weekend to have her, Shannon thought. "Tabitha wanted her to do this today?"

"Yeah," Adam said. "She felt it had festered long enough. I'm going to run her home and come right back. Can you wait?"

She nodded. When he'd gone, she stayed on the sofa. Too much had happened, she thought. Their relationship had too many sharp edges and if she wasn't careful, she was going to end up cut and bruised.

Stepchildren were a complication. One she didn't know

how to deal with. She loved Adam—that hadn't changed. But this part of his life—she didn't know how to deal. Having children with him, or anyone, was going to be different than she imagined. Hard. Worthwhile, she was sure, but not easy.

He was back as quickly as promised. He walked over to her and pulled her to her feet, then kissed her on the mouth.

"I'm sorry," he said, holding her close. "I was so incredibly wrong about all of it. Can we talk about it?"

"Sure."

They sat down. He kept her hand in his. "After the party I was mad. Char was crying and saying you'd ruined her birthday. I hadn't been there. I felt guilty and angry."

"You didn't trust me," Shannon said, remembering how betrayed she'd felt. "You didn't bother to listen to what had happened."

"She was crying. I had to deal with that."

"Why? She wasn't bleeding. You could have taken two minutes to let me explain what was wrong. But you didn't even consider that. You listened to half of what I had to say, assumed I'd hurt her and went to make it better."

He released her hand. "I never thought you'd hurt her."

"Yeah, you did. I appreciate the apology, Adam. Don't get me wrong. But it's not just what she did to me. She was horrible to Madison. She didn't like the girl's gift and she tormented her about it. I'm not saying that's a punishable offense, but it needs to be addressed. If she acts like that with all her friends, she's not going to have any left in a few months."

A muscle in his jaw tightened. "Shannon, I'm trying to make this right. I need you to get off Char and talk about us. I'll deal with Char later. Tabitha and I are going to talk about her and what happened. I'll ask about Madison. Now can we please talk about you and me?"

A reasonable request, she told herself. Because there was nothing she could do about Char. Char wasn't her business. He had Tabitha for that. A circumstance that was never going to change.

There was no instant family here. No way for her to step in and play at belonging. Adam, Oliver, Char and Tabitha already were a family. They might live in different places, but they were a unit. They had a history. No matter what, for the rest of her life, she would never be a part of that. If she and Adam stayed together, she would always feel like in some ways, she was on the outside, looking in.

She could make her own memories with the kids. She could love Adam, even marry him. But they would always be two separate circles with only a small area that intersected. A large part of who he was wouldn't belong to her.

"No," he said firmly, grabbing both her hands this time. "Don't do it, Shannon. Don't disappear on me."

"I'm right here."

"You're going away. I can feel it. I screwed up, okay? I'm going to make mistakes. But I love you."

"I love you, too," she admitted. "But loving each other didn't prevent the problem. It didn't make things go easier with Char."

"She did some things wrong. We all did. That has to be something we can survive. I want to talk about it. I want to set up some strategies so this doesn't happen again."

He held her gaze with his own. She could feel him willing her to understand. The thing was, she did understand. Even more than he did. Because she saw all the places where they could fail.

"I'm not going away," she told him, feeling her way as she spoke. "But I need to think this through. Your kids change things between us."

"For the better?" he asked hopefully.

She pulled a hand free and touched his face. "I really want this to work."

"I really want to believe you."

She kissed him. The pressure of his mouth against hers felt good. Right. She did love him, but the kid thing confused her.

"We're new at this," she said. "Give us some time to get better at it."

"I'm not worried about me running away. I'm worried about you."

"I won't run."

"You promise?"

"Yes."

She wasn't going to run, but she, like him, was going to take a little time to figure out exactly what she wanted. Adam was a package deal. She couldn't pick and choose the parts she liked. It was all or nothing.

She had thought the only question mark was whether he would be willing to have another child, and what she would do if he said no. But there was more to it than that. And while in the past she'd been the kind of woman who simply went for it, now she knew there was more on the line. Care was required. Not just to protect Adam and his children, but to protect herself, as well.

Twenty-Three

NICOLE WAS SURPRISED TO FIND HER HUSband up and sipping coffee. Normally Eric was in bed long after she'd left for her morning classes, but for some reason today he was awake and sitting at the kitchen table.

"Morning," she said. "I didn't hear you come in."

"It was late. I was going over the revised script with Jacob. He says we're a go."

"That's great. You must be excited. Congratulations."

"Thanks."

She put her travel mug on the counter. She would fill it right before she left and drink it on the way to the studio. It was early—barely five thirty. She had ten minutes to eat her breakfast and pour her coffee. Then she had a ten-minute drive to the studio and ten more minutes to get ready for class. One day she promised herself she would graduate to the place where she could live her life in fifteen-minute increments. Or even twenty.

Ah, the dreams we dream, she thought with a chuckle.

"What's so funny?" he asked.

She got a Greek yogurt out of the refrigerator and sprinkled on some of her organic granola. "Just thinking about how I live my day. Speaking of which, what do you have going on now that you've finished with the script?"

"Going back to the next one."

"Impressive dedication."

She told herself it was enough that they were having a conversation. That it didn't matter that they could have been commuters, exchanging pleasantries about the weather, for all the depth in their conversation.

"There's a party next weekend," he said. "I'd like you to go with me."

She walked over and sat across from him. "Really?" He hadn't asked her to attend anything. This was progress, she thought happily. "I'd like that."

"I'm glad. It's Saturday. Can you talk to Greta about working that night? Or get a sitter?"

"Sure."

He smiled. "I'm glad you're excited. This party is going to be so great. It's all industry, so you'll recognize some faces. You'll need to act cool. No staring."

Her good mood had been like bubbles filling the spaces in her heart. A few of them popped.

"Cool it is," she said, determined to find the good in this moment. "So what kind of party? Cocktail? Meet and mingle?"

The smile widened. "Both. There's going to be a water bar. Can you believe it?"

"A what?"

"A water bar." He stared at her like she was an idiot. "With water?"

"Okay," she said slowly. "That's interesting."

"There will be different types of water, from all over the world. You can do a tasting."

Of water? This was why it was probably for the best that she'd never gotten famous. There was no way she would appreciate all the glorious things that went with it.

"Sounds like fun."

He looked away. "You just don't get it."

"Eric, come on. It's water. But I'll be excited if that makes you happy."

"Just don't embarrass me."

"I'd never do that."

"You need to wear something nice. Not like how you usually dress. I hope you can manage that." He stood and walked out of the kitchen.

She rose as well and tossed out her yogurt, then filled her to-go mug and walked out of the house.

Pam stood in front of the ship terminal, waiting for her turn to register, or whatever it was called, before she could get on the ship. She'd arrived in Fort Lauderdale the evening before and after she'd collected her luggage, she'd been met by an older woman with a Princess Cruises clipboard.

More people had joined them and they'd eventually been whisked to a nice hotel. This morning she'd had a tour of the town and then been taken to the terminal.

While she and John had vacationed, they'd never taken a cruise. She'd underestimated how incredibly large the ships were. The Caribbean Princess rose like a beautiful, gliding superbuilding. There were rows and rows of balconies and windows and what felt like an entire village of people trying to board within a few hours of each other.

The line moved forward. She had her passport in hand.

Her luggage was being handled for her, so she only had her carry-on bags. Around her happy couples and families laughed and talked. She didn't see anyone else who was alone. She was the only one.

For a second she thought about turning back. She still could. She could get a cab back to the airport and then buy a ticket home. She could figure out the luggage problem later. She could return to her life and go on, hoping one day she would heal. Or at least be able to breathe without feeling that she was being ripped apart by grief.

Behind her a man laughed. The sound was so familiar, so wonderful, she turned. John! There'd been a miracle. A reprieve. A—

Her gaze settled on an older couple. The man was short and heavy, with dark hair and glasses. He laughed again. Pain squeezed her heart in a vicious grip that would never let go. She faced front and moved forward a few steps.

This was the answer, she reminded herself. Only a few more days and she was never going to hurt again.

The lines moved quickly. Check-in turned out to be a template of efficiency. She handed over her credit card for any additional charges, got her room key and a map, then paused to get her picture taken with several other happy people.

Proof, she told herself as she smiled broadly. Proof she'd been here, proof she was excited. Later, her children would see that picture and tell themselves that she'd been having fun. They would be fooled and that was the greatest kindness she could give them.

Even as the thought formed, a small, quiet voice whispered the greatest kindness might be to return home. To slog through the swamp that was her life without John. To be a mother and grandmother. To go when it was her time.

She shook her head and walked more quickly toward the ship. She'd made up her mind. She wasn't going to change it now.

John had booked them into a minisuite. Pam explored the efficient and comfortable space. There was a bathroom and nice-size closet, a king-size bed and beyond that a small desk and a sofa. She opened the door that led to the balcony and stepped into the warm, tropical air.

She lived in Southern California, only a few blocks from the beach. Yet somehow being on the water in Florida was completely different. Something to do with the more shallow water, she thought. Or just one of those things that nonscientific types couldn't explain.

She went back inside and quickly unpacked. There was a schedule of events for the evening, and information about their first stop at Princess Cays in the Bahamas, the next day.

She scanned what there was to do that night and decided she would go to the welcome reception and the live entertainment. In the meantime, there was a ship to explore.

Pam took her handbag with her and tucked the ship's map in the back pocket of her white cropped pants. She walked along the narrow passageway until she found her way to a bank of elevators.

She went down to the sixth floor—Plaza Deck. People filled the open space. She circled around the elevators and found herself in a huge atrium that went up several stories. There was a woman playing piano, a small café, a bar, a wine bar and a gallery with paintings and sculptures.

She wandered around, smiling and nodding as she explored. A display of pastries caught her attention.

"The éclairs are heavenly," an older woman said, then wiped her mouth with a small napkin. "I've already had two."

"Okay, then. Éclairs it is." Pam nodded at the young woman behind the counter. "An éclair."

She put it on a small plate and handed it to Pam. "Anything else?"

"I think this is plenty to ruin my dinner."

Pam paused a second, expecting the server to ask for money, then remembered that she was on a cruise. Nearly everything was included. She took a bite of the éclair and savored the sweet flavors. The crispy lightness of the pastry, along with the sweet, creamy filling, all surrounded by a whisper of chocolate.

Definitely something to have again, she thought.

She went up a couple of decks and did some window shopping. A sign said the shops would open after the ship sailed. She noted several familiar cosmetic brands and some jewelry that looked interesting. She would make sure to get everyone a souvenir, she thought. Her things would be returned to her family. Which made her think she had to make sure to send chatty emails over the next few days. Happy notes so her children would think she was having a great time.

She went back to the elevator, then up to Deck 16, the Sun Deck. She stepped into a party in progress. As the ship pulled away, live music played and people cheered. Pam sipped a tropical Mai Tai and smiled until her face hurt.

The sun was warm, the breeze gentle and all around her people laughed and waved and talked about the start of their vacation of a lifetime. Pam tried to join in. She spoke for a few minutes to a young couple from Great Britain and reunited an overly excited toddler with his mother. But it all seemed to happen from a great distance. She was there, but not there. As the moments ticked along, she felt her strength fading.

The crowd was too much, she thought. The noise. All of it.

She set her drink on an empty table, then hurried forward. She found a bank of elevators and took one down to her floor, then ran to her stateroom and ducked inside.

The thick plastic covering that had protected the bedspread from her suitcase was gone. Her room had been tidied and on the table in front of the sofa was a beautiful arrangement of pink roses.

Her legs started to give way. Pam had to hang on to the wall to stay upright. She staggered to the sofa and sank down, then reached for the card tucked into the flowers. Her fingers trembled as she opened the small envelope.

Beautiful flowers for my beautiful bride. I love you more every day. J

Not a message from the great beyond, she thought sadly. He would have ordered them when he booked the cruise. Because that was the kind of man he was.

She touched one of the rose petals, then dropped her chin to her chest and gave in to the emotion. Missing him hurt, she thought as she cried. Being without him was torture.

She collapsed onto her side and sobbed out her pain. Soon, she promised herself as she gasped for breath. Soon.

★ ★ ★

Nicole wasn't sure which shocked her more. How much her dress had cost or how little there was to it. The style was beautiful—she could easily admit that. The Alexander McQueen pleated leaf crepe dress was the most beautiful thing she'd ever worn, and that included her wedding gown. The squared-off sweetheart neckline was cut low enough to be supersexy without showing too much. The dress itself was fitted to her hips, then flared out before it ended well above her knee. But the dress had cost over twenty-three hundred *dollars*! You could get a used car for that.

She studied herself in the mirror for another second, before shrugging. Eric had rejected the first two dresses she'd brought home as not being special enough. He'd finally insisted on accompanying her to the store where she'd tried on over a dozen cocktail dresses until they'd settled on this one. When he'd gone to pay for it, she'd half expected to hear their credit card shriek in protest. Of course, when compared to what he'd been spending on clothes, the dress was completely reasonable. Which only went to show how their world had changed in the past few weeks.

She picked up the tiny clutch and then joined Eric in the living room.

Tyler smiled at her. "Mommy, you're beautiful!"

"Thank you, sweetie."

"I will have him in bed by eight," Greta promised. "You do look lovely."

"Thanks." Nicole turned to Eric. "Ready?"

"Uh-huh. Let's go."

She hugged Tyler and then followed her husband out of the house. For a second, she thought about pleading a headache. Nothing about this party sounded appealing. But she'd promised to go. Besides, she and Eric needed some time together. Not just the party, she thought. But after.

Because they weren't sure how late they were going to be, Greta was staying the night. Nicole had spent part of the afternoon tidying the guest bedroom and washing the sheets. She and Eric had booked a room at the Beverly Hills Hotel. They would be going there after the party. Their overnight bags were already in the trunk.

She wondered about their sleeping arrangements that night. She and Eric hadn't shared a bed in months. Obviously that was going to change. Would they make love, as well? She missed their intimacy, their connection. Maybe tonight would be when all that shifted back.

They went directly to the hotel and checked in. Nicole kind of wanted to see the room, but Eric was anxious to get to the party.

They drove through Beverly Hills. She lost track of where they were going, but Eric had been to the house before. It was owned by a friend of Jacob's.

They pulled into a wide, long driveway, flanked by open gates. A valet took their car and handed Eric a ticket. A second valet opened Nicole's door for her.

She got out and stared up at the three-story house. The style was Southern California Spanish, with a tiled roof and plenty of wrought iron. Floodlights illuminated the lush garden and the scent of night-blooming jasmine filled the air.

"Ready?" Eric asked as he put his hand on the small of her back.

She nodded.

They went up the front steps and into the big, open two-story foyer. Music spilled from hidden speakers. Guests mingled and servers walked around with trays of appetizers and glasses of champagne.

Everyone was above average in the looks department, she thought uneasily. Talk about a gathering of the beautiful people. She saw several stars from TV she recognized and a couple of members of One Direction. To the left, in the living room, she would swear Sandra Bullock was talking to Eric's producer friend, Jacob.

Eric took two glasses and handed her one. She thought about mentioning the "water bar" but doubted she could say the words without sounding sarcastic. She wanted tonight to go well. She was going to be the perfect party companion.

After sipping the champagne, she slipped her arm through the crook of her husband's elbow. "Let's make a circuit of the room and see who's here. Then you'll have a better idea of who you want to make sure you talk to and who can wait for later."

His brows rose. "Excellent plan."

"Thank you. I have skills."

He flashed her a smile. "Mad skills."

She laughed.

His gaze lingered on her. "You look beautiful tonight."

"I'm glad you think so." She squared her shoulders. "If anyone asks, I'm here with the hottest new writer since Matt Damon and Ben Affleck wrote *Good Will Hunting*."

"You got that right."

They plunged into the crowd. Nicole hadn't known what to expect from the party. She'd assumed it would be crowded, loud and filled with those trying to prove they belonged, while the super "in" crowd was determined to show they were too cool to have to try. That part was right.

But what she hadn't expected was how easily Eric fit in with everything going on.

They did as she suggested and made a circuit of the party. She helped him keep track of who was where. Then they ranked the list in order of importance and started the serious mingling.

Jacob came first. Nicole had briefly met the older man. He was tall, fit and well-dressed. Now he greeted her as if they'd known each other forever and kissed her on both cheeks.

"You must be proud of your husband," he said when he straightened.

"I am. Very."

"Me, too. There's a lot of people who want to be in this town. Far fewer are willing to do the work. Eric came up with a great story and turned it into an even better screenplay. We're going to have a winner with this one."

"Congratulations."

Jacob put his arm around Eric. "I have a couple of people I want you to meet." He smiled at Nicole. "Five minutes, I swear."

"No problem."

She instinctively stepped back, giving them privacy, or maybe room to walk away. They stayed close by, talking intently. Jacob gestured toward a group of young women. Two of them broke free and came over.

The casting call, Nicole thought, watching them shake hands with Eric and then stand just a little too close. There was plenty of preening and breast thrusting as they talked. Eric seemed flattered but not interested. She turned her attention to Jacob.

He was smooth, she thought, as she watched him dismiss

the girls when he was done with them. He dressed well and had a confidence about him that was appealing. She could see why Eric was happy to have him as his mentor.

She finished her champagne and replaced it with a full glass, then glanced around at the other guests. Her mother would have loved this party, she thought. Between the industry heavyweights and the stars, she would have been running around and getting autographs—which would have humiliated Eric.

Her mother had wanted this for her. How ironic it was happening to her son-in-law instead.

Nicole talked to a nice couple who were costume designers, then joined a conversation with a couple of other wives who had also been asked to wait "just a couple of minutes."

But even as she told them about Eric's screenplay and listened to them brag about their husbands, a part of her wished she was home reading Tyler his before-bedtime story. This simply wasn't her thing. She'd been influenced by her mother's dreams for her, but in her own heart, she hadn't wanted fame. Fortune, sure. Who turned that down? But the idea of being well-known, of having strangers come up to her or want her autograph? No, thanks. Which meant Eric had the best of both worlds—he was part of the in crowd, but could go to the grocery store in peace.

The "few minutes" with Jacob turned into over an hour. When Eric finally returned to her side, they circulated through the party, talking to people he knew. Jacob came by and introduced them to Steven Spielberg and his wife. Nicole listened to the conversation without joining in. She doubted Mr. Spielberg would want to hear that she'd loved *E.T.* since she was a toddler.

Sometime after midnight two guys from One Direction

joined with a couple of other singers in an impromptu jam session. Nicole found herself at the water bar, where she participated in a taste test. The ridiculousness of the concept had her giggling. Or maybe it was the champagne on an empty stomach.

By two in the morning, her butt was dragging. She'd been up since five thirty and had taught four classes. Her feet hurt, she was hungry and all she wanted to do was go home.

She searched for her husband and found him talking to Jacob. Not sure if she should join them or not, she hung back, then sank into an overstuffed chair by the French doors leading to the palatial backyard. As soon as she settled in the chair, she realized how much her feet hurt from her heels and her back ached from standing. She struggled to keep from yawning.

"Your beautiful wife is exhausted," Jacob said, smiling at her. "You should take her home." He winked at her. "If any of my wives had been half so lovely…"

She struggled to her feet. "You're too kind." She walked over to Eric and leaned against him. "Sorry," she said, yawning again. "My days start early."

Jacob nodded. "You have a boy?"

"Tyler. He's five. Full of energy."

Jacob patted Eric's shoulder. "You're a lucky man. We'll talk on Monday. Progress was made tonight. It's all good." He waved and walked away.

Eric stared after him for a second, then turned to her. "You ready to leave?"

There was something in his tone. "Not if you're not."

"There's no point in staying now." He headed for the front door.

Nicole trailed after him. She could tell he was upset,

but had no idea why. From what she'd seen, the party had been a success.

"Did you try the water bar?" she asked as they waited for the valet to bring their car. "It was interesting. The various waters really did taste different. My favorite one was from Finland. Who knew?"

Eric didn't answer. When the valet pulled up with their car, he got inside without speaking.

The short drive back to the hotel was accomplished in silence. Nicole decided to wait until they were in the hotel room to figure out what was wrong with him.

When he opened the door to their room, he pushed in without waiting for her. The closing door nearly hit her in the face. She put down her bag, stepped out of her heels, then put her hands on her hips.

"What on earth is wrong with you?" she demanded.

Eric spun toward her, his face tight with rage. "You humiliated me in front of Jacob."

"What? Are you on crack? I did no such thing."

"You were practically sleeping in that chair. You walked away from him more than once, as if to prove how uninteresting you found him. Do you know how lucky I am that he's taken me on? Do you know how unlikely it was for him to buy my script? The least you could have done was *pretend* interest, but no. That was too much for you."

She felt her mouth drop open. "You are a hundred percent wrong. I never walked away. I was giving you space. Privacy. I didn't know what you were going to talk about. I thought if I clung to you, I would be in the way. I was being polite."

"Is that what it's called?"

"Yes, and if you could take a second and breathe, you'd

see I mean what I said. Eric, I was proud of you. I was happy to be with you. I wanted to make this evening special. I did what I thought you wanted."

"By snoring in a chair?"

"I yawned. I was up early and I worked this morning. I was tired. Is that so unforgivable?" She paced to the window, then faced him again. "I'm confused. I really tried to make you happy. I mingled, I was friendly, I tried the water bar. I wasn't ignoring you or Jacob. You have to know that. What's actually going on here?"

She kept her voice gentle. She didn't want to fight with him. This was a misunderstanding. He had to know her well enough to believe she wouldn't ever try to humiliate him.

"You had your chance," he told her. "All those years ago. You had your chance and you couldn't make it. So you settled. Now you see me getting my dream and you can't stand it. You resent me for being successful."

She'd run out of ways to express shock, she thought as she gaped at him. "That isn't true. I love my life. I have the business and you and Tyler. I don't want to be in the industry. I don't want what you have but I certainly don't resent you for what you've accomplished."

"You sure didn't make it easy. You hounded me to get a job. You wanted me to stop writing."

"You quit your job without discussing it with me and then basically disappeared. You wouldn't help with anything. I had to be responsible for everything, including paying the bills."

"It's the price of art. This is who I am now."

Weariness tugged at her until all she wanted to do was collapse on a bed and sleep. She didn't want to be having this argument on what was supposed to be a special evening. She'd thought tonight might be a chance for them to make a positive change. Instead, it had turned into a disaster.

"I don't know what you want," she admitted. "I know you're angry, but I don't understand why. I'm not the bad guy here, Eric. I thought I did the right thing at the party. I'm sorry you don't agree."

She sat on the edge of the bed and shook her head. "You're so different these days. It's confusing."

"And you're exactly the same."

She raised her head. "What does that mean?"

"I've changed and you haven't. You don't want to. You like how things were. If it was up to you, you'd want things back the way they were."

"I did," she admitted. "Not anymore. You're obviously happier now. You've found your passion. You should pursue it. You—"

His words replayed in her mind. He'd changed and she hadn't. He saw her as stuck in the past and she saw him as only caring about himself. They'd reached the point where they couldn't retreat and they couldn't go forward. Not together.

For weeks she'd wondered what it would be like if she and Eric split up. She'd played with the *D* word, but hadn't actually believed it. Not in a way that meant anything.

For the first time, she stared down into the chasm that was divorce and wondered what would happen if she was forced to the other side.

"You don't want to be married to me anymore," she whispered.

His gaze met hers, his stare unflinching. She saw emotions flashing through his dark eyes and none of them were soft or loving.

"No, I don't."

Just like that. She forced herself to keep breathing, to focus on the moment. Reality would slap her hard soon enough. There was no reason to rush it.

"Is there someone else?" she asked.

"No. It's just that I don't want to be with you." He hesitated. "I'm not sure I ever loved you."

He stood there for a second, then turned to the door. "I'll go get another room for the night. You can take a cab home in the morning. I'll be by at some point to get my things."

And then he was gone.

Nicole sat on the bed and breathed slowly, staying in the moment. Because to leave it was to acknowledge that her world had just crumbled around her.

Twenty-Four

THE SINGLES MINGLE WAS THE LAST THING Pam wanted to attend. Despite calls of sun and sand, she hadn't gone on shore that day. Her balcony faced the island and she had watched the small ships—tenders, she thought they were called—take happy people across the water.

She promised herself she was going ashore in Jamaica. She had her tour all lined up and her plan to be happy and outgoing. She would ask people to take a picture with her, knowing that in return they would ask the same. That way, there would be a photographic record for later.

Planning a suicide to look like an accidental death was a lot harder than she would have thought. There were lots of complications and details to be worked out. But it had been good for her, too. She had to think about something other than how much she missed John. Which was probably the weirdest, most twisted thing ever.

She glanced at her watch and realized it was time. She got her small cross-body bag and her map, then headed out to be friendly and outgoing at the event.

She arrived at Skywalkers nightclub a few minutes later.

This was one of the highest points on the ship and the view was spectacular. A bird's-eye 360-degree view of the island they'd left and the Caribbean beyond. Both sky and water were beautifully blue.

The room itself was big, with plenty of seating and, of course, floor-to-ceiling windows. The carpet was a brightly colored swirl pattern. There were sofas and tables, lots of chairs. Music played at a comfortable pitch but she had a feeling that later in the night, it would be a whole lot louder.

Pam stopped just inside the nightclub and looked around. At first she couldn't figure out what was wrong, then the truth sank in. The meet-and-mingle she'd come to wasn't for people to meet and make friends as much as it was for singles. As in men and women. She'd been hoping for a few women her own age. Maybe someone she could make friends with.

Instead, there were lots of people in their twenties and thirties. Women in short, flirty dresses and men prowling around, eyeing the offerings.

An older man caught her gaze and winked. She immediately turned away. She couldn't do this, she thought. She had to get out of here.

She hurried to the bank of elevators and frantically pushed the down button. None of the doors opened. She pushed again and again, desperate to get out. To get away. To get back to her room. What had she been thinking? This was wrong—all of it.

The elevator doors opened. Before she could throw herself inside, she had to wait for the people already on it to exit. There were a couple of younger men who walked past her without giving her a glance, followed by three older women.

Pam practically stumbled as she rushed into the elevator. She jammed the button for her floor, pushing it over and over again. The doors couldn't close fast enough. At the last second, one of the older women stepped into the elevator with her.

"Are you all right?" she asked, her tone concerned.

"I'm fine. I don't feel well." She just had to get back to her room, she thought. Where she could sob in peace.

"Those two statements don't go together. I think it's more than that."

The elevator began to move.

The stranger moved closer. "I'm Olimpia. And you are?"

"Pam. Pam Eiland." She turned to the other woman and saw she was being watched with a combination of sympathy and understanding.

"Are you by yourself?" Olimpia asked.

Pam nodded.

"A recent widow?"

"How did you know?"

"I recognize the look. You came to the meet-and-greet thinking you could make some friends and instead you found supermodels and horndogs."

In spite of everything, Pam smiled. "Horndogs?"

"Those horrible men trying to get laid." Olimpia shuddered. "Why do men have to be like that? Why do they have to assume we want to have sex with them before we even know them? I know it's popular with young people today, but I don't understand it. Why would you want to touch a penis before you know where it's been?"

"I never thought about it like that," Pam admitted, really looking at Olimpia for the first time.

She was small, maybe five feet, and thin. She wore white

cropped pants and a yellow T-shirt with a rhinestone pink flamingo on the front. Her hair was short and dark, with a couple of red highlights. Pam would guess she was in her late fifties.

They reached Pam's floor. Several people got on. Pam started to say it had been nice to meet her when Olimpia grabbed her wrist and held her in place.

"Sixteen, please," she said to the man standing by the elevator. She turned back to Pam. "Come back upstairs with me and meet my friends. We'll go get a drink and introduce ourselves. They're nice girls. You'll like them."

Pam hesitated, then the elevator doors closed and she was on her way up again.

"The widows" as Pam thought of her new friends, turned out to be interesting women. Olimpia lived in Florida—Vero Beach. She was very proud of the fact that one of her neighbors was a famous novelist—Debbie Macomber. "The nicest woman you'd ever want to meet." Olimpia didn't have any children, but was an avid volunteer—helping out with everything from adult literacy to animal welfare.

Laura, a tall and full-figured redhead, lived in Roanoke, Virginia. She hated the winters there, but was close to her four children and nine grandchildren, so moving wasn't an option. She lived in a condo with three cats and a Swarovski figurine collection that apparently rivaled any in the country.

Eugenia was from Dallas, Texas. She had big hair, a thick accent and an ability to drink anyone under the table. She, too, wanted to move, but stayed where she was because of her children and grandchildren.

All three of them were older than Pam, but each had

been widowed. They'd met on cruises and now took two or three trips together each year.

"The Caribbean, Alaska or Mexico, then somewhere exotic," Eugenia drawled. "Last year we did a river cruise in Germany. Lots of good wine. Plus on the river, the ride's real smooth."

After Olimpia had taken Pam back upstairs and introduced her to her friends, Pam had found herself having a drink with them in the Explorers Lounge. The fact that it was the middle of the afternoon didn't seem to bother anyone. That evening she'd joined them for dinner.

Their entrées had been cleared and now they lingered over a shared chocolate soufflé and decaf coffee.

Laura nodded. "That was a good one. We're still planning our last cruise for this year. I say Italy."

Olimpia shook her head. "No way. I'm still upset about what they did to Amanda Knox."

Pam frowned. "Who?"

Eugenia rolled her eyes. "That American girl accused of murdering her roommate. The trial was all over the news. They released her, then convicted her again."

Pam glanced at Olimpia. "You know her?"

"She's never met her, or anyone in her family," Laura said. "Olimpia, honey, you're beyond weird. You know that, right? Not that I don't love you like a sister, but you are desperately strange."

"I'm old. I can be strange if I want. I'm not going to Italy."

"It's a beautiful country." Eugenia sighed. "My Roger and I had a wonderful time there. Great wine, great sex." She smiled. "The perfect combination. The people were so warm and friendly."

"You go without me," Olimpia said, and picked up her coffee. "I'll be fine on my own."

Pam wasn't sure what to make of the trio. They had obviously been friends for a long time. There was an affection and a history. She liked that.

"Roger is?" she asked cautiously.

"My late husband. It's been five years now." Eugenia smiled sadly. "He was a wonderful man. I still miss him." She nodded at the other two. "We're all widows. How long has your husband been gone?"

Pam blinked. "Nearly two months."

"He booked the cruise before he died, I'll bet," Laura murmured. "You took it, anyway." She tilted her head. "Same thing happened to me. That's how I met Olimpia."

The petite woman nodded. "I was the first. My husband died almost twenty years ago. I was supposed to go on a cruise with a girlfriend and she backed out at the last minute. I said the hell with it, and went by myself. I was lonely and I still had a good time. I went back every year until I met these two. Now we travel together. Cruises are comfortable for women our age. No luggage to carry, no worries about the hotel being safe."

Pam couldn't imagine such a thing, and yet it made perfect sense. They were able to get away, to have fun. To just be themselves. Not someone's mother or grandmother. Not that she minded either, but what she most wanted was to be John's wife again and that was impossible.

"We have a lot of fun things planned for this week," Laura said cheerfully. "You'll join us."

"Are you asking or telling?" Eugenia raised her eyebrows. "It sounded like an order to me."

"I think it was." Laura laughed. "What do you say, Pam? Want to join the widows club?"

Pam thought about her plan. Meeting these three would make it easy. She would have a visible presence on the ship. People would know her and remember her. It was perfect.

"I do," she told them, raising her cup of decaf. "To the widows club."

Nicole pressed her hand to her chest. She told herself that feeling as if she couldn't breathe wasn't the same as not being able to catch her breath. That the problem was anxiety—there wasn't anything physically wrong. Only her body didn't seem to be listening to her brain as the sense of panic increased, the sense of impending death grew, too.

She gasped, trying to draw air into her lungs. Shannon walked in from the kitchen, a bottle of wine in her hand.

"What?" she demanded the second she saw Nicole.

"I'm having a panic attack," Nicole gasped. "I can't breathe."

Shannon set the open bottle on the coffee table. "Stand up and start walking. You have to burn off the chemicals pouring into your body. Talk to me."

Nicole shook her head. She wasn't going to talk. She could barely breathe. Even though she was sucking in air, it felt as if it wasn't getting into her lungs.

"Talk," Shannon said firmly. "If you can talk, you can breathe."

"I can't," Nicole blurted, her voice a little strangled. "I can't."

But the words came a little easier.

She sucked in more air. "I'm talking. This is me talking." As she spoke, she circled the living room. "I'm a total mess."

"You're not. You're under a whole lot of stress. Which is perfectly understandable. Who wouldn't be? First you had to deal with Eric writing the screenplay and doing nothing else. Then he sold it and now this."

Nicole nodded. The vise around her chest loosened and she thought maybe she wasn't breathing so hard. She circled back to the sofa and sat down.

"Everything's a disaster," she admitted as she took the glass of wine Shannon offered. "My life, my marriage."

"Not everything," Shannon told her firmly. "You have a business you really like and you have Tyler."

Nicole sipped the wine. "You're right. Work keeps me sane. It's where I have to be every morning. It's an anchor. Tyler's just great." His happy smile and his excitement about every part of his day made putting one foot in front of the other possible. Now it felt as though Tyler was all she had and that was way too much to put on a five-year-old.

She looked at Shannon. "Eric's gone. He's really gone. I haven't heard from him in two days. He hasn't been by, we haven't spoken. He sent a text saying he was finding his own place and that he'd be in touch."

"What about the money?"

Shannon's question surprised her. "What do you mean?"

"Your joint checking account. Did he clean it out?"

The question was completely unexpected, but the implications were terrifying.

"I don't know."

Shannon pointed toward the study. "Let's go find out."

"He wouldn't do that," Nicole said, even as she got to her feet and walked across the living room to the hallway.

"Three days ago you would have said he wouldn't leave, and he has. I'm sorry to be harsh, but I've had friends go through a divorce. It's never easy and things get ugly fast. He made a lot of money selling his screenplay. Half of that is yours."

"I don't want it," Nicole said automatically.

"Sure you do. You're going to have expenses. This house for one."

The house that was only in her name, she thought. But Shannon was right. There were expenses. Greta. And even if she didn't keep the full-time nanny, there was going to be day care. She worked. With Eric gone, Tyler was solely her responsibility.

She opened her browser, then entered the address for the bank. After logging in, she checked the balance, then the history.

"He pulled out fifty thousand dollars, but the rest of it is there."

"When did he take out the money?"

"This morning."

"Tomorrow you go open a personal account and do the same. Take out exactly what he did." Shannon sat in the spare chair. "You're going to need to talk to a lawyer. I can talk you through some basics, but you need someone who knows the law. Someone who's on your side. California is a community property state. That means everything goes into a bucket and the bucket is split in half. If you had assets before the marriage or he did, then those are separate. But everything else is up for grabs. His money from the screenplay, your business."

Shannon paused, then gentled her tone. "I'm sorry," she whispered. "I know this is hard."

It was only then that Nicole realized she was crying. She brushed away the tears. "I never thought this would happen.

I never thought we'd get a divorce. But he said he didn't love me." She pressed her lips together. "No. That's not true. He said he never loved me. Things have been so horrible between us lately. I thought maybe we weren't going to make it, but that was in my head, you know? Not real. Now he's gone. I haven't told Tyler. Eric spends so much time on work, he hasn't really noticed. Greta helps with that. She knows. She hasn't said anything, but I'm sure she does."

The slightly scary nanny had been more kind than usual in the past couple of days.

"I kept thinking I'd be okay on my own. That getting a divorce might not be so bad. Now I want to go back and fix things. Only I can't."

How could she fix a relationship when her husband had never wanted it in the first place?

"I'm here for you," Shannon told her. "Do you want me to stay with you for a couple of days?"

Nicole sniffed. "No. I'm not scared to be alone." She thought about what Shannon had said earlier about the community property. "Do you think I should talk to a lawyer?"

"I do. I can get some names for you in the morning. You need to know what your rights are. You need to understand what each of you can legally do. I'm not saying Eric's a bad guy, but I don't want him taking more than he's allowed. I don't want you getting screwed."

Nicole appreciated the support even as she wished it wasn't necessary. She'd been sick to her stomach for three days now. Unable to fully grasp what had happened. Eric was gone. Their marriage was over. Even back when she'd thought things were fine, he hadn't been happy.

Which made her wonder if everything about their relationship had been a lie. He'd obviously been going through the motions and she'd been completely fooled.

Shannon pulled into the church parking lot and wished that Pam was back from her trip. While she was glad her friend was away and hopefully having a good time, right now a little wise counsel sounded good.

Before John had died, everything had been going so well for all of them, Shannon thought as she stared at the building in front of her. Eric had just sold his screenplay, things were great with Adam and Pam was her normal, happy, stable self. Then it had all gone to hell.

Nicole was in shock about Eric leaving. Shannon was surprised things had unraveled so quickly, but not totally stunned by the outcome. Adding to that was the reality that when one partner hit it big in nearly any field, there were stresses added to the relationship. In this case the million-dollar deal was both a blessing and curse. Now Eric could afford to walk away. He didn't need to be supported.

Shannon told herself there had to be other reasons for the breakup. Obviously there had been other problems. Every couple had them. Look at her and Adam. Or maybe it was better not to look.

She was avoiding him. He'd tried to set up dinner or even just a walk on the beach, but she kept saying she needed time. Which was true. She wasn't sure where their relationship was going. Despite his apologies and explanations about what had happened with Char, she wasn't sure she could do it. Be a part of his family.

Some of it was getting involved with a family that already existed. She wasn't sure where she would fit. Learning the rules, being "the other," all frightened her.

There were other considerations, as well. In truth, she'd spent the past twenty years only being responsible for herself. She'd done what she wanted, when she wanted. She'd made her own rules. Some of her decisions had been bad or wrong, but the only consequences were to herself.

If she stayed with Adam, if they kept going on their current path, then she wasn't going to be the only one in the room. There would be other considerations. Other people who had to be consulted, and not just the children. Tabitha would be a part of her life. This woman that Shannon had yet to meet would get one of the votes.

If she stayed with Adam, she would be the second wife. Whatever they did, he would have done it before with someone else. A wedding, a honeymoon, even having a child. She knew he wouldn't ever say it, but she wondered if he would be thinking it. Been there, done that.

She got out of the car and headed into the church. An easel with a sign pointed her down the hall. She entered what looked like a multipurpose room. A few high windows and a dozen or so chairs set out in a circle.

There were about ten women in the room already. They were talking to each other. A few stood together while others had already taken a seat. Shannon approached the woman behind the desk near the door.

"Hi," she said. "I'm Shannon Rigg. I called."

"Of course. Welcome." The woman's name tag said Alice. "You're welcome to be a guest at two meetings. We ask that you observe without speaking." Alice shrugged. "We've had problems with people showing up, dominating the time to get their questions answered, then disappearing."

"Sure. That makes sense." Shannon could respect the

concept of having to earn her way into the group. Assuming she wanted to belong.

"Once you join, you'll be given access to our resource network. There's an annual fee that covers maintaining the website and the referral service."

All of which Shannon already knew. She took the name tag Alice offered her, then got a cup of coffee from the tray in the back of the room. She walked over to the circle and settled in a chair.

The women in the room were all in their thirties and forties. One of them had a sleeping baby in her arms. The others watched the baby with varying expressions of longing. Madge, the group leader she'd spoken to on the phone, had explained that some women stayed on, even after having a child. They had made friendships that were important to them.

Shannon sipped her coffee and waited for the meeting to start. She didn't think she would join. She was here to observe and learn. While she was figuring things out when it came to her relationship with Adam, she'd thought maybe it was time to figure out a few things for herself. Like why hadn't she had a child on her own?

She'd been so determined to have it all or not have any of it. What was up with that? Part of her attempt to answer that question had been to come here. To a support group for women over thirty-five trying to have a child.

Some were married with fertility problems, others were single. The topics included traditional pregnancy, surrogacy and adoption.

A tall woman in a business suit walked over and sat next to Shannon.

"I'm Madge," she said with a welcoming smile. "Nice

to meet you in person. I'm glad you could make it to our meeting."

"Me, too."

Madge nodded at the woman with the baby. "She used a surrogate. We were all excited when she finally got her daughter."

"I can imagine."

Shannon braced herself for the inevitable and awkward questions. Why hadn't she had a baby before now? Had she considered adoption, or just getting pregnant by some random guy? But Madge didn't go there. Instead, she addressed the women and asked them to take their seats.

"We have a guest tonight. This is Shannon."

Several people called out a greeting.

Madge leaned back in her chair. "Who has something to report?"

A dark-haired woman in her forties smiled. "We've heard that we've been approved for our adoption in Ethiopia. We're flying out next week."

Everyone applauded.

She went on to talk about the process—how long it would take and what was involved. Several of the other women mentioned where they were in the process. Someone else gave an update on her IVF.

By the end of the hour, the sun had set and Shannon had a lot more information about what it would mean to have a baby on her own.

She thanked Madge for letting her visit and promised to think about joining the group. First she would have to figure out what she wanted and whether or not her interest in having a baby had anything to do with her relationship with Adam.

If she had a baby on her own, she would be dealing with a lot of logistical issues. Finding someone like Greta, for one. And if she was alone and working her usual fifty hours a week, should she really have a child? When would she see him or her?

There would be massive lifestyle changes. Was she willing to make them? To cut back on her hours? To talk to Nolan about working from home a couple of days a week?

If she stayed with Adam, then he would need to be part of the decision. There was his vasectomy to work through, assuming he was even interested in having a child with her. She was also very close to forty. Could she get pregnant the old-fashioned way?

She walked to her car and got in. Questions swirled, threatening to overwhelm her. She needed someone to talk to and at that moment, she couldn't think of a single person she could call. Pam was gone, Nicole was dealing with Eric leaving her, and Adam, well, she was confused about him.

As if wanting to help, her phone rang. She glanced at the screen and saw the familiar skull and crossbones.

Quinn, she thought. A man with no answers, but an impressive way of distracting her from whatever was wrong in her life.

"Hello?"

"Gorgeous."

"Hey. What's up?"

"Funny you should ask. I know we said we weren't going to do this anymore, but I wondered if I could change your mind."

There was something in his voice, she thought with surprise. A kind of vulnerability. Or maybe she was hearing what she wanted to hear.

Going over to Quinn's wouldn't solve anything, but it would make her feel better. She could lose herself in the moment, maybe put a little distance between herself and Adam. Emotionally if not physically.

Except it would be wrong, she thought with surprise. She and Adam were in a relationship. Things might be uncomfortable between them, but they were still together. She hadn't broken up with him. If she slept with Quinn, she would be cheating.

"That difficult a question?" he asked.

"It kind of is."

She thought about how feeling good would be followed by the drive of shame. She thought about how her nights with Quinn could very well be a metaphor for her life. Fun in the moment, but without direction or purpose, and always with more than a hint of regret at the end.

She didn't want regret. She wasn't sure where she stood on the baby front, but spending the night with Quinn didn't answer any of the questions. Even more important, she didn't like what a night with Quinn said about *her.*

"No," she told him. "I'm sorry, but I can't see you."

"Okay. You take care."

"You, too."

He hung up. She dropped her phone into her purse and started the engine. She might not know exactly where she was going to be in five years, but for tonight, she was going home.

Twenty-Five

PAM WAS SURPRISED TO DISCOVER THAT A busy social schedule made fitting in a suicide kind of difficult.

The week of the cruise had flown by. Once she made friends with Olimpia, Laura and Eugenia, she'd been busy nearly every second of every day. Together the three of them had explored Jamaica, including a very fun river cruise on a small flat-bottomed boat. Laura had brought lemon-flavored vodka for all of them and they'd ended up singing "Born to Be Wild" and frightening their tour guide.

When they'd stopped in Grand Cayman, they'd visited the turtle farm and Pam had discovered that not only did rum cake get you drunk, but if you ate enough, it could also give you a hangover. Now it was the last day—the day at sea, when she was supposed to do the deed. But so far she hadn't found a single moment to get herself ready, let alone fling herself off the ship.

She'd seen ruins in Mexico and had bought silly souvenirs for her kids. She'd attended an art auction and had actually bought a couple of pieces. There'd been movies, live shows and laughter. She'd nearly forgotten what it felt like to laugh.

The week had been so much better than she'd hoped, but it was nearly over and she had to remember why she'd come in the first place. She was going to end her life.

She couldn't do it without organizing her thoughts and making sure her room was tidy. All she needed was an hour, she told herself. She would sneak away and get it done.

But morning had turned into afternoon and now it was only an hour or so from dinner. Maybe that was better, she thought. In the dark no one would see her falling. That way it would take them longer to miss her. After dinner. She would have a last meal with her friends.

Eugenia waved a piece of paper. "Do you know how hard it is to plan a tour in Europe without going to Italy? Especially when everyone else *wants* to go to Italy?"

They sat, as they always did, in the Explorers Lounge. They even had "their" table. They'd met for cocktails before dinner.

"I'm ignoring the parts about Italy," Olimpia said. "What did you find?"

"A glorious cruise. It leaves September sixth. We start in Amsterdam and finish up in Istanbul." Eugenia looked at Laura. "That's in Turkey."

"I know where Istanbul is," Laura told her. "Wasn't there a song?"

Olimpia leaned toward Pam. "Music is where Laura gets all her information."

"I'll have ya'll know, I was very talented at one time."

"You're still talented," Pam pointed out. Because she'd learned that Laura was a classically trained pianist. And that Eugenia had published five novels. And that Olimpia had kept her husband's business going for nearly a decade after his death.

These women weren't just widows. They were bright and funny and loyal. She enjoyed their company. They had helped her get through what could have been a horrible week and she would always be grateful. In a way, she wished she could leave them a note, telling them what they meant to her. But she couldn't. Her death was supposed to be an accident.

"Back to the cruise," Eugenia said. "Are we interested?"

"We are," Olimpia said, then winked at Pam. "She always gets like this when it's her turn to plan things. Completely imperious."

Pam smiled. She'd learned that each year one of them was responsible for making the arrangements for their three cruises.

"I'm ignoring you," Eugenia said.

"Then there's no point in voicing my opinion," Olimpia murmured with a sly smile. "You'll have to vote without me."

"Not a problem," Laura said cheerfully. "Three votes is a majority. What do you think, Pam?"

Eugenia passed her the itinerary. "I've checked. There are four staterooms still available."

Pam took the piece of paper and stared blindly at it. Her go with them? That had never been discussed. Oh, there had been comments made. "You'll love Alaska." Or "Would you be willing to go to Italy? We can leave Olimpia at the airport." But she'd thought they were just being nice.

She tried to bring the tiny print into focus. Laura passed over a pair of reading glasses.

Pam slipped them on. "I've never been to Malta," she

whispered, looking at the exotic-sounding ports. "That would be nice."

"Then it's decided," Eugenia said. "I'll email all of you the information as soon as I'm home." She waved at one of the servers, and gestured that they wanted another round. "Are we eating at Sabatini's tonight?"

"We are," Olimpia said. "I made reservations. Six thirty."

Sabatini's was one of the premium restaurants on the ship. Pam had forgotten they were going there. The evening would be lovely—good food and caring company. And then… Well, she would think about that later.

By the time the four of them had finished dinner and giggled through the last night of karaoke and had a nightcap, it was close to midnight. With every passing second, Pam was aware of the ship getting closer and closer to Florida.

The evening had gone by so quickly, she thought. She'd laughed and talked and while she'd still missed John with every breath, the pain was less intense than it had been. It seemed almost…manageable.

How could that be? She'd lost her husband—she needed to be suffering. Not only to feel closer to him, but also to prove her love. Even as those thoughts appeared, she understood the wrongness of them. But that didn't take away their power.

She'd come on this cruise for only one reason and her window of opportunity was closing.

"I should get to bed," she said as she stood.

The three women exchanged a look, then Olimpia rose. "I'll walk with you." She picked up her bag. "We're all clear on where we're meeting in the morning?"

Laura wiggled her fingers. "You've told us fifteen times.

We'll be there, to say our goodbyes. Until September, right Pam?"

Pam bit her lower lip and nodded. She wanted to hug each of them. To tell them how much she'd appreciated them taking her under their collective wing. They'd made her feel welcome and they'd reminded her that life did indeed go on. She might not be willing to go through the pain of healing, but they'd allowed her to see the possibilities.

But to admit any of that would mean telling them too much. So there would be no goodbyes, no last hugs, no thanking them. Instead, she simply said, "Good night" and walked with Olimpia to the elevators.

"I've never been to Mischief Bay," Olimpia said as they waited for the elevator. "What's it like?"

"A small town tucked in the middle of Los Angeles. The weather is great."

"You're near the beach?"

"Only a few blocks away."

They stepped into the elevator. Pam pushed her floor.

"Maybe I'll come out for a visit this August," Olimpia said. "By then the humidity is making me think about relocating." She flashed a smile. "Not that I would, but I do complain and threaten."

They got off on Pam's floor. She thought about pointing out that her friend was on a different deck, but figured she wouldn't mind a little company. It wasn't that she was having second thoughts, exactly. It was just the thought of throwing herself off the ship was a little harder than she'd expected.

They got to Pam's room and stepped inside. Olimpia headed for the sofa and sat on one cushion.

"You must be excited about seeing your kids," she said as Pam set down her bag and took the chair opposite.

"I am. Of course."

"Jen's what? Four months' pregnant?"

"Yes."

Olimpia smiled. "You'll know the sex of the baby soon. That's so fun. I don't suppose twins run in your family."

"No, and don't let Jen hear you say that. She would freak out."

"Twins would be difficult. But she'll have you. And soon Steven will meet someone and settle down. Plus Brandon will be graduating. A doctor. You must be so proud."

Pam nodded because it was expected, but what she was thinking was that she wanted Olimpia to stop talking. All this conversation about her children was making her sad. She didn't want to think about all they would accomplish or experience without her being there to see it. She didn't want to imagine not holding her first grandchild, or her second or tenth.

But she had to do this, she reminded herself. It was the only thing that made sense. She had to…

"I'm not leaving," Olimpia said quietly, her gaze steady. "If I think I can't stay awake, I'm going to call Laura or Eugenia and they'll come sit with you."

Pam eyes widened. Her face flushed and she stood. "I don't know what you're talking about."

"You do, and it's all right. We've felt what you feel, Pam. We've had the long nights, the empty days, the horror that the missing won't go away and the terror that it will. We've all wrestled with going on and the knowledge that sometimes it seemed so much easier not to."

She smiled sadly. "If you want to do it, I can't stop you.

But it won't be tonight. Not on our watch. We care about you and want you to be around to travel with us."

Pam sank back in the chair. "I'm sorry."

"You don't have to be. We understand better than most. It does get better. It's never easy, it never feels completely right, but you do heal. And move on."

Pam wasn't sure what to feel. Embarrassment, maybe. Shame. Or defiance. Emotions swirled through her, none of them staying long enough to be defined.

"I didn't know how to survive without him," she admitted.

"You'll learn. And when it gets hard, remember, John wouldn't have wanted this. He would have wanted you to be happy."

Olimpia was right, she thought, a little dazed by the revelation. John *would* have wanted her to keeping moving forward. To find her place in life.

In life, she repeated to herself. Because that was the whole point of every person's journey. To be alive. To live and to keep moving forward.

"I'm not sure I'm ready for this," Adam said. "So I appreciate the company."

"Not to mention the extra free labor," Shannon added.

He grinned. "That, too."

He'd called the previous day and explained he was painting Oliver's bedroom. His son had decided he was old enough to let go of his Brad the Dragon motif and move toward "big boy" decor. According to Adam, that meant light blue walls and new bedding.

By the time she'd arrived at his house that morning, Adam had already taken the dragon bed out and loaded it into a company pickup. He would be dropping it off at Nicole's later for a very thrilled Tyler.

The dresser and desk had been pushed to the center of the room and covered with plastic. The windows and doors were taped off, as were the baseboards.

"I can cut in around the ceiling," he said. "Unless you want to."

"I've painted exactly once before in my life," she admitted. "You should give me the jobs I can't mess up."

"A novice," he said, stepping close to her. "So I get to show you the ropes."

"There are ropes? I thought we used brushes."

"Very funny."

He put his hands on her hips and drew her against him. He was casually dressed in jeans and a paint-spattered T-shirt. Both looked good on him, as did his choice not to shave that morning.

She rested her fingers on his broad chest. He was warm and being close to him made her breath hitch. She'd missed him, she thought. She'd kept herself busy enough that she wouldn't notice, but she had. So when he'd called, she'd wanted to say yes.

She still wasn't sure where they were going, but somehow being without Adam had become more difficult.

"It's nice to have you here," he said, right before he kissed her.

His mouth settled on hers. Wanting settled low in her belly. She raised her arms and wrapped them around his neck. Her breasts nestled against his chest.

They fit, she thought. In so many ways. But what about everything else?

She drew back enough to see into his eyes. She needed to put herself out there. To take a risk in love and see it through. "I don't know if I can be a good stepmother."

She ignored the fact that he hadn't asked. They were supposed to be a couple. It was the next logical step.

"Is it something you're willing to talk about?" he asked.

"I think so. I want things to work out, but I'm not sure. You and Tabitha were a family. I'll never have equal footing. I'll always be the other one. You'll want me to care about the kids as much as you do but I won't have the same say in what happens with them."

His dark gaze never wavered. "That doesn't sound very fair."

"It's not, but do you think it's untrue?"

"No." He touched her cheek. "I can't change what I bring to the table."

"I don't want you to. I'm just not sure how to make it all work. What if I want a baby from Ethiopia?"

"Do you?"

"Maybe. I'm not sure. Did Tabitha work when you had the kids?"

"No. She stayed home until Oliver was three."

Shannon tried to imagine giving up her career. She loved her work, loved her lifestyle. But was it enough? She had a feeling she already knew the answer.

"I could see taking a six-week leave. Or even a couple of months," she said slowly. But not more. She didn't want to give up that much of who she was.

Had that been the issue all along? Had she not wanted children, but been afraid to admit it? Afraid it made her a bad person? So she'd pretended it was because she couldn't find *the one*?

"I love you," Adam told her and kissed her. "Whatever you decide, I want to be with you. Losing you isn't an option." He smiled. "I mean that in a nonscary way."

He leaned his forehead against hers. "I know what happened with Char was frustrating. I'm to blame for a lot of that. You're the first woman they've met."

She straightened. "I'm pretty sure they've met other women, Adam. At the grocery store, at the park."

He groaned. "Fine. You're the first woman I've been dating that they've met. It's going to take some time for us all to figure it out." He grabbed her hand. "I want to make it work. My sister Gabby and I were talking about this. She thought maybe family counseling would help. First you and me, then with the kids. To establish ground rules that are fair for everyone. What you said before about being the outsider? I know that there are pieces of that I can't change, but I want to make it right for you. However I can."

She believed him. Because he was listening and accepting and because he was a good guy. Would there be mistakes? Sure—by both of them. That came with being human. But with some effort, and maybe a little professional help, they could make it work.

She flung herself at him. "I love you."

"I love you, too."

His mouth settled on hers. She pressed her body to his and gave herself over to the passion they generated. When he started nudging her backward, toward his bedroom, she went willingly. Because while they might not have all the answers, as long as they were willing to search for them, they were going to be just fine.

* * *

The *click-click-click* of Lulu's nails on the kitchen floor was a familiar sound. Pam reached down and picked up her little dog.

"I missed you," she told Lulu. "Was I silly to think I could leave you or what?"

Lulu kissed her chin, then snuggled close. The dog hadn't left her side in the three days she'd been home. It had always been this way when they traveled, Pam thought. Only this time she'd been the only one to come home.

The last night of the cruise had gone just as Olimpia had promised. She hadn't left Pam alone. They'd talked for hours and had fallen asleep in their chairs sometime after two. There'd been a rush for the early morning departure with plenty of hugs and promises to stay in touch.

Since she'd been home, she'd already heard from all three of them. Even more important, she'd made her reservation for the European cruise they were taking in September. It wasn't like having John back, nowhere close. But it wasn't the hell it had been. Maybe she couldn't see the light at the end of the tunnel just yet, but she knew it was there. Her job was to keep moving.

Now, with Lulu in her arms, she walked through the big house she'd lived in for so long. She went from room to room, studying the furnishings, the mementos.

In the living room was a family portrait taken about ten years ago. Brandon looked impossibly young. John was so handsome. In his study was the baseball he'd caught at a Dodger game. There were candid photos of all the kids and several of her. The mug he'd used and casually placed on the bookcase the weekend before he died was exactly where he'd left it.

The dining room held other memories. Family dinners. She and Jen had had their worst fight ever at that table. Her daughter had been seventeen and wanting to be respected as an adult while cared for as a child. Pam had wondered if they would ever get through that time where every word was misunderstood and each encounter seemed to lead to angry words and door slamming. John had been her rock through it all. He'd assured her Jen would once again become the daughter they remembered, and in time, she had.

In the hallway, Pam paused by what had been Brandon's door. How many nights had she and John stood there, not sure what to do or say as their youngest experimented with drugs and alcohol. They'd spent hundreds of hours worrying and fearing the future. But he'd gotten through it.

In the hall bath, behind the door, were the lines marking Steven's various heights. At nine, he'd been frantic he wouldn't be big enough to play professional baseball, only to discover that while he enjoyed the game, he wasn't interested in making it his entire life.

So many memories. So many good times. She'd been blessed. And while losing John would be a wound she would carry with her always, she was beginning to see that maybe, just maybe, she had the strength to go on.

"Hi, Mom. It's me!"

Lulu struggled to get down. Pam set her on the floor and the little dog went running to greet Jen. All three kids were coming by that night for a rare midweek dinner. Pam had chili in the Crock-Pot and her famous cheddar biscuits ready to bake.

She went toward the kitchen and found her daughter holding Lulu.

"Mom!" Jen put down the dog and hurried to greet her.

"I'm so glad you had a good time on the cruise, but I missed you. It was hard having you gone."

They hugged. Jen hung on a little tighter than usual. Pam gave a brief prayer of thanks for whatever angel had arranged for her to meet her three friends. Without them, she wouldn't have made it back. She knew that. And what a waste of a blessed life.

Pam cupped her daughter's face in her hands. "Look at you. You really are glowing. You've always been beautiful, but now it's kind of unfair to the rest of us."

"Oh, Mom." Jen's eyes filled with tears. "I had my ultrasound while you were gone. Kirk was with me. The baby is healthy and I'm doing well. You're the first to know, aside from Kirk, of course. We're having a boy."

Warm, bubbling happiness filled her. Pam hung on to it, even as the pain of loss tempered the edges of the joy. It would always be like this, she thought. But it was okay. There would be good days and bad days. And John would always be in her heart.

"Congratulations. A boy. Kirk must be thrilled. He's always had that macho streak."

Jen laughed. "I know. He's really excited." Her daughter sniffed. "We want to call him John, if you're okay with that."

Pam had to take a breath before she could speak. "That would be wonderful, but you know you don't have to."

"I know. We want to. I miss Daddy so much. Not like you do, I'm sure."

They walked into the family room and sat down on the sofa. Lulu jumped up and settled between them. She curled up against Pam but kept her gaze on Jen, as if making sure no one was going anywhere.

"I'm glad you made friends on your cruise," Jen said. "Those three ladies sound great."

"They are. I'm joining them in September. We're going to Europe together. The four of us."

"Wow. Impressive. Look at you, traveling the world."

Pam smiled. "I'll be nervous, but I won't be alone. Then I'm staying put until you have your baby."

"Good, because I want you with me for every second the whole first year."

"You say that now, but you'll do great. Of course, I'll help when you need it, but I'm not worried about you." She looked around at the big room, the giant TV John had loved so much. "I want to talk to you about something."

Jen's eyes widened. "What? Are you okay?"

"I'm fine. I've just been thinking. This house is so big and—"

The tears returned to Jen's eyes. "No, Mom. You can't sell it. We need this house in our family. The memories. Don't all the books say you have to wait a year before doing anything big? Wait. We'll help. Didn't Steven do a spreadsheet for maintenance and stuff? We can all pitch in."

Pam shook her head. "Hear me out. It's okay. Yes, your brother put together a spreadsheet of what has to happen when. I have a list of vendors to call. I can take care of the house—I just don't want to anymore. I've talked to your brothers about this and they agree with you. The house has to stay in the family."

Jen shot to her feet. "Is Steven taking it? Because he would not treat this house right. He's a single guy. There's no way Brandon would want it."

Pam patted the sofa. "Sit. Listen."

Jen's mouth twitched. "Now you're talking to me like I'm Lulu."

"She is better behaved than you."

Jen laughed and sat. "Okay. I'm listening."

"The boys agree that the house should stay in the family. We have so many memories here. Like the Memorial Day barbecue in a couple of weeks." An annual tradition where friends and family came over for a big celebration of the start of summer. On the flight home Pam had realized she had to continue the tradition. At least this one last time.

"You're right about Brandon and Steven not wanting the house. But you do. You and Kirk."

Jen's eyes widened. "Mom, that would be incredible, but there is no way we can afford it. I'm a public school teacher and Kirk's a cop. On our best day, we barely make the rent on our apartment."

"I know. If you want the house, you can have it. Think of it as an early inheritance. I would transfer title to you and Kirk. I would put an amount equal to the value of the house into the boys' trusts."

"What would you do?"

"Buy a condo. My friend Shannon has a lovely place right on the beach. I'm going to look in her building. I'd be five minutes away." She smiled at her daughter. "You think about it and talk to Kirk. I'd love to see you two and your children here. But it means hosting the family events and carrying on traditions. I'd help with the cooking, but the bulk of it would fall to you."

Jen hugged her. Lulu wiggled between the two of them and gave plenty of kisses.

"Mom, I don't know what to say. I'd love it. I'll talk to Kirk, but I'm pretty sure he'll agree. This house is so amazing." She drew back. "But not right away. You have to think about it, too. You and Daddy lived here for so long. You have to be sure you want to give that up."

"It's okay," Pam told her. "Wherever I go, John is with me. We had a wonderful life here. There's a lot of good energy in these walls. A lot of happiness. I know he'd want this for all of us."

Twenty-Six

PAM WAITED UNTIL BOTH SHANNON AND Nicole had their Cosmos before raising her glass. "To friends. Thank you both for being there for me after John died. I don't think I ever thanked you."

"You did," Shannon told her.

"You're being kind."

Shannon wrinkled her nose. "Not possible. I'm a career-driven harpy. Haven't you heard?"

Despite her words, Shannon was practically floating. Her eyes were bright and her skin glowed. There was a softness about her and an air of mystery. She was keeping secrets, Pam thought. The good kind.

"Another article on successful women breaking barriers?" Nicole asked.

"You know it," Shannon said and took a sip of her drink. "There's an entire paragraph on my unmarried and childless state."

"Fuck 'em if they can't take a joke," Pam said.

Both women stared at her.

"I've never heard you say the *F* word," Nicole admitted. "It makes me like you so much more."

Pam grinned at her, even as she worried about her friend. Shannon had already called and told her about what happened with Eric. While Shannon was all happy smiles, Nicole seemed smaller somehow, and shell-shocked. As if the reality of what was happening hadn't set in yet.

Pam knew the feeling. She'd felt like the walking dead for a couple of months after John's death. Pretty much until the cruise, she thought. Most of her heart was still in hibernation, but there was the hint of coming spring. A bud or two. And for now, that was enough.

"Tell us about the cruise," Shannon said. "It sounded like you had a good time."

"I did. Better than I expected."

They were in the bar at Pescadores. Their reservation for dinner was in an hour, giving them plenty of time to chat at a quiet table in the back of the bar. It was relatively early on a Wednesday evening. There weren't many other patrons. Even so Pam lowered her voice as she spoke.

"I'm not going to share this with anyone else, but I want you two to know the truth." She sipped her drink. "I went on the cruise to kill myself. I thought I couldn't survive losing John."

Both Nicole and Shannon stared at her.

"Oh, my God," Shannon murmured. "Pam, I had no idea. I'm sorry you felt so alone."

"No. Don't blame yourself. I meant what I said before. You were both there for me. Everyone was willing to help the first couple of weeks, but you two went so beyond that. I wouldn't have made it through without you." She rested her elbows on the table and told them about how she'd picked the day and the means.

"It's hard to explain. The loss, I mean. I haven't been anyone but John's wife for thirty years. I didn't want to try to find out what being on my own would be like. I was selfish and weak. John would have been so ashamed of me."

She thought about the man who had been the best part of her. He wouldn't have understood, she thought. "This may sound strange, but I'm so grateful for what I went through. I'm glad I came up with the ridiculous plan and tried to see it through. To be honest, I have no idea if I could have done it or not. What I do know is I was extraordinarily fortunate to meet the women I did on that ship. That last night, when Olimpia wouldn't leave me on my own, I felt as if God touched me."

She wrinkled her nose. "I don't mean that in a weird way. Just that I was given another chance. It's not any easier without John, but somehow I can deal with it better. I can breathe. I couldn't breathe before. Jen's going to have a baby. One day Steven will fall in love. Brandon is going to be a wonderful doctor. I want to see all that."

She turned to Shannon. "I want to see what happens with Adam and watch you continue to kick business ass." She touched Nicole's arm. "I want to be around as Tyler grows up and you figure out what's next. But mostly I want to thank you for being my friends."

"I am not crying," Shannon said firmly. "You're not going to make me."

Nicole wiped away tears. "I'm not even trying not to. Pam, I've said this before and I hope you know it's a compliment, but I so want to be you when I grow up."

"Aim higher," Pam told her.

Nicole shook her head. "Not possible."

"I need you to prepare a list of all your assets and all your debts, both personally and for the business."

"Should I be taking notes?" Nicole asked.

Her lawyer, Nancy, a sensible-looking woman in a suit, shook her head. "No. I'll be sending you home with a lot of paperwork for you to look over. There are some information sheets and a list of what you'll bring to the next meeting."

Nicole didn't understand how she'd gotten here. Oh, not to the meeting itself. That was simple. Pam had driven her. But to this place in her life. She and Eric were getting a divorce.

They still hadn't talked. Nor had she seen him. He'd been by a couple of times to pick up clothing and his computer. She only knew because Greta mentioned it. Three days ago he'd sent a text saying he was retaining a lawyer and suggesting she do the same.

Shouldn't they have a conversation? Talk about what had gone wrong or even try to fix it? His answer was easy to figure out, she thought, still too surprised by everything happening to feel anything. She moved through her days as if her life was happening to someone else and she was just the observer.

"Nicole owns her own business," Pam said. "And Eric recently sold a screenplay for a sizeable sum."

"Everything comes into play," the lawyer said. "California is a community property state. That means all joint assets are shared. Did you own anything before you were married?"

"My house," Nicole murmured. "I bought it myself and Eric isn't on the title."

"Did he put any money down on it or pay for any improvements?"

She shook her head.

"Eric hasn't worked in over a year," Pam told the lawyer. "He quit his job to write his screenplay. Nicole's been paying all the bills."

"That helps," Nancy said as she took notes. "You'll need to prepare a P-and-L for your business."

Nicole looked at Pam. "A what?"

"Profit-and-loss statement," her friend told her. "It's in your bookkeeping program. I'll show you. It's not hard. Basically everything will be added up. The value of your business, less any debts, what you owe on credit cards and how much money you have. Life insurance and the like. Then it's split down the middle."

"Exactly," the lawyer said with a smile. "You've been through this before."

"Not personally," Pam told her. "But a few friends had difficult divorces."

Nancy nodded and looked at Nicole. "What about your son?" She glanced at her notes. "Tyler."

Nicole shrugged. "Eric and I haven't talked. He hasn't seen Tyler since he moved out. I want to retain custody. We have a nanny—Greta. I don't think I can afford her on my own, but without her, there will be day care expenses. Could Eric help with that?"

The last thing she wanted was her son having even more disruptions.

"Absolutely. Once I meet with his attorney, I'll know

what he expects as far as custody. His abandonment of the family works in your favor."

Nicole wondered if it had to be phrased that way. Eric had left them. Wasn't that different? Or maybe when it came to a divorce, it didn't matter.

"If you're the custodial parent, he'll be paying child support. With your share of his screenwriting money and child support, you should be able to afford Greta, or some other arrangement." Nancy gave her a sympathetic smile. "I know this is overwhelming. You need to understand it's going to get worse before it gets better. Divorce isn't easy, but it is survivable. You have a support network. I suggest you take advantage of that. This is the time to reach out to your friends."

Pam squeezed her hand. "We're all here for you."

"Thank you."

Nancy returned to her notes. "Don't make any major purchases. It's fine to buy food and replace clothing, but don't get a new car. Also, I'll need copies of all recent bank statements. Neither of you is allowed to transfer out money from the joint account beyond necessities for living expenses. You're not still having sex with Eric, are you?"

Nicole blinked. "Ah, no."

"Good. Keep it that way. It's possible he may try to get back into the marriage bed as a way to manipulate you into agreeing to a lesser settlement."

The idea was practically comical, Nicole thought. Eric hadn't slept with her for months. No way would he try to do it now, she thought.

"I think I'm pretty safe," she said. "But I'll remember your advice."

They discussed more logistics, then wrapped up the meeting. Nancy handed over paperwork and Nicole gave her a check to retain her services.

When they were in the office building parking lot, Pam gave her a hug.

"I won't ask how you're doing."

"Good, because I don't have an answer," Nicole admitted. "None of this is real. Everything happened so fast. We were struggling, then Eric sold his screenplay and now we're getting a divorce. How is that possible?"

"I only have clichés to offer. People change and grow apart. It's not your fault."

While Nicole appreciated the vote of confidence, she was less sure. For things to fall apart so quickly, there had to have been underlying problems. Things she hadn't noticed or maybe hadn't wanted to see. While it took two to make a relationship successful, she had a feeling that it also took two for it to fail. So where had she gone wrong?

"You are the weirdest man," Shannon said.

"You love that I'm weird," Adam told her, his voice cheerful.

He was right, she thought, looking into his dark eyes and knowing that whatever course they chose, she wanted them on it together.

She still didn't have answers to the kid question. Nor was she a hundred-percent sure she was decent stepmother material. But she was willing to try. With patience and maybe some outside help, they could make it.

It was Sunday morning. The warm temperatures had meant breakfast out on her deck overlooking the POP and the ocean beyond. Already joggers and cyclists were out, earnestly exercising. In the distance, she could see a couple of dogs in the dog park.

Adam had spent the night. They had a lazy afternoon planned, then dinner with friends. The kids were with their mother this weekend. If she and Adam stayed together, this would be what it was like, she thought. Every other weekend would be just the two of them. Unless they had a baby. Or adopted.

"Why are you frowning?" he asked. "I walked three miles in the snow to get you croissants."

She laughed. "There is no snow and Latte-Da is two blocks away."

"Still. I hunted and brought you back my prize kill."

She raised her latte and toasted him. "I appreciate it."

"So why the frown?"

"I don't know what to think about having a baby," she admitted. "I'm very capable. If I wanted children, wouldn't I have taken care of that by now? Yet, if I don't do something soon, I won't have the chance later. It's complicated. I want to make the right decision and I don't know what that is."

He surprised her by standing. "Hold that thought."

He disappeared into her condo, only to return a couple of seconds later with a briefcase. He sat across from her and started pulling out folders.

He handed her one. "Information from my urologist."

She stared at him. "You have a urologist?"

"I do now. I've been to see him about reversing the vasectomy. Because my vasectomy is less than ten years old, the expected success rate is ninety percent. It's an outpatient procedure with an easy recovery." He shrugged. "No sex for three weeks, but then we can go for it."

"You'd do that for me?"

"Of course. I love you, Shannon." He nodded at the folder. "All the information is in there."

He pulled out a second folder. "International adoption. I talked to my sister Gabby."

"She's an immigration lawyer."

"Right, but she has friends who handle adoption. There are a lot of opportunities, and not just in Ethiopia. Although if that's your favorite country, we should go for it."

She opened her mouth, then closed it. Speech was impossible. This man, this amazing man, only wanted to make her happy. She pressed her lips together.

"It doesn't have to be Ethiopia."

"Good to know."

He set a third folder on the pile. "This is kind of from left field, but hear me out. You love your work. You want kids, but I don't see you taking off six months to do the stay-at-home mom thing." He held up both hands. "An observation, not a judgment."

"Keep talking."

He tapped the folder. "Foster kids. There are hundreds who need a home. We could provide that. A place for them to feel safe. Maybe even adopt a couple. We'd have our own family, you'd get to be a mom and it would be good for Char and Oliver. Plus, if we went with older kids, you wouldn't have to give up any part of your career. Everybody wins."

Foster children? The idea had never crossed her mind. "We'd have to get approved or certified or whatever first."

"Sure, but I think we'd make it through the process." He reached in his briefcase again and pulled out a turquoise blue jewelry box.

Her gaze locked on it, then slowly rose to his face. He

smiled at her. "I love you, Shannon. I swear, the first time I saw you, I couldn't believe I was that lucky. As I got to know you, I realized that the beautiful package on the outside was nothing when compared to who you are on the inside. You're smart, funny, caring and for reasons that delight me constantly, you love me. And every time I'm with you, I'm more sure of my love for you. I want to spend the rest of my life being with you. I want us to create a family that makes you happy and I don't care what form it takes. As long as you're with me."

He drew in a breath. "I come with some baggage and I'm not saying it will be easy. But I promise to be there, no matter what. Will you marry me?"

She didn't remember standing, but suddenly she was on her feet and circling the table. He pulled her into his arms and held her close.

"Yes," she whispered. "I love you and I want to marry you, Adam. I'm all in."

Twenty-Seven

"IT'S ALL VERY FAIR," NANCY SAID. "I'LL ADMIT it. Eric surprised me."

"Me, too," Nicole murmured.

Her lawyer glanced at her. "I won't ask if you're okay. But do you need a minute?"

Nicole shook her head. There was nothing left to think about. It was done.

She thought about reading the documents one more time, but didn't have it in her. She trusted her lawyer and even if she didn't, she was too exhausted and numb to fight.

Eric had agreed to divide everything down the middle. The house was hers, because it always had been. The modest value of her business had been added to the money he'd made on his screenplay, less taxes and agent fees. Their debts had been subtracted from that amount and that final amount had been divided in two.

From her half, Nicole had bought him out of her business. The final lump sum would be deposited in her new only-hers checking account. She now owned her business herself and soon would have a nest egg sitting in a money market.

Of that two hundred thousand dollars, she would put half away for Tyler's college and keep the other half for herself. It wasn't enough to live on forever. Not even close. But it was there. A nice, comfortable safety net.

In addition, they'd agreed on child support payments. The amount allowed Nicole to keep Greta. Eric would see Tyler every other weekend, while she retained full custody.

Nancy had brought up asking for alimony, but Nicole had refused. She was young and healthy. She could support herself. Asking for anything else seemed greedy.

She signed the documents where Nancy indicated. In a matter of minutes it was done. Her divorce would be final, according to the state of California, in six months. But she knew the marriage had been over for years.

She thanked her attorney and headed for home. Eric had said he would come by at two to get his things and she wanted to be there.

When she rounded the corner, his car was already in the driveway. She parked across the street and walked toward the house.

"It's me," she called as she walked in the front door.

"I'm back here."

From the sound of his voice, she would guess he was in his office.

There were just the two of them in the house. She'd asked Greta to take Tyler out for the afternoon so they wouldn't be here. Not that Nicole was expecting anything to happen. Even so there was no need for their son to witness the last gasps of their failed marriage.

She went down the hall. The door to Eric's office stood open. He was putting books into boxes. He glanced up and smiled at her.

"Hi. I shouldn't be too long."

"When's the truck coming?"

"What truck?"

"The moving truck. For your things. Aren't you taking some of the furniture?"

He looked around at the small office. "No. I don't need it. The only thing I bought was that." He nodded at the futon. "While it has sentimental value, I'm not interested in finding a place for it. Let me know if you need help getting rid of it."

She'd thought he would want at least some of the furniture. Now that she thought about it, she realized they'd never discussed what he would and wouldn't need for his new place.

"You have things for the kitchen and a sofa and stuff?" she asked.

"I'm living in a furnished place. I'm not sure where I want to settle. I'm close to the studio, so convenient for now, but after I sell my next screenplay, I might move to the Hills."

Hollywood Hills, she thought. Where houses perched like eagles' nests had views from downtown to the ocean.

"You'll want lots of entertaining space," she said quietly. "For your movie-star parties."

He grinned. "You know it."

Nothing about this felt like it was really happening, she thought as he picked up the full box and carried it out to his car. Not him leaving, not the empty space that separated them. She honestly couldn't think of a single thing to say to him. How could they have been married for less than six years and have already run out of words?

Not sure what else to do, she filled a second box with the rest of his books.

"Thanks," he said, when he returned. "I still have a few things in the bedroom."

She took one of the boxes, walked out of the office and into the living room. She'd already sorted the DVDs and Blu-ray disks. She put them in the box, then collected a couple of magazines, and a plate Tyler had decorated for him last Father's Day.

In the kitchen, she added a couple of pens from the junk drawer and a few pictures of him and Tyler.

There were some T-shirts and board shorts stacked on the washer. She got those and added them to the box, along with an iPod and headphones.

He walked into the kitchen. "I think I have everything."

She pointed to the box. "You'll want that."

He glanced inside. "Thank you."

They stared at each other. Although he looked exactly the same as he had the last time she'd seen him, and the time before, in so many ways, he was a stranger. She no longer knew him and wondered if she ever had. Their relationship had been nothing but an illusion. They'd both played at being in love, and neither of them had done a very good job.

"If you want to see Tyler more, just call me and we'll set something up."

"I'm going to be busy," he said, picking up the last box. "The every other weekend thing is about all I can handle and I might need you to understand if I have to miss a few times."

She wanted to protest—to point out that a boy needed his father. That Tyler missed him. Only Eric had started leaving long before he'd moved out. So much so that their son barely mentioned him. Tyler had friends and preschool.

Come September he would be in kindergarten. Eric would matter less and less.

One day Eric might regret that. One day he might try to reconcile with his son. Until then, her job was to give Tyler the most stable home she could. To love him so much he wouldn't notice the absent father.

"I have a meeting," Eric told her. "I have to go. Once my lawyer gets the signed papers, he'll arrange to have the money sent over to your account."

She nodded.

He gave her a quick, impersonal smile. "Okay, then. I'll see you."

He walked out of the kitchen. Seconds later, the front door closed.

She stood in the quiet house and steadied her breathing. It was done. The paperwork was signed. In six months the lawyers would go to court and a judge would sign some papers and she would be divorced.

She looked around the kitchen, at the painted cabinets and the tile she'd chosen shortly after she'd bought the house. Through the window she could see the backyard. All the plants she'd nursed back to health and the ones she's bought. She'd always loved this house. The bright colors, the light, how she'd decorated…

Nicole slowly turned in a circle, taking in every corner of the kitchen. There was the stove she'd replaced and the door handles she'd bought. In the laundry room were the washer and dryer that had been replaced just before Eric had quit. A washer and dryer she'd bought on her own because he didn't care about that kind of thing.

She ran into the living room and stared at the sofa, the chairs, even the TV. She'd picked them all. In the bedroom was the set she'd bought at an estate sale the same month she'd closed on the house. It had taken her two months to refinish the wood and stain it. She'd been so proud of the outcome and when Eric had first seen them, he'd been impressed by her hard work.

Slowly, she walked to Eric's office. Even there she'd been the one to find the old desk at the Habitat for Humanity store. Eric had liked it fine, but he hadn't picked it. No wonder he'd only needed a few boxes to move out. There was nothing of him in this house.

She leaned against the hall wall and slowly sank to the floor. After pulling her legs up to her chest, she rested her head on her knees and told herself to keep breathing.

But the truth was insistent. Like a lonely dog determined to be petted, it nudged at her, slipping in when she let down her guard.

She and Eric had never known each other. Not really. And because she hadn't known him, she couldn't love him. Not really. Not in a way that was meaningful to him.

He'd been the one to leave. He'd been the one to step away from their marriage, but she hadn't given him any reason to stay. The past six years of his life fit in a handful of boxes. No part of their life had been his.

She was to blame, she thought, her stomach twisting until she was afraid she was going to throw up. Not completely, but she had a pretty equal share.

She'd never seen it. Making everything his fault had been so very easy. She'd never noticed how she was also responsible. She wasn't sure she wanted to be married to Eric anymore, but by her actions, she hadn't given either of them a choice.

Now it was done. There was no going back. There was

only moving forward. Right now that unknown path was more than a little terrifying. And the kicker was, she'd done it to herself.

The sun flooded the backyard with warmth and light. Pam had made sure there were plenty of chairs in the shade, not that anyone was using them, she thought happily. Her guests were too busy laughing and talking to do something as mundane as sit.

She'd already made a pest of herself with the sunscreen, especially for the children. It was the first unofficial day of summer. She didn't want anyone getting a sunburn. Brandon had taken her aside and told her to lighten up. He'd then kissed her cheek and handed her a margarita. She'd decided to take his advice.

The Eiland family Memorial Day barbecue was a tradition. It had started two weeks after she and John had moved into this house. She'd been pregnant with Brandon, exhausted from unpacking and too big to sleep more than thirty minutes at a stretch and tired of not being able to see her feet. She'd been swollen, achy and the last thing she'd wanted was a party.

But John had promised he would handle everything and to her surprise, he had. When the guests had arrived, they'd swarmed the house and seen to the last of the unpacking. In less than an hour the books were in the bookcase, the baby-to-be's room was in order and all the boxes were lying flattened in the garage. A good thing, because right after the burgers had been served, her water had broken. Six hours later, Brandon entered the world.

The following year, they'd had the party again. Mostly

to thank their guests who had cleaned up after the party and put the leftovers in the refrigerator.

And so it had begun.

The party had grown as she and John had made new friends. Later, their children's friends had joined in. Some people had moved away or found traditions of their own. But the core of the party, the celebration of friends and summer and all that went with both, had continued.

Pam stood in front of the kitchen window, watching her guests and sipping her margarita. Eugenia had called that morning to confirm the travel arrangements to London. The four women were meeting there for three days of sightseeing, before leaving for Amsterdam, where they would start their cruise.

Pam was already checking out the Chico's website for their easy travel clothes. Hayley would take Lulu for the three weeks Pam would be gone.

Jen walked into the kitchen. Her daughter glowed in a simple red T-shirt and shorts. She was showing already and counting the days until summer vacation started.

"Kirk says he's starving," Jen said with a laugh. "That man can eat. I'm going to take out the burgers so the boys can get started cooking."

The boys being her brothers, Pam thought. She put down her margarita. "Let me help."

"Mom, I can carry a platter of meat."

"Yes, and I'll take care of the chicken and the ribs. You be sure to wash your hands when you're done."

"Oh, Mom."

The words were filled with a combination of affection and frustration. Because Pam would always be a worrier and her family would have to live with that fact.

Come mid-July, Jen and Kirk would move into the big house. The title was in the process of being transferred. Pam still had to decide how much furniture she was taking with her and how much she was going to buy. She thought a combination of familiar and new would be best.

Pam and Jen walked out into the backyard. Shannon and Adam stood talking with Gabby, Adam's sister. Char, Adam's daughter, leaned against Shannon. Shannon absently stroked the girl's hair.

They were a family now, Pam thought, glancing at the other woman's sparkling diamond engagement ring. Shannon had used her business-honed efficiency to plan a wedding for the last week of June. Three days before, escrow would close on Shannon's beachfront condo. While they were on their honeymoon, Pam would move Shannon's things into Adam's house and her own things into Shannon's former, aka her new, condo. Once engaged, Shannon had wanted to sell and Pam had wanted to buy. Taking care of the move was her wedding gift to her friend.

Jen handed the plate of burgers to her husband. "Better?" she asked.

Kirk kissed her. "Now that you're here."

Pam set the chicken and ribs by the barbecue. Her children were happy, she thought with pleasure. Brandon was gearing up for finals, but enjoying every second of medical school. Steven had come into his own with the business. There were days when the responsibility weighed on him, but he got through it.

She watched him talk to Hayley. Rob, Hayley's husband, was traveling on business.

Steven tucked a strand of hair behind Hayley's ear as he laughed at something she said. Pam watched them, wondering if there was something going on, then dismissed the notion. Hayley was married. Steven would never get in the way of that.

She turned her attention to the rest of her guests. Fraser Ingersoll and his partner talked with a couple of guys from John's business. Lulu cuddled happily in her vet's arms. Children ran through the trees, laughing and shrieking. Tyler was with them.

Pam looked for Nicole. She stood with several other women. Although she nodded and smiled, there was still a sadness in her eyes. She'd gotten thinner since Eric had moved out. Quieter. Pam didn't know what it was like to get a divorce, but she knew plenty about grieving. She would be there for her friend. Help her as best she could.

Violet and Bea, from the angel fund, were part of the group of women. Pam had committed to join them. She still couldn't believe how much money she was putting on the line, yet she knew she'd made the right decision. She wanted to be a part of something bigger than herself.

So much had changed, she thought. She was moving, she was going to travel, she would be working several days a week.

In a perfect world, John would still with her. He would be standing at the barbecue, cooking the burgers and telling jokes. He would catch her eye and wink at her and she would smile back.

She thought about all that had happened since his death. All he had missed. The nights without him and how she still thought she had to call and tell him something, only to remember she couldn't. Not anymore.

She would give anything to have him back, even for a minute. Just one more hug, she thought. One more whisper of his voice. She would give anything, but that wasn't an option. So she had begun to heal. To move forward. Because it was what he would have wanted.

Sometimes life was hard, she thought, walking across the grass to be with her friends. Just when you least expected it, you had to start over. There was pain in that, but also satisfaction. With or without her wanting it to, life moved on. And she would, too.

* * * * *

THE GIRLS OF MISCHIEF BAY

SUSAN MALLERY

Reader's Guide

Bookclub Menu Suggestion:

To Drink: A California Chardonnay
To Eat: The Farm Table's Chicken-Spinach Salad with Strawberries and Maple Vinaigrette (recipe follows)

1. Nicole, Shannon and Pam are very different. Why do you think they're friends? What do they have in common? Do you think age matters when it comes to friendship? Do you have a close friend from a different generation? What makes your friendship work?

2. What did you think of the setting of Mischief Bay, California? Did the setting affect the characters and the story and, if so, how?

3. Nicole was angry with her husband for quitting his job in order to pursue his dream of writing a screenplay. Did she have a right to be angry? Did your feelings change as the story progressed? How should Nicole and Eric have handled things differently?

4. As you were reading, did you feel that Shannon really wanted children? Why or why not? How

would you have handled Char at her birthday party?

5. Pam does something surprising to breathe new life into her marriage with John. What did you think of the couple's retreat? How did their relationship change after that? Would you ever sign up for a weekend like that?

6. What did you think of Pam's plan when she went on the cruise that John had booked? What surprised you about the cruise?

7. Which heroine did you relate to the most, Nicole, Shannon or Pam? Why?

8. How did each woman change by the end of the book? What were the turning points that prompted these changes?

9. Susan Mallery's working title for this book was *The Beginners Class*. "Every time you learn something new, you have to start in the beginners class," Nicole says in Chapter Thirteen. How is this relevant to each woman's story? How is it relevant in your life?

10. Nicole will be a main character in the next Mischief Bay novel. What do you hope will happen?

RECIPE

The Farm Table's Chicken-Spinach Salad with Strawberries and Maple Vinaigrette

Vinaigrette:

1/3 cup vegetable oil

1/3 cup maple syrup

3 tbsp. balsamic vinegar

1 tbsp. Dijon mustard

1 tbsp. lemon juice

1/2 tsp. salt

1/4 tsp. pepper

Salad:

1 lb. boneless, skinless chicken breasts

5 oz. baby spinach

8 oz. strawberries, quartered

4 green onions, sliced

1/2 cup slivered almonds, roasted 30 seconds in a dry pan

Whisk together the vinaigrette ingredients and refrigerate.

Grill the chicken breasts until thoroughly cooked. Slice on the diagonal. Mix all salad ingredients in a bowl. Serve with maple vinaigrette. Makes 4-6 main dish salads.

Find more recipes from the restaurants of Mischief Bay at www.mischiefbay.com!